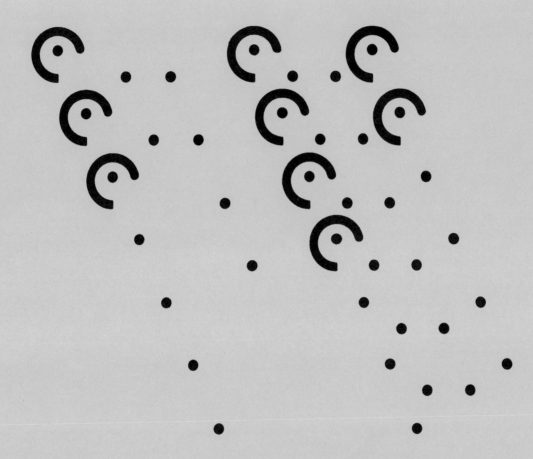

**Hermeneia
—A Critical
and Historical
Commentary
on the Bible**

Zephaniah

A Commentary

by Marvin A. Sweeney

Edited by
Paul D. Hanson

**Fortress
Press** Minneapolis

Zephaniah
A Commentary

Cover and interior design by Kenneth Hiebert
Typesetting and page composition by
The HK Scriptorium

ISBN 0-8006-6049-8 (alk. paper)

The paper used in this publication meets the mini-
mum requirements of American National Standard
for Information Sciences—Permanence of paper for
Printed Library Materials, ANSI Z329.48–1984.

Manufactured in the U.S.A.

07   06   05   04   03   1   2   3   4   5   6   7   8   9   10

■ FOR RICK

The Author

Marvin A. Sweeney is Professor of Hebrew Bible at the
Claremont School of Theology and Claremont Graduate
School in Claremont, California. His recent books
include *Isaiah 1–39, with an Introduction to Prophetic
Literature* (FOTL, 1996), *The Twelve Prophets* (2 vols., Berit
Olam, 2000), and *King Josiah of Judah: The Lost Messiah of
Israel* (2001). He is Vice-President and CEO of the
Ancient Biblical Manuscript Center for Preservation and
Research and editor of the *Review of Biblical Literature*.
He has held research fellowships at the Hebrew
University of Jerusalem, the W. F. Albright Institute for
Archaeological Research, and the Lilly Theological
Research Fund.

Contents
Zephaniah

The name *Hermeneia*, Greek ἑρμηνεία, has been chosen as the title of the commentary series to which this volume belongs. The word *Hermeneia* has a rich background in the history of biblical interpretation as a term used in the ancient Greek-speaking world for the detailed, systematic exposition of a scriptural work. It is hoped that the series, like its name, will carry forward this old and venerable tradition. A second, entirely practical reason for selecting the name lies in the desire to avoid a long descriptive title and its inevitable acronym, or worse, an unpronounceable abbreviation.

The series is designed to be a critical and historical commentary to the Bible without arbitrary limits in size or scope. It will utilize the full range of philological and historical tools, including textual criticism (often slighted in modern commentaries), the methods of the history of tradition (including genre and prosodic analysis), and the history of religion.

Hermeneia is designed for the serious student of the Bible. It will make full use of ancient Semitic and classical languages; at the same time, English translations of all comparative materials—Greek, Latin, Canaanite, or Akkadian—will be supplied alongside the citation of the source in its original language. Insofar as possible, the aim is to provide the student or scholar with full critical discussion of each problem of interpretation and with the primary data upon which the discussion is based.

Hermeneia is designed to be international and interconfessional in the selection of authors; its editorial boards were formed with this end in view. Occasionally the series will offer translations of distinguished commentaries which originally appeared in languages other than English. Published volumes of the series will be revised continually, and eventually, new commentaries will replace older works in order to preserve the currency of the series. Commentaries are also being assigned for important literary works in the categories of apocryphal and pseudepigraphical works relating to the Old and New Testaments, including some of Essene or Gnostic authorship.

The editors of *Hermeneia* impose no systematic-theological perspective upon the series (directly, or indirectly by selection of authors). It is expected that authors will struggle to lay bare the ancient meaning of a biblical work or pericope. In this way the text's human relevance should become transparent, as is always the case in competent historical discourse. However, the series eschews for itself homiletical translation of the Bible.

The editors are heavily indebted to Fortress Press for its energy and courage in taking up an expensive, long-term project, the rewards of which will accrue chiefly to the field of biblical scholarship.

The editor responsible for this volume is Paul D. Hanson of Harvard University.

Frank Moore Cross	*Helmut Koester*
For the Old Testament	For the New Testament
Editorial Board	Editorial Board

Acknowledgments

The manuscript for this commentary was written during the calendar years 1999 and 2000. Although I did not have a research leave or grant support during this period, the commentary is deeply rooted in earlier research leaves and grants for which I would like to express my appreciation. A 1988 research grant from the University of Miami funded a summer's work at the Hebrew University of Jerusalem that enabled me to produce the first draft of my initial study on Zephaniah ("A Form-Critical Reassessment of the Book of Zephaniah," *CBQ* 53 [1991] 388–408). The Dorot Research Foundation provided the funds for my 1993–94 appointment as the Dorot Research Professor at the W. F. Albright Institute for Archaeological Research, Jerusalem, Israel. This enabled me to begin work on my study, *King Josiah of Judah: The Lost Messiah of Israel* (New York: Oxford Univ. Press, 2001), in which Zephaniah figures prominently. A 1997–98 Lilly Theological Research Grant enabled me to spend a year working on my commentary on the book of the Twelve Prophets (*The Twelve Prophets* [2 vols.; Berit Olam; Collegeville, Minn.: Liturgical Press, 2000]), which is the immediate predecessor to the present commentary. The Institute for Antiquity and Christianity of the Claremont Graduate University, the Society of Biblical Literature, and the Ancient Biblical Manuscript Center of the Claremont School of Theology have provided various forms of support that have advanced this project as well.

I would like to thank the editors of the Hermeneia commentary series for their invitation to contribute this volume to such a distinguished series. I am especially grateful for the free hand they have granted me to pursue all topics that I consider essential to the interpretation of Zephaniah. I am particularly indebted to Paul D. Hanson, the editor of this volume, whose sharp and judicious eye as volume editor has "saved me from the wolves" at many points. I have learned much from him and his writings through our common interest in the book of Isaiah. Any problems that might remain are my responsibility. I would also like to thank my student assistant, Mr. Gi-soo Song, for his work on this volume.

My colleagues in Hebrew Bible, Tammi Schneider and Kristin De Troyer, and my students at the Claremont School of Theology and the Claremont Graduate University, particularly those from my Zephaniah seminars in 1996 and 1999, have provided constant sources of collegiality and insight. It is a pleasure and a privilege to be associated with such fine scholars.

My wife, Muna, and my daughter, Leah, have given me the love and support that have kept me on an even keel during the course of work on this project. Nothing is possible without the love and joy that they bring into my life.

Finally, I would like to dedicate this work to my brother, Rick, who continually demonstrates his tenacity in overcoming life's challenges.

San Dimas, California
Erev Rosh ha-Shanah,
29 Elul, 5762/
6 September, 2002

Marvin A. Sweeney

Author's note: In keeping with some circles in Jewish tradition, I have chosen to employ the expressions YHWH, G-d, L-rd, and so on in rendering the name of G-d. The use of *qop* in the various forms of Hebrew *ʾeloqim* is also deliberate. It is a way to avoid writing out the Hebrew equivalent for G-d. Such practice is intended to express the sanctity of the divine name.

Reference Codes

1. Abbreviations

AASOR	Annual of the American Schools of Oriental Research
AB	Anchor Bible
ABD	*Anchor Bible Dictionary*, ed. D. N. Freedman et al.
ABS	Archeology and Biblical Studies
AHw	*Akkadisches Handwörterbuch*, by W. von Soden
AION	*Annali dell' istituto orientali di Napoli*
AJBI	*Annual of the Japanese Biblical Institute*
AnBib	Analecta biblica
ANEP	*The Ancient Near East in Pictures Relating to the Old Testament*, ed. J. B. Pritchard
ANET	*Ancient Near Eastern Texts Relating to the Old Testament*, ed. J. B. Pritchard
AOAT	Alter Orient und Altes Testament
ARAB	*Ancient Records of Assyria and Babylonia*, ed. D. D. Luckenbill
ASTI	*Annual of the Swedish Theological Institute*
ATD	Das Alte Testament Deutsch
ATSAT	Arbeiten zu Text und Sprache im Alten Testament
BA	*Biblical Archaeologist*
BARev	*Biblical Archaeology Review*
BASOR	*Bulletin of the American School of Oriental Research*
BBET	Beiträge zur biblischen Exegese und Theologie
BCE	Before the Common Era
BDB	*Hebrew and English Lexicon of the Old Testament*, by F. Brown, S. R. Driver, and C. A. Briggs
BEATAJ	Beiträge zur Erforschung des Alten Testaments und des antiken Judentums
BEvTh	Beiträge zur evangelischen Theologie
BHK	*Biblia hebraica*, ed. Rudolph Kittel
BHS	*Biblia hebraica stuttgartensia*, edited by Karl Elliger and Wilhelm Rudolph
Bib	*Biblica*
BibIntSer	Biblical Interpretation Series
BibOr	Biblica et orientalia
BibSem	Biblical Seminar
BIOSCS	*Bulletin of the International Organization of Septuagint and Cognate Studies*
BJS	Brown Judaic Studies
BK	*Bibel und Kirche*
BLS	Bible and Literature Series
BN	*Biblische Notizen*
BSac	*Bibliotheca sacra*
BTS	Biblisch-theologische Studien
BZ	*Biblische Zeitschrift*
BZAW	Beihefte zur Zeitschrift für die alttestamentliche Wissenschaft
CAD	*The Assyrian Dictionary of the Oriental Institute of the University of Chicago.* Chicago, 1956–
CAH	*Cambridge Ancient History*
CAT	Commentaire de l'Ancien Testament
CBQ	*Catholic Biblical Quarterly*
CBQMS	Catholic Biblical Quarterly Monograph Series
CE	Common Era
ConBOT	Coniectaneia Biblica, Old Testament Series
CRINT	Compendia Rerum Iudaicarum ad Novum Testamentum
CurBS	*Currents in Research: Biblical Studies*
DDD²	*Dictionary of Deities and Demons in the Bible*, ed. K. van der Toorn, B. Becking, and P. van der Horst. 2nd edition
DJD	Discoveries in the Judaean Desert
EB	Études bibliques
EncJud	*Encyclopaedia Judaica*, ed. Cecil J. Roth et al.
ErIsr	*Eretz Israel*
EThL	*Ephemerides theologicae lovanienses*
EvTh	*Evangelische Theologie*
ExpT	*Expository Times*
FAT	Forschungen zum alten Testament
Fest.	Festschrift
FOTL	Forms of the Old Testament Literature Commentary Series
FRLANT	Forschungen zur Religion des Alten und Neuen Testaments
GBS	Guides to Biblical Scholarship
GCT	Gender, Culture, and Theory Monograph Series
GKC	*Gesenius' Hebrew Grammar*, ed. E. Kautzsch; trans. A. E. Cowley
HALOT	*Hebrew and Aramaic Lexicon of the Old Testament,* L. Koehler et al.
HAR	*Hebrew Annual Review*

HAT	Handbuch zum Alten Testament	OTG	Old Testament Guides
HBD	*HarperCollins Bible Dictionary*, ed. P. Achtemeier et al. 2d edition	OTL	Old Testament Library Commentary Series
HKAT	Handkommentar zum Alten Testament	*OTP*	*Old Testament Pseudepigrapha*, ed. J. H. Charlesworth
HSAT	Die Heilige Schrift des Alten Testaments	*OTS*	*Oudtestamentische Studiën*
HSM	Harvard Semitic Monographs	POT	De Prediking van het Oude Testament
HSS	Harvard Semitic Studies	PTMS	Pittsburgh Theological Monograph Series
HUCA	*Hebrew Union College Annual*		
ICC	International Critical Commentary	*RB*	*Revue biblique*
		RevQ	*Revue de Qumran*
IDB	*Interpreter's Dictionary of the Bible*, ed. G. Buttrick	*RevScRel*	*Revue de sciences religieuses*
		SBLABS	Society of Biblical Literature Archaeology and Biblical Studies
IDBSup	*Interpreter's Dictionary of the Bible: Supplementary Volume*, ed. K. Crim	SBLDS	Society of Biblical Literature Dissertation Series
IEJ	*Israel Exploration Journal*	SBLMS	Society of Biblical Literature Monograph Series
Int	*Interpretation*		
JAOS	*Journal of the American Oriental Society*	*SBLSP*	*Society of Biblical Literature Seminar Papers*
JARCE	*Journal of the American Research Center in Egypt*	SBLSymS	Society of Biblical Literature Symposium Series
JBL	*Journal of Biblical Literature*	SBS	Stuttgarter Bibelstudien
JCS	*Journal of Cuneiform Studies*	SBT	Studies in Biblical Theology
JNES	*Journal of Near Eastern Studies*	*SEÅ*	*Svensk exegetisk årsbok*
JNSL	*Journal of Northwest Semitic Languages*	SJLA	Studies in Judaism in Late Antiquity
JR	*Journal of Religion*	*SJOT*	*Scandinavian Journal of the Old Testament*
JRT	*Journal of Religious Thought*		
JSOT	*Journal for the Study of the Old Testament*	SWBA	Social World of Biblical Antiquity
JSOTSup	Journal for the Study of the Old Testament, Supplement Series	*TA*	*Tel Aviv*
		TB	Theologische Bücherei
JSS	*Journal of Semitic Studies*	*TD*	*Theology Digest*
JTS	*Journal of Theological Studies*	*TDOT*	*Theological Dictionary of the Old Testament*, ed. H. Ringgren et al.
KAT	Kommentar zum Alten Testament		
KHAT	Kurzer Hand-Commentar zum Alten Testament	*ThStK*	*Theologische Studien und Kritiken*
		TJ	Targum Jonathan
KS	*Kleine Schriften*, by Albrecht Alt	*UF*	*Ugarit-Forschungen*
LXX	Septuagint	Vg	Vulgate
MS(S)	manuscript(s)	*VT*	*Vetus Testamentum*
MT	Masoretic text	VTSup	Vetus Testamentum Supplements
Mus	*Muséon*	WBC	Word Biblical Commentary
n.	note	WMANT	Wissenschaftliche Monographien zum Alten und Neuen Testament
NEAEHL	*New Encyclopedia of Archaeological Excavations in the Holy Land*, ed. E. Stern et al.	*WZKM*	*Wiener Zeitschrift für die Kunde des Morgenlandes*
NEASB	*Near Eastern Archeological Society Bulletin*	*ZAW*	*Zeitschrift für die Alttestamentliche Wissenschaft*
NIB	*New Interpreter's Bible*	ZBK	Zürcher Bibelkommentar
NedThT	*Nederlands theologisch tjidschrift*	*ZDMG*	*Zeitschrift der deutschen morgenländischen Gesellschaft*
OBO	Orbis biblicus et orientalis		
ÖBSt	Österreichische biblische Studien	*ZDPV*	*Zeitschrift des deutschen Palästina Vereins*
		ZThK	*Zeitschrift für Theologie und Kirche*

2. Short Titles of Frequently Cited Literature

Avigad, *Discovering Jerusalem*
Nahman Avigad, *Discovering Jerusalem* (Nashville: Nelson, 1983).

Avigad, *Hebrew Bullae*
Nahman Avigad, *Hebrew Bullae from the Time of Jeremiah: Remnants of a Burnt Archive* (Jerusalem: Israel Exploration Society, 1986).

Ball, *Zephaniah*
Ivan J. Ball Jr., *Zephaniah: A Rhetorical Study* (1972; reprinted Berkeley: BIBAL, 1988).

Barthélemy, *Critique textuelle*
Dominique Barthélemy et al., *Critique textuelle de l'ancien testament*, vol. 3: *Ézéchiel, Daniel et les 12 Prophètes* (OBO 50/3; Göttingen: Vandenhoeck & Ruprecht, 1992).

Barthélemy, *Devanciers*
Dominique Barthélemy, *Les devanciers d'Aquila* (VTSup 10; Leiden: Brill, 1963).

Ben Zvi, *Zephaniah*
Ehud Ben Zvi, *A Historical-Critical Study of the Book of Zephaniah* (BZAW 198; Berlin: de Gruyter, 1991).

Bennett, "Zephaniah"
Robert A. Bennett, "The Book of Zephaniah," *NIB* 7:657–704.

Berger, *Histoire*
Samuel Berger, *Histoire de la Vulgate pendant les premiers siècles du moyen age* (1893; reprinted New York: Franklin, 1958).

Berlin, *Zephaniah*
Adele Berlin, *Zephaniah* (AB 25A; New York: Doubleday, 1994).

Brin, "Title"
Gershon Brin, "The Title בן (ה)מלך and Its Parallels: The Significance and Evaluation of an Official Title," *AION* 29 (1969) 432–65.

Cathcart and Gordon, *Targum*
Kevin J. Cathcart and Robert P. Gordon, *The Targum to the Minor Prophets: Translated with a Critical Introduction, Apparatus, and Notes* (Aramaic Bible 14; Wilmington, Del.: Glazier, 1989).

Childs, *Crisis*
Brevard S. Childs, *Isaiah and the Assyrian Crisis* (SBT II/3; London: SCM, 1967).

Churgin, *Targum Jonathan*
Pinkhos Churgin, *Targum Jonathan to the Prophets* (1927; reprinted New York: KTAV, 1983).

Dearman, *Studies*
J. Andrew Dearman, ed., *Studies in the Mesha Inscription and Moab* (SBLABS 2; Atlanta: Scholars Press, 1989).

DeVries, *From Old Revelation*
Simon J. DeVries, *From Old Revelation to New: A Tradition-Historical and Redaction-Critical Study of the Temporal Transitions in Prophetic Prediction* (Grand Rapids: Eerdmans, 1995).

Edler, *Kerygma*
Rainer Edler, *Das Kerygma des Propheten Zefanja* (Freiburger theologische Studien 126; Freiburg: Herder, 1984).

Elliger, *Zephanja*
Karl Elliger, *Die Propheten Nahum, Habakuk, Zephanja, Haggai, Sacharja, Maleachi* (ATD 25/2; Göttingen: Vandenhoeck & Ruprecht, ¹1949, ⁸1982).

Finkelstein, "Archaeology"
Israel Finkelstein, "The Archaeology of the Days of Manasseh," pp. 169–87 in Michael D. Coogan, J. Cheryl Exum, and Lawrence E. Stager, eds., *Scripture and Other Artifacts: Essays on the Bible and Archaeology in Honor of Philip J. King* (Louisville: Westminster John Knox, 1994).

Floyd, *Minor Prophets*
Michael H. Floyd, *Minor Prophets, Part 2* (FOTL 22; Grand Rapids: Eerdmans, 2000).

Fuller, "Twelve"
Russell E. Fuller, "The Twelve," pp. 221–318 in Eugene Ulrich et al., *Qumran Cave 4. X: The Prophets* (DJD 15; Oxford: Clarendon, 1997).

Gaster, *Myth*
Theodore Gaster, *Myth, Legend, and Custom in the Old Testament* (New York: Harper & Row, 1969).

Gelston, *Peshitta*
Anthony Gelston, *The Peshitta of the Twelve Prophets* (Oxford: Clarendon, 1987).

Gerleman, *Zephanja*
Gillis Gerleman, *Zephanja textkritisch und literarkritisch untersucht* (Lund: Gleerup, 1942).

Gerstenberger, *Psalms, Part 1*
Erhard Gerstenberger, *Psalms, Part 1; with an Introduction to Cultic Poetry* (FOTL 14; Grand Rapids: Eerdmans, 1988).

Gitin, "Tel Miqne-Ekron"
Seymour Gitin, "Tel Miqne-Ekron: A Type-Site for the Inner Coastal Plain in the Iron Age II Period," pp. 23–58 in Seymour Gitin and William Dever, eds., *Recent Excavations in Israel: Studies in Iron Age Archaeology* (AASOR 49; Winona Lake, Ind.: Eisenbrauns, 1989).

Hallo and Simpson, *Ancient Near East*
William W. Hallo and William K. Simpson, *The Ancient Near East: A History* (New York: Harcourt, Brace, Jovanovich, 1971).

Hillers, "Hôy"
Delbert Hillers, "Hôy and Hôy-Oracles: A Neglected Syntactic Aspect," pp. 185–88 in Carol L. Meyers and Michael O'Connor, eds., *The Word of the Lord Shall Go Forth* (Fest. D. N. Freedman; Winona Lake, Ind.: Eisenbrauns, 1983).

Horgan, *Pesharim*
Maurya Horgan, *Pesharim: Qumran Interpretation of Biblical Books* (CBQMS 8; Washington, D.C.: Catholic Biblical Association, 1979).

Horst, *Propheten*
Th. H. Robinson and F. Horst, *Die Zwölf Kleinen Propheten* (3d ed.; HAT 14; Tübingen: Mohr [Siebeck], 1964).

Hunter, *Seek the Lord*
A. Vanlier Hunter, *Seek the Lord! A Study of the Meaning and Function of the Exhortations in Amos, Isaiah, Micah, and Zephaniah* (Baltimore: St. Mary's Seminary and University, 1982).

Irsigler, *Gottesgericht*
Hubert Irsigler, *Gottesgericht und Jahwetag. Die Komposition Zef 1,1–2,3, untersucht auf der Grundlage der Literarkritik des Zefanjabuches* (ATSAT 3; St. Ottilien, EOS, 1977).

Jastrow, *Dictionary*
Marcus Jastrow, *A Dictionary of the Targumim, the Talmud Babli and Yerushalmi, and the Midrashic Literature* (2 vols.; Brooklyn: Shalom, 1967).

Jellicoe, *Septuagint*
Sidney Jellicoe, *The Septuagint and Modern Study* (Oxford: Clarendon, 1968).

Junker, *Sophonia*
Hubert Junker, *Die Zwölf Kleinen Propheten. II. Hälfte: Nahum, Habakuk, Sophonia, Aggäus, Zacharias, Malachis* (HSAT VIII/3.II; Bonn: Hanstein, 1938).

Kapelrud, *Message*
Arvid S. Kapelrud, *The Message of the Prophet Zephaniah: Morphology and Ideas* (Oslo: Universitetsforlaget, 1975).

Keller, *Sophonie*
René Vuilleumier and Carl-A. Keller, *Michée, Nahoum, Habacuc, Sophonie* (CAT XIb; Neuchâtel: Delachaux et Niestlé, 1971).

Knierim, *Text*
Rolf P. Knierim, *Text and Concept in Leviticus 1:1-9* (FAT 2; Tübingen: Mohr [Siebeck], 1992).

Krašovec, *Merismus*
J. Krašovec, *Der Merismus in biblisch-hebräischen und nordwestsemitischen* (BibOr 33; Rome: Biblical Institute Press, 1977).

Kuhrt, *Ancient Near East*
Amélie Kuhrt, *The Ancient Near East, c. 3000–330 B.C.* (2 vols.; London: Routledge, 1997).

Langhor, "Sophonie"
Guy Langhor, "Le livre de Sophonie et la critique d'authencité," *EThL* 52 (1976) 1-27.

Levenson, *Sinai*
Jon D. Levenson, *Sinai and Zion: An Entry into the Jewish Bible* (Minneapolis: Winston, 1985).

Levenson, "Temple"
Jon D. Levenson, "The Temple and the World," *JR* 64 (1984) 275-98.

Marti, *Dodekapropheton*
Karl Marti, *Das Dodekapropheton* (KHAT XIII; Tübingen: Mohr [Siebeck], 1904).

Mazar, *Archaeology*
Amihai Mazar, *Archaeology of the Land of the Bible, 10,000–586 B.C.E.* (New York: Doubleday, 1990).

Mulder, *Mikra*
Martin Jan Mulder, ed., *Mikra: Text, Translation, Reading and Interpretation of the Hebrew Bible in Ancient Judaism and Early Christianity* (CRINT II/1; Philadelphia: Fortress Press, 1988).

Milik, *Murabbaʿat*
P. Benoit, J. T. Milik, and R. de Vaux, *Les Grottes de Murabba'at* (2 vols.; DJD 2; Oxford: Clarendon, 1961).

Nowack, *Propheten*
W. Nowack, *Die Kleinen Propheten* (HKAT III/4; Göttingen: Vandenhoeck & Ruprecht, 1922).

Redford, *Egypt*
Donald B. Redford, *Egypt, Canaan, and Israel in Ancient Times* (Princeton: Princeton Univ. Press, 1992).

Renaud, *Sophonie*
B. Renaud, *Michée–Sophonie–Nahum* (Sources bibliques; Paris: Gabalda, 1987).

Renaud, "Sophonie"
B. Renaud, "Le livre de Sophonie: Le jour de YHWH thème structurant de la synthèse rédactionelle," *RevScRel* 60 (1986) 1–33.

Roberts, *Zephaniah*
J. J. M. Roberts, *Nahum, Habakkuk, and Zephaniah* (OTL; Louisville: Westminster John Knox, 1991).

Rudolph, *Zephanja*
Wilhelm Rudolph, *Micha–Nahum–Habakuk–Zephanja* (KAT XIII/3; Gütersloh: Mohn, 1975).

Ryou, *Zephaniah's Oracles*
Daniel Hojoon Ryou, *Zephaniah's Oracles against the Nations: A Synchronic and Diachronic Study of Zephaniah 2:1–3:8* (BibIntSer 13; Leiden: Brill, 1995).

Sabottka, *Zephanja*
Liudger Sabottka, *Zephanja. Versuch einer Neuübersetzung mit philologischem Kommentar* (BibOr 25; Rome: Biblical Institute Press, 1972).

Sæbø, *Antiquity*
Magne Sæbø, ed., *Hebrew Bible/Old Testament*, vol. I/1: *Antiquity* (Göttingen: Vandenhoeck & Ruprecht, 1996).

Schürer, *History*
Emil Schürer, *History of the Jewish People in the Age of Jesus Christ (175 B.C.–A.D. 135)*. Vol. 1. Revised and edited by Geza Vermes, Fergus Millar and Matthew Black (rev. ed.; Edinburgh: T & T Clark, 1973).

Schwally, "Sefanjâ"
Schwally, "Das Buch Sefanjâ, eine historisch-kritische Untersuchung," *ZAW* 10 (1890) 165–240.

Segal, *Grammar*
M. H. Segal, *A Grammar of Mishnaic Hebrew* (Oxford: Clarendon, 1978).

Sellin, *Zwölfprophetenbuch*
Ernst Sellin, *Das Zwölfprophetenbuch* (2d-3d ed.; 2 vols.; KAT XII; Leipzig: Deichert, 1930).

Seybold, *Zephanja*

    Klaus Seybold, *Nahum, Habakuk, Zephanja* (ZBK 24.2; Zurich: Theologischer Verlag, 1991).

Seybold, *Satirische Prophetie*

    Klaus Seybold, *Satirische Prophetie: Studien zum Buch Zefanja* (SBS 120; Stuttgart: Katholisches Bibelwerk, 1985).

Smallwood, *Jews*

    E. Mary Smallwood, *The Jews under Roman Rule: From Pompey to Diocletian* (SJLA 20; Leiden: Brill, 1976).

J. M. P. Smith, *Zephaniah*

    John Merlin Powis Smith, William Hayes Ward, and Julius A. Bewer, *A Critical and Exegetical Commentary on Micah, Zephaniah, Nahum, Habakkuk, Obadiah, and Joel* (1911; ICC; reprinted Edinburgh: T & T Clark, 1985).

R. L. Smith, *Micah–Malachi*

    Ralph L. Smith, *Micah–Malachi* (WBC 32; Waco: Word, 1984).

Smolar and Aberbach, *Studies*

    Leivy Smolar and Moses Aberbach, *Studies in Targum Jonathan to the Prophets* (New York: KTAV, 1983).

Steck, "Zu Zef 3,9-10"

    Odil Hannes Steck, "Zu Zef 3,9-10," *BZ* 34 (1990) 90–95.

Striek, *Zephanjabuch*

    Marco Striek, *Das vordeuteronomistische Zephanjabuch* (BBET 29; Frankfurt am Main: Lang, 1999).

Strugnell, "Notes"

    John Strugnell, "Notes en marge du volume V des 'Discoveries in the Judaean Desert of Jordan,'" *RevQ* 7 (1969) 163–275.

Sweeney, "Form-Critical Reassessment"

    Marvin A. Sweeney, "A Form-Critical Reassessment of the Book of Zephaniah," *CBQ* 53 (1991) 388–408.

Sweeney, *Isaiah 1–39*

    Marvin A. Sweeney, *Isaiah 1–39; with an Introduction to Prophetic Literature* (FOTL 16; Grand Rapids: Eerdmans, 1996).

Sweeney, *King Josiah*

    Marvin A. Sweeney, *King Josiah of Judah: The Lost Messiah of Israel* (Oxford: Oxford Univ. Press, 2001).

Sweeney, "Sequence"

    Marvin A. Sweeney, "Sequence and Interpretation in the Book of the Twelve," in James D. Nogalski and Marvin A. Sweeney, eds., *Reading and Hearing the Book of the Twelve* (SBLSymS 15; Atlanta: Society of Biblical Literature, 2000) 49–64.

Sweeney, *Twelve Prophets*

    Marvin A. Sweeney, *The Twelve Prophets* (2 vols.; Berit Olam; Collegeville, Minn.: Liturgical Press, 2000).

Swete, *Introduction*

    Henry Barclay Swete, *An Introduction to the Old Testament in Greek* (1902; reprinted New York: KTAV, 1968).

Tov, *Greek Minor Prophets*

    Emanuel Tov, *The Greek Minor Prophets Scroll from Naḥal Ḥever (8ḤevXIIgr)* (DJD 8; Oxford: Clarendon, 1990).

Tucker, "Prophetic Superscriptions"

    Gene M. Tucker, "Prophetic Superscriptions and the Growth of the Canon," pp. 56–70 in George W. Coats and Burke O. Long, eds., *Canon and Authority: Essays in Old Testament Religion and Theology* (Philadelphia: Fortress Press, 1977).

van der Woude, *Zefanja*

    A. S. van der Woude, *Habakuk, Zefanja* (POT; Nijkerk: Callenbach, 1978).

van Hoonacker, *Prophètes*

    A. van Hoonacker, *Les Douze Petits Prophètes* (ÉB; Paris: Gabalda, 1908).

Vlaardingerbroek, *Zephaniah*

    Johannes Vlaardingerbroek, *Zephaniah* (Historical Commentary on the Old Testament; Leuven: Peeters, 1999).

Weigl, *Zephanja*

    Michael Weigl, *Zephanja und das "Israel der Armen." Eine Untersuchung zur Theologie des Buches Zefanja* (ÖBSt 13; Klosterneuburg: Österreichisches Katholisches Bibelwerk, 1994).

Weitzman, *Syriac Version*

    Michael Weitzman, *The Syriac Version of the Old Testament: An Introduction* (Univ. of Cambridge Oriental Publications 56; Cambridge: Cambridge Univ. Press, 1999).

Wellhausen, *Propheten*

    Julius Wellhausen, *Die Kleinen Propheten* (Berlin: de Gruyter, ^{3}1898, ^{4}1963).

Whedbee, *Isaiah and Wisdom*

    J. William Whedbee, *Isaiah and Wisdom* (Nashville: Abingdon, 1971).

Willey, *Remember*

    Patricia Tull Willey, *Remember the Former Things: The Recollection of Previous Texts in Second Isaiah* (SBLDS 161; Atlanta: Scholars Press, 1997).

Yadin, *Bar Kochba*

    Yigael Yadin, *Bar Kochba: The Rediscovery of the Legendary Hero of the Second Jewish Revolt against Rome* (New York: Random House, 1971).

Zalcman, "Ambiguity"

    Lawrence Zalcman, "Ambiguity and Assonance in Zephaniah ii 4," *VT* 36 (1986) 365–71.

Ziegler, *Duodecim Prophetae*

    Joseph Ziegler, *Septuaginta: Vetus Testamentum Graecum*, vol. 13: *Duodecim Prophetae* (3d ed.; Göttingen: Vandenhoeck & Ruprecht, 1984).

Zimmerli, *Ezekiel 1*

    Walter Zimmerli, *Ezekiel 1: A Commentary on the Book of the Prophet Ezekiel, Chapters 1–24* (Hermeneia; Philadelphia: Fortress Press, 1979).

The endpapers of this volume display fragments of 4QXII[b], a leather scroll of the Book of the Twelve Prophets dated to the early Hasmonean period (ca. 150– 125 B.C.E.) found in Qumran Cave 4. The fragments pictured include portions of Zeph 1:1-2; 2:13-15; 3:19-20; and Hag 1:1-2. The photograph (PAM 43.087) was provided by the Ancient Biblical Manuscript Center for Preservation and Research, Claremont, California, with the permission of the Israel Antiquities Authority.

The book of Zephaniah constitutes a veritable micro-cosm for the study of the prophetic books. Despite its small size and relative obscurity in relation to better-known books such as Isaiah, Jeremiah, Hosea, and Amos, it presents a full range of exegetical and hermeneutical issues.[1] On the one hand, it is frequently read as an eschatological scenario of judgment and restoration for Israel and the nations of the world on the Day of YHWH. On the other hand, it is also frequently read as a historically based presentation of Zephaniah's attempts to marshal support for King Josiah's program of religious reform and national restoration in seventh-century Judah. In these respects, it poses fundamental interpretive and hermeneutical issues both for a reader-centered, synchronic under-standing of the book as a whole in relation to the con-texts in which it is read, and for an author-centered, diachronic understanding of its contents in relation to the sociohistorical and literary matrices that prompted and influenced its composition. In short, Zephaniah pre-sents an ideal text for constructive theological reflection in the Sacred Scriptures of Judaism and Christianity and for reconstructive historical-critical research on the socioreligious and political realities of late-monarchic period Judah.

According to the superscription for the book in 1:1, the prophet spoke in the time of King Josiah of Judah, who ruled from 640 to 609 BCE and undertook a major program of religious reform and national restoration fol-lowing the decline of Assyrian hegemony in southwest-ern Asia. Nevertheless, the placement of the book of Zephaniah in the sequence of the Twelve Prophets of the Hebrew Bible suggests a different understanding of the setting of the book that profoundly influences its interpretation. Zephaniah is the ninth book in all major versions of the book of the Twelve Prophets, including the Masoretic text (MT), the Septuagint (LXX), the Murabbaʿat manuscript of the Twelve Prophets from the Judean wilderness (Mur), Targum Jonathan on the Prophets (TJ), the Peshitta, the Vulgate, and presumably the Naḥal Ḥever manuscript of the Twelve Prophets from the Judean wilderness.[2] Although the sequence of the Twelve Prophets in the LXX differs from that of the other traditions based on a markedly different herme-neutical perspective in the reading of the Twelve as a whole,[3] Zephaniah occupies the same position and therefore plays a similar role in both sequences. It fol-lows Habakkuk, which takes up Judah's subjugation to the Neo-Babylonian Empire in the late seventh century BCE, and it precedes Haggai, which calls for the rebuild-

---

1   Cf. Rex Mason, *Zephaniah, Habakkuk, Joel* (OTG; Sheffield: JSOT Press, 1994) 16–18.

2   Because of its fragmentary nature, the Naḥal Ḥever MS of the Twelve Prophets preserves text only from the books of Joel, Micah, Nahum, Habakkuk, Zephaniah, Haggai, and Zechariah (see Emanuel Tov, *The Greek Minor Prophets Scroll from Naḥal Ḥever (8ḤevXIIgr)* [DJD 8; Oxford: Clarendon, 1990]). The sequence of books preserved in the scroll corre-sponds to the sequence found in the MT, and the missing books would have appeared at the begin-ning (i.e., Hosea, Amos, Obadiah, Jonah) and at the end of the scroll (i.e., Malachi). There is therefore little reason to claim that the Naḥal Ḥever scroll represents an alternative sequence of books. It is noteworthy, however, that 4QXII[a] clearly represents a sequence of Malachi–Jonah, which deviates from any other known sequence of the book of the Twelve (see Russell E. Fuller's edition of this MS, "The Twelve," in Ulrich et al., *Qumran Cave 4: The Prophets* [DJD 15; Oxford: Clarendon, 1997] 221–32). Because Jonah and Malachi are entirely missing in the Naḥal Ḥever MS, it is theoretically possible that a similar sequence originally appeared there as

well, but clear evidence for such a claim is lacking. Nevertheless, this does not have an impact on the reading of Zephaniah, as it continues to follow Habakkuk and precede Haggai. Otherwise, the frag-mentary 4QXII MSS show no variation from the masoretic order of the text. Variant sequences of the Twelve appear in 4 Ezra 1:39-40; *Asc. Isa.* 4:22; and the *Lives of the Prophets* (see Ehud Ben Zvi, "Twelve Prophetic Books or 'The Twelve': A Few Preliminary Considerations," in James W. Watts and Paul R. House, eds., *Forming Prophetic Literature: Essays on Isaiah and the Twelve in Honor of John D. W. Watts* [JSOTSup 235; Sheffield: Sheffield Academic Press, 1996] 124–56, 134 n. 24). Zephaniah appears following Haggai and preceding Zechariah in *Asc. Isa.* 4:22, which would further reinforce a nonhistor-ical and eschatological reading of the book.

3   For full discussion of this issue, see Marvin A. Sweeney, "Sequence and Interpretation in the Book of the Twelve," in James D. Nogalski and Marvin A. Sweeney, eds., *Reading and Hearing the Book of the*

ing of the Jerusalem Temple in the early Persian period immediately following the end of the Babylonian exile. Such a sequence suggests that the book of Zephaniah, which is fundamentally concerned with the threat of judgment posed to Jerusalem and Judah on the so-called Day of YHWH, is to be read not in relation to King Josiah's efforts at religious reform and national restoration in the late seventh century BCE,[4] but instead in relation to the Babylonian destruction of Jerusalem, Judah, and the First Temple and the exile of major elements of the Judean population in the early sixth century BCE.

Indeed, this understanding of Zephaniah's placement in the sequence of the Twelve Prophets conflicts with the chronology stated in the superscription of the book. The issue is complicated by claims that the present form of the book is the product of extensive exilic or post-exilic redaction, which added a great deal of material concerned with worldwide eschatological punishment and salvation in an effort to transform the book from one concerned only with the fate of Jerusalem and Judah in the days of King Josiah to one concerned with the fate of the entire world in the Second Temple period and beyond.[5] Consequently, many interpreters claim that the structure of the present form of Zephaniah comprises three major parts: oracles concerned with judgment against Jerusalem and Judah in 1:2–2:3; oracles concerned with judgment against the nations at large in 2:4-15/3:1-8; and oracles concerned with the coming salvation of Jerusalem/Judah and the nations of the world in 3:1-8/3:9-20.[6]

Of course, such a conceptualization of Zephaniah fits well with the theological claims of the New Testament (NT) and subsequent Christian theology for the salvation of humankind,[7] but a close reading of the linguistic and rhetorical features of MT Zephaniah, including both its syntactic/semantic characteristics and the means by which it is organized to address its reading/hearing audience, demonstrates that such a pattern does not constitute the structure of the book. Instead, the structure of Zephaniah reflects an interest in presenting a prophetic discourse that calls on its audience to turn to YHWH before the threatened purge of apostasy in the nation takes place on the Day of YHWH. Although the book contains many statements that express a universalist perspective concerning all creation, they reflect the role of the temple as the holy center of creation in ancient Judean theology.[8] This does not indicate that the threefold concern with judgment against Jerusalem/Judah, judgment against nations, and blessing for Jerusalem/Judah/Israel and the nations is absent from Zephaniah. Instead, it indicates that these concerns are part of the so-called deep or conceptual structure of the book and that they serve the overarching concern to persuade the hearing/reading audience to identify with

Twelve (SBLSymS 15; Atlanta: Society of Biblical Literature, 2000) 49–64; idem, *The Twelve Prophets* (2 vols.; Berit Olam; Collegeville, Minn.: Liturgical Press, 2000) 1:xv–xxix.

4 See Marvin A. Sweeney, *King Josiah of Judah: The Lost Messiah of Israel* (Oxford: Oxford Univ. Press, 2001), for full discussion of Josiah's reign and its impact on the reading and composition of historical and prophetic literature in the Hebrew Bible.

5 In addition to my commentary on the Twelve Prophets and study on Josiah noted above, see Marvin A. Sweeney, "A Form-Critical Reassessment of the Book of Zephaniah," *CBQ* 53 (1991) 388–408. For an assessment of earlier scholarship on Zephaniah with a particular emphasis on this issue, see idem, "Zephaniah: A Paradigm for the Study of the Prophetic Books," *CurBS* 7 (1999) 119–45. Other key surveys of research on Zephaniah include Hubert Irsigler, *Gottesgericht und Jahwetag. Die Komposition Zef 1,1–2,3, untersucht auf der Grundlage der Literarkritik des Zefanjabuches* (ATSAT 3; St. Ottilien:

EOS, 1977) 71–93; Mason, *Zephaniah, Habakkuk, Joel,* 16–58; and Michael Weigl, *Zefanja und das "Israel der Armen." Eine Untersuchung zur Theologie des Buches Zefanja* (ÖBSt 13; Klosterneuburg: Österreichisches Katholisches Bibelwerk, 1994) 230–42.

6 See also Weigl, *Zefanja,* 230–31, for discussion of the problem and bibliographical listing.

7 Note especially how the Day of YHWH motif from the Hebrew Bible was taken up in the NT epistles to portray the eschatological Day of the L-rd or Day of Christ, e.g., 1 Thess 5:2; 2 Thess 2:2; cf. Rom 2:16; 1 Cor 3:13; 2 Tim 1:12, 18; 4:8 (for discussion see Richard Hiers, "Day of Christ," *ABD* 2:76–79).

8 For discussion of the Jerusalem Temple as the holy center of creation in ancient Judean thought, see esp. Jon D. Levenson, "The Temple and the World," *JR* 64 (1984) 275–98; idem, "The Jerusalem Temple in Devotional and Visionary Experience," in Arthur

YHWH and thereby to avoid the punishment to be realized on the Day of YHWH when the nation will be purged of those who are considered to be apostate.[9]

Nevertheless, the chronological displacement of the book of Zephaniah within the sequence of the book of the Twelve Prophets continues to play a role in influencing its interpretation, especially since such displacement provides some justification for reading the book in relation to sets of concerns that it was not written to address. The issue is exacerbated by the fact that the wording of the text differs throughout the masoretic and LXX versions of the book. Although the differences are subtly expressed, they profoundly influence the overall evaluation of the book, particularly in relation to 2:1-3, the basic exhortation of the book that stands at the center of discussion concerning the overall structure, generic character, and interpretation of Zephaniah. Whereas the language of the MT and its related traditions reflects an address that calls on its audience to change and presupposes that it has not yet done so, the LXX and its derivative traditions reflect an address that likewise calls on the audience to change but presupposes that it is unwilling or unable to do so.

These differences result in a very different reading of each version. The MT and its related versions represent an exhortative text that is designed to persuade its audience to adapt a new course of action to adhere to YHWH. It thereby portrays punishment as a threat and restoration as a promise that are designed to encourage the audience to make the choice advocated in the book to adhere to YHWH. Such a reading presupposes the situation of the nation in seventh-century Judah when the audience is to make a choice. It likewise functions similarly when read in later contexts when such choices stand before the readers of Zephaniah.

The LXX and its related versions, however, represent a judgmental text that calls on its audience to adhere to YHWH but presupposes that the audience will not do so. It therefore presents judgment as a coming reality

and restoration as an event that will take place throughout the world only after the punishment has been realized. Such a reading presupposes that choice is no longer possible, as the events have already taken place. It attempts to justify past punishment and suffering by Jerusalem/Judah/Israel as an act of G-d that was prompted by the nation's sin in declining to adhere to YHWH. It thereby addresses the needs of an audience that wishes to look back on history, perhaps because it sees itself in a similar situation of choice and hopes to avoid purported mistakes of the past or perhaps because it no longer identifies with seventh-century Judeans and seeks to understand the reasons why they were punished.

It is therefore essential to analyze the overall textual features, such as the use of language, structure, generic characteristics, settings, and rhetorical strategies, of each of the versions of the book of Zephaniah in order to assess its unique interpretive and communicative perspectives.

I. The Masoretic Version

A. Textual Features

The basic Hebrew text of the book of Zephaniah appears as part of the larger MT of the Hebrew Bible. The MT is actually a product of Jewish textual specialists from the periods of late antiquity and the Middle Ages known as *ba'ălê hammāsôrâ*, "masters of the tradition," or Masoretes, who supplied the vowel pointing and accentuation to a standardized consonantal Hebrew text in order to establish an authoritative reading of the Hebrew Bible.[10] This includes both the proper interpretation and pronunciation of the individual words that comprise the text as well as the marking of the individual verses based on an assessment of the syntactical interrelationships between the individual words. The numbers that designate each verse were not set by the Masoretes, but derive from the numbering employed in

Green, ed., *Jewish Spirituality: From the Bible to the Middle Ages* (New York: Crossroad, 1988) 32–61; idem, *Sinai and Zion: An Entry into the Jewish Bible* (Minneapolis: Winston, 1985).

9   For discussion of the "deep" or "conceptual" structure of biblical literature, see esp. Rolf Knierim, "Old Testament Form Criticism Reconsidered," *Int*

27 (1973) 435–68; idem, *Text and Concept in Leviticus 1:1-9* (FAT 2; Tübingen: Mohr [Siebeck], 1992).

10   For full discussion of the masoretic tradition, see Israel Yeivin, *Introduction to the Tiberian Masorah* (Society of Biblical Literature Masoretic Studies 5; Missoula, Mont.: Scholars Press, 1980); Aaron Dotan, "Masorah," *EncJud* 16:1401–82; Christian D.

the Vulgate manuscript tradition. In addition, the masoretic version employs a system of gaps in the text, including both the "open section" lines *(pārāšâ pĕtûḥâ),* that is, blank spaces from the conclusion of the verse to the end of the line to indicate a large structural division in the text, and the "closed section" lines *(pārāšâ sĕtûmâ),* that is, a short space from the conclusion of one verse until the beginning of the next to indicate a structural subdivision within the larger *pĕtûḥôt.*[11] It should be noted that masoretic manuscripts are not always consistent in their use of *pĕtûḥôt* and *sĕtûmôt,* and printed editions of rabbinic Bibles *(Miqra'ot Gedolot)* do not even employ them at all. The chapter numbers that appear in contemporary critical text editions, rabbinic Bibles, and translations were established by the thirteenth-century archbishop of Canterbury, Stephen Langton.

The earliest extant texts of the masoretic tradition date to the ninth-eleventh centuries CE, and include the Cairo Codex of the Prophets (896 CE), originally copied and pointed by Moshe ben Asher;[12] the Aleppo Codex of the Bible produced by Aaron ben Asher (915 CE), once considered by Maimonides to be the most authoritative codex of the Bible;[13] and the Leningrad or St. Petersburg Codex of the Bible (1009 CE), which constitutes the oldest complete copy of the Bible in existence.[14] Although the Leningrad Codex represents a masoretic tradition slightly different from that of the Aleppo Codex, it was corrected according to the most exact texts of Ben Asher. The Leningrad Codex therefore stands as the basis for modern critical editions of the Hebrew text.[15] The Bomberg or Second Rabbinic Bible printed by Jacob ben Hayyim in Venice (1524–1525) represents another important witness to the masoretic textual tradition.[16] Most scholars maintain that the present form of the MT is based on a Tiberian system of vowel pointing and accentuation that was developed between the sixth and eighth centuries CE. In addition, scholars maintain that the present form of the

Ginsburg, *Introduction to the Massoretico-Critical Edition of the Hebrew Bible* (reprinted New York: KTAV, 1966). For an introductory discussion; see also Page H. Kelley, Daniel S. Mynatt, and Timothy G. Crawford, *The Masorah of Biblia Hebraica Stuttgartensia: Introduction and Annotated Glossary* (Grand Rapids: Eerdmans, 1998). For discussion of the text-critical study of the Hebrew Bible, see Emanuel Tov, *Textual Criticism of the Hebrew Bible* (2d ed.; Minneapolis: Fortress Press, 2001); Martin Jan Mulder, "The Transmission of the Biblical Text," in Martin J. Mulder, ed., *Mikra: Text, Translation, Reading and Interpretation of the Hebrew Bible in Ancient Judaism and Early Christianity* (CRINT II/1; Philadelphia: Fortress Press, 1988) 87–135; E. Tov, "The History and Significance of a Standard Text of the Hebrew Bible," in Magne Sæbø, ed., *Hebrew Bible/Old Testament: The History of Its Interpretation,* vol. I/1: *Antiquity* (Göttingen: Vandenhoeck & Ruprecht, 1996) 49–66; Ernst Würthwein, *The Text of the Old Testament: An Introduction to the Biblia Hebraica* (2d ed.; Grand Rapids: Eerdmans, 1995).

11 For full discussion, see Josef M. Oesch, *Petucha und Setuma. Untersuchungen zu einer überlieferten Gliederung im hebräischen Text des AT* (OBO 27; Göttingen: Vandenhoeck & Ruprecht, 1979).

12 For a facsimile edition of this text, see D. S. Loewinger (Jerusalem: Maror, 1971). A printed edition appears in F. Pérez Castro, *El codice de Profetas de el Cairo,* 8 vols. (Madrid: CSIC, 1979–1992).

13 For a facsimile edition of the Aleppo Codex, see

Moshe H. Goshen-Gottstein, *The Aleppo Codex: I. Facsimile* (Jerusalem: Magnes Press for the Hebrew University Bible Project, 1976). The Aleppo Codex was housed relatively intact in the Synagogue of Aleppo, Syria, until 1948, when it was partially destroyed by fire in anti-Jewish rioting by the local Syrian population. Although the codex was originally thought to have been completely destroyed, approximately three-quarters of the manuscript were saved from the flames and taken to Israel, where it now resides in the Israel Museum, Jerusalem. For background on the Aleppo Codex, see Moshe H. Goshen-Gottstein, "The Aleppo Codex and the Rise of the Massoretic Bible Text," *BA* 42 (1979) 145–63; Israel Penkower, "Maimonides and the Aleppo Codex," *Textus* 9 (1981) 39–128. Maimonides' comments on the codex appear in his *Mishneh Torah,* II: *Hilkot Sefer Torah* 8:4.

14 For a facsimile edition and introduction, see now David Noel Freedman et al., eds., *The Leningrad Codex: A Facsimile Edition* (Grand Rapids: Eerdmans, 1998). The Leningrad Codex (B 19A) is housed at the Russian National Library (formerly Saltykov-Shchedrin State Public Library), St. Petersburg, Russia (formerly Leningrad, U.S.S.R.).

15 E.g., Karl Elliger and Wilhelm Rudolph, eds., *Biblia hebraica stuttgartensia* (Stuttgart: Deutsche Bibelgesellschaft, 1977).

16 See Mulder, "Transmission," 133–34, for bibliographical data and a full listing of printed editions of the Hebrew Bible.

MT presupposes an earlier proto-masoretic tradition that served as the standard text of the Bible in antiquity. Certainly, the close affinities between the masoretic tradition and the Wadi Murabbaʿat Scroll of the Twelve Prophets from the Judean wilderness lend credence to such a view. Uncritical acceptance of this view is hardly warranted, however, and interpreters must be prepared to examine the variety of textual traditions available in order to reconstruct the earliest demonstrable form(s) of the Hebrew text. Nevertheless, the present commentary indicates that, with only very few exceptions, the MT represents the earliest form of the Hebrew text of Zephaniah.

The *BHS* edition of Zephaniah and the facsimile edition of the Leningrad Codex indicate that the text contains no *pĕtûḥôt*, but that *sĕtûmôt* appear after 1:9; 1:18; 2:4; 2:15; and 3:13 to indicate the masoretic reading of the structure of the book. Consequently, the Leningrad Codex indicates that the structure of the book of Zephaniah comprises six basic segments: 1:1-9; 1:10-18; 2:1-4; 2:5-15; 3:1-13; and 3:14-20.[17] Although explanations for these divisions are not available, they appear to be based on a combination of thematic and linguistic factors. Thus 1:1-9 focuses on the condemnation of apostasy. Zephaniah 1:10-18 begins with the introductory temporal statement, ״וְהָיָה בַיּוֹם הַהוּא נְאֻם ה, "and it shall come to pass on that day, utterance of YHWH," and focuses on the Day of YHWH as a day of punishment and suffering. Zephaniah 2:1-4 begins with the imperative address הִתְקוֹשְׁשׁוּ וָקוֹשּׁוּ הַגּוֹי לֹא נִכְסָף, "gather and assemble, o worthless nation," to introduce an exhortation that calls on the people to seek YHWH before the punishment comes. Zephaniah 2:5-15 begins with the exclamation הוֹי, "Woe!" which introduces a series of oracles concerning foreign nations. Zephaniah 3:1-13 likewise begins with הוֹי, which introduces a section concerned with YHWH's punishment of Jerusalem and Israel at large. Finally, 3:14-20 begins with the imperative address רָנִּי בַת-צִיּוֹן הָרִיעוּ יִשְׂרָאֵל, "Sing, O Daughter Zion! Shout, O Israel!" which introduces a depiction of YHWH's future blessing and restoration for Jerusalem and Israel at large.

Divisions in the other major masoretic manuscripts, however, differ. The Aleppo Codex divides the text as 1:1-11, 12-18; 2:1-4, 5-15; 3:1-13, 14-15, 16-20, employing criteria like that of the Leningrad Codex, that is, the formula וְהָיָה בָּעֵת הַהִיא, "and it shall come to pass at that time," in 1:12, and בַּיּוֹם הַהוּא, "in that day," in 3:16. Likewise, the Cairo Codex divides the text as 1:1-7, 8-9, 10-11, 12-18; 2:1-4, 5-15; 3:1-13, 14-20, employing the statement ״וְהָיָה בְּיוֹם זֶבַח ה, "and it shall come to pass on the day of YHWH's sacrifice," in 1:8.[18]

B. Formal Features: Structure, Genre, and Rhetorical Function

Although the masoretic structure of Zephaniah appears to take valid criteria into consideration, it does not take full account of the linguistic features of this text.[19] Overall, the various divisions represented in the masoretic structures of the text appear to reflect an interest in dividing the text into basic subunits that convey very general themes and syntactical organization. For example, the Leningrad Codex thereby leads the reader through a sequence of texts that convey generally a movement from initial concern with judgment against those who are apostate in Jerusalem and Judah, a call for repentance prior to the judgment, judgment against various nations, judgment against Jerusalem and Israel, and restoration for Jerusalem and Israel. Such a structure, as well as those of the Aleppo and Cairo Codices, may well facilitate a reading of this text in a public liturgical or study setting, but it does not account for the full range of linguistic features, such as syntactic, semantic, and generic characteristics of the text, that form the book of Zephaniah into a well-structured linguistic entity that communicates with its reading or hearing audience. A full assessment of the linguistic structure and communicative functions of Zephaniah must take these features into consideration.

---

17 Although *BHS* indicates the masoretic *sĕtûmôt*, it arranges the text according to very different criteria concerning the editor's view of the structure of the text.

18 See Adele Berlin, *Zephaniah* (AB 25A; New York: Doubleday, 1994) 18.

19 See, e.g., ibid., 19, who simply accepts the masoretic divisions of the text as the basis for her discussion of textual structure.

The following commentary discusses the formal characteristics of Zephaniah in detail, but an overview of the MT form of Zephaniah, including its literary structure, genre, use of prior tradition, and settings, facilitates the overall interpretation of the book.[20]

Although the threefold thematic concerns with judgment against Jerusalem or Israel, judgment against the nations, and (eschatological) salvation for Israel and the nations frequently dominate discussion of the structure of the book, such concerns do not correlate with the linguistic features of the text. Readers must recognize at the outset that a fundamental structural and generic distinction appears between the superscription of the book in 1:1 and the body of the book in 1:2–3:20. The fictive speaker in 1:1 is not the prophet himself, but another anonymous speaker who communicates to the reader information that introduces and identifies the following material that is attributed to the prophet.[21] In that this material is invariably narrative and functions as an introduction to the book as a whole that sets the parameters of its reading, the superscription constitutes the initial statement of the fictive narrator who presents the entire book to the reader. Thus the superscription provides

information concerning the generic character of the book as prophetic oracular material (i.e., "the word of YHWH that was unto Zephaniah"), the identity of the prophet (i.e., "Zephaniah ben Cushi ben Gedaliah ben Amariah ben Hezekiah"), and the historical setting in which the prophecy purportedly took place (i.e., "in the days of Josiah ben Amon, king of Judah"). As a genre, the superscriptions for prophetic books presuppose the social setting of the scribal circles of ancient Judah that preserved the prophetic traditions, composed them into their present forms, and made them available to readers.[22]

Prophetic books frequently contain additional narrative material that, whether or not it was written by the same hand as that of the superscription, constitutes additional statements by the fictive narrator of the book who continues to provide information that will be of use in shaping the reader's perspective and understanding the book's presentation of the prophet (e.g., Isa 7:1-25; 36–39; Hos 1:2—2:3; Amos 7:10-17; Jonah; etc.). In the case of Zephaniah, however, no additional anonymous narrative material appears. Rather, the balance of the book in Zeph 1:2—3:20 is formulated as the words of the

20   For the methodological principles employed here, see Marvin A. Sweeney, "Form Criticism," in Steven L. McKenzie and Stephen R. Haynes, eds., *To Each Its Own Meaning: An Introduction to Biblical Criticisms and Their Application* (Louisville: Westminster John Knox, 1999) 58–89; idem, "Formation and Form in Prophetic Literature," in James L. Mays, David L. Petersen, and Kent H. Richards, eds., *Old Testament Interpretation: Past, Present and Future* (Fest. Gene M. Tucker; Nashville: Abingdon, 1995) 113–26; Rolf Knierim, "Old Testament Form Criticism Reconsidered," *Int* 27 (1973) 435–68; idem, "Criticism of Literary Features, Form, Tradition, and Redaction," in Douglas A. Knight and Gene M. Tucker, eds., *The Hebrew Bible and Its Modern Interpreters* (Chico, Calif.: Scholars Press, 1985) 123–65; idem, *Text*; Walter Gross, *Die Satzteilfolge im Verbalsatz alttestamentlicher Prosa* (FAT 17; Tübingen: Mohr [Siebeck], 1996); Harald Schweizer, *Metaphorische Grammatik. Wege zur Integration von Grammatik und Textinterpretation in der Exegese* (ATSAT 15; St. Ottilien: EOS, 1981); Wolfgang Richter, *Exegese als Literaturwissenschaft. Entwurf einer alttestamentlichen Literaturtheorie und Methodologie* (Göttingen: Vandenhoeck & Ruprecht, 1971); Patricia Tull, "Rhetorical Criticism and Intertextuality," in McKenzie and Haynes, eds.,

To Each Its Own Meaning, 156–80; Phyllis Trible, *Rhetorical Criticism: Context, Method, and the Book of Jonah* (GBS; Minneapolis: Fortress Press, 1994). For studies that attempt to apply these methodological principles to the study of Zephaniah, see esp. Irsigler, *Gottesgericht*; Sweeney, "Form-Critical Reassessment"; Weigl, *Zefanja*; Daniel Hojoon Ryou, *Zephaniah's Oracles Against the Nations: A Synchronic and Diachronic Study of Zephaniah 2:1–3:8* (BibInt 13; Leiden: Brill, 1995); Michael H. Floyd, *Minor Prophets, Part 2* (FOTL 22; Grand Rapids: Eerdmans, 2000) 163–250.

21   Cf. Ehud Ben Zvi, *A Historical-Critical Study of the Book of Zephaniah* (BZAW 198; Berlin: de Gruyter, 1991), esp. 1–20, whose analysis attempts to account for the fictive character of the book's presentation of the narrator and the prophet in Zephaniah. On the basis of his analysis, he maintains that the book must be read as a very late composition.

22   See Gene M. Tucker, "Prophetic Superscriptions and the Growth of the Canon," in George W. Coats and Burke O. Long, eds., *Canon and Authority* (Philadelphia: Fortress Press, 1977) 56–70; Marvin A. Sweeney, *Isaiah 1–39; with an Introduction to Prophetic Literature* (FOTL 16; Grand Rapids: Eerdmans, 1996) 539–40.

prophet Zephaniah, regardless of whether he actually wrote these words in whole or in part.

The reader must pay particular attention to the means by which the text is organized to address its fictive audience in assessing the overall presentation and structure of the prophet's words. Important features include a combination of syntax and semantics as well as the purported speaker, addressee(s), and object(s) of the prophetic speech. Because the text presents Zephaniah as the speaker throughout, identification of the addressee(s) and the object(s) emerge as primary considerations in relation to syntax and semantics. Consideration of these features indicates that the book of Zephaniah constitutes a presentation of the prophet's parenetic address to the people of Jerusalem and Judah/Israel in which he calls on the people to seek YHWH so that they will not be included in the coming punishment on the Day of YHWH of those who are charged with having abandoned the Deity. The text clearly comprises two basic components: the prophet's announcement of the Day of YHWH in 1:2-18, and the prophet's parenetic address to the people in 2:1–3:20 calling on them to seek YHWH before the punishment comes.[23]

The prophet's announcement of the Day of YHWH in 1:2-18 is clearly identified by a combination of linguistic and thematic factors, including speaker, addressee, object of the prophet's speech, and the organization and interrelationship of its basic syntactical subunits. Zephaniah 1:2-18 explicitly identifies no particular addressee; the reader is left to infer from the overall literary context that the prophet addresses the people of Jerusalem and Judah (see v. 4) although he does not employ direct address forms, that is, second person or imperative verbs and pronouns, or state that he is speaking to the people. The text includes three syntactically self-contained subunits to present the sequence of the prophet's speech. First, the prophet relates YHWH's oracles, which speak about those who have abandoned YHWH for foreign gods and practices in vv. 2-6. Second, the prophet speaks about the anticipated punishment that will come to such

persons on the Day of YHWH in vv. 7-13. Third, the prophet reinforces the topic of the preceding subunit by stressing that the Day of YHWH is near while continuing to describe the consequences of apostasy in vv. 14-18. Although each of these subunits is syntactically self-contained, they are related together as a single unit because of the consistent presumption that the people of Jerusalem and Judah are the addressees and their consistent focus on the Day of YHWH as a day of punishment for those who have abandoned YHWH. Altogether, the prophet's announcement of the coming Day of YHWH in 1:2-18 prepares the fictive audience of the prophet's speech—and the reader—for the parenetic address that follows in 2:1–3:20.

The second major unit of the presentation of the prophet's words is the parenetic address to the people of Jerusalem and Judah/Israel in 2:1–3:20. The addressee is identified by the use of second person and imperative plural verbs as well as second person plural pronouns in 2:1-3. Similar forms appear once again in 3:5-13 and 3:14-20 to characterize Jerusalem/Bat Zion and Israel, who are explicitly named as the addressees in 3:14 and elsewhere. It is noteworthy that the characterization of Jerusalem as Bat Zion, "Daughter Zion," entails the use of second feminine singular address forms together with the masculine plural forms that support the characterization of Israel. The use of such direct forms for Jerusalem and Judah/Israel, however, does not appear throughout this text. Nevertheless, the entire text is held together by a combination of thematic and linguistic factors analogous to those of 1:2-18.

First, the shift in address forms at 2:1 coincides with a major syntactical break in the text, that is, 2:1-3 is not joined by a syntactical connector to the preceding material; rather, the imperative address הִתְקוֹשְׁשׁוּ וָקוֹשּׁוּ הַגּוֹי לֹא נִכְסָף, "gather and assemble, O worthless nation," marks the beginning of a new communicative event within the prophet's address, especially since, unlike 1:2-18, 2:1-3 demands a response from the audience, that is, to seek YHWH.

---

23   Contra Floyd, *Minor Prophets*, 171–73, whose strict definition of genres in the text of Zephaniah prompts him to miss how they work together to produce a text that is informed throughout by its dominant parenetic character. Although the parenesis proper appears strictly speaking in 2:1-3, it determines the overall generic character of the prophet's address as represented in Zephaniah.

Second, 2:1-3 is linked syntactically to a brief statement that employs language pertaining to a husband's divorce of his wife to depict the desolation of the four Philistine cities in 2:4. The link is established initially by a syntactically conjunctive causative כִּי, "because," which indicates that the audience's knowledge of the current plight of the Philistines provides a reason why they should respond to the prophet's call. The relationship between 2:1-3 and 2:4 is particularly important because 2:4 then plays a role in joining the two following sections, the oracles concerning the nations in 2:5-15 and the oracles concerning the punishment and restoration of Jerusalem and Judah/Israel in 3:1-20, each of which begins with a הוֹי, "woe," address form, to the parenetic address in 2:1-3. Zephaniah 2:4 clearly relates to the following oracles concerning the nations because of its concern with the Philistine cities, especially since the oracle concerning Philistia begins the sequence of four nations: Philistia, Moab and Ammon, Cush/Ethiopia, and Assyria, in 2:5-15. Only two of the nations within the sequence are directly addressed with second person language—Philistia and Cush/Ethiopia. The oracles concerning Moab–Ammon and Assyria refer to their subjects only with third person language. The inconsistency in address forms indicates that there is not an immediate concern to address the nations themselves; rather, the text is concerned with the underlying addressee of these oracles, which must be the people of Jerusalem and Judah, as indicated in 2:1-3. These oracles are not intended to convey direct threats to the nations mentioned within—it is highly unlikely that anyone in these nations during the late seventh century BCE could be realistically expected to be listening; rather, the oracles are intended to persuade the Jerusalemite and Judean/Israelite audience of YHWH's efficacy in the world so that the people might heed the prophet's call to seek YHWH.

Similar considerations apply to 3:1-20, which comprises three syntactically independent subunits in vv. 1-4, 5-13, and 14-20. The first is a woe oracle addressed to the contentious, defiled city that did not listen to, take instruction from, or trust in her G-d. The city is not explicitly named, but the reference to "her G-d" makes clear that it is Jerusalem. Although the oracle employs third person feminine singular language to portray the city, the initial הוֹי form is generally recognized as a direct address.[24] The feminine singular characterization of the city carries over into the second subunit, vv. 5-13, which attempts to explain that YHWH is doing justice in the world that will include punishment for the nations that punished Jerusalem. Ultimately, the prophet states that the city will fear YHWH and take instruction, and he calls on the people to wait until the time when YHWH will arise to carry out that justice. The feminine singular characterization carries over once again into the third subunit, vv. 14-20, which calls on Jerusalem and Israel to rejoice when the restoration takes place. The characterization of Jerusalem as a bride to whom the husband, YHWH, returns contrasts with the portrayal of the four Philistine cities of 2:4 that are portrayed as divorced wives.[25] By this means, the text attempts to justify Jerusalem's and Judah's/Israel's suffering by claiming that they were subject to punishment for their deeds, but that YHWH is restoring them now that the punishment is completed. Zephaniah 3:1-20 therefore functions analogously to 2:5-15 to persuade the prophet's addressees to accept his initial appeal to seek YHWH in 2:1-3.

This has three important implications for understanding the generic character of the prophet's speech and the book of Zephaniah as a whole. Scholars frequently isolate 2:1-3 as a self-contained formal unit and identify it as an exhortation.[26] First, 2:1-3 must be properly characterized as parenesis, not simply as exhortation, in that it employs both exhortation and admonition in an attempt to persuade its audience; that is, it exhorts the audience to seek YHWH and admonishes the audience by portraying the punishment of the Day of YHWH as

---

24 Sweeney, *Isaiah 1–39*, 543; Delbert Hillers, "*Hôy* and *Hôy*-Oracles: A Neglected Syntactic Aspect," in Carol L. Meyers and Michael O'Connor, eds., *The Word of the Lord Shall Go Forth* (Fest. D. N. Freedman; Winona Lake, Ind.: Eisenbrauns, 1983) 185–88. For a full assessment of the communicative or textual aspects of the "woe" oracle form, see esp.

Christof Hardmeier, *Texttheorie und biblische Exegese. Zur rhetorischen Function der Trauermetaphorik in der Prophetie* (BEvTh 79; Munich: Kaiser, 1978).

25 For discussion of the language of divorce in 2:4, see Lawrence Zalcman, "Ambiguity and Assonance in Zephaniah ii 4," *VT* 36 (1986) 365–71.

26 E.g., A. Vanlier Hunter, *Seek the Lord! A Study of the*

the consequence for failing to do so.[27] Second, 2:1-3 cannot be read in isolation as a self-contained unit. It is clear that 2:1-3 constitutes the basic unit of the prophet's speech as a whole to which the other elements of the speech are subsumed both structurally and generically. Although the announcement of the Day of YHWH in 1:2-18 does not call on the audience to undertake any action, nor does it address the audience directly, this passage nevertheless serves the persuasive task of the whole to convince the audience to accept the prophet's call to seek YHWH in 2:1-3. Likewise, the two הוֹי sequences concerning the nations in 2:5-15 and Jerusalem/Israel in 3:1-20 serve the persuasive agenda that informs 2:1-3 by providing further reasons why the audience should act, that is, YHWH is punishing the nations and YHWH will restore Jerusalem/Israel once the punishment is complete. Zephaniah 2:4 provides the link that makes such a persuasive agenda possible, that is, it articulates YHWH's punishment of a nation as a prelude to the other nations, and it characterizes that nation as a divorced wife to prepare for the metaphorical portrayal of YHWH's return to Jerusalem/Israel as husband to a previously abandoned wife. Although each of these other textual blocks is generically distinct from 2:1-3 when viewed in isolation as a self-contained unit, together they serve the overall agenda of 2:1-3 and therefore must be recognized as components of an essentially parenetic speech.

Third, although the body of the book of Zephaniah may be characterized as the prophet's parenetic speech to the people of Jerusalem and Judah/Israel, this hardly identifies the overarching genre of the book as a whole. As noted above, the superscription in 1:1 introduces the following material and identifies it as a prophetic or oracular speech by Zephaniah in the days of Josiah.

Clearly, the superscription can neither be ignored nor lumped together with the following material. Rather, it constitutes a distinct structural and generic element within the book as a whole, and its position at the head of the book enables it to define the book's overall character. Unfortunately, we do not know the identity of the party that makes this presentation, although the formal features of the superscription indicate an archival and presentational interest that would likely derive from a scribal setting in which texts would be produced for purposes of archiving, instruction, and so on.[28] Because the generic function of the superscription is to introduce or present the following material, the genre of Zephaniah must be recognized as "the presentation of Zephaniah's parenetic speech to Jerusalem/Judah" in which the prophet calls on the audience to seek YHWH. The following diagram represents the structure and generic character of the book and its major subunits:

Presentation of Zephaniah's Parenetic Speech to Jerusalem/Judah in the Days of Josiah:

Parenesis to Seek YHWH   1:1–3:20
  I. Superscription: The Word of YHWH to
     Zephaniah in the Days of Josiah   1:1
 II. The Body of the Book: Zephaniah's
     Parenetic Speech: Seek YHWH   1:2–3:20
    A. Announcement of the Day of YHWH   1:2-18
      1. Report of YHWH's oracular speeches
        concerning punishment of those who
        have abandoned YHWH   1:2-6

Meaning and Function of the Exhortations in Amos, Isaiah, Micah, and Zephaniah (Baltimore: St. Mary's Seminary and University, 1982) 259–70; cf. K. Arvid Tångberg, *Die prophetische Mahnrede: Form- und traditionsgeschichtliche Studien zum prophetischen Umkehrruf* (FRLANT 143; Göttingen: Vandenhoeck & Ruprecht, 1987), esp. 102–3.

27 See Sweeney, *Isaiah 1–39*, 527, for discussion of parenesis. See also Rex Mason, *Preaching the Tradition: Homily and Hermeneutics after the Exile* (Cambridge: Cambridge Univ. Press, 1990), for a discussion of sermonic forms in biblical literature.

28 See David W. Jamieson-Drake, *Scribes and Schools in Monarchic Judah: A Socio-Archeological Approach* (JSOTSup 109; SWBA 9; Sheffield: Almond/ Sheffield Academic Press, 1991). See also Nahman Avigad, *Hebrew Bullae from the Time of Jeremiah: Remnants of a Burnt Archive* (Jerusalem: Israel Exploration Society, 1986), who provides discussion concerning scribal institutions in late-monarchic-period Jerusalem as part of his overall presentation of the bullae found in the ruins of a scribal house purportedly destroyed by the Babylonians in 587/586 BCE (cf. Jeremiah 36).

2. Announcement of the Day of YHWH
   proper   1:7-18
   a. The Day of YHWH is a day of
      punishment   1:7-13
   b. The Day of YHWH is near   1:14-18
B. Parenesis: Seek YHWH and Avoid
  Punishment on the Day of YHWH   2:1–3:20
  1. Parenesis with reason   2:1-4
   a. Parenesis proper   2:1-3
   b. Reason: YHWH has divorced/
      abandoned Philistia   2:4
  2. Elaboration of reason   2:5–3:20
   a. Woe speech illustrating YHWH's
      punishment of nations   2:5-15
   b. Woe speech illustrating YHWH's
      restoration of "wife" Jerusalem/
      Israel once punishment is
      complete   3:1-20

C. The Literary and Sociohistorical Settings of the Text and Its Interpretation

The book of Zephaniah functions in relation to several fundamental literary and sociohistorical settings that play important roles in shaping the interpretation of the book by its readers as well as in facilitating understanding its compositional history and the agendas of its authors.

1. The Masoretic Text Tradition

First and foremost, interpreters must recognize the context in which the primary manuscripts that represent the masoretic version were produced.[29] As noted above, the Aleppo and Leningrad manuscripts were produced respectively in the tenth and early eleventh centuries CE. The Aleppo Codex was pointed by Aaron ben Asher, and the Leningrad Codex was pointed largely in accor-

dance with the teachings of Aaron ben Asher. Aaron ben Asher and his father, Moshe ben Asher, are two of the most respected medieval masoretic scribal authorities. It is uncertain whether the Ben Asher family were associated with the Karaite movement or with rabbinic Judaism in this period.[30] Nevertheless, their work—including the earlier Cairo Codex of the Prophets pointed by Moshe ben Asher—took place at a time when accurate versions of biblical manuscripts were a key issue, both in relation to discussion within Judaism as well as between Judaism and Islam or Christianity. From the time of the rise of Islam in the late seventh century CE and beyond, Muslim theologians had challenged the validity of Judaism and Christianity on various grounds, most notably that the revelation of the Qurʾan represented the most complete and accurate representation of the will of G-d and that the earlier Scriptures of Judaism and Christianity were somehow defective.[31] One dimension of this discussion is the absolutely scrupulous attention by Muslim scribes to the accuracy of the Qurʾanic text. By contrast, the wide variety of manuscript traditions in Christianity, including Greek, Latin, Syriac, Hebrew, and other versions, as well as disputed readings in the Hebrew text of Judaism and the rereadings in the targumic and midrashic literature, would tend to call the authority of these scriptural texts into question on the grounds that such variation demonstrated that they were not fully accurate. Likewise, the emergence of Karaite Judaism beginning in the eighth century, which rejected the talmudic tradition of rabbinic Judaism and called for an understanding of Judaism based on a strict construction derived solely from the biblical text, also

---

29   For current discussion of the masoretic text tradition, see Dominique Barthélemy et al., *Critique textuelle de l'ancien testament,* vol. 3: *Ézéchiel, Daniel, et les 12 Prophètes* (OBO 50/3; Vandenhoeck & Ruprecht, 1992) i–cxvi.

30   See the contrasting viewpoints of Zeev Ben-Hayyim, "Ben-Asher, Aaron ben Moses," *EncJud* 4:465–67; Barthélemy, *Critique textuelle,* xvi–xvii, who hold that the Ben Ashers were Karaites, and Aaron Dothan, "Ben-Asher, Moses," *EncJud* 4:467–69, who holds that Moshe ben Asher could not have been a Karaite. The issue depends in part on an assessment

of Saadiah Gaon's "Essa Meshali," written in reply to a Karaite opponent named Ben Asher that some identify with Aaron ben Asher. It also depends on a poem known as the "Song of the Vine," attributed to Moses ben Asher and found in the Leningrad Codex and several other MSS, which metaphorically portrays Israel as a vine that brings forth the prophets and the sages.

31   For discussion of Muslim disputations with Judaism and Christianity, see Salo Wittmayer Baron, *A Social and Religious History of the Jews,* vol. 5: *High Middle Ages (500–1200): Religious Controls and Dissensions*

prompted concern with the accurate copying of biblical manuscripts.[32] Thus the Aleppo manuscript was written in 925 by the scribe Shelomoh ben Buyaʿa and pointed by Aaron ben Asher to provide such an accurate and authoritative version of the Jewish Bible. It would therefore have been written during the lifetime of Saadiah ben Joseph al-Fayyumi (892–942 CE), Gaon of Sura in Babylonia, who was known for his attempts to refute the arguments of the Karaites.[33] The colophons of the Leningrad Codex (folios 1r, 474r, 478v, 479r, 489r, 491r), on the other hand, indicate that the manuscript was written in Cairo by Shemuel ben Jacob in the month of Sivan, 4,770 years from creation, 1,444 years from Jehoiachin's exile, 1,319 years from the "Greek dominion, 940 years from the destruction of the Temple, and 399 years from the Hijrah of Muhammed."[34] Although there are minor discrepancies among these various calculations of the date, they indicate a date between 1008 and 1010 CE. Shemuel ben Jacob wrote, vocalized, and annotated the manuscript in accordance with the teachings of Aaron ben Asher for a purchaser identified as Meborak ha-Kohen ben Netanʾel, also known as Ozdad ha-Kohen. These manuscripts would have served their respective communities for centuries as authoritative versions of the entire Bible.

2. The Masoretic Book of the Twelve Prophets

Clearly, the time of the production of the masoretic codices is a period much later than the time of the composition of Zephaniah, but no "original" manuscript of Zephaniah exists. The above-noted Wadi Murabbaʿat manuscript of the Twelve Prophets from the second century BCE corresponds largely to the masoretic consonantal text, and thereby provides confirmation of the antiquity of the consonantal text represented in the MT. Particularly noteworthy is the above-mentioned position of the book of Zephaniah within the literary sequence of the masoretic version of the book of the Twelve Prophets. Zephaniah is clearly formulated as a self-contained prophetic book, but it is presented as part of a larger collection of short prophetic books known in Jewish tradition as תרי עשר, "the Twelve," that is, the book of the Twelve Prophets or the Minor Prophets. Although modern scholars have generally focused on the individual books of the Twelve Prophets as discrete literary compositions in isolation from each other, many interpreters have more recently come to recognize that the twelve individual prophetic books have been deliberately placed together so that they will function as a single prophetic book that contains the works of twelve individual prophets.[35]

The sequence of the Twelve Prophets varies markedly between the MT and LXX versions of the book, but each

(2d ed.; Philadelphia: Jewish Publication Society, 1957) 82–94; Daniel J. Lasker, "Polemics," in R. J. Zwi Werblowsky and Geofrey Wigoder, eds., *The Oxford Dictionary of the Jewish Religion* (Oxford: Oxford Univ. Press, 1997) 538–39, and the bibliography cited there. Discussion of disputes between Christianity and Judaism during the Middle Ages appears in Baron, *History*, 5:95–137.

32   For discussion of the Karaite movement in medieval Judaism, see Baron, *History*, 5:209–85; Daniel J. Lasker, "Rabbinism and Karaism: The Contest for Supremacy," in Raphael Jospe and Stanley M. Wagner, eds., *Great Schisms in Jewish History* (New York: KTAV, 1981) 47–72; Nathan Schur, *History of the Karaites* (New York: Lang, 1992). For a selection of Karaite texts that illustrate their outlook, development, and differences with rabbinic Judaism, see Leon Nemoy, ed., *Karaite Anthology* (Yale Judaica Series 7; New Haven: Yale Univ. Press, 1952).

33   In addition to the treatment in Baron, *History*,

5:275–84; idem, *A Social and Religious History of the Jews*, vol. 6: *High Middle Ages (500–1200): Laws, Homilies, and the Bible* (2d ed.; Philadelphia: Jewish Publication Society, 1958) 235–313, see esp. Henry Malter, *Saadia Gaon: His Life and Works* (Philadelphia: Jewish Publication Society, 1942).

34   See the discussion by Victor Lebedev, "The Oldest Complete Codex of the Hebrew Bible," in Freedman et al., eds., *Leningrad Codex*, xxi–xxviii.

35   See, e.g., Sweeney, *Twelve Prophets*; Nogalski and Sweeney, eds., *Reading and Hearing the Book of the Twelve*; James D. Nogalski, *Literary Precursors to the Book of the Twelve* (BZAW 217; Berlin: de Gruyter, 1993); idem, *Redactional Processes in the Book of the Twelve* (BZAW 218; Berlin: de Gruyter, 1993); Barry Alan Jones, *The Formation of the Book of the Twelve: A Study in Text and Canon* (SBLDS 149; Atlanta: Scholars Press, 1995); Aaron Schart, *Die Entstehung des Zwölfprophetenbuchs* (BZAW 260; Berlin: de Gruyter, 1998).

sequence appears to reflect a unique hermeneutical perspective.[36] The LXX orders the books as Hosea, Amos, Micah, Joel, Obadiah, Jonah, Nahum, Habakkuk, Zephaniah, Haggai, Zechariah, and Malachi, which reflects a concern to present prophets who addressed issues pertaining to the northern kingdom of Israel (i.e., Hosea, Amos, Micah), which fell to the Assyrian Empire in 722/721 BCE, prior to those books that address issues pertaining to Jerusalem and Judah from the monarchic period through the Babylonian period and the restoration of the Second Temple. In such a sequence, the experience of the northern kingdom of Israel becomes a model for that of Jerusalem and the southern kingdom of Judah. Such an agenda is especially evident in the placement of Micah, which explicitly draws an analogy between northern Israel and southern Judah, as the third of the three books that take up northern Israel immediately prior to Joel, which focuses specifically on Jerusalem and heads the sequence of the balance of the Twelve.

The MT, however, presents the sequence Hosea, Joel, Amos, Obadiah, Jonah, Micah, Nahum, Habakkuk, Zephaniah, Haggai, Zechariah, and Malachi, which places books that address the northern kingdom of Israel in the midst of those that address Jerusalem and Judah. Thus the masoretic version of the Twelve focuses specifically on Jerusalem from the outset, especially since Hosea maintains that northern Israel's repentance and restoration entails unification with Judah under the rule of a single Davidic monarch (see esp. Hosea 3; 14). It thereby presents a process whereby Jerusalem is punished for the actions of the people of Israel and Judah so that it will be purged to serve as the holy center for YHWH's sovereignty over all the nations and creation at large.

Although the sequence of the Twelve differs in the MT and LXX versions of the book, Zephaniah occupies the same position in both as the ninth of the Twelve Prophets, immediately following Habakkuk and preceding Haggai. This is especially noteworthy because Habakkuk addresses the threat posed to Jerusalem and Judah by the Neo-Babylonian Empire, which became a factor only in 605 BCE when the Babylonians defeated Egypt and took control of Judah. Likewise, Haggai takes up issues pertaining to the rebuilding of the temple in Jerusalem, which reflects the early Persian period in 520–515 BCE when Jews returning to Jerusalem in the aftermath of the Babylonian Empire undertook the building of the Second Temple. A chronological reading of this sequence would suggest that Zephaniah addresses the intervening period between that of Habakkuk and that of Haggai when the Babylonians attacked and destroyed Jerusalem and carried off major elements of the surviving population into exile. Nevertheless, the superscription of the book clearly places Zephaniah in the reign of King Josiah of Judah (640–609 BCE), who ruled during the period prior to the Babylonian subjugation and destruction of Judah. Insofar as Zephaniah calls for the people of Jerusalem and Judah to return to YHWH in order to avoid the punishment of the Day of YHWH, the placement of the book between Habakkuk and Haggai suggests a hermeneutical perspective that would maintain that the people of Jerusalem and Judah failed to heed to prophet's call and thereby suffered the consequences as G-d brought the Babylonians upon the nation as a means to carry out the punishment threatened in Zephaniah.

3. The Sociohistorical Settings of the Book of the Twelve Prophets

The organization of the final forms of both the MT and LXX versions of the Twelve also raises questions concerning their respective sociohistorical contexts and history of composition. The MT version of the Twelve Prophets, with its focus on Jerusalem throughout, appears to presuppose a setting in which Jerusalem is viewed as the undisputed center of Jewish life and the world at large. Such a perspective appears to presuppose the reestablishment of Jerusalem and the building of the Second Temple during the first part of the Second Temple period, from the time of the rebuilding of the temple under the high priest Joshua ben Jehozadak and Zerubbabel, the Davidic governor of Judah, through the time of the restoration of Jerusalem and the temple as the center of Judean life in the times of Nehemiah and Ezra

---

36 For full discussion, see Sweeney, "Sequence"; idem, *Twelve Prophets,* xv–xxix; idem, "The Place and Function of Joel in the Book of the Twelve," *SBLSP,* *1999* (Atlanta: Society of Biblical Literature, 1999) 570–95.

during the later fifth and early fourth centuries BCE. Indeed, the production of a Jerusalem-centered book of the Twelve Prophets during this period would correspond with the production of the full form of the book of Isaiah,[37] the masoretic version of the book of Jeremiah,[38] and the books of Ezekiel, Ezra-Nehemiah, and 1-2 Chronicles, all of which focus especially on Jerusalem and were produced through the fourth century BCE.[39] The focus on the fate of the northern kingdom of Israel as a model for that of Judah corresponds with the perspectives of the so-called Deuteronomistic History in Joshua, Judges, 1-2 Samuel, and 1-2 Kings; the late-seventh-century edition of the book of Isaiah; and the LXX version of the book of Jeremiah, each of which emphasizes that the experience of the northern kingdom of Israel provides a model for Jerusalem and Judah.[40] The composition of each of these works appears to reflect the earlier concerns of the reign of King Josiah, who apparently sought to solidify his rule over Judah and extend it over the north by stressing the need to reform Judah and northern Israel from past actions that were portrayed as contrary to YHWH's will. The composition of all three works extends into the period of the Babylonian exile, and reflects an interest in explaining Jerusalem's and Judah's demise in relation to the people's failure to learn the lessons taught by the experience of the northern kingdom under the Assyrians.

It is especially noteworthy, therefore, that interpreters have noticed a correlation between the books of Hosea, Amos, Micah, and Zephaniah, in that their respective superscriptions appear to be formulated similarly.[41] Hosea 1:1; Amos 1:1; Mic 1:1; and Zeph 1:1 each employs a compositional scheme, distinct from that of the other prophets among the Twelve, that combines a generic designation for the words or oracles of the prophet, identification of the prophet by name and ancestry, and a chronology statement that places the prophet's activity in relation to a set of named kings of Judah (and Israel). This correlation has implications for establishing the possibility that an early form of the book of the Twelve included only the works of these four prophets. This is especially intriguing when one considers that Zephaniah is presented as a composition from the time of Josiah and that Hosea, Amos, and Micah are all placed in the late eighth century. Nevertheless, Hosea, Amos, and Micah each would have been available for reading in some form during the seventh century, and each clearly underwent a process of redactional recomposition that enabled them to address later periods in Judean history. Although the present forms of these books are frequently read as exilic or postexilic compositions, their respective foci on the restoration of northern Israel under the rule of a righteous Davidic monarch clearly serves the interests of King Josiah's program of religious reform and national restoration. The hypothesis must be considered tentative, but it appears possible that a combination of these four books in some earlier form may well have constituted a Josianic edition of the four "minor" prophets. Such a collection would have provided prophetic support for the king's reform program that could be traced back to the eighth-century prophets as well as to Zephaniah. Such support would have included calls for repentance and a return to YHWH as well as the rule of a righteous Davidic king over a unified people in keeping with the overall goals of Josiah's reform.

---

37 See Sweeney, *Isaiah 1–39*; Christopher R. Seitz, *Zion's Final Destiny: The Development of the Book of Isaiah* (Minneapolis: Fortress Press, 1991).

38 See Hermann-Josef Stipp, *Das masoretische und alexandrinische Sondergut des Jeremiabuches: Textgeschichtlicher Rang, Eigenarten, Triebkräfte* (OBO 136; Göttingen: Vandenhoeck & Ruprecht, 1994); Jack R. Lundbom, *Jeremiah 1–20* (AB 21A; New York: Doubleday, 1999).

39 See Walther Zimmerli, *Ezekiel* (2 vols.; Hermeneia; Philadelphia: Fortress Press, 1979–1983); Joseph Blenkinsopp, *Ezra-Nehemiah: A Commentary* (OTL; Philadelphia: Westminster, 1988); Sara Japhet, *1 & 2 Chronicles: A Commentary* (OTL; Louisville: Westminster John Knox, 1993).

40 See Sweeney, *King Josiah*; Stipp, *Sondergut*; Lundbom, *Jeremiah 1–20*.

41 See Aaron Schart, *Die Entstehung des Zwölfprophetenbuchs. Neubearbeitungen von Amos im Rahmen schriftenübergreifender Redaktionsprozesse* (BZAW 260; Berlin: de Gruyter, 1998), esp. 31–49.

4. The Sociohistorical Setting of the Book of Zephaniah

These concerns also raise questions about the compositional history of the book of Zephaniah itself. Many scholars maintain that the present form of the book is the product of extensive exilic or postexilic redaction that produced the threefold eschatologically informed structure of punishment against Jerusalem/Judah/Israel, punishment against the nations, and restoration/salvation for Israel and the nations.[42] Clearly, the position of Zephaniah in both the MT and LXX versions of the book of the Twelve indicates that the book can be read in relation to the destruction of Jerusalem and the Babylonian exile and all of its implications for further constructive theological reflection concerning divine action in human history for both Judaism and Christianity. Nevertheless, such a reading of Zephaniah entails only that the book can be read in this fashion; it does not require that the book be redactionally reformulated for such a scheme. Indeed, examination of the structure of the book indicates that it is not structured according to this threefold scheme at all. Furthermore, the so-called universal elements of the book, such as the references to the destruction of animals and human beings at the outset in 1:2-3 and the oracles against the nations in 2:(4)5-15, must be qualified. The references to creation reflect the role of the temple as the center of creation in ancient Judean thought from the outset; the references to creation at large do not presuppose postexilic redaction.[43] YHWH's role as creator is evident throughout preexilic works such as the J traditions of the Pentateuch, Deuteronomy, the first part of Isaiah, Hosea, and so on, as well as in later works, such as Second Isaiah, Ezekiel, and the P tradition of the Pentateuch. Furthermore, the nations mentioned in Zephaniah, that is,

Philistia, Moab and Ammon, Cush, and Assyria, do not represent a universal compendium of all the nations of the earth; they are simply the nations that most directly concern Judah and the prophet's hermeneutical perspective in the late seventh century.[44] The nations are cited because they are of direct interest to a Josian setting, as nations bordering Judah/Israel that held portions of the Israelite/Judean population or its territory (Philistia, Moab and Ammon), or nations whose demise, whether past or impending, demonstrates YHWH's efficacy in the world (Cush, Assyria).

Overall, the presence of a superscription in 1:1 demonstrates that the book was subject to redactional activity in that it clearly reflects the hand and interests of a writer other than the prophet himself. But as the above considerations indicate, that writer was likely a scribe from the time of King Josiah who wrote to introduce and identify the oracles of Zephaniah and perhaps placed them together with Hosea, Amos, and Micah as an early version of the book of the four "minor" prophets. Unlike what one finds in Hosea, Amos, and Micah, or larger prophetic works such as Isaiah and Jeremiah, the following commentary demonstrates no major redactional work in the book of Zephaniah. Only minor instances of glossing for various reasons appear in Zeph 1:3aβ ("and those who cause the righteous to stumble"), perhaps 1:4bβ[4-5] ("with the priests"), and perhaps 3:20. Of course, modern readers can never confirm with absolute certainty that all of 1:2—3:20 (with the exception of potential glosses) represents the words of the historical prophet Zephaniah, but analysis of the overall form and content of the book indicates that this is very likely the case.

The superscription for the book places the prophet in the reign of King Josiah ben Amon of Judah (640–609

---

42 For an overview of recent discussion, see Sweeney, *CurBS* 7 (1999) 119–45. See esp. G. Langhor, "Le livre de Sophonie et la critique d'authenticité," *EThL* 52 (1976) 1–27; idem, "Rédaction et composition du livre de Sophonie," *Mus* 89 (1976) 51–73; B. Renaud, *Michée–Sophonie–Nahum* (Sources bibliques; Paris: Gabalda, 1987); idem, "Le livre de Sophonie: Le jour de YHWH thème structurant de la synthèse rédactionnelle," *RevScRel* 60 (1986) 1–33; Klaus Seybold, *Satirische Prophetie: Studien zum Buch Zefanja* (SBS 120; Stuttgart: Katholisches Bibelwerk, 1985); idem, *Nahum–Habakuk–Zephanja* (ZBK 24.2; Zurich:

Theologischer Verlag, 1991).

43 Cf. Floyd, *Minor Prophets,* 173–79.

44 E.g., Duane Christensen, "Zephaniah 2:4-15: A Theological Basis for Josiah's Program of Political Expansion," *CBQ* 46 (1984) 669–82.

BCE), who came to the throne at the age of eight following the assassination of his father Amon ben Manasseh (see 2 Kgs 21:19-26; 2 Chr 33:21-25). At the time of the young king's ascent to the throne, Judah had been a vassal of the Assyrian Empire for nearly a century from the time of Ahaz's submission to Assyria during the course of the Syro-Ephraimite War (735–732 BCE; see 2 Kings 16; 2 Chronicles 28; Isaiah 7), the destruction of the northern kingdom of Israel (2 Kings 17), the revolt of Hezekiah (2 Kings 18–20; 2 Chronicles 29–32), and the long rule of Manasseh, who was known for suppressing dissent in the kingdom (2 Kgs 21:1-18; 2 Chr 33:1-20).[45] At the time of the death of Manasseh in 642, however, Assyria's long history of hegemony in western Asia was coming to an end. Although the Assyrians had succeeded in subduing Egypt during the reigns of Esarhaddon and Ashurbanipal beginning in 671, the Assyrians found that they were unable to maintain full control of Egypt on their own. The nature of the arrangement is not entirely clear, but it appears that the Assyrians established the Saite Dynasty of northern Egypt to rule the country on their behalf following the Assyrian defeat of the Twenty-fifth Ethiopian Dynasty. The Saite Pharaoh Psamtek I was able to unite Egypt under his rule by 656, but he appears to have done so as a vassal or ally of Assyria; his subsequent rule shows a decided interest in supporting both his own interests as well as those of his Assyrian overlords or allies. The Assyrians for their part were apparently occupied with problems of their own. Under the rule of Ashurbanipal's brother Shamash-shum-ukin, Babylonia revolted in 652, and Ashurbanipal was forced to put down the revolt in a bloody war that lasted until 648. By 646 Ashurbanipal had also subdued his late brother's Elamite allies, but the Babylonian revolt marked the beginning of Assyria's decline. Assyria

remained secure for the balance of Ashurbanipal's life, but with the death of the king, at some time between 631 or 627, the Assyrian Empire began to come apart. Although the sequence of events is not entirely clear, it appears that Babylon, supported by the Medes, revolted once again under the rule of Nabopolassar at some point between 626 and 616. By 614 the Babylonians and Medes destroyed the ancient Assyrian capital at Ashur. Nineveh fell in 612, the remnants of the Assyrian army were destroyed in 609 at Haran. Although Pharaoh Neco II of Egypt, the son of Psamtek, attempted to support his Babylonian allies, he was apparently delayed at Megiddo by an encounter with King Josiah. Neco put Josiah to death at Megiddo (2 Kgs 23:28-30; 2 Chr 35:20-27), but the encounter prevented his reaching Haran in time to join the battle.

The causes and circumstances of Amon's assassination are not entirely clear, but there is speculation that it was prompted by a faction of the royal court that called for revolt against Assyria following the long period of submission to Assyrian hegemony under Manasseh.[46] Indeed, the Assyrian withdrawal from Egypt and the difficulties faced by the Assyrians in putting down the Babylonian revolt of 652–648 may well have prompted such an action. Judah appears to have remained quiet during the early years of Josiah's reign, but the biblical sources indicate that the young king began to seek G-d in his eighth year (2 Chr 34:3) and undertake religious reforms in either his twelfth (2 Chr 34:3) or eighteenth year (2 Kgs 22:3; 2 Chr 34:8). Josiah's eighth year would have been 632, immediately prior to Ashurbanipal's death; his twelfth year would have been 628, when it was clear that Assyria was in a weakened position; and his eighteenth year would have been 622, by which time the Babylonian revolt under Nabopolassar would have been

45 For overviews of Judean history during these periods, see the essays by Herbert Donner, "The Separate States of Israel and Judah," and Bustenay Oded, "Judah and the Exile," in John H. Hayes and J. Maxwell Miller, eds., *Israelite and Judaean History* (OTL; Philadelphia: Westminster, 1977) 381–434, 435–88. For treatment of general ancient Near Eastern history during these periods, see Amélie Kuhrt, *The Ancient Near East, c. 3000–330 BC* (London: Routledge, 1998) 456–546, 573–646; William W. Hallo and William Kelley Simpson, *The Ancient Near East: A History* (New York: Harcourt, Brace, Jova-

novich, 1971) 125–49, 284–98; Donald B. Redford, *Egypt, Canaan, and Israel in Ancient Times* (Princeton: Princeton Univ. Press, 1992) 338–64, 430–69; John Brinkman in *CAH* III/2:143–45.

46 See Oded, "Judah and the Exile," in Hayes and Miller, eds., *History,* 456; and esp. Abraham Malamat, "The Historical Background of the Assassination of Amon King of Judah," *IEJ* 3 (1953) 26–29.

organized and perhaps underway. Despite the uncertainties of the situation, it appears that Josiah's religious reforms were motivated in part by an interest in establishing Judah's independence from Assyrian control and in reestablishing the Davidic dynasty's rule over all of the territory of the twelve tribes of Israel. The writing of biblical literature during this period, including the production of a Josian edition of the so-called Deuteronomistic History in Joshua, Judges, Samuel, and Kings, and the redaction of earlier eighth-century prophetic writings by Isaiah, Hosea, Amos, and perhaps Micah, indicate an interest in portraying Josiah as the righteous Davidic monarch who would purge the land of its idolatry and restore YHWH as the G-d of all Israel worshiped in Jerusalem.[47]

The parenetic nature of Zephaniah's speech, with its call to purge Jerusalem and Judah of syncretistic religious practice, presupposes a setting of public discourse in which the prophet would have called on the people to seek YHWH and reject pagan religious practice. Indeed, Zephaniah appears to cite or allude to earlier biblical tradition to support his own call for adherence to YHWH. Many have noted the allusions to the creation traditions of Genesis at the outset of the book in Zeph 1:2-3, although the terminology suggests that Zephaniah did not employ the present text of Genesis. Many have also noted that Zephaniah's calls for the rejection of pagan religious practice and the threats of punishment for continued apostasy dovetails with the general perspective of Deuteronomy, although there is little in the way of specific citation of texts. Like Hosea (chaps. 1–3), Jeremiah (chap. 2), and later Second Isaiah (chap. 54) and Ezekiel (chap. 16), the prophet employs the metaphor of a marriage relationship to depict the nation as the bride of YHWH to whom YHWH is returning after a period of separation (see esp. Zeph 3:14-20; cf. 2:4; contra Deut 24:1-4).[48] Perhaps the most noteworthy use of earlier tradition by the prophet is his clear dependence on the language and ideas of Isaiah, including his

use of the "outstretched hand" of YHWH (Zeph 1:4; cf. Isa 5:25; 9:11, 16, 20; 10:4); the Day of YHWH tradition (Zeph 1:7, 14-16, 18; 2:1-3; 3:8; cf. Isa 2:6-21; 13; 22; 34) and the related references to "that day" (Zeph 1:8, 10; 3:11, 16) and "that time" (1:12; 3:19, 20) that also appear throughout First Isaiah; the oracles concerning the nations (2:4, 5-15; Isaiah 13–23), particularly the condemnation of Assyria (Zeph 2:13-15; Isa 10:5-34; 14:24-27); the depiction of the apostate as drunks (Zeph 1:12-13; cf. Isa 5:8-24); the decimation of the people into a poor and humble remnant (Zeph 3:12-13; cf. Isa 1:9; 6:12-13; 7:1-9; 10:20-24; cf. 3:14, 15; 10:2; 11:4; 29:19); the dispersion of the people beyond the rivers of Cush (Zeph 3:10; cf. Isa 18:1); the downfall of the haughty and proudly exultant (Zeph 3:11; cf. Isa 2:6-21; 13); the restoration of Jerusalem the mother and bride (Zeph 3:14-20; contra Isa 3:25—4:1; 8:5-10), and so on.[49] It would appear that Zephaniah saw himself in continuity with Isaiah, perhaps indicating that the time for the full fulfillment of the eighth-century prophet's oracles had now arrived. Given his above-noted depiction of Jerusalem as the restored bride of YHWH and the restoration of the exiles, Zephaniah may also provide a link in the development of the Isaian tradition in Second and Third Isaiah.

The specific concern with the purity of the temple as the holy center of creation and the use of sacrificial imagery on the Day of YHWH to purge the nation of idolatry indicate that the temple would be a likely setting for the prophet's speech, because of its central role in the religious life and theological perspective of the nation and because it is the most likely place to find people assembled for the public celebration of festivals. Indeed, Jeremiah's famous temple sermon, presented in Jeremiah 7 (cf. Jeremiah 26), in which he argued that the presence of the temple alone did not ensure the security

47   For full discussion of the Deuteronomistic and prophetic literature during this period, see Sweeney, *King Josiah*.

48   For treatment of the marriage metaphor in prophetic literature, see now Gerlinde Baumann, *Liebe und Gewalt: Die Ehe als Metaphor für das Verhältnis JHWH–Israel in den Prophetenbüchern* (SBS 185;

Stuttgart: Katholisches Bibelwerk, 2000). Like other scholars who treat this topic, she does not discuss Zephaniah.

49   Cf. H. L. Ginsberg, "Gleanings in First Isaiah," in Moshe Davis, ed., *Mordecai M. Kaplan Jubilee Volume on the Occasion of His Seventieth Birthday* (New York: Jewish Theological Seminary of America, 1953)

of Jerusalem and Judah, provides a fitting analogy to Zephaniah's discourse.[50] The cycle of speeches presented in the book of Amos represents a similar prophetic effort to speak publically in the ancient Israelite temple at Bethel, although the prophet's goals were to call for the destruction of the Bethel temple, the downfall of the ruling Israelite monarch, and the restoration of Davidic rule over the northern kingdom of Israel.[51] Other prophetic sermons may well represent similar prophetic temple addresses (e.g., Isa 1:10-20).

These considerations suggest that Zephaniah spoke in support of King Josiah's reform program during the early years of the king's reign. Some features of the book, however, have prompted interpreters to question this view, but the objections can be answered in each case. First, although the book calls for the purge of syncretistic religious practice, the reference to the removal of "the remnant of Baal" in Zeph 1:4 suggests that Josiah's reform had failed; that is, the presence of a "remnant of Baal" indicates that syncretistic elements had survived the king's efforts to reemerge following his death in 609 BCE.[52] Such a view is unwarranted, however, in that the phrase "remnant of Baal" simply indicates idiomatic usage of the term to convey the complete eradication of Baal worship down to the last remnant.[53]

Second, although many interpreters view the oracles concerning the nations in 2:(4)5-15 as a portrayal of eschatological world judgment that must derive from the postexilic period, the very selective listing of nations, Philistia, Moab and Ammon, Cush, and Assyria, hardly point to a worldwide scenario.[54] Instead, they list nations

that are of direct concern to Josiah's Judah because they control Israelites and Judeans and occupy Israelite/Judean territory (Philistia, Moab and Edom) or because they are the suzerain state that is about to fall (Assyria). Cush poses problems because the Assyrians and their Saite allies had defeated the Twenty-fifth Ethiopian Dynasty some thirty years prior to Josiah's reign. The demise of Cush indicates YHWH's power in the world, and it appears that Josiah's Judah initially saw the Egyptian defeat of Cush and its advance against Philistia in the late seventh century as a sign of the impending downfall of Assyria. Although some scholars maintain that Josiah acted as a loyal ally of Assyria throughout his reign and dutifully submitted to Egyptian rule in keeping with its perception of Egypt's role as Assyria's ally, Josiah's death at the hands of Neco at Megiddo in 609 hardly represents the recognition of Josiah's loyalty.[55] Rather, it appears that Josiah saw in Egypt's rise the demise of Assyria and the opportunity to establish Judean independence, but he apparently miscalculated and lost his life as a result. The alliance of Josiah's great-grandfather Hezekiah with Babylon (see Isaiah 39; 2 Kgs 20:12-19) and Neco's removal of his son Jehoahaz to be replaced by the pro-Egyptian Jehoiakim after Josiah's death indicates that Josiah went to Megiddo as a Babylonian ally. Josiah's goal would have been to stop the Egyptians before they would be able to support their Assyrian allies against the Babylonians.

Third, many interpreters see the references to Israelite or Judean exiles in Cush in 3:10 and to "remnant of Israel" that will be left in 3:12-13 as clear indica-

245–59, esp. 258–59. For specific discussion of Zephaniah's use of Isaiah, see the following commentary.

50   For discussion of Jeremiah's temple sermon, see esp. Jay A. Wilcoxen, "The Political Background of Jeremiah's Temple Sermon," in Arthur L. Merrill and Thomas W. Overholt, eds., *Scripture in History and Theology: Essays in Honor of J. Coert Rylaarsdam* (PTMS 17; Pittsburgh: Pickwick, 1977) 151–66.

51   See Sweeney, *Twelve Prophets*, 189–276; idem, "Formation and Form in Prophetic Literature," in Mays, Petersen, and Richards, eds., *Old Testament Interpretation*, 113–26.

52   E.g., J. Philip Hyatt, "The Date and Background of Zephaniah," *JNES* 7 (1948) 25–29; Donald L. Williams, "The Date of Zephaniah," *JBL* 82 (1963) 77–88.

53   Cf. Johannes Vlaardingerbroek, *Zephaniah* (Historical Commentary on the Old Testament; Leuven: Peeters, 1999) 13–17.

54   See Berlin, *Zephaniah*, 117–24, who understands the four nations listed to represent the cardinal points of the compass and thus all of the nations.

55   E.g., J. Maxwell Miller and John H. Hayes, *A History of Ancient Israel and Judah* (Philadelphia: Westminster, 1986) 363–402, esp. 387–402; Gösta W. Ahlström, *The History of Ancient Palestine* (Minneapolis: Fortress Press, 1993) 763–69. Ahlström's contention that Josiah was a vassal or ally of Egypt is based on the references to Judah's submission to Egypt and Assyria in Jer 2:18, 36. Ahlström misses the point that Jeremiah 2 depicts Judah's relations with Egypt and Assyria at the outset of Josiah's program of religious reform and national restoration.

tions of a postexilic perspective.[56] Readers must bear in mind, however, the role that the Babylonian exile plays in shaping the perspectives of later readers of this and other biblical texts. Although the Babylonian exile was clearly the definitive event in Judean experience from the sixth century on, both Israel and Judah had experienced exile from the ninth through the seventh centuries. Israel lost the Transjordan to Moab and Aram in the ninth century so that the tribes of Reuben, Gad, and half of Manasseh came under foreign control at this time.[57] Furthermore, the Assyrian annexation of former Israelite territory in the Transjordan, Galilee, and Mediterranean coast as Assyrian provinces in the aftermath of the Syro-Ephraimite War would continue the exile of Israelites under foreign rule.[58] The later Assyrian exile of Israelites following the destruction of the kingdom in 722/721, either to Mesopotamia and Media as 2 Kgs 17:5-6 maintains or to Philistia as archeological excavation of Tel Miqne (i.e., Philistine Ekron) indicates, likewise demonstrates that references to Israelite or Judean exiles and concern with their recovery was likely in the seventh century.[59] Although Judah was not destroyed by the Assyrians, many Judeans would have been moved to Philistia as well in the aftermath of Sennacherib's invasion of 701 in which he ravaged the Judean Shephelah and turned much of its territory and population over to the control of his loyal Philistine vassals. Many other Israelites and Judeans would have fled to Egypt to escape the carnage brought upon their respective nations by the Assyrians. Josiah's program represented an attempt not only to reform the religious practice of the nation by restoring the centrality of the worship of YHWH at the Jerusalem Temple, but also to restore the integrity of the twelve tribes of Israel under the rule of a righteous Davidic monarch. The key step in such a program would be to recover the territories and population lost to Assyria and its Phoenician, Moabite, and Ammonite allies and thereby to attract the return of those who had taken sanctuary in lands as far away as Cush or elsewhere.

Zephaniah's parenetic speech calls for repentance and a renewed commitment to YHWH, and holds out the possibility of national restoration and the return of the exiles as the outcome of such a commitment. Although the prophet's scenario of impending punishment and restoration fits well with Deuteronomy's overall portrayal of reward and punishment for adherence to YHWH's expectations, the absence of specific reference to Deuteronomy suggests that the prophet's speech might well be placed in the early years of Josiah's reign and reform, prior to the discovery of the "book of Torah," that is, most likely an early form of Deuteronomy, in Josiah's eighteenth year (2 Kgs 22:3; 2 Chr 34:8; cf. 2 Chr 34:3, which traces aspects of Josiah's reform to his eighth and twelfth years). Zephaniah, therefore, would have served as an early voice calling for support at the outset of Josiah's reform program.

The prophet refers to these relations in the context of a call to return to YHWH (4:1-4); such a return entails rejection of Judah's alliances with Egypt and Assyria that had been maintained from the time that Assyria, with the assistance of the Saite Dynasty, had taken control of Egypt. For discussion of this text, see Sweeney, "Structure and Redaction in Jeremiah 2–6," in A. R. Pete Diamond, Kathleen M. O'Connor, and Louis Stuhlman, eds., *Troubling Jeremiah* (JSOTSup 260; Sheffield: Sheffield Academic Press, 1999) 200–218; idem, *King Josiah*.

56 See, e.g., Vlaardingerbroek, *Zephaniah*, 189–94.

57 The mid-ninth-century Moabite Stone announces Moab's victory over Israel and dispossession of Israelite territory east of the Jordan. For translation and discussion, see *ANET*, 320–21; Andrew Dearman, ed., *Studies in the Mesha Inscription and Moab* (SBLABS 2; Atlanta: Scholars Press, 1989).

58 See esp. Albrecht Alt, "Das System der assyrischen Provinzen auf dem Boden des Reiches Israel," *KS* 2:188–205.

59 See Seymour Gitin, "Tel Miqne-Ekron: A Type-Site for the Inner Coastal Plain in the Iron Age II Period," in Seymour Gitin and William G. Dever, eds., *Recent Excavations in Israel: Studies in Iron Age Archaeology* (AASOR 49; Winona Lake: Eisenbrauns, 1989) 23–58; idem, "Incense Altars from Ekron, Israel, and Judah," *ErIsr* 20 (1989) 52*–67*; idem, "Seventh-Century B.C.E. Cultic Elements at Ekron," *Biblical Archaeology Today, 1990: Proceedings of the Second International Conference on Biblical Archaeology* (Jerusalem: Israel Exploration Society, 1993) 248–

II. The Septuagint Version

A. Origins

The basic Greek text of the book of Zephaniah appears as part of the larger *Dodekapropheton* or book of the Twelve Prophets in the LXX text of the Christian Old Testament (OT).[60] Although the oldest currently extant manuscripts of the LXX are clearly written by later Christian scribes, the so-called Alexandrian version of the LXX is believed to have originated in the Greek-speaking Jewish community of Alexandria in the mid-third century BCE. According to the *Letter of Aristeas,* a second-century BCE Jewish pseudepigraph that was written to explain the origins of the LXX,[61] the Ptolemaic Egyptian monarch Ptolemy II Philadelphus (reigned 285–247 BCE) commissioned a Greek translation of the Jewish Torah as part of his efforts to include all known books of the world in his famed library at Alexandria. At Ptolemy's request, Eleazar, the high priest in Jerusalem, sent to Alexandria seventy-two scholars, six from each of the tribes of Israel, who worked on the island of Pharos for a period of seventy-two days to complete the translation. The completed work was approved by both the Alexandrian Jewish community and by the king, and both purportedly took measures to see that the translation would be scrupulously preserved. Later Christian patristic tradition maintains that the seventy-two (or seventy according to some) scholars worked separately, but provided identical translations because they were divinely inspired. Patristic literature also maintains that the "Seventy" translated the entire Bible.

Although the *Aristeas* account and the traditions derived from it are clearly legendary, interpreters maintain that they indicate the likelihood of the Ptolemaic Egyptian origins of the Greek translation of Jewish Scripture beginning in the third century BCE. Jews first settled in Alexandria, perhaps as early as the foundation of the city under Alexander the Great in 331 BCE,[62] and generally flourished under the rule of the Ptolemies until the beginning of the Roman era in 30 BCE when their economic position and relations with the Greek population began to deteriorate due to Roman tax measures and questions concerning their status as citizens. The *Letter of Aristeas* and later comments by Philo and Josephus point to the high esteem in which the LXX, so-called because of the tradition of the seventy-two scholars, was held by the Egyptian Jewish community. Most scholars maintain that the LXX originated in the practice of providing Greek translations of the Torah and other texts for liturgical and instructional use in the synagogues of Alexandrian Judaism and perhaps other locations in Hellenistic Egypt. The appearance of characteristic Egyptian Greek terminology indicates that the Torah was indeed translated in Egypt, perhaps by Judean or Judean-trained scholars, as early as the third century BCE, and references to "the Prophets and the other books" in the prologue to Ben Sirach indicate that the Prophets and at least some of the Writings followed in the second century BCE. Scholars likewise agree that the LXX is a composite work in that the translation technique varies throughout the various books of the Bible. They differ, however, as to the process by which the LXX

58; idem, "Ekron of the Philistines, Part II: Olive Oil Suppliers to the World," *BARev* 16 (1990) 32–42, 59.

60   For critical editions of the LXX text of Zephaniah, see Joseph Ziegler, *Septuaginta: Vetus Testamentum Graecum,* vol. 13: *Duodecim Prophetae* (3d ed.; Göttingen: Vandenhoeck & Ruprecht, 1984); and Alfred Rahlfs, *Septuaginta* (2 vols.; 9th ed.; Stuttgart: Württembergische Bibelanstalt, 1935). For full discussion of the LXX, its derivative versions, and the issues taken up below, see Henry Barclay Swete, *An Introduction to the Old Testament in Greek* (1902; reprinted New York: KTAV, 1968); Sidney Jellicoe, *The Septuagint and Modern Study* (Oxford: Clarendon, 1968); Emanuel Tov, "The Septuagint," in *Mikra,* 161–88; Melvin K. H. Peters, "Septuagint," *ABD* 5:1093–1104.

61   A critical edition of the Greek text of *Aristeas* with introduction appears in Swete, *Introduction,* 533–606. For an authoritative translation and discussion of *Aristeas,* see R. J. H. Shutt, "Letter of Aristeas," *OTP* 2:7–34. Cf. Jellicoe, *Septuagint,* 29–58.

62   See Josephus *Bell.* 2.487; *Ap.* 2.35. For discussion of the Jewish community in Ptolemaic Egypt and the Hellenistic world in general, see Victor Tcherikover, *Hellenistic Civilization and the Jews* (New York: Atheneum, 1982) 269–377; Elias J. Bickerman, *The Jews in the Greek Age* (Cambridge: Harvard Univ. Press, 1988) 69–129; Harald Hegermann, "The Diaspora in the Hellenistic Age," in W. D. Davies and Louis Finkelstein, eds., *The Cambridge History of Judaism,* vol. 2: *The Hellenistic Age* (Cambridge: Cambridge Univ. Press, 1989) 115–66.

was produced. Kahle maintains that various Greek translations or "Greek targums" were made to meet the needs of specific Jewish communities.[63] Lagarde maintains that there was an original Greek version of each book of the Bible from which variant Greek text traditions derive.[64] Tov argues for a multistaged process in which an original single translation prompted many corrected manuscripts that were produced to bring the Greek text into closer conformity with the Hebrew.[65] A period of textual stabilization followed in the first-second centuries CE, and the production of later revisions by Origen and Lucian followed again in the third and fourth centuries CE.

B. Manuscripts

No manuscript of the original Alexandrian versions of the LXX exists, and the many corrections found in existing manuscripts make clear that the Greek texts were extensively revised from the outset. The reasons for such revision are rooted in errors and translational or stylistic liberties taken by the original translators as well as in the subsequent use of the LXX by early Christians in polemics against Jews. Much of the revision was intended to bring the Greek text into closer conformity with the Hebrew, either by Jews interested in producing a more accurate translation or by Christians intent on advancing their apologetics against Jews. An early edition of the LXX was undertaken in 128 CE by Aquila, a Jewish proselyte and former disciple of Rabbi Akiba whom many identify with the translator of Targum Onqelos for the Torah. Aquila's version is a literal rendition of the Hebrew text based on principles of Jewish interpretation. Symmachus, identified either as an Ebionite Christian or a Samaritan convert to Judaism, produced a late-second-century CE revision that attempts to combine literal accuracy and good idiomatic Greek. Theodotion, identified as an Ephesian convert to Judaism or an Ebionite, produced a distinctive text in the late second or early third century CE that may derive from an early-first-century BCE

version different from the standard Alexandrian version. The discovery of a late-first-century BCE/early-first-century CE Greek manuscript of the Twelve Prophets at Naḥal Ḥever has prompted some interpreters to argue that the purported Proto-Theodotion material represents a much earlier text that provided the basis for Aquila and Symmachus. In order to prepare Christian apologists for disputes with Jews, the church father Origen prepared in 230–240 CE a six-column biblical text known as Origen's Hexapla, which contained the Hebrew text of the Bible, a Greek transliteration of the Hebrew text, Aquila, Symmachus, the LXX, and Theodotion. Origen's Hexapla was the basis on which the later fourth-century manuscripts of the LXX were prepared. Origen's Hexapla also provided the basis for the Syro-Hexaplar, a Syriac translation of the LXX prepared in 618–619 by Paul, bishop of Tella, and later recensions by Hesychius, perhaps identified with the Vatican Codex, and Lucian, a Christian martyr who died in 312.

Reconstruction of the Alexandrian LXX and its derivative versions necessarily depends on later Christian manuscripts since the earliest complete manuscripts of the LXX date to the fourth century. The manuscript most commonly employed for critical editions of the LXX is Codex Vaticanus (Vatican Greek MS 1209), which apart from a number of missing leaves, contains the entire text of the Greek Old and New Testaments.[66] Although many early LXX scholars maintain that Vaticanus was one of the fifty copies of the Bible prepared by Eusebius at the behest of Constantine for the churches of his new capital in the late fourth century, more recent study indicates that it was produced in Egypt during the mid-fourth century. Codex Sinaiticus (British Library Additional 43725) was located beginning in 1844 at St. Catherine's Monastery, Mount Sinai, by A. F. C. von Tischendorf, who witnessed monks burning its leaves as tinder for fire.[67] Von Tischendorff was able to rescue much of the manuscript in the following years. Like Vaticanus, many believed that Sinaiticus was one of the manuscripts prepared by Eusebius for

63 Paul Kahle, *The Cairo Genizah* (Oxford: Blackwell, 1959), esp. 236, 247, 251.

64 Paul De Lagarde, *Anmerkungen zur griechischen Übersetzung der Proverbien* (Leipzig: Brockhaus, 1863) 1–4; idem, *Mittheilungen I* (Göttingen: Dieterich, 1884) 19–26.

65 See esp. Emanuel Tov, *The Text-Critical Use of the Sep-* *tuagint in Biblical Research* (2d ed.; Jerusalem: Simor, 1997) 6–8.

66 For discussion of Vaticanus, see Swete, *Introduction*, 126–28; Jellicoe, *Septuagint*, 177–79.

67 See Swete, *Introduction*, 129–31; Jellicoe, *Septuagint*, 180–83. For a facsimile edition, see Constantinus Tischendorf, *Bibliorum Codex Sinaiticus Petropoli-*

Constantine, but later study has placed its origins in Caesarea in the early fourth century or in Alexandria. Codex Alexandrinus (British Library Royal I.D.) dates to the fifth or sixth century.[68] It has been extensively corrected with erasures, although many of the corrections are contemporaneous with the writing of the codex and may represent source materials of the scribe.

Other early manuscripts contain only the OT or some of its portions. Codex Venetus, now located in the library of St. Mark, Venice, is the second part of a single manuscript of only the OT that originally included Codex Basiliano-Vaticanus (now located in the Vatican Library).[69] The manuscript dates to the eighth or ninth century. It presents a distinctive text of Habakkuk 3, and the order of books among the Twelve Prophets differs from the standard LXX order in that the first six books are Hosea, Amos, Joel, Obadiah, Jonah, and Micah. Codex Marchalianus, now located in the Vatican Library, is a sixth-century manuscript of the Prophets written in Egypt.[70] Its margins contain many readings of Hexaplaric material. The Freer Manuscript, now located in the Smithsonian Museum, Washington, D.C., is a mid- to late-third-century papyrus of the Minor Prophets.[71] The Freer manuscript contains many readings that agree with or have been assimilated to the Hebrew text, probably in an effort to correct the Alexandrian text under the influence of Theodotion, Aquila, or Symmachus.

C. Literary Setting, Textual Features, and Viewpoint

The LXX Zephaniah is part of the larger LXX version of the *Dodekapropheton*, the book of the Twelve Prophets, which appears to have been translated by a single translator at some time from the late third to the late second century BCE.[72] As noted in the discussion of the placement of Zephaniah within the sequence of the MT book of the Twelve Prophets, LXX Zephaniah occupies the same position among the Twelve as that of MT Zephaniah, that is, the ninth position immediately following Habakkuk and preceding Haggai.[73] Because Habakkuk relates the rise of the Neo-Babylonian Empire in the late monarchic period and Haggai calls for the rebuilding of the temple in the early Persian period, it appears that the threats of punishment and the promises of impending restoration in Zephaniah are read in relation to the Babylonian destruction of the temple in 587/586. Although Zephaniah appears in the same position in both the LXX and MT sequences of the book of the Twelve, interpreters cannot presuppose that the Twelve Prophets functioned similarly in the two versions of the book. As noted in the discussion of the MT version of the book of the Twelve, the MT and LXX sequences for the first six books differ. Whereas the MT sequence begins with Hosea, Joel, Amos, Obadiah, Jonah, and

tanus (St. Petersburg: Published under the authority of Czar Alexander II, 1862).

68 Swete, *Introduction,* 125–26; Jellicoe, *Septuagint,* 183–88. For a facsimile edition, see *The Codex Alexandrinus (Royal MS. 1 D v-viii) in Reduced Photographic Facsimile. Old Testament,* part III: *Hosea–Judith* (London: British Museum, 1936).

69 Swete, *Introduction,* 131–32; Jellicoe, *Septuagint,* 197–99.

70 Swete, *Introduction,* 144–45; Jellicoe, *Septuagint,* 201–2.

71 Jellicoe, *Septuagint,* 233–34; Henry A. Sanders and Carl Schmidt, *The Minor Prophets in the Freer Collection and the Berlin Fragment of Genesis* (Univ. of Michigan Studies, Humanistic Series, 21; New York: Macmillan, 1927) 1–229.

72 Although attempts have been made to argue that the LXX version of the Twelve Prophets is the work of multiple translators (see Johannes Hermann and Friedrich Baumgärtel, "Die Septuaginta zum Zwölfprophetenbuch das Werk zweier Übersetzer," in

Johannes Hermann and Friedrich Baumgärtel, eds., *Beiträge zur Entstehungsgeschichte der Septuaginta* [Beiträge zur Wissenschaft von Alten Testament 5; Berlin: Kohlhammer, 1923] 32–38; C. R. Harrison Jr., "The Unity of the Minor Prophets in the Septuagint," *BIOSCS* 21 [1988] 55–72), the arguments have been refuted in favor of the view that LXX Twelve Prophets is the work of a single translator (see Joseph Ziegler, "Die Einheit der Septuaginta zum Zwölfprophetenbuch," in *Sylloge: Gesammelte Aufsätze zur Septuaginta* [Göttingen: Vandenhoeck & Ruprecht, 1971] 29–42; originally published in *Beilage zum Vorlesungsverzeichnis der Staatliche Akademie zur Braunsberg* [1934–35] 1–16; Takamitsu Muraoka, "In Defence of the Unity of the Septuagint Minor Prophets," *AJBI* 15 [1989] 25–37).

73 For a full discussion of the significance of the sequence of the books that comprise both the MT and LXX orders of the book of the Twelve, see Sweeney, "Sequence"; idem, *Twelve Prophets,* xv–xxix.

Micah, which emphasizes concern with the city of Jerusalem from the outset of the book, the LXX sequence begins with Hosea, Amos, Micah, Joel, Obadiah, and Jonah, which indicates an interest in reading the experience of the northern kingdom of Israel as a model for the later experience of Jerusalem and Judah. In this case, the LXX version of Zephaniah would provide justification for the destruction of Jerusalem by the Babylonians, that is, just as Samaria and the northern kingdom of Israel were destroyed as punishment for apostasy against YHWH (Hosea) at the Bethel sanctuary (Amos), so Jerusalem would be punished as Samaria was (Micah). Joel then initiates the sequence of books that relate the threats to Jerusalem by the nations (Joel, Obadiah, Jonah, Nahum, Habakkuk) culminating in Zephaniah's indictment of Jerusalem and Judah for apostasy against G-d. Haggai, Zechariah, and Malachi then take up issues pertaining to the restoration promised once the punishment is complete.

Although scholars frequently use the LXX as a source for reconstructing the "original" Hebrew text that must have preceded the MT, Zephaniah provides little evidence for such an enterprise. This is not to say that such work is unwarranted in principle; certainly the LXX texts of books such as 1-2 Samuel, 1-2 Kings, Jeremiah, and so on, indicate that the LXX frequently preserves readings earlier than those of the MT. Nevertheless, the nearly consistent agreement of the MT with the second-century CE Hebrew manuscript of the book of the Twelve from Wadi Murabbaʿat and the first-century CE Greek manuscript of the Twelve from Naḥal Ḥever indicates that the MT represents substantially at least the earliest consonantal Hebrew text of Zephaniah. There are a number of variant readings in the LXX form of Zephaniah, but in nearly every case they are the result of efforts to provide a stylistically consistent and idiomatic Greek text or to alter the reading of the text in accordance with the interpretive viewpoint of the translator. The initial oracle of the book in 1:2-6 provides some particularly important examples of both types of changes. Stylistic alterations appear in 1:2, in which the MT phrase, "I will utterly destroy everything," appears in LXX as "let (everything) be utterly destroyed"; 1:3, which eliminates the problematic MT reading "and those who cause the wicked to stumble" from the LXX text; and 1:5, which eliminates the second MT occurrence of the phrase, "and those

who prostrate themselves," in the LXX text. Examples of interpretive alterations appear in 1:4, which changes the MT phrase "the remnant of Baal" to "the name of Baal" in the LXX text to eliminate problems posed by the continued existence of Baal worshipers after they had supposedly been purged; again in 1:4, in which the Lucianic text of the LXX changes the phrase "by their king" to "by Milcom" to highlight the name of a pagan deity. In some cases, the LXX translator simply did not understand the Hebrew text, as in 1:10-11, where the references to gate or place names in Jerusalem, that is, "the fish gate," "the Mishneh (second quarter)," and "the Maktesh (mortar)" are read in LXX as "the gate of those slaying," "the second," and "the area broken into pieces/coined into money." Full discussion of these and the other examples throughout the book appear in the following commentary.

For the most part, these alterations do not markedly change the character of the book; LXX Zephaniah is clearly an example of translation literature in which the translator has left a distinctive mark or viewpoint at various points throughout the text. However, there is one particularly important pericope, 2:1-4, in which the LXX translator made changes that substantially alter the text of the passage and the overall character of the book. The passage is well recognized as a parenetic or exhortative statement in which the prophet calls on the audience to gather and seek YHWH before YHWH's wrath comes upon them on the Day of YHWH as punishment. The differences between the MT and LXX versions of the text appear in the means by which the prophet addresses the audience. The MT employs a text that portrays the audience in fundamental agreement with the prophet in an effort to draw in support for his calls to identify with YHWH and adhere to YHWH's expectations. In this manner, MT presents a scenario in which the nation will presumably follow the prophet's advice. Thus MT 2:3 reads: "Seek YHWH, all you humble of the land who have carried out his law. Seek righteousness, seek humility, perhaps you will be hidden in the day of the wrath of YHWH." The LXX reads the text rather differently: "Seek YHWH, work at law, and seek righteousness and answer/testify to them. In such manner you will be hidden in the day of the wrath of YHWH." In contrast to the MT, the LXX reading presupposes an apostate or potentially apostate audience that must be convinced to turn from its apostasy to follow YHWH. The LXX reading thereby strengthens the exhortative or parenetic character of this text, and presents a scenario in which the audience's reaction is in question as it is far more resistant to the prophet's appeal than in the MT. Whereas the MT presumes the audience's agreement with or acquiescence to Josiah's state-sponsored reform program, the LXX presupposes an audience that will resist a call to adhere to YHWH.

D. Sociohistorical Settings

Such a perspective is especially important when considering LXX Zephaniah in relation to its literary and sociohistorical settings in which the book was read. The LXX reading of the text presupposes this role, and shapes the text to fit it by pointing to the people's rejection of YHWH. As noted above, the placement of Zephaniah in both the LXX and MT sequences of the book of the Twelve presupposes the reality of the destruction of Jerusalem. In that the LXX reworks the text of 2:3 to emphasize the people's resistance to the prophet's appeal to turn to YHWH, it points to the people's resistance to YHWH as the cause for Jerusalem's destruction. Consequently not only does the LXX strengthen the exhortative or parenetic perspective of the text, it highlights the question of theodicy in relation to the cause for the destruction of Jerusalem in 587/586 BCE, that is, Jerusalem and the temple were destroyed not because YHWH was absent, impotent, defeated, or evil, but because the people rejected YHWH and thereby brought punishment upon themselves.

Such a viewpoint would be particularly pertinent throughout the Greco-Roman period and beyond, from the time of the initial translation of the LXX in Ptolemaic Egypt from the mid-third century BCE through the rise of Christianity in the eastern Mediterranean through the fourth century CE and following. Although the origins of anti-Semitism are frequently traced to Ptolemaic Egypt and perhaps even to pre-Hellenistic Egyptian culture,[74]

Jews were able to settle in Alexandria from its foundation and produced a flourishing community through the beginning of the Roman period. Given the overwhelming influence of the dominant Hellenistic culture, Egyptian Jews would have found themselves in a somewhat conflicted cultural climate in which they would have to navigate between the cultural (and religious) assimilation that stood at the base of Hellenistic culture in Egypt (and indeed throughout the Mediterranean world) and adherence to traditional Jewish religion centered in the Jerusalem Temple and the Torah. Indeed, Egyptian Jews were generally known for declining to support the pagan liturgies of Alexandria and other Hellenistic cities as well as for sending funds to support the Jerusalem Temple. In such a situation, the LXX text of Zephaniah, with its calls to resist pagan religious practice and to turn to G-d—and presumably to support of G-d's temple in Jerusalem—would play some role in encouraging such practice.

This question would become particularly acute in the second century BCE when the Seleucid Empire defeated Ptolemaic Egypt in 198 BCE and took control of Jerusalem. The Seleucid monarch Antiochus IV Epiphanes (176–163) was especially well known for his interference in the affairs of the Jerusalem Temple, that is, manipulating the office of the high priest and ultimately turning the temple into a shrine for the worship of Zeus, in his efforts to raise support for his continuing war against Ptolemaic Egypt.[75] Given both the cultural assimilation of the priestly class favored by Antiochus and the continuing state of hostilities between Seleucid Syria and Ptolemaic Egypt, the LXX version of the book of Zephaniah would clearly point to the threat of paganism posed to the Jerusalem Temple by the Seleucid monarchy. Ptolemaic Egyptian Jewish readers of the book would see it as a call to oppose both the religious policies of the Seleucid Empire and indeed the empire itself.

The issue would have been exacerbated further in the Roman period, beginning in 68 BCE when the Romans

---

74   See Tcherikover, *Hellenistic Civilization*, 344–77; Louis H. Feldman, *Jew and Gentile in the Ancient World: Attitudes and Interactions from Alexander to Justinian* (Princeton: Princeton Univ. Press, 1993) 84–176; and esp. Peter Schäfer, *Judeophobia: Attitudes toward the Jews in the Ancient World* (Cambridge: Harvard Univ. Press, 1997).

75   For discussion of Antiochus IV and Seleucid policy in general, see Tcherikover, *Hellenistic Civilization*, 39–203; Elias Bickerman, *From Ezra to the Last of the Maccabees: Foundations of Postbiblical Judaism* (New York: Schocken, 1962) 93–135; Emil Schürer, *The History of the Jewish People in the Age of Jesus Christ*, vol. 1 (rev. and ed. Geza Vermes, Fergus Millar, and

took control of Judea and again in 30 BCE when they took control of Egypt.[76] Although the Romans initially allowed the Hasmonean dynasty to rule Judea through 37 CE, the shifting policies of Roman rule, first under the Idumean monarch Herod, who was married to the Hasmonean princess Mariamne, and later as the Romans incorporated Judea as a province of the Roman Empire under direct Roman rule, saw increasing resistance to Roman rule in Judea. Analogous resistance emerged in Egypt as the beginning of Roman rule under Augustus saw the imposition of the *laographia* or poll tax that was imposed on all non-Greeks. Although Jews were largely acculturated to hellenization, the imposition of the poll tax was both an economic burden and a deliberate insult as non-Greeks were considered akin to barbarians. LXX Zephaniah would have been read as a call to maintain Jewish identity in the face of an increasingly hostile pagan state. Ultimately, Jews revolted against Rome on at least three occasions: in 66–74 CE when the Zealot revolt against Rome failed, resulting in the destruction of the Second Temple; in 114–117 CE when Jews in the diaspora, especially Crete and Egypt, failed in an effort to challenge Roman rule; and again in 132–135 CE when Simon Bar Kosiba (Bar Kochba) attempted to overthrow Roman rule and resulted in the destruction of much of the Jewish population of Judea. The last revolt is particularly pertinent to the concerns of LXX Zephaniah, as it was sparked in part by the perception that the Roman emperor Hadrian had reneged on his promise to rebuild the Jerusalem Temple and planned to build a temple to the Roman god Jupiter instead. Once the revolt was put down, Hadrian proceeded with his plans for the pagan shrine and the eradication of a Jewish presence in the land. Hadrian was known for banning Jews from Jerusalem and renaming the city Aelia Capitolina. He likewise renamed Judea as Palestine, banned the practice of Judaism in the land, and executed a number of Jewish luminaries, such as Rabbi Akiba, to further his efforts to eradicate Judaism.

Finally, the role of LXX Zephaniah in the newly emerging Christian canon must also be considered, especially since the prophet's charges of apostasy against the people of Jerusalem and Judah would play a role in Christian polemics against Judaism. Such a charge would support Christian claims that Jews had sinned against G-d, and that Christianity represented the true Israel that had been established by G-d to bring salvation to the entire world following the destruction of Jerusalem. Insofar as LXX Zephaniah is read in relation to G-d's eschatological restoration of Jerusalem following the period of punishment, the book would have supported early Christian expectations for the second coming of Christ. Through the course of the fourth century CE when Christianity emerged as the dominant religion of the Roman Empire,[77] LXX Zephaniah would have been read in support of state-sponsored restrictions or sanctions against Jews who were increasingly portrayed in opposition to G-d, the church, and the state. As noted above, Codex Vaticanus and Codex Sinaiticus, the earliest manuscript witnesses to the LXX as a whole, were written during this period.

III. The Scrolls from the Judean Wilderness

Portions of the book of Zephaniah appear in four of the scrolls from the Judean wilderness, including a second-century CE Hebrew version of the book of the Twelve Prophets from Wadi Murabbaʿat (Mur 88); a late-first-century BCE Greek version of the book of the Twelve Prophets from Naḥal Ḥever (8HevXIIgr); a second-

Matthew Black; Edinburgh: T & T Clark, 1973) 125–63; Otto Mørkholm, "Antiochus IV," *Cambridge History of Judaism* 2:278–91.

76   For discussion of Roman rule over Jews in Judea and Egypt, see E. Mary Smallwood, *The Jews under Roman Rule: From Pompey to Diocletian* (SJLA 20; Leiden: Brill, 1976); Schürer, *History*, 243–557; S. Appelbaum, "The Legal Status of Jewish Communities in the Diaspora," and "The Organization of Jewish Communities in the Diaspora," in S. Safrai and M. Stern, eds., *The Jewish People in the First Century: Historical Geography, Political History, Social,*

Cultural and Religious Life and Institution (CRINT I; Philadelphia: Fortress Press, 1974) 420–63, 464–503; Aryeh Kasher, *The Jews in Hellenistic and Roman Egypt: The Struggle for Equal Rights* (Tübingen: Mohr, 1985).

77   For discussion of relations between Jews and Rome in the aftermath of the Bar Kochba revolt and during the rise of Christianity in the Roman Empire, see esp. Michael Avi-Yonah, *The Jews under Roman and Byzantine Rule: A Political History of Palestine from the Bar Kochba War to the Arab Conquest* (Jerusalem: Magnes, 1984).

century BCE Hebrew manuscript of the book of the Twelve from Qumran (4QXII[b]); and a pesher or commentary on Zephaniah from Qumran (4QpZeph).

A. The Scroll of the Twelve Prophets from Murabbaʿat

The Scroll of the Twelve Prophets from Wadi Murabbaʿat (Mur 88) constitutes the most extensive witness to the pre-masoretic Hebrew text of the book of the Twelve Prophets. The caves at Wadi Murabbaʿat, located about 18 km. or 11 mi. south of Wadi Qumran and 26 km. or 16 mi. southeast of Jerusalem, have yielded a considerable quantity of material remains and manuscript fragments from the time of their initial discovery in 1951 by the Taʿamre bedouin.[78] The first four caves, explored in early 1952 by a team led by G. L. Harding and R. de Vaux, showed traces of occupation from the Chalcolithic Age (fourth millennium BCE), the Middle Bronze Age (ca. 2000–1500 BCE), the Iron Age (eighth–seventh centuries BCE), the Hellenistic period, the Roman period, and the Arab period. Written documents were discovered from the last four of these periods, the best known of which are several letters written by Simon ben Kosiba, also known as Bar Kochba, to Joshua ben Galgula. Bar Kochba is the leader of the ill-fated second Judean revolt against Rome in 132–135 CE.[79] Ben Galgula apparently was one of his commanders who sought refuge in the Murabbaʿat caves during the course of the war. A fifth cave was discovered in 1955 by Taʿamre shepherds, who found the Scroll of the Twelve Prophets.

The Murabbaʿat scroll originally constituted a full Hebrew version of the book of the Twelve Prophets that was buried in a sepulchre together with the body of a man and various artifacts. This indicates that the burial is an example of a tomb genizah, in which a man may be buried with holy books placed next to his coffin (see *b. B. Qam.* 17a; *Meg.* 26b). This differs from the better-known practice of burying sacred writings that are no longer usable due to wear or damage in a manner like

that of human beings (*m. Shab.* 16:1; 9:6; *Lev. Rab.* 21:12; *b. Meg.* 26b). It has been severely damaged since its original burial.

The Murabbaʿat scroll originally would have measured about 355 mm. high, 4.9 m. long, and contained forty columns of text. It appears to have been written "some decades after the fixation of the received text," that is, during the early second century CE prior to the Bar Kochba revolt.[80] The original scroll apparently presented all of the Twelve Prophets in the order of the present-day MT. Due to the considerable damage suffered by the scroll, it now contains Joel 2:20; Joel 2:6–4:16; Amos 1:5–2:1; 7:3–8:7; 8:11–9:15; Obad 1-21; Jonah 1:1–3:2; Jonah 3:2–Mic 1:5; Mic 1:5–3:4; 3:4–4:12; 4:12–6:7; 6:11–7:17; 7:17–Nah 2:12; Nah 2:12–3:19; Hab 1:3–2:11; Hab 2:18–Zeph 1:1; Zeph 1:11–3:6; Zeph 3:8–Hag 1:11; Hag 1:12–2:10; and Hag 2:12–Zech 1:4. In keeping with the stipulations laid down in talmudic literature, it leaves three lines between each of the books found within the Twelve Prophets, whereas biblical books normally are separated by four lines (*b. B. Batra* 13b). This indicates the dual status of the Twelve Prophets as twelve prophetic books that simultaneously function as one book.

The text of Mur 88 is virtually identical with the MT, although there are a number of orthographic changes, corrections, and other minor variations. In the case of Zephaniah, there are five differences: (1) Zeph 2:1; Mur 20:11 התקשׁשׁו MT // הִתְקוֹשְׁשׁוּ; (2) Zeph 2:1; Mur 20:11 וקשׁו MT // וָקוֹשּׁוּ; (3) Zeph 2:3; Mur 20:13 ארץ MT // הָאָרֶץ; (4) Zeph 3:9; Mur 21:3 על העמים MT // אֶל עַמִּים; (5) Zeph 3:11; Mur 21:5 עלילותיך MT // עֲלִילֹתַיִךְ. The two differences in Zeph 2:1 and in 3:11 are merely orthographic. Zephaniah 2:3 apparently represents an attempt to read the *hapax legomenon* כָּל־עַנְוֵי הָאָרֶץ (but see also Amos 8:4) as the more common כָּל־עַנְוֵי אֶרֶץ in keeping with Ps 76:10 (cf. Isa 11:4; Job 24:4). Zephaniah 3:9 represents a more stylistically consistent text. In addi-

---

78 See P. Benoit, J. T. Milik, and R. de Vaux, *Les Grottes de Murabbaʾat* (DJD 2/1-2; Oxford: Clarendon, 1961).

79 For discussion of Bar Kochba, see Schürer, *History,* 1:514-57; Smallwood, *Jews,* 428-66; Yigael Yadin, *Bar Kochba: The Rediscovery of the Legendary Hero of the Second Jewish Revolt against Rome* (New York: Random House, 1971).

80 See the discussion by Milik, *Murabbaʾat,* 181-84.

tion, Mur 88 places *sĕtûmôt* or *pĕtûḥôt* at the same locations as those found in the Leningrad Codex, that is, between 1:18 and 2:1 (*sĕtûmâ*); between 2:4 and 2:5 (*pĕtûḥâ*); between 2:15 and 3:1 (one full line); and between 3:13 and 3:14 (*petûḥâ*). The only other place at which a *setûmâ* appears in the Leningrad Codex, that is, between 1:9 and 1:10, is lost in Mur 88 due to damage to the scroll. Unfortunately, the absence of vowel pointing or other means of vocalization make it impossible to determine the exact reading of this text. Nevertheless, the close correspondence between Mur 88 and MT prompts most scholars to conclude that Mur 88 is an example of the proto-MT.[81]

One may only speculate as to how Mur 88 Zephaniah would have been read in the early second century CE. It seems likely, however, that Zephaniah's call to purge the nation of idolatry prior to the coming Day of YHWH may well have been read in relation to the earlier Zealot revolt against Rome (66–74 CE) in which the Second Temple was destroyed. Bar Kochba and his followers, many of whom saw him as the messiah,[82] prepared for some years prior to the outbreak of the revolt by training and gathering weapons in secret. Having seen the nation punished, they would have looked forward to the purge of foreign or Roman elements from the nation prior to the restoration of Jerusalem and the rebuilding of the (third) temple. Virtually nothing is known of the identity of the man with whom the scroll was buried, but it seems that he died at some point shortly before, during, or after the Bar Kochba revolt.

B. The Naḥal Ḥever Greek Twelve Prophets Scroll

The Naḥal Ḥever Greek Scroll of the Twelve Prophets (8HevXIIgr) constitutes the oldest known witness to the Greek text of the Twelve Prophets.[83] The caves at Naḥal Ḥever, located some 22 1/2 mi. or 36 km. south of Qumran, have also yielded artifacts and manuscripts that date to the Bar Kochba revolt of 132–135 CE.[84] In 1952 Taʿamre bedouin brought the bulk of the fragmentary Greek Twelve Prophets scroll to the French archeological school in Jerusalem (l'École biblique française), then located in territory seized by Jordan following the 1948 War for Independence. Several other fragments followed in 1953. Since the Naḥal Ḥever caves were located in Israeli territory, Yohanan Aharoni surveyed the region in late 1953. The Hebrew University, Israel Department of Antiquities, and the Israel Exploration Society subsequently mounted full-scale expeditions in 1960 and 1961, divided into four groups. Expedition A, led by Nahman Avigad, explored the Ein Gedi area, including Second Temple period burial caves and the "Cave of the Pool" used by Bar Kochba era refugees. Expedition B, led by Yohanan Aharoni, examined the caves at Naḥal Zeʾelim, which yielded some biblical texts and Greek papyri. Aharoni's expedition also examined the "Cave of Horror" on the southern bank of Naḥal Ḥever in which some forty Bar Kochba period refugees died for lack of water as a result of the Roman siege. Some remaining fragments of the Naḥal Ḥever Scroll of the Twelve Prophets were found in this cave that established the "Cave of Horror" as the location of the scroll. Expedition C, led by Pessah Bar-Adon, examined the "Cave of Treasure" in the Mishmar Valley that yielded Chalcolithic period tools, ritual objects, and so on. Expedition D, led by Yigael Yadin, examined the "Cave of Letters" on the north bank of the Naḥal Ḥever; it contained many documents, including the Babatha archive and letters from Bar Kochba to his commanders in Ein Gedi.

---

81 See Tov, *Textual Criticism*, 29–38; Barthélemy, *Critique textuelle*, c–cii.

82 See the famous rebuke of R. Akiba's contention that Bar Kochba was the messiah. Following Akiba's statement that Bar Kochba was "king messiah," Johanan ben Torta retorts, "Akiba, grass will grow from your cheeks [i.e., he will be dead and buried] and the son of David still will not have come" (TJ to Num 24:17; *y. Taʿan.* 4:8).

83 See Tov, *Greek Minor Prophets Scroll*.

84 For accounts of the archeological expeditions, see Nahman Avigad et al., "The Expedition to the Judaean Desert, 1960," *IEJ* 11 (1961) 3–72; idem, "The Expedition to the Judaean Desert, 1961," *IEJ* 12 (1962) 167–262; Yigael Yadin, *The Finds from the Bar Kochba Period in the Cave of Letters* (Jerusalem: Israel Exploration Society, 1963); idem, *Bar Kochba*, 1971; "Judaean Desert Caves," *NEAEHL* 3:816–37.

The Naḥal Ḥever Greek manuscript of the Twelve Prophets originally contained a complete Greek version of the book of the Twelve Prophets.[85] The order of books extant in the manuscript indicates that it employed the same order of books as the MT. It was apparently among the possessions of the forty refugees who hid in the "Cave of Horror." A Roman military camp was located on a cliff above their position, which apparently served as the base for the soldiers besieging the Jews trapped in the cave. The group buried those who succumbed during the course of the Roman siege, and they burned many of their possessions. They apparently chose to die rather than surrender.

The Naḥal Ḥever manuscript was originally about 9.64 to 10.07 m. long, making it the longest manuscript found in the Judean wilderness. The height of the leather was 35.2 cm. for hand A (see below), but data for hand B is lacking. The original would have contained some fifty-five columns of text, of which twenty-five or twenty-six are extant. The manuscript was written by two hands: hand A was originally responsible for thirty-seven columns, presumably beginning with Hosea and covering the now extant portions of the books of Jonah, Micah, Nahum, Habakkuk, Zephaniah, and Zech 1:1–8:18. Hand B was responsible for eighteen columns, covering Zech 8:18–Malachi. The extant fragments include text for Jonah 1:14–2:7; 3:2-5; 3:7–4:2; 4:5; Mic 1:1-8; 2:7-8; 3:5-6; 4:3-5; 4:6-10; 5:1(2)-6(7); Nah 1:13-14; 2:5-10; 2:13-14; 3:3; 3:6-17; Hab 1:5-11; 1:14–2:8; 2:13-20; 3:8-15; Zeph 1:1-6; 1:13-18; 2:9-10; 3:6-7; Zech 1:1-4; 1:12-15; 2:2-4(1:19-21); 2:6-12(2-8); 2:16(12)–3:2; 3:4-7; 8:19-21; 8:23–9:5. The columns produced by hand A generally contain forty-two lines, and those produced by hand B contain thirty-three lines. There are six blank lines prior to the book of Micah (cf. the three lines stipulated for the books of the Twelve in *b. B. Batra* 13b). The scroll employs a system of *pĕtûḥôt* and *sĕtûmôt* analogous to those of the masoretic system, although none appears for the book of Zephaniah. There are spaces in the middle of some verses where MT places the accent *athnach* (see Mic 1:5; 5:4; Hab 1:15; 2:3; Zeph 3:7; Zech 3:4). The

Tetragrammaton appears in Paleo-Hebrew for both hands A and B. The practice indicates special treatment of the divine name. The script employed by hand A dates to the late first century BCE, and that employed by hand B dates to the late first century BCE or perhaps the early first century CE.

Overall, the Greek appears to be a literal translation of a Hebrew text that corresponds closely to the later MT. The *Vorlage* for this manuscript would therefore be a proto-MT.[86] A number of variations appear in the text, including minor changes in the definite article, *lamed* plus infinitive, construct words, pronominal suffixes, articles before proper nouns, the rendition of the direct object marker, verb tenses, and other stylistic features. A full listing of variations, including those pertaining to the text of Zephaniah, appears in Tov's edition of 8HevXIIgr.[87] In all cases but one, the changes that appear in 8HevXIIgr may be explained not as a variation in the Hebrew *Vorlage* of the Greek text, but as the result of the Greek translator's attempt to provide a literal and stylistically coherent Greek translation. The one exception appears in 3:7, for which the MT reads מְעוֹנָהּ, "her habitation," LXX reads ἐξ ὀφθαλμῶν (Heb. מְעֵינֶיהָ or מְעֵינָה), "from her/its eye/s," and 8HevXIIgr reads ἡ πηγὴ αὐτῆς (Heb. מַעְיְנָה), "her water." Given the frequent confusion between the Hebrew letters *yod* and *waw* in a consonantal text, it appears that the differences between the three texts do not require different Hebrew text traditions, but only differences in reading the same Hebrew text.

Based on the peculiarities of the Greek rendition of 8HevXIIgr, Barthélemy argues that 8HevXIIgr represents a proto-Theodotion or *kaige*-Theodotion version that constitutes an early attempt to revise the original LXX text.[88] The basis for his conclusion is the correspondence of textual features in 8HevXIIgr to features of Aquila, Symmachus, the fifth column of the Hexapla cited by Jerome, the Greek text quoted by Justin in his Dialogues, the LXX Codex W, and the Coptic translations. Such features include the literal rendition of the conjunctive particle גַּם or וְגַם as καὶ γε, "and also"; the

---

85   For the following, see the discussion by Tov and his collaborators, Robert A. Kraft and Peter J. Parsons, in Tov, *Greek Minor Prophets*, 1–26.

86   See Barthélemy et al., *Critique textuelle*, cxl.

87   See Tov, *Greek Minor Prophets*, 99–158.

88   Dominique Barthélemy, *Les devanciers d'Aquila* (VTSup 10; Leiden: Brill, 1963).

use of ἀνήρ rather than ἕκαστος (for Heb. שִׁיא, "man"); the use of ἐπάνωϑεν/ἀπάνωϑεν instead of LXX ἀπό or ἐπάνω to render Hebrew מֵעַל, "from upon"; the elimination of the historical present in favor of the aorist to render Hebrew *waw*-consecutive imperfect verbs; the emphasis on the atemporal nature of Hebrew אֵין by translating as Greek οὐκ ἐστιν; the translation of Hebrew אָנֹכִי as ἐγώ εἰμι to distinguish it from אֲנִי; avoidance of εἰς ἀπάντησιν as a translation of Hebrew לִקְרַאת; a tendency to transliterate unknown words; a tendency to systematize Greek equivalents of Hebrew expressions, and so on.[89] Barthélemy argues that the *kaige*-Theodotion recension originated in Judean circles linked to rabbinic modes of exegesis, and identifies the proto-Theodotion translator as Jonathan ben Uzziel, to whom the Aramaic Targum for the Prophets is attributed.[90] Although the identification of Jonathan ben Uzziel as the translator is somewhat speculative, 8HevXIIgr does point to the existence of the purported proto-Theodotionic revision of the LXX in Judea. Its literal rendition of the text indicates that it was produced for use by those unable to read the Hebrew text. Unfortunately, its fragmentary character does not allow for an analysis of its overall perspective in reading the book of Zephaniah.

C. The Minor Prophets Scrolls from Cave 4

The discovery of Qumran Cave 4 in 1952 ultimately yielded portions or fragments of over five hundred manuscripts, including biblical manuscripts, pesharim or commentaries on biblical books, and many nonbiblical compositions.[91] Among the biblical manuscripts are fragments from eight copies of the book of the Twelve Prophets.[92] The manuscripts, identified as 4QXII[a-g]/ 4Q76–82 and 4QMicah, range in date from the mid-

second century BCE through the late first century CE. The contents and textual character vary. 4QXII[a] (4Q76), dated ca. 150 BCE, begins with Zech 14:18 and contains portions of Malachi and Jonah. It appears to be an independent textual witness in that it may follow MT or LXX, or present its own reading. A unique feature of this manuscript is its placement of Jonah after Malachi, which may indicate an alternative order of the book of the Twelve. 4QXII[b] (4Q77), dated to the mid-second century BCE, is a proto-MT that contains fragments of Zephaniah and Haggai. 4QXII[c] (4Q78), dated ca. 75 BCE, represents the presumed LXX *Vorlage* and contains portions of Hosea, Joel, Amos, Zephaniah, and Malachi. 4QXII[d] (4Q79), dated to the second half of the first century CE, contains proto-masoretic fragments of Hosea. 4QXII[e] (4Q80), dated ca. 75 BCE, contains fragments of Haggai and Zechariah that stand close to the LXX text tradition. 4QXII[f] (4Q81) contains presumably proto-masoretic fragments of Jonah. 4QMicah, a single fragment that contains Mic 5:1-2, may be a part of 4QXII[f]. 4QXII[g] (4Q82), dated to the latter half of the first century BCE, contains portions of Hosea, Joel, Amos, Obadiah, Jonah, Micah, Nahum, Habakkuk, Zephaniah, and Zechariah; it varies textually although it stands closest to the masoretic tradition.

Of the eight manuscripts from the book of the Twelve, two are of special interest for the study of Zephaniah. 4QXII[b] contains fragments of 1:1-2; 2:13-15; and 3:19-20. There is only one major variation from the MT: in 2:13 it reads ויא in place of MT וְיֹאבֵד, "and he will destroy." It is possible, albeit unlikely, that the scroll presents a deliberate rereading of the verb as the root אבה, "to be willing" or אבי/אבב, "to press." Unfortunately, the scroll preserves insufficient text to make such a determination. Furthermore, no other textual tradition indi-

89 See ibid., 198–202.

90 See ibid., 144–57.

91 For accounts of the discovery of Qumran Cave 4, see R. de Vaux in M. Baillet et al., *Les "Petites Grottes" de Qumran* (DJD 3; Oxford: Clarendon, 1962) 3–36; and in R. de Vaux and J. T. Milik, *Qumran, Grotte 4, II* (DJD 6; Oxford: Clarendon, 1977) 3–29.

92 For the diplomatic edition of these MSS, see Fuller, "Twelve," 221–318. See also idem, "The Minor Prophets Manuscripts from Qumrân" (Ph.D. diss.; Harvard University, 1988); idem, "The Text of the Twelve Minor Prophets," *CurBS* 7 (1999) 81–95; idem, "The Form and Formation of the Book of the Twelve," in James W. Watts and Paul R. House, eds., *Forming Prophetic Literature: Essays on Isaiah and the Twelve in Honor of John D. W. Watts* (JSOTSup 235; Sheffield: Sheffield Academic Press, 1996) 86–101.

cates a basis for accepting this reading as a textual variation. It is more likely an error, as Fuller suggests.[93] There
is a one-line gap between the end of Zephaniah (3:20)
and the beginning of Haggai (1:1). The Zephaniah fragment of 4QXII[g] contains only a few letters from 3:3-5,
that is, ע from ערב; חמ from חמסו; and לא from לא גרמו.
Although the manuscript sometimes disagrees with the
MT and LXX, there is no basis for concluding that the
text varies from the MT in Zephaniah.

D. The Zephaniah Pesher from Qumran Cave 4

Qumran Cave 4 also yielded fragments of a pesher or
commentary on Zephaniah (4QpZeph; 4Q170).[94] The
text includes only elements from 1:12-13, and it concludes with the term פשרו, "its pesher/interpretation
(is)," leaving little indication of the Qumran commentator's understanding of the passage.[95] There is only one
minor textual variation from the MT: 4QpZeph reads
למ[שוסה in place of MT לְמְשַׁסָּה, "plunder."[96] This is
merely an orthographic variation that indicates no substantive difference in the text.

E. The Zephaniah Pesher from Qumran Cave 1

Qumran Cave 1 yielded one fragment of a pesher or
commentary on Zephaniah (1QpZeph; 1Q15).[97] The text
includes elements of 1:18—2:2, and a few words from the
following commentary introduced by the term פשר

(*pešer*), "interpretation." The interpretation makes reference to "the land of Judah," and the editor of the manuscript presumes that the pesher relates the prophet's
statement to all the inhabitants of the land of Judah.
Unfortunately, too little text survives to make any kind
of determination concerning the pesher's understanding
of the prophet's statement. The text of 1:18—2:2 provides little information, other than the plene spelling of
the word כמוץ, "like chaff," from 2:2 and the possibility
that a gap might follow the word.[98] In any case, the
orthographic variation does not influence the interpretation of the verse, and the reasons for the possibility of
a gap following כמוץ are not clear.

IV. Targum Zephaniah

A. Origins

The basic Aramaic text of the book of Zephaniah is part
of the larger text of Targum Jonathan for the Prophets,
which includes all of the Former and Latter Prophets
of the masoretic canon (Joshua, Judges, 1-2 Samuel,
1-2 Kings, Isaiah, Jeremiah, Ezekiel, Twelve Prophets).[99]
The attribution of the Targum to the Prophets to Jonathan appears in *b. Meg.* 3a, which states that "the Targum of the Prophets was composed by Jonathan ben
Uzziel from the mouth of Haggai, Zechariah, and
Malachi." Jonathan ben Uzziel is identified in rabbinic

93 See Fuller, "Twelve," 233.

94 John M. Allegro, *Qumrân Cave 4: I (4Q158–4Q186)*
(DJD 5; Oxford: Clarendon, 1968) 42; see also John
Strugnell, "Notes en marge du volume V des 'Dis-
coveries in the Judaean Desert of Jordan,'" *RevQ* 7
(1969) 163–275, esp. 210–11; Maurya P. Horgan,
Pesharim: Qumran Interpretation of Biblical Books
(CBQMS 8; Washington, D.C.: Catholic Biblical
Association, 1979) 191–92.

95 Cf. Strugnell, "Notes," 210–11, who properly
arranges the fragments so that a few words of the
pesher or interpretation follow the initial quote
from Zeph 1:12. Nevertheless, the surviving text
provides little basis for a reconstruction of the
author's comment.

96 See Strugnell, "Notes," 211. Allegro mistakenly read
למ[שיסה, but the photograph supports Strugnell's
reading.

97 Dominique Barthélemy and J. T. Milik, *Qumran
Cave I* (DJD 1; Oxford: Clarendon, 1955) 80; Horgan, *Pesharim*, 63–65.

98 Unfortunately, the photograph does not provide a
clear reading of this term.

99 For general discussions of targumic literature, see
Philip S. Alexander, "Targum, Targumim," *ABD*
6:320–31; idem, "Jewish Aramaic Translations of
Hebrew Scripture," in *Mikra*, 217–53; Étan Levine,
"The Targums: Their Interpretative Character and
Their Place in Jewish Text Tradition," in Sæbø,
Antiquity, 323–31. For discussion of the Targum for
the Prophets, see Pinkhos Churgin, *Targum Jona-
than to the Prophets* (1927; reprinted New York:
KTAV, 1983); Leivy Smolar and Moses Aberbach,
Studies in Targum Jonathan to the Prophets (New York:
KTAV, 1983) 1–227. For studies of the Targum to
the Twelve Prophets, see Kevin J. Cathcart and
Robert P. Gordon, *The Targum of the Minor Prophets:
Translated with a Critical Introduction, Apparatus, and
Notes* (Aramaic Bible 14; Wilmington, Del.: Glazier,
1989); Robert P. Gordon, *Studies in the Targum to the
Twelve Prophets: From Nahum to Malachi* (VTSup 51;
Leiden: Brill, 1994).

tradition as a pupil of Rabbi Hillel (*b. Suk.* 28a; *B. Batra* 134a; *ʾAbot R. Nat.* A14, 29a), which would suggest that he lived some time during the period in which Hillel was active, that is, ca. 30 BCE–10 CE. Scholars have noted that Jonathan may be a hebraicized version of the name Theodotion, to whom an early Greek "targum" is ascribed,[100] or Theodotion may be a graecized version of the name Jonathan,[101] much as the names Onqelos, to whom the primary Targum for the Torah is ascribed, and Aquila, who produced an early LXX version, are equated (cf. *y. Meg.* 1:9). Elsewhere, the tradition cites the Targum of the Prophets together with the statement, "as Rab Joseph translates" (*b. Pesaḥ.* 68a = *Tg.* Isa 5:15; *b. B. Batra* 3b = *Tg.* Obad 6; *b. Yoma* 32b = *Tg.* Jer 46:20), thereby identifying Rab Joseph ben Hiyya (ca. 270–333 CE), head of the rabbinic academy at Pumbeditha in Babylonia, as the source of the Targum. The attributions to Rab Joseph, however, state that he would not have been able to understand the verse in question without the Targum to the Prophets (*b. Meg.* 3a; *Moʿed Qaṭ.* 28b = *Tg.* Zech 12:11), indicating that he consulted the Targum as a well-established tradition in his time.[102]

It seems clear that the targumic tradition in general, and TJ in particular, originated in the social setting of the synagogues and the schools or yeshivot. Scholars have noted the close association of the synagogues and the schools, particularly since the worship function of the synagogue appears to have developed out of the *bet midrash,* or house of study.[103] The origins of the synagogue as an institution in Judaism are not entirely clear. Some trace its beginnings to the Jewish community exiled to Babylonia beginning in 597 BCE by noting the gathering of people for worship and instruction in Ezek 14:1; 20:1 (see also the reference to the "little sanctuary" in 11:16, which is interpreted as a reference to a synagogue in *b. Meg.* 29a). The first archeological evidence for a synagogue appears in Schedia, near Alexandria in Egypt, in the third century BCE. Although no synagogues are clearly attested during the period of Ezra and

Nehemiah (late fifth and early fourth centuries BCE), the tradition traces the practice of translating Scripture from Hebrew into Aramaic during a public reading to Ezra's reading of the Torah to the people of Jerusalem (Nehemiah 8; *b. B. Qam.* 82a; *Ber.* 33a; *Meg.* 17b). According to Neh 8:7, the Levites helped the people to understand the Torah by interpreting or giving meaning to the words. Of course, the Hebrew verb תרגם, "to translate," does not appear here, although it does appear in Ezra 4:7 as מְתֻרְגָּם, "translated," in reference to the letter written by the opponents of Judah and Benjamin to King Artaxerxes of Persia in their efforts to stop the building of the Second Temple (cf. Ezra 4:18, which employs Aramaic מְפָרַשׁ, "interpreted," in reference to the translated letter).

The course of development of such public translation of Scripture in the synagogues necessarily remains uncertain, but synagogues flourished throughout the land of Israel and the diaspora by the first century CE. The Mishnah (second century CE) makes reference to such translation in *Meg.* 2:1, which stipulates that a man who hears Scripture read in Hebrew may then read it in a foreign language, and *Meg.* 4:4, which stipulates the means by which the interpreter (מתורגמן) may read texts from the Torah and the Prophets. Many later targumic texts of the Prophets include only the *Haphtarot* readings, that is, selections from the Prophets read together with the Torah portion of the week or the festival, which indicates the importance of the targumic tradition to a synagogue setting in which Jews in antiquity would come for worship and study.[104] Such a setting would explain the development of official Targumim, that is, Targum Onqelos for the Torah and Targum Jonathan for the Prophets.

Although the practice of reading some form of targum for the Torah and the Prophets appears to have emerged relatively early in the Second Temple period, the development of the official Targumim appears to be later. At first, there was no set text or translation, as the

---

100 Abraham Geiger, *Urschrift und Übersetzung der Bibel* (2d ed.; Frankfurt: Madda, 1928) 163–64.

101 Barthélemy, *Devanciers,* 148–56.

102 See esp. Churgin, *Targum Jonathan,* 13–15/241–43, for discussion of this point.

103 For discussion of the origins and functions of ancient synagogues, see Eric M. Meyers, "Syna-

gogue," *ABD* 6:251–60; Louis Isaac Rabinowitz, "Synagogue," *EncJud* 15:579–84; Joseph Gutmann, ed., *The Synagogue: Studies in Origins, Archaeology, and Architecture* (New York: KTAV, 1975); idem, *Ancient Synagogues: The State of Research* (Chico, Calif.: Scholars Press, 1981).

104 For discussion of the reading of the Torah and the

reader chose his own rendering of the passage at the time of the reading. Thus Churgin maintains that the congregation was the original author of the Targum.[105] The standard Targumim emerged by the late first or early second centuries CE, however, as Rabbi Akiba's homily on Zech 12:1 demonstrates that he knew the official Targum for the verse (see *b. Mo'ed Qaṭ.* 28a).[106] Indeed, Churgin points to a wide variety of references throughout TJ that presuppose the Roman period and the destruction of the Second Temple in 70 CE.[107] He is also able to point to one instance in Isa 21:9 that refers to the *future* downfall of Babylon, which he understands as a reference to the downfall of the Sassanian Persian Empire that ruled Babylonia in the second century CE and beyond. Churgin detects no references to the Arabs, which indicates that the Targum was completed prior to the rise of Islam in the seventh century. Churgin represents the majority of scholars in concluding that TJ took shape gradually from the Roman period, immediately prior to the destruction of the Second Temple, through the completion of the Talmudic period, immediately prior to the rise of Islam.

B. Manuscripts

The manuscripts on which the critical edition of TJ for Zephaniah is based are relatively late.[108] The basic text for Sperber's edition of the Twelve Prophets is British Library Manuscript Oriental 2211. This text is a Yemenite manuscript, which dates to approximately the fifteenth or sixteenth century and contains the Latter Prophets. This manuscript represents the supralinear vocalization of the Targum, which scholars maintain is among those manuscripts that best attest to the early-fourth-fifth-century CE Babylonian vocalization of the Aramaic text.[109] As the last leaves of Ms. Or. 2211 are partially damaged, Sperber employed another Yemenite manuscript with supralinear pointing, British Library Manuscript Oriental 1474, to replace lost text for Mal 3:3-7, 16-23. Sperber also used British Library Manuscript Oriental 1470, a manuscript that contains *Haphtarot,* but this manuscript does not include any portions of Zephaniah.

Two manuscripts represent the western Tiberian system of vocalization. Manuscript p. 116 of the Jew's College, London, contains text for 1 Samuel–Malachi (the manuscript is bound with another that contains Psalms, Job, and Proverbs). The colophon of the manuscript states that it was "finished on the new moon day of Shebat in the year 5247," which Sperber calculates as December 26, 1486.[110] Ms. p. 116 is distinguished by a number of additions (Tosephta) that are written into the text and identified in marginal notations by a later hand. The more noteworthy manuscript with Tiberian pointing is Codex Reuchlinianus, now housed in the Badische Landesbibliothek, Karlsruhe.[111] This is the oldest dated manuscript of Targum Jonathan to the Prophets; its colophon indicates a date of 1105 CE. It, too, contains a large number of variations and marginal notes. As many are identified by distinctive sigla, Sperber concluded that they point to six manuscripts consulted by the annotator of the codex.[112] Bacher's 1874 study of the marginalia in this codex concludes that they were largely

Prophets in the synagogues, see Charles Perrot, "The Reading of the Bible in the Synagogue," in *Mikra,* 137–59, and the bibliography cited there.

105 Churgin, *Targum Jonathan,* 40/268.

106 Ibid., 42/270.

107 For discussion of the historical references in TJ, see ibid., 22–30/250–58. See also Gordon, *Studies,* whose studies of these passages lead to similar conclusions.

108 The critical edition of the Targum for the Twelve Prophets appears in Alexander Sperber, *The Bible in Aramaic,* vol. 3: *The Latter Prophets according to Targum Jonathan* (Leiden: Brill, 1962).

109 See Cathcart and Gordon, *Targum,* 18, who note that these texts actually represent a western Tiberian system of pointing that has been transposed into

a Babylonian supralinear system (they cite M. F. Martin, "The Babylonian Tradition and the Targum," in R. de Langhe, ed., *Le Psautier* [Louvain: Publications Universitaires, 1962] 446–51).

110 Alexander Sperber, *The Bible in Aramaic,* vol. 4B: *The Targum and the Hebrew Bible* (Leiden: Brill, 1973) 139–40.

111 See Alexander Sperber, *The Prophets according to Codex Reuchlinianus* (Leiden: Brill, 1969).

112 Sperber, *Bible in Aramaic,* 3:x.

derived from the Talmuds and midrashim, but that some elements represent early pre-Babylonian readings of the targum for the Prophets.[113]

C. Textual Features and Viewpoint

Although the Aramaic formulation of Targum Jonathan to the Twelve Prophets often differs markedly from the Hebrew text of the masoretic tradition, it provides little basis for reconstructing a distinct Hebrew *Vorlage*. Rather, the differences between the Targum and the MT, particularly in the book of Zephaniah, may be explained as expressions of the translational and interpretive techniques of the targumic translator, who sought to render the text in accordance with the theological outlook and sociohistorical setting of early rabbinic Jewish circles in the first-second centuries CE.

First and foremost, the targumist takes special care to convey the holiness of G-d. In general, the Targum attempts to avoid portraying G-d in direct relationship to human beings, but instead employs a number of devices that suggest some distance or intermediation between G-d and human beings.[114] One of the best-known techniques is the use of the term ממרא, "word," in relation to the name of G-d, that is, "the word (ממרא) of YHWH" (3:2; cf. 3:8, 11). The term appears to derive from Biblical Hebrew statements concerning "the word of YHWH" spoken to Moses, the prophets, the priests, and so on, through which G-d acts in the world. The use of such a device both conveys the revelatory character and effective power of divine interaction with human beings while simultaneously avoiding the possibility of direct human experience or rejection of G-d, that is, if human beings reject the ממרא of G-d, then they do not reject G-d per se. Likewise, they do not directly relate to or experience the presence of G-d (like Ezekiel in Ezekiel 1), but they experience the ממרא as an intermediary as well. Similar concerns are expressed by the use of the term שכינה, "presence," as an expression of divine presence or manifestation in the world without compromising divine transcendence (Zeph 3:5, 15, 17).[115] Other devices include use of the expressions מן קדם, "from before (YHWH)," to convey the distinction between

divine and finite reality (e.g., 1:1, 6, 7, 8; 3:5); the "name" of YHWH (e.g., 1:5); the "service" of YHWH (e.g., 1:6; 3:2); the "fear" of YHWH (e.g., 1:6; 2:11); and "the plague/stroke of my power" in place of anthropomorphisms such as "my hand" (e.g., 1:4; cf. 2:13). Rather than portray G-d as the one who searches Jerusalem with lights in 1:12, Targum Zephaniah reads: "I will appoint searchers and they shall search the inhabitants of Jerusalem as men search with a torch."

The targumist also expresses a clear sense of divine judgment against the wicked of the world, and views idolatry as the chief expression of such wickedness in that idolatry represents the ultimate rejection of G-d. Thus Targum Zephaniah frequently changes the text to emphasize that all the wicked of the earth or only the wicked of the earth will suffer divine punishment, for example, "all the wicked have come to an end from before YHWH G-d" in place of "silence from before the L-rd YHWH" in 1:7, or "all the wicked of the earth will perish" in place of "all the earth will be consumed" in 3:8. The guilt of the people who commit wickedness is expressed through a number of modifications, such as the rendition of "O worthless nation [i.e., Judah]," in 2:1 as "the generation that does not desire to return to Torah"; the reading of "the people who deserve to be destroyed" in place of the ambiguous "nation of Kerethites" in 2:5; and the reading of "(you shall not be ashamed of) all your evil deeds" in place of "your deeds" in 3:11.

The targumist's emphasis on idolatry as the basis for human wickedness appears in the reading of "those who swear in the name of their idols" in place of "those who swear in the name of their king" in 1:5; "all those who throng to worship idols" in place of "all those wearing foreign attire" in 1:8; "all who walk by the laws of the Philistines" in place of "all leaping over the threshold" in 1:9; "all the peoples whose deeds are like the deeds of the people of Canaan" in place of "they resemble the people of Canaan" in 1:11; and "he [G-d] has abased all the idols of the earth" in place of "he has abased all the gods of the earth" in 2:11. The targumist also modifies the text of Zephaniah to introduce other causes for

---

113 See Wilhelm Bacher, "Kritische Untersuchungen zum Prophetentargum," *ZDMG* 28 (1874) 1–72.

114 See Smolar and Aberbach, *Studies*, 130–37 (see also

137–50); Cathcart and Gordon, *Targum*, 4–9.

115 See also Ephraim E. Urbach, *The Sages: Their Concepts and Beliefs* (Jerusalem: Magnes, 1979) 37–65.

wrongdoing, such as the acquisition of wealth or property, presumably by the Romans and those who collaborate with them,[116] for example, reading "the taxes of the wicked have multiplied" in place of "causing the wicked to stumble" in 1:3; "all those rich in possessions (have been destroyed)" in place of "all those bearing silver" in 1:11; "who lie at ease over their wealth" in place of "who congeal over their dregs" in 1:12; and "their palaces" in place of "their houses" in 1:13. The targumist also charges that the people did not listen to G-d's prophets in 3:2; alternatively, the targumist points to the teachings or influence of false prophets among the people in 3:4 or false judges in 3:15.

Despite the emphasis on human idolatry, wealth, and falsehood as the causes of punishment, the targumist also modifies the text at various points to emphasize divine redemption, restoration, or return from exile. Thus 2:7 reads: "for their record shall go up for good before YHWH their G-d, and he shall restore their exiles," in place of "for YHWH their G-d shall redeem them and he shall restore their fortunes/exile" (cf. 3:20). Zephaniah 3:1 reads: "Woe to her [Jerusalem] who hurries and is redeemed," in place of "Woe, O contentious and defiled one." Zephaniah 3:17 reads: "he will pardon your sins in his mercy," in place of the enigmatic "he will plow/be silent in his love."

At various points, the targumist clearly struggles to understand the text. Thus Targum Zeph 1:10 refers to "the Ophel,"[117] that is, the site of the royal palace complex in the monarchic period, apparently because the targumist does not understand the reference to the "Mishneh," the name for the district of the Western Hill to which the city of Jerusalem expanded in the eighth century BCE. The targumist also reads "the Kidron Valley" in place of the reference to the "Maktesh" (mortar) in 1:11, apparently misunderstanding the reference to the Tyropoean Valley that ran along the western edge of the City of David. The Tyropoean Valley had been partially filled in over the centuries due to continuous dumping and building in and around the site, whereas

the "mortar"-like depression of the Kidron Valley along the eastern edge of the City of David continues to serve as a defining feature of the city. The expression in Zeph 2:2, "like chaff (that) has passed in a day," apparently prompted considerable difficulty, as the Targum presents a reading that combines two major interpretations of these words: "like chaff from the threshing floor that the wind carries away and like the dew that passes before the day."

In other cases, the targumist changes the meaning of the text in accordance with his own viewpoints; for example, Targum Zeph 1:7 emphasizes that the "Day of YHWH" will come in the future, which may suggest that the revolt had not yet taken place, or (more likely) that the targumist viewed the "Day of YHWH" as a day of retribution against the Romans for their destruction of the temple. The targumist renders the "Day of YHWH" as a day of "killing" rather than as a day of "sacrifice," apparently resisting the notion that those who died (or will die) are to be considered as martyrs or as expiating sin. Likewise, Targum Zeph 1:14 reads "there the mighty men shall be killed" in place of "there the mighty men cry out," in keeping with its understanding of the Day of YHWH as a day of killing (cf. Zeph 1:7). Targum Zephaniah 3:13 eliminates references to the remnant of Israel as sheep, and Targum Zeph 3:14 specifies that the "daughter of Zion" is the "congregation/synagogue of Zion." Targum Zephaniah 3:9 specifies that the nations will "pray" rather than simply "call on" YHWH, and Targum Zeph 3:10 indicates that the exiles of Israel will return from India rather than from Cush. In some cases, the change is merely a clarification, for example, Targum Zeph 2:12 makes sure that the address to the Cushim/Ethiopians is grammatically consistent, reading "also you, O Cushim, you shall be slain by the sword," in place of "also you, O Cushim, slain by the sword are they." Similarly, Targum Zeph 2:14 specifies that the "voice" or "sound" in the window is a "bird," and that "her ceilings will be torn down" rather than "her cedar work shall be uncovered."

---

116 For an analysis of the relationship between the Romans and the Judean elite class as a causative factor in the Zealot revolt of 66–74 CE, see Martin Goodman, *The Ruling Class of Judaea: The Origins of the Jewish Revolt against Rome, A.D. 66–70* (Cambridge: Cambridge Univ. Press, 1993).

117 Cf. 2 Chr 33:14, which places the Fish Gate and Ophel together. Some MSS read "bird" (עוֹף) instead of Ophel (עוֹפֶל), apparently dropping the letter *lamed*.

An especially interesting case appears in Targum Zeph 3:18, for which two texts are preserved.[118] The MT reads, "those who were oppressed from the appointed time (נוּגֵי מִמּוֹעֵד) when I gathered from you were a burden upon her, a shame." Standard editions of the Targum render this statement, "those who were delaying among you the times of your festivals, I have removed from your midst, for they were taking up arms against you and reviling you." The targumist apparently read the expression נוּגֵי מִמּוֹעֵד as a reference to Roman interference with the high priesthood and temple in Jerusalem prior to the outbreak of the Zealot revolt, and employed the text of Zephaniah as a basis to announce the coming punishment of Rome for taking up arms against Judea. In the Talmud, however, b. Ber. 28a quotes a different Aramaic version of this verse, "destruction comes upon the enemies of the house of Israel because they delayed the times of the appointed seasons [festivals] that were in Jerusalem." The Talmud cites this verse in relation to a discussion concerning the delay of praying the *Musaf Tefillah* (Additional Prayer Service), which indicates that the verse is understood in reference to an internal issue among Jews concerning proper observance of Jewish liturgy. Although the statement is attributed to R. Joshua ben Levi of the third century CE, most scholars consider the talmudic reference to be older because it does not appear in the standard texts of the Targum. This would suggest that although the earlier (talmudic) text anticipated punishment for those within Judaism who were involved in delaying elements of the Jewish worship service, the standard Targum text is directed against the enemies of Judaism, most likely the Romans, who took up arms against Jews.[119] Scholars have been troubled by the Targum's perspective that the enemies of Israel have *already* been removed. The collapse of Roman Byzantine authority as a result of the Persian conquest of Palestine in 614 and the subsequent establishment of Islamic authority in 634 would provide a fitting background for such a statement at the close of the period when most scholars maintain that the Targum was edited into its present form.[120]

V. The Peshitta

A. Origins

The Syriac text of the book of Zephaniah appears as part of the *Dodekapropheton* (the book of the Twelve Prophets) in the Peshitta version of the Christian OT. The Peshitta functions as Sacred Scripture for the eastern Syriac churches, including the Syrian Orthodox and Maronite churches, as well as the Church of the East.[121] Although the Peshitta version clearly dates to a much earlier period, the term "Peshitta" first appears in the ninth century CE in the Hexameron of Moses bar Kefa (813–903) and in his introduction to the Psalms. It is a passive feminine participle form of the verbal root *pšṭ*, which means "to stretch out, extend, make straight." The passive participle form of *pšṭ* often functions with the meaning, "simple, common," in reference to the "simple" or "common" people. Scholars generally maintain that the term refers to the Peshitta as the version that is commonly employed by the eastern Syriac churches

---

118 For full discussion of this issue, see Gordon, *Studies*, 49–52; cf. Churgin, *Targum Jonathan*, 148/376.

119 Interpreters generally speculate that the talmudic quotation indicates that the words חברא אתי, "destruction comes," were originally part of the targumic text (see Gordon, *Studies*, 49–50; Churgin, *Targum Jonathan*, 148/376), but the notion of coming destruction may be inferred from the overall context of the book of Zephaniah (e.g., Zeph 1:7) and need not indicate that these terms were quoted from the text. Note that the talmudic "quotation" is not a quotation at all but a rendition of the interpretation of the verse. Rather, the essential difference is that the targumic version, in contrast to the talmudic version, identifies those who would delay the appointed times as those who also took up arms against Jews. The talmudic quotation of this verse in relation to the time that *Musaf Tefillah* is prayed need have nothing to do with the motivations of the targumic writer of this statement.

120 See Avi-Yonah, *Jews under Byzantine and Roman Rule*, 257–78.

121 See esp. Michael Weitzman, *The Syriac Version of the Old Testament: An Introduction* (Univ. of Cambridge Oriental Publications 56; Cambridge: Cambridge Univ. Press, 1999), esp. 1–14; Peter B. Dirksen, "The Old Testament Peshitta," in *Mikra*, 254–97; A. Gelston, *The Peshitta of the Twelve Prophets* (Oxford: Clarendon, 1987); cf. Michael Weitzman, "The Interpretative Character of the Syriac Old Testament," in Sæbø, *Antiquity*, 587–611.

(much like the Vulgate of the western Roman Catholic Church) in contrast to the rival Syro-Hexaplaric version of the OT made by Paul of Tella in 617–618 and the Harklean version of the NT.[122] An alternative explanation understands the term "Peshitta" as a reference to Scripture that is "widespread," again as an analogy to the Vulgate commonly employed in the Roman Catholic Church. Unfortunately, no such usage of the term is attested.

The origins of the Peshitta are clouded in legend.[123] Ishodad of Merw (ninth century) claims that some of the OT books were translated into Syriac during the time of King Solomon at the behest of King Hiram of Tyre, and other books were translated during the time of Addai the apostle and Abgar, king of Edessa, who was considered to be a contemporary of Jesus (see also Jacob of Edessa, ca. 700, quoted by Moses bar Kefa). He also mentions the opinion of others that the translation was made by the priest Asya, who was sent to Samaria by the Assyrians following the destruction of the northern kingdom of Israel. The dominant tradition is that the evangelist Mark translated the OT from Hebrew to Syriac, presented the translation before Jacob the brother of Jesus, and the other apostles, who in turn approved it and gave it to the people of Syria. Afterward, Mark wrote the Gospel together with Peter in Rome.[124]

The earliest documented references to the Peshitta appear in the works of fourth-fifth-century CE Syriac-speaking Christians, such as Aphrahat (336–345), Ephraim Syrus (d. 373), and Theodore of Mopsuestia (350–428). Most scholars maintain that the Peshitta dates to the first or second century CE.[125] Indeed, Weitzman's analysis considers the Syrian traditions of the Peshitta's origins, references to contemporary events, citations of the Peshitta by outside writers, citations of outside works

in the Peshitta, vocabulary, and grammar, in arguing that the Peshitta likely originated in Edessa during 150–200 CE. Scholars have generally been divided as to whether the Peshitta reflects Jewish or Christian origins.[126] Based on the Peshitta's textual affinities especially to the MT (but with influence from the LXX as well), Jewish modes of interpretation, and an emphasis on prayer in contrast to sacrifice, Weitzman offers a mediating position by arguing that the Peshitta was produced in nonrabbinic Jewish circles located in Edessa that later came to adopt Christianity.[127] On the basis of his analysis of the text of the *Dodekapropheton* in relation to the MT, the LXX, the Targum, and the quotation of the Twelve in the NT, Gelston maintains that the Peshitta version of the *Dodekapropheton* was produced within a Jewish community at some point during the latter part of the first century CE. Especially important factors in his assessment are the clear dependence on the proto-MT, the extensive use made of the LXX, and affinities in exegetical technique and linguistic features with the Targum.[128]

B. Manuscripts

The primary manuscripts employed for the critical edition of the Peshitta version of the *Dodekapropheton* date to the sixth, seventh, and eighth centuries, some four to six hundred years after the Peshitta was completed.[129] Gelston's critical edition of the text is based on Ms. B 21 Inferiore, Ambrosian Library, Milan, folios 194b–206b. The manuscript is written in an Estrangela script, and dates to the seventh century. It contains a nearly complete text of the *Dodekapropheton*. Some damage to the manuscript results in the loss of text in Hab 2:5-10 and Zeph 3:7-8. It also contains a number of unique readings, including Zeph 1:8 (reading *dlbyšyn* in place of the

---

122 It should be noted that the Targumic Aramaic verb פשׁט, "to be simple, straight," functions from the eleventh century on as "to interpret," apparently based on the use of the root in reference to the simple or plain meaning of the text (see Weitzman, *Syriac Version*, 2–3). This might suggest that the Syriac term also refers to "interpretation," much like the later Arabic term *tafsīr*, "interpretation, translation."

123 See Dirksen, "Old Testament Peshitta," in *Mikra*, 255; Weitzman, *Syriac Version*, 248.

124 Weitzman, *Syriac Version*, 248.

125 See esp. ibid., 206–62, esp. 248–58.

126 See Dirksen, "Old Testament Peshitta," 261–64.

127 See Weitzman, *Syriac Version*, 258–62.

128 See Gelston, *Peshitta*, 111–97, esp. 195.

129 For the critical edition of the Peshitta *Dodekapropheton*, see the Peshitta Institute, Leiden, *The Old Testament in Syriac According to the Peshitta Version*, part III, fascicle 4: *Dodekapropheton-Daniel-Bel-Draco* (Leiden: Brill, 1980). The *Dodekapropheton* was prepared by A. Gelston. See also his *Peshitta*, 65–67, where he argues for a somewhat different basis for assessing the text of the *Dodekapropheton*.

expected *dlbšyn*), 11 (reading *šqly* in place of the expected *šqyly*), and unique errors, including Zeph 2:9 (reading *dtḥlṭ* in place of *dʾtḥblṭ*). A second early manuscript employed by Gelston is British Library Additional Ms. 14.443, folios 99a–144a. This manuscript is also written in an Estrangela script, and dates to the sixth century. The text of the *Dodekapropheton* is incomplete, however, extending only from Nah 1:4 to the end of the *Dodekapropheton*. The manuscript contains three errors shared with other manuscripts, such as that in Zeph 1:2, and various corrected errors, such as 3:6 (wrong occurrence of a word), 2:9 (transposition), and 1:15 (haplography). The third early manuscript is National Library, Paris, Syriaque Ms. 341, folios 174a–185a. The manuscript is written in Estrangela (although missing leaves and corrections are written in Nestorian script), and it dates to the eighth century. It contains a complete text of the *Dodekapropheton*, although the text is obscured at several points including Zeph 1:18; 2:9, 11-12; 2:15–3:2. In addition to these three primary manuscripts, Gelston employs a large number of later manuscripts that are described in his introduction.[130]

C. Textual Features and Viewpoint

Scholars have generally recognized that the Peshitta of the Twelve Prophets presupposes a Hebrew *Vorlage* that must have been very close to that of the MT.[131] The order of books in the Peshitta *Dodekapropheton* follows the order of the proto-masoretic and masoretic texts. It is not a slavishly literal translation of the Hebrew, however, as the translators apparently took liberties to produce a coherent text, perhaps because the Hebrew text employed by the translators was damaged or obscure.[132] The translators frequently turned to the LXX in their rendering of the Hebrew,[133] but they clearly did not follow the LXX throughout. There is little evidence for direct dependence on the Targum.[134] At various points, the Peshitta makes its own interpretive decisions. Although the reasons for the Peshitta's readings are frequently stylistic and represent a serious attempt to understand the Hebrew text (with the aid of the Greek text), the Peshitta's reading shows a marked interest in understanding Zephaniah as a prophet who announced a scenario of universal, eschatological judgment followed by restoration.

A number of examples illustrate the Peshitta's dependence on the proto-masoretic tradition in contrast to the LXX. Whereas the LXX lacks text for "and causes the wicked to stumble" in 1:3, the Peshitta reads, "and there are stumbling blocks upon the wicked." The LXX reads, "and the names of Baal and the names of the priests," in 1:4; the Peshitta reads, "the remnant of Baal, and the name of the cultic attendants with the priests," much like the MT. Whereas the LXX lacks the second occurrence of the expression, "and those who prostrate themselves," found in MT 1:5, the Peshitta includes it. The LXX reads 2:2 as "and seek righteousness, and testify/answer to them," and the Peshitta reads, "and seek righteousness and humility," apparently offering only a slight stylistic improvement over the MT. Whereas the LXX reads 2:9 as "and Damascus abandoned like a heap of salt," the Peshitta reads, "and their plantings shall be destroyed and their leaders shall perish," apparently employing a text like the MT as the basis for its own interpretation of the passage. The LXX reads 2:14 as "and all the wild animals of the land," and the Peshitta reads, "and all the animals of the nations," again offering only a slight stylistic improvement over the MT. The LXX reads, "ravens in its gateways," in 2:15, but the Peshitta reads, "and destruction in its gates," with the MT. Finally, whereas the LXX reads the problematic expression "their shame" in 3:19 as the introduction to the following statement in 3:20, the Peshitta reads, "in all the land where they were shamed," much like the MT. There are other examples, but these demonstrate the Peshitta's clear dependence on the proto-MT.

Despite its numerous agreements with the MT over against the LXX, the Peshitta frequently reads with the LXX over against the MT. Again, examples appear throughout the book. The Peshitta follows the LXX in reading "from the gate of those hurting" in 1:10 instead of MT "from the fish gate," and "from the other" in

---

130 See his *Dodekapropheton*, vii–xxxi; see also idem, *Peshitta*, 3–25; cf. 26–64.

131 Gelston, *Peshitta*, 111–30.

132 See ibid., 131–59.

133 Ibid., 160–77.

134 Ibid., 178–90.

place of MT "from the Mishneh." The Peshitta reinterprets LXX 1:12, reading "upon the men who despise their advocate" in place of MT "those who linger over their winedregs." The Peshitta follows the LXX in reading 2:1, "O, unchastised/uninstructed nation," in place of MT "O, unwanted/worthless nation." The Peshitta generally follows the LXX in reading 2:6, "and the seacoast shall become a fold and Crete a house of pasture for the dewlaps of sheep," in contrast to MT "and the seacoast shall become pasturelands of the wells of shepherds and folds for sheep." The Peshitta follows the LXX in reading 2:11, "the L-rd has revealed himself over them," in contrast to MT "YHWH is fearsome against them" (see also 3:15). The Peshitta follows the LXX in reading 3:7, "and there shall not be destroyed from her eyes [i.e., and she shall not fail to see]," in place of MT "and her inhabitation shall not be cut off." The Peshitta follows the LXX in reading 3:17, "and he renews you with his love," in place of MT "and he plows/is silent with his love." There are other examples as well, but these should suffice to demonstrate the Peshitta's frequent use of the LXX.

Finally, the Peshitta translators frequently make their own decisions, independent of the proto-masoretic and LXX texts, in rendering Zephaniah. Again, examples abound. The Peshitta reads "son of Hilkiah" instead of "son of Hezekiah" in 1:1, apparently to resolve genealogical issues prompted by the claim that Zephaniah might be a descendant of King Hezekiah. In 1:5 the Peshitta reads "by Milcom" in place of "by their king," and thereby agrees with the Lucianic Greek text over against the MT and LXX. The Peshitta reads 1:9 as "all who are robbers and plunderers," apparently to address problems caused by the reading, "all who leap over the threshold." The Peshitta adds a verb in 2:10, reading "this shall be to them" in place of the MT "this (is) to them." The Peshitta reads "when he destroyed all the kings of the earth" in 2:11 in place of "because he has diminished all the gods of the earth," much as the Targum employed the term "idols," apparently objecting to the use of the term "gods" in the MT and LXX. Such a modification points to the Peshitta's concern with the downfall of temporal power, which must herald the revelation of G-d/Christ in the world at large. The Peshitta reads, "even you, O Cushites, are killed by the sword," in 2:12, providing a stylistic improvement over the MT and LXX. The Peshitta independently adds "and shall say" at

the conclusion of 2:15 to introduce the following material as a quote by those witnessing the destruction of Nineveh. The Peshitta reads "the city of Jonah" in 3:1 in place of MT "the oppressing city" and LXX "the city of the dove." The Peshitta thereby reads the oracle concerning the city in 3:1-4 as an address concerning Nineveh, not as an address concerning Jerusalem. Thus it reads Zephaniah in relation to Nahum, and points once again to the impending downfall of temporal power in the world at large as an act of G-d. Again, there are other examples, but these should suffice to demonstrate the Peshitta's independence of both the proto-masoretic and LXX texts.

The present text of the Peshitta indicates that its translators were interested in presenting a clear and understandable rendition of the Hebrew text of Zephaniah aided by the Greek version of the book. Nevertheless, the rendition of 2:11, with its statements concerning the revelation of G-d in the world and the downfall of its kings, indicates that there is a clear tendency to emphasize divine judgment against temporal power in the world. A similar perspective is evident in the Peshitta's rendition of 2:9 in which it employs a pun on the Syriac word *mlwḥ*, "salt, leader," to introduce a statement condemning Moab's and Ammon's leaders. The introduction of the phrase "and say" following 2:15 likewise indicates an interest in reading 3:1-4 as a continuation of the oracle against Assyria/Nineveh in 2:13-15. This modification reinforces the view that the Peshitta understands Zephaniah as a prophecy of divine judgment against the entire world, in which judgment against Jerusalem/Judah is the prelude for judgment against the powers of the world at large. Given the worldwide scenario of judgment with which the book begins, it is likely that the Peshitta translator viewed Zephaniah as a prophecy of eschatological punishment and restoration. Although the Peshitta may well have originated in Jewish circles of the first or second century CE, it was later read in the context of Syrian Christianity and its NT. The eschatological and universal scenario of judgment against the temporal powers of the world outlined in the Peshitta version of Zephaniah would therefore be read by Syrian Christians in relation to their expectations concerning the revelation of Jesus.

VI. The Vulgate and Old Latin Texts

A. Origins

The basic Latin text of the book of Zephaniah appears as part of the Twelve Prophets in the Vulgate version of the Christian OT.[135] The Vulgate was produced by St. Jerome (ca. 347–420 CE), who was commissioned by Pope Damasus in 382 to produce a standard Latin text of the Bible. Jerome began by revising the Latin Gospels and the Psalter, and later attempted a Latin translation of Origen's Hexaplaric edition of the LXX. After these initial forays, he translated the entire OT (with the exception of most of the deuterocanonical or apocryphal books) from Hebrew into Latin during 390–405 while residing in Bethlehem. Jerome apparently began his work with the Psalter, and then turned to the prophetic books at a relatively early time (ca. 390–392), as these books were considered to have the most theological importance.

Jerome's work was motivated by problems in the use of OT Scripture in the early church. The church initially employed the LXX as the basic text of the OT, but this text differs markedly from the Hebrew text of the Tanak employed within Judaism, which of course would raise questions concerning the church's understanding of these scriptures. The problem would have been exacerbated by the production of Origen's Hexapla, which highlighted the differences among the various Greek versions as well as with the Hebrew text. As Latin increasingly emerged as the language of the Roman Catholic Church, Latin translations of the Greek text were produced, probably from the first century CE as indicated by Tertullian's (ca. 160–220) quotations of Latin texts. The Old Latin text is known only from fragmentary sources, that is, patristic quotations, fragmentary and palimpsest manuscripts, Carolingian and medieval Bibles, glosses to the Vulgate, and liturgical texts.[136] The Old Latin text appears to display great diversity in its rendition of the Greek text, which would further exacerbate the problems in establishing the OT text as an authoritative basis for the early church.

By translating the entire Hebrew Bible into Latin, Jerome apparently sought to provide a stable Latin text that would closely conform to the original Hebrew. He considered the Hebrew text to be Sacred Scripture and Hebrew to be "the progenitress of all the other languages."[137] Indeed, he ultimately came to question the inspired character of the LXX, claiming that the legend of its origins was a lie and distinguishing between the work of the "seventy" translators and that of the original authors of the Hebrew text.[138] His Hebrew text was apparently very close to that of the MT, and he assumed that the Hebrew text underlying the Greek versions of the OT was identical to the Hebrew text current in his day. He was aware of Hebrew variants, including the tradition of the *Tiqqune Soferim*, "Emendations of the Scribes," and he sometimes strayed from the vocalization of the Hebrew text.[139] He also depended on older sources, such as the Old Latin text as well as the Greek texts of Aquila, Symmachus, and Theodotion, and he

---

135 A critical edition of the Vulgate appears in Robertus Weber, OSB, *Biblia Sacra iuxta vulgatum versionem* (Stuttgart: Deutsche Bibelgesellschaft, 1983). For the Twelve Prophets, see also *Biblia Sacra iuxta Latinam vulgatum versionem ad coducum fidem. XVII: Liber Duodecim Prophetarum ex interpretatione Sancti Hieronymi* (Rome: Libreria Editrice Vaticana, 1987). For discussion of the Old Latin and the Vulgate, see Benjamin Kedar, "The Latin Translations," in Mulder, *Mikra*, 299–338; Eva Schulz-Flügel, "The Latin Old Testament Tradition," in Sæbø, *Antiquity*, 642–62; René Kieffer, "Jerome: His Exegesis and Hermeneutics," in Sæbø, *Antiquity*, 663–81. For an edition of a palimpsest containing portions of the Old Latin version of Zephaniah, see Alban Dold, *Neue St. Galler vorhieronymische Propheten-Fragmente der St. Galler Sammelhandschrift 1398b zugehörig* (Texte und

Arbeiten I/31; Beuron: Erzabtei Beuron, 1940).

136 An edition of the Old Latin book of Zephaniah, available only in quotations of individual verses from patristic sources, appears in Sidney Zandstra, *The Witness of the Vulgate, Peshitta and Septuagint to the Text of Zephaniah* (1909; Contributions to Oriental History and Philology 4; reprinted New York: AMS, 1966) 13–15. Swete, *Introduction*, 97, notes a palimpsest located at the Vatican that apparently contains the Old Latin text for Zeph 3:13–20 (cf. Zandstra, *Witness*, 11 n. 1).

137 Kedar, "Latin Translations," 315.

138 See Schulz-Flügel, "Latin Old Testament Tradition," 653, who cites Jerome's remarks from Jerome's preface to the Pentateuch.

139 See Kedar, "Latin Translations," 322–23.

sometimes allowed his theological principles to govern his translation. For example, his translation of Isa 19:3-15 includes eight references to Jesus, and he generally avoided the term *synagoga* because of his rejection of Judaism. Nevertheless, he is known for his philological expertise in rendering the Hebrew text into Latin, and he frequently consulted Jewish authorities during the course of his work. But he is also known for his haste at some points in producing the translation for his benefactors.

Although there was considerable resistance to Jerome's translation during his lifetime, it was gradually accepted and became the standard text when Alcuin (735–804) incorporated it into his Bible during the reign of Charlemagne. Both the Old Latin and Jerome's translation were used within the Roman Church for centuries following Jerome's death. His translation was accorded official status only at the Council of Trent in 1546, after which it was known as the *Biblia Vulgata,* that is, the commonly used and authoritative edition of the Bible in the Roman Catholic Church.[140]

B. Manuscripts

Because the Vulgate serves as the authorized text of the Roman Catholic Church, a very large number of manuscripts (about 8,000) are available. Nevertheless, the manuscript tradition points to the continuous adaptation and revision of the Vulgate text as it was copied over the course of centuries. There have been various attempts to revise and standardize the text of the Vulgate. Major revisions were undertaken during the reign of Charlemagne by Theodulph of Orleans and Alcuin. Alcuin's text proved to be the more influential, and ultimately provided the basis for the Paris text of the thirteenth century. The Paris text in turn became the basis for the first printed texts of the Vulgate and later the official Roman edition published under the authority of Pope Clement VIII in 1592.

Geographical distribution is very important in considering manuscript witnesses to the Vulgate. The Irish and Spanish manuscripts are generally considered to represent the purest forms of the text; because of Ireland's and Spain's relative isolation from the rest of Europe, the manuscripts produced in these regions were copied less frequently and therefore subject to less textual corruption. The oldest known manuscript of the complete Vulgate OT (including Zephaniah) is Codex Amiatinus. Written in Northumbria early in the eighth century, and now located in Florence, it reflects the Irish text.[141] Amiatinus serves, together with Codex Cavensis, an eighth- or ninth-century Spanish text now in Salerno, as the primary witness for the critical editions of the Vulgate.[142] Other key texts for Zephaniah include the Toletanus Codex (tenth century, Spain),[143] Legionensis (960, Spain),[144] Sangallensis (eighth century, Italy),[145] examples of the Alcuin Bible,[146] and the Clementine Bible noted above.[147] A sixth-century palimpsest containing portions of the prophets from the Vulgate, including 3:13-20, has also been published.[148]

C. Textual Features and Viewpoint

Although the Vulgate tends to adhere relatively closely to a proto-MT, it does exhibit a great deal of independence due to Jerome's use of the Old Latin text, Greek traditions, and even his own theological viewpoints. Various examples illustrate each of these tendencies.

The Vulgate's adherence to the Hebrew, for example, appears in its reading of the problematic statement in 1:3, "and the wicked will be ruined," in place of the Hebrew, "and causing the wicked to stumble." The

---

140 See ibid., 321; E. F. Sutcliffe, "The Name 'Vulgate,'" *Bib* 29 (1948) 345–52.

141 For discussion of this MS, see Samuel Berger, *Histoire de la Vulgate pendant les premiers siècles du moyen age* (1893; reprinted New York: Franklin, 1958) 37–38; see Bonifatius Fischer, "Codex Amiatinus und Cassiodor," in *Lateinische Bibelhandschriften im Frühen Mittelalter* (Freiburg: Herder, 1985) 11–34 (originally published in *BZ* 6 [1962] 57–79).

142 See Berger, *Histoire,* 14–15.

143 Ibid., 12–14, who notes that some date it to the eighth century.

144 Ibid., 18–21.

145 See ibid., 123.

146 See Bonifatius Fischer, "Die Alkuin-Biblen," in *Lateinische Bibelhandschriften,* 203–403.

147 For full discussion of the Vulgate MS tradition, see Berger, *Histoire,* and the essays published in Fischer, *Lateinische Bibelhandschriften.*

148 Alban Dold, *Prophetentexte in Vulgata-Übersetzung nach den ältesten Handschriften-Überlieferung der St. Galler Palimpseste No 193 und No 567* (Texte und Arbeiten I 1/2; Beuron: Erzabtei Beuron, 1917).

phrase is missing in the LXX, but the Vulgate retains it and attempts to make sense of it. The reference to the Philistines as "the destroyed nation" in 2:5 apparently draws on the root of the gentilic name Kerethites (see both MT and LXX). In that the Hebrew root of the term Kerethites is כרת, "to cut (off)," the Vulgate reads it as a term that characterizes the Philistines rather than as a gentilic (cf. Targum, "O, people that deserves to be cast out"). Another example of such interpretation of the Hebrew text appears in 2:13, where the Vulgate reads "Nineveh" as "the splendor," based on the meaning of the root נוה, "beautiful."

The Vulgate's dependence on Greek tradition appears in 1:5, where it reads "and swear to Milcom (*Melchom*) in place of the MT and LXX readings, "and swear to their king." The reference to the Moabite deity, Milcom, appears in the Lucian Greek and Peshitta texts. It reads the reference to the "Mishneh" quarter in 1:10 as "the second," much like the LXX, although it understands the preceding Hebrew reference to the "Fish Gate," rather than reading the expression as "from the gate of those stabbing/slaying" with the LXX. The Vulgate reads 2:12, "and you, O Ethiopians, shall be slain by my sword," with the LXX in place of the problematic MT, "and you, O Cushites, slain by the sword are they." It reads "a raven in the doorframes" in 2:14 with the LXX in place of the Hebrew, "desolation in the doorframe" (see also Peshitta). Finally, it follows the LXX in 3:1, reading "and redeemed city of the dove," in place of the Hebrew, "and defiled one, the city of the dove."

The Vulgate sometimes combines both Hebrew and Greek readings in a single translation. It reads 1:9, "and I will visit all who arrogantly step over the threshold," apparently reflecting both the MT, "and I will punish all who leap (הַדּוֹלֵג) over the threshold," and the LXX, "and I will punish all openly [reading Hebrew הַדּוֹלֵג as הַדֹּלֵק 'burn for'] concerning the vestibule."

Finally, the Vulgate's theological outlook or interpretation becomes clear by considering some of its key readings. Zephaniah 1:2 (cf. v. 3) reads *congregans congregabo*, "gathering, I shall gather," which many take as an indication that Jerome read the problematic Hebrew

expression אָסֹף אָסֵף as examples of the Hebrew root אסף, "to gather," rather than as סוף, "to destroy." There appears to be a theological element to his reasoning, however, in that he employs the same Latin verb for a different expression in 2:1, *convenite congregamini*, "assemble, be gathered (הִתְקוֹשְׁשׁוּ וָקוֹשּׁוּ)." This is particularly noteworthy in that it reads against the Hebrew ("I will surely destroy"), the LXX ("let there be indeed pass away"), and even the Old Latin (*defectione deficiat*, "let there indeed be failed/abandoned"). This allows him to create an analogy between the "gathering" of all creation in 1:2-6 and the "gathering" of the "unloved nation," Judah, in 2:1-3. Whereas the former has generally been understood as a portrayal of universal divine judgment and the latter as a portrayal of the prophet's exhortation to the people of Jerusalem and Judah, Jerome's text points to a sequence in which all creation and Jerusalem/Judah will witness G-d's actions of judgment and restoration, culminating in the Day of the L-rd. Whereas the Hebrew text of Zephaniah (and the others as well) portrays the Day of YHWH as a day of sacrifice and judgment against the wicked who will be purged from the land (see esp. 1:7-18; cf. 2:1-3, 4-15), Jerome portrays it as the day that Christ's resurrection will be manifest to all. This is evident in his reading of 3:8, "therefore wait for me, says the L-rd, in the day of my future resurrection (*in die resurrectionis meae in futuram*)," in place of the Hebrew expression, "therefore wait for me, utterance of YHWH, for the day of my rising as a witness." Jerome's choice of words at the outset of the book in 1:2-3, when read in relation to key statements in 2:1 and 3:8, make clear that he understands Zephaniah as a prophet who points to the coming eschatological revelation of Jesus to the world.

VII. Other Textual Traditions

In addition to the textual traditions discussed above, text editions of the book of Zephaniah have been published for a Coptic Akhmimic version,[149] an anonymous late-

---

149 Walter C. Till, *Die Achmimische Version der Zwölf Kleinen Propheten (Codex Rainerianus, Wien)* (Hauniae: Gyldendalske Boghandel-Nordisk Forlag,

1927). For collations of Coptic MSS pertaining to Zephaniah, see Willem Grousow, *The Coptic Versions of the Minor Prophets: A Contribution to the Study of the*

twelfth-century Judeo-Arabic Tafsir,[150] and a fourteenth-century Ethiopic version.[151]

VIII. Zephaniah in Later Traditions

Zephaniah also appears in a number of postbiblical Jewish and Christian traditions. The *Apocalypse of Zephaniah* is known by a citation in the *Stromata* (5.11) of Clement of Alexandria (late second century CE) and a fifth-century Sahidic papyrus.[152] The reference by Clement relates that the prophet was taken by a spirit to the fifth level of heaven, where he saw the angels singing hymns of praise to G-d. The Sahidic text relates that the prophet saw a human soul being flogged in the lower world by angels for sins from which it had not repented. When Zephaniah is confronted by angels bearing records of his evil and good deeds, he prays for deliverance, witnesses the transformation of his angelic guide, and ultimately joins the angelic host. The work is clearly designed to outline the two choices open to human beings, evil and righteousness, by pointing to the consequences of each. Scholars maintain that the *Apocalypse of Zephaniah* dates originally to Egyptian Jewish circles of the first century BCE to the first century CE.

The NT does not directly quote Zephaniah, but the Nestle-Aland edition of the NT suggests that it alludes to statements from the book four times.[153] The reference to the causes of sin in Matt 13:41 apparently alludes to the phrase, "and causes the wicked to stumble," in Zeph 1:3, although it is noteworthy that the phrase is missing in the LXX. The mention of "the great day of their wrath" in Rev 6:17 apparently alludes to the portrayal of the Day of YHWH as a day of wrath in Zeph 1:14-16. A similar reference to divine wrath in Rev 16:1 alludes to the outpouring of YHWH's wrath in Zeph 3:8. Finally, the

portrayal of the redeemed of the earth in Rev 14:5 alludes to the redeemed remnant of Israel mentioned in Zeph 3:11.

The first-century CE *Lives of the Prophets,* which describes the names of the prophets, where they are from, and where they are buried, includes a brief section on Zephaniah in *Liv. Pro.* 13:1-3.[154] It identifies Zephaniah as a member of the tribe of Simeon from the countryside of Sabaratha, that is, Biriath Satia, about 3.5 km. (2.1 mi.) north of Beit Jibrin (Eleutheropolis). It claims that Zephaniah prophesied about the city, the end of the Gentiles, and the shaming of the impious, and that he was buried at Sabaratha. Although this text likely originated in Judean Jewish circles, it was preserved in Christian sources, where it played a role in prompting the veneration of saints.

Rabbinic tradition identifies Zephaniah as the great-grandson of Hezekiah and a contemporary of Jeremiah and Huldah. According to *Seder Olam Rabbah* 20,[155] a midrashic chronological work ascribed to the second-century Tannaitic Rabbi Yose ben Halafta (*b. Yeb.* 82b; *Nid.* 46b), Zephaniah spoke (in the days of Josiah) after the time of Habakkuk (who spoke in the time of Manasseh) and at the beginning of the time of Jeremiah. He was therefore one of the many prophets who appeared in relation to the destruction of the temple in the days of Nebuchadnezzar. Zephaniah was a righteous man (*b. Meg.* 15a), and the teacher of Jeremiah. Whereas Jeremiah spoke on the streets of Jerusalem, Zephaniah preached in the synagogues and Huldah preached to the women (*Pesiq. R.* 26, 129b).

Septuagint (Monumenta biblica et ecclesiastica 3; Rome: Pontifical Biblical Institute Press, 1938) 73–76.

150 Abr. Heisz, *Eine anonyme arabische Uebersetzung und Erklärung der Propheten Zephanja, Haggai und Zecharja* (Berlin: Itzkowski, 1902).

151 Oscar Löfgren, *Jona, Nahum, Habakuk, Zephanja, Haggai, Sacharja und Maleachi Äthiopisch* (Uppsala: Almqvist & Wiksells, 1930).

152 See O. S. Wintermute, "Apocalypse of Zephaniah," *OTP* 1:497–507.

153 Eberhard Nestle, *Novum Testamentum Graece* (25th

ed.; London: United Bible Society, 1971) 670.

154 See D. R. A. Hare, "The Lives of the Prophets," *OTP* 2:379–99, esp. 394.

155 Samuel K. Mirsky, *Midrash Seder Olam* (Jerusalem: H. Vegshel/Tal Orot, 1988).

Zephaniah

1

Translation

1   **The word of YHWH[a] that was unto[b] Zepha-niah son of Cushi son of Gedaliah son of Amariah son of Hezekiah[c] in the days of Josiah son of Amon, king of Judah.[d]**

a   TJ reads, פתגם נבואה מן קדם יוי, "the word of prophecy from before YHWH." The use of קדם is designed to show respect for YHWH by portraying actions or entities "before" YHWH rather than in direct association with the Deity. The preposition is employed similarly in relation to kings and courtiers in Biblical Aramaic (see Ezra 4:18; 7:14; Dan 2:10; 5:17). For discussion, see Cathcart and Gordon, *Targum*, 5.

b   TJ reads, עם, "with"; Peshitta reads, ʿl, "upon."

c   Peshitta reads, br ʾmryʾ brh dḥlqyʾ, "son of Amariah the son of Hilkiah." For discussion, see the commentary below.

d   TJ reads, מלך שבטא דבית יהודה, "king of the tribe of the house of Judah."

Form and Setting

The superscription for the book of Zephaniah appears in 1:1. Superscriptions are statements prefixed to the body of a literary work (as opposed to subscriptions, which follow the body of the literary work), such as a book, a collection of songs, oracles, wisdom sayings, and so on, that are designed to introduce the following material to the reading or listening audience of the text.[1] They may include a combination of elements, such as the actual or purported author(s) of the work, its addressees, its generic character or literary type, some indication of its contents or topics, its historical or social setting, its purpose(s), and so on. They may function as the titles of literary works (e.g., Isa 1:1; Jer 1:1-3; Hos 1:1; Joel 1:1; Amos 1:1; Obad 1a; Mic 1:1; Nah 1:1; Hab 1:1; Mal 1:1; Prov 1:1; Cant 1:1; Qoh 1:1; Neh 1:1a), although they are not necessarily the same, since titles serve only as the distinguishing name of a work (see, e.g., the citation of חֲזוֹן יְשַׁעְיָהוּ בֶן־אָמוֹץ, "the vision of Isaiah ben Amoz," from Isa 1:1 as the title of the book of Isaiah in 2 Chr 32:32) and since superscriptions may appear within the body of a book to introduce a more limited textual block (e.g., Gen 2:4a; 5:1a; Lev 7:1; 7:11; Deut 12:1; Isa 2:1; 13:1; 15:1; 38:9; Jer 11:1; 45:1; 46:1; Hab 3:1; Zech 12:1; Pss 3:1; 4:1; Prov 30:1; 31:1). Super-scriptions find their social settings in the literary activity of the tradents of ancient literature who composed, preserved, studied, interpreted, and transmitted the works to which superscriptions were added to their various reading or listening audiences. Such tradents might include archivists, teachers, or even creative authors who sought to identify and classify prophetic literature so that it might be preserved for various uses, or provide the basis for further composition. An example of such a tradent appears in the figure of Baruch ben Neriah, Jeremiah's scribe, who recorded the prophet's words and sometimes conveyed them to others (e.g., Jeremiah 36).[2] Because of their introductory character and function, superscriptions are generically and structurally distinct from the material that they introduce. The superscription in Zeph 1:1 therefore constitutes the first major structural block or subunit of the book of Zephaniah, and the body of the book in 1:2–3:20 constitutes the second major structural block.

---

1   Sweeney, *Isaiah 1–39,* 539–40; Tucker, "Prophetic Superscriptions."

2   See Avigad, *Hebrew Bullae,* who publishes a collection of Hebrew bullae from the late monarchic period. Avigad's collection includes one "belonging to Berekyahu ben Neriyahu, the scribe (לברכיהו בן נריהו הספר)," which appears to be the name of

Jeremiah's scribe (see Avigad, *Hebrew Bullae,* 28–29; idem, "Baruch the Scribe and Jerahmeel the King's Son," *IEJ* 28 [1978] 52–56). Avigad's bullae were purchased from a Jerusalem antiquities dealer in 1975, which leaves scholars unable to confirm the archeological context in which they were found. Subsequent excavations at the City of David uncov-

The superscriptions of the prophetic books display a variety of formulations. All provide some generic identification of the contents of the book together with the name of the prophet, and many refer to the historical setting of the prophet's activities. Generic identification includes the characterization of the book as "the vision" (חָזוֹן) of the prophet (e.g., Isa 1:1; Obad 1a; Nah 1:1); "the words of" (דִּבְרֵי) the prophet (e.g., Jer 1:1; Amos 1:1; see also Prov 30:1; 31:1; Qoh 1:1; Neh 1:1a, which introduce wisdom compositions or memoirs); "the word of YHWH that was unto" (דְּבַר־ה׳ אֲשֶׁר הָיָה אֶל־) the prophet (e.g., Hos 1:1; Joel 1:1; Mic 1:1; Zeph 1:1; see also the variant in Mal 1:1 and Jer 1:2; Ezek 1:3; Jonah 1:1; Hag 1:1; Zech 1:1 in which this formulation or its variants appear in narrative form); and "the pronouncement of" (מַשָּׂא) the object of the prophet's concern (e.g., Nah 1:1; Mal 1:1) or simply "the pronouncement" that the prophet saw (e.g., Hab 1:1; see also Prov 30:1). The formulation of Zeph 1:1, דְּבַר־ה׳ אֲשֶׁר הָיָה אֶל־צְפַנְיָה בֶּן־כּוּשִׁי בֶּן־גְּדַלְיָה בֶּן־אֲמַרְיָה בֶּן־חִזְקִיָּה בִּימֵי יֹאשִׁיָּהוּ בֶן־אָמוֹן מֶלֶךְ יְהוּדָה, "the word of YHWH that was unto Zephaniah ben Cushi ben Gedaliah ben Amariah ben Hezekiah in the days of Josiah ben Amon, king of Judah," employs a combination of the prophetic word formula, the prophet's name together with a four-generation genealogy that identifies his ancestry, and a reference to the days of King Josiah ben Amon of Judah as the setting for the prophet's words. The prophetic word formula typically employs a reference to "the word of YHWH" (דְּבַר־ה׳) together with a form of the verb היה, "to be," and the preposition אֶל, "unto," to designate the party to whom the word of YHWH is communicated.[3] It appears commonly in narrative contexts to indicate the reception of a prophetic communication (e.g., 1 Sam 15:10; 1 Kgs 6:11) as well as in superscriptions (as noted above), both at the begin-

ning of prophetic books and within prophetic compositions, to identify the following material as the word of YHWH communicated to the prophet. It may also be employed in first person autobiographical accounts in which a prophet relates his or her own reception of a prophetic word from YHWH (e.g., Jer 1:4, 11; 2:1; Ezek 6:1; 7:1).

The present formulation of the superscription in Zeph 1:1 corresponds closely to the superscriptions in Hos 1:1 and Mic 1:1 (see also Joel 1:1, which lacks reference to the historical setting of the prophet's activities). The Greek text of Jer 1:1 (in LXX) appears to presuppose an analogous Hebrew *Vorlage* (i.e., τὸ ῥῆμα τοῦ Θεοῦ ὃ ἐγένετο ἐπὶ Ιερεμιαν τὸν τοῦ Χελκιου ἐκ τῶν ἱερέων ὃς κατῴκει ἐν Αναθωθ ἐν γῇ Βενιαμιν [דְּבַר־ה׳ אֲשֶׁר הָיָה אֶל יִרְמְיָהוּ בֶּן חִלְקִיָּהוּ מִן הַכֹּהֲנִים אֲשֶׁר בַּעֲנָתוֹת בְּאֶרֶץ בִּנְיָמִן]). In addition, Jer 1:1-3 (in MT) and Amos 1:1 appear to be variants of the same basic formulation that incorporate a reference to "the words of" (דִּבְרֵי) the prophet at the beginning. Although the superscription of Zephaniah places the prophet's activity in the late-seventh-century reign of Josiah and the superscriptions of Hosea, Amos, and Micah place their respective prophets in the late eighth century, the formal similarity suggests that these prophetic works were intended to be read together. There has been some speculation, based on the similarities of form in Hos 1:1; Amos 1:1; Mic 1:1; and Zeph 1:1 as well as on the common interest in establishing the historical settings of the prophets in question, that these books constituted some sort of a Deuteronomistically oriented early collection within the book of the Twelve.[4]

Indeed, the issue involves much more than only the compositional history of the book of the Twelve. It appears that there was a great deal of interest in establishing prophetic collections during the reign of King

ered a house destroyed by the Babylonians in 587/586 BCE that contained an archive of such bullae. Apparently, the house was the location of an archive or scribal office during the years immediately prior to the Babylonian destruction of Jerusalem. For discussion of the social dimensions of scribal activity in ancient Judah, see now David W. Jamieson-Drake, *Scribes and Schools in Monarchic Judah: A Socio-Archeological Approach* (JSOTSup 109; SWBA 9; Sheffield: Almond, 1991); cf. Floyd, *Minor Prophets*, 181–82.

3   Sweeney, *Isaiah 1–39*, 546–47; see also Samuel A.

Meier, *Speaking of Speaking: Marking Direct Discourse in the Hebrew Bible* (VTSup 46; Leiden: Brill, 1992) 314–19.

4   See Aaron Schart, *Die Entstehung des Zwölfprophetenbuchs. Neubearbeitungen von Amos im Rahmen schriftenübergreifender Redaktionsprozesse* (BZAW 260; Berlin: de Gruyter, 1998) 30–46, 157, who examines the similar formation of the superscriptions in Hos 1:1; Amos 1:1; Mic 1:1; and Zeph 1:1, and argues that they indicate a collection of prophetic books that represent an early stage in the compositional history of the book of the Twelve that he labels the

Josiah of Judah, who was also responsible for the composition of an early version of the Deuteronomistic History (Deuteronomy, Joshua, Judges, Samuel, Kings).[5] Apparently, the late-seventh-century version of the Deuteronomistic History was intended to point to Josiah as the ideal monarch of Israel, who would undo the past abuses of Israel's and Judah's kings and reunite the people under the rule of the Davidic dynasty. Various prophetic compositions, including early versions of Hosea, Amos, Micah, Isaiah, Zephaniah, and Jeremiah, were produced in order to present the young monarch's reign, with its program of national restoration and religious reform in the aftermath of the collapse of the Assyrian Empire, as the fulfillment of prophetic expectations, both past and present, of an ideal period of Davidic rule and national restoration that follow a period of punishment by the Assyrians. Apparently, the book of Zephaniah was composed to support Josiah's efforts at religious reform.

■ **1** The name Zephaniah derives from the Hebrew root צפן, "to conceal, hide, treasure," which is frequently employed in reference to YHWH's treasured saints (Ps 83:4), the concealment of YHWH's servants from evil (Pss 27:5; 31:21), or even as a designation for YHWH's "treasured" or "cherished" city of Jerusalem (Ezek 7:22). The name apparently means "YHWH has concealed/treasured," or the like, and would refer to YHWH's protection of the bearer of the name. The proposal to understand the name in reference to the Canaanite divine name, *b'l spn*, "Baal Zaphon," seems unlikely.[6] The proposal is based on a reading of the root צפן in relation to the noun צפון, "north," and the appearance of the *omicron* in the LXX's rendition of the name as Σοφονιας. Such a rendition would require that the name mean "Zaphon is YHWH," which presupposes a reference to the "north" as the mythological home of the Canaanite gods in Ugaritic literature. There is little evidence that such fifteenth-fourteenth-century names from

the Phoenician and north Syrian coast would have appeared in seventh-century Judah,[7] nor does it appear likely that the Greek form represents an earlier or original form of the name. The initial *omicron* or *o*-class vowel of Σοφονιας would hardly appear as the first vowel of *spn* in either Ugaritic or Hebrew. More importantly, the verbal sentence represented by the rendition of the name as "YHWH protects/conceals" constitutes a well-recognized common basis for forming personal names in Judah during the late monarchic period.

In addition to the prophet, the name Zephaniah is borne by three other figures in the Hebrew Bible. Zephaniah ben Maaseiah was a priest who served in the temple during the reign of King Zedekiah ben Josiah in the early sixth century, immediately prior to the Babylonian destruction of Jerusalem. According to Jer 21:1-10, the prophet Jeremiah delivered an oracle to Zephaniah ben Maaseiah and the priest Pashhur ben Malchiah that was to be conveyed to King Zedekiah in which YHWH stated plans to side with the Babylonians against Judah and the king. According to Jer 37:1-10, Zedekiah sent Zephaniah ben Maaseiah and Jehucal ben Shelemiah to Jeremiah to request that the prophet pray to YHWH on Judah's behalf. Jeremiah's response in this instance was that the Egyptians, who had pledged support to Judah, would return to Egypt and that the Chaldeans (neo-Babylonians) would take Jerusalem. Jer 52:24-27 identifies Zephaniah as "the second priest" who was put to death together with other Judean officials by Nebuchadnezzar at Riblah following the fall of Jerusalem. 1 Chr 6:33-38 identifies Zephaniah ben Tahath as the seventh-generation descendant of Levi and the twelfth-generation ancestor of the prophet Samuel. Zech 6:10-14 identifies Zephaniah as the father of Josiah (no known relation to the seventh-century monarch), in whose house the high priest Joshua ben Jehozadak would be crowned as a royal figure known as

"deuteronomic-deuteronomistic corpus." See also idem, "Reconstructing the Redaction History of the Twelve Prophets: Problems and Models," in James D. Nogalski and Marvin A. Sweeney, eds., *Reading and Hearing the Book of the Twelve* (SBLSymS 15; Atlanta: Society of Biblical Literature, 2000) 34–48; idem, "Redactional Models: Comparisons, Contrasts, Agreements, Disagreements," *SBLSP, 1998* (Atlanta: Scholars Press, 1998) 893–908.

5   For a full discussion of this issue, see Sweeney, *King Josiah*.

6   Liudger Sabottka, *Zephanja: Versuch einer Neuübersetzung mit philologischem Kommentar* (BibOr 25; Rome: Biblical Institute Press, 1972) 1–3.

7   See F. Schwally, "Das Buch Sefanjâ, eine historisch-kritische Untersuchung," *ZAW* 10 (1890) 165–66, who also points to the use of the root in Carthaginian names.

the "Branch" (cf. Isa 11:1-16; Jer 23:5-8; 33:14-26) and designated as the man to build the Temple of YHWH.

The prophet's genealogy, which traces his ancestry back to four generations, has provoked considerable comment, as it is very unusual, apart from the genealogies in Chronicles and Ezra-Nehemiah, to provide such a lengthy pedigree.[8] Many have speculated that the reason for such a lengthy genealogy is that his great-great-grandfather, Hezekiah, is to be identified as the late-eighth-century King Hezekiah ben Ahaz of Judah. Such an identification was made by the twelfth-century Spanish-Jewish commentator Abraham Ibn Ezra, who argued that Amariah ben Hezekiah must have been the brother of the Judean King Manasseh ben Hezekiah and who demonstrated that the chronology of four generations is appropriate for a prophet who spoke during Josiah's reign. This view was disputed by the twelfth-thirteenth-century commentator David Kimhi of Provencal (RaDaK), who argued simply that the prophet's ancestors are mentioned because they are (presumably all) noteworthy (lit. גְּדוֹלִים, "great ones"). Key to the issue is the identification of Amariah as the son of Hezekiah and older brother of Manasseh. Unfortunately, no son of Hezekiah named Amariah is known, although 2 Chr 31:15 lists an Amariah as one of the Levites appointed by Hezekiah to distribute freewill offerings in the cities of the priests. Manasseh was only twelve years old when he succeeded his father as king in Jerusalem (2 Kgs 21:1), which indicates that Hezekiah fathered him at the age of forty-two, following his revolt against Sennacherib (cf. 2 Kgs 18:1-2, which states that Hezekiah was twenty-five when he became king and ruled for twenty-nine years). It is likely that Hezekiah had other sons prior to Manasseh, and Sennacherib refers to taking daughters of Hezekiah into captivity.[9] Unfortunately, the lack of clear evidence requires that the matter be left open.

Interestingly, the Peshitta reads Hezekiah (*hzqyh*) as Hilkiah (*hlqyh*), and employs a combination of possessive pronominal suffix and the preposition *d* instead of the construct state employed for the other names to identify Amariah as the son of Hilkiah (i.e., "the son of Amariah the son of Hilkiah"; *br ʾmryʾ brh dhlqyʾ*). Such a construc-

tion emphasizes the genitive relationship between the two names. No other version or ancient manuscript presents such a reading. The shift in the reading of the names requires only a slight modification of the Syriac letter *zain* to *lamad*, as the two appear to be somewhat similar in the Estrangela script. Gerleman notes that the reading is probably to be attributed to the thirteenth-century Syrian archbishop, Bar Hebraeus, who identifies Hilkiah as the father of the prophet Jeremiah (see Jer 1:1) and maintains that Zephaniah and Jeremiah were relatives.[10] Gerleman correctly notes that Bar Hebraeus did not consider the chronological difficulties of such an assertion. Although Zephaniah and Jeremiah are presumably contemporaries who lived during the reign of Josiah, Zephaniah would be the great-great-grandson of Hilkiah whereas Jeremiah was Hilkiah's son. It is noteworthy, however, that Neh 8:4 lists a Hilkiah as one of the persons standing on the platform together with Ezra as he reads the Torah to the people, but 1 Esdr 9:43, which presumably presents the same list, identifies him as Hezekiah. Because several forms of Old Aramaic scripts indicate some similarities between *zayin* and *lamed*, and thus potential for confusion between the two letters, it is entirely possible that the shift in names in the Peshitta reflects an early mistaken reading that was rationalized by the observation that Hilkiah would have been the common ancestor of both Zephaniah and Jeremiah. Alternatively, the reading may reflect an attempt within the Syrian tradition or its precursors to resolve the problem of Zephaniah's potential royal descent, especially in view of the absence of any evidence that Hezekiah had a son named Amariah, by identifying him instead as a descendant of Hezekiah's priest Amariah and thus as Jeremiah's relative.

There has also been considerable discussion of Zephaniah's father, Cushi.[11] Although Cushi is presented here as a proper name, it appears in the common gentilic form that refers to Ethiopians, Nubians, or people from the land of Cush (for gentilic uses of the term, see Num 12:1; 2 Sam 18:21, 22, 23, 31, 32; Jer 13:23; 38:7, 10, 12; 39:16). Insofar as Ethiopians are black and apparently recognized as such in the Bible (see Jer 13:23, "can

8   For discussion see esp. Ben Zvi, *Zephaniah,* 41–51.
9   See Sennacherib's account of his campaign against Judah in 701 as recorded on the Taylor Prism in *ANET,* 287–88.
10   Gillis Gerleman, *Zephanja textkritisch und literarkritisch untersucht* (Lund: Gleerup, 1942) 1.
11   See esp. Roger W. Anderson Jr., "Zephaniah ben

Cushites change their skin?"), this raises the possibility that the prophet Zephaniah was of African ancestry. It was certainly possible for Judeans or Israelites to have African ancestry; one need only note the traditions that "a mixed crowd," generally understood as people who were the descendants of intermarriages with the Egyptians, accompanied Israel on the exodus from Egypt (see Exod 12:38; cf. Lev 24:10-23, which indicates the blasphemy of a man descended from an Israelite mother and an Egyptian father; Deut 23:7-8, which indicates that third-generation descendants of the Egyptians [and the Edomites] are to be admitted to the assembly of YHWH), Moses' marriage to a Cushite wife (Num 12:1; perhaps a reference to Zipporah's Midianite background; cf. Hab 3:7, which equates Cushan with Midian), Solomon's marriage to the daughter of Pharaoh (1 Kgs 3:1) and his liaison with the Queen of Sheba, generally identified as an east African or south Arabian kingdom. According to the fourteenth-century Ethiopian chronicle, *Kebra Negast* ("Glory of the Kings"), the Queen of Sheba's meeting with Solomon resulted in the birth of Menelik, the ancestor of the subsequent line of Ethiopian kings until the death of Haile Selassie in 1975 (1 Kings 10).[12] Hezekiah's alliance with the Ethiopians or the Egyptians is also noteworthy (Isaiah 30; 31; cf. Isaiah 18; 19–20; 36:6; 37:9; 2 Kgs 18:21; 19:9). Such an alliance would commonly be sealed with a marriage between the royal families in keeping with the customs of the day. Nevertheless, there are indications that the term "Cushi" was employed as a personal name as well. Jer 36:14 identifies Jehudi ben Nethaniah ben Shelemiah ben Cushi as a royal official sent to summon Baruch ben Neriah so that he might read Jeremiah's words before the king's officials. Likewise, Ps 7:1 labels the following

song as one sung by David to YHWH concerning Cush, a Benjaminite. Although some have questioned whether either of these instances may be understood as personal names, it seems unlikely that such an ethnic or racial epithet would function as a personal name in such a genealogy. Even those instances in which individuals are identified as Cushites employ the definite article so that Ebed-melech in Jeremiah 38–39 and the Cushite in 2 Samuel 18 are identified as "*the* Cushite" (הַכּוּשִׁי)[13] and Moses' wife is identified in Num 12:1 as "*the* Cushite woman" (הָאִשָּׁה הַכֻּשִׁית). Keller is undoubtedly correct in his observation that the intense discussion of this question is probably to be attributed to the European preoccupation with race.[14]

Finally, the superscription places Zephaniah's activity "in the days of Josiah ben Amon, king of Judah" (reigned 639–609 BCE). This indicates that Zephaniah spoke during the reign of the monarch who attempted to restore Judah during the late seventh century as an independent state in the aftermath of the collapse of the Assyrian Empire. Such efforts entailed purification of the Temple in Jerusalem and its establishment as the central institution for worship and the collection of the nation's economic resources as well as an attempt to reestablish Davidic rule over all the land and people of the northern tribes of Israel. The attempt apparently failed and led to King Josiah's death at Megiddo by the hand of Pharaoh Neco of Egypt, but Zephaniah's prophetic words appear to be composed as an exhortation that was designed to convince people to abandon pagan ways and provide support to the young king's program of restoration with its central focus on worship of YHWH alone at the Jerusalem Temple.

Cushi and Cush of Benjamin: Traces of Cushite Presence in Syria-Palestine," in S. W. Holloway and L. K. Handy, eds., *The Pitcher Is Broken: Memorial Essays for Gösta W. Ahlström* (JSOTSup 190; Sheffield: Sheffield Academic Press, 1995) 45–70; J. Heller, "Zephanjas Ahnenreihe (Eine redaktionsgeschichtliche Bemerkung zu Zeph. I 1)," *VT* 21 (1971) 102–4; G. Rice, "The African Roots of the Prophet Zephaniah," *JRT* 36 (1979) 21–31; Robert A. Bennett, "The Book of Zephaniah," *NIB* 7:670–72.

12   See E. Ullendorf, "The Queen of Sheba in Ethiopian Tradition," in J. B. Pritchard, ed., *Solomon*

and Sheba (London: Praeger, 1974) 104–14; Stephen D. Ricks, "Sheba, Queen of," *ABD* 5:1170–71.

13   The second reference to כּוּשִׁי in 2 Sam 18:21 lacks the definite article, which could suggest that the term functions as a proper name. All other instances of the term in this context, however, include the definite article, which indicates that it functions as a gentilic designation.

14   Carl-A. Keller, in René Vuilleumier and Keller, *Michée, Nahoum, Habacuc, Sophonie* (CAT XIb; Neuchâtel: Delachaux et Niestlé, 1971) 187 n. 2.

Because Zeph 1:2—3:20 follows the superscription in 1:1, it constitutes the second major structural component of the book. The passage is distinguished from the superscription both structurally and generically. Whereas 1:1 constitutes the editor's or narrator's introduction to the book as a whole that identifies the following material as the word of YHWH to Zephaniah, 1:2—3:20 constitutes YHWH's word to the prophet, as indicated by the superscription.[1] Zephaniah 1:1 presupposes an audience that reads or hears the book at some time after the prophet's initial address to his audience in seventh-century BCE Jerusalem and Judah, while 1:2—3:20 presupposes an audience that hears the prophet's words either at the time of the prophet's initial address or at later times when the book is heard or read. And 1:1 is formulated with objective reporting language that is designed to convey information about the book to the book's reading or listening audience, but 1:2—3:20 is formulated as a parenetic address that is designed to persuade its audience to seek YHWH and to avoid the consequences that will befall those who fail to do so, irrespective of whether the audience is to be identified as the audience of the book or the audience of the prophet. In these respects, 1:2—3:20 functions both as the words of the prophet Zephaniah and as the words of the book Zephaniah.

Parenesis is an address form that is employed to persuade an audience to adopt a particular set of beliefs or attitudes and/or to pursue a particular course of action.[2] Parenesis also includes a dissuasive element in that it is designed to convince its audience to give up an opposing set of beliefs or attitudes and to avoid an opposing course of action. It therefore comprises both exhortation, which constitutes the persuasive elements of parenesis, and admonition, which constitutes the dissuasive

elements of parenesis. Although both exhortation and admonition may appear separately as independent address forms, they are closely related and generally appear together as the two major components of parenesis.[3] Examples of parenetic address forms appear in Deuteronomy 6–11, which is designed to persuade the audience to observe YHWH's legal instruction that follows in Deuteronomy 12–26 and thereby to avoid the consequences inherent in a failure to observe YHWH's expectations.[4] It also appears in Isaiah 1 and 31, both of which are designed to convince the audience to change its behavior as YHWH prepares to cleanse Jerusalem and Judah by removing those who act contrary to YHWH's will.[5] Whereas Isaiah 1 is formulated generally, Isaiah 31 calls upon its audience to abandon plans to rely on Egyptian aid against Assyria and instead to rely solely on YHWH as the guarantor of Jerusalem's and Judah's security. Parenesis, exhortation, and admonition apparently derive from the general sphere of instruction, and appear to be rooted especially in the wisdom literature. Some examples from the sphere of wisdom appear in Prov 1:8-19, in which a parent instructs a child in proper conduct, or in literature that presupposes a cultic setting, such as Psalm 1, which calls on its audience to follow the instruction or Torah of YHWH, or Psalm 50, which impels its audience to call on YHWH in a time of distress.

The parenetic character of Zeph 1:2—3:20 is particularly evident in 2:1-3, which calls on the nation of Judah to seek YHWH and thereby to avoid divine wrath on the Day of YHWH.[6] Zephaniah 2:1-3 constitutes the rhetorical center of the book in that it defines and expresses its basic premise or purpose.[7] Many scholars group it together with 1:2-18 on thematic grounds because both 1:2-18 and 2:1-3 are concerned with the Day of YHWH.[8]

1   For discussion of the structural and generic distinctions between superscriptions and the material that they are intended to introduce, see Tucker, "Prophetic Superscriptions"; Sweeney, *Isaiah 1–39,* 539–40.

2   For discussion of the formal characteristics of parenesis, see Sweeney, *Isaiah 1–39,* 527.

3   See esp. Hunter, *Seek the Lord;* K. A. Tångberg, *Die prophetische Mahnrede* (FRLANT 143; Göttingen: Vandenhoeck & Ruprecht, 1987); T. M. Raitt, "The Prophetic Summons to Repentance," *ZAW* 83 (1971) 30–49; G. Warmuth, *Das Mahnwort* (BBET 1; Frank-

furt: Lang, 1976); H. W. Wolff, "Das Thema 'Umkehr' in der alttestamentlichen Prophetie," *ZThK* 48 (1951) 129–48; Sweeney, *Isaiah 1–39,* 513, 520.

4   For an analysis of the exhortative framework of Deuteronomy, see esp. Gerhard von Rad, *Studies in Deuteronomy* (SBT I/9; London: SCM, 1953) 11–24.

5   For discussion of these texts, see Sweeney, *Isaiah 1–39,* 63–87, 401–8.

6   Hunter, *Seek the Lord,* 259–70.

7   See Sweeney, "Form-Critical Reassessment."

8   E.g., Wilhelm Rudolph, *Micha–Nahum–Habakuk–*

Consequently 1:2—2:3 would form the first basic structural subunit of the book. Such a view is mistaken, however, because it fails to take account of the formal and rhetorical features of the text in relation to its thematic content. Zephaniah 2:1-3 is formulated with imperative verbs that are designed to address the audience directly and to call on it to take action, in this case to gather together, to seek YHWH, to seek righteousness, and to seek humility, as the Day of YHWH comes near. The imperative verbs are syntactically disjunctive, and draw the audience's attention away from the prophet's reporting and announcement language in 1:2-18, in which he reports YHWH's oracles (1:2-6) and announces that the Day of YHWH is about to come (1:7-18). The absence of a direct syntactical link to 1:2-18 heightens the foundational role of 2:1-3 within the book and identifies it as the fundamental premise of the entire book. Whereas 1:2-18 prepares the audience to expect the Day of YHWH with all of its consequences for those who have acted contrary to YHWH's will, 2:1-3 addresses the audience directly to demand their decision and action when the Day of YHWH actually takes place. Zephaniah 2:1-3 is thereby formulated to insure that the people in the audience realize that the consequences will apply to them if they do not make the correct decision now. The basis for such parenesis then appears in 2:4—3:20, which is syntactically joined to 2:1-3 by an introductory כִּי, "therefore," and which then lays out the reasons why the people should gather themselves to seek YHWH. As the following material in 2:4—3:20 indicates, YHWH's punishment of the nations (2:4-15) and YHWH's restoration of Jerusalem following its own period of punishment (3:1-20) provide ample reason to heed the prophet's call to adhere to YHWH's demands as the day of divine punishment against the wicked and restoration of the righteous draws near.

Zephaniah 1:2-18 then constitutes the prophet's announcement of the Day of YHWH within the overall context of Zephaniah's parenetic address to the people that calls on them to seek YHWH. Although it contains no overt exhortative or admonitory elements, it functions as an introduction to the formal parenetic address in 2:1—3:20 in that it introduces the Day of YHWH as the time at which YHWH will take action against those who act contrary to divine expectations. It therefore serves the admonitory aspects of the parenesis in that it prepares the audience to think of the Day of YHWH as a time when YHWH will unleash punishment against the wicked. The passage also therefore prepares the audience to respond positively to the exhortation to seek YHWH in 2:1—3:20; presumably, the lurid portrayal of the consequences of the Day of YHWH for those who reject YHWH will play an important role in persuading the audience to accept the prophet's proposal and thereby to avoid the punishment outlined in 1:2-18.

In order to serve this function, 1:2-18 employs the largely objective language of report and announcement to convey the images of the consequences that will befall the wicked on the Day of YHWH. The text begins in 1:2-6 with the prophet's report of YHWH's two oracular speeches in vv. 2-3a and 3b-6 concerning the Deity's intentions to destroy those within Jerusalem and Judah who have abandoned YHWH in order to pursue other deities. Although YHWH's identity as speaker is evident in the first person singular formulation of the speeches in vv. 2-3a and 3b-4, the prophet's role as the conveyor of YHWH's words is evident in the two instances of the formula נְאֻם־יְהוָה, "utterance/oracle of YHWH," within YHWH's words at the ends of v. 2 and v. 3. The prophet's role is also evident in the third person references to YHWH in vv. 5 and 6, although it is not entirely clear in vv. 3b-6 at what point YHWH's words conclude and the prophet's words begin. Many have argued that the universal language of vv. 2-3, in which YHWH threatens life in the whole of creation, stands in stark contrast to the explicit concern with Judah and Jerusalem in vv. 4-6, and that the universal language must be the product of a later hand that was interested in universalizing or eschatologizing the words of the prophet in the period of the Babylonian exile or the

Zephanja (KAT XIII/3; Gütersloh: Mohn, 1975) 255–56; Irsigler, *Gottesgericht*; Seybold, *Zephanja*, 92–104; J. J. M. Roberts, *Nahum, Habakkuk, and Zephaniah* (OTL; Louisville: Westminster John Knox, 1991) 161–63; Bennett, "Zephaniah," 662–67; Vlaardingerbroek, *Zephaniah*, 33–123.

postexilic restoration.[9] Such a view fails to consider that the Jerusalem Temple was conceived to be the holy center of creation in ancient Judean thought and that such universal references provide the context from which YHWH threatens those who have turned to other gods.[10] YHWH is conceived as the creator, and the Jerusalem Temple as the site from which creation proceeds. Those in Judah and Jerusalem who deny YHWH in order to turn to other gods therefore deny the very basis of YHWH's relationship with Jerusalem and Judah and the foundation for Jerusalem's and Judah's existence; YHWH is the creator, who places Jerusalem and Judah at the center of creation. To deny YHWH is to deny creation, including Jerusalem and Judah, itself.

Zephaniah 1:7-18 then turns to the prophet's announcement of the Day of YHWH. Once again, YHWH's words appear in vv. 8-9, 10-11, and 12-13 in the form of first person addresses in which the Deity threatens punishment against various parties among the people who reject YHWH to pursue pagan practices. Nevertheless, the prophet's role as the conveyor and interpreter of YHWH's speeches is once again evident in the third person references to YHWH that appear throughout the passage, such as the command for silence in v. 7, the reference to YHWH's sacrifice in v. 8, the appearance of the formula נְאֻם־יהוה, "oracle/utterance of YHWH," in v. 10, and the third person references to YHWH throughout the prophet's portrayal of the Day of YHWH in vv. 14-18. This passage comprises two basic components, each of which begins with the prophet's direct address to the audience concerning the approaching Day of YHWH. In vv. 7-13 the prophet begins with a command for silence because the Day of YHWH draws near, and he then proceeds to present YHWH's state-ments that threaten punishment against those who have abandoned the Deity. The prophet begins once again in vv. 14-18 with a direct address to the audience in which he announces that the Day of YHWH draws near. He then proceeds in vv. 14-16 to describe the bitterness and wrath of the Day of YHWH, and continues in vv. 17-18 with his depiction of the consequences for the people. Altogether, 1:7-18 is designed to build apprehension of the Day of YHWH in the audience as the people contemplate their own action in relation to the announced threat.

Zephaniah 1:2-18 clearly employs the Day of YHWH motif as part of a general scenario of threatened punishment to prepare the audience for the exhortation to seek YHWH in the following material. Scholars have extensively discussed the significance of the Day of YHWH and its setting in the life of ancient Israel or Judah.[11] Most agree that the Day of YHWH derives from the liturgical setting of the Israelite/Judean New Year or autumn festival in which YHWH's kingship over creation is recognized and renewed for the coming year. Indeed, the motifs of the renewal of divine sovereignty and the purification or resanctification of the world are inherent in the Jewish festivals of Rosh ha-Shanah (New Year, 1 Tishri), Yom Kippur (Day of Atonement, 10 Tishri), and Sukkot (Booths or Tabernacles, 15-23 Tishri), which are celebrated during the month of Tishri, roughly September-October, at the beginning of the autumn season. Rosh ha-Shanah marks the formal beginning of the New Year;[12] Yom Kippur is the Day of Atonement in which human beings ask forgiveness for wrongdoing, as their fate for the coming year is deter-

---

9 E.g., Renaud, *Sophonie*, 175–259; idem, "Sophonie."

10 For discussion of the concept of Jerusalem as the holy center of creation, see esp. Levenson, "Temple."

11 For overviews of the discussion, see K. J. Cathcart, "Day of Yahweh," *ABD* 2:84–85; Richard H. Hiers, "Day of the Lord," *ABD* 2:82–83; A. J. Everson, "Day of the Lord," *IDBSup* 209–10; Jacob Licht, "Day of the Lord," *EncJud* 5:1387-8. More specialized studies include Sigmund Mowinckel, *Psalmenstudien II* (Kristiana: Dybwad, 1922); Ladislav Černý, *The Day of Yahweh and Some Relevant Problems* (Prague: Nákladem Filosofické Fakulty University Karlovy, 1948); Gerhard von Rad, "The Origin of the Concept of the Day of Yahweh," *JSS* 4 (1959) 97–108; Meir Weiss, "The Origin of 'the Day of the Lord'—Reconsidered," *HUCA* 37 (1966) 29–60; John Gray, "The Day of Yahweh in Cultic Experience and Eschatological Prospect," *SEÅ* 39 (1974) 5–37; A. J. Everson, "The Days of Yahweh," *JBL* 93 (1974) 329–37; Yair Hoffmann, "The Day of the Lord as a Concept and a Term in the Prophetic Literature," *ZAW* 93 (1981) 37–50.

12 See Louis Jacobs, "Rosh Ha-Shanah," *EncJud* 14:305–10.

mined by G-d;[13] and Sukkot commemorates the period of wilderness wandering in the exodus traditions as the people were prepared for their entry into the promised land.[14] This period also marks the end of the dry hot summer and the beginning of the fall-winter rainy season, and thus it commemorates the renewal of creation as the fall rains bring the vegetation of the land back to life. It also marks the time of the late summer harvest in which the people go out into the fields and orchards and live in temporary dwellings or סֻכּוֹת, "booths," in order to bring in the year's harvest of grapes, olive oil, and other fruits that mature at this time.

In that the rule of the Davidic monarch is authorized by YHWH and rooted in the created order of the cosmos,[15] it is believed that the Davidic monarch's reign was symbolically renewed each year at this time so that the nation would be secure at the center of the cosmos. Indeed, many of the extant texts in the prophetic books of the Bible that take up the motif of the Day of YHWH portray YHWH's defense of Jerusalem/Israel from the enemy nations that threaten the existence of the nation and its role in the Deity's created world order.[16] In many cases, however, prophets portray the Day of YHWH as a day of threat against those in Israel or Judah who are considered to have rejected YHWH's expectations.[17] Interestingly, the often-cited example in Amos 5:18-20 appears to presuppose that the Day of YHWH is widely considered to be a day of blessing or light for Israel, but the prophet clearly portrays it as a day of threat or darkness in which the nation will be punished for the wrongdoing with which Amos charges it. In this respect, the Day of YHWH functions as a day of punishment or purification, both for creation at large and for Israel or Judah in particular. Both creation and its center in Israel or Jerusalem are thus purified and renewed for the coming year.

The Day of YHWH is thus presented throughout Zeph 1:2-18 as a day of sacrifice and purification of Jerusalem and Judah. Some see this as a sign of a later hand interested in introducing postexilic ritual concerns into the text.[18] One should note, however, that sacrifice and repentance function together in ancient Judah as the primary means to maintain or restore the relationship between the people of Jerusalem/Judah and YHWH in the context of all creation. It functions especially as part of a purification process in which the people and all creation are cleansed of impurity and wrongdoing so that the holiness of creation might be achieved or realized. In this respect, the Day of YHWH must be viewed as part of the process by which Jerusalem and Judah—and indeed, all creation—are purified and restored to a holy relationship with YHWH.

Insofar as King Josiah's religious reform was designed for such national purification and restoration, it would appear that Zeph 1:2-18 was written to support Josiah's program and efforts.[19] Although many see the continued references to pagan practice in this chapter as a sign that perhaps Josiah's reform had failed,[20] such practices are best understood as the very targets of the religious elements of the young king's reforms. This would require that Zephaniah's words reflect the situation in Jerusalem and Judah at the outset of the king's reforms, very likely about the twelfth year of his reign (i.e., 628–627 BCE; see 2 Chr 34:3; contra 2 Kgs 22:3, which marks the beginning of Josiah's reforms in his eighteenth year [622–621] following the discovery of the book of Torah in the temple), which coincides with the year of Nabopolassar's accession to the Babylonian throne and its revolt against Assyria following Ashurbanipal's death. In keeping with Hezekiah's former alliance

---

13 See M. D. Herr and J. Milgrom, "Day of Atonement," *EncJud* 5:1376–87.

14 See Ernst Kutsch and Louis Jacobs, "Sukkot," *EncJud* 15:495–502.

15 See Psalm 89; 2 Sam 23:1-7.

16 E.g., Isaiah 13; 34; Joel; Obadiah.

17 E.g., Ezek 13:5; Amos 5:18-20; Zephaniah 1; Mal 3:19; cf. Isa 2:6-21, in which the Day of YHWH is directed against those who are arrogant throughout the world, whether from Israel or from the nations.

18 E.g., Renaud, *Sophonie,* 189–91; idem, "Sophonie."

19 For a full discussion of Josiah's program of religious reform and national restoration, including the role played by prophetic literature, see Sweeney, *King Josiah.*

20 See Donald Williams, "The Date of Zephaniah," *JBL* 82 (1963) 77–88.

21 See Isaiah 39/2 Kgs 20:12-19. For discussion of

with the Babylonian prince Merodach-baladan against Sennacherib in the late eighth century, Josiah appears to have allied with Nabopolassar against Assyria in the late seventh century.[21] Josiah's religious reform was part of a larger program of national restoration that was designed to reunite all of Israel under Davidic rule. Zephaniah's prophecy would have been delivered to support that effort.

Merodach-baladan and his alliances, see esp. J. A. Brinkman, "Merodach Baladan II," in R. D. Biggs and J. A. Brinkman, eds., *Studies Presented to A. Leo Oppenheim, June 7, 1964* (Chicago: Oriental Institute, 1964) 6–53; Sweeney, *Isaiah 1–39,* 505–11; idem, *King Josiah,* ad loc.

1

Translation

2 "I will utterly destroy[a] everything[b] from
upon the face of the ground,"
utterance of YHWH.
"I will destroy[c] human and animal;

3 I will destroy[d] the bird of the heavens,
and the fish of the sea,
and those who cause the wicked to stumble."[e]
"And I will cut off[f] humanity from upon the
face of the ground,"
utterance of YHWH,

4 "and I will stretch out my hand[g] against
Judah
and against all the inhabitants of
Jerusalem,
and I will cut off from this place the remnant of Baal
and the name of the cultic attendants
with the priests[h]

5 and those who prostrate themselves
upon the rooftops[i]
to the host of heaven
and those who prostrate themselves[j] who
are sworn[k] to YHWH[l]
and who are sworn by their king[m]

6 and those who turn aside from after
YHWH,[n]
and who do not seek YHWH[o] and do not
inquire[p] of him."

a MT reads, אָסֹף אָסֵף; cf. TJ, שיצאה אשיצי, "I will
utterly destroy." Contra LXX, Ἐκλείψει ἐκλιπέτω,
"let there indeed pass away," אָסֹף הֵאָסֵף, "indeed, be
gathered"); 8HevXIIgr, συναγωγῇ συναγω, "let
there surely be gathered (אָסֹף הֵאָסֵף, "indeed, be
gathered"); Peshitta, mᶜbrw mᶜbr ʾnʾ, "I am surely
removing," אָסֹף אֹסֵף; Vulgate, congregans congregabo,
"gathering, I will gather; Old Latin, defectione
deficiat, "let there indeed pass away."

b Lacking in LXX and 8HevXIIgr, but implied in the
statements, Ἐκλείψει ἐκλιπέτω, "let (all) indeed
pass away (all)" (LXX); συναγωγῇ συναγω, "let (all)
surely be gathered" (8HevXIIgr).

c MT reads, אָסֵף; cf. TJ, אסיף, "I will remove." Contra
LXX, ἐκλιπέτω, "let there pass away" (אָסֵף or הֵאָסֵף,
"be gathered"); 8HevXIIgr lacks a reading due to
scroll damage; Peshitta, mᶜbr ʾnʾ, "I am removing,"
(אֹסֵף); Vulgate, congregans, "gathering"; Old Latin,
deficiat, "passing away."

d Again MT reads, אָסֵף; cf. TJ, אסיף, "I will remove."
Contra LXX, ἐκλιπέτω, "let there pass away" (אָסֵף or
הֵאָסֵף, "be gathered"); 8HevXIIgr lacks a reading
due to scroll damage; Peshitta, mᶜbr ʾnʾ, "I am
removing" (אֹסֵף); Vulgate, congregans, "gathering";
Old Latin, deficiat, "passing away."

e MT reads, וְהַמַּכְשֵׁלוֹת אֶת־הָרְשָׁעִים; cf. Peshitta, wtwqltʾ
ʾytʾ ᶜl ḥtyʾ, "and stumbling blocks there are upon the
sinners/wicked"; Vulgate, et ruinae impiorum erunt,
"and ruined will be the wicked." The phrase is lacking in the LXX and Old Latin. Although the phrase
is also lacking in 8HevXIIgr due to scroll damage,
Tov maintains that there is room for a Greek rendition of the phrase to have appeared (Tov, *Greek Minor
Prophets*, 94). TJ reads, על דאסגיאה תקלת רשיעיא,
"because the taxes of the wicked have increased."
See the discussion of v. 3 below.

f MT reads, וְהִכְרַתִּי; cf. LXX, καὶ ἐξαρῶ, "and I will lift
off"; TJ, ואשיצי, "and I will destroy": Peshitta, wʾwbd,
"and I will destroy"; Vulgate, disperdam, "and I will
destroy"; Old Latin, et auferam, "and I will remove."

g MT reads, יָדִי, "my hand." Cf. TJ, מחת גבורתי, "the
stroke/plague of my power."

h MT reads, אֶת־שְׁאָר הַבַּעַל אֶת־שֵׁם הַכְּמָרִים עִם־הַכֹּהֲנִים.
See also Peshitta, šᵊʾrbh dbᶜlʾ wšm dkwmrʾ ᶜm dkhnʾ,
"the remnant of Baal, and the name of the cultic
attendants with the priests"; TJ, ית שאר בעלא ית שום
פלחיהון עם כומרתהון, "the remnant of Baal, the
name of their worshipers with their (pagan)
priests"; Vulgate, reliquias Baal et nomina aedituorum
cum sacerdotibus, "the remnant of Baal and the name
of the temple attendants with the priests." Cf. LXX,
τοῦ τὰ ὀνόματα τῆς Βααλ καὶ τὰ ὀνόματα τῶν
ἱερέων, "and the names of Baal and the names of
the priests"; 8HevXIIgr, τὸ] ὑπ[όλειμμα]Βααλ τὸ
ὄνομα τῶ[ν χωμα]ρειμ μ[ετὰ τῶν ἱ]ερέων, "the]

re[mnant of] Baal, the name of the Ko[ma-]rim w[ith the p]riests."

i MT reads, עַל־הַגַּגּוֹת; cf. LXX, ἐπὶ τὰ δώματα, "upon the houses."

j MT reads, וְאֶת־הַמִּשְׁתַּחֲוִים, which reduplicates the initial expression of v. 5; cf. LXX, which eliminates this occurrence of the expression, apparently for stylistic reasons. The expression is retained in TJ, Peshitta, and Vulgate. Although it is lacking in 8HevXIIgr due to scroll damage, there is apparently sufficient space to include a rendition of the phrase.

k MT reads, וְהַנִּשְׁבָּעִים, "and those who swear/are sworn (to)." Cf. Peshitta, wymyn, "and those who are firm/faithful (with)."

l TJ adds, בשמא, "in the name [of YHWH]."

m MT reads, בְּמַלְכָּם, "by their king"; cf. LXX, κατὰ τοῦ βασιλέως αὐτῶν, "by their king." The Lucianic Greek tradition reads, κατὰ τοῦ Μελχομ, "by Mil-

com"; cf. Peshitta, bmlkwm, "by Milcom"; Vulgate, in Melchom, "by Milcom." TJ reads, תבין שום פתכריהון, "and returning in the name of their idols," which apparently renders the expression in reference to the pagan god, Milcom. Although the reading is lacking in 8HevXIIgr, Tov proposes that it should read ἐν τῷ μελχομ, "in Milcom," due to space considerations (Greek Minor Prophets, 95).

n TJ adds, פולחנא "the service [of YHWH]."

o TJ adds דחלתא, "the fear (of YHWH)."

p MT reads, וְלֹא דְרָשֻׁהוּ "and (they) did not seek him." Cf. LXX, καὶ τοὺς μὴ ἀντεχομένους τοῦ κυρίου "and those not clinging to the L-rd"; TJ, ולא בעו מן קדמוהי, "and they did not ask from before him"; Peshitta, wlʾ mʿqbin ʿlwh, "and are not following upon him"; Vulgate, nec investigaverunt eum, "nor inquire of him."

Form and Setting

Zephaniah 1:2-6 constitutes a distinctive formal subunit within the larger context of 1:2-18 in which the prophet presents YHWH's oracular speeches prior to the announcement of the Day of YHWH in vv. 7-18. Verses 2-6 comprise two oracular speech reports in vv. 2 and 3-6 in which the prophet conveys and elaborates on YHWH's statements concerning the upcoming punishment of those in Jerusalem and Judah who engage in syncretistic religious practice. The oracular formula נְאֻם־ה׳, "utterance of YHWH," appears within each of these texts, at the end of v. 2 and at the end of v. 3b, to identify the prophet as the speaker and to indicate that he speaks on behalf of YHWH and conveys YHWH's own statements. The use of this technical language suggests that Zephaniah may well have been a professional prophet or oracle diviner who worked either within or in relation to the temple or another holy site.[1] YHWH's

statements appear clearly in first person singular form throughout both passages in vv. 2 and 3-5a, but the shift to third person form—including several third person references to YHWH—indicates that the prophet emerges once again in vv. 5b-6 with his own words in an effort to specify the targets of YHWH's punitive statements in vv. 4-5a. Altogether, the two oracular reports prepare the audience for the announcement of the Day of YHWH, which will be a day of judgment and purification directed against those who have abandoned YHWH, in vv. 7-18.

The first oracular speech report appears in v. 2. As noted above, it comprises a first person statement by YHWH together with an example of the oracular formula that identifies Zephaniah as the speaker who quotes and conveys YHWH's words. This particular text is demarcated on both generic and syntactical grounds. It is clearly not part of the preceding superscription in v. 1, and it lacks any syntactical connector at the outset

---

1   Examples include Moses, who delivered oracles to the people of Israel based on his experience of YHWH while secluded in the tent of meeting (Exod 33:7-11); Isaiah, who apparently delivered YHWH's oracle concerning Sennacherib to Hezekiah in the temple (2 Kgs 19:1-34; Isa 37:1-35); or Huldah, who resided in Jerusalem's Mishneh quarter, but delivered an oracle concerning the discovery of a Torah scroll in the temple (2 Kgs 22:11-20). Although Balaam is presented satirically in Numbers 22–24, his actions are sometimes described as those of a Mesopotamian baru priest or oracle diviner who

discerns the message of the gods by reading signs produced by divinatory procedures (S. Daiches, "Balaam—a Babylonian bārū," in H. V. Hilprecht Anniversary Volume [Leipzig: Hinrichs, 1909] 60–70; contra Abraham Malamat, "A Forerunner of Biblical Prophecy: The Mari Documents," in Patrick D. Miller, Paul D. Hanson, and S. Dean McBride, eds., Ancient Israelite Religion: Essays in Honor of Frank Moore Cross [Philadelphia: Fortress Press, 1987] 33–52, esp. 49–50 n. 20, who considers Balaam perhaps to be an example of the āpilum, "answerer," prophet found at Mari). Ezekiel may also reflect the

that would join it to the superscription. Likewise, there is no syntactical join with the following material in v. 3, although the repeated appearance of the verb אָסֵף, "I will destroy," in v. 3aα[1] and 3aα[4] reiterates the initial verbal expression of v. 2, אָסֹף אָסֵף, "I will utterly destroy" (for discussion of this expression, see the commentary on vv. 2, 3 below). This indicates that the following material beginning in v. 3 must be read together with that of v. 2 as a subunit that continues and builds on the line of thought presented in v. 2. Essentially, v. 2 presents YHWH's basic statement indicating the intention to destroy everything in the land. It serves as the basic premise for the following material in vv. 3-6 in which YHWH progressively narrows the focus of divine punishment to those in Jerusalem and Judah who have engaged in syncretistic religious practice and therefore have abandoned YHWH.

Many scholars claim that this verse (and v. 3) must be a late composition because of its universal perspective and its correspondence to the portrayal of creation in the P material of Gen 1:1–2:3.[2] Nevertheless, one must recognize that the Temple in Jerusalem was the fundamental religious institution of ancient Judah from the time of Solomon and that the temple was conceived to be the holy center of all creation in ancient Judean thought.[3] Because YHWH is posited as the creator and the Jerusalem Temple as YHWH's sanctuary, the threat to begin a purge of creation that would focus on Jerusalem and Judah in particular makes a great deal of sense, especially since such a program corresponds to the aims of Josiah's reforms.

The prophet's second oracular speech report appears in vv. 3-6. The oracular formula appears in the midst of the subunit at the end of v. 3. Otherwise, these verses comprise first person speech by YHWH in vv. 3-5a and the prophet's elaboration on YHWH's words in vv. 5b-6. Although two examples of the verb אָסֵף, "I will destroy," appear in v. 3aα, which indicates continuity with the initial verbal expression אָסֹף אָסֵף, "I will utterly destroy," in v. 2, the absence of a syntactical connector indicates that v. 3 begins a second subunit that follows and builds on the initial subunit of v. 2. In this respect, YHWH's dual statements, "I will destroy human and animal" in v. 3aα[1-3] and "I will destroy the bird of the heavens and the fish of the sea" in v. 3a[4-8], specify YHWH's intention to utterly destroy everything on the face of the ground in v. 2. Verse 3aα, "and those who cause the wicked to stumble," is generally recognized as a gloss, but in the present form of the text it further defines the objects of YHWH's wrath as those entities that prompt the people to engage in wicked or improper practice (see below for detailed discussion of this statement).

The impetus to further specification of YHWH's statements continues in vv. 3b-5. The appearance of the oracular formula at the end of v. 3 and the first person perspective of vv. 3b-4 indicate that the prophet continues to convey YHWH's speech. The *waw*-consecutive construction of the initial verb of v. 3b, וְהִכְרַתִּי, "and I will cut off," establishes a syntactical link between the presentation of YHWH's statements in v. 3a and the material that begins in v. 3b. Indeed, the appearance of first person *waw*-consecutive verbs at the beginning of v. 4a and v. 4b indicates that these verbs form a syntactical chain that begins with the finite verbal forms, that is, the two occurrences of אָסֵף, "I will destroy," in v. 3a. Likewise, the conjunctive *waw*s that appear at the begin-

---

role of an oracle diviner in that the people come to consult him concerning the word of YHWH (e.g., Ezek 3:12-27; 14:1-23; 20:1-44). For discussion of prophecy and oracle divination in Israel and the ancient Near East, see Frederick H. Cryer, *Divination in Ancient Israel and Its Ancient Near Eastern Environment: A Socio-Historical Investigation* (JSOTSup 142; Sheffield: Sheffield Academic Press, 1994); Lester Grabbe, "Prophets, Priests, Diviners and Sages in Ancient Israel," in Heather A. McKay and David J. A. Clines, eds., *Of Prophets' Visions and the Wisdom of Sages: Essays in Honour of R. Norman Whybray on His Seventieth Birthday* (JSOTSup 162; Sheffield: JSOT Press, 1993) 43–62.

2 E.g., Renaud, *Sophonie,* 196–97; idem, "Sophonie," esp. 4–10; Marco Striek, *Das vordeuteronomistische Zephanjabuch* (BBET 29: Frankfurt am Main: Lang, 1999) 84–91. For a convenient summary of the discussion, see Michael De Roche, "Zephaniah I 2-3: The 'Sweeping' of Creation," *VT* 30 (1980) 104–9. Although De Roche notes the dependence of these verses on both the P and J creation account in Genesis 1–3, he opines that P must perhaps be dated to a period earlier than the exile.

3 See Levenson, "Temple."

ning of the third person statements in vv. 5a, 5bα, 5bβ, 6a, 6bα, and 6bβ establish a syntactical link between these statements by the prophet and the preceding statements by YHWH.[4] Altogether, vv. 3b-6 form a formal block that continues and develops the earlier statements in v. 3a.

Verses 3b-6 comprise a sequence of three first person *waw*-consecutive statements by YHWH that are presented and expanded by the prophet. The first returns to the initial premise of v. 3a, that YHWH intends to destroy human beings, and thereby initiates the sequence of statements that specify which human beings will be the targets of YHWH's punishment. Indeed, the statement also picks up the language of v. 2 by indicating that these persons will be "cut off . . . from upon the face of the ground." The oracular formula insures that the readers understand that the prophet presents YHWH's words. The second statement in the sequence begins in v. 4a with YHWH's threat, "and I will extend my hand against," and further specifies the target of YHWH's wrath as "Judah" and "all the inhabitants of Jerusalem." The implication is that these persons are the specific group within humanity that are to be cut off from the land. The third statement in the sequence begins in v. 5b and further specifies YHWH's targets as "the remnant of Baal" and "the name of the cultic attendants with the priests." These terms will be discussed in more detail below, but at this point it is clear that they refer to those in Jerusalem and Judah who engage in apostasy or syncretistic behavior insofar as they are identified with Baal. Certainly, the statement that they will be cut off "from this place," an expression frequently employed in reference to the temple,[5] supports such a view and suggests cultic purification. As noted above, the absence in v. 5a of first person language that identi-

fies YHWH as the speaker as well as third person references to YHWH make it difficult to determine whether this statement is a part of YHWH's or the prophet's speech. In any case, the statement further defines the somewhat ambiguous "cultic attendants" as those who worship the "host of heaven" upon the rooftops.

As noted above, the third person references to YHWH in vv. 5b-6 indicate clearly that YHWH is no longer the speaker and that the prophet has begun to speak once again. Furthermore, the sequence of *waw*s in these verses, particularly those connected to the direct object particle אֵת in vv. 5b and 6a, indicates that these statements are to be read as part of the formal subunit in vv. 3b-6 as part of the prophet's presentation of YHWH's speech. The initial expression of v. 5b, וְאֵת הַמִּשְׁתַּחֲוִים, "and those who worship," reduplicates that of v. 5a, and indicates that these verses represent the prophet's own effort further to specify the objects of YHWH's wrath as delineated in v. 5a (which in turn specify the preceding statements). In this case, the prophet's remarks point to the simultaneous swearing of fidelity to YHWH and to the pagan god Milcom, the turning away from YHWH, and the refusal to seek YHWH. All of these actions represent clear acts of syncretism and apostasy that both YHWH and the prophet intend to condemn.

■ **2** The initial expression of this verse, אָסֹף אָסֵף, "I will utterly destroy," has proved to be extremely difficult to explain.[6] In the present form of the MT, it comprises a combination of the infinitive absolute form of the verbal root אָסַף, "to gather," and a first person common singular *hiphil* imperfect form of the verbal root סוּף, "to destroy."[7] Although the appearance of an infinitive absolute verb before a finite verbal form is a common means to express emphasis or intensity in Biblical

4   Note that although v. 5a is somewhat ambiguous in that it is not clearly formulated in first person language, it appears to continue YHWH's statements in v. 4b by specifying that "the remnant of Baal" and "the cultic attendants" are to be identified as "those who worship on the rooftops to the host of heaven." The third person references to YHWH in vv. 5b-6 indicate clearly that these verses are to be read as statements by the prophet that elaborate on the meaning of v. 5a. For further discussion, see below.

5   E.g., 1 Kgs 8:29, 30, 35; 2 Chr 6:20, 21, 26; Jer

27:22. For a full listing of references, see BDB, 880, §4.

6   See esp. the discussions in Vlaardingerbroek, *Zephaniah*, 57–59; Ben Zvi, *Zephaniah*, 51–53; Irsigler, *Gottesgericht*, 6–11; Sabottka, *Zephanja*, 5–7; Gerleman, *Zephanja*, 2–3.

7   Notably, examples of the verb סוּף are rare in Biblical Hebrew, appearing elsewhere in the *qal* only in Isa 66:7; Amos 3:15; Ps 73:19; and Esth 9:28. The *hiphil* examples of the verb in Zeph 1:3 (twice, see below) and Jer 8:13 are identical to that of the present verse, and indeed, Jer 8:13 employs a combina-

Hebrew, the use of an infinitive absolute derived from a verb other than that of the following finite form has never been adequately demonstrated.[8] Three other potential examples are known in Biblical Hebrew. Jer 8:13, אָסֹף אֲסִיפֵם, "I will utterly destroy them," presents a variation of the same construction as that of the present verse. Isa 28:28, אָדוֹשׁ יְדוּשֶׁנּוּ, "he surely threshes it," presents a different set of problems as the infinitive absolute אָדוֹשׁ appears to derive from the verbal root אדשׁ, "to thresh(?)," as opposed to the root דושׁ, "to thresh," of יְדוּשֶׁנּוּ. There is no other known usage of a verbal root אדשׁ. There have been attempts to argue that both אָדוֹשׁ and אָסֹף represent unique *hiphil* infinitive absolute forms of the verbal roots דושׁ and סוף, respectively, analogous to the Aramaic *aphel* infinitive forms of middle weak verbs such as קום, but there is no other evidence for such forms in Biblical Hebrew.[9] 2 Sam 1:6, נִקְרֹא נִקְרֵיתִי, "I happened to be," combines the *niphal* infinitive absolute form of the root קרא, "to meet, call," with the *niphal* first person singular perfect form of the root נקה, "to happen, occur," but most scholars argue that נִקְרֹא is an erroneous rendition of נִקְרֹה as *lamed-ʾalep* and *lamed-he* verbs are frequently confused.[10] Notably, all of these examples involve instances in which the two roots share two root letters, which perhaps plays a role in prompting their association.

The problem is exacerbated by the appearance of the expression אָסֹף אֶאֱסֹף, "I will surely gather," in Mic 2:12, which is a combination of the infinitive absolute and the first person common singular *qal* imperfect forms of the verbal root אסף, "to gather." This example demonstrates that the expected combination of forms from the same verbal root does occur in Biblical Hebrew. It therefore has provoked attempts to argue that the two verbal forms of Zeph 1:1 (and Jer 8:13) are indeed both derived from the root אסף, but this inevitably requires emendation of אָסֹף.[11] As the example in Mic 2:12 demonstrates, the standard first person singular common *qal* imperfect form of אסף is אֶאֱסֹף. Some have argued that אָסֹף must be read as an example of the *qal* form in which the initial vowels *segol* and *shewa* have elided into a single long vowel *qames*, just as they elide into the long vowel *holem* in *qal* imperfect verbs such as אֹמַר (from אֶאֱמֹר), "I will say," or אֹכַל (אֶאֱכֹל), "I will eat."[12] The appearance of the *sere* is explained by reference to the second person common singular *qal* imperfect form of the root אסף in Ps 104:29, תֹּסֵף, "you will gather." Of course, there is no other secure example of a *qal* imperfect form of אסף in which the *qames* appears with an initial *ʾalep*, and most proponents of this solution are forced to emend אָסֹף to אֹסֵף in order to make the argument work.[13] Although attractive in some respects, this does not explain how

tion similar to that of Zeph 1:2 (see the discussion below).

8   For discussion see GKC, 344 n. 3.

9   See Jacob Barth, *Die Nominalbildung in den semitischen Sprachen* (2d ed.; Hildesheim: Olms, 1894) 73. See also A. van Hoonacker, *Les douze petits prophètes* (EB; Paris: Gabalda, 1908) 508; J. M. P. Smith, W. H. Ward, and J. A. Bewer, *A Critical and Exegetical Commentary on Micah, Zephaniah, Nahum, Habakkuk, Obadiah, and Jonah* (1911; ICC; reprinted Edinburgh: T & T Clark, 1985) 191; and Gerleman, *Zephanja*, 3.

10   See GKC, §75rr; Paul Dhorme, *Les livres de Samuel* (EB; Paris: Gabalda, 1910) 265; S. R. Driver, *Notes on the Hebrew Text and Topography of the Books of Samuel* (2d ed.; Oxford: Clarendon, 1913) 232.

11   See Roberts, *Zephaniah*, 167; Rudolph, *Zephanja*, 261; Ernst Sellin, *Das Zwölfprophetenbuch* (2d-3d ed.; 2 vols.; KAT XII; Leipzig: Deichert, 1930) 420, 421; Karl Marti, *Das Dodekapropheton* (KHC XIII; Tübingen: Mohr [Siebeck], 1904) 361-62.

12   The argument goes back to Rashi. See also F. Horst, *Die Zwölf Kleinen Propheten* (3d ed.; HAT 14; Tübin-

gen: Mohr [Siebeck], 1964) 190; Sellin, *Zwölfprophetenbuch*, 420, 421; Wilhelm Nowack, *Die Kleinen Propheten* (HKAT III/4; Göttingen: Vandenhoeck & Ruprecht, 1922) 292; Marti, *Dodekapropheton*, 361-62; Julius Wellhausen, *Die Kleinen Propheten* (Berlin: de Gruyter, ³1898; ⁴1963) 150.

13   E. Lipiński, review of A. S. Kapelrud, *The Message of the Prophet Zephaniah*, VT 25 (1975) 688-90, reads אָסֹף as a *qal* first person singular imperfect form based on the analogy of וַיֵּאָצֶל, "and he withdrew," in Num 11:25. Although וַיֵּאָצֶל appears to represent a *hiphil* form of the verb, Gesenius points out that the verb appears elsewhere only in *qal* and *niphal* forms (GKC, §68f). According to Lipiński's analysis, the initial *qames* of אסף (and וַיֵּאָצֶל) did not shift to *holem* due to the elision of the *ʾalep*, as is usually the case in *qal* examples of imperfect *pe-ʾalep* verbal forms, but preserves an archaic form instead. He further argues that *sere/segol* of both forms may be explained by reference to תֹּסֵף, "you will gather/remove," in Ps 104:29 in which the *sere* appears in place of the expected *holem*. Although attractive,

the Masoretes would have understood the form or why they would have changed the initial *ḥolem* to *qameṣ* in אָסֵף.[14]

An alternative would be to read אָסֵף as an example of the first person common singular *hiphil* imperfect form of אסף.[15] The contention requires that the initial *pataḥ* and *ḥatep pataḥ* of the expected form אַאֲסִיף would have to elide into the long *qameṣ* and that the long *ḥireq* would have to appear as *ṣere*. Of course, no such form is known is Biblical Hebrew, and the verbal root אסף does not even appear at all in a *hiphil* form in Biblical Hebrew.[16]

The versions appear to have wrestled with the problem in various ways. The LXX reading, Ἐκλείψει ἐκλιπέτω, "let there indeed pass away," appears to presuppose a Hebrew text that would read אָסֹף הֵאָסֵף/אָסֹף, "indeed, be gathered." The same reading appears to underlie the Greek of 8HevXIIgr, συναγωγή συναγω, "let there surely be gathered," and the Old Latin, *defectione deficiat*, "let there indeed pass away." The form אָסֹף could be *pual* imperative of אסף, but there is no attestation for such a form in Biblical Hebrew. The form הֵאָסֵף is a *niphal* masculine singular imperative of the root אסף, but no *he* appears in the consonantal text to support such a reading. One might argue that the LXX translators understood the initial *he* and *ṣere* to have elided into the following ʾ*alep* and *qameṣ*, but there is no other attestation for such a phenomenon. It is also possible to argue

that a *qal* masculine singular imperative form of אסף, that is, אֱסֹף, "gather," underlies the two Greek and the Old Latin texts, but such a contention does not explain the third person forms of any of these texts and it leaves the problem of the MT unresolved. This would suggest that both the Greek and the Old Latin translations exercised some poetic license in their attempts to make sense of the Hebrew.

Targum Jonathan renders the expression as שיצאה אשיצי, "I will utterly destroy," which apparently translates literally the text that now appears in the MT. The Peshitta renders the verse as *mᶜbrw mᶜbr ʾnʾ*, "I am surely removing," which presupposes Hebrew אָסֹף אָסֵף. It apparently reads אָסֵף as the *qal* participle אֹסֵף, "gathering/removing," in an effort to make sense of the text. Such a reading might presuppose that the long *qameṣ* or *a*-class vowel be read as a short *qameṣ* or *o*-class vowel.

The Vulgate reading, *congregans congregabo*, "let there be gathered," is based on the understanding that the expression combines two forms of the root אסף. It is especially notable in view of the Old Latin reading noted above, so that the Vulgate represents Jerome's attempt to clarify or correct the text in relation to the Hebrew. It is also noteworthy in relation to the Vulgate's rendition of Zeph 2:1, in which the expression *convenite congregamini*, "come, assemble," translates the Hebrew expression הִתְקוֹשְׁשׁוּ וָקוֹשּׁוּ, "assemble and gather." The

---

Lipiński's theory suffers from the lack of adequate attestation for the root אצל. There are only three examples of the root in *qal*, all of which are perfect forms of the verb (Gen 27:36; Num 11:17; Qoh 2:10), and one *niphal* perfect (Ezek 42:6). It remains disputed whether the example in Num 11:25 is actually *qal* or *hiphil* (see BDB, 69).

14 It is noteworthy that the *qal* imperfect forms of the root אסף employ a variety of vowel combinations with the prefix and initial root letter ʾ*alep*. The standard form of the verb would employ a combination of *segol* and *shewa* as in the אֶאֱסֹף of Mic 2:12 (cf. הֵאָסֵף in Deut 28:38; Ps 26:9; יֶאֱסֹף in 2 Kgs 5:3; Job 34:14; 39:12; and תֶּאֱסֹף in Lev 25:20). But as noted above, the initial root consonant ʾ*alep* sometimes elides into the preformative and the *segol/shewa* combination shifts to a *ḥolem* as in the תֹסֵף of Ps 104:29 (cf. אֹסְפֵך in 1 Sam 15:6; אֹסְפָה in Mic 4:6; and וַיֹּסֵף in 2 Sam 6:1). A number of instances of the imperfect form, all with suffixes, appear with a double *pataḥ* under the preformative and the initial

root consonant ʾ*alep* as in תַּאַסְפֵם in Josh 2:18 (cf. יַאַסְפֵנִי, Ps 27:10; יַאַסְפֶךָ, Isa 58:8; וְיַאַסְפֵהוּ, Hab 1:15; וַיַּאַסְפֵהוּ, 1 Sam 14:52; וַיַּאַסְפֵהוּ, 2 Sam 11:27; וַיַּאַסְפֵם, 2 Chr 29:4; and the many occurrences of וַיֵּאָסֵף, Exod 4:29; Num 11:32; etc.). Although a secure first person imperfect form is lacking, these examples point to the possibility that an original אַאֲסִיף could have elided into the present אָסֵף of Zeph 1:2, 3 and that it would have been preserved alongside imperfect forms that employ a combination of *segol/shewa* or *ḥolem*. Cf. the discussion in GKC, §68.

15 The argument goes back to Radak. See now van Hoonacker, *Prophètes*, 508; J. M. P. Smith, *Zephaniah*, 191.

16 Sabottka's recent proposal to read אָסֹף אָסֵף as אָסֹף אֹסֵף, "I would again sweep away," must be rejected (*Zephanja*, 6–7; cf. Arvid S. Kapelrud, *The Message of the Prophet Zephaniah: Morphology and Ideas* [Oslo: Universitetsforlaget, 1975] 21). The emendation presupposes a combination of the verbal roots אסף, "to gather," and יסף, "to add." Both

use of the verb *congregamini* for וְקוֹשׁוּ suggests that Jerome attempted to draw a parallel between the two passages,[17] apparently in an attempt to portray them as two stages in which first all creation and then Jerusalem and Judah would assemble to witness the day of the L-rd, understood by Jerome to be the day of Jesus' coming resurrection (see esp. Vulgate 3:8).

The difficulties posed by the extant form of the expression in the MT indicates that the MT form is likely the intended reading of this text. It is noteworthy that the only examples of אָסֵף appear in 1:2, 3 (twice), and Jer 8:13, all of which employ the infinitive absolute together with the imperfect *hiphil* of סוּף, although it is possible that אָסֵף represents a variant first person *qal* imperfect form of the root אסף.[18] Certainly, the appearance of the similar form of the expression in Jer 8:13 attests to its authenticity. Likewise, the various attempts of the versions to make some sense of the expression, often based on a somewhat different rendition of the phrase, support such a conclusion. In light of this evidence it would appear that the expression אָסֹף אָסֵף is an idiom that combines forms of the verbs אסף and סוּף to express complete and utter destruction.[19]

Such an expression apparently plays especially on both the positive and negative meanings of the root אסף, "to gather." On the one hand, the verb אסף refers to gathering the harvest, and indeed, the root stands as the basis of the noun אָסִיף, "ingathering, harvest," which is employed in Exod 34:22 as an apparently early name for the Festival of Sukkot (cf. the similar use of the term אָסֹף in Exod 23:16). Sukkot, or Booths/Tabernacles, is celebrated for seven days beginning on the fifteenth day of the seventh month (Tishri) as the concluding harvest festival of the Judean agricultural and cultic year (see Exod 23:16; 34:22; Lev 23:33-43; Num 29:12-38; Deut 16:13-15). The festival takes place in the fall (September-October), immediately prior to the onset of the rainy season in the land of Israel, and celebrates the harvest of fruits in the land such as grapes, figs, olives, and so on. It follows Pesach or Passover, which marks the beginning of the grain harvest in the first month (Nisan, March-April; see Lev 23:5-8; Num 28:16-25), and Shavuot or Weeks, which marks the conclusion of the grain harvest some fifty days later in the third month (Sivan, May-June; see Lev 23:15-22; Num 28:26-31). Sukkot therefore constitutes one of the three primary temple festivals in which the produce of the land is gathered and all males are required to appear at the temple to bring their annual offerings and to participate in the national celebration of the harvest (Exod 23:14-19; 34:18-26; Deut 16:1-17). Bringing in the harvest entails the destruction or at least the cutting of the vines and trees as the grapes, figs, olives, and other fruits are gathered (see esp. Jer 8:13, which refers to the gathering of grapes and figs), and thus the term frequently serves as an indication of destruction (see also 1 Sam 15:6, in which Saul uses the verb אסף to threaten the Kenites with destruction if they remain with the Amalekites; and Ezek 34:29, in which the term is employed to express the potential destruction of the sheep or people of Israel by hunger). Such an emphasis on the verb אסף, "to gather," and its association with the *hiphil* form of the verb סוּף, "to

---

verbs can appear as אסף, which contributes to the wordplay. Sabottka fails to address the grammatical problem of the combination of two different verbal roots, i.e., "I will again, I will sweep away/gather," or to explain adequately the form אֹסֵף, apparently a masculine imperative or an infinitive construct of אסף. There are also problems with understanding the role of אֹסֵף, "again, I will add." Kapelrud maintains that it refers back to YHWH's initial destruction of the world by flood, but the present text makes no allusion to YHWH's prior destruction of the world. Furthermore, the Genesis tradition preserves YHWH's promise never to bring such destruction again (Gen 9:8-17). If Zephaniah is indeed dependent on the Genesis traditions, this would be an egregious oversight.

17 Note that the Old Latin text for 2:1 reads, *convenite et congregamini*, "come and assemble," which suggests that Jerome's rendition of this verse relied heavily upon the Old Latin text, whereas his rendition of 1:2, 3 departed markedly from it.

18 Note the use of the *niphal* form of אסף in Hos 4:3, "and also the fish of the sea will be gathered (יֵאָסֵפוּ)," which indicates that the root אסף can be employed in relation to the destruction of the creatures of the world mentioned in Zeph 1:3. See Gerleman, *Zephanja*, 3; Ben Zvi, *Zephaniah*, 53.

19 Cf. Berlin, *Zephaniah*, 72; Ben Zvi, *Zephaniah*, 51–53.

destroy," suggests that the statement presupposes a setting in relation to the Festival of Sukkot in which the prophet employs the imagery of harvest to announce the potential destruction of everything in the land. Sukkot would be an ideal occasion for the prophet to address the people, as the entire nation would gather at the Jerusalem Temple for the festival.[20]

The expression כָּל מֵעַל פְּנֵי הָאֲדָמָה, "everything from upon the face of the ground," lends itself to such a scenario. Indeed, although the term אֲדָמָה, "ground, land," may be employed generally for land or the earth (Gen 1:25; 6:20; 47:19; Lev 20:24; Isa 19:17; Ezek 11:17, etc.), it is also frequently employed in reference to tillable land (Gen 2:5, 9; 3:17, 23; 4:2, 3, 12; Exod 23:19; 34:26; Deut 26:2, 10, 15; Isa 1:7; 28:24; Jer 7:20, etc.). Because Sukkot is the concluding harvest festival of the year, it completes the harvest and therefore presupposes the removal of the entire range of agricultural produce from the land. Such a metaphor lends itself easily to the prophet's rhetorical strategy, in which he posits the complete destruction or punishment of the whole land should the people choose not to heed his call for adherence to YHWH.

The appearance of the oracular formula נְאֻם־ה״, "utterance of YHWH," at the end of the verse identifies the prophet's statements as statements from YHWH.[21] The formula therefore identifies the prophet as an oracular spokesperson for YHWH, in that he delivers YHWH's own statements to the people, and aids in lending authority to his words. The formula appears frequently in prophetic texts. The appearance of the expression in Num 24:3, 15, which relates Balaam's attempts to deliver divine oracles against Israel, points to its function in relation to oracular divination. The term is normally construed as a noun, although the form

may well derive from a passive participle of the root נאם. The appearance of the root as a verb in Jer 23:31 in Jeremiah's diatribe against false or lying prophets likewise suggests that the term functions in reference to oracular divination or prophecy.

■ **3** Although many consider v. 3 together with v. 2 because of the twofold recurrence of the verb אָסֵף, "I will destroy," and YHWH's statements concerning the destruction of all creation, the absence of a syntactical connector that would join v. 3 to v. 2 indicates that it is the beginning of a new subunit distinct from v. 2. The presence of *waw*-consecutive verbs and conjunctive *waw*s at the beginning of each major clause throughout vv. 3b-6 indicates that v. 3a is the initial statement and premise of the subunit in vv. 3-6 on which the following vv. 3b-6 build (see the discussion of the form and setting of 1:2-6 above).

Despite its role as the beginning of a new subunit, v. 3a clearly builds on v. 2 by specifying the initial statement, "I will utterly destroy everything from upon the face of the ground." In the present case, the references to "human and animal," "bird of the heavens and fish of the sea," and "those who cause the wicked to stumble" define the meaning of "everything" in v. 2. This relationship is clear not only from the contents of vv. 2 and 3a, but from their respective forms as well. Like v. 2, v. 3a is formulated as a first person speech by YHWH, and the presence of the oracular formula, נְאֻם־ה״, "utterance of YHWH," in v. 3b demonstrates that the whole is the prophet's presentation of YHWH's oracular speech.

On the basis of YHWH's stated intention to destroy human, animal, bird, and fish from the land, a number of scholars have concluded that this passage refers to the flood traditions of the book of Genesis.[22] Especially noteworthy in this discussion is YHWH's statement con-

---

20 Cf. Theodore Gaster, *Myth, Legend, and Custom in the Old Testament* (New York: Harper & Row, 1969) 679. Note also Ivan J. Ball Jr., *Zephaniah: A Rhetorical Study* (1972; reprinted Berkeley: BIBAL, 1988) 16–17, who attempts to demonstrate that אָסֹף אָסֵף deliberately attempts a play on words between the roots סוּף and אסף to convey the interrelation of the themes of punishment/destruction and restoration/gathering that appear throughout the book.

21 Friedrich Baumgärtel, "Die Formel *nĕʾum jahwe*," *ZAW* 73 (1961) 277–90; Samuel Meier, *Speaking of Speaking: Marking Direct Discourse in the Hebrew Bible*

(VTSup 46; Leiden: Brill, 1992) 298–314; Rolf Rendtorff, "Zum Gebrauch der Formel *nĕʾûm jahwe* im Jeremiabuch," *ZAW* 66 (1954) 27–37; Sweeney, *Isaiah 1–39*, 546.

22 For an overview of this discussion, see De Roche, *VT* 30 (1980) 104–9.

cerning the intention to destroy humanity from upon the face of the ground in Gen 6:7, "And YHWH said, 'I will blot out humanity, which I created from upon the face of the ground, from human to animal to creeping creature and to the bird of the heavens, for I have repented that I made them.'" Also relevant to the issue are the statements in Gen 7:4 and 8:8 that refer to the destruction of everything "from upon the face of the ground" (מֵעַל פְּנֵי הָאֲדָמָה), which corresponds precisely to the formulation of the phrase in Zeph 1:2. Some have argued that this dependence on the Genesis flood tradition, generally viewed to be the product of the postexilic Priestly stratum of the Pentateuch, indicates the presence of a postexilic redaction that sought to universalize and eschatologize the words of the seventh-century prophet Zephaniah.[23]

Nevertheless, there is good reason to question Zephaniah's dependence on the Genesis flood tradition and the concomitant claim that Zeph 1:3 (and 1:2) is the product of a postexilic eschatologizing redaction. Although there is a great deal of correspondence between Zephaniah's specification of the life that is to be destroyed by YHWH and that to be destroyed in the flood, the identification of fish in 1:3 indicates that this verse is hardly dependent textually on Gen 6:7—or any other text in the flood tradition for that matter—as Gen 6:7 does not mention fish nor would one expect that a flood over all the earth would destroy the fish as well as those creatures normally found on the ground or in the air. Instead, the enumeration of humans, animals, birds, and fish points to an interest in portraying the destruction of all life in creation, as these references identify humans and representative creatures that appear in all three of the major regions of the created world, that is, on the ground, in the air, and in the water. Ben Zvi

notes that this tripartite division of the world appears throughout biblical tradition (cf. Pss 69:36; 96:11; Job 12:7-8; Deut 30:11-13), so it cannot be ascribed only to the flood or the creation traditions in Genesis.[24] Instead of textual dependence, these references convey the totality of creation that YHWH intends to destroy.

Furthermore, the terminology employed in Zeph 1:3 is likewise not restricted to Genesis. The expression אָדָם וּבְהֵמָה, "human and animal," is a common merism in the Hebrew Bible that is employed in reference to everyone and everything that stands between human and beast.[25] The references to the bird of the heaven and the fish of the sea do not constitute a similar merism, but function only as a means to indicate that YHWH's projected destruction will encompass all of creation, including the heavens and the waters as well as the earth, and therefore be comprehensive. This combination also appears in Hos 4:3, "therefore, the earth will mourn and every inhabitant in it will wither, together with the creature of the field (בְּחַיַּת הַשָּׂדֶה), and with the bird of the heavens (וּבְעוֹף הַשָּׁמַיִם), and even the fish of the sea will be gathered (וְגַם דְּגֵי הַיָּם יֵאָסֵפוּ)." Interestingly, the reference to the comprehensive nature of the destruction is intended to focus especially on human beings that inhabit the land in Hosea 4 (see Hos 4:1), and most especially on the prophets and priests who are responsible for instructing the people in proper conduct in the midst of creation. From the perspective of Hosea 4, all creation suffers from human misconduct, and the priests and prophets are ultimately responsible for educating the people in their responsibilities, not only to themselves but to all creation at large.[26] This has implications for the portrayal of YHWH's intended destruction of all creation, particularly since the statements in Zeph 1:3a and 3b(-6) emphasize human beings by plac-

---

23 E.g., Gaster, *Myth*, 679; Sabottka, *Zephanja*, 8–14; Renaud, *Sophonie*, 196–97.

24 Ben Zvi, *Zephaniah*, 56; cf. J. Krašovec, *Der Merismus im biblisch-hebräischen und nordwestsemitischen* (BibOr 33; Rome: Biblical Institute Press, 1977) 35, who points to two major entities in creation.

25 Krašovec, *Merismus*, 65–73, 75; Ben Zvi, *Zephaniah*, 56. For this combination of terms, see Gen 6:7; 7:23; Exod 8:13, 14; 9:9, 10, 19, 22, 25; 12:12; 13:2, 15; Lev 7:21; 27:28; Num 3:13; 8:17; 18:15; 31:11, 26, 47; Jer 7:20; 21:26; 27:5; 31:27; 32:43; 33:10, 12; 36:29; 50:3; 51:62; Ezek 14:13, 17; 19:21; 25:13;

29:8; 36:11; Jonah 3:7, 8; Hag 1:11; Zech 2:8; Pss 36:7; 135:8; Qoh 3:19.

26 Cf. Jer 4:22-26, in which the lack of understanding on the part of human beings is also responsible for the suffering of all creation (for discussion see William Holladay, *Jeremiah 1* [Hermeneia; Philadelphia: Fortress Press, 1986] 163–64). Likewise, Isa 24:1-23 portrays disaster throughout all creation, as the people who live in the land have violated their covenant with YHWH in part because their priests have failed to give proper instruction (see Sweeney, *Isaiah 1–39*, 325–32).

ing human beings at the head of the list in v. 3a and pointedly repeating the reference to humans, without mention of the other creatures, in v. 3b. The balance of the material in vv. 4-6 then takes up exclusively human subjects. It would appear that the portrayal of the destruction of all creation is intended to target human beings specifically.

Zephaniah's interest in human beings is highlighted additionally by the explicit reference to "those who cause the wicked to stumble" at the end of v. 3a. The expression appears as the phrase וְהַמַּכְשֵׁלוֹת אֶת־הָרְשָׁעִים, which has prompted many attempts at emendation in an effort to make the phrase conform to the first person singular statements by YHWH in the rest of the verse. The most common emendation is וְהִכְשַׁלְתִּי, "and I shall cause (the wicked) to stumble,"[27] although one also finds וְכִשַּׁלְתִּי, "and I will cause to stumble";[28] וְהִשְׁמַדְתִּי, "and I will destroy";[29] והמכשלתי, "and (I will) bring to ruin";[30] וְיִמַּחוּ שְׁמוֹ רְשָׁעִים, "and I will erase the names of the wicked";[31] and others.[32] Attempts to emend the text into a first person verbal form are, however, entirely unwarranted. There is not a shred of evidence for such a form in the versions. Moreover, the present form of the expression fits perfectly as one more direct object of the verb אָסֵף in v. 3a[4], that is, "I will destroy the bird of the heavens, the fish of the sea, and those who cause the wicked to stumble." There is no need to emend the text in its present form.

This does not mean that the reading is without problems. The meaning of the feminine plural noun וְהַמַּכְשֵׁלוֹת, "and the stumbling blocks," is not clear as the phrase would have to translate as the nonsensical, "and the stumbling blocks with the wicked," reading אֶת as the preposition "with" rather than as the direct object marker. The term מַכְשֵׁלָה (singular form) appears

elsewhere only in Isa 3:6, where it refers to "the ruin" (הַמַּכְשֵׁלָה), that is, the devastated city in which the people of Jerusalem will live. Most scholars read אֶת immediately following as the direct object marker, and read וְהַמַּכְשֵׁלוֹת as a *hiphil* feminine plural participle, "and those who cause (the wicked) to stumble."[33] Normally, the expected form would be וְהַמַּכְשִׁילוֹת, although it is not unusual for *hiphil* forms, such as the feminine second/third person plural imperfect, to employ a *ṣere* in place of the expected *ḥireq* when a heavy suffix is added, for example, יַקְטִיל and תִּקְטֵלְנָה. Nevertheless, the appearance of a *ṣere* in *hiphil* feminine plural participles is not otherwise attested.

A further problem is the identification of the referent or the antecedent for the term when it is read as a *hiphil* participle; who or what causes the wicked to stumble? Although בְּהֵמָה, "animal," is a feminine noun, both עוֹף, "bird," and דָּג, "fish," are masculine. Some scholars have suggested that the term refers to images of feminine deities that have led the people astray (see 2 Kings 21, which describes Manasseh's erection of an Asherah for the people to worship), but there is no evidence for such a claim and it apparently reads some rather unwarranted gender presuppositions into this text. Berlin suggests that the phrase alludes to Deut 4:16-18, which warns against making any replica (תַּבְנִית, feminine singular noun) of man, woman, animal, bird, crawling creature, or fish for the purpose of worship.[34] Such images would be conceived as stumbling blocks for the people that lead them into illicit worship. Although attractive, this proposal must remain speculative, especially since the term מַכְשֵׁלָה/וֹת appears nowhere in the passage.

The versions appear to have had their difficulties with the term as well. The expression does not appear in the LXX at all, which has prompted many claims that it

27 Van Hoonacker, *Prophètes*, 508–9; J. M. P. Smith, *Zephaniah*, 191; Nowack, *Propheten*, 292; Sellin, *Zwölfprophetenbuch*, 421–22; Horst, *Propheten*, 190.

28 Schwally, "Sefanjâ," 168–69.

29 Marti, *Dodekapropheton*, 362.

30 Sabottka, *Zephanja*, 8, claims this to be a mixed form of מוך/מכך (sink) and כשל (stumble).

31 J. Bachmann, "Zur Textkritik des Propheten Zephania," *ThStK* 67 (1894) 641.

32 See Irsigler, *Gottesgericht*, 11–14; Vlaardingerbroek, *Zephaniah*, 55.

33 Lipiński, *VT* 25 (1975) 688–90; Rudolph, *Zephanja*, 261–62; Roberts, *Zephaniah*, 167; Ben Zvi, *Zephaniah*, 58–60.

34 Berlin, *Zephaniah*, 73–74.

must be recognized as a later gloss. It does appear in later Greek versions, however, which undermines such a claim. Although 8HevXIIgr is heavily damaged at this point in the text so that the term does not appear, there is clearly sufficient space for some rendition of the expression. The Peshitta renders the phrase as *wtwqlt* *ʾytʾ ʿl ḥṭyʾ*, "and stumbling blocks there are upon the wicked," which clearly represents an attempt to make the phrase understandable while adhering as closely as possible to the extant Hebrew text. Targum Jonathan demonstrates an innovative approach, reading תקלת רשיעיא על דאסגיאה, "because the taxes of the wicked have increased." This reading is achieved by rendering Aramaic תקלא (*taqlāʾ/taqqālāʾ*), "stumbling block," as תקלתא (*tĕqaltāʾ*), "taxes," apparently in an effort to relate the verse to the Roman policy of imposing heavy taxes in Judea during the first and second centuries CE.[35] If the phrase is a gloss, it must have appeared in the text at a very early time, perhaps prior to the writing of the LXX.[36]

The difficulties posed by the expression וְהַמַּכְשֵׁלוֹת אֶת־הָרְשָׁעִים suggest that it is indeed an early gloss. It is apparently designed to specify which human beings are to be destroyed by YHWH, as indicated by YHWH's statements in v. 3a and 3b, particularly since the following material in vv. 4-6—and indeed throughout the rest of the book—indicates that YHWH's actions are directed against those among the people who are wicked, that is, who constitute the "remnant of Baal," who worship the hosts of heaven on the rooftops, who are sworn to YHWH but turn aside from YHWH, who do not seek YHWH, and so on. The presumed author of such a gloss was apparently disturbed by the blanket condemnation of humanity and all creation at the outset of the passage, and chose to indicate that those who were turning the people to wickedness were to be targeted for destruc-

tion by YHWH. The feminine plural form of the expression remains an anomaly, which indicates the tentative nature of this proposal.

The prophet's presentation of YHWH's statement in v. 3b, "and I will cut off humanity from upon the face of the ground," then begins the above-noted sequence in vv. 3b-6, which focus on the human targets of YHWH's punishment. The expression "and I will cut off" (וְהִכְרַתִּי) appears frequently throughout biblical literature in statements of YHWH's intention to punish a particular party by destruction or expulsion.[37] There are several noteworthy parallels. 1 Kgs 9:7 states, "and I will cut off Israel from upon the face of the ground," as part of YHWH's statements to Solomon concerning the potential consequences of failure to observe the Deity's commandments and statutes. Isa 14:22 states, "and I will cut off from Babylon name and remnant, offspring and posterity," as part of YHWH's oracle of judgment against Babylon. Finally, Ezek 14:13 states, "and I will cut off from it human beings and animals," as part of YHWH's promises to punish a land that sins (cf. Ezek 14:17; 25:13). Each of these cases employs language closely parallel to that of Zeph 1:3 (and 1:2), which indicates that the present context employs a relatively common expression of YHWH's intentions to bring punishment for apostasy. Verse 3b therefore forms an appropriate introduction to the sequence in vv. 3b-6, especially since these verses target those who have abandoned YHWH or failed to meet YHWH's expectations. The rhetorical function of the text as exhortation must be noted, particularly since it may be formulated to persuade its audience to abide by YHWH's expectations rather than only to announce punishment for those who have already engaged in apostasy.

35 Cf. Churgin, *Targum Jonathan*, 22–23, who notes this issue in relation to TJ's rendition of Hab 3:17; contra the reservations of Robert P. Gordon, *Studies in the Targum to the Twelve Prophets: From Nahum to Malachi* (VTSup 51; Leiden: Brill, 1994) 44–49.

36 It must be recognized that the earliest MSS of the LXX, i.e., Vaticanus and Sinaiticus, are early Christian MSS that date to the third or fourth centuries CE (see Swete, *Introduction*, 126–28, 129–31), which raises questions concerning their attestation of readings in the third century BCE. In any case, the omission of the phrase may be due to stylistic reasons, a common occurrence in the LXX.

37 See Lev 17:10; 20:3, 5, 6; 26:30; 1 Kgs 9:7; 14:10; 21:21; 2 Kgs 9:8; Isa 14:22; Ezek 14:13, 17; 21:8; 25:13, 16; 29:8; 30:15; 35:7; Amos 1:5, 8; 2:3; Mic 5:9, 10, 11, 12; Nah 2:14; Zech 9:6, 10.

■ 4 The *waw*-consecutive statement in v. 4a, "and I will stretch out my hand (וְנָטִיתִי יָדִי) against Judah and against all the inhabitants of Jerusalem," constitutes the second element in the sequence of statements that begins in v. 3b. Like וְהִכְרַתִּי in v. 3b, וְנָטִיתִי יָדִי and other forms of the expression appear often throughout biblical literature to express YHWH's punitive action against a particular party. It is especially characteristic of the plague tradition in Exodus, where Moses and Aaron are the primary figures who carry out such action,[38] but it also appears frequently in the prophets, where YHWH is the primary actant.[39] Several of the passages in Ezekiel associate the expression with הִכְרַתִּי (Ezek 14:13; 25:7, 13, 16) and target human beings and animals in particular (Ezek 14:13; 25:13). It is noteworthy that the formula is most frequently associated with priestly figures. References to YHWH's "outstretched hand" (against Israel or Assyria) also appear in Isa 5:25; 9:11, 16, 21; 10:4, and Crenshaw has argued that the repetitive nature of these references indicates a background in a liturgical form.[40] Indeed, the "outstretched hand" formula may be a variation of the formula, "and with a strong hand and outstretched arm (וּבְיָד חֲזָקָה וּבִזְרוֹעַ נְטוּיָה),," which appears frequently in liturgical contexts.[41] The priestly and liturgical background of this expression suggests that the present text in Zephaniah is also intended to function in a cultic setting such as the Temple in Jerusalem. This would fit well with the specification of Jerusalem and the inhabitants of Judah as the objects of YHWH's punishment, since the Jerusalem Temple is the cultic center of both Jerusalem and Judah.

The *waw*-consecutive verb, וְהִכְרַתִּי, "and I will cut off," in v. 4b constitutes the basis of the third statement in the sequence of vv. 3b-6. The appearance of the *waw*-conjunctive together with the direct object marker at the beginning of vv. 5a, 5b, and 6 indicates that these verses further specify the objects of YHWH's punishment as articulated in v. 4b.

The expression "from this place" (מִן־הַמָּקוֹם הַזֶּה) has prompted considerable discussion. There has been much speculation concerning the identity of this place. Some maintain that it must refer to Jerusalem (cf. Jer 19:12) or the land of Judah as indicated by the preceding statement in v. 4a. Others maintain that it is a reference to the Jerusalem Temple, particularly because Deuteronomy frequently refers to YHWH's sanctuary as "the place" where YHWH will cause the divine name to dwell, and because it also sometimes serves as a technical term for the temple elsewhere in biblical and postbiblical Jewish literature.[42] Although the expression has a wide range of meanings, the emphasis on cultic matters and adherence to YHWH in the present context indicates that it refers to the Jerusalem Temple, which in turn stands as the holy center of Jerusalem and Judah.

Many have also suggested that the expression "from this place" is a gloss that was added to the present form of the text. The basic reasons for this claim are metrical, in that the expression seems to overload the verse, and questions concerning the setting of Zephaniah's oracles, that is, did he speak out in the temple in support of Josiah's reforms? The metrical argument hardly constitutes the basis for textual excision or emendation; schol-

---

38   Exod 8:1, 2; 9:22; 10:12, 21 (cf. 8:12-13) in J; Exod 7:19; 14:16, 21, 27 in P (see Ben Zvi, *Zephaniah*, 60 n. 79).

39   See Isa 23:11; Jer 51:25; Ezek 6:14; 14:9, 13; 16:27; 25:7, 13, 16; 35:3 (see Ben Zvi, *Zephaniah*, 60–61).

40   James L. Crenshaw, "A Liturgy of Wasted Opportunity (Amos 4:6-12; Isaiah 9:7–10:4; 5:25-29)," *Semitics* 1 (1970) 27–37. The Isaian passages appear to function as a literary motif and do not presently constitute a liturgical text, although the form may derive from a liturgy (see Sweeney, *Isaiah 1–39*, 192; William P. Brown, "The So-Called Refrain in Isaiah 5:25-30 and 9:7–10:4," *CBQ* 52 [1990] 432–33).

41   See Exod 6:6; Deut 4:34; 5:15; 7:19; 9:29; 11:2; 26:8; 1 Kgs 8:42; 2 Kgs 17:36; Jer 21:5; 27:5; 32:17, 21; Ezek 20:33, 34; Ps 136:12; 1 Chr 6:32.

42   See Hag 2:9; Neh 1:9; 1 Kgs 8:29, 30, 35; 2 Chr 6:20, 21, 26; Jer 27:22; Isa 18:7; Ezek 43:7; Jer 17:12; Isa 60:3; Ezra 9:8; Ps 24:3; see also Gustav H. Dalman, *Aramäisch-Neuhebräisches Handwörterbuch zu Targum, Talmud und Midrasch* (reprinted Hildesheim: Olms, 1987) 249; Marcus Jastrow, *A Dictionary of the Targumim, the Talmud Babli and Yerushalmi, and the Midrashic Literature* (2 vols.; reprinted Brooklyn: Shalom, 1967) 1:829–30, who indicate that the term in Rabbinic Hebrew can refer to a sanctuary or even to G-d.

ars have been unable to demonstrate that ancient Judean or Israelite poets adhered strictly to any given metrical pattern. Furthermore, the expression appears in all textual versions of Zephaniah. The question concerning the setting of Zephaniah's oracles owes much to the following reference to YHWH's actions against "the remnant of Baal," that is, if only a remnant is left, then Zephaniah must have spoken after the reform had already been carried out. This has no bearing on the question of whether the expression מִן־הַמָּקוֹם הַזֶּה constitutes a gloss, since the context indicates a setting in the cult that corresponds well with a potential reference to the temple. Even if Zephaniah spoke after Josiah's reform and even if Josiah's reforms failed, the temple would provide the most logical setting for the presentation of his oracles.

The appearance of the direct object marker in the phrase "the remnant of Baal" (אֶת־שְׁאָר הַבַּעַל) indicates that this expression forms the first object of YHWH's punishment in vv. 4b-6. As noted above, the expression has created some difficulties, especially since the reference to the "remnant" of Baal suggests a prior purge of Canaanite religious practice. This has prompted some to claim that Zephaniah's prophecies were delivered at some time after Josiah's religious reforms and that perhaps those reforms had failed in that they did not completely eradicate the influence of the Canaanite deity.[43] Such a contention is bolstered by the discovery of many goddess figurines throughout Jerusalem and Judah in the late monarchic period that indicate widespread veneration of Canaanite goddesses such as Asherah throughout the period of Josiah's reign.[44] Yet such a contention conflicts with the superscription of the book that places Zephaniah's career "in the days of Josiah ben Amon, king of Judah." Indeed, the LXX apparently perceived a problem in the statement that a "remnant" of

Baal existed in Jerusalem in the days of Josiah, as it alters the passage to read, "the name of Baal" (τὰ ὀνόματα τῆς βααλ). Such a rendition would be warranted by the association between the terms "name" (שֵׁם) and "remnant" (שְׁאָר/שְׁאֵרִית) in the Bible that indicates parallel meaning (see 2 Sam 14:7; Isa 14:22). The Peshitta reads שְׁאָר as šrbʾ, "family," "tribe," or "nation." This reading would have derived from שְׁאֵר, "flesh," and apparently presented a means to avoid the problems associated with the term "remnant" when Josiah's reform should have eliminated idolatrous worship from Judah. Although Sabottka accepts this reading,[45] it must be rejected as a later attempt to make sense out of a difficult text.

The text explicitly names "the remnant of Baal" as the target of YHWH's punishment, but there is little indication that people in ancient Judah turned wholeheartedly away from YHWH to worship foreign deities. The studies by Cogan and McKay on Assyrian religious policy indicate that the Assyrians did not promote the worship of Assyrian gods in subject territories.[46] Instead, the common pattern in the ancient world was to identify the gods of one culture with those of another, that is, YHWH might be conceived as a manifestation of the Assyrian Ashur or the Aramean Hadad. Furthermore, there is little reason to believe that Baal would somehow supplant YHWH in Jerusalem, as the major centers for the worship of Baal were located on the Phoenician coast rather than in the Judean or Israelite hill country. Likewise, studies of Judean personal names in the late monarchic period indicate that no names appear with the theophoric element Baal, but many appear with the theophoric element YHWH.[47] Indeed, many have noted the tendency of biblical traditions to employ the language of the Canaanite cult to polemicize against

43   J. P. Hyatt, "The Date and Background of Zephaniah," *JNES* 7 (1948) 25–29; D. Williams, "The Date of Zephaniah," *JBL* 82 (1963) 77–88.

44   See, e.g., William G. Dever, "The Silence of the Text: An Archaeological Commentary on 2 Kings 23," in M. D. Coogan, J. C. Exum, and L. E. Stager, eds., *Scripture and Other Artifacts: Essays on the Bible and Archaeology in Honor of Philip J. King* (Louisville: Westminster John Knox, 1994) 143–68.

45   See his discussion in *Zephanja*, 14, 15–18, where he reads the term as a reference to "the family of Baal"; cf. Irsigler, *Gottesgericht*, 16–17, who accepts

Sabottka's emendation.

46   Mordecai Cogan, *Imperialism and Religion: Assyria, Judah, and Israel in the Eighth and Seventh Centuries B.C.E.* (SBLMS 19; Missoula, Mont.: Scholars Press, 1974); J. W. MacKay, *Religion in Judah under the Assyrians 732–609 B.C.* (SBT II/26; London: SCM, 1973).

47   See Ben Zvi, *Zephaniah*, 68–69 n. 114; cf. J. Tigay, *You Shall Have No Other Gods: Israelite Religion in the Light of Hebrew Inscriptions* (HSS 31; Atlanta: Scholars Press, 1986); Avigad, *Hebrew Bullae*.

YHWHistic practices that were not considered to be legitimate. Note, for example, the Kuntillet Ajrud inscriptions that mention YHWH's Asherah.[48] Such a portrayal presents YHWH as a Baal-like figure with a consort, but the parties who created these inscriptions probably saw themselves not as devotees of Baal but as worshipers of YHWH. They simply conceived YHWH differently than did those in Jerusalem who were responsible for writing the Deuteronomistic History or elements of the prophetic tradition.[49]

It is therefore noteworthy that the term שְׁאָר, "remnant," is not used elsewhere in reference to a deity, but it is frequently employed in reference to people, such as the remnant of Moab (Isa 16:14), Aram (17:3), the archers of Kedar (21:17), Israel (10:20, 21, 22; 11:11, 16; 28:5), or people in general (1 Chr 16:41; Ezra 3:8; 4:3, 7; Neh 10:29; 11:1, 20; Esth 9:16). This would suggest that "the remnant of Baal" refers to those in Jerusalem who are engaged in illegitimate worship of YHWH, so that the term may function as a précis for the following references to the cultic attendants and priests, that is, those religious functionaries who represented YHWH incorrectly in the eyes of Zephaniah. If Zephaniah was indeed speaking on behalf of Josiah's reform, such an expression would target priests and other figures in the Jerusalem Temple who were to be purged or who were expected to reform their practices as the temple was purified. Certainly, the illegitimate cultic practice in the Jerusalem Temple reported in 2 Kings 21 and 2 Chronicles 33 during the reign of Manasseh (and perhaps Amon) would have provided the targets for Zephaniah's words.

The use of the expression אֶת־שֵׁם הַכְּמָרִים, "the name of the cultic attendants," as a second designation for the objects of YHWH's punishments supports such a view.

Scholars universally recognize that כֹּמֶר is a loanword in Biblical Hebrew to refer to idolatrous or illegitimate priests. The term appears widely throughout the ancient Near East as a designation for priests in Akkadian, Aramaic, Punic, Nabatean, Palmyrene, and Syriac,[50] which has prompted some suggestions that the term refers to foreign priests who were operating in Judah during the late monarchic period.[51] The term appears elsewhere in the Hebrew Bible only in Hos 10:5 and 2 Kgs 23:5. In both instances it refers not to foreign priests, but to Israelite or Judean priests who serve at sanctuaries in the land of Israel, that is, either at Bethel in the case of Hos 10:5 or throughout the cities of Judah in 2 Kgs 23:5. In both cases, the כְּמָרִים are YHWHistic priests who act— or are accused of acting—illegitimately. In this respect, it is noteworthy that the Hebrew Bible regularly employs the term כֹּהֵן, "priest," both for legitimate Israelite or Judean priests and for foreign priests of pagan gods (Gen 47:22; Exod 2:16; 1 Sam 5:5; 6:2; Jer 48:7; 49:3).[52] It appears likely that the term refers to Judean priests of YHWH who were engaged in—or accused of engaging in—illegitimate YHWHistic worship, perhaps like that represented in the Kuntillet Ajrud inscriptions.[53]

Because of the difficulties associated with the expression "the name of cultic attendants," many view the following expression, אֶם־הַכֹּהֲנִים, "with the priests," as a later gloss that is designed to explain the meaning of the former term. The argument is based in part on the semantic equivalence of the prepositions אֵם and אֵת to "with" and כְּמָרִים and כֹּהֲנִים to "priests." It is also based in part on the reading of the LXX, καὶ τὰ ὀνόματα τῶν ἱερέων, "and the names of the priests," which eliminates the problem of the potentially dual reference in Hebrew. Both terms are present, however, in 8HevXIIgr, TJ, Peshitta, and the Vulgate, which undermines attempts to

48 Zeev Meshel, "Kuntillet ʿAjrud," *ABD* 4:103–9.
49 See Ben Zvi, *Zephaniah*, 66.
50 See "kumru," "kumirtu," *CAD* 8:534–35, 8:532–33; "kumru," *AHw* 1:506; "כמרII," in C.-F. Jean and J. Hoftijzer, *Dictionnaire des inscriptions sémitiques de l'Ouest* (Leiden: Brill, 1965) 122.
51 E.g., Hermann Spieckermann, *Juda unter Assur in der Sargonidenzeit* (FRLANT 129; Göttingen: Vandenhoeck & Ruprecht, 1982) 85–86; Mordecai Cogan and Hayim Tadmor, *II Kings* (AB 11; Garden City, N.Y.: Doubleday, 1988) 285–86; J. M. P. Smith, *Zephaniah,* 187; Sellin, *Zwölfprophetenbuch,* 422;

Horst, *Propheten,* 191–92; R. L. Smith, *Micah–Malachi* (WBC 32; Waco: Word, 1984) 126; Renaud, *Sophonie,* 201–2; Roberts, *Zephaniah,* 172.
52 Ben Zvi, *Zephaniah*, 68.
53 Cf. van Hoonacker, *Prophètes,* 509–10; Nowack, *Propheten,* 292; Berlin, *Zephaniah,* 74.

identify the phrase as an early gloss. It is far more likely that the LXX translation represents an attempt to smooth out a difficult text by merging the two expressions into one, especially since the LXX has a great deal of difficulty in rendering the term כְּמָרִים. It translates וּכְמָרָיו in Hos 10:5 as καὶ καθὼς παρεπίκραναν αὐτόν, "and as they provoked him," apparently reading the Hebrew as וּכְמָרוּ עָלָיו, which involves only the elimination of the *yod* from וּכְמָרָיו and minor repointing. It simply transliterates כְּמָרִים in 2 Kgs 23:5, apparently for lack of an adequate translation.[54] It would appear that the LXX translation is a stylistic emendation or translation of the underlying Hebrew text.[55]

Targum Jonathan likewise "emended the text" through translation as "the name of their worshipers (פלחיהון) with their (pagan) priests (כומריהון)." The use of כומריהון, the Aramaic equivalent of כְּמָרִים, in place of כֹּהֲנִים clearly indicates the Targum's attempt to eliminate the problem by eliding the latter in favor of כְּמָרִים.

The phrase אֶת־הַכֹּהֲנִים could well be an early gloss, but in the present form of the text, it indicates that among the legitimate priests of YHWH were those who were practicing illegitimately. YHWH's stated intention to cut off those "cultic attendants" indicates the announcement of a purge in the priesthood or at least a rhetorical attempt to prompt such priests to reform or purify their practice so as to avoid punitive action. The use of the term כְּמָרִים, known as a reference to foreign or illegitimate priests, would then serve such a rhetorical strategy by labeling offenders as foreign or illegitimate, therefore justifying action against them.

■ **5** Verse 5 continues YHWH's first person statement in v. 4b concerning the intention to "cut off" the remnant of Baal and the cultic attendants. The introductory direct object markers (with *waw*-conjunctives) in v. 5a and 5b indicate that these clauses continue the specification of the objects of YHWH's actions begun in v. 4bα. The absence of a *waw*-conjunctive for the direct object marker of the phrase "the name of the cultic attendants

with the priests" indicates that v. 5a and 5b specify this phrase in particular; that is, v. 5 further defines the cultic attendants mentioned in v. 4bα. Furthermore, v. 5 lacks the explicit first person perspective evident in YHWH's statements in the preceding verses. Verse 5a also lacks third person references to YHWH and could therefore be considered a direct continuation of YHWH's speech. Verse 5b, however, includes a third person reference to YHWH and must be considered as a speech by the prophet. Although this raises redaction-critical issues that will be addressed below, v. 5b reinforces the textual perspective that the prophet presents YHWH's speeches to his listening (or reading) audience.

Verse 5a begins by further specifying the כְּמָרִים as "and those who prostrate themselves upon the rooftops to the host of heaven." The participle מִשְׁתַּחֲוִים, "prostrate themselves," is a unique *eshtaphel* verbal form of the root חוה, "to coil," which generally refers to bowing down or prostrating oneself for worship or to show respect to a superior.[56] The mention of worship of the host of heaven upon the rooftops apparently refers to the worship of astral deities (cf. Jer 19:13), such as those of the Mesopotamian or the Syro-Canaanite pantheons. Although the hosts of heaven are commonly associated with foreign deities, they apparently have a background in early Israelite religion, which portrays YHWH as a divine warrior at the head of a heavenly army.[57] This is indicated by the military connotations of the term צָבָא, "host, army," and the many references to YHWH's heavenly armies (Num 10:35-36; Deut 33:2-5, 26-29; Josh 5:13-15; Judg 5:23; Isa 13:1-5; Joel 4:11b; Ps 68:8-13, 18; etc.). As noted above there is no clear indication that the Assyrians forced the worship of their deities on Judah, but such synchronistic practice would likely be motivated in part by Judah's subjugation to Assyria during the late eighth through the late seventh centuries, and the concomitant tendency to identify YHWH and other divine figures, such as YHWH's council (see 1 Kgs 22:19/2 Chr 18:18; cf. Isaiah 6; Psalm 82), with Assyrian

---

54 Note that 8HevXIIgr likewise transliterates כְּמָרִים. Although the text is fragmentary at this point, the letters ρειμ, apparently a transliteration of רִים from כְּמָרִים, appear at the beginning of col. 20, line 37 (see Tov, *Greek Minor Prophets*, 58–59 and plate XIV).

55 Cf. Gerleman, *Zephanja*, 6.

56 See *HALOT* 1:295–96.

57 See E. Theodore Mullen Jr., "Hosts, Host of Heaven," *ABD* 3:301–4; H. Niehr, "Host of Heaven," *DDD*², 428–30.

figures. Worship of the host of heaven is condemned in Deuteronomistic and prophetic literature (see Deut 7:3; 2 Kgs 17:16; 21:3; 23:4-5; Jer 19:13). The prohibition of such syncretistic practice formed the basis for King Josiah's reform program (see esp. 2 Kgs 23:1-5), which was especially concerned with focusing worship and veneration exclusively on YHWH in order to concentrate support on YHWH's designated institutions, the Jerusalem Temple and the Davidic monarchy.[58]

The second conjunctive direct object clause in v. 5b likewise begins with וְאֶת־הַמִּשְׁתַּחֲוִים, "and those who prostrate themselves," as in v. 5a, which has prompted considerable speculation that it is the product of a later hand.[59] This contention is supported not only by the reduplication of וְאֶת־הַמִּשְׁתַּחֲוִים from v. 5a, but by the somewhat awkward syntactical relationship with the following participle clause, הַנִּשְׁבָּעִים לַה׳, "those sworn to YHWH." The relationship must be understood either as appositional, "and those who prostrate themselves, that is, those sworn to YHWH, and so on," or as a verbless clause, "and those who prostrate themselves are sworn to YHWH, and so on." Furthermore, v. 5b clearly shifts away from a first person speech by YHWH, as indicated by the third person reference to YHWH, and therefore must be considered as speech by the prophet. A number of scholars maintain that הַנִּשְׁבָּעִים must be secondary,[60] and some argue that the terms הַמִּשְׁתַּחֲוִים and הַנִּשְׁבָּעִים represent the preservation of two variant readings in the same text.[61] Finally, one might be tempted to argue that the whole of v. 5b (and 6) must be secondary because it clearly no longer represents speech by YHWH.

The textual versions vary somewhat. The LXX does not preserve a second occurrence of וְאֶת־הַמִּשְׁתַּחֲוִים at the beginning of v. 5b, but otherwise preserves a text like that of the MT, "and those swearing to the L-rd and those swearing to their king." As noted in other instances above, however, this could well be a stylistic emendation. Although the expression does not appear in the extant text of 8HevXIIgr due to scroll damage, there is sufficient space for it.[62] Both וְאֶת־הַמִּשְׁתַּחֲוִים and הַנִּשְׁבָּעִים apparently underlie the readings of TJ and the Peshitta.

There are also problems involving the phrase, "those sworn to YHWH and those sworn by their king." The statement בְּמַלְכָּם, "by their king," is read as κατὰ τοῦ Μελχομ, "by Milcom," in the Lucianic Greek version, and this reading is reflected in the Peshitta and Vulgate as well. Milcom is the name of the god of the Ammonites, and proponents of this reading maintain that Milcom appears in this text as an example of the various gods that the syncretists (or apostates) were worshiping. It should be noted, however, that Milcom is only one of the foreign deities targeted by Josiah's reform (2 Kgs 23:13 lists Milcom together with Ashtoreth/Astarte, goddess of Tyre, and Chemosh, god of Moab), and there is little reason to believe that Milcom in particular should have been mentioned by Zephaniah to the exclusion of other deities. Other possibilities include the argument that בְּמַלְכָּם must refer to Molek, the Canaanite deity to whom children were reportedly sacrificed in the Hinnom Valley just southwest of Jerusalem (see 2 Kgs 16:3; 21:6; 23:10),[63] or that "by their king" must refer to Baal.[64] Nevertheless, these suggestions raise questions similar to the single focus on Milcom.

The differentiation between the prepositions immediately following each instance of הַנִּשְׁבָּעִים is especially noteworthy because they indicate different roles for the indirect objects of each.[65] Whereas the first instance indicates "those sworn to YHWH (לַה׳)," the second indicates "those sworn by their king (בְּמַלְכָּם)." In most

58 See Sweeney, *King Josiah*.

59 Wellhausen, *Propheten*, 151; Rudolph, *Zephanja*, 262; Irsigler, *Gottesrecht*, 23.

60 Van Hoonacker, *Prophètes*, 510; J. M. P. Smith, *Zephaniah*, 192; Marti, *Dodekapropheton*, 363; Nowack, *Propheten*, 292; Sellin, *Zwölfprophetenbuch*, 422; Horst, *Propheten*, 190, 191; René Vuilleumier and Carl-A. Keller, *Michée, Nahoum, Habacuc, Sophonie* (CAT XIb; Neuchâtel: Delachaux et Niestlé, 1971) 188; Roberts, *Zephaniah*, 168; Vlaardingerbroek, *Zephaniah*, 63, 76.

61 Gerleman, *Zephanja*, 7.

62 Tov, *Greek Minor Prophets*, 95.

63 See Ben Zvi, *Zephaniah*, 76–77. On Molek, see G. C. Heider, "Molech," *DDD*[2], 581–85.

64 Ben Zvi, *Zephaniah*, 76.

65 Interestingly, LXX, TJ, Vulgate, and Peshitta all employ the same prepositions for both terms.

cases where the verb שׁבע, "to swear," is employed to indicate an oath to someone, the preposition לְ, "to," designates the party to whom the oath is made, and the preposition בְּ, "by," designates the party that authorizes or guarantees compliance with the oath; for example, "swear now to me by YHWH" (Josh 2:12; 9:19); "and you, swear to me by YHWH" (1 Sam 24:22); "and Saul swore to her by YHWH" (1 Sam 28:10); "and you shall swear by YHWH to your maidservant" (1 Kgs 1:17); "and I swore to him by YHWH, saying" (1 Kgs 2:8). In the present case, v. 5b indicates those who have sworn an oath to YHWH by the agency of their king. Berlin states that such a case would be "strange" because swearing an oath by a king (or other human being) is otherwise unknown in the Bible.[66] Although the specific terminology is not used, examples appear in Josiah's concluding a covenant between the people and YHWH in 2 Kgs 23:1-5, Joshua's conclusion of a covenant between YHWH and the people in Josh 8:30-35, Moses' concluding a covenant between YHWH and the people in Deuteronomy 27–30; Exodus 24; 34. Indeed, the covenant made between the people and YHWH by Ezra in Nehemiah 8–11 explicitly mentions the "oath" (שְׁבוּעָה) of the people in Neh 10:30 (see also Ezra 10:5). Asa's conclusion of a covenant between the people and YHWH likewise explicitly mentions the oath of the people (2 Chr 15:14), and Isa 19:18 indicates that cities may be sworn to YHWH. In all cases, a leader of the people of Israel or Judah serves as the agent by which the people swear to observe YHWH's expectations; indeed, the example of Josiah's covenant is particularly important, since it would be contemporary to the time of the prophet Zephaniah.

Additional evidence appears in the three statements that indicate that cursing G-d and the king is a crime in ancient Israel: "you shall not disparage G-d, and the prince (נָשִׂיא) you shall not curse" (Exod 22:27); "and they witnessed against him, saying, 'you have cursed (בֵּרַכְתָּ) G-d and king,' and they took him out, and they stoned him, and he died" (1 Kgs 21:10); and "and they shall curse their G-d and their king and turn to rebellion" (Isa 8:21). All three statements indicate the close relationship between G-d and king in ancient Israel, especially since YHWH authorizes kingship and the selection of kings (1 Samuel 8–12; 16; 2 Samuel 2; 7; 1 Kings 11; Psalms 2; 89) and the kings build temples to worship YHWH (2 Samuel 6; 24; 1 Kings 6–8; 12–13). Furthermore, both statements indicate the implications of a reversal of an oath to G-d and king as expressed in Zeph 1:5; both G-d and king are bound up together as the objects of the people's loyalty. Such a situation prevailed in Israel and Judah during the monarchic period; but following the Babylonian exile, Judah was not ruled by a native king again until the short-lived Hasmonean dynasty of the late second and early first century BCE. Given the disruption of the relationship between G-d and king in the Second Temple period, it is only natural that various textual versions would read this statement as a reference to a foreign god rather than to the king, especially since the consonants for "king" (מֶלֶךְ) and for "Milcom" are the same in Hebrew.

In view of this evidence, it seems best to conclude that v. 5b represents a second attempt to elaborate on the statements in vv. 4b and 5a concerning the character or identity of those who are identified as engaging in sycretistic practice according to YHWH's speech. In this case, v. 5b provides a further definition of the expression וְאֶת־הַמִּשְׁתַּחֲוִים from v. 5a. It is difficult to specify the identity of the writer or the writer's setting, although the following statement that those who prostrate themselves are to be identified as those sworn to YHWH and sworn by their king suggests an author who would presuppose the interrelationship between YHWH and king that would have been predominant throughout the monarchic period in which YHWH authorized the Davidic monarch (see Psalms 2; 89) and the Davidic monarch supported YHWH and maintained the temple (see Psalm 132). Insofar as Zephaniah presents YHWH's oracular statements throughout the book, the writer could well be Zephaniah.

---

66   Berlin, *Zephaniah*, 76. She does indicate that such practice is known in Akkadian texts, and that Isa 8:21 may support such a contention. Indeed, it does, as the passage reads, "and they shall curse their G-d and their king and turn to rebellion" (see Sweeney, *Isaiah 1–39*, 175–88, esp. 185; idem, "A Philological and Form-Critical Reevaluation of Isaiah 8:16–9:6," *HAR* 14 [1994] 215–31).

■ **6** A number of scholars argue that v. 6 must be considered as a secondary addition to the text, based on the disruption of the metrical pattern of the preceding verses and the clear third person references to YHWH that indicate that YHWH is no longer the speaker.[67] As noted above, metrical considerations hardly constitute the basis for such decisions, and the shift to the third person indicates the prophet's role as the transmitter of YHWH's speech.[68] In the present form of the text, the introductory conjunctive *waw* and direct object marker, וְאֵת, is the third in the sequence of such clauses in vv. 5a, 5b, and 6, that build on the object phrase, "(אֵת) the name of the cultic attendants with the priests," in v. 4bα. Verse 6 thereby continues the sequence of direct object clauses in vv. 4bα-6 that specify the objects of YHWH's action in v. 4bα. Rather than point to those who are engaged in syncretistic practice, this verse points to those who reject YHWH outright. Thus the expression, "and those who turn aside from after YHWH," employs the *niphal* form of the verb סוג, "to be moved away, backslide, turn oneself away," which appears in Isa 50:5; 59:13; Pss 44:19; and 78:57 as a means to express apostasy from YHWH. Renaud sees this as a Deuteronomistic phrase,[69] apparently because of its reference to turning away from YHWH, but these references indicate that the expression does not appear in Deuteronomistic literature.[70]

The nature of the apostasy is defined by the relative pronoun clause in v. 6b as "and who (וַאֲשֶׁר) do not seek YHWH and do not inquire of him."[71] Both of the verbs employed in this phrase, בקשׁ, "to seek," and דרשׁ, "to inquire," appear frequently in cultic contexts in reference to prayer and oracular inquiry.[72]

---

67 E.g., Marti, *Dodekapropheton,* 363; Nowack, *Propheten,* 292–93; Sellin, *Zwölfprophetenbuch,* 423; Keller, *Sophonie,* 187, 189; Guy Langhor, "Le livre de Sophonie et la critique d'authencité," *EThL* 52 (1976) 6; Rainer Edler, *Das Kerygma des Propheten Zefanja* (Freiburger theologische Studien 126; Freiburg: Herder, 1984) 79–80; Renaud, *Sophonie,* 202–3. Horst, *Propheten,* 190, emends the text so that it is formulated as a first person speech by YHWH, but there are no grounds for this in the versions.

68 A number of scholars reject the contention that v. 6 is secondary, e.g., J. M. P. Smith, *Zephaniah,* 190–91; Vlaardingerbroek, *Zephaniah,* 63–64; cf. Hubert Junker, *Die zwölf kleinen Propheten. II Hälfte: Nahum, Habakuk, Sophonia, Aggäus, Zacharias, Malachis* (HSAT VIII/3.II; Bonn: Hanstein, 1938) 70; Rudolph, *Zephanja,* 266; Roberts, *Zephaniah,* 173; Berlin, *Zephaniah,* 77–78.

69 Renaud, *Sophonie,* 202–3; idem, "Sophonie," 5.

70 Cf. Ben Zvi, *Zephaniah,* 78.

71 Cf. Berlin, *Zephaniah,* 77–78, who argues that the verbs continue the participle of v. 6a and that they should be translated in the same tense.

72 For examples of בקשׁ in reference to prayer or a general seeking of YHWH, see Hos 5:15; 1 Chr 6:11/Ps 105:4; 2 Chr 7:14; 2 Sam 21:1; Pss 24:6; 27:8; Deut 4:29; Hos 3:3; 5:6; Exod 33:7; 1 Chr 16:10/Ps 105:3; 2 Chr 11:16; 20:4; Isa 51:1; Prov 28:5; Zech 8:21, 22; Jer 50:4, etc. For an example of בקשׁ in reference to seeking the word of YHWH, see Amos 8:12. For examples of דרשׁ in reference to prayer, see Deut 4:29; Hos 10:12; Amos 5:4, 6; Isa 9:12; 31:1; 55:6; 58:2; 65:10; Jer 10:21; 29:13; Lam 3:25; 1 Chr 16:11/Ps 105:4; 1 Chr 28:9; 2 Chr 12:14; 14:3, 6; 15:2, 12; 16:12; 22:9; 26:5; Pss 9:11; 22:27; 34:5, 11; 119:2, 12, etc.; for examples of דרשׁ in reference to oracular inquiry, see Gen 25:22; Exod 18:25; 1 Sam 9:9; 1 Kgs 22:8; 2 Kgs 3:11; 8:8; 22:13, 18; 1 Chr 15:13; 21:30; 2 Chr 18:7; 34:21; Pss 24:6; 78:34; Jer 21:2; 37:7; Ezek 20:1, 3, etc. Cf. Roberts, *Zephaniah,* 173; Ben Zvi, *Zephaniah,* 79; Vlaardingerbroek, *Zephaniah,* 77–78.

Translation

7 Silence!^a from before my L-rd, YHWH,
   for the Day of YHWH is near;^b
   for YHWH has prepared a sacrifice;^c he
      has sanctified^d his invitees.

8 And it shall come to pass on the day of
   YHWH's sacrifice,^e
   "And I shall punish^f the officers and the
      sons of the king^g
   and all who are dressed in foreign attire.^h

9 And I shall punishⁱ those who cross^j over
      the threshold^k in that day,
   those who fill the house of their lord with
      violence^l and deceit."

10 And it shall come to pass on that day, utterance of YHWH,
   "The sound of outcry from the Fish Gate^m
      and wailing from the Mishnehⁿ and
      great tumult from the hills.

11 The inhabitants of the Maktesh^o wail,
      because all the people of Canaan are
      destroyed,^p
      all who weigh out money^q are cut off."

12 And it shall come to pass at that time,
   "I will search out Jerusalem with lamps,^r
   and I shall review the people,
      those who linger over their wine
         dregs,^s
      who say in their heart, 'YHWH does no
         good, and he does no evil,'

13 and their wealth^t shall become plunder
      and their houses^u desolation,
   and they shall build houses, but they shall
      not dwell in them,
   and they shall plant vineyards, but they
      shall not drink their wine."

14 The great Day of YHWH is near! Near and
   coming very fast!
   The sound of the Day of YHWH is bitter,
      a warrior cries out there.^v

15 That day is a day of fury,
   a day of distress and stress,
   a day of destruction and devastation,
   a day of darkness and gloom,
   a day of cloud and dark fog,

16 a day of shofar and trumpet
      against the fortified cities and
      against the high towers.^w

17 "And I shall afflict humankind,
   and they shall walk like the blind,
      because they have sinned against
         YHWH,
   and their blood shall be spilled out like
      dust,
   and their guts^x like dung."^y

18 Neither their silver nor their gold shall be
   able to save them
   on the day of the wrath of YHWH,
   and by the fire of his jealousy, all the land
      shall be consumed
   because destruction, indeed, sudden
      devastation,
   he shall make for all the inhabitants of
      the land.

a LXX reads, Εὐλαβεῖσθε, "beware!"; TJ reads, ספו כל
   רשׁיעיא, "all the wicked have perished"; Peshitta
   reads, dḥlw, "be afraid!"

b TJ reads, ארי קריב יומא דעתיד למיתי מן קדם יוי, "for
   near is the future day for coming from before
   YHWH."

c LXX reads, τὴν θυσίαν αὐτοῦ, "his offering." TJ
   reads, , "a slaying/killing."

d TJ reads, ערע, "he has summoned."

e TJ reads, ביום קטלא דעתיד למיתי מן קדם יוי, "on the
   future day of killing to come from before YHWH."

f LXX reads, καὶ ἐδικήσω ἐπὶ, "and I will bring punishment upon."

g LXX reads, τὸν οἶκον τοῦ βασιλέως, "the house of
   the king."

h TJ reads, ועל כל דמתרגשׁין למפלח לטעותא, "and upon
   all who are stirred to worship idols."

i LXX reads, καὶ ἐδικήσω ἐπὶ, "and I will bring punishment upon."

j LXX reads, ἐμφανῶς, "openly," in place of MT הַדּוֹלֵג,
   "(all) who cross." It appears that LXX took the word
   assonantally as הַדּוֹלֵק, "(all) who burn for/are eager
   for." Vulgate appears to have combined both readings with its translation, omenem qui arroganter
   ingreditur super limnen in die illa, "all who arrogantly
   step over the threshold in that day," in that arroganter appears to render הַדּוֹלֵק and ingreditur renders
   הַדּוֹלֵג. For a full discussion of this text, see Irsigler,
   Gottesgericht, 35–49.

k TJ reads, כל דמהלכין בנמוסי פלשׁתאי, "all who fol-
   low/walk in the laws/religion of the Philistines."
   Peshitta reads, klhwn ḥṭwpᵓ wbzwzᵓ, "all who are robbers and plunderers."

l LXX reads, ἀσεβείς, "impiety/profaneness."

m LXX reads, ἀπὸ πύλης ἀποκεντούντων, "from the
   gate of those stabbing/slaying," apparently reading
   Heb. מִשַּׁעַר הַדָּגִים, "from the gate of fish," as, מִשַּׁעַר
   הֹרְגִים, "from the gate of those slaying" (cf. Gerleman, *Zephanja*, 14; Rudolph, *Zephanja*, 262).
   Peshitta reads, mn trᶜ dsydᵓ, "from the gate of those
   hurting," apparently following the LXX reading.

n LXX reads, ἀπὸ τῆς δευτέρας, "from the second,"
   apparently a literal translation of Heb. מִן־הַמִּשְׁנֶה,
   "from the Mishneh." TJ reads, מן עופלא, "from the
   Ophel." A number of Targum MSS read, מן עופא,
   "from the bird (gate)," apparently rendering an interpretation of the "Mishneh/Second" gate in terms
   analogous to that of the Fish Gate (see Sperber, *The
   Bible in Aramaic*, 3:465, note to v. 10; Rudolph,
   Zephanja, 262–63; Cathcart and Gordon, *Targum*,
   166). Peshitta reads, mn ᵓḥrnᵓ, "from the other"; and
   Vulgate reads, a secunda, "from the second."

o LXX reads, τὴν κατακεκομμένην, "(the inhabitants
   of) the area broken into pieces/coined into money,"
   apparently an attempt to render Heb. הַמַּכְתֵּשׁ, "the

mortar," which derived from the verbal root כתש, "to pound." Mur88 20:1 reads, ה[מ]כתש כי נדמה, like MT; cf. Vulgate *habitores pilae*, "inhabitants of the mortar." TJ reads, בנחלון דקדרון, "in the Kidron Valley" (cf. Gerleman, *Zephanja,* 15; Smoler and Aberbach, *Studies,* 111; contra Rudolph, *Zephanja,* 263; and Cathcart and Gordon, *Targum,* 166, who suppose that the Maktesh cannot refer to the Kidron Valley because a commercial area would have to be in the city. Archeologists likewise surmise that the Maktesh must refer to the area of the Tyropoean Valley to the west of the City of David because of its association with the Mishneh quarter, also located west of the city. Certainly, a western location makes sense, not only because the area of the Tyropoean Valley would have been shaped as a mortar-like depression, but also because the city's commercial centers would more likely be situated to the west, which was closer to the roads leading to the coastal plain and the Mediterranean Sea (see A. Mazar, *Archaeology of the Land of the Bible, 10,000–586 B.C.E.* [New York: Doubleday, 1990] 424; Y. Shiloh, "Jerusalem," *NEAEHL* 2:708). A major gate for Jerusalem faced the Kidron Valley during the monarchic period (cf. Isa 7:3; 36:2/2 Kgs 18:17) and Second Temple times, and it is possible that TJ read these verses as an address to all the quarters of Jerusalem.

p LXX reads, ὡμοιώθη, "are like," apparently reading Heb. נדמה, "destroyed" (דמה II, "to destroy"), as a form of the root דמה I, "to speak in parables, to compare" (see Rudolph, *Zephanja,* 263). TJ follows suit in reading, "because all the people whose works are like the works (לעובדי דדמן עובדיהון) of the people of the land of Canaan" (see Cathcart and Gordon, *Targum,* 166). Vulgate reads, *conticuit omnis populus Chanaan,* "silent are all the people of Canaan," reading Heb. נדמה as a form of the root, דמם I, "to be dumb, silent."

q TJ reads, עתירי נכסיא, "rich in property."

r TJ reads, "I shall appoint searchers and they shall search the inhabitants of Jerusalem as (people) search with a lamp." Apparently TJ protects divine sanctity by portraying human searchers, appointed by G-d (cf. Gerleman, *Zephanja,* 15; Cathcart and Gordon, *Targum,* 167). The basis for this expansion is the Hebrew phrase בנרות, "with lamps," in which the preposition בְּ, "with," indicates agency.

s LXX reads, ἐπὶ τοὺς ἄνδρας τοὺς καταφρονοῦντας ἐπὶ τὰ φυλάγματα, "upon the men who despise their charges," apparently reading Heb. שמריהם, "their dregs" (from שֶׁמֶר/שָׁמָר), as "their watchings" (from שׁמר). Cf. Vulgate, which reads, *defixos in fecibus suis,* "who fix upon their charges." TJ reads, על גבריא דשלן שליוא על נכסיהון, "upon the men who are quietly at ease upon their wealth." TJ apparently

employs a pun on Aram. שליוא, which means both "dregs" and "unconcerned." It also apparently draws on Heb. חֵילָם, "their wealth," from v. 13 in that it employs נכסיהון, "their wealth," for שמריהם, "their dregs ." Peshitta reads, ʿl gbrʾ dšylyn lyṭwrhwn, "upon the men who despise their advocate," reading lyṭwrhwn, "their advocate," for שמריהם, "the one who watches them," in a manner analogous to LXX. Cf. the discussions in Gerleman, *Zephanja,* 16–17; Rudolph, *Zephanja,* 263; Cathcart and Gordon, *Targum,* 167.

t TJ reads, בתיהון, "their houses," for חֵילָם, "their wealth," having employed the latter in its rendition of v. 12 (see note s above).

u TJ reads, ובירניתהון, "and their palaces." See notes t and s above.

v LXX reads, καὶ σκληρὰ τέτακται δυνατή, "and harsh, he has appointed power." Apparently, LXX had difficulty with the present form of the Hebrew text and read צֹרֵחַ, "shrieking/outcry," as צָרַח, "harsh," and שָׁם גִּבּוֹר, "there (שָׁם) a warrior," as "he appointed (שָׂם) power/a warrior." 8HevXIIgr 21:29 reads ἐπισ[ ], apparently preserving a form of the verb ἐπιστένω, "to groan" (cf. Tov, *Greek Minor Prophets,* 95, who cites Barthélemy's reading, ἐπισ[ημος (*Devanciers,* 177). Apparently, TJ also had some difficulties with the phrase, as indicated by its rendition, "the sound of the day that is appointed to come from before YHWH, on which is trouble and outcry; there, the warriors are being killed." Like LXX, TJ reads, צֹרֵחַ, "shrieking/outcry," together with the preceding מַר, "bitter," but adds מתקטלין, "are being killed/are killing themselves" (apparently on the basis of TJ's reference to the Day of YHWH as a day of "slaughter" or "killing" in v. 7), to explain the phrase שָׁם גִּבּוֹר "there (שָׁם) a warrior." The Peshitta simplifies the matter by deleting שָׁם, "there," altogether and reading "the sound of the day of the L-rd is bitter and hard and strong (mryr wqšʾ wʿšyn)." Vulgate reads, *tribulabitur ibi fortis,* "afflicting the strong." Cf. the discussions in Gerleman, *Zephanja,* 20–21; Rudolph, *Zephanja,* 263.

w TJ reads, ועל רמתא מנטלתא, "and concerning the high/uplifted heights," apparently expressing a pun between Aram. מנטלתא, "uplifted," and Heb. נְטִילֵי כָסֶף, "those bearing money," as both מנטלתא and נְטִילֵי derive from the same verbal root, נטל, "to lift, bear."

x LXX reads, τὰς σάρκας αὐτῶν, "their flesh"; 8HevXIIgr 21:38-9 reads, π[τώ]μα[τ]α [αὐτῶν], "their corpses" (cf. Tov, *Greek Minor Prophets,* 95); TJ reads, ונבילתחון, "and their corpses"; and Peshitta reads, wbsrhwn, "and their flesh." Cf. Gerleman, *Zephanja,* 21.

y TJ reads, כסחותא, "like sweepings/refuse."

Form and Setting

Zephaniah 1:7-18 constitutes a discrete formal subunit within the larger context of 1:2-18, immediately following the prophet's presentation of YHWH's oracular speeches concerning the impending Day of YHWH in vv. 2-6. The absence of a syntactic join at v. 7, the appearance of the exclamatory הַס, "Silence!" at the beginning of the verse, and the shift in theme from the punishment of apostasy to the Day of YHWH, mark v. 7 as the beginning of the subunit that calls for the audience's attention to the prophet's (and YHWH's) statements concerning the Day of YHWH. The call to gather at the beginning of 2:1, the absence of a syntactical connector to the preceding material, and the prophet's appeal for decisive action on the part of the audience rather than for its attention signal the beginning of a subsequent unit.

Because vv. 2-6 prepare the reading or listening audience for what is to follow, vv. 7-18 constitute the prophet's formal announcement of the Day of YHWH. Although these verses once again contain first person statements by YHWH in vv. 8aα-9 and 10aα⁶⁻⁹-13, the third person references to YHWH in v. 7, vv. 8aα and 10aα¹⁻⁵, and throughout vv. 14-18, indicate that the prophet is the speaker who conveys YHWH's statements to the audience, as in vv. 2-6. Some might argue that v. 12aα must also be considered a statement by the prophet,[1] but the absence of any clear third person reference to YHWH suggests that no change in speaker takes place. The shift in formula, from "and it shall come to pass in that day" to "and it shall come to pass at that time," in v. 12aα likewise indicates a distinction from the formulae in vv. 8aα and 10aα¹⁻⁵, which are clearly attributable to the prophet. The appearance of the oracular formula נְאֻם־ה׳, "utterance of YHWH," in v. 10aα⁴⁻⁵ demonstrates a setting in which the prophet presents and interprets oracular speech from YHWH.

A major syntactic break at v. 14 and the prophet's repeated references to the Day of YHWH at the outset of the passage in v. 7 and again in v. 14 suggest that the passage comprises two major portions: the prophet's presentation of YHWH's oracular statements concerning the Day of YHWH in vv. 7-13, and the prophet's explanation of the significance of the Day of YHWH in vv. 14-18.

The literary structure of 1:7-13 clearly demonstrates the rhetorical aim to capture the audience's attention and direct it to YHWH's oracular announcements concerning the Day of YHWH. This is clear from the initial statement in v. 7, which presents the prophet's exclamatory demand for silence before YHWH (v. 7a), followed by two כִּי clauses that provide reasons for the demand for silence: the Day of YHWH is near (v. 7bα), and YHWH has prepared a sacrifice and sanctified those who are called/invited to attend (v. 7bα). The call for silence is particularly important in relation to the characterization of the Day of YHWH as a day of sacrifice because strict silence is observed by the priests who officiate at the altar as they carry out their sacrificial functions.[2] The introductory formulae, וְהָיָה בְּיוֹם/בַּיּוֹם הַהוּא, "and it shall come to pass in the day of/that day," in vv. 8aα and 10aα¹⁻⁵ are both linked syntactically to v. 7 by the *waw*-consecutive verb formation, וְהָיָה, "and it shall come to pass." They also introduce subunits in vv. 8-9 and 10-13 in which the prophet presents YHWH's oracular announcements concerning the divine intention to punish those considered apostate on the Day of YHWH. In this sense, vv. 7-13/14-18 build on the earlier material in 1:2-6. The association suggests that those who are to be punished are also those who are to be sacrificed. In ancient Judean thought, such a conceptualization builds on the role of sacrifice as a means of purification and sanctification that restores the proper relationship between the heavenly and earthly realms.[3]

The introductory formula, "and it shall come to pass on the day of the sacrifice of YHWH," makes this equation clear in that the characterization of the Day of YHWH as one of sacrifice introduces YHWH's statements concerning the punishment of those who have

---

1 E.g., Renaud, *Sophonie*, 209–10; Irsigler, *Gottesgericht*, 95–96, 108–13.

2 See, e.g., Israel Knohl, *The Sanctuary of Silence: The Priestly Torah and the Holiness School* (Minneapolis: Fortress Press, 1994); Knierim, *Text*.

3 See esp. Gary A. Anderson, "Sacrifice and Sacrificial Offerings (OT)," *ABD* 5:870–86, and the literature cited there.

apostatized against YHWH. YHWH's statements are evident in the pair of first person, *waw*-consecutive verbs, וּפָקַדְתִּי, "and I will punish/review," at the beginning of vv. 8aα and 9. Indeed, each appearance of וּפָקַדְתִּי introduces the two basic statements by the Deity that define the basis for this textual subunit. The first appears in v. 8aα-b, in which YHWH states the intention to "review" or "punish" three different parties: the officers, the sons of the king, and all those who are attired in foreign garments. Such a threat encompasses those in Jerusalem/Judah who are entrusted with political authority: the officers include the nation's military and administrative figures, the sons of the king include the king's inner council of advisors,[4] and those who are dressed in foreign attire indicate those at the upper levels of Judean society who can afford to dress in such garments and by doing so choose to identify with the foreign nations that rule Judah and/or engage in trade with Judah.

Verse 8aα-b offers no explicit charges against the three objects of YHWH's punishment other than the implication that those to be punished by YHWH must somehow deserve that punishment. Verse 9, on the other hand, makes the basis for punishment clear by the manner in which those who will suffer punishment are described. Verse 9 includes two objects of YHWH's punishment: those who leap over the threshold and those who fill the house of their masters/lords with violence and deceit. The practice of leaping over a threshold constitutes a form of apostasy in that it is identified with the Philistine practice of refraining from stepping on the threshold of the temple of the god Dagon (see 1 Sam 5:5). Bringing violence and deceit into the house of one's master, whether the master or lord is human or divine, is self-explanatory. Thus YHWH's statements move from the mere suggestion of improper action to an explicit charge of wrongdoing.

The prophet's second report of YHWH's announcements in vv. 10-13 begins with the introductory formula, "and it shall come to pass on that day, utterance of YHWH," which explicitly identifies the following statements as oracular statements by YHWH. The general pattern of YHWH's statements is based on the prophetic judgment speech,[5] which conveys impending punishment or disaster and attempts to identify the cause for such disaster in the wrongdoing of the people. It thus characterizes the disaster suffered by the people as a punishment brought on them by YHWH as a consequence of their improper actions.

YHWH's statements begin in vv. 10aα[6-9]-11 with a depiction of disaster overtaking the people of Jerusalem (and perhaps Judah). It begins in v. 10aα[6-9]-b with a portrayal of outcry and wailing throughout the various quarters of the city, including outcry from the Fish Gate, located apparently on the north side of Jerusalem,[6] the wailing from the Mishneh quarter, the new portion of the city built on the hill immediately to the west of the Temple Mount and the City of David,[7] and the crashing noise that is heard among the hills that surround Jerusalem. Verse 11 continues with a portrayal of the wailing of the inhabitants of the Maktesh, "Mortar," an area believed by most to encompass the region of the Tyropoean Valley that lies between the Western Hill and the City of David.[8] The כִּי clause in v. 11b states that the cause of such wailing is the demise of the "people of Canaan," a term often employed for traders or merchants and those who handle money.

Having described the general scenario of wailing and suffering, vv. 12-13 then identify YHWH as the cause, insofar as YHWH states the intention to search Jerusalem for apostates and to punish accordingly. The intro-

---

4   Cf. 2 Kgs 10:1-11, which refers to the seventy sons of Ahab killed by Jehu in his revolt against the house of Omri, and Judg 8:30 and 9:1-6, which refer to the seventy sons of Gideon killed by Abimelech in his bid for power. For discussion of the political character of the "sons of the king," see G. Brin, "The Title בן המלך and Its Parallels: The Significance and Evaluation of a Cultic Title," *AION* 29 (1969) 432-65.

5   Sweeney, *Isaiah 1-39*, 533-34; Claus Westermann, *Basic Forms of Prophetic Speech* (1967; reprinted Louisville: Westminster John Knox, 1991) 129-209.

6   Neh 3:3; 12:38-39 (cf. 13:16). See D. C. Liid, "Fish Gate," *ABD* 2:797-98.

7   See Yigal Shiloh, "Jerusalem: The Early Periods and the First Temple Period," *NEAEHL* 2:698-712, esp. 704-9, and the literature cited on 716; Philip J. King, "Jerusalem," *ABD* 3:747-66, esp. 755; Nahman Avigad, *Discovering Jerusalem* (Nashville: Nelson, 1983) 23-60.

8   See textual note o and n. 7 above for references.

ductory formula, "and it shall come to pass at that time," indicates continuity with the preceding material by virtue of its *waw*-consecutive verbal formation (וְהָיָה בָּעֵת הַהִיא) that conveys both a syntactical and temporal link. Two first person statements presuppose YHWH's role as the speaker who states the intention to search out Jerusalem with lamps and to punish those who sit over their wine dregs uttering statements that deny YHWH efficacy: "YHWH does neither good nor evil." Verse 13 then employs the *waw*-consecutive verb וְהָיָה, "and it shall come to pass," to describe the consequences for such apostasy: their wealth shall be plundered and their houses laid waste; they shall build houses and not live in them and plant vineyards and not drink their wine.

Following the above-noted syntactical break at v. 14, vv. 14-18 present the prophet's explanation of the significance of the Day of YHWH. The third person references to YHWH throughout these verses indicate that the prophet is the speaker. Although the first person address in v. 17aα, "and I shall afflict humankind, and they shall walk like the blind," might indicate that YHWH is the speaker,[9] the following כִּי clause in v. 17aα, "for they have sinned to YHWH," suggests that the prophet is the speaker who promises to afflict human beings.

The literary structure of 1:14-18 well serves its explanatory character. The passage begins in v. 14a with a pair of syntactically independent statements that are related together by their common concern with naming the Day of YHWH and making assertions concerning its imminence. By naming the Day of YHWH and announcing that it is "near" (קָרוֹב), the prophet revisits the statements in v. 7 that call for silence before YHWH on the approaching Day of YHWH, thereby alerting the audience. Thus v. 14a directs the audience's attention once again to the basic theme of the passage so that the prophet is now able to offer his own explanation concerning the significance of the day. The references to the nearness of the day and the speed with which it will come aid in capturing the audience's attention for the following explanation. The prophet's explanation then appears in vv. 14b-18 with a series of statements that characterize the day as one of YHWH's anger and threat against the nation (vv. 14b-16) followed by the prophet's statement concerning the consequences of the day for those who are to be punished (vv. 17-18).

The prophet's characterization of the day begins with the initial statement in v. 14b, a syntactically independent assertion that once again identifies the Day of YHWH by name, thereby marking its role as the premise from which the following statements will proceed, and characterizes it as bitter based on the sound of warriors crying out or shrieking in a time of grave danger. Verses 15-16 then build on this characterization by first presenting six statements, each beginning with the word יוֹם, "a day," that present the various attributes of the day. The term יוֹם of course does not repeat the full name "Day of YHWH," but merely alludes to the name presented in v. 14b. The six attributes combine elements of YHWH's presence and anger that commonly appear in theophanic texts: anger (v. 15a), affliction (v. 15bα[1-3]), destruction (v. 15bα[4-6]), darkness (v. 15bα), cloud (v. 15bα), and shofar or trumpet blast (v. 16a). The concluding clause in v. 16b twice employs the preposition עַל, "against," to identify the objects of the Day of YHWH as described in the preceding statements as "fortified cities" (v. 16bα) and "high towers" (v. 16bα).

The initial *waw*-consecutive verbal formation, וַהֲצֵרֹתִי, "and I shall afflict," syntactically joins the prophet's statement in v. 17 concerning the cause of the people's suffering and a graphic portrayal of the consequences: they will be stricken blind because they have sinned against YHWH, and their blood and guts will be spilled out. The verb recalls the prophet's earlier characterization of the day as a day of "distress" (צָרָה), which is based on a related verbal root. Such a portrayal revisits the characterization in v. 7 of the Day of YHWH as a sacrifice, since the entrails of a sacrificial animal must first be removed before the animal is ready for burning at the altar.[10] Verse 18a, joined syntactically to v. 17 by

---

9   E.g., Irsigler, *Gottesgericht*, 99, 110–11; Renaud, *Sophonie*, 214–15; Ben Zvi, *Zephaniah*, 127.

10   See, e.g., Leviticus 1, which specifies that the entrails of the whole burnt offering (עֹלָה) must first be removed and washed in water prior to the sacrifice (for discussion see Knierim, *Text*, esp. 58–64).

77

the initial particle גַּם, "also, indeed," revisits the assertions of v. 11 that the traders and merchants of Jerusalem would suffer on the Day of YHWH by asserting that neither their silver nor their gold would save them. Finally, the prophet's concluding statement in v. 18b refers to the day as one of YHWH's wrath (עֶבְרַת ה״) and thereby revisits the prophet's characterization of the day in v. 15a. The following assertion that all the land will be consumed in the fire of YHWH's zeal continues the underlying image of sacrifice by employing the metaphor of an animal being consumed by flames on the altar. The כִּי clause reiterates this theme by pointing to the complete destruction of all the inhabitants of the land, metaphorically destroyed by YHWH like a whole burnt offering.

1:7-13

■ 7 Zephaniah 1:7 constitutes the prophet's exclamatory demand for silence at the beginning of the presentation of YHWH's oracular statements that announce the coming Day of YHWH. The basic demand for silence in the presence of YHWH appears in v. 7a, which is based on the exclamation, הַס, "Silence!" Some scholars correctly point out that the three verbs of v. 7b provide the basis for defining three additional clauses that continue the prophet's exclamation.[11] Nevertheless, the appearance of the introductory particle כִּי, "for, because," at the beginning of v. 7bα and v. 7bβ indicates a syntactical structure in which two explanatory clauses state the reasons for the prophet's demand for silence: the Day of YHWH is near (v. 7bα), and YHWH has prepared a sacrifice for which those who are "called" or "invited" have been sanctified (v. 7bβ). In the case of v. 7bα, the two subclauses, "for YHWH has prepared a

sacrifice" (v. 7bα[1-4]), and "he has sanctified his invitees" (v. 7bα[5-6]), constitute parallel statements in that they relate YHWH's preparation of two parties that are essential to the sacrifice, that is, the sacrifice itself and those who are to attend the sacrifice. Indeed, as the passage develops, the distinction between these two parties seems somewhat blurred, as those who are invited to observe or attend to the sacrifice are indeed those who are themselves to be sacrificed.

The reference to YHWH's preparations for sacrifice in v. 7bα has proved to be particularly important to the interpretation of this passage; many have claimed that the prophet's demand for silence and announcement of the approaching Day of YHWH must be typical elements of an overall cultic scenario in which sacrifice takes place on the aforementioned Day of YHWH.[12] Although they clearly function as elements of such a scenario in the present context, it is somewhat questionable whether they constitute typical elements of such a scenario.[13]

The demand for silence before YHWH is a case in point. The particle הַס, "Silence!" is clearly an onomatopoeic element that represents the typical human attempt to "hush" others who are making noise of any sort. Although its basic form appears to be a particle, it is conjugated as a verb in several instances. Its appearance in various cultic contexts apparently reflects the practice by the priests of maintaining silence while carrying out sacrificial ritual at the altar.[14] Such a practice apparently stands behind the narrative in Neh 8:11, in which the Levites hush the people at the temple on Sukkot as Ezra prepares to read the Torah to them: "so the Levites stilled the people, saying, 'Silence (הַסּוּ)!' for this day is holy; do not be grieved."

11   E.g., Ben Zvi, *Zephaniah*, 83–85; cf. Ball, *Zephaniah*, 63.

12   Rudolph, *Zephanja*, 266, designates it formally as a "cultic call"; cf. Floyd, *Minor Prophets*, 193; Roberts, *Zephaniah*, 177; Seybold, *Zephanja*, 95; Keller, *Sophonie*, 190; Sabottka, *Zephanja*, 31–32; Horst, *Propheten*, 192; Junker, *Sophonia*, 70; Sellin, *Zwölfprophetenbuch*, 425–26; J. M. P. Smith, *Zephaniah*, 194; Marti, *Dodekapropheton*, 363. Schwally, "Sefanjâ," 171, notes that such calls for silence were characteristic of Roman sacrifice (cf. Horace *Odes* 3.1.2; Virgil *Aeneid* 5.71).

13   Cf. Vlaardingerbroek, *Zephaniah*, 82.

14   See note 2 above.

Other instances are somewhat ambiguous, however, such as the prophet's statement in Hab 2:20, "and YHWH is in his holy palace/temple, 'silence before him, all the land!'" Although the context of YHWH's holy temple would certainly reflect the conceptualization of the temple as the place of YHWH's abode and the place where sacrifice is made for YHWH, the prophet's statement appears as part of the prophet's summation following the presentation of a series of woe oracles in 2:5-20 in which the prophet announces judgment against the Babylonians for oppressive treatment of Judah.[15] It is not clear that 2:20 appears in the context of cultic sacrifice. Likewise, Zech 2:17, "Be silent (הַס), all people, before YHWH; for he has roused himself from his holy dwelling," employs the imagery of YHWH's holy temple in its call for silence from the people. Nevertheless, the context does not portray a scene of cultic sacrifice; instead, it portrays YHWH's efforts to gather the exiles of Judah and return them to Zion.[16] Amos 8:3, "the dead bodies shall be many, cast out in every place. Be silent! (הָס)," likewise appears in a context in which the temple is present; indeed, 8:1-3a make clear that the presentation of fruit offerings at the altar is a part of the overall scenario. But the call for silence does not appear to be necessary to the sacrificial presentation; rather, it is issued on account of the many dead who will be the victims of YHWH's wrath in 8:1-14. Indeed, the appearance of the particle in 6:10 makes clear that the demand for silence is related to a refusal to utter the name of YHWH in the presence of the dead. Perhaps such a concern lies in part behind the priestly silence at the altar while handling the slaughter and sacrifice of animals deemed holy to YHWH.

Finally, two instances of the term indicate its use in contexts that have little to do with sacrifice. In Num 13:30 Caleb "quiets" (וַיַּהַס) the people who are disturbed by the reports of the spies that Joshua sent to the land of Canaan. In Judg 3:19 Eglon calls for "Silence! (הָס)" so that he might receive the "secret message" that Ehud brings him. The term is apparently used commonly in Hebrew for situations in which one might call for silence. Its appearance in contexts related to sacrifice does not appear to identify it as any sort of technical language.

The phrase "for the Day of YHWH is near (קָרוֹב)" appears frequently in contexts that announce the Day of YHWH (Isa 13:6; Ezek 30:3; Joel 1:15; 2:1; 4:14; Obad 15; cf. Zeph 1:14 below; see also Ezek 7:7, 12).[17] Although this suggests a certain typicality to the form, it appears to function as a device to convey the threat occasioned by the nearness of the day, especially since the Day of YHWH is conceived as a time of YHWH's threat against the enemies of Judah/Israel or YHWH (e.g., Isa 13:6, 9; Jer 46:10; Ezek 30:3; Joel 4:14; Obad 15; cf. Isaiah 34; 61:1-3; 63:1-6) or against Judah/Jerusalem/ Israel itself (e.g., Ezek 7:19; 13:5; Joel 1:15; 2:1, 11; 3:4; cf. Amos 5:18-20; Isa 2:6-21; Mal 3:19-24; Lamentations 1–2) or even against first Jerusalem/Judah and then the nations that threaten them (e.g., Zech 14:1-21). A few scholars have argued that some or most of these texts are dependent on Zephaniah's formulation,[18] but such a contention appears to be unnecessary by virtue of the general threat conveyed in all representations of the day.

Many scholars see the reference to the Day of YHWH in this text as evidence of later redaction in that it eschatologizes Zephaniah's message to point to a time beyond historical experience when all the enemies of YHWH, that is, all who are evil in the world, are to be destroyed as the kingdom of G-d is manifested on earth.[19] Such contentions are perhaps unduly influenced by NT con-

15 For discussion of the place of Hab 2:20 in relation to its literary context, see Marvin A. Sweeney, "Structure, Genre, and Intent in the Book of Habakkuk," *VT* 41 (1991) 63–83; idem, *Twelve Prophets*, 478.

16 See Sweeney, *Twelve Prophets*, 584–92.

17 For overviews of discussion concerning the Day of YHWH, see K. J. Cathcart, "Day of Yahweh," *ABD* 2:84–85; Richard H. Hiers, "Day of the Lord," *ABD* 2:82–83; A. J. Everson, "Day of the Lord," *IDBSup* 209–10.

18 See Vlaardingerbroek, *Zephaniah*, 83, who attributes this position to van der Woude et al.

19 E.g., Vlaardingerbroek, *Zephaniah*, 80–82; Renaud, *Sophonie*, 189–91; Seybold, *Zephanja*, 89–90; idem, *Satirische Prophetie*, 23–25.

cepts of eschatology, particularly the end of human history inherent in the second coming of Christ as the culmination of a linear progression of time. But one must consider the conceptualization of time in the context of the ancient Jerusalem Temple and its festival system. Time is not only linear but also cyclical; it progresses linearly throughout the year from one New Year to the next, and it progresses cyclically as each year repeats itself with the same system of holidays.[20] Furthermore, as noted earlier, the Jerusalem Temple is the locus of creation in ancient Judean thought and the place where heaven and earth come together or exist simultaneously. Insofar as creation originally took place at the temple, it continues to take place at the temple at each major cultic observance.[21] This includes not only the annual or seasonal festivals, such as Passover, Shavuot, and Sukkot, but the weekly observance of Sabbath as well, which is conceived as a time for the renewal of creation. In this sense, creation takes place not only at the beginning of earthly history or time but also repeatedly through time—it is ritually reenacted each day as sunrise symbolizes the repeated creation of the first element, light, followed by the emergence of order once again in the created world. The temple holidays and Sabbaths therefore mark the suspension of normal, linear time.

This conceptualization of time is particularly important in relation to the Day of YHWH and its association with sacrifice. The Day of YHWH is regularly presented as a day on which YHWH defeats enemies, whether those enemies are conceived as enemy nations that threaten Jerusalem/Judah/Israel or those within Jerusalem/Judah/Israel who act contrary to YHWH's expectations. In this respect, the correlation between creation and the defeat of YHWH's enemies throughout biblical tradition is noteworthy: YHWH defeats Pharaoh and Egypt by employing the element of nature or creation in the form of plagues and the Red (or Reed) Sea in Exodus 1–15; YHWH defeats Sisera and Hazor in the time of Deborah by employing the stars and the Wadi Kishon in Judges 5; YHWH's defeat of the Assyrians and protection for Jerusalem and the house of David is evident in the cyclical patterns of the growth of a tree in Isaiah 6 and 10–11; YHWH's reversal of Job's misfortunes is analogous to YHWH's defeat of Behemoth or Rahab by which creation was placed in order in Job 38–42; and so on. Indeed, YHWH's guarantee of security from enemies to Jerusalem (Psalm 46; Isaiah 40:1-11, 12-31; 51:9-23; cf. Psalms 47; 48), the Davidic King (Psalm 89; cf. Psalm 2), and Israel at large (Jer 31:31-37) is rooted in YHWH's role as creator. The overcoming of evil or enemies is conceived as an act of creation throughout the Hebrew Bible.[22]

The time for such action takes place in the cultic observance of each day, each weekly Sabbath, and each annual (and cyclical) festival. With respect to the reference to the sacrifice that YHWH has prepared in Zeph 1:7b, it is particularly noteworthy that sacrifice constitutes a central element in the ritual observance of each day, Sabbath, and festival (see Numbers 28–29). Mowinckel correctly associated the Day of YHWH with the cultic observance of the temple, although perhaps he conceived of the observance too narrowly by limiting

---

20   For a study that focuses on the linear aspects of time in the Bible, see Bertil Albrektson, *History and the Gods: An Essay on the Idea of Historical Events as Divine Manifestations in the Ancient Near East and in Israel* (ConBOT 1; Lund: Gleerup, 1967); cf. Gerhard von Rad, *Old Testament Theology* (2 vols.; New York: Harper & Row, 1962–1965); V. R. Gold, "Time," *IDB* 4:642–49, who states, "On the whole, then, one must probably assume that the OT had an unconsidered chronological, linear conception of time" (p. 646). For observations on the cyclical character of time in the Bible, see Marvin A. Sweeney, "Tanak versus Old Testament: Concerning the Foundation for a Jewish Theology of the Bible," in Henry T. C. Sun et al., eds., *Problems in Biblical Theology: Essays in Honor of Rolf Knierim* (Grand

Rapids: Eerdmans, 1997) 353–72, esp. 366–68 (note: the observation goes back to Knierim's perspectives on Deuteronomy 26). On cyclical time in general, see Mircea Eliade, *The Myth of the Eternal Return, or Cosmos and History* (Princeton: Princeton Univ. Press, 1971).

21   See Levenson, "Temple"; idem, *Sinai*.

22   For discussion of this point, see esp. Jon D. Levenson, *Creation and the Persistence of Evil: The Jewish Drama of Divine Omnipotence* (New York: Harper & Row, 1988).

it to the New Year/Sukkot Festival because of his interest in the motif of YHWH's kingship as well as YHWH's creation.[23] Nevertheless, the association of the Day of YHWH with the Jerusalem festival system points to a fundamental feature of the Day of YHWH, that is, its conceptualization of YHWH's creation or re-creation through the defeat of enemies does not entail an eschatological scenario of the end of earthly or linear time; it constitutes a repeated event that is ritually reenacted at every temple observance when the forces of evil that would threaten creation are defeated once again as the power of YHWH is manifested or celebrated in sacrifice and ritual. The Day of YHWH does not represent the end of time; it represents an ideal scenario of what might take place within time and within human events, whether it is expressed through the defeat of the Assyrians, the restoration of Davidic kingship over all Israel, the security of the nation from outside threat, or the purification of its religious observance from within.

Finally, the reference to those "called" or "invited" whom YHWH has sanctified requires attention. Although various texts in Deuteronomy indicate that all of the people were able to share in the eating of temple sacrifices together with the Levitical priests (see Deut 12:2-27; 14:22-29; 15:19-23; 16:1-17; 18:1-8), a number of texts indicate that persons could be specially invited to take part in a sacrificial ritual. Examples include Samuel's invitation to Saul, who was placed at the head of those invited to indicate his status as the man to be anointed as king (1 Sam 9:22-24; cf. 9:13); Jesse and his sons, from whom Samuel was to select one to become king after Saul (16:1-5); the two hundred men from Jerusalem who were invited by Absalom to accompany him to Hebron for sacrifice (2 Sam 15:7-12); and those invited by Adonijah to witness the sacrifices that would take place on the occasion of his presumed accession to the throne (1 Kgs 1:5-10, 41-53). Other examples might include Moses, Aaron, Nadab, Abihu, and the seventy elders of Israel who are invited to participate in a banquet with YHWH at Mount Sinai (Exod 24:9-11), the

nations who are invited to a banquet with YHWH at Mount Zion (Isa 25:6-10a), or the birds and animals who are to be invited to YHWH's sacrifice of the mighty on the mountains of Israel (Ezek 39:17-20). Likewise, just as the priests had to purify or consecrate themselves for holy service at the altar (e.g., Exod 19:22; 1 Chr 15:12, 14; 2 Chr 5:11; 29:5, 15, 34; 30:3, 15, 34; 31:18; 35:6), so the people in general had to consecrate themselves for sacrifice (e.g., Num 11:18; Josh 3:5; 7:13; Isa 30:29; 66:17; Ezek 44:19; 46:20; 2 Chr 30:17) as did the specially invited guests (1 Sam 16:5). Such consecration would include washing with water (Exod 19:10, 14), abstinence from sexual relations (Exod 19:15), and perhaps other requirements that are otherwise unknown.

There is a certain element of irony in the reference to the consecration of those invited to the sacrifice on the Day of YHWH in Zeph 1:7. As the above examples indicate, those invited to the sacrifice normally come to participate in the celebration and to consume a portion of the sacrificial meal. The following material in vv. 8-13 and 14-18 indicates, however, that those who are invited to the sacrifice are those who will be punished and destroyed if they are evil, thereby becoming the sacrifices themselves. This represents quite a play on the notion of purification or consecration for sacrifice.[24] Normally, such persons would have consecrated themselves properly for such a ritual occasion, but Zephaniah apparently chooses to portray those in Judah who are guilty of the apostasy portrayed throughout chap. 1 as ritually defiled and therefore in need of purification. Since sacrifice is the culminating action of the process of purification, the prophet conceives of the punishment and destruction of such persons as the purification or consecration of the people at large.

Although the language of the MT indicates clearly a concern with portraying the Day of YHWH as YHWH's sacrifice of those who are evil, the versions provide various nuances. For example, the LXX and Peshitta read the initial call for silence as a warning: LXX εὐλαβεῖσθε, "Beware!" and Peshitta *dhlw*, "Be afraid!" Both appar-

---

23   See Sigmund Mowinckel, *Psalmenstudien II. Das Thronbesteigungsfest Jahwäs und der Ursprung der Eschatologie* (Kristiana: Dybwad, 1922).

24   Cf. Seybold, *Satirische Prophetie,* 25, who refers to v. 7 as an example of Zephaniah's "parody of a sacrificial meal" (*Opfermahlparodie*).

ently presuppose the general context of threat and warning that is inherent in the usage of the particle הַס in Hab 2:20 and Zech 2:17. Targum Jonathan highlights the destruction of the wicked by reading the initial demand for silence as the exclamation, "all the wicked have perished (סָפוּ) from before the L-rd, G-d," apparently playing upon the initial statements by YHWH in v. 3 promising that, "I will destroy (אָסִיף) the humans . . . from the face of the land." The Targum does not characterize YHWH's action as a sacrifice (דבחא) in v. 7, however, but as a "slaying" or "killing" (קטול), perhaps because a sacrifice would have to be sacred, but those who were to be punished by YHWH clearly were not.[25]

■ **8** Many scholars have argued that v. 8aα, "and it shall come to pass on the day of YHWH's sacrifice," must be a later editorial insertion in the original words of the prophet Zephaniah.[26] Several reasons are mustered to support such a claim. There is a disruption in the form of the passage in that the statement makes a third person reference to YHWH, but the following material is clearly formulated as a first person speech by YHWH. This change of speaker also creates tension between the *waw*-consecutive וְהָיָה, "and it shall come to pass," that appears at the beginning of v. 8aα and the *waw*-consecutive וּפָקַדְתִּי, "and I shall visit/punish," that begins YHWH's speech. The formulation of the statement is a variation of the formula "and it shall come to pass on that day (וְהָיָה בַּיּוֹם הַהוּא)," which is widely regarded as a formulaic signal of later redaction that is particularly concerned with relating an earlier text to later eschatological concerns.[27] The reference to YHWH's sacrifice

appears to play little role in relation to the following material, which does not mention sacrifice again but focuses on various classes of people in Jerusalem/Judah who apparently will be subject to punishment by YHWH on the Day of YHWH. The reference to "sacrifice" (זֶבַח) does repeat the concern with YHWH's sacrifice in the preceding verse, suggesting that the author of v. 8aα modeled this statement on v. 7. Overall, v. 8aα appears to be an element that plays a role in organizing the prophet's words rather than an essential element of the prophet's speech.

Nevertheless, these arguments do not support the contention that v. 8aα constitutes a later editorial insertion in this text. An important element in the decision to consider it as redactional is the view that original units of prophetic speech are relatively short and may be identified by their generic or formal consistency. Thus the first person speech by YHWH in vv. 8aα-9 must constitute the original or authentic prophetic speech unit, and v. 8aα must be secondary because it disrupts the speech form. But such an argument misses several crucial points. First, the present form of Zephaniah is not a prophetic speech, but a prophetic book or text that presents or portrays prophetic speech. Thus Zephaniah is fundamentally written literature, not oral speech. Second, the book portrays the prophet Zephaniah as the one who presents or transmits speeches by YHWH that had presumably been communicated to him so that he might in turn convey them to his audience. In this case, the third person form of v. 8aα identifies it as a statement by the prophet that introduces his presentation or

25 Cf. Cathcart and Gordon, *Targum*, 166 nn. 18, 19.

26 Seybold, *Satirische Prophetie*, 25–26; idem, *Zephanja*, 96; Vlaardingerbroek, *Zephaniah*, 85; Roberts, *Zephaniah*, 178; Edler, *Kerygma*, 103–6; Irsigler, *Gottesgericht*, 95–96; Langohr, "Sophonie," 7; Renaud, "Sophonie," 10; idem, *Sophonie*, 205; Rudolph, *Zephanja*, 264, 267; Kapelrud, *Message*, 29–30; Sabottka, *Zephanja*, 35–36; H. Donner, "Die Schwellenhüpfer: Beobachtungen zu Zephanja 1,8f," *JSS* 15 (1970) 42–55, esp. 42–43; Sellin, *Zwölfprophetenbuch*, 423; Nowack, *Propheten*, 293; J. M. P. Smith, *Zephaniah*, 196; Marti, *Dodekapropheton*, 363.

27 In addition to the literature cited above, see Hugo Gressmann, *Der Messias* (FRLANT 43; Göttingen: Vandenhoeck & Ruprecht, 1929), esp. 82–84; Peter A. Munch, *The Expression bajjom hahwᵓ–Is It an Eschatological Terminus Technicus?* (Oslo: Dybwad, 1936); Simon J. DeVries, *Yesterday, Today, and Tomorrow: Time and History in the Old Testament* (Grand Rapids: Eerdmans, 1975) 55–136, 279–331; idem, *From Old Revelation to New: A Tradition-Historical and Redaction-Critical Study of the Temporal Transitions in Prophetic Prediction* (Grand Rapids: Eerdmans, 1995) 38–63, 248.

quotation of a statement by YHWH. It is to be expected that such a statement plays an important role in organizing and interpreting the first person speeches by YHWH. The reader must remember that the book of Zephaniah presents the prophet Zephaniah as the primary speaker throughout this text, even when he quotes a word attributed to YHWH.[28] Third, there is nothing inherently eschatological about the formula, "and it shall come to pass on the day of YHWH's sacrifice"; it merely refers to an event that will take place in the future, irrespective of whether that event is eschatological. Furthermore, the formula "and it shall come to pass in that day" carries no inherent eschatological meaning. Such meaning depends on the context in which the phrase is employed; it simply refers to the future. Fourth, the reference to YHWH's sacrifice indicates that those who are condemned or threatened in the following statements by YHWH are those who are to be "sacrificed" on the Day of YHWH, that is, if they do not change their behavior, the Day of YHWH will become the day of their punishment rather than a day on which they will participate in a sacrifice to celebrate the Day of YHWH. The reversal of the Day of YHWH, from a day of YHWH's defeat of Israel's enemies to a day on which Israel is punished, is a motif that appears at various points in prophetic literature (e.g., Amos 5:18-20; Joel 1–2).

In sum, v. 8aα is not the product of later redaction. It simply represents the formal and rhetorical framework of the passage in which the prophet introduces, interprets, and presents statements by YHWH to his reading or listening audience.

YHWH's statement in vv. 8aα-9 begins with the verb וּפָקַדְתִּי, "and I shall visit/punish." Interpreters correctly read this verb as a statement of YHWH's intent to punish the parties that are then delineated, but they miss the irony inherent in the use of this term. The fundamental meaning of the verbal root פקד is "to attend to, visit, muster, appoint." Although such meanings easily lend themselves to contexts in which YHWH "attends

to" or "visits" a given party in order to "appoint" punishment, the verb frequently refers to the "appointment" of a given party to a specific office, task, or role. Examples include Moses' call for YHWH to appoint someone (i.e., Joshua) to lead the people in the wilderness (Num 27:16); the captain of the guard's appointment of Joseph as the custodian of the Egyptian cupbearer and baker while he was in prison (Gen 40:4); YHWH's call to appoint a marshal to command the forces that will attack Babylon (Jer 51:27); the commanders or officers who are appointed to take charge of the people in time of war (Num 31:14, 48; Deut 20:9; 2 Kgs 11:15; 2 Chr 23:14). This last category is particularly important in relation to Zeph 1:8, because the officers "appointed" over the people are generally referred to as שָׂרִים, which is the same term that appears in YHWH's statement in v. 8aα[1-3], "and I will visit punishment upon the officers/officials (הַשָּׂרִים)." It would seem that YHWH's statement contributes to the irony of a sacrifice in which those invited (see v. 7) are indeed those who are to be sacrificed; that is, those officials who were "appointed" (פקד) to their roles are now "appointed" (פקד) for sacrifice or punishment. In this case, the "officials" (הַשָּׂרִים) would have to refer to those who were charged with administrative leadership over the people in the kingdom of Judah, which might include military figures (Deut 20:9; 1 Kgs 2:5; 1 Chr 27:3; 2 Sam 24:2; 2 Kgs 9:5; etc.); religious leaders (Ezra 8:24, 29; 10:5; 2 Chr 35:14; 1 Chr 15:16, 22; etc.); judicial figures (Exod 2:14; 18:21; Deut 1:15; Hos 5:10; Mic 7:3; etc.); professional classes (Gen 37:36; 40:2); the magistrate or administrator of a city (Judg 9:30; Neh 7:2) or district (1 Kgs 20:14, 15; Esth 1:3; 8:9); and so on. Zephaniah 1:8 provides no clear indication of the specific roles of these officials, but they evidently represent the administrative bureaucracy of the Davidic kingdom.[29]

The reference to "the sons of the king" in v. 8aα[4-6] among those who will potentially suffer YHWH's punishment has prompted considerable debate as to

---

28 Cf. DeVries, *From Old Revelation*, 248, who maintains that the editorial framework in this passage could be the work of the prophet or a disciple-editor.

29 For studies of the administrative officials and practices of ancient Israel and Judah, see T. N. D. Mettinger, *Solomonic State Officials: A Study of the Civil*

Government of the Israelite Monarchy (ConBOT 5; Lund: Gleerup, 1971); G. W. Ahlström, *Royal Administration and National Religion in Ancient Palestine* (Leiden: Brill, 1982).

whether they refer literally to the biological offspring of the Davidic monarch or only to figures who are appointed to serve the king in some capacity.[30] There is certainly no shortage of references to the biological sons of the king in the Hebrew Bible, but the term raises some difficulties when it is read in relation to the historical setting of King Josiah's reign as specified in the superscription for the book (Zeph 1:1). According to 2 Kgs 21:19-26/2 Chr 33:21-25; 2 Kgs 22:1-2/2 Chr 34:1-2, King Josiah came to the throne ca. 640 BCE at the age of eight following the assassination of his twenty-four-year-old father, Amon, by members of the royal court. Although it is not impossible that Josiah had brothers, no other sons of Amon (or of his father Manasseh) are mentioned. Furthermore, Josiah's oldest known son was Jehoiakim, who would have been born when Josiah was fourteen, leaving him presumably too young to be condemned by the prophet Zephaniah early in Josiah's reign. It is certainly possible that the reference to "the sons of the king" in this verse refers literally to sons of Manasseh, Amon, or Josiah, but the absence of any mention of such sons elsewhere in biblical literature perhaps stands behind the LXX's reading of this phrase as "the house of the king," that is, the royal family, rather than as "the sons of the king."

This has prompted some speculation that perhaps the phrase refers to administrative officials who are not members of the royal family but who are appointed to serve the king.[31] Certainly the parallel reference to הַשָּׂרִים, "the officials," in v. 8a lends itself to such an interpretation. Furthermore, the references to the seventy sons of Gideon in Judg 8:29 and 9:5 and the seventy sons of Ahab in 2 Kgs 20:1-17 are sometimes equated with the seventy-member council of elders that held authority in Israel (see Exod 24:1, 9; Num 11:16-17, 24-25; cf. 2 Sam 5:3), particularly since these figures are killed by Abimelech and Jehu, respectively, during the course of their attempts to seize royal power. Nevertheless, the narratives in both cases make clear that these seventy sons are indeed the biological sons of Gideon/Jerubaal and Ahab, respectively.

Four additional figures in the Bible identified as "the son of the king," have been brought forward: "Joash, the son of the king" (1 Kgs 22:26-27; 2 Chr 18:25-26); "Jerahmeel, the son of the king" (Jer 36:26); Malchiah, the son of the king" (Jer 38:6); and "Maaseiah, the son of the king" (2 Chr 28:7).[32] The first three figures are mentioned in contexts in which they have the authority to imprison someone, which indicates their official capacities, and Maaseiah is listed as killed during an attempt by Zichri of Ephraim to revolt against King Ahaz. Although each instance indicates official capacity, nothing precludes the identification of each figure as a biological son of the king.

The hypothesis persists, however, because several seals from monarchic-period Judah have been discovered that identify their owners as "the son of the king": "(to) Elshama, the son of the king"; "(to) Gealyahu the son of the king"; "(to) Manasseh, the son of the king"; and "(to) Yehoahaz, the son of the king."[33] Supporters of this hypothesis resort to the use of the title "son of the king" and its variants in Egypt, Mari, Ugarit, and the Amarna archive apparently to refer to administrative officials who are not necessarily descendants of the king.[34] Likewise, the term בֶּן־הַמֶּלֶךְ, "son," frequently denotes membership in some sort of professional or social class in Biblical Hebrew, such as the army (1 Sam 14:52; 2 Chr 25:13), the prophets (2 Kgs 2:3; Amos 7:14), the priests (Ezra 10:18; 1 Chr 9:30), the wise (Isa 19:11), people of importance (Neh 11:14), servants of the household (Qoh 2:7).[35]

Although the term clearly indicates a professional or social role that would include some official capacity for service to the king, biblical literature lacks a clear example in which the term הַשָּׂרִים refers only to an official capacity and not also to biological descent from the king. Since ambiguities remain concerning the existence of additional sons of Manasseh or Amon during the reign of Josiah and the birth of sons to Josiah himself beginning in approximately the sixth year of his reign, one must conclude that the phrase "sons of the king" refers literally to the king's biological sons. The use of

---

30   For a full summary and discussion of the evidence, see Brin, "Title."
31   See ibid., 433–34, for references.
32   Ibid., 434–35.
33   See ibid., 435–40.
34   Ibid., 440–51.
35   Ibid., 451–59.

the term as a title, however, and its parallel with הַשָּׂרִים, "officials," indicates that the sons of the king had some official capacity, which is signaled by their inclusion in this text as those whom YHWH will punish.[36]

Finally, v. 8b lists persons who dress in "foreign attire" (מַלְבּוּשׁ נָכְרִי) among those who are potentially to be punished by YHWH. While at first glance such a contention might seem trivial, several references make clear that the term refers to some sort of official or ceremonial attire, such as that worn by Solomon's officials and servants during the visit of the Queen of Sheba (1 Kgs 10:5; 2 Chr 9:4), the worshipers of Baal who were killed by Jehu during his revolt against the house of Omri (2 Kgs 10:22), YHWH's garments worn while slaughtering the Edomites (Isa 63:3), the rich garments given by YHWH to Jerusalem when she was ready for marriage (Ezek 16:13), and the rich clothing of the wicked (Job 27:16). The term clearly does not refer to ordinary clothing, but to rich clothing worn to signify official capacity or high social standing. In the context of late-seventh-century Judah, such foreign attire might well signify identification with the Assyrian Empire that had ruled Judah from the late eighth century until the reign of King Josiah. The threat to punish those so attired represents an attempt to purge the nation, particularly its leadership or highest classes, of any ties to the Assyrian state.

The question would remain, however, why the king himself is not singled out in the list of persons to be punished. After all, the prophets in general are hardly shy in their criticism of the Israelite and Judean monarchs. The narratives concerning Josiah's reign in 2 Kings 22–23 and 2 Chronicles 34–35 make clear that Josiah is the sponsor of reform in Jerusalem and Judah during his reign.[37] In that the reform represents Josiah's attempt to purge the nation of foreign influence and solidify the position of the house of David and the temple as the central political and religious authorities of the nation, Zephaniah would hardly target the king himself. Instead, it appears that the prophet's words are delivered in sup-

port of Josiah's reform, and that they are intended to convince people to abandon foreign allegiances and practices in order to rally support around Josiah, the Davidic monarch, and the Jerusalem Temple as the central institutions of authority in late-seventh-century Judah and perhaps Israel at large.

■ 9 Zephaniah 1:9 constitutes the second of the paired first person statements by YHWH in vv. 8aα-9 concerning YHWH's intention to "punish" various officials who are deemed somehow to have abused their offices.[38] Like v. 8aα-b, v. 9 begins with the verb וּפָקַדְתִּי, "and I will visit/punish," which conveys irony in that the verb פקד is also employed to mean "to appoint," that is, to some official capacity. Whereas v. 8aα-b focuses on civil or political offices, such as the general "officials" or the "sons of the king," v. 9 appears to focus on cultic functionaries or "all those who 'leap' over the threshold."

The expression "all those who leap over the threshold" (כָּל־הַדּוֹלֵג עַל־הַמִּפְתָּן) has created many difficulties for interpreters, beginning with the authors of the various versions of Zephaniah in the LXX, TJ, Peshitta, and Vulgate.[39] As noted above, the LXX reads the phrase as "and I shall exact punishment upon all eagerly/openly (ἐμφανῶς) upon the vestibule (in that day)," apparently reading Hebrew הַדּוֹלֵג, "those leaping," as הַדּוֹלֵק, "burning, eager," to indicate the eagerness or openness of those who are upon the threshold of a pagan temple. This understanding is based on the analogy of this verse with the reference to the threshold of the temple of the Philistine god Dagon in 1 Sam 5:4-5, upon which the Philistine priests do not tread. A somewhat similar understanding of the reference appears in TJ, which translates, "and I shall visit punishment upon all who tread upon/follow the laws/religion of the Philistines in that time," apparently drawing on the language and imagery of 1 Sam 5:4-5. The Peshitta sidesteps the problem by reading the phrase in relation to the following reference to those who fill the house of their master with violence and deceit: "and I shall visit punishment upon all who are robbers and plunderers in that day."

36 Cf. Ben Zvi, *Zephaniah*, 92–93.
37 For a full discussion of texts and issues related to Josiah's reform, see Sweeney, *King Josiah*.
38 Cf. Irsigler, *Gottesgericht*, 233–43, for discussion of formal issues in this verse.
39 For discussion see esp. Gerleman, *Zephanja*, 8–13;

Ben Zvi, *Zephaniah*, 95–102; Vlaardingerbroek, *Zephaniah*, 87–90.

The Vulgate combines the two understandings of the verb by reading, "who arrogantly step over the threshold in that day."

Most contemporary interpreters follow the LXX and TJ in reading the phrase as a reference to the pagan religious practices of those who are to be punished by YHWH.[40] Thus "all those who leap over the threshold" are viewed as somehow engaging in pagan religious practice much like the Philistine priests who are imagined to leap over the threshold of the temple of Dagon in 1 Sam 5:4-5. Yet it is striking that 1 Sam 5:5 makes no explicit reference to "leaping" over the threshold, but merely refers to the practice of not stepping upon the threshold of the temple: "therefore, the priests of Dagon and all who enter house of Dagon do not tread/step (לֹא יִדְרְכוּ) upon the threshold of Dagon in Ashdod until this day." 1 Sam 5:5 is sometimes read with LXX 1 Kgdms 5:5, "therefore the priests of Dagon and everyone that enters into the house of Dagon do not tread upon the threshold of Dagon in Azotus until this day, for they step over." The addition of the phrase "for they step over" apparently presupposes Hebrew כִּי אִם דָּלֹג יִדְלְגוּ, but most interpreters see this as an addition to the text influenced by the present verse, Zeph 1:9.[41]

Interpreters who read this verse in relation to the aforementioned Philistine practice generally maintain that the threshold of a temple or even a house embodies some sort of magical significance that presents a danger to humans and therefore precludes contact.[42] But it is striking that the phrase is a direct object of the verb, "and I shall punish," and occupies the same position within the sentence as the references to "the officials" and "the sons of the king" in v. 8a. There is no inherent guilt associated with these offices; the implication of guilt appears only in v. 8b, which refers to those who

wear foreign clothing and suggests identification with those nations that rule Judah and stand as an obstacle to its independence and self-determination. Likewise the phrase, "those who fill the house of their master/lord with violence and deceit," clearly indicates wrongdoing, but can the same be said of "all those who leap across the threshold"? Clearly, the reading of v. 9 requires close examination.

A major element in the association of v. 9 with the reference to the Philistine practice in 1 Sam 5:4-5 lies in the appearance of the terms "threshold" (מִפְתָּן) and "the one who leaps" (הַדּוֹלֵג). Although the term "threshold" (מִפְתָּן) appears in 1 Sam 5:4-5 in reference to a pagan cultic establishment, it also appears in Ezekiel's references to the first Jerusalem Temple and to his vision of the future temple. In Ezek 9:3; 10:4, 18, the "threshold" is mentioned in relation to Ezekiel's depiction of the movement of "the glory of YHWH," which rises up from the cherubim and moves to the threshold of the temple. In 46:2 the threshold of the eastern gate to the inner courtyard of the temple is the place where the Davidic prince will bow down before YHWH while the priests offer his whole burnt offering and his Shelamim (well-being) offering at the altar of the temple. In 47:1 water flows from under the threshold of the temple toward the east and south to water the entire land. Some have attempted to argue that Hebrew מִפְתָּן refers to some sort of pedestal or elevated platform on which either the ark of the covenant or the entire temple rested.[43] Such an interpretation is based in part on the meaning of the Akkadian cognate verb *patānu*, "to protect," and the common structure of temples and royal palaces in ancient Syria that included a raised platform below the Holy of Holies/throne room or even below the entire temple/palace structure. Nevertheless, the sense of protection

40 E.g., Vlaardingerbroek, *Zephaniah,* 87–89; Berlin, *Zephaniah,* 79–80; Roberts, *Zephaniah,* 179; Seybold, *Zephanja,* 97; Renaud, *Sophonie,* 208; Irsigler, *Gottesgericht,* 238–43; Rudolph, *Zephanja,* 267–68.

41 See, e.g., S. R. Driver, *Notes on the Hebrew Text and Topography of the Books of Samuel* (2d ed.; Oxford: Clarendon, 1913) 51; K. Budde, *Die Bücher Samuel* (KHAT VIII; Tübingen: Mohr [Siebeck], 1902) 40; P. Dhorme, *Les livres de Samuel* (EB; Paris: Gabalda, 1910) 56; H.-J. Stoebe, *Das Erste Buch Samuelis* (KAT VIII/1; Gütersloh: Mohn, 1973) 139.

42 See J. M. P. Smith, *Zephaniah,* 197–98.

43 H. Winckler, "Miftan," *Altorientalischer Forschungen* 3 (1905) 381–84; Herbert Donner, "Die Schwellenhüpfer: Beobachtungen zu Zephanja 1,8f," *JSS* 15 (1970) 42–55.

need not refer only to a raised platform that elevates an object of veneration and thereby protects it from its profane surroundings; the threshold of an entrance to a temple easily fills a similar role. Likewise, the term מִפְתָּן never clearly applies to the inner room of such a structure, which is called הָעֲלִיָּה, "the upper/raised (chamber)," in the narrative concerning Ehud's encounter with Eglon in Judg 3:12-31, esp. vv. 24, 20.[44] The מִפְתָּן clearly refers to a threshold in Ezek 46:2, since it is associated with the gate to the inner courtyard of the temple. Some view it as the platform of the Holy of Holies in Ezek 9:3; 10:4, 18 because it is associated with cherubim that stand over the ark,[45] but each of these verses depicts the movement of "the glory of YHWH" from the cherubim, that is, the ark or the Holy of Holies, to a place where "the glory of YHWH" then has access to the entire world as it departs from the Jerusalem Temple. In 47:1 the מִפְתָּן is associated with the entrance to the temple on the eastern side, and the water flowing from under the מִפְתָּן flows only to the east and south, suggesting that the מִפְתָּן is not a platform for the entire temple but merely a feature associated with the eastern entrance.[46] In all cases, the מִפְתָּן best refers to a threshold at a gate or door of the temple and its courtyards rather than to a raised platform for either the Holy of Holies or for the entire temple structure.

The verb דלג, "to leap," appears four times in the Hebrew Bible besides the present reference in Zeph 1:9. Its basic meaning derives from Isa 35:6, where it is employed metaphorically to describe the leaping of the lame like a deer at the time that YHWH returns the redeemed exiles of Israel to Zion. A similar metaphor appears in Cant 2:8, where דלג portrays the approach of the lover leaping (מְדַלֵּג) upon the mountains and bounding (מְקַפֵּץ) over the hills like a gazelle or young stag (cf.

Cant 2:9). Of course, the parallel with the verb קפץ, "to spring," aids in establishing the meaning of דלג as "to leap." It also appears in 2 Sam 22:30/Ps 18:30 in reference to the psalmist's ability to leap over a wall with YHWH's help. Some have attempted to argue that the verb refers simply to scaling or climbing over the wall in 2 Sam 22:30/Ps 18:30, but the metaphorical references to deer, gazelle, and so on make clear the meaning of the term as "to leap."

Because דלג means "to leap" in its other four occurrences in the Bible as well as in later Hebrew and Aramaic, most interpreters are content to read it as "to leap" in Zeph 1:9.[47] Such a reading strategy is supported by the above-mentioned reference in 1 Sam 5:5 to the Philistine priests who do not tread upon the threshold of the temple of Dagon. But as noted above, their action does not constitute the rather unusual act of leaping over the threshold; rather, it only portrays avoidance of stepping on the threshold. In this respect, it is noteworthy that the appearance of the verb דלג in Zeph 1:9 is the only example of a *qal* form of the verb. The other four forms are all *piel*, which indicates an intensive meaning for the root. This might suggest that the *qal* form of the root means something less intensive, such as "to cross/step over," rather than the *piel* meaning, "to leap." Donner has attempted to establish this meaning by reference to the root דרג, "to step, walk," in Biblical Hebrew and various cognates in other Semitic languages by arguing that the consonant *lamed* represents a common dissimilation of the *resh*.[48] Although his hypothesis is not widely accepted because other sufficiently clear examples of the shift in דרג/דלג are not readily apparent, the meaning of *qal* דרג, "to step," in the present instance would make a great deal of sense. In this case, 1:9 would refer to "all those who cross/step over the threshold" of

---

44 For discussion of this upper chamber in Judges 3 and as a characteristic feature of ancient Israelite/Syrian temples and palaces, see Baruch Halpern, *The First Historians: The Hebrew Bible and History* (San Francisco: Harper & Row, 1988) 39–75, esp. 46–54.

45 See Winckler, "Miftan"; and Donner, "Schwellenhüpfer."

46 Cf. W. Zimmerli, *Ezekiel 2: A Commentary on the Book of the Prophet Ezekiel 25–48* (Hermeneia; Philadelphia: Fortress Press, 1983) 511, who considers it to be an "(elevated) threshold," because it must be an

architectural element visible to the prophet from the outside.

47 See, e.g., the discussion by Ben Zvi, *Zephaniah*, 96.

48 Donner, "Schwellenhüpfer," 45–49.

the temple, that is, to the priests who serve in the temple and who alone are granted access to its interior. In keeping with the references to "the officials" and "the sons of the king" in v. 8aα, the present reference to "all those who cross/step over the threshold" would refer only to the official positions of those who are targeted for punishment by YHWH, that is, the priests. As in v. 8b, the specific accusation of wrongdoing would appear in the second half of the verse.

Although many have argued that the reference to "in that day" indicates eschatological significance, the term is merely a reference to the time in the future when the Day of YHWH will take place.[49]

Finally, v. 9b contains the specific accusation that serves as the basis for YHWH's punishment in v. 9: "those who fill the house of their master/lord with violence and deceit." Some have argued that the reference to "the house of their master/lord" refers to the Davidic monarch,[50] but this position is based on the reference to "the sons of the king" in v. 8 and the use of the common term אֲדֹנֵיהֶם, "their master/lord," rather than the divine name, YHWH. But the reference to "the sons of the king" appears in a syntactically distinct statement in v. 8 and does not necessarily determine the meaning of the following statement in v. 9. Likewise, the title אֲדֹנָי, "my/the L-rd," has already appeared in v. 7 in reference to YHWH. In that "all those who cross/step over the threshold" refers to the priests, the phrase "those who fill the house of their L-rd with violence and deceit" refers to the reasons for which they are to be punished. The role of the priest is to establish holiness and righteousness in the world and among the people (see Hosea 4; Numbers 18; Deut 16:18–17:13; 1 Sam 2:22-36). "Violence" (חָמָס) breaks out when the world is in disarray and appears frequently in the complaints by psalmists and others who seek YHWH's aid in restoring order (e.g., Ps 18:3/2 Sam 22:3; Mic 6:12; Hab 1:2, 9; 2:8, 17; Pss 55:10; 7:17; 11:5; 73:6; 140:2, 5, 12; Job 16:17; cf. Deut 19:16; Ps 35:11). "Deceit" (מִרְמָה) likewise appears

frequently in contexts that portray the disruption of creation and its moral norms (e.g., Amos 8:5; Hos 12:8; Mic 6:11; Prov 11:1; 20:23; 12:5, 17, 20; 14:8; 26:24; Pss 52:6; 109:2; 35:20; 24:4; 10:7; 34:14; 36:4; 38:13; 59:19; 55:12; Job 15:35; 31:5).

■ **10** Verse 10 opens the second segment of the prophet's presentation in vv. 10-13 of YHWH's announcements concerning the intention to punish those who are apostate on the Day of YHWH. The third person reference to YHWH in the introductory formula, "and it shall come to pass on that day, utterance of YHWH," indicates that the prophet is the speaker at this point and that the following statements are the prophet's presentation of YHWH's oracular statements. Many have argued that this statement is redactional because of its clear third person reference to YHWH and because it serves as a transitional link between YHWH's words in vv. 8aα-9 and 10aα⁶⁻¹⁰-11(12-13).[51] Nevertheless, it is noteworthy that some identify the prophet as the redactor of the "original" statements by YHWH.[52] The phrase is redactional only in that it serves as a literary link or transition between textual units that are presented as speeches by YHWH, but this does not require the conclusion that it is a secondary addition to an original text. There is no clear evidence that the prophet first recorded or composed an original speech of YHWH and then later added his own editorial comments. Rather, the present form of the text suggests that the author or prophet employed his/her own third person editorial and explanatory comments from the outset as a means to provide an overall framework for the presentation of YHWH's words. Although the first person perspective characteristic of the speeches by YHWH in this text does not appear until v. 12aα, the oracular formula נְאֻם־ה׳, "utterance of YHWH," always marks either the preceding or following material as divine oracular speech. Since the reference to YHWH in the preceding statement precludes its identification as speech by YHWH, the divine speech must follow.

---

49 DeVries, *From Old Revelation,* 38–63, although he considers the reference in Zeph 1:9 to be a scribal gloss (p. 40).

50 E.g., Seybold, *Zephanja,* 97; Ben Zvi, *Zephaniah,* 100–102; Renaud, *Sophonie,* 207; Rudolph, *Zephanja,* 268. Berlin, *Zephaniah,* 80; and Roberts, *Zephaniah,* 179, are unable to decide.

51 E.g., Irsigler, *Gottesgericht,* 95–96, 109–11; Edler, *Kerygma,* 103–6; Renaud, *Sophonie,* 207; idem, "Sophonie," 10; Seybold, *Zephanja,* 98.

52 Vlaardingerbroek, *Zephaniah,* 91; cf. Roberts, *Zephaniah,* 179–80.

The initial statement by YHWH appears in v. 10aα[6-10]α-b as a three-part exclamation that relates the outcry, wailing, and general commotion throughout Jerusalem as the calamity of the Day of YHWH becomes apparent. Each of the three elements in v. 10aα[6-10], 10aα, and 10b is linked together by a conjunctive *waw*, which together with the character of their respective contents ensures that they form a single textual subunit.

The first element is the exclamation, "the sound of outcry from the Fish Gate!" The initial noun, קוֹל, frequently means "voice," but often designates "sound" as well. When קוֹל stands together with a following genitive at the beginning of a statement, it frequently functions as an exclamation: "Listen! Outcry from the Fish Gate!" A similar case appears in Gen 4:10, "Listen! Your brother's blood cries out" (cf. Isa 13:4; 66:8; see also Isa 40:3; 52:8; Jer 10:22; Mic 6:9; Cant 2:8).[53] The Fish Gate is mentioned in the Chronicler's account of Manasseh's reign, in which the king constructs "an outer wall for the city of David west of Gihon, in the valley, reaching the entrance at the Fish Gate; he carried it around to Ophel, and raised it to a very great height" (2 Chr 33:14). It also appears in the accounts of Nehemiah's rebuilding of the walls of Jerusalem, where it is situated near the Tower of Hananel and the Tower of the Hundred (Neh 3:3; 12:38-39). Insofar as these towers are located at the northwestern corner of the Temple Mount area,[54] it is likely that the Fish Gate was located along the northern wall of the city to the west of the Temple Mount.[55] It is sometimes identified with the Ephraim Gate (2 Kgs 14:13; 2 Chr 25:23), which is also situated along the northern wall.[56] The name of the Fish Gate suggests that it was the site of the Jerusalem fish market mentioned in Neh 13:16 in which the Tyrians who lived in the city sold fish and other goods on the Sabbath. This would suggest that the

Fish Gate provided access to the main road descending from Jerusalem to the coastal plain via Beth Horon and Ayala. It might also provide access to the northern roads leading to Samaria and beyond. As noted above, the LXX and Peshitta read Hebrew הַדָּגִים, "fish," as הֹרְגִים, "those slaying," which may be explained by the similarity of the Hebrew letters *dalet* and *reš*. This suggests that the LXX translator was not familiar with the gate names of monarchic-period Jerusalem[57] or that the translator deliberately reread the text to highlight the motif of slaughter.

The second element mentions "wailing from the Mishneh." The "Mishneh" or "second quarter" refers to the Western Hill of Jerusalem, immediately to the west of the City of David and the Temple Mount across the Tyropoean Valley, that was settled and fortified by King Hezekiah in the late eighth century BCE. Apparently, Jerusalem expanded rapidly in the aftermath of the Assyrian conquest of northern Israel as many Israelites moved southward to escape the devastation brought about by the Assyrian army and the subsequent incorporation of northern Israel as an Assyrian province.[58] According to 2 Kgs 22:14, the prophetess Huldah resided in the Mishneh quarter during the reign of Josiah. The LXX renders "the Mishneh" literally as "the second," and the Peshitta follows suit by referring to it as "the other," apparently because the translators lacked familiarity with monarchic-period Jerusalem. Targum Jonathan renders it as "the Ophel," apparently in reference to 2 Chr 33:14, which indicates that Manasseh's wall extended from the Fish Gate to the Ophel, which suggested to TJ that the Mishneh was the next location in Manasseh's wall.[59]

Finally, the third element refers to "great tumult from the hills." The Hebrew term שֶׁבֶר means literally "break-

---

53   See GKC, §146b; C. Peters, "Hebräisches קוֹל als Interjektion," *Bib* 1 (1939) 288-93.

54   See the discussion in M. Avi-Yonah, "The Walls of Nehemiah—A Minimalist View," *IEJ* 4 (1954) 239-48, esp. 241-42; Tamara Cohn Eskenazi, "Hananel, Tower of," *ABD* 3:45; Dale C. Liid, "Hundred, Tower of," *ABD* 3:333-34. The Hananel Tower is also mentioned in Jer 31:38 and Zech 14:10. For general discussion of the walls of Jerusalem in this period, see Shiloh, "Jerusalem," *NEAEHL* 2:704-9; Avigad, *Discovering Jerusalem*, 23-60.

55   In addition to the literature cited in the preceding

note, see Dale C. Liid, "Fish Gate," *ABD* 2:797-98.

56   Dale C. Liid, "Ephraim Gate," *ABD* 2:556.

57   Ben Zvi, *Zephaniah*, 104 n. 251.

58   For discussion of this expansion, see Shiloh, "Jerusalem," *NEAEHL* 2:704-9; Avigad, *Discovering Jerusalem*, 23-60; Amihai Mazar, *Archaeology of the Land of the Bible, 10,000-586 B.C.E.* (New York: Doubleday, 1990) 417-24.

59   See the textual notes on this reading above, which indicates that some TJ MSS read the statement as "the bird," apparently in an attempt to name the "second" in a manner analogous to the Fish Gate.

ing" or "crashing," and refers to the sound of breaking or great commotion caused by troops as they wreak havoc throughout the land. The reference to "the hills" refers to the hills that surround Jerusalem in all directions, especially to the north and west. Jerusalem is most vulnerable to attack from the north, where the city is not protected by the Hinnom, Tyropoean, and Kidron valleys that define the western, southern, and eastern boundaries of the city. As the accounts of Sennacherib's invasion of Judah demonstrate, the Assyrian army focused on the destruction of the entire land of Judah prior to any attempt to assault Jerusalem.[60]

■ 11 Verse 11 constitutes the initial element of the second portion of YHWH's announcement concerning the anticipated punishment of the apostate on the Day of YHWH. Although v. 11 is generally considered to be a self-standing complement to v. 10, it is linked syntactically to vv. 12-13 by the formula וְהָיָה בָּעֵת הַהִיא, "and it shall come to pass at that time," in which YHWH graphically specifies the means by which Jerusalem will be searched and those who are apostate will be identified and punished.

Verse 11 does indeed recap the major themes of v. 10 by continuing the portrayal of the calamity that is about to overtake Jerusalem. Like v. 10, it lacks any explicit indication that YHWH is the speaker, but the appearance of the oracular formula נְאֻם־ה″, "utterance of YHWH," in v. 10a[5-6] indicates that the following material constitutes the prophet's presentation of speech by YHWH.

The initial statement of the verse, הֵילִילוּ יֹשְׁבֵי הַמַּכְתֵּשׁ, is somewhat ambiguous because the verb הֵילִילוּ can function either as the masculine plural imperative, "Wail! (O inhabitants of the Maktesh)," or as the *hiphil* third masculine singular perfect, "(the inhabitants of the Maktesh) wail/wailed." Most interpreters follow LXX, TJ, and Peshitta in understanding the verb as an imperative, particularly since the above-noted exclamatory force of the initial קוֹל, "sound," of v. 10 and the following state-

ments of the verse suggest the immediacy of the threat. Likewise, the language of the verse appears to reflect the typical form of the "call to public lament" identified by Wolff.[61] The language itself need not be tied exclusively to a liturgical form of public lament, since it apparently rises out of a situation of imminent disaster in which calls to mourn would be uttered as part of a general effort to warn people of an approaching calamity. The imperative form would convey YHWH's warning of imminent punishment or disaster to the population of Jerusalem. Nevertheless, the verb can be read easily as a perfect, which, like the nominal statements in v. 10aα[7-]10α-b, conveys the general situation of terror among the people of Jerusalem as the threat becomes apparent.

The precise location of the area of Jerusalem known in antiquity as the "Maktesh" is uncertain. The Hebrew word מַכְתֵּשׁ means "mortar," and is derived from the root כתש, "to pound, pound fine" (Prov 27:22). It apparently describes a geographical depression or hollow in the city, based on the analogy of its use in Judg 15:19 to designate the location of the spring at Lehi as a low-lying area or hollow. Most archeologists identify it as the low-lying area of the Tyropoean Valley between the Temple Mount and City of David to the east and the Mishneh/Western Hill or the newer quarter of Jerusalem to the west.[62] The justification for this identification includes not only the geographical features of the city, but the presumption that the Tyropoean Valley would constitute a commercial area as well. Certainly, the northern extension of this area constitutes a major thoroughfare in the present-day Old City of Jerusalem from the Damascus Gate to the Temple Mount. Furthermore, excavations in the valley west of the Temple Mount indicate that it served a similar function as early as the Hasmonean period or late Second Temple period.[63]

The versions reflect some difficulties in understanding this reference. The LXX refers to הַמַּכְתֵּשׁ as τὴν κατα-κεκομμένην, "the area broken into pieces/coined into money," employing a participle form of the verb κατα-

---

60 See 2 Kings 18–19; Isaiah 36–37; *ANET,* 287–88.
61 Hans Walter Wolff, "Der Aufruf zur Volksklage," *ZAW* 76 (1964) 48–56, esp. 52.
62 See Avigad, *Discovering Jerusalem,* 24, 28, 54, 58; Shiloh, "Jerusalem," *NEAEHL* 2:708.
63 See Hillel Geva, "Jerusalem: The Second Temple Period," *NEAEHL* 2:740–42.

κόπτω, "to break into pieces" or "to coin into money." Apparently, this plays on the meaning of the root of מַכְתֵּשׁ and the following reference in v. 11 to those who bear or handle silver. Targum Jonathan renders מַכְתֵּשׁ as נחלון דקדרון, "the Kidron Valley," which runs along the eastern side of the Temple Mount and City of David. The Targum's rendition may well depend on the general topographical layout of this area, which would also resemble a mortar. The Kidron is hardly an area where one would expect heavy commercial activity because it provides little direct access to roads that would take travelers to major trading areas in the land of Israel and beyond.[64] The Targum's decision may well reflect the mention of the Kidron as the place where Josiah destroyed idolatrous vessels from the temple (2 Kgs 23:4-6) and its understanding that the Canaanites mentioned later in the verse refer to the pagan people of Canaan rather than to traders. The Peshitta simply transliterates the term as *mktš*.

The introductory כִּי, "because," may provide some emphasis to v. 11b, but it also indicates that the following statements provide the reasons for the wailing in v. 11a and perhaps also the commotion depicted in v. 10. The statement in v. 11bα, "for all the people of Canaan are destroyed," provides a very interesting play on words. On the one hand, "the people of Canaan" may be taken literally as a reference to the Canaanite inhabitants of the land of Israel. In this case, the statement would convey a dual message. First, it suggests that the pagan people who live outside Jerusalem and Judah have been destroyed, that is, the approaching threat has already overtaken the Canaanites who live in the outlying areas of the land of Israel. Second, it is a rhetorical device that suggests the destruction of the Canaanites, whether they are identified as the pagan peoples of the land of Israel or those within Jerusalem and Judah whom the prophet wishes to accuse of apostasy, whether they are actually of Canaanite background or not. On the other hand, the term "Canaanite" is frequently employed as a reference to "merchants" or "traders" in the Hebrew Bible (see Isa 23:8, 9; Ezek 16:29; 17:4; Hos 12:8; Zech 14:21; Job 40:30; Prov 31:24). Such an understanding would relate well to the following mention of the destruction of all those handling/bearing silver. Once again, YHWH/Zephaniah refers to the audience as Canaanites, not necessary because all merchants are guilty of sin and should be destroyed, but because of a rhetorical strategy that is designed to convince the audience to adapt their behavior to a recommended course of action. It is becoming increasingly clear that the Assyrian Empire expanded into Syria, Israel, and Philistia in the late eighth and seventh centuries in order to develop trade contacts with Egypt and the eastern Mediterranean in general.[65] Excavations at Tel Miqne, identified conclusively as Philistine Ekron, indicate that the Assyrians built an extensive olive oil industry on the site and moved large numbers of northern Israelites (and perhaps others) to Ekron in order to work at producing olive oil to supply the needs of the entire empire.[66] In such a scenario, merchants and traders would naturally be associated with the Assyrians, who subjugated Judah during this period and whose rule Josiah's reform was intended to overthrow. Those tar-

---

64 Contra Smolar and Aberbach, *Studies,* 111.

65 Albrecht Alt, "Neue Assyrische Nachrichten über Palästina," *KS* 2:226–41; H. Tadmor, "Philistia under Assyrian Rule," *BA* 29 (1966) 86–102; A. Spalinger, "The Year 712 B.C. and Its Implications for Egyptian History," *JARCE* 10 (1973) 95–101; Moshe Elat, "The Economic Relations of the Neo-Assyrian Empire with Egypt," *JAOS* 98 (1978) 20–34; Nadav Naᶜaman, "The Brook of Egypt and Assyrian Policy on the Border of Egypt," *TA* 6 (1979) 68–90; G. L. Mattingly, "An Archeological Analysis of Sargon's 712 Campaign against Ashdod," *NEASB* 17 (1981) 47–64.

66 See Trude Dothan and Seymour Gitin, "Miqne, Tel (Ekron)," *NEAEHL* 3:1051–59; Gitin, "Tel Miqne-Ekron"; idem, "Ekron of the Philistines. Part II: Olive Oil Suppliers to the World," *BARev* 16/2 (1990) 32–42, 59; idem, "Incense Altars from Ekron, Israel, and Judah," *ErIsr* 20 (1989) 52*–67*; idem, "New Incense Altars from Ekron: Context, Typology, and Function," *ErIsr* 23 (1992) 43*–49*; idem, "Seventh-Century B.C.E. Cultic Elements at Ekron," *Biblical Archaeology Today, 1990: Proceedings of the Second International Congress on Biblical Archaeology* (Jerusalem: Israel Exploration Society, 1993) 248–58; Seymour Gitin, Trude Dothan, and Joseph Naveh, "A Royal Dedicatory Inscription from Ekron," *IEJ* 47 (1997) 1–16.

geted by YHWH's speech would most likely be those who engaged in trade in support of Assyrian economic policies, and the depiction of impending threat would be designed to convince them to give up such associations in order to lend support to Judah's own interests as defined in Josiah's reform. Overall, the passage employs the term "Canaanites" to convey a combination of ethnic, religious, and economic associations, in an effort to prompt the audience to dissociate itself with everything that the term "Canaanite" entails and to identify more closely with Judean interests as articulated by Zephaniah and Josiah's reform.

Again, the versions indicate differences in the interpretation of this passage, in part because of the above-mentioned ambiguities of the references to the Canaanites and because of ambiguities involving the interpretation of the verb נִדְמָה, "is destroyed." The verb נִדְמָה is a *niphal* masculine singular perfect or participle form of the root דמה, which means either "to cease, cause to cease," or "to resemble." Although the meaning "is destroyed, ceased" is clear from the parallel with the following verb, נִכְרְתוּ, "is cut off," the ambiguities of the reference to the Canaanites have prompted speculation that the verb should be rendered "resemble" in so far as the charge that the people would "resemble" Canaanites would support the prophet's charges of apostasy among the people. Thus the LXX renders the phrase, ὅτι ὁμοιώθη πᾶς ὁ λαὸς Χανααν ἐξωλεθρεύθησαν πάντες οἱ ἐπηρμένοι ἀργυρίῳ, "for all the people resemble Canaan; all who exalt silver are cut off." Targum Jonathan reads, "because all the people whose works are like (דמן) the works of the people of the land of Canaan are utterly destroyed (אשתיציאו), all those rich in property," apparently preserving both interpretations of נִדְמָה. The Peshitta renders the verse, "because all the people of Canaan are confounded (*twr*)," apparently playing off the meaning of the verb נִדְמָה, from the related root, דמם, "to grow dumb, silent, still, astound," and the literal meaning of "Canaanites." The Vulgate likewise reads, *conticuit omnis populus Chanaan*, "silent are all the people of Canaan."

Verse 11bα, נִכְרְתוּ כָּל־נְטִילֵי כָסֶף, "all who weigh out silver are cut off," is generally taken as a parallel statement to the preceding phrase, "all the people of Canaan are destroyed," that aids in establishing the meaning of the latter. Again, the phrase suggests the demise of those who engage in trade, presumably as part of the imperial Assyrian economic system. The reference to "silver" or "money" (כֶּסֶף) is particularly important because coinage is believed to have begun in Asia Minor during the seventh century BCE,[67] and the Assyrians are frequently credited with having established a cash basis for trade during the period of their rule, which certainly would facilitate the economic goals and bases of their empire.

Again, the versions show a variety of readings, based in part on their readings of the preceding references to the Canaanites. The LXX perhaps implies a value judgment on those who are greedy for money, that is, "all those who lift up/exalt (ἐπηρμένοι) silver," based on the root meaning of נְטִילֵי as "to lift, bear." TJ renders the phrase as "(they) are utterly destroyed, all those rich in property (כל עתירי נכסיא)." As noted above, this reading reflects an attempt to present both meanings of נִדְמָה. It also expands the reference to כֶּסֶף to include all manner of wealth or property. The Peshitta simply reads, "and all those carrying/weighing silver are destroyed," which mainly follows the Hebrew, but the use of the verb שקל indicates both "bearing" and "weighing."

■ **12** Many consider the introductory temporal formula in v. 12aα, וְהָיָה בָּעֵת הַהִיא, "and it shall come to pass at that time," to be a redactional addition to the text of Zephaniah that, together with the temporal formulae in vv. 8aα and 10aα[1-5], provides an editorial framework for the first person speeches by YHWH in vv. 8-13.[68] The justification for such a view rests on several arguments: (1) the analogy of this formula to the temporal formula, "and it shall come to pass on that day," which is frequently considered to be redactional; (2) the perceived eschatological character of such temporal statements, which points to the milieu of the exilic or postexilic period; (3) and the third person form of the formula in the context of first person speeches by YHWH.

---

67   See John W. Betlyon, "Coinage," *ABD* 1:1076–89.

68   See Irsigler, *Gottesgericht*, 96; Renaud, *Sophonie*, 209–10; idem, "Sophonie," 10; Edler, *Kerygma*, 103–6; Seybold, *Zephanja*, 99.

None of these arguments justifies the conclusion that the formula is the product of later redaction. First, studies of the temporal formulae in general note that in many cases they are indeed redactional, but this does not warrant the conclusion that all such cases are the product of later redaction.[69] One may note, for example, the frequent appearance of the expression "in that day" (בַּיּוֹם הַהוּא) within the context of first person speech by a prophet or YHWH.[70] Second, studies of the temporal formulae in the Hebrew Bible have long indicated that they do not necessarily point to eschatological scenarios.[71] Nothing in the formula inherently marks eschatological interest; it simply points to a future time regardless of whether it is eschatological. Such eschatological scenarios can only be justified by the contexts in which the temporal formulae function. As noted above, the references to the "day of YHWH" in the present context designate the occasion on which YHWH will take action, but the "day of YHWH" entails no inherently eschatological scenario in that it does not relate the end of the world or of history; it merely points to the time when YHWH will purge Jerusalem of those who are apostate. Third, the present analysis of the overall form of Zeph 1:2-18 and of vv. 7-13 in particular notes that the passage is constituted generically as the prophet's presentation of YHWH's oracular speeches. The appearance of third person material in this context is to be expected since the prophet would quote YHWH's first person speeches but formulate his own words in the third person to provide the framework for YHWH's oracles. It is noteworthy that the present formula includes no third person references to YHWH like those that appear in vv. 7, 8aα, and 10aα$^{1-5}$. Furthermore, the formula facilitates the transition between YHWH's speech in vv. 10aα$^{6-9}$-11 and that in vv. 12aα-13. The formula can stand easily as part of YHWH's speech that points to the future actions of YHWH to search out and punish those who are apostate in Jerusalem. In that it is linked syntactically to v. 11, it introduces YHWH's speech in vv. 12-13 that explains why the Canaanites/

traders are destroyed and why all who handle money are cut off, that is, YHWH is about to take action against them.

Verse 12aα-b constitutes YHWH's statement of the actions to be taken against the apostate, and v. 13 states the consequences that they will suffer as a result of YHWH's actions. YHWH's statement of action falls into two basic parts as indicated by the use of the two first person finite verbs, "I will search (אֲחַפֵּשׂ)" and "and I will punish (וּפָקַדְתִּי)," which are linked syntactically by the *waw*-consecutive formulation of the latter. They consequently form parallel or consecutive statements of the sequence of YHWH's actions.

The first statement in v. 12aα, "I will search Jerusalem with lamps," clearly constitutes a metaphorical statement that conveys the thoroughness of YHWH's efforts to scrutinize Jerusalem and to identify all those who will be subject to punishment on the "day of YHWH." It is possible that the statement reflects some contemporary social practice in the city, that is, perhaps there was some form of constabulary or other group that stood watch and employed lamps to ensure the security of the city at night, but such a contention must necessarily be speculative in the absence of hard evidence. The same metaphor appears in Prov 20:27, "the human soul is the lamp of YHWH (נֵר ה׳) searching (חֹפֵשׂ) all the inner rooms," which conveys the imagery of YHWH's employing lamps to search the innermost reaches of the human being. A somewhat analogous image, although with different vocabulary, appears in Jer 17:10, "I YHWH test the mind [lit. 'heart'] and search the heart [lit. 'kidneys'] to give to each according to his ways, according to the fruit of his actions." The lamp also symbolizes diligence as indicated in the portrayal of the ideal woman in Prov 31:18, "she perceives that her merchandise is profitable; her lamp does not go out at night." The metaphorical image of YHWH searching Jerusalem with lamps lends

---

69 A number of scholars consider the phrase to be an original redactional composition, i.e., it was written by Zephaniah to organize the words of YHWH; see Roberts, *Zephaniah*, 180; DeVries, *From Old Revelation*, 248; Keller, *Sophonie*, 189–90; Vlaardingerbroek, *Zephaniah*, 96–97.

70 See DeVries's discussion of integral transitions in his study, *From Old Revelation*, passim.

71 DeVries, *Yesterday, Today, and Tomorrow*; idem, *From Old Revelation*.

itself well to the following image of drunkenness, particularly since night time is the most likely time to find those who are "lingering over their wine dregs," that is, beginning to pass out after having drunk more than their fill.

The versions employ a variety of forms for understanding the metaphor of lamps. The use of the definite article in the phrase בַּנֵּרוֹת, "with the lamps," is enigmatic, although it is possible that the Masoretes understood the metaphor as a reference to the lamps in the Temple of Jerusalem (see Lev 24:4; Exod 25:37; 39:37; 1 Chr 28:15; 2 Chr 4:20), especially since Zech 4:2 portrays the lights of the temple menorah/lampstand as the "eyes of YHWH which range through the whole land." The Murabbaʿat scroll clearly employs the plural form, but without vowel pointing it is impossible to know if it read the definite article. The LXX and Peshitta translators were apparently bothered by the reference to multiple lamps and simply change the noun to a singular, that is, "I will search Jerusalem with a lamp." Targum Jonathan understands the term in the plural, but protects the holiness of G-d by introducing searchers who act on G-d's behalf: "I shall appoint searchers and they shall search the inhabitants of Jerusalem as people search with a lamp."

Verse 10b constitutes YHWH's clear and unambiguous statement of the intention to punish those who are apostate. The image of those to be punished as "those who linger over their wine dregs" clearly employs the metaphor of drunkenness, which in the prophetic and wisdom literature frequently portrays those who do not think clearly and correctly (e.g., Isa 5:11-13, 22-24; 28:7-13; Jer 51:7-8; Hab 2:5, 15-17; Prov 4:14-16; 20:1; 23:29-35; 31:4-7). Indeed, Prov 23:29-30 states, "Who has woe? Who has sorrow? Who has strife? Who has complaining? Who has wounds without cause? Who has redness of eyes? Those who linger late over wine, those who come to investigate mixed wines." The verb קפא, "to congeal," is employed in Exod 15:8 to describe the congealing of the waters as the Red/Reed Sea divided to allow the passage of the Israelites at the time of the exodus. Otherwise, it refers to freezing water (Zech 14:6) or to the

formation of a fetus in the womb (Job 10:10). It constitutes an apt metaphor in the present context, as one who becomes steadily drunk is less and less able to move or think clearly while slipping gradually into a stupor. The use of the term שֶׁמֶר, "lees, dregs," is also apt; it refers to the ancient method of making wine by letting grapes sit and ferment in water until they form a thick, sticky, and unmoving conglomeration that must be mixed with water before it can be drunk. In effect, those who drink the wine become exactly like the wine that they drink.

Indeed, the term שֶׁמֶר provides the basis for a number of different interpretations of this passage in the versions, because the root שמר means "to observe, watch."[72] When applied to "dregs," it refers to the making of wine by letting grapes ferment over time, which requires that they be watched. The LXX reads, "and I will bring punishment upon the men who despise their charges," in which שִׁמְרֵיהֶם, "their dregs," is read as the root שמר, "to observe, watch," to indicate their failure to fulfill their responsibilities to observe YHWH's requirements. Targum Jonathan reads, "and I shall visit punishment upon the men who are at ease upon their herds/wealth," again reading שִׁמְרֵיהֶם as an expression of the root שמר, "to watch," in reference to the guarding of possessions, herds, or wealth. The Peshitta reads, "and I will visit punishment upon the men who despise their advocate," reading שִׁמְרֵיהֶם once again as an expression of the root שמר, "to watch," but in reference to G-d who watches over them and protects them. The Vulgate reads, "and I will visit (punishment) upon men who fix upon their charges," again reading שִׁמְרֵיהֶם as an expression of the root שמר, "to watch," but in reference to one's own responsibilities.

The connotations of sloth, immobility, and confused thinking then facilitate the portrayal of the drunks as "those who say in their hearts, 'YHWH does not do good, and he does not do evil,'" that is, YHWH lacks the power or capacity to do anything in the world.[73] The charge that YHWH lacks efficacy also appears in Isaiah's portrayal of drunks who view YHWH as of little consequence, "who say, 'Let him [YHWH] make haste, let him speed his work that we may see it; let the plan of the

---

72 Cf. Gerleman, *Zephanja*, 17.
73 Cf. Jer 48:11, which employs the imagery of quietness over dregs to express Moab's complacency.

Holy One of Israel hasten to fulfillment that we may know it'" (Isa 5:18-24, esp. 19). The basic combination of "good" and "evil" is a common merism in Biblical Hebrew that points to the most fundamental aspects of knowledge (cf. Isa 41:23; Gen 2:9, 17; 3:5, 22; Deut 1:39; 2 Sam 13:22; 14:17; 1 Kgs 3:9; Qoh 12:14).[74] The lack of such fundamental knowledge concerning YHWH's capacity to act in the world becomes the basis for apostasy.

■ **13** The presentation of YHWH's speech in vv. 10aα[6-9]-13 continues in v. 13 with YHWH's statement of the consequences that will befall the apostate. As noted in the discussion of v. 12, this statement follows YHWH's announcement of action to be taken against the apostates in v. 12aα-b. The introductory וְהָיָה, "and it shall come to pass," facilitates the transition from the statement of actions to be taken against the apostates to the statement of the consequences that will befall them.

The statement falls into two basic parts. Verse 13a constitutes the first part, in which YHWH relates images of plundered wealth and destroyed houses to convey the punishment that the apostate will experience. Although Zephaniah is frequently read in relation to the later Babylonian destruction of Jerusalem, there is nothing in this verse that points to the despoliation or destruction of the entire city; it merely relates the anticipated punishment of those within Jerusalem and Judah who are identified as having abandoned YHWH or turned to other gods. Insofar as the rhetorical intent of the prophet's presentation of YHWH's words is to convince them not to be among those who will suffer punishment for apostasy against YHWH, v. 13a must be considered as a form of threat that is designed to facilitate the persuasive goals of the prophet's discourse. When read in the context of late-seventh-century Jerusalem during the period of Josiah's reform, it would have to refer specifically to those who submitted to Assyrian authority and gained their wealth by cooperating with the Assyrians in their extensive trade network. Josiah's reform was not only religiously based; it was also economically based in that it was designed to declare Judah's political and economic independence from the Assyrians.

The second part of the statement appears in v. 13b, in which YHWH states that the people will not dwell in the houses that they have built nor drink the wine produced from the vineyards that they have planted. Because of the correspondence of this threat with similarly worded or conceived texts in Amos 5:11; Deut 28:30-34, 38-42; Lev 26:16; and Mic 6:15, many scholars consider the verse to be a secondary addition to the text of Zephaniah.[75] The argument is bolstered by the observation that the building of houses and planting of vineyards will take place in the future, which indicates some disruption in the temporal sequence of v. 13.

This conclusion is unnecessary, however, as such "futility" images are characteristic of the pervasive influence of treaty curses in biblical and particularly prophetic texts.[76] Hillers notes that such statements appear frequently in the prophetic literature. In addition to the above cited examples, see Hos 4:10: "they shall eat but not be satisfied; they shall play the harlot but not increase" (cf. Hos 5:6; 8:7; 9:12, 16); Amos 8:12: "they shall run to and fro seeking the word of YHWH, but they shall not find it" (cf. Amos 4:8); Hag 1:6: "you have sown much, and harvested little; you eat, but you never have enough; you drink, but you never have your fill; you clothe yourselves, but no one is warm; and you that earn wages earn wages to put them into a bag with holes" (cf. Mal 1:4). Such curses also appear in contemporary ancient Near Eastern treaty texts; for example, the mid-eighth-century BCE Aramean Sefire inscription, which relates the treaty between Bargayah, king of Ktk, and

74 See J. Krašovec, *Der Merismus in biblisch-hebräischen und norwestsemitischen* (BibOr 33: Rome: Biblical Institute Press, 1977) 102–3, 106.

75 E.g., Irsigler, *Gottesgericht*, 105–6; Renaud, *Sophonie*, 210; Edler, *Kerygma*, 81–82; Seybold, *Zephanja*, 99; idem, *Satirische Prophetie*, 33; J. M. P. Smith, *Zephaniah*, 203; Marti, *Dodekapropheton*, 365; Sellin, *Zwölfprophetenbuch*, 424; Nowack, *Propheten*, 294; Schwally, "Sefanjâ," 175; Karl Elliger, *Die Propheten*

Nahum, Habakuk, Zephanja, Haggai, Sacharja, Maleachi (ATD 25/2; Göttingen: Vandenhoeck & Ruprecht, 1982) 65; Vlaardingerbroek, *Zephaniah*, 97, 101–2.

76 Delbert R. Hillers, *Treaty-Curses and the Old Testament Prophets* (BibOr 16; Rome: Pontifical Biblical Institute Press, 1964) 28–29; cf. van Hoonacker, *Prophètes*, 514; Roberts, *Zephaniah*, 181; Berlin, *Zephaniah*, 88–89; Keller, *Sophonie*, 194; Ben Zvi,

themes of Zeph 1:14-16, Ezek 30:3 states, "for a day is near (קָרוֹב), the day of YHWH is near (קָרוֹב); it will be a day of clouds, a time of nations," as a prelude to the prophet's condemnation of Egypt, Ethiopia, and other nations associated with them. Joel states repeatedly, "for the day of YHWH is near (קָרוֹב)," in the context of the prophet's announcement of YHWH's announcements of the threats posed by the nations to Jerusalem (Joel 1:15) or YHWH's actions against the nations that threaten Jerusalem (4:14). Joel also states, "for the day of YHWH is coming, it is near (קָרוֹב), a day of darkness and gloom, a day of clouds and thick darkness," in the context of announcing the threat of the nations against Jerusalem (2:1-2). Obadiah 15 likewise employs the phrase, "for the day of YHWH is near (קָרוֹב)," when announcing YHWH's actions against the nations that have abused Zion and Jacob, that is, Jerusalem and Israel. Some of these texts may actually draw on the others, for example, Joel quotes extensively from Obadiah,[79] but the frequent use of this terminology suggests that the announcement that the Day of YHWH is near (קָרוֹב) also constitutes a stereotypical statement of the Day of YHWH tradition, whether employed against Jerusalem/Israel or the nations that threaten Jerusalem/Israel, on which Zephaniah draws. Insofar as many argue that Zephaniah is the earliest of these prophetic texts, Zephaniah may well have originated the expression that then served as a model for the later texts in Isaiah, Ezekiel, Joel, and Obadiah.[80] In this respect, Zephaniah's above-mentioned ironic use of language must be noted in relation to Ps 145:18, "YHWH is near (קָרוֹב) to all who call upon him [קֹרְאָיו; cf. קְרֻאָיו, "his invited/called ones" in v. 7]," which appears in the context of an acrostic hymn of praise for YHWH's capacity to act on behalf of the people.[81] It is uncertain whether this psalm stems from the monarchic

period, but it certainly employs our term, קָרוֹב, to express the notion of YHWH's protection of the nation. Although Zephaniah is not the first prophet to direct the notion of the Day of YHWH against Israel (cf. Amos 5:18-20; Isa 2:6-21), it appears that Zephaniah draws on the characteristic language of the tradition as well as its motifs to articulate YHWH's judgment against those in Jerusalem and Judah who are charged with abandoning their G-d.

The second strophe in v. 14aα, "near and very fast," repeats the term קָרוֹב and adds וּמַהֵר מְאֹד, "and very fast," apparently to strengthen the contention that the Day of YHWH is imminent. Some have argued that the adjective מַהֵר must be emended to a *piel* participle form, מְמַהֵר, in order better to convey the active character of the approach of the Day of YHWH.[82] This argument is based on the contention that the initial *mem* of מְמַהֵר has elided to produce the form מַהֵר (cf. Gen 41:32). This is unnecessary, however, as מַהֵר is a *piel* infinitive absolute form of the root מַהֵר that functions adverbially to provide a fitting parallel for the infinitive absolute קָרוֹב.[83]

Verse 14b then shifts from the motif of imminence and speed to the motif of bitterness and threat. The initial statement, "the sound of the Day of YHWH is bitter," draws on the imagery of a hastily approaching army that would threaten Jerusalem. Some read the initial קוֹל, "voice, sound," as an interjection, "Hark! Listen!"[84] In that Jerusalem is surrounded by hills, it would likely be the case that the first clue of an approaching threat would be the sounds made by a marching army as it rapidly made its way toward the city; a visual sighting would come after the initial warning of the commotion. In this respect, v. 14b draws on the earlier announcements by YHWH in v. 10 of noise, wailing, and commotion throughout the city and the surrounding hills as the

79   See Siegfried Bergler, *Joel als Schriftinterpret* (BEATAJ 16; Frankfurt am Main: Lang, 1988); Sweeney, *Twelve Prophets*, 145–87.

80   For the dating of Isaiah, Joel, and Obadiah, see Sweeney, *Isaiah 1–39*, 51–60; idem, *Twelve Prophets*, 147–52, 279–85.

81   For discussion of the generic character of Psalm 145, see Erhard Gerstenberger, *Psalms, Part 2* (FOTL XIV/2; Grand Rapids: Eerdmans, 2001) 436.

82   Gerleman, *Zephanja*, 18–19; Rudolph, *Zephanja*, 263; van Hoonacker, *Prophètes*, 515; Nowack,

Propheten, 295; Horst, *Propheten,* 192; Sellin, *Zwölf-prophetenbuch,* 426; Marti, *Dodekapropheton,* 365; Wellhausen, *Propheten,* 152; J. M. P. Smith, *Zephaniah,* 209; Schwally, "Sefanjâ," 176; see also GKC, §52s.

83   See Ben Zvi, *Zephaniah,* 117; Keller, *Sophonie,* 194; Irsigler, *Gottesgericht,* 49–50; Roberts, *Zephaniah,* 182; Vlaardingerbroek, *Zephaniah,* 146; see esp. Sabottka, *Zephanja,* 50–52.

84   Vlaardingerbroek, *Zephaniah,* 106–7; Ben Zvi, *Zephaniah,* 118–19; Berlin, *Zephaniah,* 189; Rudolph, *Zephanja,* 263.

Mattiel, king of Arpad, states, "seven rams shall tup a ewe, and she shall not become pregnant; seven wet-nurses shall anoint their breasts and suckle a boy, and he shall not be sated; seven mares shall suckle a colt, and he shall not be sated; seven ewes shall suckle a lamb, and it shall not be sated; his [i.e., Mattiel's] seven daughters shall go in search of food, and they shall not arouse concern."[77] Ashurbanipal's annals from the mid-seventh century BCE relate similar curses suffered by his enemies for violating the terms of their treaties with him.[78]

The appearance of similar statements in Deut 28:30-34, 38-42, and Lev 26:16, which constitute portions of the blessings and curses sections at the end of their respective books, clearly indicates that such language appears within the context of the Hebrew Bible's statements of YHWH's expectations and that it apparently influences the prophets who charge the people with failing to abide by the requirements of their relationship with YHWH. The contention that v. 13b somehow disrupts the temporal sequence of the portrayal of consequences is hardly an indication of later redaction as the entire scenario is placed in the future.

1:14-18

■ **14** The third person references to YHWH in vv. 14, 17, and 18 indicate that the text presents the prophet as speaker once again in vv. 14-18. As noted above, this corresponds to the primary role of the prophet in vv. 7-13 in which he presents YHWH's oracular statements to the reading or listening audience of the text. Essentially, the prophet resumes his statements in v. 7, in which he announced the theme of the "Day of YHWH" as a day of sacrifice to introduce YHWH's oracles of threat against those who are accused of abandoning G-d. But whereas the prophet presents YHWH's oracles concerning the Day of YHWH in vv. 7-13, he now turns to an exposition of the significance of the Day of YHWH as a time of YHWH's threat against the land at large and its inhabitants. As in vv. 2-6, the language indicates YHWH's threat against "human beings" (v. 17), "all the land/earth" (v. 18a), and "all the inhabitants of the earth/land" (v. 18b), but the statement in v. 17b, "because they

have sinned against YHWH," indicates that the threat is directed against those who are defined as apostate in vv. 2-6 and 7-13.

The prophet begins his exposition in v. 14, in which he articulates the two basic premises on which he will elaborate in the following verses: the Day of YHWH is imminent, and it is a day of threat. The syntactical features of the verse allow it to comprise two basic strophes that respectively convey these premises. Each strophe is further subdivided into two constituent subunits that together present the images that convey the basic premise. Thus v. 14a focuses on the imminence of the Day of YHWH, and v. 14b focuses on the threatening character of the Day of YHWH.

The prophet's initial statement in v. 14aα, "near is the great day of YHWH," employs the infinitive absolute form קָרוֹב, "near," as an adjective to convey the imminence of the day. The use of this term is noteworthy not only in relation to its role in presenting the concern with the imminence of the day but with its role in establishing a relationship to the larger literary context, both in relation to Zephaniah and to the larger prophetic corpus that takes up the motif of the Day of YHWH. First, it relates to the prophet's previous statement in v. 7, "silence from before my L-rd YHWH, for near (קָרוֹב) is the day of YHWH." As noted above, v. 7 likewise conveys the imminence of the day as a prelude to identifying it as a day of sacrifice. But whereas v. 7 is somewhat ambiguous as to the role of the people in relation to the sacrifice—it identifies them as YHWH's invited guests, which suggests that they will take part in consuming the sacrifice rather than actually constituting the sacrificial victims themselves—v. 14 begins to articulate clearly the threatening nature of the day that removes the ambiguity of v. 7.

Furthermore, the use of the term קָרוֹב, "near," relates to many other passages in the prophetic literature that announce the coming of the Day of YHWH. Isa 13:6 states, "Wail, for the Day of YHWH is near (קָרוֹב), it will come like destruction from Shaddai/the Almighty," in the context of an announcement that YHWH's holy warriors will attack and bring down Babylon for its iniquity. In a text that takes up much of the terminology and

---

Zephaniah, 116; Junker, *Sophonia,* 73; Bennett, "Zephaniah," 679–80.

77 See *ANET,* 659.
78 See *ANET,* 300.

threat became apparent. The verse may also draw on Isaiah's portrayal of the rapid approach of the Assyrian army, called by YHWH to punish Israel on a day of distress and darkness (see Isa 5:26-30). The emphasis on the speed of the approach, "and behold, rapidly (מְהֵרָה), swiftly they come," strengthens the parallel with Zephaniah and suggests the prophet's dependence on the earlier book.

Finally, v. 14bβ, צֹרֵחַ שָׁם גִּבּוֹר, "there, the warrior shrieks," has prompted a great deal of discussion from the time of the LXX translation to the present.[85] In the present context, the statement builds on the audial imagery of v. 14bα in that the shrieks or outcries of warriors, whether those who were attacking and plundering the land or those who were defending and dying as they attempted to stop the enemy, would be among the sounds that one would hear as an invading army approached. Nevertheless, there are some problems in understanding the statement, especially since the referent for שָׁם, "there," is not entirely clear. When read in relation to the larger literary context, it could refer to the districts of Jerusalem or the surrounding hill country, but such references do not appear in the immediate context. Consequently, the LXX translates v. 14b, "the sound of the day of the L-rd is bitter and harsh, he has made/appointed power." This reading presupposes some rereading of the Hebrew text in that the Greek σκληρά, "harsh," likely presupposes the Hebrew צָרָה, "hostile" (from the root צרר, "to besiege, show hostility"), rather than צֹרֵחַ, "shrieking." It also requires that שָׁם, "there," be read as the verb שָׂם, "he placed, appointed." It is noteworthy, however, that 8HevXIIgr reads צֹרֵחַ as ἐπισ[, apparently a fragment of the word ἐπίσημος, "groans," which supports the MT reading.[86] Targum Jonathan reads, "Near and hastening very much is the sound of the day that is appointed to come from before YHWH, which is trouble and outcry; there, the warriors are being killed." This reading apparently reflects some controversy over the understanding of the

word צֹרֵחַ, "shrieking," as the Targum apparently renders the word twice, first as וצוח, "and outcry," and then as מקטלין, "are being killed/are killing themselves." The latter reading apparently presupposes a transposition of letters from the root צרח, "to shriek," to the root רצח, "to murder, kill." The Peshitta follows the LXX in part by reading, "the sound of the day of the L-rd is bitter and hard and strong," which reads צֹרֵחַ, "shrieking," as צָרָה, "hard, hostile" (Syriac wqṣᵓ), but it also eliminates שָׁם, "there," so that גִּבּוֹר, "warrior," simply functions according to its root meaning as "strong" (wᶜšyn). The Vulgate reads צֹרֵחַ as a transitive verb with גִּבּוֹר as the object, "afflicting there the strong." In each case, the versions attempt to clarify the ambiguity inherent in the underlying Hebrew text.

■ **15** Following the statement of the prophet's premises in v. 14 that the Day of YHWH is imminent and a threat, vv. 15-17 then turn to a more detailed exposition of the threatening nature of the day. Verses 15-16 employ a series of eight paired strophic statements, in which the first six statements employ a basic construct formation of the noun יוֹם, "day," together with either one or a pair of nouns that characterizes the threatening nature of the day, and the final two statements relate the objects against which the Day of YHWH is directed. Ball suggests that the six strophes together constitute a hymn that depicts the day of wrath, but this formal conclusion appears to be influenced by the role that v. 15a plays as the opening stanza of the medieval hymn "*Dies irae dies illa*," which was once employed in the Roman Catholic Requiem Mass.[87] The use of such a phrase appears in the narrative concerning Sennacherib's siege of Jerusalem in which Hezekiah's officers declare to Isaiah that "this day is a day of distress and rebuke and disgrace (יוֹם־צָרָה וְתוֹכֵחָה וּנְאָצָה)" (Isa 37:3; 2 Kgs 19:3), which suggests that it is only a construction to characterize a time of distress. The repetitive nature of the strophes in Zephaniah, however, points to an interest in employing repetition as a means to drive the point home to the

85   The statement shares some vocabulary with Isa 42:13, which could suggest the latter's dependence on Zeph 1:14.

86   See Tov, *Greek Minor Prophets*, 61, 95.

87   Ball, *Zephaniah*, 84; note that the Latin title derives from the Vulgate's rendition of v. 15a. See also Vlaardingerbroek, *Zephaniah*, 103–4, who cites Cornelis Vellekoop, *Dies irae dies illa. Studien zur Frühgeschichte einer Sequenz* (Bilthoven: Creyghton, 1978).

audience of this text. Verses 17-18 are joined syntactically to vv. 15-16 by the initial *waw*-consecutive verbal formation, וְהַצֵּרֹתִי, "and I shall afflict," and lay out the consequences for those who are the targets of YHWH's wrath on the Day of YHWH.

The first statement in the series, "a day of wrath is that day" (יֹום עֶבְרָה הַיֹּום הַהוּא), sets the theme for the following five statements by pointing to the wrathful and thus the threatening nature of the day. In contrast to the following five statements that employ pairs of nouns in the construct formulation to characterize the nature of the day, v. 15a employs only one noun, "wrath" (עֶבְרָה), both to set the basic theme and to accommodate the following phrase "is that day," which stands as the implied completion of the succeeding five statements. Ben Zvi notes that the noun "wrath" appears in other contexts associated with the Day of YHWH or related themes (e.g., Isa 9:18; 13:9, 13; Ezek 22:21, 31; 38:19; Lam 2:2), but the expression appears not to be characteristic of the Day of YHWH tradition. Rather, it suggests an interest in defining the day ironically as a day of divine judgment against Jerusalem or Judah rather than against the enemies of Jerusalem, Judah, or Israel. In this respect, the ironic characterization of the Day of YHWH as a day of wrath against Jerusalem appears to continue a theme that first appears in Amos's use of the Day of YHWH motif as a means to announce YHWH's judgment against Israel (see Amos 5:18-20).[88] It is noteworthy that Amos's characterization of the day employs the motif of darkness together with threat, which suggests an analogy with strophes four and five below.

The second strophe of the series in v. 15bα[1-3], "a day of stress and distress" (יֹום צָרָה וּמְצוּקָה), builds on the initial theme of v. 15a by pointing to its effects on those who are the targets of YHWH's wrath. Ben Zvi notes

that the expression "day of stress" (יֹום צָרָה) appears frequently in the Hebrew Bible,[89] but only one of those citations indicates a context in the Day of YHWH tradition (Obad 14). The use of the term מְצוּקָה, "stress," to characterize a day is unique to Zeph 1:15, although adjectives based on the same root are employed together with references to darkness in Isa 8:22 to describe the stress of the land at the approach of the Assyrians, who are to carry out divine judgment: "and unto the land he shall gaze, and behold, stress and darkness (צָרָה וַחֲשֵׁכָה), the gloom of anguish (מְעוּף צוּקָה) and it [the people] is thrust into deep darkness (אֲפֵלָה)."[90] As in the preceding strophe, the use of such language does not reflect a long-standing traditional portrayal of the Day of YHWH; rather it once again represents an attempt to portray the Day of YHWH ironically as a day of threat against Jerusalem.

The third strophe in the series appears in v. 15bα[4-6], "a day of destruction and desolation" (יֹום שֹׁאָה וּמְשֹׁואָה). It continues the sequence of the preceding two strophes by pointing to complete destruction as the consequence or aftermath of divine wrath and human stress. The use of these terms to characterize a day are unique in the Hebrew Bible,[91] which once again points to the absence of a clear, linguistically defined tradition for the portrayal of the Day of YHWH as a day of threat against Jerusalem. Both terms, שֹׁאָה and מְשֹׁואָה, are based on the same root and convey destruction. Although the distinctive nuances of each term are not certain, their appearance together in this context conveys the meaning of complete destruction. It is noteworthy that שֹׁאָה, "Shoah," is now employed in place of "Holocaust" to designate the murder of some six million Jews and others by the Nazis and their sympathizers in World War II.[92]

88 See Hans Spieckermann, "Dies irae: Der alttestamentliche Befund und seine Vorgeschichte," *VT* 39 (1989) 194–208. Spieckermann also notes that the motif of YHWH's wrath may draw on Mesopotamian omen traditions of divine anger or days of wrath, darkness, and evil. A direct relationship between these texts and Zephaniah is not entirely clear, although it is possible that such concerns had an impact on Judah during the late eighth and seventh centuries when Assyria dominated the region. Zephaniah's use of the motif could well constitute an adaptation of such a con-

ceptualization for his Jerusalemite/Judean audience.

89 *Zephaniah,* 122.

90 For discussion of Isa 8:22, see Marvin A. Sweeney, "A Philological and Form-Critical Reevaluation of Isaiah 8:16—9:6," *HAR* 14 (1994) 215–31; idem, *Isaiah 1–39,* 175–88.

91 Ben Zvi, *Zephaniah,* 123.

92 The English term "holocaust" denotes the whole burnt offering sacrificed on the temple altar as a means to atone for wrongdoing (see Leviticus 1). Since it implies wrongdoing on the part of the per-

The fourth and fifth strophes in the series, "a day of darkness and gloom (יוֹם חֹשֶׁךְ וַאֲפֵלָה); a day of cloud and dark fog (יוֹם עָנָן וַעֲרָפֶל)," appear both in v. 15bα and 15bβ and in Joel 2:2aα, where it follows a call to blow the shofar to announce the coming Day of YHWH. Because Joel is generally considered to be a composition from the late fourth century BCE that cites extensively from earlier biblical literature, the text of Joel is apparently dependent on that of Zephaniah, especially since the motifs of the shofar and the statement of the imminent Day of YHWH employs the same terminology as Zeph 1:7, 14, 15-16.[93] The language and imagery of darkness in the present text of Zephaniah appear frequently in theophanic reports that attempt to depict the presence of YHWH (e.g., Exod 19:16; 20:18; Deut 4:11; 5:22; 1 Kgs 8:12; Nah 1:3; Ps 97:2; 2 Chr 6:1; cf. Isa 8:22-23; Joel 2:2). 1 Kgs 8:12/2 Chr 6:1 are especially instructive in this regard because they relate a portion from Solomon's speech at the dedication of the Temple in Jerusalem in which he recounts the imagery of YHWH surrounded by darkness: "Then Solomon said, 'YHWH has said that he would dwell in thick darkness (בָּעֲרָפֶל). I have built you an exalted house, a place for you to dwell forever and ever.'" This statement suggests that the thick darkness is associated with the Holy of Holies in the Jerusalem Temple in which the ark of the covenant, symbolizing the throne or presence of YHWH, was located (see 1 Kgs 8:1-11/2 Chr 5:2-14). 1 Kgs 6:31-32 reports that the Holy of Holies was shielded by olivewood doors carved with cherubim, palm trees, and open flowers and overlaid with gold to insure the darkness and seclusion of the Holy of Holies at times when the temple was not open for public worship. Such imagery also appears in Ps 97:2, "Clouds and thick darkness (עָנָן וַעֲרָפֶל) are all around him [YHWH]; righteousness and justice are the

foundation of his throne," in a context in which YHWH's throne would be represented by the ark of the covenant that resides in the Holy of Holies in the temple. "Heavy cloud" (עָנָן כָּבֵד) also appears together with "shofar" at the Sinai theophany, which is often identified with manifestations of YHWH's presence at the Jerusalem Temple.[94] Indeed, the representation of darkness in Zephaniah's presentation of the Day of YHWH draws on the imagery of YHWH's presence in the Holy of Holies in the Jerusalem Temple and thereby aids in establishing the ironic character of the event. The Day of YHWH and the Jerusalem Temple no longer signify YHWH's protection for Jerusalem; instead, these symbols signify the threat of judgment that YHWH brings against the city.

■ 16 The sixth strophe in the series appears in v. 16a, "a day of shofar and trumpet (יוֹם שׁוֹפָר וּתְרוּעָה)," which focuses on the alarms that are sounded to warn the people and assemble them at the time of threat. The shofar is a trumpet or horn fashioned from a ram's horn, and it is still employed for liturgical purposes in modern Judaism.[95] Trumpets, referred to as חֲצֹצְרוֹת in Num 10:1-10, were made of hammered silver. The shofar and trumpets were employed in biblical times to call the people to arms against enemies (Josh 6:4-5; Judg 3:27; cf. Amos 2:2; 3:6; Jer 4:19; 49:2; Job 39:25), to signal cultic celebration (Pss 47:6; 98:6; 150:2-5; 2 Sam 6:15; 1 Chr 15:28), to proclaim the reign of a new king (2 Sam 15:10); and its use was portrayed as a signal for the return of exiled Jews to Jerusalem (Isa 27:13). References to blowing the shofar and the trumpet blast appear in theophanic portrayals of the divine presence at Mount Sinai (Exod 19:16) and the Day of YHWH (Joel 2:1). The ironic portrayal of their use in relation to the present depiction of the Day of YHWH becomes evident

son making the offering, it is an inappropriate designation for the murder of Jews in the Nazi era. Consequently, "Shoah," which simply denotes destruction, is now employed in this capacity. For discussion see Zev Garber and Bruce Zuckerman, "Why Do We Call the Holocaust 'the Holocaust?' An Inquiry Into the Psychology of Labels," *Modern Judaism* 9 (1989) 197–211; reprinted in Zev Garber, ed., *Shoah: The Paradigmatic Genocide* (Studies in the Shoah 8; Lanham, Md.: University Press of America, 1994) 51–66.

93 See esp. Siegfried Bergler, *Joel als Schriftinterpret,*

153–69; Irsigler, *Gottesgericht,* 106–7; H. W. Wolff, *Joel and Amos: A Commentary* (Hermeneia; Philadelphia: Fortress Press, 1977) 10–12, 43–44; James L. Crenshaw, *Joel* (AB 24C; New York: Doubleday, 1995) 119; Sweeney, *Twelve Prophets,* 145–87. See also Rudolph, *Joel, Amos, Obadja, Jona* (KAT XIII/2; Gütersloh: Mohn, 1971) 54–55, who considers Joel to be a contemporary of Zephaniah.

94 See Levenson, *Sinai,* esp. 187–217.

95 A. L. Lewis, "Shofar," *EncJud* 14:1442–47.

when one considers that shofar and trumpet blast also signaled the celebration of the New Year in the Jerusalem Temple (Num 29:1; cf. Lev 23:24; Num 10:10) and the Jubilee Year (Lev 25:9). In that these festivals celebrated the renewal of creation and YHWH's sovereignty over the world, they would be seen as events that fostered the notion of Jerusalem's role as the holy center of creation and cosmic stability. Nevertheless, the shofar and trumpet blast in the present context signal YHWH's threat against Jerusalem, and thus the reversal of their expected roles.

Finally, v. 16b concludes the series by stating that the Day of YHWH is directed "against the fortified cities (עַל הֶעָרִים הַבְּצֻרוֹת) and against the high towers (וְעַל הַפִּנּוֹת הַגְּבֹהוֹת)." The expressions "fortified cities" and "high towers" are relatively common expressions in the Bible (see Hos 8:14; Neh 9:25; 2 Chr 32:1; 33:14; and Zeph 3:6; 2 Chr 26:15; Neh 3:24, 31, 32, respectively). The defensive character of this imagery indicates, however, that the fortified cities of Judah, particularly Jerusalem, are the targets of YHWH's wrath. Once again, this indicates the ironic character of Zephaniah's portrayal of the Day of YHWH, since the normal target of YHWH's wrath would be the enemy nations that threatened those very fortifications rather than the fortifications themselves. Indeed, the irony is conveyed with reference to tradition, since the term "fortified cities" appears in the narrative concerning Sennacherib's threats against the fortified cities of Judah during the course of his assault against Judah in 701 BCE (see 2 Kgs 19:25; Isa 37:26). The irony is compounded by the fact that the term is employed to describe the fortified cities of the Canaanites in Num 13:28; Deut 1:28; 3:5; 9:1, which would suggest that Judah has taken the role played by Canaan in the time of Joshua. Finally, the depiction of the Day of YHWH directed against the fortified cities and high towers of Jerusalem and Judah is analogous to the portrayal of the Day of YHWH in Isa 2:6-21.[96] The Isaian text appears to be directed generally against all that is lifted

up, high, or arrogant in the land, although it is not always clear whether the passage refers only to the land of Israel or to the entire earth. The preceding references to the nations streaming to Zion (2:2-4) and to humanity in general (2:9, 11, 17, 20) suggest that the latter is the case. Nevertheless, the Isaian text is also ironic in that Israel/Judah appears to be included in the worldwide judgment, especially since the passage is included in a larger block (Isaiah 2–4) that is ultimately concerned with Jerusalem. Especially noteworthy are the references in 2:(12-)15 to high fortifications that will be the target of YHWH's actions: "for the Day of YHWH is against all that is high and lifted up . . . and against every high tower (וְעַל כָּל־מִגְדָּל גָּבֹהַ) and against every fortified wall (וְעַל כָּל־חוֹמָה בְּצוּרָה)," since the passage employs language that is somewhat similar to that of Zeph 1:16b. It would appear that the Zephanian text draws on Isaiah to a certain extent to portray its understanding that the previously threatened Day of YHWH from the time of Isaiah is about to take place. Furthermore, any ambiguities about whether the day is targeted against the entire world or only against Jerusalem are removed in the Zephanian text.

■ **17** Verses 17-18 the provide a detailed portrayal of the consequences of the Day of YHWH's wrath for those who have sinned against YHWH. Many have argued that the first person formulation of v. 17aα, "and I shall afflict humanity, and they shall walk like the blind," demonstrates that the verse is to be read as a first person statement by YHWH, analogous to those found throughout chap. 1 (see vv. 2-4, 8aα-9, 10aα6-9-13).[97] As a consequence of this view, v. 17aβ, "for they have sinned to YHWH," is frequently considered to be a gloss because it disrupts the first person formulation of the rest of the verse. Furthermore, many see the reference to "humanity" (אָדָם) as an indication of the universal concerns of this text that therefore stands as evidence that the entire verse must be a secondary expansion of the text designed to provide an eschatolog-

---

96   For treatment of this passage, see Sweeney, *Isaiah 1–39*, 100–104.

97   For full discussion, see Irsigler, *Gottesgericht*, 429; Rudolph, *Zephanja*, 270; Seybold, *Satirische Prophetie*, 34; Edler, *Kerygma*, 199–204; Renaud, *Sophonie*, 214–16; Keller, *Sophonie*, 196; Vlaardingerbroek, *Zephaniah*, 104; Ben Zvi, *Zephaniah*, 127–30;

Roberts, *Zephaniah*, 184–85; Berlin, *Zephaniah*, 90–91; Floyd, *Minor Prophets*, 195–200; Horst, *Propheten*, 194–95; Nowack, *Propheten*, 295–96; Sellin, *Zwölfprophetenbuch*, 427–28; Marti, *Dodekapropheton*, 366; J. M. P. Smith, *Zephaniah*, 205–6; Elliger, *Zephanja*, 66–67; van Hoonacker, *Prophètes*, 515.

ical dimension to the text that would stem from the post-exilic period.[98]

Two considerations undermine this view. First, there is no reason to read the reference to "humanity" as an indication that the concern of this text has shifted from Jerusalem/Judah to humanity at large, or that it indicates an eschatological scenario.[99] As noted above in relation to similar statements in vv. 2-6, references to humanity or the larger world of creation must be related to the role of the Jerusalem Temple as the holy center of creation in ancient Judean thought. Indeed, the shift from the language of humanity or creation at large to that of the inhabitants of Jerusalem/Judah who have sinned demonstrates such a conceptualization in that it points to a disruption at the very center of creation. There is little reason to consider v. 17 to be secondary on these grounds.

Second, it appears likely that v. 17 was written to convey a statement by YHWH, based on the consistent identification of first person statements throughout the rest of Zephaniah as those by YHWH whereas third person statements are either those of the prophet or the narrator of the book. It is noteworthy that a similar expression appears as a statement by YHWH in Jer 10:18, "I am going to sling out the inhabitants of the land at this time, and I will bring distress on them so that they shall feel it" (cf. Deut 28:52; 1 Kgs 8:37/2 Chr 6:28; Neh 9:27; cf. also 2 Chr 28:20, 22; 33:12). These considerations do not require that v. 17aα be considered a gloss, however, as prior examples in Zephaniah demonstrate a stylistic tendency for the prophet to complete first person statements by YHWH with his own third person statements that expand on or clarify the divine speech. A clear example of this tendency appears in Zeph 1:2-6. In this instance, vv. 1-4 are clearly first person speech by YHWH, and vv. 5b-6 are clearly statements by the prophet, as indicated by the third person references to YHWH. The specification of the direct object of the preceding statement by YHWH in v. 5a is ambiguous, however, because it lacks both indications of first person speech and third person references to YHWH. Despite this clear shift in the perspective of the speaker, vv. 5b-6

continue the specification of the direct object of v. 4b that is begun in v. 5a. The identity of YHWH as speaker fades and that of the prophet as speaker emerges within a single syntactically coherent unit. Similar ambiguities appear in vv. 10-13, in which the third person reference to YHWH in v. 10aα[1-5] clearly marks this statement as the work of the prophet or the narrator, and the first person formulation of vv. 12-13 clearly marks these verses as a statement by YHWH. Verses 10a[1-5]-b lack both a third person reference to YHWH and a first person formulation, and therefore blur the distinction between YHWH and prophet/narrator as speaker within this segment.

Much the same phenomenon appears in v. 17, except that at no point is there any explicit indication that YHWH is the speaker in v. 17aα and 17b. Although it may well have been the intention that YHWH appear as the speaker in v. 17aα and perhaps in v. 17b as well, a synchronic reading of this verse requires that the prophet be viewed as the speaker throughout. Consequently, it is the prophet who threatens to afflict human beings for sinning against YHWH, and it is the prophet who describes the disembowelment of YHWH's victims in such grotesque terms. Such a conceptualization is consistent with the identification of the prophet as speaker throughout vv. 14-18, and the stylistic tendency to portray the prophet as one who elaborates on and explains the preceding words by YHWH. Indeed, it is consistent with texts such as 3:1-5 in which the prophet employs a woe oracle form to announce the possibility of punishment for Jerusalem.

The statement, "for they have sinned to YHWH" (כִּי לַה' חָטָאוּ), is significant both because it specifies those who are to be targeted by YHWH or the prophet for punishment and because it points to the overall conceptualization of the Day of YHWH as a day of sacrifice in keeping with the statements made in v. 7. Sacrifice in ancient Judean religion is part of the means to maintain the natural and moral order of the cosmos; that is, it aids in ensuring the stability of creation and in restoring the stability of creation when that stability is disrupted by improper action.[100] In that those targeted by YHWH

---

98 E.g., Renaud, *Sophonie*, 214–16.
99 Cf. Ben Zvi, *Zephaniah*, 127–28; Roberts, *Zephaniah*, 182.

100 See esp. J. Milgrom, "Sacrifices and Offerings, OT," *IDBSup* 763–71; idem, *Cult and Conscience* (Leiden: Brill, 1976); idem, *Studies in Cultic Theol-*

are said to have sinned, their actions have disrupted the cosmos, and sacrifice is necessary to restore that order. Sacrifice is an inherently purifying act; thus those who will actually administer the sacrifice must be ritually pure before they perform the sacrificial ritual, and the ritual killing and burning of those who will constitute the sacrifice symbolizes the purification of the cosmos or the removal of that which has disrupted it.

This allows for further ambiguity and irony in the depiction of the sacrifice for the Day of YHWH in Zephaniah 1. As noted in the discussion of v. 7 above, those who were "called" or "invited" to participate in the sacrifice, presumably to take part in eating the sacrifice, are in fact those who are designated to constitute the sacrifice. The role of the sacrificial victim becomes clear in v. 17b as well. Although much of the discussion of this verse has centered on its grotesque imagery, particularly in relation to attempts to render its depiction of intestines spilling out like dung on the ground, the primary function of the verse is to depict the gutting of the sacrificial victims and the removal of their intestines and internal organs as part of the process by which sacrificial animals are prepared for burning on the altar. Such a procedure is clear throughout the instructions in Leviticus for the preparation of animal sacrifices as the whole burnt offering: "Aaron's sons shall arrange the parts, with the head and the suet, on the wood that is on the fire on the altar; but its entrails and its legs shall be washed with water.[101] Then the priest shall turn the whole into smoke on the altar as a burnt offering, an offering by fire of pleasing odor to YHWH" (Lev 1:8-9; cf. 1:12-13). Similar procedures apply to the offering of well-being (3:1-5, 6-11, 12-16) and purification offerings (4:3-12, 13-21, 22-26, 27-31, 32-35).

The Hebrew text apparently has caused some problems due to its graphic portrayal of the disembowelment of the victims: "and their blood shall be poured out like dust, and their guts like dung." The term לְחֻם, "bowels, intestines," appears also in Job 20:23, "To fill their belly

to the full, he [G-d] will send his fierce anger into them and rain it upon them into their bowels." The meaning of the term is somewhat uncertain, however, because it derives from the root לחם, "to use as food, eat," or "to fight." The former root seems clearly to apply, and the derived meaning of "intestines" seems appropriate to the context of sacrificial disembowelment. The terms גְּלָלִים and גֵּל are commonly employed for "dung" or "turds" (see 1 Kgs 14:10; Ezek 4:12, 15; Job 20:7). This terminology apparently caused some embarrassment among the versions, which sometimes employ more temperate language. The LXX reads, "and their blood will pour out like dust and their flesh like dung" (καὶ τὰς σάρκας αὐτῶν ὡς βόλβιτα). 8HevXIIgr 21:37-39 reads, "a[n]d [their blood shall be spilled out] like [dust a]n[d their c]orp[ses like . . ." (κ[αὶ] [ἐκξεῖτο τὸ αἷμα αὐτῶ]ν ὡς [χοῦν κ]α[ὶ] πρώματα αὐτῶν ὡς. . .). Targum Jonathan reads likewise, "and their blood shall be poured out like the dust and their corpses like refuse (ונבילתחון כסחותא)." The Peshitta reads, "and their blood shall be poured out like the dust and their flesh like dung (wbsrhwn ʾik kbyʾ)." The Vulgate reads, "and their blood shall be poured out like dirt and their corpses like dung (et corpus eorum sicut stercora)."

■ 18 Verse 18 continues the portrayal of the consequences of the Day of YHWH that was initiated in v. 17. Some see here major syntactical and thematic shifts that call into question the authorship of all or parts of v. 18,[102] but closer attention to both the syntax of v. 18 and the development of its themes indicates a text that coheres well with v. 17.

The syntactical features of v. 18 point to a basic two-part structure that is joined to v. 17 by the initial particle combination גַם . . . גַם, "(n)either . . . (n)or." Although this combination indicates coordination between the two (or more) terms or phrases that the particles introduce, the conjunctive force of the particle must also be recognized.[103] Thus v. 18 follows syntactically from v. 17. Furthermore, the fundamental syntactical structure of

---

ogy and Terminology (Leiden: Brill, 1983); cf. G. A. Anderson, "Sacrifice and Sacrificial Offerings (OT)," ABD 5:870-86.

101 See esp. Knierim, Text, 59-64.

102 See Irsigler, Gottesgericht, 417-30; Seybold, Satirische Prophetie, 34; idem, Zephanja, 102; Gerleman, Zephanja, 22-23; Edler, Kerygma, 82-84; Renaud,

Sophonie, 214-16; idem, "Sophonie," 6-10; Elliger, Zephanja, 66; J. M. P. Smith, Zephaniah, 206-7; Marti, Dodekapropheton, 366; Sellin, Zwölfprophetenbuch, 428; Nowack, Propheten, 296; Horst, Propheten, 194-95; Vlaardingerbroek, Zephaniah, 113.

103 See C. J. Labuschagne, "The Emphasizing Particle Gam and Its Connotations," in W. C. van Unnik,

the verse points to two basic parts. Verse 18a constitutes a coherent syntactical unit based on the verbal formation לֹא־יוּכַל לְהַצִּילָם, "(it) will not be able to save them." Verse 18aα-b likewise constitutes a coherent syntactical unit in v. 18aα based on the verb תֵּאָכֵל, "(it) shall be eaten/consumed," and a כִּי clause in v. 18b that employs another verbal statement based on יַעֲשֶׂה, "(he) will do," to explain the purpose of YHWH's consuming fire.

Thematic factors also point to an interrelationship between vv. 17 and 18, especially in that v. 18 ultimately resumes the sacrificial imagery of v. 17. Verse 17 focuses on the prophet's affliction of those who have sinned against YHWH and portrays the victims of the Day of YHWH as the sacrifices that are to be offered on the temple altar, but v. 18aα returns to the imagery of wealth that appeared at various points throughout the chapter (cf. 1:11, 13; see also 1:8, 9). Although at first glance this might be interpreted as a shift in motif, the coordination of the themes of sacrifice on the Day of YHWH and the portrayal of apostasy and wealth throughout the preceding verses in chap. 1 point to a scenario in which those who have collaborated with the Assyrians, whether religiously through the adoption of foreign worship practice, culturally through the use of foreign dress, or economically through participation in the Assyrian imperial economy, are designated as the invited victims of YHWH's sacrifice on the Day of YHWH. The present statement focuses on the wealth of those who are to become the targets of YHWH's punitive actions in order to point to the futility of such measures in the face of YHWH's wrath. The phrase, "in the

day of the wrath of YHWH" (בְּיוֹם עֶבְרַת ה׳), of course recalls the statement in v. 15a, "a day of wrath is that day" (יוֹם עֶבְרָה הַיּוֹם הַהוּא), the initial element in a six-part series that characterized the approaching Day of YHWH. Many note the correspondence of the statement, "neither their silver nor their gold will be able to save them on the day of the wrath of YHWH," with Ezek 7:19, "their silver and their gold will not be able to save them on the day of the wrath of YHWH"; but most maintain that Ezekiel adapted the phrase from its present context in Zephaniah.[104]

Although v. 18aα turns to the motifs of silver and gold, the key concern of the statement is not the wealth of the victims that makes them guilty and thus fit for punishment, but the fact that their wealth will not be able to save them from YHWH's wrath. The statement is interested not so much in the guilt of the victims—that has already been established—but in the inevitability and the completeness of their punishment. Thus it is striking that the imagery of sacrifice resumes in v. 18aα-b with the portrayal of YHWH's zealous fire consuming the entire land in complete destruction,[105] just as a whole burnt offering is consumed entirely on the altar of the temple (see Leviticus 1). Furthermore, just as the whole burnt offering functions as a means to maintain or restore the holiness of creation or the equilibrium of the cosmos, so the complete destruction of those who are guilty in Jerusalem/Judah will function similarly in the prophet's understanding. Verse 18b makes clear that the punishment encompasses the entire land,[106] just as the preceding verses have consistently portrayed YHWH's

ed., *Studia Biblica et Semitica* (Fest. T. C. Vriezen; Wageningen: Veenman en Zonen, 1966) 193–203.

104 So Vlaardingerbroek, *Zephaniah*, 112. Cf. Walther Zimmerli, *Ezekiel 1: A Commentary on the Book of the Prophet Ezekiel, Chapters 1–24* (Hermeneia; Philadelphia: Fortress Press, 1979) 199, who notes that the statement, "their silver and their gold cannot save them on the day of YHWH's anger," is missing in LXX Ezek 7:19 and was probably added to the Hebrew text on the basis of Zeph 1:18. See also Isa 13:17, "See, I am stirring up the Medes against them, who have no regard for silver and do not delight in gold," which many correctly judge to be a late text, but this hardly provides criteria for judging the authenticity of the statement in Zeph 1:18.

105 Many argue that the clause "and by the fire of his jealousy, all the land shall be consumed," must be

secondary because the clause "for the fire of my jealousy, all the land will be consumed," appears in Zeph 3:8b (see Marti, *Dodekapropheton*, 366; J. M. P. Smith, *Zephaniah*, 206–7; Sellin, *Zwölfprophetenbuch*, 428; Edler, *Kerygma*, 82; Seybold, *Zephanja*, 102; Vlaardingerbroek, *Zephaniah*, 113. Contra Irsigler, *Gottesgericht*, 111; Ben Zvi, *Zephaniah*, 132–33.

106 Note that the versions have had some difficulties in rendering the term נִבְהָלָה, "complete/speedy destruction," in v. 18b, "because destruction, indeed sudden devastation he [YHWH] shall make for all the inhabitants of the land." LXX reads, σπουδὴν, "haste/speed"; the text of 8HevXIIgr is missing at this point; TJ reads, שיצאה, "destruction"; the Peshitta reads, *mtl ddlwhyʾ wswpnʾ ʿbr mryʾ ʿl klhwn ʿmwryh dʾrʿ*, "for fear and destruction has the L-rd made over all of them who inhabit the land";

judgment against the entire land and all humanity. It is only in 2:1-3 that one begins to see some hint that repentance may avert the punishment on the day of YHWH's anger, but even then there is little indication that the text envisions punishment—or deliverance from punishment—on an individual basis. Rather, the book of Zephaniah portrays punishment and deliverance as a corporate matter: either the entire nation is guilty and subject to punishment, or the entire nation might be redeemed if it seeks YHWH.

---

and Vulgate reads, *qui a consummationem cum festinatione*, "for complete consummation with haste (he shall make for all the inhabitants of the earth)." The verbal root בהל means both "to hasten" and "to disturb," and therefore conveys both haste and disruption, when employed together with כָּלָה, "destruction."

Zephaniah 2:1–3:20 constitutes the second major structural element of the body of the book (1:2–3:20). Following the initial Prophetic Announcement of the Day of YHWH in 1:2-18, it constitutes the Prophet's Parenetic Address to Seek YHWH.[1] Because 1:2-18 prepares the audience for the prophet's address by introducing the fundamental concern with the Day of YHWH, 2:1–3:20 builds on that premise—and the audience's concerns with both the threats and opportunities offered by the Day of YHWH—to persuade the audience to accept the prophet's contention that they should seek YHWH. In this respect, 2:1–3:20 conveys the primary purposes of the book and therefore serves as the fundamental literary unit of the entire book.

As noted in the formal overview of 1:2-18, 2:1–3:20 is distinguished by the absence of an explicit syntactical link with the preceding material and by the introduction of the direct address language in 2:1-3 in contrast to the general objective announcement language of 1:2-18. As in 1:2-18, the text presents the prophet as the primary speaker, who in turn presents statements by YHWH throughout this unit. Whereas 1:2-18 simply announces the coming Day of YHWH as part of the overall rhetorical strategy employed within the book, 2:1–3:20 employs imperative verbs, הִתְקוֹשְׁשׁוּ וָקוֹשּׁוּ, "assemble yourselves and gather," at the outset of the passage together with other second person address forms throughout the balance of the passage to demand attention, decisions, and action from the Jerusalemite/Judean audience presupposed throughout the book. The direct address forms shift from second masculine plural verbs and pronouns in 2:1-3 and 3:20 to second feminine singular forms in 3:5-13 and 3:14-19, which might suggest a different structural arrangement. The combination of the second feminine singular address verbs, אַךְ־תִּירְאִי אוֹתִי תִּקְחִי מוּסָר,

"indeed, fear me; take instruction," together with the imperative address, לָכֵן חַכּוּ־לִי, "therefore, wait for me," in the context of the prophet's presentation of YHWH's statements to Judah/Jerusalem nevertheless demonstrates the interplay of the different address forms within the unit as a whole. The return to the second masculine plural address perspective in 3:20 likewise demonstrates this shift in perspective and leaves the entire unit encased in second masculine plural address forms. The shift may be explained as an expression of the means by which the text is designed to portray the prophet's address to Judah and Jerusalem. On the one hand, the audience is addressed as the people of Jerusalem and Judah, which requires masculine plural address forms to account for the large numbers of people involved; on the other hand, Jerusalem (and Judah) is personified as בַּת־צִיּוֹן, "the daughter of Zion" (3:14), who ultimately becomes the restored bride of YHWH in 3:16-18. Such a characterization is especially important since 2:4, which constitutes the basic premise for the parenesis, metaphorically employs the language of divorce to portray the judgment against the Philistine cities.[2] Such a portrayal draws on the extensive traditions of Israel as YHWH's bride (see Hosea 1–3; Isaiah 49–54; Jeremiah 2; Ezekiel 16) to argue implicitly that YHWH had abandoned Jerusalem for a period of time to dally with other nations. Certainly, such a conceptualization would explain Jerusalem's and Judah's suffering and sense of abandonment during the period of Assyrian hegemony over Judah from the late eighth through the mid-seventh centuries BCE. A similar paradigm is employed later in Deutero-Isaiah to explain Jerusalem's suffering under the Babylonians and its restoration at the beginning of the Persian period.[3]

---

1   For discussion of parenesis, see Sweeney, *Isaiah 1–39*, 527.

2   See Zalcman, "Ambiguity."

3   See Patricia Tull Willey, "The Servant of YHWH and Daughter Zion: Alternating Visions of YHWH's Community," *SBLSP, 1995* (ed. Eugene H. Lovering Jr.; Atlanta: Scholars Press, 1995) 267–303; Mark Biddle, "The Figure of Lady Jerusalem: Identification, Deification, and Personification of Cities in the Ancient Near East," in K. L. Younger et al., eds., *The Biblical Canon in Comparative Perspective* (Lewiston: Mellen, 1991) 173–94; John Sawyer, "Daughter of Zion and Servant of the Lord in Isaiah," *JSOT* 44 (1989) 89–107. Cf. John J. Schmitt, "The Gender of Ancient Israel," *JSOT* 26 (1983) 115–25, who argues that the Hebrew Bible consistently employs the feminine singular when speaking of cities and the masculine singular for Israel.

The overall structure of 2:1—3:20 comprises three basic parts.[4] The fundamental parenetic address in 2:1-4 calls on the audience to seek YHWH before the judgment comes upon them. It includes two imperative addresses in vv. 1-3, the first of which calls on the people to assemble before the wrath of YHWH comes upon them on the Day of YHWH (vv. 1-2), and the second of which demands that they seek YHWH so that they might be hidden or spared on the day of YHWH's wrath (v. 3). The portrayal of Philistia's coming punishment in 2:4, linked syntactically to vv. 1-3 by the initial causative כִּי, "for, because," provides the basis for the prophet's parenetic demands from the audience, that is, Philistia is currently undergoing punishment, which the prophet presents as an act of YHWH.[5] If YHWH brings punishment upon Philistia—and, as the following oracles attempt to demonstrate, upon the nations culminating in Assyria as well—then Jerusalem's and Judah's restoration must be at hand.

The two successive woe addresses in 2:5-15 and 3:1-20, directed respectively to the nations and to Jerusalem/Judah, are designed to support the rhetorical goals of this text with an elaboration on the basic parenesis defined in 2:1-4. Zephaniah 2:5-15 points to YHWH's actions in the world concerning the nations with a sequence of oracles that addresses the situations of four individual nations. Although the formal woe address is formulated at first sight to address the party named in the text, that is, the Philistines in the case of 2:5, it is unlikely that this text was ever written to be read or heard by a Philistine audience. Consequently, the Philistines are only the fictive addressees; the actual addressees are the Jerusalemite and Judean audience that is addressed by the book as a whole. The sequence begins with oracles concerning both the Philistines (vv. 5-7) and the Moabites and Ammonites (vv. 8-9). No particular reason is given for the punishment of the Philistines, but Egyptian advances against Philistia in the mid-seventh century BCE point to their impending down-

fall and the possibility that Judah will be able to regain territory lost to Philistia as a consequence of the Assyrian assault against Judah in 701. The Moabites and Ammonites are portrayed as nations that expanded their territory at Judah's and Israel's expense, beginning in the mid-ninth century and again under the auspices of the Assyrians in the late eighth through mid-seventh centuries. The attacks against Moab and Ammon by nomadic Arab tribes—very likely with the support of Assyria's foe, Babylonia—apparently provided the occasion for the prophet to claim that YHWH was acting against these nations as well. Verses 10-11, formulated by means of the summary-appraisal genre, make this point clear,[6] and provide the occasion to define YHWH's action in the broader world. The summary-appraisal therefore provides the platform for recalling the defeat of the Ethiopian Dynasty by Assyria and its Saite Egyptian allies (v. 12)—again as a testimony to YHWH's actions in the world—and then turns to a projection of YHWH's coming judgment against the Assyrian Empire (vv. 13-15). This last oracle provides a key basis for the contention in the following woe speech that YHWH will restore Jerusalem and Judah/Israel.

The second woe speech in 3:1-20 is designed to demonstrate that YHWH is acting to restore Jerusalem/Israel. In order to do so, however, it must first come to grips with the reality of Jerusalem's suffering under the rule of the Assyrians. It therefore begins with a woe oracle in 3:1-4 that articulates the reasons for Jerusalem's punishment: it did not listen to YHWH; it did not accept instruction; it did not trust in YHWH; it did not draw near to its G-d; its officials, judges, prophets, and priests were corrupt; and so on. The oracle is designed to demonstrate that Jerusalem and Judah were in need of punishment and that YHWH was justified in bringing punishment upon them. All of this of course serves the overarching rhetorical goals of the passage, however, in that 3:5-13 is designed to announce that the time of punishment is now over and that YHWH is about to act to

---

4   For a discussion of the overall structure of these chapters, see Sweeney, "Form-Critical Reassessment," 397–403; contra Floyd, *Minor Prophets*, 201–14, 237–42. For detailed discussion of the passages see the following commentary.

5   Contra Sweeney, "Form-Critical Reassessment," 397. See Floyd, *Minor Prophets*, 215–17; Ryou, *Zephaniah's*

Oracles, 186–207; and the following commentary.

6   For discussion of the summary-appraisal form, see Sweeney, *Isaiah 1–39*, 539; Brevard S. Childs, *Isaiah and the Assyrian Crisis* (SBT II/3; London: SCM, 1967) 128–36; J. W. Whedbee, *Isaiah and Wisdom* (Nashville: Abingdon, 1971) 75–79.

restore Jerusalem and Israel. Verse 5 is a syntactically independent statement by the prophet that asserts YHWH's righteousness. It thereby functions as the prophet's programmatic introduction to the following speech by YHWH in vv. 6-13 that makes several fundamental contentions: YHWH has punished the nations in order to convince Jerusalem to fear or respect its G-d and to accept instruction; YHWH is acting to purify the nations so that they will all recognize YHWH as their G-d; Jerusalem/Israel shall be purged of its own wickedness in keeping with the contentions of 1:2-18; and the humble remnant of Israel will be secure in its own land. The final subunit of the passage appears in the syntactically independent subunit in 3:14-20. The prophet presents YHWH's direct address to "the daughter of Zion" that is designed to convince her that YHWH is about to restore her as the divine wife, rejoicing over her, dealing with her oppressors, bringing her home, and restoring her honor and fortunes in the sight of the entire world.

In this manner, 2:1–3:20 is designed to convince the audience to accept the fundamental premise of the whole, that is, to seek YHWH. Although the text itself does not specify what this means exactly, the historical placement of this text in relation to the early years of Josiah's reign suggests that it calls on the Jerusalemite and Judean audience to support the program of King Josiah for Judean religious reform and national restoration. Josiah's program calls for the establishment of the Jerusalem Temple as the sole legitimate worship site for the entire kingdom of Israel, the purification of the temple from foreign religious influence, and the restoration of Davidic rule over all Israel, including both Judah and the territory of the former northern kingdom of Israel.[7]

The settings for such a text remains the same as that for 1:2-18, that is, the social setting of the Festival of Sukkot celebrated in the ancient Jerusalem Temple and the historical setting of the early reign of King Josiah at the outset of his program of religious reform and national restoration. As noted above, the Festival of Sukkot, celebrated for seven days beginning on the fifteenth day of the seventh month, marks the conclusion of the agricultural year when the grape and olive harvests are brought in immediately prior to the onset of the rainy season in the fall.[8] It also marks the occasion when the temple altar is dedicated for divine service (see 1 Kings 8; 2 Chr 6:1–7:11; Ezra 3:1-7; cf. 1 Kgs 12:25-33 in which Jeroboam ben Nebat institutes a new Festival of Sukkot in the eighth month in order to dedicate the altar at Bethel; see also 1 Macc 4:36-59 in which the Hasmonean dedication of the temple altar in the month of Kislev [Hanukkah] is modeled on the celebration of Sukkot). In that the conclusion of the harvest marks the completion of YHWH's provision of food for the nation, the festival celebrates YHWH's kingship in the world and serves as a means for the legitimation of the institutions that represent YHWH's kingship and care for the nation, the temple, and the monarchy. Sukkot therefore celebrates YHWH's role as the source of life, holiness, and righteousness in the kingdom. It is only natural that the festival is associated with the beginning of the new year,[9] or the celebration of the creation of the world, on the first day of the seventh month and the Day of Atonement,[10] or the day on which the nation asks forgiveness and attempts to purge itself from wrongdoing, on the tenth day of the seventh month. Such a combination presents a fitting setting for 2:1–3:20, which essentially calls on the people of Jerusalem and Judah to purge themselves of wrongdoing in order to prepare for YHWH's restoration of the nation following a period of punishment.

The early years of Josiah's reign saw the possibility of the collapse of the Assyrian Empire, which had controlled Judah as a vassal state since the end of the eighth century BCE. A series of important events had taken place during the seventh century—the waning of Assyrian influence in Egypt, the rise of the Saite Egyptian

---

7   For discussion of Josiah's reform and the literature associated with it, see Sweeney, *King Josiah*.

8   See Lev 23:33-43; Num 29:12-38; E. Kutsch and L. Jacobs, "Sukkot," *EncJud* 15:495–502; Sigmund Mowinckel, *Psalmenstudien II* (Kristiana: Dybwad, 1922).

9   Lev 23:23-25; Num 28:26-31; 29:1-6; L. Jacobs, "Rosh ha-Shanah," *EncJud* 14:305–10.

10 Lev 23:26-32; Num 29:7-11; M. D. Herr and J. Milgrom, "Day of Atonement," *EncJud* 5:1376–87.

Dynasty and its attempts to move against Philistia, the death of Ashurbanipal sometime between 631 and 627, the Babylonian revolts against Assyria in 652–648 and 626—that would support the prophet's contentions that Assyria was about to fall and that the restoration of Jerusalem was at hand. Again, the beginnings of Josiah's reform in the twelfth year of his reign (628–627) through the full implementation of the reform in his eighteenth year (622–621) constitutes the likely historical setting for the prophet's appeals to Jerusalem and Judah to purge themselves from evil and idolatry and to seek YHWH once again, as the nation was about to be restored to its former glory.

2

Translation

1 Assemble yourselves and gather,[a] O worthless nation,[b]

2   before the decree is born, (and) like chaff,
the day has passed,[c]

    before there comes upon you the angry
wrath of YHWH,[d]

    before there comes upon you the day of
the wrath of YHWH.

3 Seek YHWH, all you humble of the land[e]
who have carried out his law.[f]

Seek righteousness; seek humility;[g]
    perhaps[h] you will be hidden in the day of
the wrath of YHWH.

4 For Gaza shall be forsaken, and Ashkelon
desolate;

Ashdod, by noon they shall drive her out,
and Ekron shall be uprooted.[i]

a   Although the MT employs two imperative forms of the same root, i.e., הִתְקוֹשְׁשׁוּ וָקוֹשּׁוּ, lit. "gather your-selves and gather" (cf. Mur, התקשש וקשו), the versions employ combinations of two or more different verbs in order to distinguish their respective seman-tic functions: LXX, Συνάχϑητε καὶ συνδέϑητε, "gather together and unite"; TJ, אתכנשו ואיתו ואתקרבו, "gather yourselves, and come, and draw yourselves near"; Peshitta, ʾtknšw wtʾsrw, "gather yourselves and assemble"; Vulgate, convenite con-gregamini, "assemble, be gathered."

b   MT reads, הַגּוֹי לֹא נִכְסָף, "O unwanted/worthless nation" (cf. Mur, הגוי לא), but the versions wrestle with the meaning of the expression, i.e., LXX, τὸ ἔϑνος τὸ ἀπαίδευτον, "O boorish/undisciplined nation"; TJ, עם דרא דלא חמיד למתב לאוריתא, "O nation of the generation that does not desire to return to instruction/Torah"; Peshitta, ʿmʾ dlʾ rdʾ, "O unchastised/uninstructed nation"; Vulgate, gens non amabilis, "O unlovable/undesirable nation."

c   MT reads, בְּטֶרֶם לֶדֶת חֹק כְּמֹץ עָבַר יוֹם, lit. "before bearing a statute, like chaff a day has passed" (cf. Mur, כמץ עבר י]ום). The versions present several different renditions of this text: LXX, πρὸ τοῦ γενέσϑαι ὑμᾶς ὡς ἄνϑος παραπορευόμενον, "before you become like a passing flower"; TJ, לא תפוק עליכון גזירת בית דינא ותהון דמן לכמוצא מאידרא דנסבא רוחא וכסלא עדי מן קדם יומא, "before there comes upon you the decree of the lawcourt and you become resembling chaff from the thresh-ing floor that the wind carries away and like the dew that passes away from before the day"; Peshitta, ʿdʾ thwwn ʾyk ʿwrʾ dʾbr, "until you shall be as chaff that has passed"; Vulgate, priusquam pariat iussio quasi pulverem transeuntem diem, "before judgment comes forth like dust (clouds) passing (in a) day."

d   Cf. TJ, "before there comes upon you the strength (תקוף) of the anger of YHWH."

e   MT reads, כָּל־עַנְוֵי הָאָרֶץ, "all the humble of the land," apparently a unique formulation in the Hebrew Bible (but cf. עַנְוֵי אֶרֶץ in Amos 8:4). Although Milik follows MT in part by reading Mur 20:13 as כל[ע]נוי ארץ, examination of the photo-graph indicates that the text should read כל]ע[נ]יי ארץ, which corresponds to the reading of this expression in Ps 76:10 (cf. Isa 11:4; Job 24:4). It would appear that the scribe either corrected the text or erred in reading the expression with Ps 76:10.

f   MT reads, אֲשֶׁר מִשְׁפָּטוֹ פָּעָלוּ, "who have done his law," clearly taking פָּעָלוּ as a perfect pausal form of the verb פָּעַל, "to do" (cf. Mur, אשר משפטו פ]עלו). Because the accent athnach requires a strengthening of the vowels patah and patah hatup, the verb may also be read as a pausal form of the masculine plural imperative, פַּעֲלוּ, "do"; cf. LXX, κρίμα ἐργά-ζεσθε, "work at law" (lit. "law, work at"); Peshitta, wᶜbdw dynᵓ, "and do/perform the law." TJ and Vulgate generally read the expression like the MT.

g MT reads, בַּקְּשׁוּ־צֶדֶק בַּקְּשׁוּ עֲנָוָה, "seek righteousness, seek humility" (cf. Mur, צודקן בקשון ענוה בקשו). LXX rereads the phrase as καὶ δικαιοσύνην ζητέσατε καὶ ἀποκρίνεσθε αὐτά, "and seek righteousness, and answer/testify to them," which presupposes a slightly different reading of the Hebrew as וּבַקְּשׁוּ צֶדֶק וְעָנֻם. It is unlikely that LXX read a different *Vorlage*; rather, it appears to have reread the entirety of v. 3 in an effort to strengthen its exhortative character, remove the problem inherent in the Hebrew that the text addresses those who already do YHWH's will, and provide a stylistically more consistent text. The other versions read the text generally along the lines of the MT: TJ, "seek truth (קושטא), seek humility"; Peshitta, wbᶜw zdiqwtᵓ wmkykwtᵓ, "and seek righteousness and humility," apparently a stylistic improvement over the MT; Vulgate, *quaerite iudicium quaerite mansuetum*, "seek justice, seek gentleness."

h MT reads, אוּלַי, "perhaps" (see also Mur, אולי); cf. LXX, ὅπως (, "as, how, in such manner," which apparently eliminates the ambiguity of the Hebrew term in an effort to strengthen the exhortative character of the text.

i Note the assonantal character of this text; each verb is selected to reflect elements of the pronunciation of the name of each city: עַזָּה עֲזוּבָה תִהְיֶה (ᶜazzâ ᶜzûbâ tihyeh), "Gaza will be abandoned"; וְאַשְׁקְלוֹן לִשְׁמָמָה (wĕᵓašqĕlôn lišmāmâ), "and Ashkelon (will be) for desolation"; אַשְׁדּוֹד בַּצָּהֳרַיִם יְגָרְשׁוּהָ (ᵓašdôd baṣṣohŏrayim yĕgārĕšûhâ), "Ashdod, by noon, they will drive her out"; וְעֶקְרוֹן תֵּעָקֵר (wĕᶜeqrôn tēᶜāqēr), "and Ekron will be uprooted." The versions, of course, are limited in their ability to reproduce this assonance, since it is dependent on the original language. The LXX, TJ, and Peshitta make attempts, however, in their renditions of the statement concerning Ekron, "and Ekron shall be uprooted": LXX, καὶ Ακκαρων ἐκριζωθήσεται; TJ, ועקרון תתעקר; Peshitta, wᶜqrwn ttᶜqr.

Form and Setting

Zephaniah 2:1-4 constitutes the formal core of Zephaniah, on which the overall syntactical and rhetorical structure of the book as well as its generic character are based. Most scholars employ generic observations to define the fundamental unit as an exhortative address in 2:1-3,[1] but the syntactical structure of the passage points to the inclusion of v. 4 as well.[2] The passage is demarcated at the outset by the initial masculine plural imperatives הִתְקוֹשְׁשׁוּ וָקוֹשּׁוּ, "assemble yourselves and gather," in v. 1, which lack any syntactical connection to the preceding announcement by the prophet of the day of YHWH in 1:2-18. The imperative address to the nation at large and the third person references to YHWH and the day

of YHWH in vv. 2 and 3 indicate that the passage presupposes the prophet as the speaker in this passage and that he continues to address the people of Jerusalem and Judah as in 1:2-18. The masculine plural imperative and imperfect verbal address forms in v. 3 indicate the continuation of this perspective.

Nevertheless, the cessation of the masculine plural address forms in v. 3 do not indicate the complete closure of the textual subunit. Instead, the conjunctive function of the introductory כִּי in v. 4 must be considered. Most scholars consider the portrayal of impending disaster for the four Philistine cities in v. 4 to be part of the formal oracles concerning the nations that appear through the balance of Zephaniah 2. Consequently, the initial כִּי is judged to have an emphatic function, but it

1 See, e.g., Hunter, *Seek the Lord*, 259–71; Irsigler, *Gottesgericht*, 113–17, 312–18; Ben Zvi, *Zephaniah*, 295–98; Vlaardingerbroek, *Zephaniah*, 214–16; Floyd, *Minor Prophets*, 215–18; Sweeney, "Form-Critical Reassessment," 399; Seybold, *Zephanja*, 102–4; Renaud, *Sophonie*, 218–22; Keller, 197–99; Rudolph, *Zephanja*, 271–75; Ball, *Zephaniah*, 114–20; Horst, *Propheten*, 195; Elliger, *Zephanja*, 67–69; Nowack, *Propheten*, 296–97; Sellin, *Zwölfprophetenbuch*, 428–30; J. M. P. Smith, *Zephaniah*, 211–15; van Hoonacker, *Prophètes*, 516; Marti, *Dodekaphopheton*, 367–68.

2 See Ryou, *Zephaniah's Oracles*, 186–207, esp. 186 n. 44, 294–96; Bennett, "Zephaniah," 684–86; Berlin, *Zephaniah*, 99, 101–2. Note also the presence of a masoretic *sĕtûmâ* (closed section) following v. 4, which indicates that the Masoretes read vv. 1-4 as a single unit and v. 5 as the beginning of the next unit. A similar division appears in the text of the Peshitta.

plays no conjunctive role.[3] Although such a conclusion is warranted on thematic grounds, the formal syntactical features of the text point to a different conclusion. First, כִּי may indeed function in an emphatic role, but it never relinquishes its conjunctive or subordinating character. Even when it does appear at the head of a formally defined unit, its subordinating or conjunctive role is present; for example, "for (כִּי) in the night that Ar was laid waste, Moab was undone," indicates a circumstance for the main concern with Moab (Isa 15:1); "for (כִּי) my lord YHWH does nothing without revealing his secret to his servants the prophets" (Amos 3:7) provides the climax and conclusion to the prior wisdom analogy in Amos 3:3-6;[4] "what is his name and what is the name of his son; for (כִּי) you know" (Prov 30:4) indicates the resulting presupposition that the addressee does indeed know the name of the person in question. When one considers the conjunctive force of the כִּי in v. 4, it provides a reason why the prophet's audience should heed his calls to gather and seek YHWH; that is, the impending destruction of the Philistine cities indicates the potential consequences for Jerusalem and Judah if the people do not return to YHWH.

This observation is reinforced by the third person descriptive character of v. 4, that is, no shift in addressee is apparent from vv. 1-3 to v. 4. Indeed, a change in the identification of the prophet's addressees is not evident until v. 5, in which the second person address forms indicate that the prophet's הוֹי ("woe") oracle is addressed to the Philistines.[5] Although the content of v. 4 indicates a concern with the Philistines like that of vv. 5-7, the absence of a clear shift in addressee until v. 5 indicates that v. 4 is intended to be read together with the address to the Jerusalemite/Judean nation in vv. 1-3, whereas v. 5 marks a shift in address to the Philistines

themselves.[6] At no point in the balance of the oracles concerning the nations in 2:5-15 does the address shift once more to Jerusalem/Judah.

Overall, the generic characteristics of vv. 1-3 and 4 and the causative function of the initial כִּי of v. 4 point to the basic syntactical structure and rhetorical function of this passage. The two sets of imperative address forms in vv. 1-2 and 3 clearly indicate that vv. 1-3 as a whole are designed to call on the audience to do something—gather and seek YHWH. The subordinate clauses that follow each set of imperatives, that is, the בְּטֶרֶם, "before," clauses in v. 2 and the אוּלַי, "perhaps," clause in v. 3bβ, provide both positive and negative reasons that are designed to persuade the audience to follow the instructions of the prophet (e.g., "before the decree is born . . . before the angry wrath of YHWH comes upon you . . ."; "perhaps you will be hidden in the day of YHWH's wrath"). But these clauses present only theoretical possibilities concerning the imagined scenario of the day of YHWH's wrath. Verse 4, with its definitive statement of the impending threat to the Philistine cities, provides an unambiguous demonstration of YHWH's intentions; that is, the fate of the Philistines portends the fate of Jerusalem and Judah if the people do not follow the prophet's instructions.

Thus vv. 1-3 are clearly exhortative—or more properly parenetic—in character because they hold out the possibility of negative or positive consequences depending on the audience's choice of action. There is, of course, a presumption that the audience is sympathetic to the prophet's overtures, since he characterizes them both as "the worthless/unvalued nation" and as those "who have carried out his [YHWH's] law," presumably to suggest to them that their time of action has come. Verse 4 is demonstrative because it points to the unambiguous

---

3   For discussion of the functions of כִּי, see Anneli Aejmelaeus, "Function and Interpretation of כִּי in Biblical Hebrew," *JBL* 105 (1986) 193–209; Anton Schoors, "The Particle כִּי," *OTS* 21 (1981) 240–76; James Muilenburg, "The Linguistic and Rhetorical Usages of the Particle כִּי in the Old Testament," *HUCA* 32 (1961) 135–60.

4   See my discussion of this passage in Sweeney, *Twelve Prophets*, 220–21.

5   For discussion of the syntactical analysis of woe oracles as address forms, see Hillers, "*Hôy*."

6   Contra Roberts, *Zephaniah*, 196, who argues that v.

4 must originally have been read after v. 5, but that it was transposed to its present position to provide an editorial link between 1:2–2:3 and 2:4-15. His position is based on a rigid view of genre as the basic constituent of texts rather than the recognition that texts are uniquely formulated and employ generic language within texts to serve more immediate rhetorical goals.

reality of the impending threat against the Philistine cities as a means to convince the audience to follow the prophet's instructions. When these two elements are placed together to form the larger textual entity of vv. 1-4, the parenetic character of the texts emerges as the dominant generic characteristic in that the demonstrative character of v. 4 is designed to serve the parenetic function of vv. 1-3. Overall, 2:1-4 constitutes a parenetic address that is designed to convince the prophet's Jerusalemite/Judean audience to gather and seek YHWH. It includes both the parenetic address proper in vv. 1-3 and the basic reason or motivation for the prophet's appeal to the people in v. 4. Furthermore, the parenetic character of these verses influences the generic character of the entire body of the book in 1:2–3:20, in that the preceding announcement of the day of YHWH in 1:2-18 and the following oracles concerning the nations and Jerusalem/Judah, respectively, in 2:5-15 and 3:1-20 are also designed to reinforce the rhetorical goal of convincing the people to turn to YHWH as a means of avoiding the consequences of the Day of YHWH and realizing the benefits of the restoration projected for Jerusalem/Israel.

The setting for such an address must appear in the early reign of Josiah, at a time when his program of religious reform and national restoration was just getting underway. Although the specific referents of the appeals to seek YHWH, justice, and humility are unclear from the present form of this text, such appeals would support Josiah's efforts at purifying the temple as the religious center of the nation and at extending Davidic rule over all of the territory of Israel and Judah. According to 1 Kgs 22:3 and 2 Chr 34:8, Josiah's reforms began in the eighteenth year of his reign (622 BCE). 2 Chr 34:3, however, indicates that Josiah began to seek YHWH in the eighth year of his reign (632) and that he began to purge Jerusalem and Judah of foreign or syncretistic religious influence in the twelfth year of his reign (628). This last date is particularly important because it appears to coincide with the beginnings of the Babylonian revolt against Assyria in 627. This suggests that Josiah may well have coordinated his actions with those of the Babylonians, who had been allies of the house of David from the time of Hezekiah's revolt against Assyria in the late eighth century.[7] It would appear from this that the prophet Zephaniah was instrumental in attempting to raise support for the king's program among the people of Jerusalem and Judah during the early years of his reign.

The versions, of course, would read this text somewhat differently based on the historical circumstances and presuppositions of their own respective periods. As the textual notes indicate, the LXX does not presuppose a potentially sympathetic audience, as it reads the phrase "(those) who have carried out his law" as an imperative, "work at law," which suggests the need of the audience to begin doing something that they have not done before. Likewise, the LXX's reading of the command "seek righteousness, seek humility," as "seek righteousness and answer/testify to them" serves a similar purpose. Finally, the LXX's reading of "perhaps (you will be hidden)" as "in such manner (you will be hidden)" reinforces the certainty of a positive outcome should the people choose to seek YHWH and observe YHWH's laws. In this manner, the LXX reading appears designed to strengthen the exhortative character of the passage by attempting to convince the audience to change its course of action from nonobservance of YHWH's laws to observance. Such a concern might well reflect the reading of this passage in relation to the circumstances of Hellenistic Alexandria or even Judea from the third/second century BCE on through the second/third century CE, in which elements of the Jewish population had abandoned a strictly observant Jewish lifestyle to become assimilated to the dominant Hellenistic or Greco-Roman culture. In the aftermath of the destruction of the temple in 70 CE and the failed Bar Kochba revolt of 132–135 CE, the LXX text of Zephaniah would have provided a theological perspective to explain why such judgment had taken place: the people had failed to heed the prophet's call. This perspective is certainly dominant in early Christianity in the centuries following the Roman destruction of the temple and Judea.

---

7   See Kuhrt, *Ancient Near East*, 589–90; T. C. Mitchell, *CAH*, vol. III/2: *The Assyrian and Babylonian Empires and Other States of the Near East, from the Eighth to the* Sixth Centuries B.C. (Cambridge: Cambridge Univ. Press, 1991) 390–91.

Targum Jonathan does not present textual rereadings as extensive as those of the LXX, but it does appear to presuppose the Roman destruction of the temple and Judea. By reading the initial reference to "the unwanted nation" as "the people of the generation that does not desire to return to the instruction/Torah of YHWH," it presents the view that those who fomented the revolts against Rome were guilty of abandoning Torah and thus brought punishment upon themselves. Such a characterization implicitly calls on the readers of the Targum not to repeat the mistakes of that generation and to heed the call of the prophet to follow YHWH's will—and thus to adhere to YHWH's Torah.

The Peshitta and Vulgate show little substantive change in the reading of these verses. Nevertheless, both originate as Christian translations that would presuppose that the prophet's call is directed to Christians in the aftermath of the destruction of the Jerusalem Temple and its significance for understanding the origins of Christianity.

■ **1** The initial imperative combination of v. 1a, הִתְקוֹשְׁשׁוּ וָקוֹשּׁוּ, here translated as "assemble yourselves and gather," has been very controversial in exegetical discussion.[8] There is some disagreement concerning the presentation of the imperative forms, as the Murabbaʿat Scroll reads them as התקששו וקשו, clearly omitting the plene *waw* of the first imperative and the reduplicated *šin* of the second, but the reading of the forms in 1QpZeph corresponds to the masoretic reading of the verbs. Most interpreters agree in deriving both of the imperative forms from the verbal root קשׁשׁ, identifying the first instance as a *hithpolel* form of the verb and the second as *polel*.[9] Apparently, the masoretic placement of a *dageš* in the *šin* of the second imperative, קוֹשּׁוּ, makes this clear, since the root would otherwise be read as an

imperative form of קוּשׁ or יקשׁ, that is, קוֹשׁוּ, "lay bait" or "lay a trap," which would change the meaning of the command completely.[10] Normally, the root קשׁשׁ refers to the gathering of sticks or stubble, as indicated by its use in Exod 5:7, 12, where it describes the gathering of stubble by the Hebrew slaves to make bricks for the Egyptians; Num 15:32, 33, where it describes the actions of a man who gathers sticks on the Sabbath and therefore desecrates the holy day by working; and 1 Kgs 17:10, 12, where it describes the gathering of sticks by the widow of Zarephath who intends to cook a meal for herself and her son. In each case, the verb refers to the action of gathering, but it is always associated with sticks or stubble. The appearance in Biblical Hebrew of the noun קשׁ, "stubble" or "chaff," which derives from this root, indicates that stubble or chaff is inherent in the meaning of the root. Such an association seems inappropriate in the present context, which speaks of the gathering of people rather than of stubble or chaff, and therefore commentators have puzzled over the meaning of these terms. Indeed, the verb קשׁשׁ is never used elsewhere to describe the simple gathering or assembly of people.

Nevertheless, the use of the verb and its inherent relation to the gathering of sticks or chaff appears to be a deliberate choice in this context because of the general metaphorical portrayal of the sacrifice that is to be carried out on the Day of YHWH. The commentary on 1:7-18 above notes the metaphorical and ironic role that sacrifice plays in 1:7-18, especially since the people are invited to a sacrifice in which they expect to participate as worshipers, but in fact they are intended to serve as sacrificial victims. The gathering of sticks or wood is an essential element of the preparation of the sacrificial altar, and the prophet's use of these verbs in the command to gather builds on this metaphorical and ironic

8   See esp. Ben Zvi, *Zephaniah*, 137–39, for a summary of discussion.

9   Ben Zvi, *Zephaniah*, 137 n. 386; Renaud, *Sophonie*, 216; Marti, *Dodekapropheton*, 367; cf. Roberts, *Zephaniah*, 186–87; Horst, *Propheten*, 192; van Hoonacker, *Prophètes*, 516; Ball, *Zephaniah*, 97. Berlin, *Zephaniah*, 196–97; Ryou, *Zephaniah's Oracles*, 17–20; Sellin, *Zwölfprophetenbuch*, 428; J. M. P. Smith, *Zephaniah*, 221, consider the forms to be a combination of *hithpolel* and *qal*. Vlaardingerbroek, *Zephaniah*, 117, is unable to translate the statement; Nowack, *Propheten*, 296, considers it to be hopeless; Keller,

Sophonie, 197, follows the versions. Junker, *Sophonia*, 75; Gerleman, *Zephanja*, 23–24, derive the second imperative from the root קשׁה, "be firm."

10 The latter derivation and meaning are proposed by Rudolph, *Zephanja*, 271; Sabottka, *Zephanja*, 60–62.

strategy by portraying the gathering of the people as the gathering of the very sticks that are to be burned up as part of the sacrifice on the Day of YHWH. By this means, the implicit meaning of the prophet's summons becomes clear. The people are not summoned to consume the sacrifice; they are summoned to constitute the sacrifice. The rhetorical strategy of the prophet is therefore conveyed by the choice of the verb קשש to describe the people's assembly and the threat that the Day of YHWH actually poses to them. The combination of *hithpolel* and *polel* forms reinforces this strategy. The reflexive *hithpolel* form indicates that the action of the people is to be focused on gathering themselves. The *polel* form, however, is commonly used for the gathering of wood or chaff in the passages cited above, and conveys the normal expectations that they are to gather wood for the sacrifice.

The versions render this in different ways. Targum Jonathan, the Peshitta, and the Vulgate understand the verbs to convey the simple act of assembly. Thus TJ employs three imperatives, אתכנשו ואיתו ואתקרבו, "gather yourselves and come and draw near," to render the commands. The Peshitta employs two, ʾtknšw wʾlʾsrw, "gather yourselves and assemble," and the Vulgate reads, *convenite congregamnini*, "come together, assemble." The LXX, however, attempts to employ the imagery of sheaves of grain that are gathered and bound together simultaneously with the imagery of a gathering crowd, συνάχθητε καὶ συνδέθητε, "gather together and unite/bind together."

The reference to the prophet's addressees as לֹא נִכְסָף, here translated, "O worthless [nation]," also presents problems. The verbal root כסף generally means "to long for," "to desire" (see Gen 31:30; Ps 84:3; cf. Job 14:15; Ps 17:12), which apparently underlies the use of the root for the noun כֶּסֶף, "silver, money." In later forms of Hebrew, however, the root carries the meaning "to be disappointed, pale, white," and it is frequently understood to mean "to be ashamed," based on Aramaic and Arabic cognates. It is possible to render the expression here as "O shameless nation," based on the general context of condemnation of the people by the prophet.[11]

The understanding of the root in relation to the absence of shame appears to have informed the transla-

tion of several of the versions. Thus the LXX reads τὸ ἔθνος τὸ ἀπαίδευτον, "the boorish/uneducated nation," which relates the meaning of shamelessness to the lack of education or training that would make one aware of responsibility or self-presentation. A similar rendition appears in the Peshitta, ʿmʾ dlʾ rdʾ, "O unchastised/uninstructed nation." Targum Jonathan introduces an element of accusation that is designed to point to the ignorance and rebelliousness of the generation that suffered the destruction of the temple by the Romans: עם דרא דלא חמיד למתב לאוריתא, "O people of the generation that did not desire to return to the Torah/instruction." This, of course, is in keeping with the view of the Targumists that only those who had committed wrongdoing could be subject to divine punishment. The Vulgate, however, renders the term in relation to the desirability of the nation to G-d, *gens non amabilis*, "O unloved nation," which indicates an element of divine judgment against the nation.

The use of the verb לֹא נִכְסָף seems once again a deliberate choice on the part of the author of this passage to convey metaphorically the irony of the people's situation. By employing the verb כסף, the same root that stands as the basis for כֶּסֶף, "silver," the author plays on the earlier characterization of the people as the "nation of Canaanite/traders" and "those who handle money (כֶּסֶף)" in 1:11. In this manner, the earlier accusations leveled against the people, that is, that they value prosperity but not YHWH, then come into play as they are considered "worthless" or "undesirable" even though they are accused of pursuing wealth. Such a ploy of course parallels the previously mentioned characterization of their assembly as a command to gather wood in preparation for a sacrifice for which they will unknowingly serve as the sacrificial victims.

■ **2** Verse 2 contains a sequence of three dependent temporal clauses, which are apparently intended to convey to the audience the urgency and necessity of following the prophet's appeal in v. 1 to assemble. Each is introduced by a form of the particle בְּטֶרֶם, which is usually employed adverbially to express time, that is, "before," "ere." In general, the verse is designed to warn the audience that they should take action quickly before the punishment of the Day of YHWH is realized. To

11   Gerleman, *Zephanja*, 24.

clarify the formulation and interpretation of the verse, however, one must address a number of textual and philological problems.

Several such issues appear in v. 2a, presently read in the MT as בְּטֶרֶם לֶדֶת חֹק כְּמֹץ עָבַר יוֹם, and translated, "before the decree is born and (like) chaff, the day has passed."

The first involves the phrase לֶדֶת חֹק, literally "to bear a decree/statute." The appearance of the infinitive construct of ילד, "to bear (a child)," following בְּטֶרֶם is unusual in that an infinitive construct never follows בְּטֶרֶם elsewhere in the Hebrew Bible. It is not impossible, as substantives follow בְּטֶרֶם in Isa 17:14, "before morning (בְּטֶרֶם בֹּקֶר), they are no more"; and Isa 28:4, "(it is) like the first ripe fruit before summer (בְּטֶרֶם קַיִץ)"; and an infinitive construction, albeit without the preposition ל, "to, for," follows מִטֶּרֶם in Hag 2:15, "before stone is placed upon stone (מִטֶּרֶם שׂוּם אֶל־אָבֶן) in the temple of YHWH." Nevertheless, the construction remains difficult, as the preposition ל plus infinitive construct never follows בְּטֶרֶם. Normally, an imperfect verb form follows the expression.

Furthermore, the phrase לֶדֶת חֹק is itself problematic; the verb ילד is normally employed in reference to the birth of new life, but the use in relation to a decree is unique. The verb can be used metaphorically to refer to the "birth" of wickedness (Ps 7:15; Job 15:35; Isa 33:11); of vain efforts depicted as bringing forth wind (Isa 26:18), or as a day that "brings forth" events (Prov 27:1). It is therefore not impossible to allow the text to stand as it appears in the MT.

Nevertheless, the phrase bears little relation to the language pertaining to the gathering of the harvest that appears in the immediate context of Zeph 2:1-3 and the larger context of 1:2-18. Scholars have proposed any number of emendations that would demonstrate such a relationship, for example, תִּנָּדֵפוּ, "you will be expelled/ driven away";[12] לֹא תִהְיוּ, "you will not be (like chaff)";[13] לִדֹק תִּהְיוּ, "you will be dust";[14] לֹא תִדַּקְּכֶם, "you are crushed (like passing chaff)";[15] לֹא תִהְיוּ כְדַק, "you will not become like dust";[16] לֹא תֵרָחֵק, "you [singular] will not be removed";[17] לֹא תִדָּחֲקוּ, "you will not be oppressed";[18] לֹא תֵרָחֲקוּ, "you [plural] will not be removed";[19] לֶדֶת חֵק, "before your lap gives birth to worthless chaff";[20] and לֹא תִדָּחֲקוּ, "you will not be driven away."[21] Although many scholars follow the emendation suggested by *BHK* and *BHS*, לֹא תִדָּחֲקוּ, "you will not be oppressed," apparently originally proposed by Köhler,[22] an increasing number are reading the text as it stands in the MT because of the apparent lack of consensus and because the MT, despite its difficulties, appears to make some sense.[23] It is not impossible that some form of the verb דחק, "to oppress, squeeze, impel," lies behind this text, perhaps a reflexive infinitive form like the *ithpeal* form in Aramaic,[24] but clear evidence is lacking. Consequently, it seems best to read the MT as it stands. In this case, the expression warns the audience to gather and take action before YHWH's decree of judgment against them is metaphorically "born" or comes into being.

A third problem involves the phrase כְּמֹץ עָבַר יוֹם, "like chaff, a/the day has passed," or "like chaff that passes (in a) day." The primary problem appears to be the exact

12 Schwally, "Sephanjâ," 182.
13 Marti, *Dodekapropheton*, 368; Wellhausen, *Propheten*, 152.
14 J. M. P. Smith, *Zephaniah*, 222.
15 Van Hoonacker, *Prophètes*, 518.
16 Nowack, *Propheten*, 297.
17 Sellin, *Zwölfprophetenbuch*, 429.
18 *BHK*; *BHS*; Junker, *Sophonia*, 76; Elliger, *Zephanja*, 67; Keller, *Sophonie*, 197; Irsigler, *Gottesgericht*, 63; Renaud, *Sophonie*, 218.
19 Horst, *Propheten*, 192.
20 Sabottka, *Zephanja*, 64.
21 Roberts, *Zephaniah*, 185, 188.
22 Ludwig Köhler, "Emendationen," in Karl Budde, ed., *Vom Alten Testament, Karl Marti zum siebzigsten Geburtstage Gewidmet* (BZAW 37; Giessen: Töpelmann, 1925) 173–80, esp. 176.

23 See Gerleman, *Zephanja*, 25; Rudolph, *Zephanja*, 272; Ball, *Zephanja*, 98–100; Hunter, *Seek the Lord*, 263–64; Seybold, *Zephanja*, 102, 103 (contra idem, *Satirische Prophetie*, 35–38; idem, "Text und Textauslegung in Zef 2,1-3," BN 25 [1984] 49–54); Ben Zvi, *Zephaniah*, 143; Berlin, *Zephaniah*, 97; Ryou, *Zephaniah's Oracles*, 23–24; cf. Vlaardingerbroek, *Zephaniah*, 119–21.
24 Jastrow, *Dictionary*, 1:293.

interpretation of the syntax of the phrase. If יוֹם, "day," is read as the subject, "like chaff, a/the day has passed," it refers to the fleeting opportunity to assemble and respond to the prophet's demand to seek YHWH that appears in the following verse. If מֹץ, "chaff," it is read as the subject, "like chaff that passes (in a) day," it would convey the imminence of the previously mentioned decree of YHWH. The absence of clearly defined syntactical criteria in this expression enables it to convey either meaning. It can therefore be read both in relation to the prophet's prior presentation of the Day of YHWH and the prophet's coming exhortation that the people seek YHWH.

Finally, scholars have noted the enigmatic use of בְּטֶרֶם לֹא, literally "before not," in the two subordinate clauses of v. 2b. Both clauses convey the immediacy of the threat of YHWH that might come upon the people if they do not act, expressed first in relation to the "angry wrath of YHWH" (חֲרוֹן אַף־ה׳) and then in relation to the "day of YHWH's anger" (יוֹם אַף־ה׳). In this manner, the prophet ties the exhortation back into the theme of the Day of YHWH, which appeared previously in 1:2-18 and which will appear momentarily in the next verse. The expression בְּטֶרֶם never appears with לֹא elsewhere in the Hebrew Bible.[25] Although unusual, the appearance of לֹא immediately following בְּטֶרֶם conveys the prophet's rhetorical strategy to convince the audience that the consequences of the day of YHWH are something to be avoided. Gesenius-Kautzsch notes these statements as double negations in the same sentence that do not neutralize each other, but instead provide emphasis.[26] In this manner, the prophet prepares the audience for the primary exhortation that appears in v. 3.

The versions apply several different approaches in their respective readings of this verse. The LXX reads, "Before you become like a passing flower; before the anger of the L-rd comes upon you; before the day of the wrath of the L-rd comes upon you." Apparently, the LXX eliminates the problem of לֶדֶת חֹק by reading πρὸ τοῦ γενέσθαι ὑμας ὡς ἄνθος, "before you become like a flower." Although this reading has prompted those who have emended the Hebrew to read תִּהְיוּ, "you shall

be/become," the Greek verb γίνομαι also means, "to come into being" or "to be born," and therefore indicates the translator's attempt to account for the verb לֶדֶת, "to bear," in the text. The choice of the term ἄνθος, "flower," shows a similar attempt to play on the use of מֹץ, "chaff," in the Hebrew, as ἄνθος (means, "flower, dust, scum, froth, anything thrown out." Overall, the LXX characteristically attempts to present a much smoother text. By removing the reference to the decree, it also focuses on the consequences for the people themselves and therefore stresses the immediacy of the threat and the need to make a decision quickly concerning the threat at hand.

Targum Jonathan reads, "Before there comes upon you the decree of the court and you become like/resemble chaff from the threshing floor that the wind carries away and like the dew that passes away from before the day; before there shall come upon you the strength of the anger of YHWH; before there shall come upon you the day of the anger of YHWH." The Targumist emphasizes the role of the divine decree represented in the book, but reads the Hebrew verb לֶדֶת, "to bear," as לְדַת, "for law/judgment." This, of course, allows for a smoother reading and facilitates the reading of the following simile as a statement of what the people will become, that is, like passing chaff, if they do not take action. The Targumist plays on the meaning of מֹץ, however, as the roots מֹץ/מצץ mean "to suck dry," in reference either to water itself or to plants that require water. Consequently, the Aramaic reads the phrase in relation to both the chaff of the threshing floor and to dew that evaporates in the morning sun. In this manner, the two readings account for both the verb עָבַר, "(it) has passed," and the noun יוֹם, "day," and resolves the problems mentioned above concerning how to read them together in the same statement.

The Peshitta adopts a reading much like the LXX: "Until you shall be as chaff that has passed and until there shall come upon you the angry wrath of the L-rd and until there is come upon you the day of the wrath of the L-rd." Like the LXX, it reads the verb לֶדֶת much like γίνομαι in its use of the Syriac verb thwwn, "you shall become." It also eliminates like the LXX the reference to

---

25 See Ben Zvi, *Zephaniah*, 143–44.
26 GKC, §152y.

the decree so that the text reads much more smoothly. Also like the LXX, it drops the reference to the "day" that had caused so much confusion as noted above. Indeed, the text reads much like the LXX in focusing on the judgment that will come upon the people.

The Vulgate reads, "before judgment comes forth like dust clouds passing in a day; before there comes over you the raging anger of the L-rd; before there comes over you the day of the anger of the L-rd." Jerome apparently finds a way to retain both the reference to the decree and to the verb לֶדֶת. The decree becomes *iussio*, "law" or "judgment," as in TJ, and the verb ילד is then rendered less graphically as *pario*, "to bring forth." Jerome also protects the verb עבר, "to pass," and the reference to the "day." The result is a reading of the passage that emphasizes the immediacy of the divine decree of judgment.

The Murabbaʿat text is fragmentary, but corresponds precisely to that of the MT. 1QpZeph offers only orthographic variants.

■ **3** Verse 3 presents the primary statements of the prophet's exhortation, in which he calls on his audience to seek YHWH. Whereas vv. 1-2 employed one imperative statement to call on the audience to assemble and three subordinate clauses to provide motivation by warning the audience of the impending threat posed by the Day of YHWH, v. 3 employs three imperatives to call on the audience to seek YHWH, righteousness, and humility, and one subordinate clause to provide motivation in reference to the day of YHWH's wrath. Altogether, the prophet's statements call on the people to take part in King Josiah's efforts to purify Jerusalem from the foreign influence and religious syncretism that would have accompanied Assyrian hegemony over the region.

The primary interpretive problems of this verse concern as much its contents as its addressees.[27] The addressees are identified as "all the humble of the land who have done/performed his [YHWH's] law," which is somewhat anomalous because it suggests that the prophet's appeal is directed to those who are already doing what he asks. Furthermore, this identification of the audience appears to clash with the prior reference to the audience as "the worthless nations" in v. 1, which suggests an audience that does not carry out YHWH's will as understood by the prophet.

The problem is engendered, however, by some rather wooden readings of these verses that assume that the prophet knows whether he is speaking to a sympathetic or a hostile crowd. In order to understand these references, the interpreter must take account of the rhetorical situation of such speech, in which the prophet attempts to convince his audience to adopt his viewpoint and carry out the actions that he recommends. In such a situation, it is unlikely that he knows fully where each member of his audience stands on the issue, and even if he does know whether the audience at large is sympathetic, he still must appeal to its sense of self-identity to achieve his goals.

In such a situation of persuasion, the characterization of the audience plays a crucial role. The prophet first refers to the audience in vv. 1-2 with language that suggests its failure to identify with YHWH's or the prophet's recommended course of action. This characterization appears with the prophet's threatening language of the coming day of YHWH's wrath and the appeal to assemble. In such a context, the negative characterization of the audience serves his rhetorical goals in that it identifies the audience as those who are subject to YHWH's threat; they therefore need to hear his appeal and consider his appeal to return to YHWH. The prophet then refers to the audience in v. 3, which reference suggests that the audience has already adopted his viewpoint and will carry out his recommendation to seek YHWH. In this regard, he employs the designation of the audience as "all the humble of the land who do his law" to prompt the audience to identify with his message and therefore to make the choice to follow his recommended course of action.

The prophet's strategy is facilitated by the vague nature of his imperative appeals. The basic demand appears in the first command, "seek YHWH" (בַּקְּשׁוּ אֶת־יהוה). The verb בקשׁ is sometimes understood to be a

27   For summaries of the discussion, see Hunter, *Seek the Lord*, 264–70; Ben Zvi, *Zephaniah*, 144; Ryou, *Zephaniah's Oracles*, 25–26; Rudolph, *Zephanja*, 273–74; Vlaardingerbroek, *Zephaniah*, 115–16; Irsigler, *Gottesgericht*, 113–17; Floyd, *Minor Prophets*, 215–16.

technical term that refers to oracular divination or cultic inquiry, but the present context requires only that it function in its general sense of seeking or turning to YHWH. Of course, this statement contrasts with that in 1:6, which charges that people in Jerusalem/Judah have turned away from YHWH and neither "seek" YHWH nor "inquire" of YHWH. Most interpreters recognize that such a demand, of course, entails the rejection of syncretistic or foreign religious practice, such as that outlined in 1:2-18, but one must consider the context of religious syncretism in which those who engaged in such practice likely considered themselves to be adherents of YHWH. They simply engaged in practices that tended to identify YHWH with pagan or non-Judean religious symbols and practices. Indeed, the presupposition of identification with YHWH would further serve the prophet's rhetorical goals, as he might presume that the audience already does consider itself to be "seeking YHWH." He gives few details as to what he requires the audience to do, and the appeal to seek YHWH would hardly be contested. Much the same might apply to his following two imperative appeals to "seek righteousness" (בַּקְּשׁוּ צֶדֶק) and to "seek humility" (בַּקְּשׁוּ עֲנָוָה), neither of which would provoke much resistance from the audience. Of course, neither demand states exactly what the prophet means by "righteousness" or "humility." His immediate strategy is to persuade the audience to identify with him and to accept his program. The details will follow later.

The prophet returns to the initial premise of his appeal to the people in the final statement of the verse (3bβ), the impending threat of the day of YHWH. The statement is formulated to appeal to the audience's fear of potential consequences by the initial particle, אוּלַי, "perhaps," followed by the suggestion that the people might be hidden and thus spared on the day of YHWH's wrath. Of course, this recalls the basic theme of the prophet's parenesis in 2:1-4 and his announcement in 1:2-18: the Day of YHWH and the threat that it poses to Jerusalem and Judah.

The versions display several different readings of this verse. Chief among them is the LXX, which reads the text very differently from the MT: "Seek the L-rd, all the humble of the land; work at law and seek righteousness and mark/answer them; in such manner you shall be sheltered in the day of the L-rd's wrath." This reading at first appearance seems to presuppose some major textual changes or errors,[28] but a closer examination of LXX's language indicates that it is reading the same text as MT. The first is the threefold imperative chain, κρίμα ἐργάζεσθε καὶ δικαιοσύνην ζητήσατε καὶ ἀποκρίνεσθε αὐτά" law work at and righteousness seek and answer/mark them." Many scholars note the strikingly different reading of the Hebrew, אֲשֶׁר מִשְׁפָּטוֹ פָּעָלוּ, "who have done/performed his law," which indicates the absence of the relative pronoun אֲשֶׁר, "who," and the pronominal suffix וֹ, "his," in מִשְׁפָּטוֹ, "his law." The change in verb form is also noted, but it is striking that the imperative ἐργάζεσθε, "work at," is actually an alternative translation of פָּעָלוּ, "they have done/worked," in the MT. The form is influenced by the accent *athnach*, which requires the pausal form of the MT, but the normal form of the verb is פָּעֲלוּ, which is nearly identical to masculine plural imperative form, פַּעֲלוּ; indeed, the pausal forms of the two verbs would be identical. It appears that the LXX translator adopted an imperative reading of פָּעֲלוּ and eliminated both אֲשֶׁר, "who," and the pronominal suffix וֹ, "his," to make the reading work.

Interestingly, the LXX also eliminates the imperative בַּקְּשׁוּ, "seek," from the phrase בַּקְּשׁוּ עֲנָוָה, "seek humility," and rereads the noun עֲנָוָה as "mark/answer them," which is the equivalent to Hebrew עֲנוּהָ, "answer it," except that the Greek presupposes a plural direct object to account for the two antecedents. The reason for such a rereading is somewhat perplexing until one realizes that the verb ענה also means, "to act as a witness/testify," in a court setting (see Gen 30:33; 1 Sam 12:3; 2 Sam 21:16; Isa 3:9; Mic 6:3; Job 15:6, etc.). This means that the LXX would have read the verb עֲנוּהָ as "testify to it," which supports its earlier appeal to "work at law" and to "seek righteousness." Thus the two imperatives, "work at law" and "seek righteousness," are followed and reinforced by a command to "witness to it (them)" or "answer to it (them)," that is, answer/testify to law and righteousness.

The LXX's reading of the verse therefore presupposes, in contrast to the MT, that the audience does not already do G-d's law. Instead, they must be persuaded to do it. This reinforces the exhortative character of the verse and resolves the difficulty with the designation of the

---

28 See Gerleman, *Zephanja*, 27.

audience as "the worthless nation" (MT) or "the unedu-cated nation" (LXX) in v. 1. The LXX also eliminates the ambiguity of the term אוּלַי, "perhaps," in the concluding statement, "perhaps you will be hidden in the day of YHWH's wrath." Instead, it employs ὅπος, "in such man-ner," which provides some measure of certainty that the audience will be spared on the day of YHWH if they fol-low the prophet's recommendations: "in such manner you shall be sheltered in the day of the L-rd's wrath."

The Peshitta appears to follow largely in the footsteps of the LXX with its rendition of the verse: "Seek the L-rd, all of you humble of the land; and do the law and seek righteousness and humility; perhaps you will be hidden in the day of the wrath of the L-rd." Like the LXX, the Peshitta renders the Hebrew phrase, "who do his law," as an imperative statement, "and do the law" (wʿbdw dynʾ), which likewise strengthens the exhortative charac-ter of the passage by removing the discrepancy in the characterization of the audience in vv. 1 and 3. The Peshitta follows the LXX by eliminating the third impera-tive, וּבַקְּשׁוּ, "seek (humility)," and reading instead, "seek righteousness and humility" (wbʿw zdyqwtʾ wmkykwtʾ), which provides a stylistically simpler text although it does not engage in the rereading of "humility" as LXX does. The ambiguity of the final statement is preserved by the use of the particle kbr, which means, "doubtless" or "perhaps."

Targum Jonathan presents a reading that follows closely the lines of the MT: "Seek/search the fear of YHWH, all you humble of the land who have done the laws of his pleasure; seek truth, seek humility; perhaps there is protection upon you in the day of the wrath of YHWH." The Vulgate likewise adheres closely to the text presupposed by the MT: "Seek the L-rd, all the tame/mild of the earth who work his law/judgment (iudicium);

seek justice (iustum), seek tameness/gentleness; suppos-ing that you will be hidden in the day of the anger of the L-rd." The use of the particle si quo, "if/supposing that," preserves the ambiguity of the last statement.

In a very rare instance, the Murabbaʿat scroll differs slightly from the MT in the reading of כָּל־עַנְוֵי הָאָרֶץ, "all the humble of the land." The expression occurs only here in the MT. The editor of the scroll reads ורי ארץ, which presupposes that the scroll has dropped the initial he or the definite article from ארץ, "land."[29] The reading would therefore be analogous to כָּל־עַנְוֵי אֶרֶץ, "all humble of the land," in Ps 76:10; Isa 11:4; and Amos 8:4 (Kethib). A closer examination of the photograph, however, indi-cates that the difference is even greater in that the initial waw of ורי, presumably the surviving fragment of כל־ענוי ארץ, is actually a yod, that is, כל־ענוי ארץ, equivalent to כָּל־עֲנִיֵּי אֶרֶץ, "all the poor of the land," in Job 24:4; Sym-machus Isa 11:4;[30] Amos 8:4 (Qere).[31] In either case, the Murabbaʿat scribe has read the expression כָּל־עַנְוֵי הָאָרֶץ as a form that appears more commonly elsewhere in the Hebrew Bible.

■ 4 Verse 4 provides additional motivation for the pare-netic appeal to seek YHWH in vv. 1-3 by pointing to the disaster that will overtake the Philistines, thereby imply-ing that Philistia's demise is an act of YHWH. Many interpreters maintain, however, that v. 4 is not to be joined structurally to vv. 1-3, but to the following woe oracle concerning the Philistines in vv. 5-7.[32] This is a decision that is based entirely on thematic grounds, but greater attention to the formal text-linguistic features of the text, especially its syntactical features, point to a dif-ferent conclusion.[33]

The first is the presence of the particle הוֹי, "woe," in v. 5. Normally, הוֹי functions as the introduction to an oracle or a series of oracles that warn the addressee of

---

29   Milik, Murabbaʿat, 201.

30   See BHS note on Isa 11:4, which indicates that Sym-machus reads πτωχούς, "poor."

31   See Milik, Murabbaʿat, plate LXX. The letter read as waw by Milik is actually very short, much like the following yod. It does not correspond to the pattern of the waw in the scroll, which tends to have a much longer shaft (see the example in the divine name two lines down on the same scroll column or the waws in וקשו two lines above). According to Milik, Murabbaʿat's reading of the expression in Amos 8:4 corresponds to the Kethib of the MT, עֲנִיֵּי אֶרֶץ

(Murabbaʿat, 187). Unfortunately, the photograph is hardly legible as published.

32   E.g., Ben Zvi, Zephaniah, 150; Roberts, Zephaniah, 195–96; Renaud, Sophonie, 222–23; cf. Rudolph, Zephanja, 279, who points to its conjunctive role and notes that it connects the oracles against the nations to 2:1-3.

33   See Ryou, Zephaniah's Oracles, 186–207; Floyd, Minor Prophets, 215–18; cf. Berlin, Zephaniah, 99, 100–102, who bases her decision primarily on the presence of

impending danger or judgment (see Isa 5:8-24; 28-33; Amos 5:18-20; Nah 3:1-17; Hab 2:6-20). Although הוֹי can appear within a larger literary unit, as in Isa 1:4, within the context of Isa 1:2-20, or Zech 2:10, 11, within the larger context of Zech 2:5-17, it invariably introduces either a self-contained literary unit or a self-contained subunit within a larger literary subunit.[34] The הוֹי of Zeph 2:5 introduces a self-contained oracle concerning the Philistines in vv. 5-7. Although the oracle concerning the Philistines may build on the theme of v. 4, it is formally distinct. Furthermore, the Philistine oracle, with its introductory הוֹי, initiates a sequence of oracles concerning the nations in 2:5-15 that is parallel to the oracles concerning Jerusalem in 3:1-20. Zephaniah 3:1-20 is likewise introduced by הוֹי.

The second is the presence of the particle כִּי, "for, because," at the beginning of v. 4. Many interpreters point to the emphatic function of כִּי in order to argue that it introduces a new structural subunit in vv. 4-7 that is concerned with the Philistines,[35] but this overlooks the conjunctive functions of כִּי. The particle כִּי at times does carry emphatic force, but it never abandons its conjunctive character when doing so. This is evident, for example, in Psalm 47:2-3, which Ben Zvi cites as an example of emphatic כִּי: "Clap your hands, all you peoples; shout to G-d with loud songs of joy. For (כִּי) YHWH, the Most High, is awesome, a great king over all the earth." Alternatively, the conjunctive force of כִּי may appear in its role as a particle that introduces a subordinate clause, as in Isa 15:1, which Ben Zvi also cites: "Pronouncement concerning Moab. Because (כִּי) Ar is laid waste, Moab is undone; because (כִּי) Kir is laid waste, Moab is undone." In this case, the initial כִּי clauses are syntactically subordinate to the following verbal statements concerning Moab, as the demise of the individual cities, Ar and Kir, points to the conclusion that the larger entity Moab, of

which the cities are a part, is also destroyed. In no case does כִּי ever begin a syntactically self-contained statement unless it is somehow subordinate or conjunctive.

In the present instance, there is no indication that the initial כִּי of v. 4 indicates syntactical subordination, but its conjunctive force is clear in that the causative nature of כִּי points to a further reason to accept the prophet's call to seek to YHWH in vv. 1-3; that is, the impending destruction of the Philistines points to YHWH's capacity for punishment on the day of YHWH. Verses 1-3 indicate that such punishment is hypothetically possible, but v. 4 conveys the reality of that possibility. This, of course, requires that the prophet can point to the reality of the threat against the Philistines in order to make his case to his audience that the threat against Jerusalem/Judah is just as real. The threat posed against Philistia by Egypt in the mid- to late seventh century BCE comes immediately to mind. According to Herodotus, "Psammetichus ruled Egypt for fifty-four years; for twenty-nine of these he sat before Azotus [Ashdod], a great city in Syria, and besieged it until he took it. Azotus held out against a siege longer than any of which I have heard."[36] The details of Herodotus's statement cannot be confirmed, but an Egyptian threat against Philistia makes a great deal of sense when considered in relation to what is known of Egypt's movements into Philistia and Syro-Israel during this period.[37] The Twenty-sixth Saite Egyptian Dynasty, of which Psamtek (Psammetichus) I was the second ruler (664–609), came to power as an ally of the Assyrian Empire during Esarhaddon's and Ashurbanipal's successful campaigns against the Twenty-fifth Ethiopian Dynasty. After the fall of Thebes to the Assyrians and their Saite allies in 663, Psamtek was able to contain the Ethiopians and establish his rule over all of Egypt. Subsequent years, however, saw the decline of Assyrian influence in Egypt, and the details of the rela-

a masoretic sĕtûmâ, which indicates a structural division between vv. 4 and 5. It is noteworthy that the Peshitta includes a similar structural division at the same location.

34 For discussion of the "woe" oracle form, see Sweeney, *Isaiah 1–39*, 543, and the literature cited there.

35 See Aejmelaeus, "Function and Interpretation of כִּי," *JBL* 105 (1986) 193–209; Schoors, "The Particle כִּי," *OTS* 21 (1981) 240–76; Muilenburg, "The Linguistic and Rhetorical Usages," *HUCA* 32 (1961) 135–60.

36 Herodotus *Persian Wars* 2.157. For the text and translation see A. D. Godley, *Herodotus, Books I-II* (Loeb Classical Library; Cambridge: Harvard Univ. Press, 1996) 468–71.

37 For discussion see Hallo and Simpson, *Ancient Near East*, 289–95; Kuhrt, *Ancient Near East*, 634–46; Redford, *Egypt*, 351–64, 430–69; A. K. Grayson, *CAH* III/2:143–45.

tionship between Psamtek and Ashurbanipal are not entirely clear. It appears that at some point, Psamtek ceased to be a dependent of the Assyrians and emerged as a full-fledged ally. Indeed, the Babylonian Chronicle indicates that by 616, the Egyptian army was operating in Mesopotamia in support of the Assyrians against the Babylonians.[38] Furthermore, by 609, Psamtek's son and successor, Necho II, put King Josiah of Judah to death as he moved northward to support his beleaguered Assyrian allies against the Babylonians. Whether Psamtek laid siege to Ashdod for twenty-nine years is uncertain, but the Egyptians were certainly moving into Philistia and the Syro-Israelite region during the latter part of the seventh century so that they might control the region, either on behalf of their Assyrian allies or on behalf of their own interests.

The uncertainties of the Egyptian role would play into perceptions in Judah. Although Psamtek had begun as an Assyrian vassal, the Assyrians left Egypt very early in his reign. Many have concluded that Egypt was compelled to leave, either by force or by recognition that they could not hold on to Egypt by themselves. In either case, the removal of the Assyrians from Egypt would be perceived throughout the Near East and in Judah in particular as a blow against Assyria, and would point to Egypt as a nation that had managed to free itself of Assyrian control. Furthermore, an Egyptian move into Philistia, an area controlled by the Assyrians, would be viewed as a potential challenge to Assyrian interests. In such a situation, Judah would look to Egypt as a potential ally that would be useful in freeing itself from Assyrian control, and view the rise of Egypt as an act of YHWH that portended the overthrow of Assyrian power. Only later would Egypt emerge as a nation that threatened Judah's aspirations to independence under Josiah. From Zephaniah's perspective, one could choose to maintain Judah's status as a vassal of Assyria and accept the consequences, or one could recognize the Egyptian moves as a sign of Assyria's impending down-

fall and as an act of YHWH. For Zephaniah, the demise of Assyria clearly served Judah's interests and testified to the power of YHWH.

Scholars generally note that only four of the five Philistine cities are mentioned; Gaza, Ashkelon, Ashdod, and Ekron are mentioned, but Gath is not. This listing also corresponds to the Philistine cities mentioned in Amos's oracle against Philistia (Amos 1:7-8), Jeremiah's reference to the Philistines (Jer 25:20), and Zechariah's mention of the Philistines at the approach of the new king (Zech 9:5-6). Scholars also have noted that Sargon II claims to have taken Gath in the eleventh year of his reign (ca. 712–711).[39] Consequently, there is a great deal of speculation that he destroyed the city and that is was not subsequently rebuilt. The matter must remain uncertain, however, as the site has never been positively identified and fully excavated.[40] The uncertainty is further compounded by Sargon's statements in the same texts that he also captured Ashdod, but Ashdod was never completely destroyed.

Verse 4 also displays some rather interesting stylistic features. The paronomastic and assonantal qualities of the verse have been long recognized. "Gaza," עַזָּה (ʿazzâ), will become "forsaken," עֲזוּבָה (ʿazûbâ); "Ashkelon," אַשְׁקְלוֹן (ʾašqĕlôn), will become "desolate," שְׁמָמָה (šĕmāmâ); "Ashdod," אַשְׁדּוֹד (ʾašdôd), will be "driven out," יְגָרְשׁוּהָ (yĕgārĕšûhā), literally "they will drive her out"; "Ekron," עֶקְרוֹן (ʿeqrôn), "shall be uprooted," תֵּעָקֵר (tēʿāqēr). Many have noted that the association of אַשְׁדּוֹד (ʾašdôd), with יְגָרְשׁוּהָ (yĕgārĕšûhā) is not completely satisfactory; the paronomastic relationship between the two terms is not as close as it is for the others, particularly the first and last pairs of the series.[41] Consequently, any number of emendations have been proposed to strengthen the relationship.[42] Especially noteworthy is Graetz's suggestion to read the verb as יִשְׁדְּדוּהָ, which means "they shall plunder her," and corresponds more closely to the name Ashdod.[43] Zalcman, however, notes this discrepancy and argues that paronomasia is only a secondary

---

38 See *ANET*, 304.

39 See *ANET*, 286; *ARAB* 2:62.

40 Gath is commonly identified as Tel Zafit (Tell eṣ-Ṣafi), although this is disputed. For discussion and bibliography, see Ephraim Stern, "Ẓafit, Tel," *NEAEHL* 4:1522–24.

41 Zalcman, "Ambiguity," 365–71.

42 See ibid., 366, for a summary.

43 Heinrich Graetz, *Emendationes in plerosque Sacrae Scripturae Veteris Testamenti Libros II* (Breslau: Schottlaender, 1893); A. B. Ehrlich, *Randglossen zur hebräischen Bibel* 5 (Leipzig: Hinrichs, 1912), cited by Zalcman, "Ambiguity," 366, 370 nn. 5, 6.

rhetorical device in this text. His study of the vocabulary indicates a conscious choice of verbs that are designed to employ double entendre to portray the Philistine cities as a wife that has been divorced and abandoned by her husband. Thus עֲזוּבָה refers to the abandonment of a wife, as indicated by its use in Isa 54:6; 60:15; 62:4; Jer 4:29. The word שְׁמָמָה refers to a woman who is left desolate in Isa 62:4, which employs it in parallel with the above noted עֲזוּבָה and contrasted with בְּעוּלָה, "married woman," in the same context (see also 2 Sam 23:20, where the term describes Tamar after she is raped and abandoned by Amnon). The verb גרשׁ is a standard term for divorce of a wife (see Lev 21:7; 21:14; 22:13; Num 30:10; Ezek 44:22; cf. Gen 21:10; Mic 2:9). The verbal root עקר is used in Rabbinic Hebrew to refer to a barren woman.[44]

Zalcman's observations are insightful and to the point,[45] but they do not explain why the author of this verse chose the metaphor of an abandoned or divorced woman to depict the plight of the Philistine cities. An answer appears, however, in the depiction of Jerusalem as the "Daughter of Zion," in Zeph 3:14-20, where she is addressed in feminine singular forms and called on to rejoice and sing as a result of her restoration. Zephaniah 3:17 is particularly poignant in this regard in that the verse portrays YHWH as a warrior who returns to rejoice over Daughter Zion and renew his relationship with Zion in love.[46] It would appear that the depiction of the Philistine cities as abandoned women is intended to be contrasted with the depiction of restored Jerusalem in 3:14-20 as a woman whose husband, YHWH, has come home (cf. Isaiah 54; see also Isa 3:25—4:1). The structural placement of these two passages is also noteworthy. Zephaniah 2:4 is placed together with the initial parenesis to seek YHWH in 2:1-4 as a means to provide motivation to the audience, that is, the Philistines have been abandoned by YHWH. Zephaniah 3:14-20 appears at the conclusion of the book following the woe oracles directed to the nations in 2:5-17 and to Jerusalem in 3:1-13. The marriage metaphor becomes the basis by which to portray Jerusalem's restoration at the end of the book and to contrast her fate to that of the Philistines.

---

44 See the examples y. Ber. 6:3 ("they sought to abolish this immersion on account of the women of Galilee who became barren because of the cold") and b. ʿAbod. Zar. 22a ("a heathen has regard for his animal lest it become barren"), cited by Zalcman, "Ambiguity," 369, 371 n. 14.

45 See also R. Gordis, "A Rising Tide of Misery: A Note on a Note on Zephaniah ii 4," VT 37 (1987) 487–90.

46 See the discussion of Zeph 3:17 in the commentary below. Note that the difficult phrase, "he shall be silent (יַחֲרִישׁ) in his love," actually means, "he shall plow in his love," which is a metaphor for sexual relations (cf. Judg 14:18; see also Tammi J. Schneider, Judges [Berit Olam; Collegeville, Minn.: Liturgical, 2000] 211–12; Marvin A. Sweeney, "Metaphor and Rhetorical Strategy in Zephaniah," forthcoming in Timothy J. Sandoval and Carleen Mandolfo, eds., Relating to the Text: Interdisciplinary and Form-Critical Insights on the Bible (JSOTSup; Sheffield: Sheffield Academic Press).

2

Translation

5 Woe! O inhabitants of the seacoast, O nation of Kerethites;[a]
The word of YHWH is upon you, O Canaan, land of the Philistines,[b]
"and I will destroy you, leaving no inhabitant,

6 and the seacoast will become pasturelands of the wells of shepherds, and folds for sheep,[c]

7 and the coast[d] shall be for the remnant of the house of Judah,
upon them they shall graze,[e]
in the houses of Ashkelon at evening they shall lie down,"[f]
because YHWH their G-d shall visit them[g] and restore their captivity.[h]

a MT reads, גּוֹי כְּרֵתִים; cf. Mur 20:16, [גּ]וֹי כרתים; LXX, πάροικοι Κρητῶν, "O, neighbors of the Cretans"; TJ, עמא דחייבין לאשתיצאה, "O, people that deserves to be cast out"; Peshitta, wlʿm² dqrt², "and to the nation of the Cretans"; Vulgate, *gens perditorum*, "O destroyed nation."

b Cf. LXX, γῆ ἀλλοφύλων, lit. "land of foreigners," although the term ἀλλοφύλων is employed generally in the LXX as a designation for the Philistines.

c MT reads, וְהָיְתָה חֶבֶל הַיָּם נְוֹת כְּרֹת רֹעִים וְגִדְרוֹת צֹאן; cf. Mur 20:17-18, [צאן] נוֹת כרות [וְחִתָה חבל הים; LXX, καὶ ἔσται Κρήτη νομὴ ποιμνίων καὶ μάνδρα προβάτων, "and Crete shall be a pasture/district of flocks and fold of cattle"; TJ, ויהי ספר ימא דירוות בית משרי רעין וחטרין דען, "and the coast of the sea shall be the dwelling places of a house of camps of shepherds and folds of sheep"; Peshitta, wnhws ḥbl ymʾ dirʾ wqrtʾ byt mrʿntʾ lgnrʾ dʿnʾ, "and the seacoast shall become a fold and Crete a house of pasture for the dewlaps of sheep"; Vulgate, *et erit funiculus maris requies pastorum et caulae pecorum*, "and the coast of the sea will be a resting place of herds/shepherds and a sheepfold of cattle."

d MT, חֶבֶל, "district, coast"; cf. TJ, עדבא, "the lot/share"; LXX, τὸ σχοίνισμα τῆς θαλάσσης, "the coast of the sea."

e MT, יִרְעוּן, "they shall graze"; cf. LXX, νεμήσονται, "they hold sway/dwell/pasture/graze."

f Cf. Vulgate, *et erit funiculus eius qui remanserit de domo Iuda ibi pascentur in domibus Ascalonis*, "and the same coast that remains for the house of Judah, there they shall feed in the houses of Ashkelon."

g MT, יִרְבָּצוּן, "they will lodge/lie down"; cf. LXX, καταλύσουσιν ἀπὸ προσώπου υἱῶν Ιουδα, "they will lodge from before the sons of Judah."

h Cf. TJ, ארי ייעול דוכרנהון לטבא קדם יוי אלקהון, "because their record will go up for good before YHWH their G-d."

i *Qere*, וְשָׁב שְׁבִיתָם, "and he shall return their captivity"; *Kethib*, וְשָׁב שְׁבוּתָם, "and he shall restore their fortune." The versions follow the *Qere* reading.

Form and Setting

Zephaniah 2:5-7 constitutes an example of the woe oracle form in which the prophet presents YHWH's announcement of punishment against the Philistines.[1] It is demarcated initially by the prophet's הוֹי, "Woe," address to the seacoast, later identified with the Philistines, in v. 5a-bα, and it concludes with the prophet's statements that YHWH will visit them (i.e., Judah) and restore their (i.e., Judah's) captivity in v. 7bβ. The concluding concern with Judah relates to the announcement of punishment against the Philistines in that the so-called remnant of Judah will occupy homes and territory left vacant by YHWH's punishment of the

---

1 For discussion of the woe oracle form, see Sweeney, *Isaiah 1–39*, 543, and the literature cited there, esp.

Claus Westermann, *Basic Forms of Prophetic Speech* (1967; reprinted Louisville: Westminster John Knox,

Philistines. The syntactically disjunctive first person statement by YHWH in v. 8 opens a new subunit that is concerned with the Moabites and Ammonites.

The basic structure of 2:5-7 is evident in the identification of the speakers in each component of the text.[2] The text presents the prophet as the primary speaker who in turn presents a first person statement by YHWH concerning the Philistines.

The prophet's initial statements appear in v. 5a-bα in which he employs a form of the "woe" address directed to the seacoast or Philistines in order to introduce the following statement by YHWH. The "woe" address typically begins with the particle הוֹי, "Woe!" followed by a noun or participle construction that identifies and frequently characterizes the party addressed by the speaker. In general, the form is construed as a direct address to the relevant party.[3]

In the present case, the initial address by the prophet consists of two parallel statements in v. 5a and 5bα. The first (v. 5a) comprises a typical הוֹי address form in which the particle הוֹי introduces the prophet's statement and the following noun clauses, "inhabitants of the seacoast" and "nation of Kerethites," identifies the addressees. Although the cause or nature of the danger is not yet specified, the initial הוֹי implies that some threat to the addressee exists, especially since the particle is employed elsewhere to warn of impending danger (Zech 2:10). The prophet's second statement then follows in v. 5b, in which the ambiguities of the preceding statements are clarified. First, the threatening character of the address is made explicit by the statement that "the word of YHWH is upon/against you," although the specific nature or cause of the threat is not identified. Second, the second person masculine plural pronoun indicates that the prophet's statements constitute a direct address to the threatened parties. Third, the ambiguous identifications of "inhabitants of the seacoast" and "nation of Kerethites" is specified by the identification of the addressees as "Canaan" and "land of the Philistines." Of course, these identifications build on the listing of the four Philistine cities in 2:4.

YHWH's own announcement of punishment against the Philistines appears in vv. 5bα-6. It is joined syntactically to the prophet's preceding statement by the initial *waw*-consecutive formulation, וְהַאֲבַדְתִּיךְ, "and I will destroy you," although it is distinguished by the first person common singular subject, "I," which identifies YHWH as the speaker, and the second feminine singular suffix pronoun, "you," which identifies YHWH's statement as an address to the seacoast, previously identified as the Philistines. Although no further first person pronoun subject appears, the feminine singular *waw*-consecutive formation, וְהָיְתָה, "and it/she shall be," ties v. 6 syntactically to v. 5bα and continues the characterization of the object of the statement as feminine singular. At this point, YHWH's statement makes the threat against the seacoast or Philistines very clear; that is, YHWH proposes to destroy the seacoast or Philistia so that it is left without inhabitants to become a place for grazing and keeping sheep. YHWH's statement provides no particular reason or justification for this proposed action; it confines itself only to the consequences that the seacoast or Philistines will suffer.

The prophet's elaboration on YHWH's statement then follows in v. 7. The passage is tied syntactically to YHWH's preceding statement by the *waw*-consecutive formation, וְהָיָה, "and it/he shall be," and no change in speaker is clearly evident until v. 7bα, when YHWH is mentioned in the third person, which indicates that the speaker is the prophet once again. Nevertheless, the shift in the gender of the verb formation from the feminine וְהָיְתָה to the masculine וְהָיָה suggests a shift in speaker, especially since the subject of the verb remains the same. Although the identification of the speaker in v. 7a-bα must remain somewhat uncertain, several additional factors support the contention that the prophet speaks in v. 7a-bα as well as in v. 7bα. First, the subject matter shifts from punishment against the Philistines in vv. 5bα-6 to the resulting benefits for the remnant of Judah in v. 7. Second, the third person masculine singular subjects of the verbs יִרְעוּן, "they will graze," and

---

1991) 190–98; Christof Hardmeier, *Texttheorie und biblische Exegesis* (BEvTh 79; Munich: Kaiser, 1978).

2   Contra Ryou, *Zephaniah's Oracles*, 207–22; and Floyd, *Minor Prophets*, 218–21, who do not distinguish the speakers in their discussions of the formal

characteristics of this text.

3   For discussion of the syntactical features of the "woe" statement and its character as a direct address form, see Hillers, "*Hôy*."

יִרְבָּצוּן, "they will lie down," in v. 7a-bα clearly refer to the remnant of Judah, and they correspond to the three third person masculine suffix pronouns of v. 7bα, viz., יִפְקְדֵם, "he will visit them," אֱלֹקיהם, "their G-d," and שְׁבִיתָם, "their captivity," all of which must also refer to the remnant of Judah.

The setting of this "woe" speech lies in the attempt to call the audience's attention to an actual or impending threat (see esp. Zech 2:10). Although the text explicitly identifies the seacoast or the Philistines as the addressees of the prophet's and YHWH's words, it is unlikely that this text was written so that it might be read by the Philistines. Rather, it appears to have been written with a Jerusalemite/Judean audience in mind. Since it does not identify the reasons that YHWH is bringing punishment against the Philistines but only articulates the punishment itself and the resulting benefits that will accrue to the remnant of Judah, its purpose apparently lies in an attempt to communicate something to the Jerusalemite/Judean audience. The guilt of the Philistines is not at issue here; rather, the reality of the threat posed against them, whether present or impending, is at issue. Furthermore, the identification of YHWH as the source of the threat appears to be a fundamental facet of the texts' communicative purpose; that is, 2:5-7 is designed to convince its audience, either mid- to late-seventh-century Jerusalemite/Judeans or later readers of the text, that YHWH is bringing punishment against the Philistines.

Such a contention is especially pertinent in the mid- to late-seventh-century period when King Josiah was attempting to launch a reform program that was designed to see to the restoration of an independent Judean kingdom centered around the ruling house of David and the Jerusalem Temple. Judah had been subject to the Assyrian Empire since the late eighth century, and such subjugation to Assyria would have suggested to ancient Judah either that YHWH was powerless to resist the Assyrians or that YHWH had chosen to allow their rule. The contentions that YHWH was bringing punishment against the Philistines and that such punishment would enable Judah to expand into Philistine territory would signal an end to at least one aspect of the period of Assyrian hegemony during which the Assyrians had placed portions of Judean territory under Philistine rule in the aftermath of Hezekiah's attempted revolt against Sennacherib. Discussion of the specific occasion for the prophet's portrayal of YHWH's threat against the Philistines appears in the commentary on 2:4.

■ 5 As noted in the discussion of form and setting above, the prophet's two-part introduction to YHWH's announcement of punishment against the Philistines appears in v. 5a-bα. The prophet's initial statement is formulated as a woe address directed to "the inhabitants of the seacoast" and the "nation of Kerethites."

Interpreters frequently note that the expression חֶבֶל הַיָּם, generally translated as "seacoast" or "coast of the sea," is unique to 2:5-7.[4] More commonly, the term חוֹף הַיָּם is employed to designate the seacoast (see Deut 1:7; Josh 9:1; Judg 5:17; Jer 47:7; Ezek 25:16; cf. חוֹף הַיַּמִּים, "coast of seas," and חוֹף אֳנִיּוֹת, "coast of ships"). Although there has been an attempt to rationalize the use of this term by identifying it as a political term in contrast to the geographic term חוֹף הַיָּם,[5] the choice of the unique terminology here appears to serve Zephaniah's well-represented sense of irony and wordplay. The term חֶבֶל and the root חבל on which the noun is based have a variety of meanings. The root חבל I means "to bind, pledge," and frequently appears in contexts in which two parties arrive at some sort of an economic agreement or contract to which each is bound. Most often, the agreement pertains to a loan in which the debtor pledges to repay a debt and puts up some form of property as collateral (Exod 22:25; Deut 24:6, 17; Ezek 18:16; Amos 2:8; Prov 20:16; 27:13; Job 22:6; 24:3, 9) although it may refer more generally to a relationship that unites Israel and Judah (Zech 11:7, 14). This meaning apparently stands behind the noun חֶבֶל, which means "cord" or "territory." The meaning of "cord" or "rope, line," and so on appears frequently in relation to binding captives (1 Kgs 20:31, 32), the wicked (Ps 119:61; Isa 5:18), and the dead (Ps 18:6/2 Sam 22:6). It can also be employed in relation to a measuring cord (Zech 2:5; 2 Sam 8:2; Amos 7:17; Mic 2:5; Ps 78:55) that might be used to measure property (e.g., Job 21:17). Hence the noun is also employed in reference to land that is inherited or allot-

---

4   E.g., Ben Zvi, *Zephaniah,* 152.
5   Sabottka, *Zephanja,* 73.

ted (Deut 32:9; 1 Chr 16:18; Josh 17:5, 14; 19:9; Ezek 47:13). In this sense, the term חֶבֶל conveys the strip of land along the seacoast where the Philistines lived in Gaza, Ashkelon, and Ashdod. But חבל II means "to act ruinously, corruptly" (Job 34:31; Neh 1:7) or "to destroy" in *piel* (Mic 2:10; Isa 13:5; 32:7; 54:16; Cant 2:15). The noun חֶבֶל can therefore mean "destruction" (Mic 2:10), and חֵבֶל can refer to the "cords" or "pains" of childbirth (Isa 13:8; 26:17; 66:7; Jer 13:21; 22:23; 49:24; Hos 13:13; Job 39:3). Indeed, the references in Isa 13:5, 8; 26:17; 66:7 employ a play on the root to convey both the destruction of the old world and the labor pains involved in the birth of the new world. Given the various meanings and the poetic license associated with the term, חֶבֶל here apparently conveys both the meaning of a narrow strip of land along the seacoast and the potential for destruction and transformation as the Philistines are removed and the land is given to Judah for inhabitation.

The expression גּוֹי כְּרֵתִים, "nation of Kerethites," has prompted a great deal of difficulty because the meaning of the term is not entirely certain. It appears to be a reference to Philistia, however, especially since it parallels a reference to the Philistines in Ezek 25:16, and 1 Sam 30:14 refers to "the Negev of the Kerethites," which would be a region of the Negev desert west of Judah, that is, in Philistia. It appears most frequently in reference to mercenary soldiers in David's personal army (see 2 Sam 8:18; 15:18; 20:7; 1 Kgs 1:38, 44; 1 Chr 18:17), although it should be noted that David's stronghold in Ziklag was granted to him by the Philistine ruler, Achish of Gath (1 Samuel 28; 30). This would indicate that Ziklag was in Philistine territory, and its location in the Negev would suggest that it was part of the land of the Kerethites. Hence David's Kerethite warriors likely would have come from this region.

Based on the assonance of the term כְּרֵתִים with Κρήτη, the LXX and Peshitta identify the term as a reference to Crete. This would suggest that the LXX translator does consider the term as a reference to the Philistine nations, since Amos 9:7, which identifies Caphtor as the original home of the Philistines (cf. Deut 2:23; Jer 47:4),

appearas in the LXX as a reference to Cappadocia (cf. LXX Deut 2:23, but contra LXX Jer 29:4). Targum Jonathan and the Vulgate play on the basic meaning of the root כרת, "to cut (off), destroy." In both cases, the term would also play on the meaning of the above-mentioned root, חבל, as "to destroy." The Targum renders the expression, "O people that deserves to be cast out [cut off]," apparently reading ahead to the scenario in which the Philistines are destroyed, enabling the remnant of Judah to take over their territory and homes. The Vulgate likewise reads, "O destroyed [cut off] nation," apparently in reference to the historical disappearance of the Philistines as a distinct people in the period following the Judean exile to Babylon. The readings by TJ and Vulgate suggest that the choice of the term כרתים may have been a deliberate wordplay in the Hebrew, since the root of the term, כרת, "to cut (off)," recalls the notion of Philistia's destruction, much like חבל.[6]

As noted above, the second statement of the prophet's introduction to YHWH's announcement of punishment against the Philistines appears in v. 5bα, which removes the ambiguities of the preceding statement. The initial statement, "the word of YHWH is upon/against you," indicates that the prophet is the speaker, since it refers to YHWH in the third person. The second person masculine plural pronominal suffix characterizes the prophet's speech as a direct address to the seacoast inhabitants. It also indicates that YHWH is the source of the threat for which the prophet warns the seacoast in v. 5a. The following statements by YHWH in vv. 5bα-6 constitute the word of YHWH mentioned here. At this point, the ambiguities created by the prophet's use of language suggestive of destruction, that is, חֶבֶל and כְּרֵתִים, are resolved by the prophet's identification of the addressees as "Canaan" and "land of the Philistines." Most commentators note that the term "Canaan" is rarely applied to the Philistines in the Hebrew Bible,[7] but the prophet's penchant for wordplay may again be at work. As noted in the discussion of 1:11, "Canaan" is employed in reference to "merchants" or "traders," who "handle silver/money." Insofar as the Philistine territories played an important economic role

---

6   Cf. Gerleman, *Zephanja*, 29.
7   Ben Zvi, *Zephaniah*, 155; Vlaardingerbroek, *Zephaniah*, 139.

in the Pax Assyriaca of the seventh century BCE—Ekron, for example, was turned into a major production facility to manufacture olive oil for distribution throughout the Assyrian Empire[8]—the appellation of "Canaan/merchant" for the Philistines would be fitting.

Finally, YHWH's statement, identified by its first person pronoun and second feminine singular addressee, conveys YHWH's basic intention to destroy Philistia so that it is left without inhabitant. The first person pronoun clearly refers to YHWH as the agent who brings destruction upon the Philistines. The second person feminine address form for the Philistines apparently plays on the language of divorce that was employed in 2:4 to portray the fate of the four Philistine cities, who were metaphorically "divorced" and left "destitute" by YHWH.

■ **6** Following YHWH's direct threat against the Philistines in v. 5bα, v. 6 continues with YHWH's statement that the seacoast will become an empty place suitable for the care and grazing of sheep. The third person feminine singular form of the verb, וְהָיְתָה, "and it/she shall be/come to pass," is anomalous, especially since both elements of the subject, חֶבֶל הַיָּם, "seacoast," are masculine. This has prompted proposals that חֶבֶל הַיָּם is a gloss that should be removed or emended to a feminine noun such as הָאָרֶץ, "the land,"[9] but there is no substantive evidence for these proposals. Some maintain that the three feminine plural objects of the verb, נְוֹת, "pasturages," כְּרֹת, "wells," and גְּדֵרוֹת, "(sheep)folds," may play a role in the feminine formulation of the verb, but this does not explain the singular formulation.[10] It seems best to note YHWH's second feminine singular direct address to the seacoast in v. 5bα, which apparently builds on the characterization of the four Philistine cities in v. 4 as a wife rejected or divorced by YHWH. This would explain the feminine singular verb in v. 6, and perhaps indicate that the expression חֶבֶל הַיָּם functions as a proper name for the land, which function would support its feminine singular characterization.

The appearance of the terms נְוֹת, "pasturages," and כְּרֹת, "wells," is problematic because it results in a three-part construct chain נְוֹת כְּרֹת רֹעִים, "the pasturages of the wells of the shepherds." Although construct noun formulations normally allow for only two nouns, longer chains of three (Gen 47:9), four (Job 12:24), five (Isa 10:12), and perhaps six nouns (Isa 21:17) are possible.[11] Nevertheless, the formulation is somewhat awkward, and the similarities in meaning between נְוֹת, "pasturages," and כְּרֹת, "wells," have suggested to some scholars that one is a gloss meant to explain the other.[12] It is noteworthy, therefore, that כְּרֹת, "wells," is a *hapax legomenon* in the Hebrew Bible and that its consonants, כרת, correspond to those of כְּרֵתִים, "Kerethites," in v. 5. Otherwise, the noun כָּר means "pasturage" (Isa 30:23) or even "sheep" (Isa 16:1), but plural examples of the term appear only in the masculine form (Pss 37:20; 65:14 ["pasturage"]; Amos 6:4; 1 Sam 15:9; 2 Kgs 3:4, etc. ["sheep, lambs"]). This would suggest that the term was deliberately employed to create a pun with the reference to "the nation of the Kerethites (כְּרֵתִים)" so that the Kerethites will now become the location of "shepherds' wells" (כְּרֹת רֹעִים). This would further suggest that the feminine plural construct form, נְוֹת, "pasturages," is indeed a gloss that was introduced to explain the *hapax* כְּרֹת. In this regard, it is noteworthy that the plural construct of נָוֶה, "pasture, meadow," normally appears as נְאוֹת. Apparently, the *ʾalep* elides to produce the unique form of the word in Zeph 1:6. It is also noteworthy that Amos 1:2 includes the phrase נְאוֹת הָרֹעִים, "pasturages of the shepherds," which may have provided a model for the insertion of נְוֹת in Zeph 1:6. This would suggest that the elision of the *ʾalep* was deliberate so that the נְוֹת would provide a form morphologically similar to the likewise unique כְּרֹת. In any case, the introduction of נְוֹת as a gloss would have been done at a relatively early time as both

---

8   Gitin, "Tel Miqne-Ekron"; idem, "Ekron of the Philistines, Part II: Olive-Oil Suppliers to the World," *BARev* 16/2 (1990) 32–42, 59.

9   Schwally, "Sefanjâ," 185; Wellhausen, *Propheten,* 153; Marti, *Dodekapropheton,* 369; Nowack, *Propheten,* 298; Sellin, *Zwölfprophetenbuch,* 432; Rudolph, *Zephanja,* 277; Berlin, *Zephaniah,* 106.

10   E.g., Vlaardingerbroek, *Zephaniah,* 140 (who notes the difficulties with the proposal).

11   GKC, §128a.

12   E.g., Ben Zvi, *Zephaniah,* 157–58.

expressions appear fragmentarily in Mur 20:17 as . . . ‏[נות כרת‏ . . . , precisely as in the MT.

The versions apparently had a great deal of difficulty with this verse, and render it with great latitude.[13] The LXX reads, "and Crete (*Κρήτη*) shall be a pasture/district (*νομή*) of flocks and a fold of cattle." Apparently, the LXX resolved the difficulties of this text by eliminating ‏חֶבֶל הַיָּם‏, "seacoast," and reading ‏כְּרֹת‏, "wells," as a reference to Crete in its place on the basis of its consonants, ‏כרת‏. It is noteworthy therefore that the noun ‏חֶבֶל‏, "coast, land, inheritance," appears to have played some role in the rendition of ‏נְוֺת‏, "pasturages," as *νομή*, "pasturage, district." Apparently, the Greek noun *νομός*, "law, custom," derives its meaning from its basic reference to land or property, which would provide the double meanings of "pasturage" and "district," thus enabling the LXX to convey both Hebrew ‏חֶבֶל‏ and ‏נְוֺת‏ with the same Greek term.

Targum Jonathan reads, "and the coast of the sea shall be dwelling places (‏דירוות‏), a house (‏בית‏) of the camps of shepherds and folds of sheep." This expanded formulation appears to be an attempt to explain the meaning of the Hebrew text in relation to the dwellings of shepherds, apparently with an eye to the following statements in v. 7 that "the remnant of the house of Judah" will dwell in the abandoned houses of Ashkelon.

The Peshitta reads, "and the seacoast shall be a fold/dwelling (*dyrʾ*) and Crete a house of pasture for the dewlaps of cattle/sheep." This reading appears to combine features of both LXX and TJ. The term ‏נְוֺת‏, for example, is rendered as *dyrʾ*, "fold, dwelling," much like ‏דירוות‏, "dwelling places," in TJ. The term ‏כְּרֹת‏ is rendered *wqrtʾ byt mrˁntʾ*, "and Crete a house of pasture," which combines both the LXX reading of *Κρήτη* and TJ's interest in the houses of the shepherds based on the following statements in v. 7. Apparently, the Peshitta translators faced an interpretive difficulty here and chose to combine both understandings in their own rendition of the text.

Finally, the Vulgate reads, "and the coast of the sea will be a resting place of herds/shepherds (*pastorum*) and a sheepfold for cattle." One might argue that this translation eliminates the problematic ‏כְּרֹת‏ entirely, but the Latin *pastorum* conveys both "herd" and "shepherd," apparently in an attempt to convey both ‏כְּרֹת‏, "sheep," and ‏רֹעִים‏, "shepherds."

■ **7** As noted above, v. 7 constitutes the prophet's elaboration on YHWH's preceding statement in vv. 5bα-6. Although the third person references to YHWH that indicate the prophet's role as speaker do not appear until v. 7bα, several features of the verse as a whole point to this conclusion. The second and third person feminine singular characterization of "the seacoast" or Philistines now shifts to a third person masculine singular and plural characterization in keeping with the prophet's initial statements in v. 5a-bα. Furthermore, v. 7 appears to elaborate on the meaning of YHWH's statement in vv. 5bα-6 by focusing on the image of the seacoast or Philistia destitute of its human population and by portraying Judah's settlement in the region with language suggestive of grazing sheep. Nevertheless, several features of this verse require further discussion.

The first is the shift to the third person characterization of the seacoast as indicated in the expression ‏וְהָיָה חֶבֶל‏, "and the district/coast shall be." A number of scholars have argued that this phrase is the source of the enigmatic ‏וְהָיְתָה חֶבֶל הַיָּם‏, "and the seacoast shall be," in that the masculine subject was introduced into v. 6 in place of an originally feminine subject, such as ‏הָאָרֶץ‏, "the land," or the like.[14] The absence of ‏הַיָּם‏ in v. 7 speaks against such a proposal, however, and there is little reason to emend v. 7 to supply the term, as many scholars have proposed.[15] Rather, it seems best to retain the phrase in v. 7 as it stands, recognizing that the shift

13 See esp. Gerleman, *Zephanja*, 30–33.
14 See n. 9 above.
15 See LXX; Peshitta; Schwally, "Sefanjâ," 187; Wellhausen, *Propheten*, 153; Marti, *Dodekapropheton*, 369; J. M. P. Smith, *Zephaniah*, 224; van Hoonacker, *Prophètes*, 521; Nowack, *Propheten*, 298; Sellin, *Zwölfprophetenbuch*, 432; Junker, *Sophonia*, 78; Elliger,

Zephanja, 69; Horst, *Propheten*, 194; Keller, *Sophonie*, 201.

in characterization is an indication of the shift in speaker from YHWH to prophet. Furthermore, the exclusive use of the term חֶבֶל, "lot, portion (of land)," rather than the earlier חֶבֶל הַיָּם, "seacoast," employs an element of wordplay to focus the prophet's interest in Judah's possession of Philistia.[16] Whereas the term חֶבֶל הַיָּם emphasizes the geographical character of Philistia as a land distinct from Judah, חֶבֶל recalls the portions of land assigned to Israel according to the accounts of the conquest of Canaan under Joshua. In this respect, it is noteworthy that although Israel did not include the territory of the Philistines according to Josh 13:1-7, Joshua 15 indicates that Judah's territory would extend to the sea just north of Philistia.[17] Furthermore, Josh 13:1-7 indicates that Philistia was among those lands yet to be possessed, so that the prophet's comments here in v. 7 outline a scenario in which Judah will accomplish that portion of the traditional mandate to possess the entire land of Canaan.

The reference to "remnant of the house of Judah" has also prompted a great deal of discussion because it is believed that the term can refer to the surviving elements of Judah only following the period of the Babylonian exile. Consequently, a number of scholars have argued that the presence of the term here indicates postexilic redactional reworking of this text.[18] This proposal overlooks the losses suffered by Judah during the course of the Assyrian occupation of the land of Israel from the late eighth century on. As noted above, Sennacherib had stripped away a great deal of territory in western Judah and given it over to Philistine control. Furthermore, just as the presence of four-horned altars at Tel Miqne/Ekron indicates that the Philistines had moved a large number of northern Israelites into Philistia to work the olive presses established there,[19] it is equally likely that

the Assyrians also moved a large number of Judeans into Philistia for the same purposes following their invasion of the kingdom and deportation of large numbers of its population. Such losses would justify the prophet's use of the term "remnant of the house of Judah" in the context of his statements that Judah would expand and restore its captivity. Insofar as the prophet envisions YHWH's actions against Judean/Jerusalemite apostates in 1:2-18 and 2:1-4, the reference to "the remnant of the house of Judah" would also indicate those who would survive YHWH's purge on the Day of YHWH and thus realize the rewards of adherence to the Deity.

An especially problematic issue is determining the antecedents of the pronouns in the phrase, "upon them they shall graze; in the houses of Ashkelon, at evening, they shall lie down," in v. 7aα-bα. The subject of the verbs, יִרְעוּן, "they shall graze," and יִרְבָּצוּן, "they shall lie down," appears to be the earlier phrase, לִשְׁאֵרִית בֵּית יְהוּדָה, "for the remnant of the house of Judah." Although "remnant" (שְׁאֵרִית) is a feminine noun and "house" (בֵּית) is a masculine singular noun, the collective notion of the phrase, "remnant of the house of Judah," appears to be presupposed by these verbs. The phrase עֲלֵיהֶם, "upon them," is much more difficult, especially since its natural antecedents in v. 6, נְוֹת כְּרֹת רֹעִים וְגִדְרוֹת צֹאן, "pasturages, wells of shepherds, and folds of sheep," are all feminine plural nouns. Nevertheless, the shift in gender indicating the beginning of the prophet's speech in contrast to the speech by YHWH must be considered here. In this case, the grammatical antecedent would not be the aforementioned nouns of v. 6; rather, it would have to be the following reference to the houses of Ashkelon

16 Cf. Renaud, *Sophonie*, 225–27; Roberts, *Zephaniah*, 192; Berlin, *Zephaniah*, 106; Vlaardingerbroek, *Zephaniah*, 132, who recognize wordplay in this verse.

17 For discussion of Judah's tribal boundaries, see Zecharia Kallai, *Historical Geography of the Bible* (Jerusalem: Magnes, 1986) 115–24, esp. 123–24.

18 See Schwally, "Sefanjâ," 223–26; Wellhausen, *Propheten*, 153; Marti, *Dodekapropheton*, 369; van Hoonacker, *Prophètes*, 521–22; J. M. P. Smith, *Zephaniah*, 219–20; Nowack, *Propheten*, 298; Junker, *Sophonia*, 78; Elliger, *Zephanja*, 69 (note the lack of bold

print for v. 7, which indicates a redactional text); Rudolph, *Zephanja*, 280; Keller, *Sophonie*, 201, 202; Renaud, *Sophonie*, 225–27; Vlaardingerbroek, *Zephaniah*, 132.

19 Gitin, "Tel Miqne-Ekron"; idem, "Incense Altars from Ekron, Israel, and Judah," *ErIsr* 23 (1992) 43*–49*; idem, "Seventh-Century B.C.E. Cultic Elements at Ekron," *Biblical Archaeology Today, 1990: Proceedings of the Second International Congress on Biblical Archaeology* (Jerusalem: Israel Exploration Society, 1993) 248–58.

in v. 7bα, "in the houses of Ashkelon they shall lie down," especially since the phrase בְּבָתֵּי אַשְׁקְלוֹן, "in the houses of Ashkelon," is based on a masculine plural noun, בָּתִּים, "houses."

The LXX appears to read this phrase somewhat differently: "upon them they shall hold sway/graze (νιμήσονται) in the houses of Ashkelon; at evening, they will lodge (καταλύσουσιν) from before/because of the sons of Judah (ἀπὸ προσώπου υἱῶν Ιουδα)." It apparently takes the aforementioned shepherds and sheep of v. 6 as the subjects of the verbs, νιμήσονται and καταλύσουσιν, as indicated by the introduction of the phrase, ἀπὸ προσώπου υἱῶν Ιουδα, which has no Hebrew *Vorlage*. It would appear that the LXX reading is the result of its attempt to wrestle with the referents of the unspecified third person masculine singular pronouns in this passage, and its conclusion that the Hebrew verbs, יִרְעוּן and יִרְבָּצוּן, must refer to the actions of the shepherds and sheep mentioned in v. 6. The other versions apparently read much like the MT.

The concluding explanatory clause in v. 7bα then provides the rationale for the entire scenario of the Philistine oracle and, indeed, for the preceding scenario of purification on the Day of YHWH, that is, YHWH is about to act on Judah's behalf and restore its captivity. The introductory particle כִּי, "for, because," conveys the explanatory character of the clause and joins it syntactically to the prophet's statement in v. 7a-bα. Although the verb פקד is frequently employed in contexts in which YHWH will "visit" or "punish" the parties who are presented as the objects of YHWH's actions, the basic meaning of the verb, "to visit, appoint," must be considered, especially since it is coupled with the statement that YHWH will "restore their captivity." In such a context, the punishment is clearly directed against the Philistines or the seacoast, which will be left uninhabited as a result of YHWH's action. The third person masculine plural suffix pronouns that appear with the verb יִפְקְדֵם, "he will visit them," with the divine name ה"

אֱלֹקיהֶם, "YHWH their G-d," and with the noun שְׁבִיתָם (*Qere*), "their captivity," can only refer to the previously mentioned "remnant of the house of Judah," like the earlier third person masculine plural references in the verbs יִרְעוּן "they shall graze," and יִרְבָּצוּן, "they shall lie down."

The phrase שְׁבִיתָם (*Qere*)/וְשָׁב שְׁבוּתָם (*Kethib*) has been the subject of much discussion, both in this context and throughout the rest of the Hebrew Bible.[20] The terms שְׁבִית and שְׁבוּת are frequently taken as variations of the same term, although the Masoretes clearly distinguished between them, as their frequent *Qere/Kethib* shifts indicate. There is also confusion concerning which verbal root the term derives from, that is, שבה, "to take captive," and שוב, "to return," so that the derived nouns could refer to "captivity" in the first instance and "fortune [i.e., that which is returned]" or "captivity [i.e., that which is returned]" in the second. It is noteworthy that either meaning, "and he shall restore their captivity" or "and he shall restore their fortunes," would fit well with the present context. The problem, of course, is exacerbated by the *lamed-he* formulation of the root שבה, and the *ʿayin-waw* formulation of the root שוב, both of which generally retain only two root letters, that is, *šin* and *bet*, in their derived forms. Unfortunately, studies in Biblical Hebrew noun morphology do not distinguish semantically between the meanings of the noun suffixes ‏ית- and ‏ות-.[21] Studies in Rabbinic Hebrew noun morphology do distinguish between them, however, so that ‏ית- is employed to express simple denominative meanings of verbs and sometimes diminutive meanings.[22] The suffix ‏ות-, however, is employed to express abstract meanings from concrete nouns.[23] This might explain the masoretic distinction between שְׁבִית, "captivity," based on the verbal root שבה, "to take captive," and the more ambiguous שְׁבוּת, "that which is returned," based perhaps on the participle form שָׁב, "(a) return," derived from the verbal

---

20 See the discussions in BDB, 988; *HALOT*, 1385–87; John M. Bracke, "*šûb šĕbût*: A Reappraisal," *ZAW* 97 (1985) 233–44, and the literature cited there. Note that Bracke does not consider the *Qere* reading of שְׁבִית.

21 See, e.g., GKC, §95t-u.

22 See M. H. Segal, *A Grammar of Mishnaic Hebrew* (reprinted Oxford: Clarendon, 1978) §271.

23 Ibid., §272.

root שׁוב, "to return." On this basis, it appears that the Masoretes deliberately read the expression as a reference to YHWH's intention to restore the captivity of Judah. The meaning of the consonantal text, however, is ambiguous: either "and he will restore their captivity" or "and he will restore their fortunes," which would have prompted masoretic intervention to specify the text.[24]

The versions, including LXX, TJ, Peshitta, and Vulgate, are unanimous in reading the phrase as an expression of YHWH's intentions to restore the captivity of Judah.[25] In any case, the presence of this expression, however it is understood, appears to convey YHWH's intentions to restore Jerusalem/Judah in the aftermath of Philistia's demise.

24 See Bracke, "šûb šᵉbût"; James Barr, *The Semantics of Biblical Language* (Oxford: Clarendon, 1961) 105–60, who critiques such etymological attempts to ascertain the meaning of a term.
25 The text of Mur 20:19 provides little insight as the crucial letter is lost, i.e., שׁבֿ[י/]חֿתֿם. The letters *waw* and *yod* are difficult enough to distinguish in Qumran Hebrew as they look very similar, but the leather provides no basis on which to determine the reading of this text.

2

Translation

8 "I have heard the insult[a] of Moab and the revilings[b] of the sons of Ammon,
 when they reproached my people, and expanded upon their border.[c]

9 Therefore, as I live," oracle of YHWH of Hosts, G-d of Israel,
 "that Moab shall be like Sodom, and the sons of Ammon like Gomorrah,
 a possession of weeds and a pit of salt[d] and eternal desolation.
 The remnant of my people shall despoil them,
 and the remainder[e] of a nation[f] shall possess them."

10 This shall happen to them[g] in place of their pride,
 because they reproached and they expanded against the people of YHWH of Hosts.[h]

11 YHWH shall be fearsome against them,[i]
 because he has diminished all the gods of the earth,[j]
 and they shall bow down to him, each from its place,
 all the islands/edges of the nations.

a MT, חֶרְפַּת, "reproach/insult of"; cf. LXX, ὀνειδισμοὺς, "reproaches/insults"; TJ, חסודי, "insults/taunts of."

b MT, וְגִדּוּפֵי, "and the revilings of"; cf. Peshitta, wgwdpʾ, "and the reviling/blasphemy of."

c MT, וַיַּגְדִּילוּ עַל־גְּבוּלָם, "and they expanded upon their border"; cf. LXX, καὶ ἐμεγαλύνοντο ἐπὶ τὰ ὅρια μου, "and they exalted themselves upon my borders."

d MT, מִמְשַׁק חָרוּל וּמִכְרֵה־מֶלַח, "a possession of weeds and a pit of salt"; cf. LXX, καὶ Δαμασκὸς ἐκλελειμμένη ὡς θημωνιὰ ἁλός, "and Damascus abandoned like a heap of salt"; TJ, ומחפורין דמלח משמט מלוחין, "an abandoned place of salt plants and mines of salt"; Peshitta, dʾtḥblt nsbthyn wʾbd mlwḥḥyn, "and their plantings shall be destroyed and their leaders shall perish"; Vulgate, siccitas spinarum et acervi salis, "a dry thorn bush and a heap of salt."

e MT, יֶתֶר, "remainder"; cf. LXX, κατάλοιποι, "remnant," which is the same term employed for יֶתֶר above; 8HevXIIgr distinguishes the two terms, however, employing κατάλοι]πο[ι, "remnant," in the first instance and ἐπίλοι[οι, "remainder," in the second instance.

f MT, גוֹי, "a nation" (Kethib); גוֹיִי, "my nation" (Qere); cf. TJ, שבטיא, "the tribes."

g MT, זֹאת לָהֶם, "this (is) to them"; cf. Peshitta, which supplies a verb to clarify the expression: hdʾ thwʾ lhwn, "this shall be to them"; Vulgate, hoc eis eveniet, "this comes forth/happens."

h Note that LXX drops the reference to עַם, "people," reading only, καὶ ἐμεγαλύνθησαν ἐπὶ τὸν κύριον τὸν παντακράτορα, "and they boasted over the L-rd Almighty"; Peshitta adds a specification that the people are Israel: wʾtrwrbw ʿl ʿmh dmrʾʾhyltnʾ ʿl ʾysryl, "and they boasted against the people of the L-rd of Hosts, against Israel."

i MT, נוֹרָא ה״ עֲלֵיהֶם, "YHWH is fearsome against them"; cf. LXX and Peshitta, which read, respectively, נורא as נראה or the like, i.e., ἐπιφανήσεται κ-ς ἐπ' αὐτούς, "the L-rd shall appear upon them"; ʾtgly mryʾ ʿlyhwn, "the L-rd has revealed himself over them." See also TJ, which emphasizes YHWH's role in redeeming the people: דחילא יוי אמר למפרקהון, "the fear of YHWH has said to redeem them."

j MT, כִּי רָזָה אֵת כָּל־אֱלֹהֵי הָאָרֶץ, "because he has diminished/subdued all the gods of the earth"; cf. LXX, καὶ ἐξολεθρεύσει πάντας τοὺς θεοὺς τῶν ἐθνῶν τῆς γῆς, "and he shall utterly destroy all the gods of the nations of the earth"; TJ, ארי אמאיך ית כל דהלת ארעא, "for he humbled all the idols of the earth"; Peshitta, dnwbd lklhwn mlkyh dʾrʿʾ, "when he destroyed all of the kings of the earth."

Form and Setting

Zephaniah 2:8-11 constitutes the prophet's presentation of YHWH's judgment speech against Moab and Ammon. It is demarcated at the beginning by the syntactically independent first person singular statements that can presuppose only YHWH as the subject, as well as by the shift in subject matter from Philistia to Moab and Ammon. Although the presentation of the judgment speech concludes with v. 9, the prophet's summary-appraisal speech in vv. 10-11 is clearly joined with vv. 8-9 by the third person masculine plural verbs in v. 8 that reiterate the actions of the Moabites and Ammonites as stated in vv. 8-9 and by the third masculine plural pronouns of v. 9 that also refer back to the Ammonites and Moabites.

As the above discussion of the form and setting of 2:5-15 indicates, vv. 8-11 are part of a larger unit that also includes the oracles concerning Ethiopia and Assyria in vv. 12 and 13-15, respectively, each of which is joined to the preceding unit by an initial conjunction, גַּם, "also, even," in v. 12 and conjunctive *waw* in v. 13. Thus the prophet's statement in v. 11 concerning YHWH's subduing of the foreign gods of the world provides both a conclusion to the Moabite/Ammonite oracle and an introduction to the oracles concerning Cush and Assyria, which will likewise submit to YHWH.

The literary structure of 2:8-11 comprises three basic components, each of which is distinguished by the absence of an explicit syntactical connector. Together, they constitute the prophet's announcement of YHWH's judgment speech against Moab and Ammon in vv. 8-9, the prophet's summary-appraisal of the judgment speech in v. 10 in which he reiterates that the judgment to be inflicted on Moab and Ammon is a consequence of their arrogance and self-aggrandizement against the people of YHWH Sebaot, and his projection in v. 11 of YHWH's fearsomeness against them because YHWH has already afflicted the gods of the nations at the ends of the earth.

The role of the prophet as the primary speaker in vv. 8-9 is clearly evident by the presence of the oracular formula in v. 9a[4-8], נְאֻם־ה׳ צְבָאוֹת אֱלֹקֵי יִשְׂרָאֵל, "oracle of YHWH of Hosts, G-d of Israel," which refers to YHWH in the third person. Otherwise, these verses comprise a first person speech by YHWH that announces judgment against Moab and Edom. YHWH's accusations against Moab and Edom appear in v. 8: they have reproached Israel and encroached upon the territory of Israel. The announcement of punishment, introduced by the particle לָכֵן, "therefore," then states the consequences for these actions: Moab and Ammon will become like Sodom and Gomorrah, a deserted land filled with weeds and salt that will ultimately be despoiled and appropriated by the remnant of YHWH's people.

Verses 10-11 then present the prophet's summary and appraisal of this oracle in two parts. The third person references to YHWH in both verses clearly indicate that the prophet is the primary speaker. The summary-appraisal form is an analytical genre based in the wisdom tradition that normally concludes a literary unit and presents the speaker's assessment of the preceding material, including an interpretation of what was stated and the projected implications or results.[1] It is normally introduced by a demonstrative article, "this," which refers back to the preceding material. The prophet in v. 10 simply reiterates YHWH's prior statements concerning Moab and Ammon in vv. 8-9, most likely due to ambiguities concerning the accusation that Moab and Ammon "had expanded upon their border." The idiom הִגְדִּיל עַל, "to make great upon," elsewhere never refers to territorial expansion, but generally to boasting.[2] The prophet's statement in v. 10 drops the reference to "their border" and therefore seems to present the idiom as it normally appears, as a reference to boasting.

---

1. For discussion of the summary-appraisal genre, see Sweeney, *Isaiah 1–39*, 539; Childs, *Crisis*, 128–36; Whedbee, *Isaiah and Wisdom*, 75–79. Other examples of the summary appraisal form appear in Prov 1:19; Job 8:13; 18:21; 20:29; Qoh 4:8; Ps 49:14; Isa 14:26; 17:14; 28:29; Jer 13:25.
2. See Jer 48:26, 42; Ezek 35:13; Pss 35:26; 38:17; 55:13; Job 19:5; see also *hithpael* forms of the verb in Isa 10:15; Dan 11:36, 37.

The prophet's statement in v. 11 draws out some important implications of YHWH's judgment oracle against Moab and Ammon: YHWH will be fearsome or awesome against them (Moab and Ammon) and thereby force the submission of all the gods of the earth from its farthest reaches. This statement then motivates those of vv. 12, 13-15, which announce YHWH's judgment against Cush/Ethiopia and Assyria, two nations that were at the edges of the earth as far as Judah was concerned. The implication is that the setbacks suffered by Cush and Assyria in the seventh century must be understood as acts of YHWH. Such a contention justifies the view that setbacks suffered by Moab and Ammon are also acts of YHWH that were prompted by their earlier actions against Israel or Judah.

The historical setting for 2:8-11 clearly presupposes some threat against Moab and Ammon that would be understood as an action by YHWH. The so-called Rassam Cylinder relates Ashurbanipal's campaigns against Arab tribes, particularly Uateᶜ, king of Arabia, because he had violated the terms of his treaty with Assyria.[3] As part of the general description of the grounds for his actions against Uateᶜ, Ashurbanipal relates that Uateᶜ had joined Shamash-shum-ukin, the regent of Babylon who was preparing for a revolt against his brother Ashurbanipal for control of the Assyrian Empire. Ashurbanipal states that his army defeated the Arabs in various areas along the western fringes of the Arabian desert, including Edom, Beth-Ammon, and Moab, as well as other locations. These events are related to Ashurbanipal's ninth campaign, estimated to have taken place immediately prior to his war with Shamash-shum-ukin of Babylon in 651.[4] Subsequent campaigns were fought in 651 against Arab forces from Qedar and elsewhere led by the brothers Abiyateᶜ and Ayamu ben Teʾri, who supported Shamash-shum-ukin, again in 646–645 against Arab federations in the vicinity of Palmyra, and perhaps once again at a later time.[5] Arab tribes apparently constituted quite a threat against Assyrian interests in the mid-seventh century, and Ammon and Moab were among their principal targets. These Arab advances against Assyrian-controlled territory along the western Arabian desert, particularly against Ammon and Moab, would seem to constitute the basis for the prophet's claims that YHWH was acting against Moab and Ammon. Such threats against Moab and Ammon, well known for their submission to Assyria,[6] would also be understood as YHWH's threats against Assyria itself.

The occasion for the charges against Ammon and Moab is not difficult to fathom. The Moabite Stone reports that as early as the mid-ninth century, King Mesha of Moab was able to take control of Israelite territory in Transjordan during the reigns of the Omride kings of Israel.[7] Although this territory would presumably have been recovered by Jeroboam ben Joash of Israel, whose territory extended from Lebo-Hamath in Syria to the Sea of the Arabah (Gulf of Aqaba; see 2 Kgs 14:25), Isaiah's oracle concerning Moab in Isaiah 15–16 depicts the advance of the Assyrian king Tiglath-pileser III into Transjordan during the Syro-Ephraimite War of 734–732.[8] The oracle indicates that the Assyrian

---

3   See *ANET*, 297–98; *ARAB* 2:817–18. See also Cylinder B (*ARAB* 2:868–70).

4   For full discussion of this material, see Israel Ephal, *The Ancient Arabs: Nomads on the Borders of the Fertile Crescent, 9th–5th Centuries B.C.* (Jerusalem: Magnes, 1984), esp. 142–55.

5   *ANET*, 298–301; *ARAB* 2:819–31; Ephal, *Ancient Arabs*, esp. 155–69.

6   See *ANET*, 301, for a fragmentary text dated sometime between the reigns of Sargon II and Esarhaddon, which reports the receipt of tribute from Bit-Ammon, Moab, Judah, and Edom. See also Cylinder C from the reign of Ashurbanipal, which reports the receipt of tribute from Musuri, king of Moab, and Ammi-nadbi, king of Beth-Ammon, among others (*ARAB* 2:876). Cf. Assyrian texts from other periods that report tribute paid by Moab to Sargon (*ARAB* 2:195), submission by Moab and Beth-Ammon to Sennacherib (*ARAB* 2:239), and assistance given by Moab and Beth-Ammon to Esarhaddon in the rebuilding of his palace at Nineveh (*ARAB* 2:690).

7   For translation and full discussion of the Moabite Stone, see *ANET*, 320–21; J. Andrew Dearman and Gerald Mattingly, "Mesha Stele," *ABD* 4:708–9; Dearman, *Studies*.

8   For full discussion of Isaiah 15–16 and its implications for understanding the Assyrian advance into Transjordan, see Sweeney, *Isaiah 1–39*, 240–52.

advance extended only as far as the Wadi Arnon, the southern border of the territory formerly belonging to Israel and the northern border of Moab proper. The Assyrians ultimately incorporated this land into the Assyrian province of Galazu. Insofar as Moab and Ammon were known to be loyal Assyrian allies during this period, it stands to reason that they were able to advance their interests against Israel by virtue of their cooperation with the Assyrians in contrast to the frequent Israelite and Judean revolts. It would seem that the prophet is aware of this history, and refers to it in his presentation of the reasons why YHWH is punishing Moab and Ammon.

■ **8** Verse 8 begins the prophet's presentation of YHWH's judgment speech against Moab and Ammon in vv. 8-9. As noted above, the prophet's role as the speaker who presents the words by YHWH appears in the oracular formula of v. 9. The judgment speech proper is cast in a first person common singular form, which when read together with the oracular formula clearly presupposes that YHWH is the speaker.

The oracle concerning Moab and Ammon differs markedly from the preceding oracle concerning the Philistines (vv. 5-7) in that it provides reasons for YHWH's decision to punish the Moabites and Ammonites. Initially, the actions of the Moabites and Ammonites that justify the punishment are portrayed in very general terms, that is, YHWH claims to have heard the "insult" or "reproach" (חֶרְפָּת/חֶרְפָּה) of Moab and the "revilings" (גִּדּוּפֵי/גִּדּוּף) of the sons of Ammon. The combination of these two roots is common throughout the Hebrew Bible; the pair occurs in various noun forms in Isa 51:7 and Ezek 5:15, and verbal forms of the pair appear in Isa 37:23/2 Kgs 19:22 and Ps 44:17. The root חרף in both its nominal and verbal forms appears frequently throughout the Hebrew Bible as a common term for reproach, insult, taunting, scorn, shame, disgrace, and so on (e.g., verb: Judg 8:15; 1 Sam 17:10, 25; Pss 42:11; 55:13; 57:4; 74:10, 18; etc.; nouns: 1 Sam 17:26; Neh 3:36; Pss 69:20, 21; 71:13; 89:51; Prov 18:3; Ezek 21:33; Lam 3:61; etc.). The root חרף appears to have a more limited and perhaps specialized sense of reviling or blasphemy (noun: Isa 43:28; verb: Isa 37:6; 2 Kgs 19:6; Num 15:30). The general nature of these terms and the close proximity of Moab and Ammon to Israel and Judah throughout their history make it difficult to spec-

ify an occasion on which such actions might have taken place.

The second half of the verse, particularly the phrase, "and they expanded upon their border" (וַיַּגְדִּילוּ עַל־גְּבוּלָם), presents some possibilities for specifying the occasion. The idiom הִגְדִּיל עַל, "to make great against/concerning," appears frequently in Biblical Hebrew, where it generally refers to boasting (see esp. Ezek 35:13, "and you magnify yourselves against me with your mouth"; see also Pss 35:26; 38:17; 55:13; Job 19:5; Jer 48:26, 42; and below in Zeph 2:10). The addition of a reference to "their territory" in the present verse is unique and potentially important because it suggests territorial expansion rather than mere boasting, catcalling, and hostile demonstrations upon the borders of Israel/Judah with Moab and Ammon. Biblical literature indicates that territorial issues apparently existed between Moab/Ammon and Israel/Judah from the earliest periods. Already, the Pentateuch indicates hostility between the Moabites and Israelites during the period in which Israel passes through Moab on its way from the wilderness into the promised land. Num 21:10-35 relates the traditions of the war between Israel and Kings Sihon of the Amorites and Og of Bashan who tried to prevent Israel from passing through their territories in Transjordan, roughly Moab and Ammon. Numbers 22–24 likewise relates the unsuccessful attempt by King Balak of Moab to use the Mesopotamian prophet Balaam to curse Israel while they were encamped in Moabite territory. Numbers 25 relates an episode of apostasy by Israel in the land of Moab when Israelite men engaged in sexual relations with Moabite and Midianite women during religious worship devoted to Baal of Peor and thereby incurred judgment. Later tradition also indicates hostilities between Israel and Ammon or Moab. 2 Samuel 8; 10–12 relates David's wars against the Moabites and especially against the Ammonites and the Arameans who apparently supported Ammon. 2 Kings 3 relates the unsuccessful war by Jehoram of Israel (849–842), Jehoshaphat of Judah (873–849), and their Edomite allies against the Moabites.

These narratives hardly constitute an entirely reliable basis for the reconstruction of history; the Balaam narratives are clearly written as satire that is designed to poke fun at a pagan prophet and magnify YHWH's reputation for power over against Moab and Balaam;[9] the David narratives are written to provide background for his affair with Bathsheba and the murder of her husband, Uriah the Hittite;[10] and the Kings narrative is presented in relation to a larger narrative complex that is designed to discredit the house of Omri.[11] Nevertheless, inscriptional evidence points to situations of historical conflict between Israel/Judah and Moab or Ammon in the ninth-eighth centuries that may well have played a role in generating these narratives. As noted above in the discussion of the form and setting of this passage, the mid-ninth-century Mesha inscription indicates that King Mesha of Moab had succeeded in taking control of Israelite territory in Transjordan occupied by the tribes of Reuben and Gad.[12] Insofar as the Mesha inscription is dated generally to the period either immediately before or soon after the death of King Ahab of Israel in combat against the Arameans at Ramoth Gilead in ca. 850, it points to a period in which Israel was pushed out of Transjordan by the Arameans and their allies to the north and the Moabites to the south. Its presence in Dhiban, not far from the Wadi Arnon, which constituted the ancient border between Israel and Moab, would constitute an example of public boasting by Moab against Israel in the context of border disputes between the two ancient nations.

The presence of the Balaam inscription in the town of Deir ʿAlla on the east bank of the Jordan River just south of the Sea of Kinneret/Galilee is another case in point.[13] Although the function of the inscription and the circumstances in which it was produced are not entirely clear, it appears to have originated at some point between 880 and 700, in the period when Moab and other nations held sway over Israelite territories in Transjordan. It is noteworthy that the Balaam inscription was displayed publicly on the wall of a sanctuary in a town that faced Israelite territory across the Jordan River. It also utters curses against an undetermined audience. Balaam is a foreign prophet and the inscription does not mention YHWH, but refers only to the Canaanite name El and other epithets. It seems entirely possible therefore that the inscription was written to justify Israel's defeat in the Transjordan. If so, the inscription could well be an example of the blasphemies attributed to Moab and Ammon in the Zephanian text.

Biblical traditions may also play a role in understanding the Zephaniah oracle against Moab and Ammon. 2 Kgs 14:25 notes that King Jeroboam ben Joash of Israel (786–746) was able to restore Israel's borders from Lebo-Hamath in northern Syria to the Sea of the Arabah (Gulf of Aqaba) in the south. Presumably, this means that he was able to recover Israel's lands in Transjordan lost to Aram/Ammon and Moab. The oracle concerning Moab in Isaiah 15–16, however, points to a scenario in which refugees in the region north of the Wadi Arnon, the traditional border between Israel and Moab, flee from before an invading enemy.[14] Although the population of the Moabite territory south of the Arnon is clearly traumatized, they do not appear to suffer direct invasion as do their neighbors to the north. This leads to the conclusion that Isaiah 15–16 depicts the invasion of the Israelite Transjordan by the Assyrian monarch Tiglath-pileser III in 734–732 during the Syro-Ephraimite War. In the immediate aftermath of the war, the Assyrians annexed the Israelite Transjordan and renamed it as the province of Galazu (i.e., Gilead). Assyrian records indicate that Moab and Ammon remained loyal to Assyria throughout the late eighth and seventh centuries, which suggests that Ammon and

9   E.g., David Marcus, *From Balaam to Jonah: Anti-Prophetic Satire in the Hebrew Bible* (BJS 301; Atlanta: Scholars Press, 1995).

10   E.g., Gilian Keys, *The Wages of Sin: A Reappraisal of the 'Succession Narrative'* (JSOTSup 221; Sheffield: Sheffield Academic Press, 1996).

11   E.g., Robert Coote, ed., *Elijah and Elisha in Socioliterary Perspective* (SBL Semeia Studies; Atlanta: Scholars Press, 1992).

12   See *ANET*, 320–21; Dearman and Mattingly, "Mesha Stele," *ABD* 4:708–9; Dearman, *Studies*.

13   For discussion see Meindert Dijkstra, "Is Balaam

Also Among the Prophets?" *JBL* 114 (1995) 43–64 and the literature cited there; see esp. P. Kyle McCarter Jr., "The Balaam Texts from Deir ʿAlla: The First Combination," *BASOR* 239 (1980) 49–60; Jo Ann Hackett, *The Balaam Text from Deir ʿAllā* (HSM 31; Chico, Calif.: Scholars Press, 1984).

14   Sweeney, *Isaiah 1–39*, 240–52.

Moab may have played a role in helping Assyria to secure and maintain its hold on this region throughout the seventh century.

Thus the inscriptional and biblical evidence points to a scenario in which Moab and perhaps Ammon were able to encroach on Israelite territory during the ninth through the seventh centuries and to erect monuments or inscriptions that trumpeted their successes. Clearly, such inscriptions would explain the use of language in Zeph 2:8 that would point to the insults or revilings of Moab and Ammon against Israel. The reference to "their border" is also understandable in light of gains made by Moab and Ammon against Israelite territory at various points during these times. In that the beginning of Josiah's reign coincided with the impending dissolution of the Assyrian Empire and the potential restoration of an autonomous Davidic state, the time would have been ripe for the recovery of Israelite or Judean territory in Transjordan that had been lost at various times to the Moabites and Ammonites, as well as to the Assyrians, during these years. It would appear then that Zephaniah looked forward to that time as part of the larger scenario of the Day of YHWH.

This background would not have entered into the presentation of this text by the textual versions. In every case, they understand the idiom, "and they made great against their border," as an indication of boasting rather than actual territorial encroachment in keeping with the normal function of the idiom, particularly in Jer 48:26, 42, which charge Moab with the statement, "because he magnified himself against YHWH." Thus the LXX renders the text, "I have heard the reproaches of Moab and the insults of the sons of Ammon, when they would reproach my people, and they exalted themselves upon my borders." Interestingly, the LXX renders גְּבוּלָם, "their border," as τὰ ὅριά μου, "my borders," in order to emphasize that the crime of the Moabites and Ammonites is against YHWH. Targum Jonathan and the Peshitta employ similar renditions, respectively: "Heard before me are the taunts of Moab and the boasts of the sons of Ammon when they taunted my people and they boasted upon their border"; and "I have heard the taunt of Moab and the blasphemy of the sons of Ammon, and

they have taunted my people, and they have boasted upon their border." The Vulgate follows suit as well: "I have heard the reproach of Moab and the blasphemy of the sons of Ammon who reproached my people and were boasting upon their border."

■ 9 Verse 9 constitutes the second portion of the prophet's presentation of YHWH's judgment speech concerning Moab and the sons of Ammon. The introductory particle, לָכֵן, "therefore," is a characteristic feature of the prophetic judgment speeches that typically introduces the announcement of punishment in the prophetic judgment speech form. The first person formulation of the speech together with the appearance of the expanded oracular formula in v. 9a[4-8], נְאָם ה" צְבָאוֹת אֱלֹקֵי יִשְׂרָאֵל, "oracle of YHWH Sebaot, G-d of Israel," indicates that the prophet is the primary speaker in this passage who conveys a statement by YHWH. This full form of the formula appears elsewhere only in 1 Sam 2:30 and Isa 17:6. In both cases, it refers to YHWH as G-d of all Israel, that is, all twelve tribes of Israel in the premonarchic period in the case of 1 Sam 2:30 or of both northern Israel and southern Judah in the late eighth century in the case of Isa 17:6. Since Josiah's program of religious reform and national restoration is designed to reunite the former northern kingdom with Judah and to centralize worship of the whole around the Jerusalem sanctuary, the addition of "G-d of Israel" makes great sense insofar as it identifies YHWH with the larger entity of all Israel. YHWH's speech in this verse presents the formal announcement of punishment against Moab and Ammon following the accusations articulated in v. 8 that provide the reasons for the announcement of punishment.

Following the introductory particle לָכֵן, the oath formula חַי-אָנִי, "as I live," both aids in identifying YHWH as the speaker and emphasizes YHWH's commitment to the course of action announced in the following statements.[15] The present form of the oath formula appears frequently in the narrative and prophetic literature of the Hebrew Bible (Num 14:21, 28; Isa 49:18; Jer 22:24; 46:18; Ezek 5:11; 14:16, 18, 20; 16:48; 17:16, 19; 18:3; 20:3, 31, 33; 33:11, 27; 34:8; 35:6, 11). Variations include: חַי-אָנֹכִי ("as I live," Deut 32:40), חַי-דֶּרֶךְ בְּאֵר שֶׁבַע

---

15   See Sweeney, *Isaiah 1–39*, 525–26, 546; Marvin H. Pope, "Oaths," *IDB* 3:5725–577; Moshe Greenberg, "The Hebrew Oath Particle Ḥay/Ḥē," *JBL* 76 (1957) 34–39.

("as the way of Beer-sheba lives," Amos 8:14), and חֵי אֱלֹהֶיךָ דָּן ("as your G-d [at] Dan lives," Amos 8:14). The formula presupposes life as an essential attribute of YHWH (see Josh 3:10; Hos 2:1; Pss 42:3; 84:3), and the formula חַי ה׳, "as YHWH lives," appears frequently in the oaths of human beings who call on YHWH as a means to bind themselves to a course of action that they propose (see Judg 8:19; Ruth 3:13; 1 Sam 14:39, 45; 1 Kgs 1:29; 2 Kgs 5:16; Hos 4:15; Jer 4:2; 5:2; etc.). The present form of the oath formula translates literally as "alive/living am I," and functions figuratively as a form of self-curse, "as I live," that indicates a guarantee to the course of action so as to avoid the implicit claim that YHWH will cease to live if the action is not carried out. There is, of course, a certain rhetorical force to this statement, as the possibility of YHWH's death is understood to be an unshakable and unconditional impossibility in the context of ancient Judean cultic life and prophecy. Consequently, the oath formula functions as an unconditional guarantee that the actions outlined here will take place. The formula may also be employed by the speaker of the oath or in reference to another person to indicate that a human life is put forward as the guarantee of the speaker's commitment to action. Of course, the life in question may be that of the king (1 Sam 17:55; 2 Sam 14:19; 15:21), the pharaoh (Gen 42:15, 16), or the priest Eli (1 Sam 1:26), indicating the rhetorical nature of the oath; that is, it appeals to the presumption of life on the part of a major public figure or the addressee as a means to guarantee the proposed action or ideas.

YHWH's announcement of punishment against Moab and Ammon draws on the Sodom and Gomorrah traditions that appear in Genesis 18–19 as well as in many other texts (see Deut 29:22; 32:32; Amos 4:11; Isa 1:9, 10; 3:9; 13:19; Jer 23:14; 49:18; 50:40; Ezek 16:46, 48, 49, 53, 55, 56; Lam 4:6). Gen 19:29-38 ties the destruction of Sodom and Gomorrah to the origins of Moab and Ammon in that the birth of their eponymous ancestors results from the incestuous relations between Lot and his daughters following the destruction of the region. A survey of the other passages indicates that Sodom and Gomorrah constitute quintessential examples of nations or peoples that are considered wicked and therefore subject to punishment by YHWH. The cities are also associated with images of total devastation as a result of their wickedness, and the present oracle draws on that imagery by citing examples of the natural phenomena that one will see in the vicinity of the Dead Sea where Sodom and Gomorrah were traditionally situated.

The first term employed to convey this devastation is מִמְשַׁק חָרוּל, frequently translated as "a possession of weeds."[16] The term מִמְשַׁק is a *hapax legomenon* in the Hebrew Bible, apparently related to another *hapax*, מֶשֶׁק, in Gen 15:2. The meaning of the term is generally derived from the latter reference, where it describes Abram's servant, Eliezer: "My L-rd, YHWH, what will you give me as I am childless, and the heir (בֶּן־מֶשֶׁק) of my house is the Damascene Eliezer [alternatively, Eliezer of Damascus]?" The understanding of מֶשֶׁק as "possession" is derived from the context, which describes Eliezer as one who has rights to the possession of Abram's estate in the absence of a biological heir. The meaning of מִמְשַׁק is established as "possession" based on the analogy of מֶשֶׁק, which derives from the same root. It appears to function in the present context as a term that simply describes territory, although the connotations of possession or inheritance might allude to the following statements in v. 9b that Israel will despoil the Moabites and Ammonites and inherit or take possession of their territory. The term חָרוּל is used elsewhere in reference to weeds that grow in the vineyards of those who are lazy and do not tend them well (Prov 24:30-31) or to the shelter of those who are outcast (Job 30:7). Thus the phrase alludes to the clumps of weeds that dot the ground in the vicinity of the Dead Sea.

The expression וּמִכְרֵה־מֶלַח, "and salt pit," is also problematic because מִכְרֵה is another *hapax legomenon*. It is generally derived from the root כרה, "to dig," and is therefore understood as a word for a pit or a place where one digs. Again, the expression relates to the region of the Dead Sea where one will find many salt formations. These formations result from the seepage of water and salt into the ground that are then forced to

---

16   See J. C. Greenfield, "A Hapax Legomenon, מִמְשַׁק חָרוּל," in S. Brunswick, ed., *Studies in Judaica, Karaitica, and Islamica Presented to Leon Nemoy on his 80th* *Birthday* (Ramat Gan; Bar Ilan Univ. Press, 1982) 79–85, for discussion of this expression.

the surface around the sea by pressure from incoming water, earthquake, volcanic activity, and other evaporation due to the extremely dry and warm conditions.[17]

The expression וּשְׁמָמָה עַד־עוֹלָם, "and desolation until eternity/forever," involves no philological or semantic problems. It merely functions as an apt phrase to describe the environs of the Dead Sea.

The versions tend to read this depiction of Moab's and Ammon's fate in relation to the Sodom/Gomorrah and other traditions concerning Abram/Abraham. Thus the LXX reads, "for Moab will be like Sodom and the sons of Ammon like Gomorrah, and Damascus (will be) abandoned like a heap of salt and destroyed forever." The reading of the term "Damascus" in place of מִמְשַׁק חָרוּל clearly draws on the identification of the בֶּן־מֶשֶׁק in Gen 15:2 as דַּמֶּשֶׂק אֱלִיעֶזֶר, "Damascene Eliezer," and the understanding of חָרוּל, "weeds," as a reference to a desolate or abandoned region that is overgrown with weeds.[18] The reading also relates to the LXX's overall concern with the relation between YHWH and the nations in Zephaniah. The reference to מִכְרֵה־מֶלַח as θημωνιὰ ἁλός, "a heap of salt," draws on similar references to Lot's wife in both the MT and LXX versions of Gen 19:26 in which she is turned into "a pillar of salt" (MT, נְצִיב מֶלַח; LXX, στήλη ἁλός). Targum Jonathan reads the passage as, "for Moab shall be like Sodom and the sons of Ammon like Gomorrah, an abandoned place of salt plants and mines of salt and desolation forever." Although Hebrew חָרוּל is sometimes read as "chickpeas," TJ employs the expression מְלוֹחִין, "salt plants," to ensure that the reader understands the phrase to refer to plants appropriate to the Dead Sea region. The Peshitta takes pains to relate the statement to an indictment of Moab's and Ammon's leaders: "that Moab shall be like Sodom and the sons of Ammon like Gomorrah, and their plantings shall be destroyed and their leaders shall perish, and they shall be destroyed forever." The rendition apparently depends on a pair of puns in Syriac. The word *nyṣbthyn*, "their plantings," relates to Hebrew נְצִיב

מֶלַח, "pillar of salt," used in Gen 19:26 to describe Lot's wife after she looked back on the destruction of the cities. Syriac *nyṣbʾ* has a range of meanings including "plants," and the derivative form *nyṣwbʾ* is employed to refer to one who "founds" or "plants" an institution or a set of ideas or doctrines. Syriac *mlwḥhyn*, "their leaders," is based on the verb *mlḥ*, which means "to salt" and metaphorically refers to governing or directing. It would appear that the Peshitta reads this text in relation to the "pillar of salt" in Gen 19:26, and employs various puns on the Hebrew term to express the downfall of Moab's and Ammon's leaders.

Finally, v. 9b describes the consequences of Moab's and Ammon's becoming desolate like Sodom and Gomorrah: their lands will be taken by the people of Judah/Israel. The use of the terms שְׁאֵרִית עַמִּי, "remnant of my people," and יֶתֶר גּוֹי, "remainder of a nation," has prompted many claims that v. 9b is a secondary addition to the text.[19] The basis for such a claim is that such "remnant" terminology must presuppose the postexilic period when only a remnant of the people Israel remained in the aftermath of the Babylonian exile. One must recall, however, that Judah saw itself as the "remnant of Israel" following the Assyrian destruction of the northern kingdom of Israel, and that Josiah's program was designed to restore all Israel following the collapse of the Assyrian Empire. In the case of Moab and Ammon, the possession of their lands would be a particularly poignant example of reversal. In that Moab and Ammon had seized Israelite territory in the past and continued to control it during the period of Assyria's hegemony over the region, it would be entirely fitting for Israel to take possession of Moabite and Ammonite territory in the aftermath of Assyria's, Moab's, and Ammon's destruction. One might note further indications of irony or double entendre in the choice of verbs that express these actions. The verb יְבֹזּוּם, "they will despoil/plunder them," derives from the root בזז, "to despoil/plunder," but it relates assonantally to the root

---

17   See esp. W. H. Morton, "Dead Sea," *IDB* 1:788–90, for a brief discussion of the physical characteristics of the Dead Sea.

18   See Gerleman, *Zephanja*, 37–38, who considers it to be an inner Greek corruption; see also Rudolph, *Zephanja*, 277; Roberts, *Zephaniah*, 192; Berlin, *Zephaniah*, 109; Ryou, *Zephaniah's Oracles*, 38.

19   Nowack, *Propheten*, 299; Sellin, *Zwölfprophetenbuch*, 433; Junker, *Sophonia*, 79; Elliger, *Zephanja*, 72–73; Keller, *Sophonie*, 203 n. 9; Rudolph, *Zephanja*, 281–82; Renaud, *Sophonie*, 229; Edler, *Kerygma*, 54–56; Seybold, *Satirische Prophetie*, 48; idem, *Zephanja*, 107.

בּוֹזֶה, "to despise," which suggests reversal in relation to the boasting and insults of the Moabites and Ammonites. The use of the verb יְנְחָלוּם, "they shall inherit them," refers specifically to the possession of land, which recalls the aforementioned territorial expansion of the Moabites and Ammonites at Israel's expense.

Although the grounds for the punishment are portrayed as past actions by the Moabites and Ammonites, the punishment itself is portrayed as a future event. This indicates that the prophet's speech is able to draw on the past (and possibly the present) experience of Moab and Ammon on the part of the audience, but it also points to anticipation of fundamental change in the situation of both Ammon/Moab and the people of Judah/Israel; that is, Israel/Judah will be able to take control of Moabite and Ammonite territory once the punishment is complete, thereby repaying them for the territorial encroachment against Israel in which they had engaged from the ninth century on.

■ **10** Verse 10 begins a summary-appraisal in vv. 10-11 that both reflects on the prior oracle concerning Moab and Ammon in vv. 8-9 and points forward to the oracles concerning Cush and Assyria that follow in vv. 12, 13-15.[20] The summary-appraisal is basically a didactic form that is designed to reflect on and analyze phenomena in the world or previously stated literary material in order to summarize and clarify its meaning. It is also designed to point to conclusions that may be drawn from such analysis of that phenomena or material. The genre is generally identified by an initial demonstrative pronoun, זֶה or זֹאת, "this," that refers back to the phenomena or previously stated material, and by a bicolon literary structure that lays out the didactic content of the form.

Many have argued that the repetitive and clarifying nature of the summary-appraisal in vv. 10-11 marks it as a secondary editorial addition to the text,[21] but this posi-

tion fails to account for its structural placement and argumentative character within Zephaniah's oracles concerning the nations.[22]

The present example of the summary-appraisal includes a reflection in v. 10 on the preceding Moabite-Ammonite oracle that points to pride as the reason for the judgment that is leveled against them. Insofar as it is formulated in narrative form with a third person reference to YHWH, it constitutes the prophet's commentary on YHWH's statement concerning Moab and Ammon in vv. 8-9. By pointing to "their pride" (גְּאוֹנָם) as the basic cause of Moab's and Ammon's actions and the reason for their punishment, v. 10 refers once again to the Isaian tradition of the Day of YHWH in Isa 2:6-21, which identifies the Day of YHWH as the time when YHWH will take action against all manifestations of pride and arrogance in the world, including both the nations (especially Assyria) and Israel/Judah (see also Isa 10:5-34; 13:1–14:27; 15:1–16:13; 17:1-14; 23:1-18; 28:1-29; 34:1-17; 36:1–37:38). As noted in the discussion of Zephaniah 1, the Day of YHWH tradition, particularly its Isaian forms, underlies Zephaniah's appeals for the purging of Jerusalem and Judah from foreign or idolatrous influence. By linking YHWH's words to the Isaian tradition in this fashion, the summary-appraisal points to past prophetic tradition as a warrant for the prophetic tradition and appeals for action in the present. It also reiterates the terminology employed to describe basic causes for YHWH's actions against Moab and Ammon as articulated in vv. 8-9: "they have reviled" (חֵרְפוּ; cf. v. 8) and "they have boasted" (וַיַּגְדִּילוּ; cf. v. 8). Some have seen the statement, "because they have reviled and boasted/magnified (themselves) against the people of YHWH Sebaot," as a modification of the oracle in vv. 8-9 due to the elimination of reference to "their border" following וַיַּגְדִּילוּ and by the specification

---

20   For discussion of the summary-appraisal form, see Sweeney, *Isaiah 1–39*, 539; Childs, *Crisis*, 128–36; Whedbee, *Isaiah and Wisdom*, 75–79.

21   See Schwally, "Sefanjâ," 226, who assigns all of vv. 5-10 to the postexilic period; cf. Marti, *Dodekapropheton*, 370; J. M. P. Smith, *Zephaniah*, 228; van Hoonacker, *Prophètes*, 523; Nowack, *Propheten*, 298–99; Sellin, *Zwölfprophetenbuch*, 433; Elliger, *Zephanja*, 73; Horst, *Propheten*, 196; Keller, *Sophonie*, 203–4; Rudolph, *Zephanja*, 282; Edler, *Kerygma*, 92;

Renaud, *Sophonie*, 229; Seybold, *Satirische Prophetie*, 48; idem, *Zephanja*, 107; Ryou, *Zephaniah's Oracles*, 302.

22   Cf. Ball, *Zephaniah*, 136–37; Roberts, *Zephaniah*, 201; Floyd, *Minor Prophets*, 224.

of "my people" as "the people of YHWH Sebaot."[23] Although the verb וַיַּגְדִּ֫ילוּ would normally be expected to mean "and they boasted," rather than "and they expanded (upon their border),"[24] the context insures that וַיַּגְדִּ֫ילוּ functions as it does in v. 8. Likewise, the shift from "my people" in v. 8 to "the people of YHWH Sebaot" in v. 10 merely makes explicit the identification of the people as articulated in YHWH's own statement.

By relating YHWH's oracle to the Isaian Day of YHWH tradition, v. 10 prepares the way for v. 11, which continues the summary-appraisal and lays the foundation for YHWH's worldwide action as articulated in vv. 12-15.

■ **11** The summary-appraisal continues in v. 11 with a projection of YHWH's fearsomeness that will be applied not only to Moab-Ammon but to the farthest reaches of the earth as well. The result will be the submission to YHWH of all the gods of the earth, which then motivates the inclusion of the oracles concerning Cush (v. 12) and Assyria (vv. 13-15), nations that are arguably at the farthest reaches of the world from the perspective of ancient Judah. Interestingly, the summary-appraisal reflects on a current situation, the threats posed to Moab and Ammon by the Arab tribes and their Babylonian supporters (and perhaps to the threat posed to Philistia by the Egyptians). Drawing on the lessons of these current situations, the prophet then turns to the past with an oracle concerning Cush or Ethiopia, which was subdued by the Twenty-fifth Egyptian Saite Dynasty in the early seventh century, and to the future with a projection of the ultimate downfall of the Assyrian Empire. Indeed, the projection of Assyria's downfall appears to be a major concern of both the summary-appraisal and of Zephaniah's oracles concerning the nations at large.

The third person plural pronoun of the initial statement in v. 11a, "fearsome (נוֹרָא) is YHWH against them," clearly indicates that the verse refers back to the statements concerning Moab and Ammon in the first element of the summary-appraisal in v. 10 as well as to the prophet's presentation of YHWH's judgment speech against these nations in vv. 8-9. Likewise, the portrayal of YHWH as "fearsome" is entirely appropriate in such a context, as it relates YHWH's wrath that will be unleashed against them as punishment for their aforementioned actions against both the people and G-d of Israel. Ben Zvi notes the parallel between this statement and that of Ps 96:4/1 Chr 16:25, "for great is YHWH and much praised; he is fearsome (נוֹרָא) against all gods," which portrays YHWH's sovereignty and superiority over the nations of the earth and their gods.[25] This observation is particularly noteworthy because it attests to this reading in a context with concerns much like those of Zephaniah, that is, it contends that YHWH is sovereign over all creation, the nations, and their gods. Whereas the MT reading of נורא is based on a *niphal* participle form of the root ירא, the LXX and Peshitta presuppose a reading of the term that is based on a *niphal* participle form of the root ראה, "to see," that is, נִרְאָה, "is seen," "appeared," or the like. Thus the LXX reads, "the L-rd shall appear (ἐπιφανήσεται) to them," and the Peshitta reads, "the L-rd has revealed himself (ʾtgly) to them." Unfortunately, none of the Judean Desert scrolls from Murabbaʿat, Naḥal Ḥever, or Qumran Cave 4 preserve readings for this term. Although most scholars would see the differences among these texts as a misreading of relatively little consequence,[26] the LXX and Peshitta seem to have deliberately read the text to present YHWH's actions in theophanic terms in keeping with traditions such as Judges 5; Habakkuk 3; Psalms 48;

---

23 See n. 21 above. Note that LXX eliminates the reference to the people to maintain that Moab and Ammon have acted directly against YHWH, i.e., "and they boasted over the L-rd Almighty." Gerleman, *Zephanja,* 39, attributes the change to haplography, but it appears to be a deliberate attempt on the part of the LXX translator to highlight YHWH's relationship with the nations at large.

24 See the commentary on v. 8 for discussion of this idiom. The LXX, TJ, and Peshitta all understand the term as a reference to boasting. The Vulgate understands it as a reference to self-magnification.

25 Ben Zvi, *Zephaniah,* 172–73.

26 E.g., Gerleman, *Zephanja,* 39; Rudolph, *Zephanja,* 277–78.

68, and other texts that portray YHWH's actions against Israel's (and YHWH's) enemies. Again, this emphasizes the LXX's overall concern with YHWH's relationship with the nations and the Peshitta's ongoing interaction with the LXX. In contrast, TJ both supports the reading of the MT and modifies the phrase to emphasize YHWH's redemptive acts on behalf of Israel: "the fear of YHWH (דחילא יוי) has said to redeem them." The Vulgate likewise supports the MT, "the fear of the L-rd (*horribilis Dominus*) is upon them."

The following explanatory clause in the balance of the verse begins with the statement, "because he has diminished (רָזָה) all the gods of the earth," which correlates YHWH's fearsomeness in punishing Moab and Ammon to YHWH's domination of the gods of the nations of the world at large. This entails a claim to YHWH's universal character, and presupposes the premise of Zephaniah 1 that the Temple in Jerusalem constitutes the holy center of creation at large. It likewise calls to mind other traditions that relate YHWH's status vis-à-vis other gods, such as Psalm 82, in which YHWH condemns the deities of the divine council to death for their failure to enact justice in the world, or Exodus 15, which relates YHWH's use of the sea to defeat Egypt before all the nations and proclaims in v. 11, "Who is like you among the gods, O YHWH?"

There is some uncertainty concerning the verb רָזָה, "he has diminished."[27] First, the literal meaning of the verb is "to make lean" as indicated by its use in Isa 17:4(-5) to indicate the leanness of flesh and the harvest of grain and olives that is employed metaphorically to describe YHWH's bringing low the glory of Jacob for its role in threatening Judah during the Ephraimite war. Likewise, the adjectival form רָזֶה is employed in Ezek 34:20 to identify the lean and fat sheep, and the noun form רָזוֹן to indicate wasting disease (Ps 106:15), a short measure (Mic 6:10), or a wasting sickness sent by YHWH against the Assyrian king's warriors (Isa 10:16). The term appears regularly in contexts that relate to the

diminishment of the object or party with which it is related. Thus the reference in v. 11 indicates that YHWH has somehow "wasted" or "diminished" the gods of the earth, that is, YHWH has overpowered them or rendered them ineffective. Second, the verb is not otherwise attested as transitive, but the only other occurrence is in Isa 17:14, which employs a *niphal* formation in relation to a grammatical subject. Third, the perfect form of the verb suggests that YHWH's action against the gods has already taken place. Some interpreters feel that this conflicts with the future orientation of v. 11 and therefore suggest that the verb be rendered as an imperfect *piel*, יְרַזֶּה, or the like.[28] No *piel* form of the verb is attested, but the LXX renders the verb in future perspective: "and he shall utterly destroy (καὶ ἐξολεθρεύσει) all the gods of the nations of the earth." This must be a stylistic modification, as the other versions all presuppose past tense renditions: "because he has humbled (אַמְאִיךְ) all the gods/idols of the earth" (TJ); "because he destroyed (*dnwbd*) all the kings of the earth" (Peshitta); and "and he has attenuated/made thin (*adtenuabit*) all the gods of the earth" (Vulgate). The Targum and Peshitta, of course, do not accept the existence of other gods and portray YHWH's actions against the idols or kings of the earth, respectively. In that the versions appear to confirm the perfect form of the verb, v. 11 apparently presupposes that YHWH's sovereignty over the gods has already been established.

This has important implications for v. 11b, which employs a simple conjunctive *waw* together with the imperfect form of the verb יִשְׁתַּחֲווּ־לוֹ, "they shall bow down to him," to portray the submission of the gods to YHWH. The statement clearly portrays the submission of the gods as the direct consequences of YHWH's actions against them, but the conjunctive *waw* indicates an element of disjunction (in contrast to a *waw*-consecutive) that marks v. 11b as a distinctive element within the syntax of the statement. Such a formulation indicates temporal discontinuity; YHWH's dominance has already

---

27   See Vlaardingerbroek, *Zephaniah*, 150; Ben Zvi, *Zephaniah*, 173; Roberts, *Zephaniah*, 193; Rudolph, *Zephanja*, 278; and esp. Ryou, *Zephaniah's Oracles*, 41–42; cf. Schwally, "Sefanjâ," 190–91.

28   Schwally, "Sefanjâ," 190–91; Marti, *Dodekapropheton*, 370; J. M. P. Smith, *Zephaniah*, 228–29, 231; van Hoonacker, *Prophètes*, 524; Nowack, *Propheten*, 300;

Sellin, *Zwölfprophetenbuch*, 433; Junker, *Sophonia*, 79; Elliger, *Zephanja*, 70; Rudolph, *Zephanja*, 278; Keller, *Sophonie*, 203; Renaud, *Sophonie*, 230; Roberts, *Zephaniah*, 193.

been established, but the full recognition of that sovereignty is yet to be realized. Such a temporal sequence relates to the following temporal portrayal of the oracles concerning Cush and Assyria in vv. 12, 13-15: Cush's fate has already been realized, but Assyria's is yet to come. It thereby serves the argumentative character of these oracles in that the prophet points first to the defeat of Cush in order to make the case that Assyria will fall as well.

Finally, the specification of the gods of the earth who bow down to YHWH as "each from his own place, all the islands of the nations," likewise points forward to the oracles concerning Cush and Assyria and thereby serves the argumentative strategy that points to the fall of Assyria as the ultimate rhetorical goal of this passage. Most interpreters understand the phrase אִיֵּי הַגּוֹיִם, "the islands of the nations," rather literally in keeping with the versions and well-established philological principles of textual interpretation. A recently published Babylonian map of the world from the late eighth or seventh century BCE, however, sheds some light on the means by which the ancients viewed the world and perhaps understood this expression.[29] The map places Babylon in the center of a land mass that includes Assyria, Urartu, Susa, and other Mesopotamian locations. This land mass is surrounded by water labeled "the ocean," and beyond the ocean are a series of small triangular land masses called *nagû* in Akkadian. The term *nagû* can have various connotations, such as "districts" or "provinces," but it is clear from Nebuchadnezzar's royal inscriptions that *nagû* are located in the midst of the sea and thus would be identified as islands.[30] Other examples, however, suggest that *nagû* are not always associated with the sea and refer basically to outlying regions at the farthest reaches of the world from a Babylonian perspective. Although Hebrew אִיִּים refers semantically to islands, it would appear that in analogy to the usage of Akkadian *nagû* the term also functions as a reference to outlying areas or the farthest reaches of the world known to Judah.[31] The following references to Cush and Assyria would qualify for such a referent, as Cush/Ethiopia represents one of the southernmost locations known to Judah, and Assyria is one of the northernmost locations.

29 For full discussion, see Wayne Horowitz, "The Babylonian Map of the World," *Mesopotamian Cosmic Geography* (Winona Lake, Ind.: Eisenbrauns, 1998) 20–42. An earlier publication appeared in his "Babylonian Map of the World," *Iraq* 50 (1988) 147–65.

30 See Horowitz, *Geography,* 30–32.

31 See Gen 10:5, where אִיֵּי הַגּוֹיִם refers to the coastland peoples descended from Japhet who spread westward through the Greek islands and Asia Minor (cf. Wayne Horowitz, "The Isles of the Nations: Genesis X and the Babylonian Geography," in J. A. Emerton, ed., *Studies in the Pentateuch* [VTSup 41; Leiden Brill, 1990] 35–43, for the equation of *nagû* with these islands of the nations). Afterward, Gen 10:6-14 relates the birth of the sons of Ham, including Cush, who founds Ethiopia and environs and in turn becomes the father of Nimrod, who founds Nineveh among other major locations in Mesopotamia.

2

Translation

12	**Also you, O Ethiopians,ᵃ slain by my swordᵇ are they!ᶜ**	a	MT, כּוּשִׁים, "Cushites/Ethiopians(?)"; LXX, Αἰθίοπες, "Ethiopia"; TJ, כושאי, "Cushites/Ethiopians"; Peshitta, *kwšyʾ*, "Cushites/Ethiopians"; Vulgate, *Aethiopes*, "Ethiopia."
		b	MT, חַרְבִּי, "my sword"; cf. Peshitta, *ḥrbʾ*, "the sword."
		c	MT, הֵמָּה, "(are) they"; cf. LXX, ἐστε, "are you"; TJ, תהון, "you shall be"; Vulgate, *eritis*, "you shall be." Peshitta drops the pronoun altogether, reading, "are killed by the sword."

Form and Setting

Zephaniah 2:12 constitutes YHWH's oracle concerning the Cushites, commonly identified as the Ethiopians. Although the first person suffix pronoun of חַרְבִּי, "my sword," identifies the verse as a statement by YHWH addressed to the Cushites, the larger context of the summary-appraisal form in vv. 10-11 and the oracles concerning the nations as a whole indicate that it is part of the prophet's presentation of YHWH's oracles concerning the nations. The oracle is demarcated initially by its generic and thematic shift as a direct address to Cush. It is also demarcated initially by the particle גַּם, "also, indeed," which establishes both a conjunctive and disjunctive syntactical relationship with the preceding statement of the summary-appraisal in v. 11. It is conjunctive in that the particle binds v. 12 to v. 11, but it is disjunctive in that גַּם also functions in an exclamatory or intensive fashion to call attention to a distinctive or new element within the larger syntactical structure of the text.[1] The conjunctive *waw* in v. 13 marks the beginning of a new oracular subunit that is concerned with the downfall of Assyria. As noted in the discussion of the summary-appraisal in vv. 10-11, vv. 12 and 13-15 are joined together syntactically to illustrate the anticipated outcome of YHWH's actions against the Moabites and Ammonites; that is, YHWH's sovereignty will be established over all the gods and nations of the earth. Insofar as the summary-appraisal envisions such recognition to the farthest reaches of the earth, the following oracles concerning Cush and Nineveh illustrate that reach. Cush would be one of the world's southernmost locations from the perspective of ancient Judah, and Nineveh or Ashur would be one of the northernmost locations.

Floyd identifies v. 12 as a "taunt" against the Cushites based on its function as a derisive utterance that insinuates defeat or inferiority.[2] He correctly maintains, however, that it is "a somewhat atypical representative of its genre"[3] in that it makes no direct accusation against the Cushites nor does it give any indication as to how their punishment might benefit Judah. Indeed, its placement in relation to the summary-appraisal and the following Assyrian oracle make that function clear insofar as the past defeat of the Ethiopians points to the impending downfall of the Assyrians. In this respect, the shift in the address perspective of the verse is noteworthy. Whereas the first half of the verse is directed to the Cushites, "also you, O Cushites," the second half refers to the Cushites in the third person, "slain by my sword are they." As noted above, the versions made attempts to correct this discrepancy, but the concern with such consistency in the address perspective overlooks the possibil-

---

1   GKC, §150; cf. Bruce K. Waltke and M. O'Connor, *An Introduction to Biblical Hebrew Syntax* (Winona Lake, Ind.: Eisenbrauns, 1990) §16.3.5b, who maintain that when a personal pronoun follows גַּם, "it has *no special emphasis* and . . . means little more than 'also'" (note that in §39.3.4d, they hold out for the possibility that גַּם can indeed be emphatic in such a circumstance).

2   Floyd, *Minor Prophets*, 225, 227–28, 649.
3   Floyd, 227.

ity that such inconsistency is deliberate and indicates the communicative intention of the text. It is very unlikely that the author of this text ever envisioned the possibility that the Cushites might read or hear this text. Although it employs a second person masculine plural direct address, it is likely intended for a Jerusalemite or Judean audience. Thus the initial address to the Cushites constitutes a fictive address that is formulated for the benefit of the Jerusalemite/Judean audience. The third person reference to the Cushites in the second half of the verse makes clear that the text speaks about the Cushites, not to them. The purpose of the text is to bring forward evidence, in this case the well-known defeat of the Cushites or Twenty-fifth Ethiopian Dynasty of Egypt in 663 BCE as evidence for the contention that YHWH would also bring about the downfall of Nineveh or Assyria.[4]

The identification of Cush with Ethiopia, however, is somewhat controversial. Some (including me) have previously identified Cush with Egypt, based on the contention that Zephaniah's oracles concerning the nations were directed against major enemies of Judah in the time of Josiah.[5] Others have correctly pointed out that such an equation is made nowhere else in the Hebrew Bible and that the Ethiopians ceased to rule Egypt following the fall of Thebes in 663.[6] Since this event took place some twenty-four years prior to the reign of Josiah, in which the prophecy of Zephaniah is placed historically (see Zeph 1:1), it is unlikely that the prophet would refer to such a distant event.

Consequently, alternatives have been put forward. The most cogent alternative is that Cush refers to the Midianites, based on the identification of Midian with the name Cushan in Hab 3: 7 and the identification of Moses' wife, presumably Zipporah the daughter of Jethro, priest of Midian, as a Cushite woman in Num 12:1.[7] Such a contention suffers from many uncertainties, such as why the Midianites would pose a threat to Judah in this period, especially since they are associated with an illustrious figure such as Moses, and the related Rechabites are held up as an example of ideal piety for YHWH in Jeremiah 35.[8] Some have speculated that the string of fortresses built along the southern borders of Judah in the Negev during the seventh century were designed to protect Judah from encroachments by various bedouin and Edomite groups.[9] Although the Arad

---

4   For discussion of the defeat of the Twenty-fifth Cushite Dynasty of Egypt and the rise of the Twenty-sixth Saite Dynasty, see Kuhrt, *Ancient Near East,* 634–46; Hallo and Simpson, *Ancient Near East,* 287–97; Redford, *Egypt,* 351–64, 430–69; A. Spalinger, "Psammetichus, King of Egypt I," *JARCE* 13 (1976) 133–47; idem, "Psammetichus, King of Egypt: II," *JARCE* 15 (1978) 49–57; idem, "Egypt, History of, 3d Intermediate-Saite Period (Dyn. 21-26)," *ABD* 2:353–64.

5   E.g., Sweeney, "Form-Critical Reassessment"; D. L. Christensen, "Zephaniah 2:4-15: A Theological Basis for Josiah's Program of Political Expansion," *CBQ* 45 (1984) 669–82; see now Vlaardingerbroek, *Zephaniah,* 152. See also Bustenay Oded, "Judah and the Exile," in John H. Hayes and J. Maxwell Miller, eds., *Israelite and Judaean History* (OTL; Philadelphia: Westminster, 1977) 458–69.

6   Robert D. Haak, "'Cush' in Zephaniah," in Steven W. Holloway and Lowell K. Handy, eds., *The Pitcher Is Broken: Memorial Essays for Gösta W. Ahlström* (JSOTSup 190; Sheffield: Sheffield Academic Press, 1995) 238–51; Ben Zvi, *Zephaniah,* 176–78.

7   Haak, "'Cush' in Zephaniah." For an overview of the proposals for understanding Cush, see Berlin, *Zephaniah,* 111–13; idem, "Zephaniah's Oracle Against the Nations and an Israelite Cultural Myth," in Andrew. A. Bartelt et al., eds., *Fortunate the Eyes That See* (Fest. D. N. Freedman; Grand Rapids: Eerdmans, 1995) 175–84. She rightly rejects identification of the Cushites with Egypt, Midian, and tribes from the Arabian peninsula for lack of clear evidence and probability. Her own proposal to identify the Cushites with the Kassite kingdom of Mesopotamia (see also Ball, *Zephaniah,* 141, 242–52), based on the observation that Gen 10:5-11 identifies Cush as the father of Nimrod who in turn founded Nineveh and Ashur, must also be rejected, as the Kassite kingdom disappeared by the end of the Bronze Age (Haak, "'Cush' in Zephaniah," 241–42).

8   Note that the Rechabites are associated with the Kenites in 1 Chr 2:55, "these are the Kenites who came from Hammath, father of the house of Rechab." Note also that Zipporah's father, Jethro, is also known as Reuel the Kenite in Num 10:29. For discussion see F. Frick, "Rechab," *ABD* 5:630–32.

9   See Amihai Mazar, *Archaeology of the Land of the Bible, 10,000–586 B.C.E.* (New York: Doubleday, 1990) 438–44; Yohanan Aharoni, *The Archaeology of the Land of Israel* (Philadelphia: Westminster, 1982) 264–79. The fortresses include Arad, Horvat ʿUza,

ostraca from this period that relate the correspondence of Judean officials responsible for the administration of the city of Arad in the Negev point to a great deal of conflict with the Edomites, evidence that the Midianites threatened Judah in this region during this period is lacking.[10] The situation is further clarified by the recognition that the fundamental reason for the construction of these fortresses lies in the demographic and economic realities of Judah during the seventh century.[11] As a result of the Assyrian invasion of Judah in the late eighth century, Judah lost substantial territory in the Shephelah region, and began to shift its population to the east and the south. During the reign of Manasseh, Judah apparently expanded into the Negev, especially in the region of Beer-sheba, in order to provide the surviving Judean population with alternative living and agricultural areas following the loss of the fertile Shephelah region. An additional motivation appears to be the control of the Negev trade routes that provided a lucrative income to the various bedouin tribal groups that lived there. Of course, the control of this region would have been of great interest to the Assyrians, whose general expansion into western Asia was motivated especially by an interest in establishing and controlling trade in the region. A further motivation lies in Assyria's interest in protecting its interests against the Egyptians, who were known to use the Negev routes at various times in history, either to invade Israel/Judah and Transjordan or to gain control of the Negev and Transjordanian trade routes for themselves.[12] In that Assyria invaded Egypt early in the seventh century, these fortresses may also have functioned to protect the southwestern borders of the Assyrian Empire and its Judean vassal against Egyptian retaliation.

Such a scenario raises questions about the contention that Zeph 2:12 depicts the results of Judean efforts to subdue the Negev bedouin. Conflict with the bedouin is certainly possible in this scenario, but Judah's conflicts appear to be with the Edomites, who were attempting to encroach upon this region. If Zephaniah was concerned with conflict in this region, it seems far more likely that he would mention Edom, which is entirely lacking in his oracles. In that Cush generally refers to Ethiopia in the Bible, it is necessary to reconsider the reasons why Zephaniah would include an oracle concerning the demise of the Ethiopians at a time when Ethiopia no longer controlled Egypt and had little opportunity to interact with Judah at all. I noted above that in dismissing the oracle's reference to Ethiopia, scholars point to the fall of the Twenty-fifth Ethiopian Dynasty with the sack of Thebes by the Assyrians in 663. It is noteworthy, however, that the Assyrians were not able to accomplish this defeat entirely on their own, but did so by establishing Egyptian allies, especially the Saite ruler Neco I (d. 664) and his son Psamtek (664–609). Although the Saites were initially Assyrian vassals, they eventually emerged as the rulers of all Egypt, as the Assyrian monarchs Essarhaddon and Ashurbanipal were forced to withdraw from Egypt in order to attend to challenges at home in Mesopotamia. The early Saite relationship is not entirely clear; they may have played a role in ensuring that the Assyrians were unable to regain full control of Egypt, but later periods see them acting in support of the Assyrians against the Babylonians.[13] Nevertheless, the rise of the Saite Dynasty in Egypt and its later advances against the Philistines during the reign of Psamtek (see above on

Tel ʿIra, ʿArorer, Tel Masos, Tel Malhata, and Beer-sheba.

10 For the Arad ostraca, see Yohanan Aharoni, *Arad Inscriptions* (Jerusalem: Israel Exploration Society, 1981). See also Itzhaq Beit-Arieh and Bruce C. Cresson, "Horvat ʿUza: A Fortified Outpost on the Eastern Negev Border," *BA* 54 (1991) 126–35, who discuss ostraca from this site that also point to an Edomite presence.

11 For a full discussion and bibliography, see Israel Finkelstein, "The Archaeology of the Days of Manasseh," in Michael D. Coogan, J. Cheryl Exum, and Lawrence E. Stager, eds., *Scripture and Other Arti-*

facts: Essays on the Bible and Archaeology in Honor of Philip J. King (Louisville: Westminster John Knox, 1994) 169–87.

12 See Redford, *Egypt,* 269–75, 348–64, 444.

13 See the Babylonian Chronicle, which places the Egyptian army in Mesopotamia by 616 when it acts in support of the Assyrians against the Babylonians (*ANET,* 303–4).

2:4, 5-7), pointed to the ultimate downfall of the Assyrian Empire. The Assyrians were no longer able to control either Egypt or western borders, and in fact became dependent on Egypt for support by the late seventh century.

This situation has implications for understanding 2:12. The verse is formulated as a verbless statement, which indicates that its depiction of Cush's demise lacks any temporal referent. It cannot be located in the past, present, or future, but instead describes an ongoing situation in which Cush is clearly subdued. Since the Saite Dynasty controlled Egypt by the early reign of Josiah, having kept Cush at bay and having seen the withdrawal from Egypt of the Assyrians, the rise of Saite Egypt and its incursions into Assyrian territory such as Philistia would be seen in Judah as a portent for the ultimate downfall of the Assyrians.[14]

■ **12** Although "Cushan" parallels "Midian" in Hab 3:7 and Num 12:1 refers to Moses' Midianite wife Zipporah as a Cushite woman, the term "Cush" appears to refer to Ethiopia throughout the rest of the Hebrew Bible (see Isa 11:11; 18:1; Ezek 29:10; Job 28:19; Esth 1:1; 8:9; Isa 20:4; Jer 46:9; Ezek 38:5; Ps 68:32; Isa 20:3, 5; 43:3; 45:14; 2 Kgs 19:9/Isa 37:9; Nah 3:9; Ezek 30:4, 5, 9; Ps 87:4). Certainly the reference to the return of Israel's/Judah's exiles from beyond the rivers of Cush indicates the recognition of YHWH from the most distant regions of the earth rather than a reference to Midianite or bedouin regions of control.

As noted above, the shift in address perspective from the second person address to Cush, "also you, O Cushites," to a third person reference, "slain by my sword are they," indicates the rhetorical perspective of this text. The Cushites are only the fictive addressees of this text. Rather, it is addressed to a Judean or Jerusalemite audience, which is expected to draw the conclusion that YHWH is ultimately responsible for the defeat of the Ethiopians. Each of the major versions provides a reading that attempts to present a stylistically consistent text. Thus the LXX reads, "And you, O Ethiopians, you are wounded by my sword." Targum Jonathan reads, "Also you, O Cushites, you shall be killed of my sword." The Peshitta reads, "Also you, O Cushites, are killed by the sword," which apparently indicates reluctance to attribute the killing to G-d when no reason for the killing is given. The Vulgate reads, "And you, however, O Ethiopians, you shall be slain by the sword," apparently reflecting a similar sentiment to that of the Peshitta.

Insofar as the defeat of Cush is known to have occurred at the time of the origins of the Saite Egyptian Dynasty, it provides evidence that YHWH will ultimately bring down the Assyrians as well in that the Saites advance toward Philistia, the southwestern edge of Assyria's empire. As the initial formulation of the following oracle concerning Assyria shows, the downfall of Assyria would be construed as a new exodus event in which the Assyrians had assumed the role of the Egyptians as the enemy of YHWH that was to suffer the effects of YHWH's hand.

---

14   Floyd, *Minor Prophets,* 226; cf. Bennett, "Zephaniah," 691.

2

Translation

13 And he shall extend his hand[a] against the north, and he shall destroy[b] Ashur; and he shall make Nineveh into a desolation, a desert like the wilderness.[c]

14 And flocks shall lie in its midst, every animal of a nation,[d]
both pelican[e] and porcupine,[f] in its capitals they shall reside;[g]
a voice sings in the window,[h] desolation in the door frame,[i]
for cedar is laid bare.[j]

15 This is the exultant[k] city that sits secure,[l] that says in its heart, "I and no other!"
How it has become a desolation, a place for animals to lie;[m]
each one who passes by[n] it will hiss, he will wave his hand.[o]

a   MT, וְיֵט יָדוֹ, "and he shall extend his hand"; cf. TJ, וירים מחת גבורתיה, "and he shall raise the plague of his might."

b   MT, וִיאַבֵּד אֶת, "and he shall destroy"; cf. 4QXII[b], fragment 2, line 1,]ויאב את[, which may be a scribal error.

c   MT, וְיָשֵׂם אֶת־נִינְוֵה לִשְׁמָמָה צִיָּה כַּמִּדְבָּר, "and he shall make Nineveh into a desolation, a desert like the wilderness"; cf. Vulgate, *et ponet speciosam in solitudinem et in invium quasi deertum*, "and he shall place splendor in solitude and impassable like a desert." The Vulgate's translation of נינוה, "Nineveh," as *speciosam*, "splendor," apparently presupposes the root נוה, "beautiful" (see Gerleman, *Zephanja*, 42; Rudolph, *Zephanja*, 278; Ryou, *Zephaniah's Oracles*, 45).

d   MT, כָל־חַיְתוֹ־גוֹי, "every animal of a nation"; cf. LXX, καὶ πάντα τὰ θηρία τῆς γῆς, "and all the wild animals of the land"; TJ, דכל חיות ברא (עדרין), "(flocks) of all the animals of the outdoors"; Peshitta, *wklhyn ḥywtʾ dʿmmʾ*, "and all the animals of the nations"; Vulgate, *omnes bestiae gentium*, "all the animals of the nations."

e   MT, קָאַת, "pelican"; LXX, χαμαιλέοντες, "chameleons"; TJ, קתין, "pelicans"; Peshitta, *qqʾ*, "pelican"; Vulgate, *onocrotalus*, "pelican."

f   MT, קִפֹּד, "porcupine"; LXX, ἐχῖνοι, "hedgehogs"; TJ, קופדין, "hedgehogs"; Peshitta, *qwpdʾ*, "owl"; Vulgate, *ericius*, "hedgehog."

g   MT, בְּכַפְתֹּרֶיהָ יָלִינוּ, "in her/its capitals, they shall reside"; LXX, ἐν τοῖς φατνώμασιν αὐτῆς κοιτασθήσονται, "(they) shall sleep in her/its ceilings"; TJ, בפיתוה תרעהא יביתיתון, "(they) shall lodge in the engraved work of her/its gates"; Peshitta, *bbtyh nbwtwn*, "(they) shall lodge in her/its houses"; Vulgate, *in liminibus eius morabuntur*, "(they) shall reside in her/its capitals."

h   MT, קוֹל יְשׁוֹרֵר בַּחַלּוֹן, "a voice/sound sings in the window"; LXX, καὶ θηρία φωνήσει ἐν τοῖς διορύγμασιν αὐτῆς, "and wild animals shall sound off in her/its breaches"; TJ, בכוהא קל עופא דמנציף, "the sound of a bird that chirps in her/its windows"; Peshitta, *whywtʾ nnhmn bgwh*, "and animals that roar in her/its midst"; Vulgate, *vox cantatis in fenestra*, "a voice sings in the window."

i   MT, חֹרֶב בַּסַּף, "desolation in the door frame"; LXX, κόρακες ἐν τοῖς πυλῶς αὐτῆς, "ravens in her/its gateways"; TJ, חרובו תרעהא, "her/its gates shall be destroyed"; Peshitta, *wḥrbʾ btrʿyh*, "and destruction in her/its gates"; Vulgate, *corvus in superliminari*, "a raven in the door frames."

j   MT, כִּי אַרְזָה עֵרָה, "because her/its cedar is laid bare"; LXX, διότι κέδρος τὸ ἀνάστημα αὐτῆς, "because a cedar was her loftiness"; TJ, וטללהא סתרו, "and her/its ceilings will be torn down";

149

Peshitta, *mtwl d'qrh 'tprsy*, "because its/her foundation is overrun"; Vulgate, *quoniam adtenuabo robur
eius*, "because I will diminish her/its strength/oak."

k   MT, הָעַלִּיזָה, "exultant"; LXX, ἡ φαυλίσρια, "disparaging"; TJ, תקיפתא, "strong"; Peshitta, ʿšyntʾ, "strong";
Vulgate, *gloriosa*, "glorious."

l   MT, לָבֶטַח, "secure"; LXX, ἐπ᾽ ἐλπίδι, "upon hope";
TJ, לרחצן, "secure"; Peshitta, *bšlyʾ*, "in quiet/peace";
Vulgate, *in confidentia*, "in confidence."

m   MT, מַרְבֵּץ לַחַיָּה, "a (place of) lying down for animals"; LXX, νομὴ θηρίν, "a district of wild animals";
TJ, בית משרי חיות ברא, "a camp house for wild animals"; Peshitta, *wbyt mrbʿ lḥywtʾ*, "and a residence
house of animals"; Vulgate, *cubile bestiae*, "a den of
animals."

n   Peshitta adds, *ntmh*, "shall be amazed."

o   Peshitta adds, *wnʾmr*, "and shall say."

Form and Setting

Zephaniah 2:13-15 constitutes the prophet's oracle concerning the downfall of Ashur or Assyria and its capital
at Nineveh. Its third person references to YHWH's hand
indicate that the prophet is the speaker of this passage,
and he relates both YHWH's actions against Assyria and
the consequences of those actions. The unit is demarcated by an initial *waw*-conjunctive verbal formation, וְיֵט,
"and he shall extend," and by the shift in subject matter
from the Cushites of v. 12 to Assyria and Nineveh beginning in v. 13. Two additional *waw*-conjunctive verbs follow in v. 13, which relate YHWH's actions against
Ashur/Assyria and Nineveh. Verse 14 employs a combination of the *waw*-consecutive perfect verb וְרָבְצוּ, "and
they shall lie," and the imperfect forms יָלִינוּ, "they shall
reside," and יְשׁוֹרֵר, "he/it sings," to depict the consequences of YHWH's actions as animals take residence in
the remains of the ruined city. Together, vv. 13-14 constitute an announcement of punishment against Assyria/
Ashur and Nineveh, but they do not state the reasons for
the punishment.[1] The reasons are implicit in the summary-appraisal form that appears in v. 15, indicated by
its initial demonstrative, זֹאת, "this," that characterizes
Nineveh as "the exultant city that sits secure" and as an
arrogant city that looks only to itself.[2] Insofar as the
summary-appraisal characterizes the city as arrogant and
portrays the scoffing of those who pass by its remains
following YHWH's punishment, v. 15 must be read

together with vv. 13-14. Altogether, vv. 13-15 constitute a
prophetic announcement of punishment against
Assyria.[3] The initial הוֹי, "Woe," form of 3:1 introduces
the following oracle sequence that is concerned with
Jerusalem's fate in relation to that of the nations outlined in the הוֹי sequence of 2:5-15.

Thus 2:13-15 constitutes the culmination of the oracles concerning the nations in 2:5-15 in that it points to
the downfall of Assyria as the projected outcome of
YHWH's current judgment against the Philistines (vv. 4,
5-7), the Moabites and Ammonites (vv. 8-9), the islands
or farthest ends of the earth (vv. 10-11), and YHWH's
past judgment against Cush (v. 12). Insofar as the rise of
Saite Egypt and perhaps also the Babylonian insurgen-
cies against Assyria stand behind these actions, the oracles concerning the nations are apparently designed to
point to past and contemporary events to project the
ultimate downfall of Assyria. This would serve the
exhortative end of convincing the Jerusalemite/Judean
audience to accept the prophet's call to seek YHWH in
2:1-4 and to purge Jerusalem/Judah of foreign influence
on the day of YHWH (1:2-18). The projected downfall of
Assyria appears prior to the oracles concerning
Jerusalem's own purging and restoration in 3:1-20. Consequently, the projected downfall of Assyria stands as a
sign that Jerusalem will be restored as YHWH's
metaphorical bride and holy center in the midst of the
nations.

1   Note that this element constitutes the second characteristic portion of the prophetic judgment speech
(see Sweeney, *Isaiah 1–39*, 530–31, 533–34).

2   For discussion of the summary-appraisal, see
Sweeney, *Isaiah 1–39*, 539; Childs, *Crisis*, 128–36;
Whedbee, *Isaiah and Wisdom*, 75–79.

3   Cf. Floyd, *Minor Prophets*, 227–28, who identifies vv.
12-15 as a prophecy of punishment against a foreign nation.

The historical setting for such a contention must lie in the early years of Josiah's reign, during the period when Philistia is threatened by the Egyptians and Moab and Ammon are threatened by Arab tribes. Such a situation appears to prevail from the beginning of Josiah's reign in 639 BCE and prior to the accession of Nabopolassar to the Babylonian throne in 627–626.[4] Although the date of Ashurbanipal's death is not entirely certain—he may have died as early as 631—such an event would serve as a fitting setting in which to project the downfall of Assyria and its consequences for Jerusalem and Judah.[5]

■ **13** Verse 13 begins the announcement of punishment against Ashur and Nineveh in vv. 13-14 and the summary-appraisal in v. 15, which states the reasons for the punishment. Although Assyria is strictly speaking to the east and north of the land of Israel, it is very difficult to travel through the Arabian desert, which stands between Assyria and Israel. Consequently, the routes of travel and communication from Assyria to the land of Israel passed through Aram, which is situated to the north.

The use of the expression וְיֵט יָדוֹ, "and he shall extend his hand," is striking in the present context, especially since the oracles concerning the nations in Zephaniah appear to presuppose the rise of the Saite Egyptian empire as an act of YHWH that will ultimately bring down the Assyrians. The idiom נָטָה יָד, "to extend (the) hand," and its variants is employed frequently in the Hebrew Bible as a general term for punitive action against a party, particularly by YHWH (see Josh 8:18; Ps 21:12; Job 15:25; Isa 23:11; Ezek 6:14; 7:5). Nevertheless, the idiom is a characteristic feature of the plague narrative in Exodus in which YHWH takes action against Egypt (see Exod 7:19; 8:1; 9:22, 23; 10:12, 13, 21, 22; 14:16, 21, 26, 27; cf. 15:12). The idiom is also employed

in Isaiah to express YHWH's actions against northern Israel (i.e., עוֹד יָדוֹ נְטוּיָה, "still his hand is stretched out"; see Isa 5:25; 9:11, 16, 20; 10:4). This usage is itself ironic in Isaiah because it employs the characteristic idiom of YHWH's actions against Egypt to depict YHWH's (and Assyria's) punishment of Israel. In this regard, it is noteworthy that Isa 10:24-26 draws an analogy between Assyria's punishment of Israel and Egypt's previous actions against Israel immediately prior to the portrayal of Assyria's downfall for arrogance against YHWH and the oppression of Israel/Jerusalem in the book of Isaiah (see 10:5-11, 16). The book of Isaiah deliberately employs a reversal of the exodus motif to express the punishment of Israel and the ultimate downfall of Assyria.[6] Zephaniah appears to employ such reversal once again by portraying Assyria as the victim of YHWH's outstretched hand, although irony enters the picture in that Egypt appears to be presupposed as a major factor in bringing about divine action against the Assyrians.

The reference to Ashur can designate the land of Assyria, the ancient capital city of Ashur, or the chief god of the Assyrian Empire.[7] Throughout the Hebrew Bible, the term tends to designate the land of Assyria (e.g., Gen 2:14; 10:11; Num 24:22, 24; Isa 10:5; 11:11, 16; 14:25; Jer 2:18, 36; Ezek 31:3; Hos 5:13; 7:11; Mic 7:12) or its eponymous ancestor (Gen 10:22), but there is no clear evidence that the term ever refers to the city or its god in the Hebrew Bible. The city of Ashur was destroyed during the last years of Josiah in 614 by the combined forces of the Babylonians and the Medes who destroyed the Assyrian Empire.

The reference to the destruction of Nineveh of course targets the capital city of the Assyrian Empire, first established by Sennacherib in the late eighth century

4   See Kuhrt, *Ancient Near East,* 589–90.
5   See ibid., 540–46, esp. 542–43, 588–89. The issue turns on whether Kandalanu, the ruler of Babylonia from 648 to 627, is a Babylonian throne name for Ashurbanipal, who would have taken direct control of Babylon following the failed revolt of his brother, Shamash-shun-ukin. For arguments that Kandalanu is Ashurbanipal, see S. Zawadski, *The Fall of Assyria and Median-Babylonian Relations in Light of the Nabopolassar Chronicle* (Posnan: Delft, 1988). For arguments against this identification, see John Brinkman, *Reallexikon für Assyriologie* 5:368–69; G.

6   Frame, *Babylonia 689–627 B.C.* (Leiden: Brill, 1992). For discussion of the Isaian passages, see Sweeney, *Isaiah 1–39,* 112–211.
7   See A. Kirk Grayson, "Asshur (Place)," *ABD* 1:500.

and used as such by all subsequent Assyrian monarchs.[8] It too was destroyed by the Babylonians and Medes during the last year of Josiah, 612. From the standpoint of the early reign of Josiah, the future orientation of the *waw*-conjunctive verbs employed in Zeph 2:13 (וְיֵט, "and he shall extend"; וִיאַבֵּד, "and he shall destroy"; וְיָשֵׂם, "and he shall appoint/place/make") of course point forward to Nineveh's destruction at some point in the future. The depiction of a desolate Nineveh that becomes dry like the desert indicates an effort to reverse the usual imagery of the city, which is well watered by virtue of its placement by the Tigris River and the canal that ran through its center. It also draws on the wilderness traditions associated with the exodus; although the wilderness responds to Israel's return to the land with rejoicing, water, and fecundity (see Exod 15:22–17:7; Num 11:31-35; 20:2-13; Ps 105:40-41; cf. Isa 40:3-5; 43:19-21; 45:8; 48:21), Nineveh by contrast will become a dry wilderness when it experiences its own "exodus" tradition at the hand of YHWH. Targum Jonathan apparently makes the association with the exodus traditions explicit when it renders the statement, "and he shall raise the plague of his might against the north." Of course the use of the term מחת גבורתיה, "plague of his might," also enables the Targumist to avoid the anthropomorphic portrayal of YHWH's hand applied against Assyria.[9]

■ **14** Verse 14 continues the prophet's announcement of punishment against Assyria or Nineveh with a depiction of the desolate city overrun with the various forms of animal life that typically take up residence in ruins. Although the syntax shifts from the imperfect conjunctive verbs of v. 13 to the initial converted perfect, וְרָבְצוּ, "and they shall lie," and the finite imperfect forms, יָלִינוּ, "they shall reside," and יְשׁוֹרֵר, "it/he shall sing/sound

off," of v. 14, the general future orientation remains. The shift may be explained by content as well since v. 13 portrays YHWH's punitive actions against Nineveh whereas v. 14 describes the consequences for the city now that YHWH has turned it into a dry, desolate ruin.

The internal structure of the verse comprises three basic syntactical units, each of which is based on one of the three verbs noted above, which convey three images of the ruined city that is now taken over by wildlife. The sequence of the images is apparently based on the view of the city to be had by one who approaches from a distance and comes gradually closer, in that they move from the larger and more numerous animals, that is, flocks of sheep or goats, that are easily seen from a distance, to the smaller animals or birds that fly or crawl about individually, to those that remain concealed within and are detected only by the noise they make in hooting, chirping, squawking, and so on, through ruined windows and doorways of buildings that are now open and exposed to the elements.

Each of these statements is beset with interpretive difficulties. Verse 14aα portrays the herds of sheep or goats that lie freely about the site now that it is abandoned by its human residents. The difficulty with this statement appears in the phrase כָל־חַיְתוֹ־גוֹי, "every animal of a nation." Although the structure of the phrase חַיְתוֹ־X is well known throughout the Hebrew Bible,[10] the second element of the construction generally appears as a noun that conveys some topographical feature associated with land, for example, אֶרֶץ, "land" (Gen 1:24; Ps 79:2), שָׂדַי, "my field" (Isa 56:9; Ps 104:11), or יַעַר, "forest" (Pss 50:10; 104:20).[11] The term גוֹי, "nation," does not appear elsewhere in this construction, and is frequently emended because it represents more of an abstract noun than the other examples just listed.[12] The versions,

8   See A. Kirk Grayson, "Nineveh," *ABD* 4:1118–19.
9   See Smolar and Aberbach, *Studies*, 137–50.
10   See GKC, §90o.
11   See Ben Zvi, *Zephaniah*, 180.
12   For the various emendations, see Marti, *Dodeka-propheton*, 371 (הָאָרֶץ, "the land"); J. M. P. Smith, *Zephaniah*, 236–37 (שָׂדַי, "my field"); van Hoonacker, *Prophètes*, 524 (גַּי, "valley, swamp"); Nowack, *Propheten*, 301 (שָׂדַי, "my field"); Sellin, *Zwölf-prophetenbuch*, 431 (גַי, "plain"); Elliger, *Zephanja*, 70 (שָׂדַי, "my field"); Horst, *Propheten*, 194 (יַעַר, "forest" or אֶרֶץ, "land"); Keller, *Sophonie*, 203 (גַי, "valley");

Rudolph, *Zephanja*, 276, 278 (נָוֶה, "field"); Seybold, *Satirische Prophetie*, 53 (גִיא, "valley"; cf. 108–9); Renaud, *Sophonie*, 232 (גַי, "valley"); Roberts, *Zephaniah*, 193 (שָׂדַי, or נָוֶה, "meadow"); Vlaardingerbroek, *Zephaniah*, 156–57 (כָל חַיָּה בְּגֵנָה, "all kinds of wild animals in it"). A number of commentators correctly retain גוֹי based on its metaphorical parallel with terminology for animals that swarm over the land in Joel 1:6; see Schwally, "Sefanjâ," 194; Gerleman, *Zephanja*, 42–43; James Barr, *Comparative*

including the LXX, which renders גּוֹי as γῆς, "land," on grounds of both assonance and content, demonstrate attempts to wrestle with the meaning of the text that now appears in the MT.[13] It should be noted that the term גּוֹי denotes an abstract social entity that is inherently associated with land. In this case, the reference to "every animal of a nation" ties in well with the concerns of the oracles of the nations in Zephaniah.

The second phrase in v. 14aα focuses on the smaller creatures, such as birds and crawling animals, that also will typically inhabit a ruined site. The difficulty here is in establishing the exact meaning of the terms employed. Although most scholars understand קָאַת as "pelican," there have been difficulties in explaining why a bird normally associated with water should appear at the site of Nineveh, which is inland along the Euphrates River.[14] The LXX has struggled as well in suggesting "chameleon," although TJ, Peshitta, and Vulgate all translate as "pelican."[15] The term קִפֹּד, generally translated as "hedgehog,"[16] is also uncertain, with other possibilities including "porcupine" and "owl."[17] The Peshitta renders as "owl," while the other versions all stay with "hedgehog." Although the reference to lodging "in its capitals" (בְּכַפְתֹּרֶיהָ) has occasioned some variations among the versions, the term makes perfect sense in the present context, as it points to the animals that will nest or sit on the ruined rafters or roof supports of the buildings. The versions appear to be occupied with attempts to embellish rather than to challenge the language; thus "they shall sleep in its ceilings" (LXX), "they shall lodge in the engraved work of its gates" (TJ), "they shall lodge in its houses" (Peshitta), and "they shall reside in its capitals" (Vulgate).

The third phrase in v. 14b focuses on animals that are concealed within the ruins and are perceived only by

their singing, chirping, squawking, or other sounds. The verb יְשׁוֹרֵר derives from the root שִׁיר, "to sing," but the unique context hardly conveys normal singing. The *polel* form of the verb conveys intensive and repetitive sound that may be employed for Levitical singers in the temple (1 Chr 6:18; 9:33; 2 Chr 29:28; cf. Job 36:24) or formal women singers (Neh 7:67; cf. Ezra 2:65). Given the formal liturgical context or setting in which the verb is normally employed and the portrayal of the once proud but now ruined imperial city that the text of Zephaniah presents, it would appear that the use of the verb in this context is deliberately intended to convey something of the irony of Nineveh's situation in which only the owls or other wildlife are left to sing of the city's splendor now that its human inhabitants are long gone.

The term חֹרֶב, "desolation," has also prompted a great deal of difficulty among the versions as the various translations indicate: "ravens" (LXX), "shall be destroyed" (TJ), "destruction" (Peshitta), and "raven" (Vulgate). The Peshitta follows the Hebrew[18] and TJ renders it as a verb. Both the LXX and Vulgate, however, point to the possibility of a wordplay in that the letter ʿayin in Hebrew עֹרֵב, "raven," can be pronounced with a guttural sound that would associate it with חֹרֶב, "desolation."[19] A reference to ravens or other scavenger birds would convey the image of destruction and devastation required by this context.

Finally, the phrase כִּי אַרְזָה עֵרָה, "for cedar is laid bare," has prompted a great deal of variation among the versions, which have had difficulty in understanding the terms employed. The term אַרְזָה is a *hapax legomenon* that is generally understood as a variation of אֶרֶז, "cedar." Hence the Vulgate attempts to read it as a first person singular imperfect form of the verb רזה, "to make lean, diminish," which also appears in v. 11, that is, "because I

Philology and the Text of the Old Testament (Oxford: Clarendon, 1968) 144, 324; Berlin, *Zephaniah*, 114–15; Ryou, *Zephaniah's Oracles*, 46–47.

13 Note that Mur 20:27 reads כֻּלּוֹ חיתו גוֹין, as does MT.

14 BDB, 866; cf. *HALOT*, 1059–60, which notes the problem and suggests goose, owl, or jackdaw as possibilities.

15 Cf. Gerleman, *Zephanja*, 43.

16 See BDB, 891.

17 *HALOT*, 1117.

18 The Peshitta text, *ḥrbʾ*, may be read either as "destruction" (with MT) or as "sword," which would

require a Hebrew text pointed as חֶרֶב. Both terms would convey the same basic understanding of the image of destruction.

19 Cf. Gerleman, *Zephanja*, 45; cf. Ryou, *Zephaniah's Oracles*, 49–50.

will diminish its oak/strength." Both TJ and Peshitta understand the association with cedar as a reference to major architectural support features in the construction of the buildings: "and its ceilings will be torn down" (TJ) or "because her foundation is overrun" (Peshitta). The term עֵרָה, "it/she is uncovered," from the root ערה, "to be naked, bare," is also difficult because of its association with nudity. The LXX reads, "because a cedar was its loftiness," apparently reading עֵרָה as a form of the root עור, "to awaken," but Roberts correctly observes that this is "gibberish."[20] The Vulgate apparently borrows the sense of אֶרֶז to render עֵרָה as "its strength/oak," but this is philologically unjustified. Both TJ and Peshitta attempt to render the term in reference to the destruction of structure based on the understanding of עֵרָה as "uncover." Although most commentators believe the phrase makes little sense in the present context,[21] it should be recalled that cedar was employed to line the inner rooms of important structures, such as palaces or temples (see 1 Kgs 6:9-36; 7:7-12; cf. Jer 22:14-15; Hag 1:4), and that cedar was sometimes overlaid with gold in such structures (1 Kgs 6:20-22). In either case, a reference to exposed cedar, whether it once lined rooms that are now exposed to the elements by the collapsed roofs and walls or it once was covered by gold that has now been stripped away, makes perfect sense in the context of a passage that depicts the ruins of a once splendid city.

■ **15** Verse 15 constitutes a summary-appraisal form that reflects on the downfall of Nineveh in relation to the preceding statements in vv. 13-14.[22] Although some have attempted to claim that it is a distinct unit because it presents Nineveh's demise as an established fact whereas vv. 13-14 anticipate the downfall of the city,[23] it must be read together with vv. 13-14 because its tempo-

ral perspective aids in establishing the certainty that Nineveh will fall.[24] Furthermore, the initial feminine singular demonstrative זֹאת, "this," clearly refers back to Nineveh in v. 13b; in turn Nineveh is clearly characterized as a feminine singular noun by its feminine singular description as שְׁמָמָה, "desolation," and צִיָּה, "desert," in v. 13b and by the pronominal suffixes of בְּתוֹכָהּ, "in her/its midst," in v. 14a and כַּפְתֹּרֶיהָ, "her/its capitals," in v. 14b. Because the basic concern of the summary-appraisal in this instance is to portray the certainty of Nineveh's demise, it employs elements of the lament or dirge form, including the so-called 3:2 *qinah* meter that is characteristic of lamentations and the exclamation אֵיךְ, "How!"[25] As part of its depiction of Nineveh's fall, it points to the city's arrogance as the reason for its punishment.

As the readings of the versions (discussed below) indicate, there has been some confusion as to the identity of the city. This is due in part to the absence of an explicit syntactical conjunction at the beginning of v. 15 and to the use of the term עַלִּיזָה, "exultant," to characterize Jerusalem in Isa 22:2 and 32:13. The latter has been especially influential in this decision because the context portrays Judean women as complacent and characterizes their city, presumably Jerusalem, as the "exultant city" that is now forsaken and overrun with animals.[26] Nevertheless, the term עַלִּיזָה may be employed in relation to foreign cities such as Tyre (Isa 23:7), and עַלִּיזִים, "exultant ones," may be used to characterize YHWH's warriors who attack Babylon (13:3), the once exultant people of the earth who have witnessed the destruction of their city, presumably Babylon (24:8),[27] and the arrogant in the midst of Jerusalem (Zeph 3:11). As the above discussion of the summary-appraisal form in this verse indicates, however, the "exultant city" must be Nineveh. The expressions employed to express the city's sense of

20 Roberts, *Zephaniah*, 194; cf. Gerleman, *Zephanja*, 45; Ryou, *Zephaniah's Oracles*, 50.

21 E.g., Vlaardingerbroek, *Zephaniah*, 156.

22 Cf. Floyd, *Minor Prophets*, 227.

23 Marti, *Dodekapropheton*, 371; J. M. P. Smith, *Zephaniah*, 234; Nowack, *Propheten*, 301–2; Sellin, *Zwölfprophetenbuch*, 434; Langohr, "Sophonie," 69; Edler, *Kerygma*, 93–94; Renaud, *Sophonie*, 235; idem, "Sophonie," 16.

24 Cf. Ryou, *Zephaniah's Oracles*, 303–4.

25 See Erhard Gerstenberger, *Psalms, Part 1; with an Introduction to Cultic Poetry* (FOTL 14; Grand Rapids: Eerdmans, 1988) 10–11; Hedwig Jahnow, *Das hebräische Leichenlied* (BZAW 36; Giessen: Töpelmann, 1923).

26 For discussion of the passage, see Sweeney, *Isaiah 1–39*, 409–20.

27 For discussion see ibid., 325–32.

security and arrogant self-confidence, "that sits secure (הַיּוֹשֶׁבֶת לָבֶטַח), that says in its/her heart, 'I and no other!' (הָאֹמְרָה בִּלְבָבָהּ אֲנִי וְאַפְסִי עוֹד)" appear word for word also in the characterization of the fallen city of Babylon in Isa 47:8a (cf. 47:10). Although past scholarship has seen Deutero-Isaiah as an entirely original prophet, more recent studies have demonstrated Deutero-Isaiah's clear dependence on earlier prophetic tradition.[28] In this case, Isaiah 47 appears to have employed Zephaniah's characterization of Nineveh as part of its own characterization of Babylon.[29]

The concluding statements in v. 15b draw heavily on the language of lamentation in characterizing Nineveh as a city that has become a desolation inhabited only by animals. Note the similar language concerning Babylon in Jer 50:23; 51:41: "how Babylon has become a horror among the nations (אֵיךְ הָיְתָה לְשַׁמָּה בָּבֶל בַּגּוֹיִם)." The concluding portrayal of passersby whistling, hissing, and making hand gestures over the ruined site is a typical portrayal of astonishment at destruction in the Hebrew Bible (see 1 Kgs 9:8; Jer 18:16; 19:8; 49:17; 50:13; Ezek 27:36; Lam 2:15; Job 27:23).[30]

Although the MT clearly reads this verse as a reference to Nineveh that concludes vv. 13-14, several versions read it in relation to the following material.[31] The LXX, for example, reads v. 15 as the first verse of chap. 3 so that it introduces the oracle concerning the oppressive city in 3:1-4. In this case, the LXX reads 2:15/LXX 3:1 as the introduction to the oracle against Jerusalem in 3:1-4/LXX 3:2-5, which speaks of G-d's presence in the midst of the city and the failure of her people and priests to maintain holiness or observe the law. In addition, it rereads the initial statement, "this is the exultant city that sits secure," as "this is the disparaging (ἡ φαυλίσρια) city that dwells upon hope/expectation (ἐπ᾽ ἐλπίδι)." The reading does not presuppose a different text, but indicates an effort to associate the term עַלִּיזָה, "exultant," with pride and arrogance. Targum Jonathan continues to read the verse as the conclusion of vv. 13-14, but rereads the initial statement as, "this is the strong (תקיפתא) city that dwells in security," apparently in an attempt to define עַלִּיזָה as the product of Nineveh's strong defenses. The Peshitta likewise reads עַלִּיזָה as ʿšynt᾽, "strong," like TJ, but it adds wn᾽mr, "and he shall say," at the end of the verse to connect it to 3:1-4. In this manner, 3:1-4, which portrays the now punished city of Jonah, that is, Nineveh,[32] becomes the statement made by passersby.

28 See Willey, *Remember;* and esp. Benjamin D. Sommer, *A Prophet Reads Scripture: Allusion in Isaiah 40–66* (Stanford: Stanford Univ. Press, 1998) 155, 245, 252, who specifically discusses the dependence of Isa 47:5-11 on Zeph 2:13-15. Note that the similarities between Zeph 2:13-15 and Isa 47:5-11 have sometimes been employed to claim that the Zephaniah text is a late redactional addition, since Isaiah 47 must have been the original text (e.g., Edler, *Kerygma,* 93–94).

29 See also the analogy drawn between Babylon and Assyria in Isa 52:3-6 and 14:24-27 (in the context of the Babylonian oracle of 13:1–14:27). For a brief discussion of 52:3-6, see P.-E. Bonnard, *Le Second Isaïe. Son disciple et leurs éditeurs. Isaïe 40–66* (EB; Paris: Gabalda, 1972) 258–59. For discussion of 14:24-27 in relation to its context, see Sweeney, *Isaiah 1–39,* 218–39. Note also the use of Nah 2:1, which celebrates the downfall of Nineveh, in Isa 52:7 (for discussion see Willey, *Remember,* 116–20).

30 Vlaardingerbroek, *Zephaniah,* 163; Ben Zvi, *Zephaniah,* 183.

31 Although the readings of v. 15 in both Murabbaʿat and 4QXII[b] are fragmentary, they show no major variation from the MT.

32 See the text-critical discussion of this section below.

3

Translation

1   **Woe, O contentious[a] and defiled one,[b]**
      the oppressing city![c]

2   **She did not listen to any voice,[d]**
      she did not take instruction;[e]
   in YHWH[f] she did not trust,
      unto her G-d[g] she did not draw near.

3   **Her officials in her midst**
      are roaring lions;
   her judges are evening wolves,[h]
      they do not leave anything until morning.[i]

4   **Her prophets are wanton,[j]**
      men of treacheries;
   her priests profane holiness,[k]
      they corrupt Torah.[l]

a   MT, מֹרְאָה, "contentious," is a *qal* feminine singular participle derived from the root מרה, "to rebel." The א apparently enters the form since ל״ה verbal forms sometimes follow the pattern of ל״א forms (GKC, §75rr). Mur 20:31 likewise reads, מראה; cf. LXX, ἡ ἐπιφανὴς, "the remarkable/noticeable one," apparently reading מראה as a form derived from the root ראה, "to see"; TJ, דמוחיא, "the one who hurries on," apparently reading מראה as a form derived from the root מהר, "to hurry"; Peshitta, *mdyntʾ ydyʿʾ*, "the famous/known city," apparently follows LXX and adds the reference to "city" for the sake of clarity; Vulgate, *provacatrix*, "the provocative one," apparently reflects the Hebrew as understood by the MT.

b   MT, וְנִגְאָלָה, "and defiled one," derives from the root גאל II, "to defile," as opposed to גאל I, "to redeem," which would result in the translation, "and the redeemed one." Mur 20:31 likewise reads וְנִגְאָלָה. The interplay in meaning between the two roots apparently influences the reading of this verse in the versions; see LXX, καὶ ἀπολελυτρωμένη, "and ransomed/redeemed (one)"; TJ ומתפרקא is generally translated, "and is redeemed," although the term can also mean, "and falls apart"; Peshitta, *wpriqʾ*, "and redeemed (city)"; Vulgate, *et redempta civitas columba*, "and redeemed city of the dove."

c   MT, הָעִיר הַיּוֹנָה, "the oppressing city"; cf. Mur 20:31, העיר היונה. The term יוֹנָה is a *qal* participle from the root ינה, "to oppress," but the form may also be read as the noun יוֹנָה, "dove," or as the name of the prophet Jonah, who prophesies against Nineveh in the book of Jonah. Again, both of these meanings play influential roles in the versions; see LXX, ἡ περιστερά, "the dove," which may be read in relation either to the preceding material: "O remarkable and redeemed city, the dove," or to the following material: "the dove has not listened to a voice"; TJ, קרתא דמסגיא, "the city that oppresses"; Peshitta, *mdynth dywnn*, "the city of Jonah"; Vulgate, *et redempta civitas columba*, "and redeemed city of the dove."

d   Cf. LXX, which may read ἡ περιστερά, "the dove," as the subject of the statement in v. 2: "the dove has not listened to a voice." See also TJ, which interprets the verse as a reference to Jerusalem's failure to heed the prophets: לא שמעת בקל עבדוהי נבייא, "she did not listen to the voice of his servants the prophets," and the Peshitta, which renders v. 2 as a relative clause in relation to v. 1: *dlʾ šmʿt bqlʾ*, "which did not listen to the voice [i.e., of G-d]."

e   MT, מוּסָר, "instruction, chastisement," which is a common term for moral instruction; cf. TJ, אלפן, "instruction," which is commonly used for elementary or school instruction.

f   TJ, במימרא דיוי, "in the *Memra* of YHWH."

g   TJ, ולפולחנא דאלקה, "and to the service of her G-d."

h   MT, זְאֵבֵי עֶרֶב, "evening wolves"; Mur 20:33 likewise reads זאבי ערב. Cf. LXX, ὡς λύκοι τῆς Ἀραβίας "(its judges are) like wolves of Arabia," which apparently rereads עֶרֶב, "evening," as a reference to עֲרָב, "Arabia."

i   MT לֹא גָרְמוּ לַבֹּקֶר is very difficult to translate, as the *hapax* גָרְמוּ is generally taken to mean "they cut off, reserved," and the noun גֶּרֶם means "bone." Nevertheless, the sense of the verse is clear, as "wolves of the evening/night" are understood to devour everything so that nothing is left by morning; cf. LXX, οὐχ ὑπελίποντο εἰς τὸ πρωί, "they do

not leave anything remaining until morning"; TJ, לא מורכין לצפרא, "(they) do not tarry until morning"; Peshitta, wlʾ mktryn lṣprʾ, "and (they) do not wait for morning"; Vulgate, *non relinquebant in mane*, "not leaving anything in the morning." Mur 20:33 likewise reads, לא גרמו לבקר.

j   Cf. TJ, נבי שקרהון, "prophets of their lies," or "false prophets."

k   MT, קֹדֶשׁ, "holiness"; cf. Peshitta, mqdšʾ, "the sanctuary."

l   Cf. Vulgate, *iniuste egerunt contra legem*, "unjustly they carry out law."

Form and Setting

Zephaniah 3:1-4 constitutes a woe speech concerning Jerusalem,[1] which accuses the city and its various classes of officials of unrighteousness and a failure to heed YHWH or divine expectations. The third person references to YHWH in v. 2 and the references to the city throughout the passage indicate that the prophet is the speaker. Within the context of 3:1-20, it functions as the basic starting point for the portrayal of YHWH's righteousness (see esp. 3:5), by which YHWH will purge both the nations (cf. 2:5-15) and Jerusalem so that Jerusalem may be restored as YHWH's "bride" or the holy center of creation in the midst of the nations.

Zephaniah 3:1-4 is demarcated initially by its introductory "woe" statement in v. 1.[2] In keeping with the typical features of the form, the initial "woe" statement begins with the particle הוֹי, "Woe!" which is syntactically unrelated to the preceding material in chap. 2. The "woe" is formulated as a direct address that employs a vocative perspective to characterize the addressee as a "contentious," "defiled," and "oppressing" city.[3] This is followed by a series of four statements in v. 2, each of which is formulated as a syntactically self-contained unit

based on a finite, perfect verb, that accuse the city of refusing to listen (presumably to G-d), failing to accept instruction or correction, failing to trust in YHWH, and refusing to draw near to its G-d. Verses 3-4 then shift to the major officials of the city, employing a combination of metaphors and direct accusations to charge the officials with misconduct in four syntactically self-contained statements. Thus the "officials" (שָׂרִים) are accused as acting like "roaring lions," employing an image of a predator that celebrates the taking of prey (cf. Amos 3:4, 8). Of course this contrasts markedly with the role of public officials who are charged with maintaining the well-being of the people (Exod 23:8; 18:21-23; Deut 16:18-20). The judges are portrayed metaphorically as "evening wolves" who sneak into inhabited areas under the cover of darkness to devour everything they can find before morning. Again, this contrasts markedly with the role of judges who are charged with doing justice for the people (see Exod 23:1-4, 6-7; 18:21-23; Deut 16:18-20). The prophets are charged with wantonness and treachery so that one cannot be assured that their statements are indeed representative of G-d (cf. Deut 18:9-22, which takes up the problem of false prophets; cf. Jer 23:9-40). Finally, the priests are accused of violating their most

---

1   For discussion of the woe speech form, see Sweeney, *Isaiah 1–39*, 543, and the literature cited there.

2   For the demarcation of this unit, see Sweeney, "Form-Critical Reassessment," 401–2.

3   For discussion of the syntactical features of the "woe" statement and its characterization as a direct address, see Hillers, "*Hôy*."

fundamental charges by profaning what is sacred and corrupting Torah or divine revelation. Although many take this listing of officials to be comprehensive, it is noteworthy that the king is not included.

Many scholars maintain that the subunit continues beyond vv. 1-4 to comprise vv. 1-5,[4] 1-7,[5] 1-8,[6] 1-13,[7] and so on.[8] This is fundamentally mistaken for several reasons. First, v. 5 is frequently judged to be a secondary redactional addition because of its hymnic characteristics,[9] but diachronic grounds hardly provide the basis for making a synchronic decision concerning the structure of the present form of the text. Second, v. 5 lacks a syntactical conjunction with the preceding material, which indicates that it constitutes the beginning of a new subunit within vv. 1-20. Third, v. 5 marks the beginning of a pronounced thematic shift in that it portrays YHWH's righteousness, whereas vv. 1-4 portray Jerusalem's lack of righteousness. Fundamentally, vv. 1-4 focus on Jerusalem, but with v. 5 the attention shifts to a new subject in YHWH and YHWH's actions vis-à-vis both Jerusalem and the nations at large. Fourth, although v. 6 begins with first person verbal forms that indicate speech by YHWH, v. 5 functions as an introduction to the speech in that it identifies YHWH as the speaker. Otherwise, the reader/hearer is left to wait for the appearance of the oracular formula in v. 8, which also identifies YHWH as the speaker. Fifth, the statement in v. 5 that "YHWH is righteous in her [Jerusalem's] midst" might be taken as a contrast to the statement in v. 3 that "her [Jerusalem's] officials in her midst are roaring lions" that is intended to link the two verses together. Nevertheless, the phrase in v. 5 points forward to the statement made by the prophet to Jerusalem in v. 18, "YHWH your G-d is in your midst," to portray the realization of YHWH's righteousness. Sixth, the contention

that YHWH is righteous forms the basic premise of the following material in vv. 6-13 and 14-20, in which YHWH is portrayed as taking action to purge both Jerusalem and the nations of the world at large to restore Jerusalem as the divine bride and thus as the holy center of all creation.

It is noteworthy that the oracle does not explicitly name Jerusalem. Furthermore, the language employed to describe the city is somewhat enigmatic; it might be taken either as a positive or as a negative portrayal of the city, that is, מֹרְאָה might be read either as "contentious" or as "fearsome," נִגְאָלָה might be read as "defiled" or as "redeemed." This, of course, raises a multitude of questions, since 2:13-15 certainly portrays Nineveh in very negative terms, whereas 3:5-20 points clearly to Jerusalem's redemption and restoration. A key element that adds to the confusion is the characterization of the city as הָעִיר הַיּוֹנָה, "the oppressing city," which naturally evokes images of Nineveh (cf. Nahum; Jonah), especially since the term יונה corresponds to the name of the prophet who condemned Nineveh only to see it redeemed when it responded to the condemnation with contrition. But יוֹנָה also means "dove," sometimes taken as a symbol of beauty (Cant 1:15; 4:1) that might be applied to Jerusalem (cf. Mark 1:10; Matt 3:16; Luke 3:22, which portray the spirit of G-d alighting on Jesus like a dove, and Isa 61:1, which portrays the descent of G-d's spirit on the servant sent to Jerusalem). Consequently, there has been some confusion in the versions.[10] As noted in the discussion of the oracle concerning Assyria and Nineveh in Zeph 2:13-15, the LXX reads 2:15 as the first verse of chap. 3 so that Nineveh becomes the city that is portrayed in 3:1-4. Likewise, the Peshitta adds the statement, "and he shall say," to the end of 2:15 so that the portrayal of the passerby

---

4   Ryou, *Zephaniah's Oracles*, 252–69; Vlaardingerbroek, *Zephaniah*, 167 (within the context of vv. 1-8; see pp. 166–67); Ben Zvi, *Zephaniah*, 315–17 (within the context of vv. 1-8); Bennett, "Zephaniah," 693–94; Seybold, *Zephanja*, 109–11 (within the larger context of vv. 1-10); Kapelrud, *Message*, 35–36; Keller, *Sophonie*, 205–8; Horst, *Propheten*, 197; Elliger, *Zephanja*, 74–76.

5   Floyd, *Minor Prophets*, 229–33; Wellhausen, *Propheten*, 156–57; van Hoonacker, *Prophètes*, 527; J. M. P. Smith, *Zephaniah*, 238–46; Marti, *Dodekapropheton*, 372–74; Ball, *Zephaniah*, 199–230.

6   Renaud, *Sophonie*, 235–45 (but vv. 1-4 form a subunit within); Rudolph, *Zephanja*, 284–90; Junker, *Sophonia*, 81–85.

7   Berlin, *Zephaniah*, 135–39; Roberts, *Zephaniah*, 204–19; Nowack, *Propheten*, 302–5; Sellin, *Zwölfprophetenbuch*, 434–40.

8   Scholars who see vv. 1-4 as the fundamental unit include Renaud, *Sophonie*, 237–40 (within the context of vv. 1-8); Edler, *Kerygma*, 147–60.

9   E.g., Renaud, *Sophonie*, 240–41.

10   See the textual notes to Zeph 3:1-4 and 2:13-15 above.

who hisses and motions his hand in astonishment at the fate of the destroyed city will state the woe oracle in vv. 1-4 as a characterization of the city of Nineveh. The identity of the city may be gleaned only by the references to YHWH as its G-d in v. 2b: "in YHWH she did not trust, unto her G-d she did not draw near." Although later readers might contend that YHWH is also the G-d of Nineveh, particularly in relation to the book of Jonah, it is unlikely that the book of Zephaniah presupposes the much later book of Jonah. Furthermore, Zephaniah's portrayal of the process by which the nations come to recognize YHWH is yet to come in the perspective of the prophet. In any case, that perspective emphasizes the nations at large, not Nineveh in particular, and their relationship to Jerusalem.

Again, the sociohistorical setting of this pericope may be placed in relation to the early years of Josiah's reform program in that it points to corruption among Jerusalem's officials that must be addressed. Clearly, the charges articulated in 3:1-4 provide the basis for a purge, which can be designed either to remove corrupt officials from office or to motivate officials to act in a manner that is consistent with the expectations of their roles. The absence of the king is particularly noteworthy. Apparently, he does not come in for the same scrutiny as the officials who serve under his authority. This would point to the fact that the king is the one who stands behind the reform and the purge that it entails.

■ **1** Verse 1 constitutes the initial statement of the "woe" oracle in vv. 1-4. It is a syntactically self-contained statement that is formulated with the characteristic introductory particle הוֹי, "Woe!" which generally conveys a sense of warning concerning some impending danger to the addressee. Reference to the addressee, in this case an unnamed city, immediately follows the הוֹי in keeping with the typical features of the genre. A series of three participles characterize the city as "contentious," "defiled," and "oppressing," but neither the initial woe statement nor the oracle as a whole indicates that any

punishment or action against the city is imminent. Rather, as the following material in vv. 5-20 indicates, the city's negative characterization will become the basis for YHWH's efforts to demonstrate divine righteousness by seeing to the purification of the city, later identified explicitly as Jerusalem, the purging of its unrighteous elements so that it might stand as the holy center of all creation.

Indeed, the choice of terminology to characterize the city is quite ambiguous, and reflects an effort to employ metaphor and irony to signal to the reading or listening audience that the negative characteristics of the city will shift into far more positive images.[11] The term מֹרְאָה, "contentious," has proved to be particularly difficult because of the presence of the letter ʾalep in the third root position of the qal feminine singular participle derived from the verbal root מרה, "to be contentious, rebel." This is the only example of this particular form in the Hebrew Bible. The pointing of the form is precisely what one would expect from a lamed-he feminine singular participle, and the presence of the ʾalep represents a common feature of such forms that often follow the pattern of lamed-ʾalep verbs.[12] But the presence of the ʾalep causes the term to resemble the masculine singular noun מוֹרָא, "fear, awe," which is widely attested throughout the Hebrew Bible (e.g., Deut 4:34; 26:8; 34:12; Isa 8:12, 13; Jer 32:21; Mal 2:5; Ps 76:12). Although no feminine form of this noun is known to exist, the resemblance of מֹרְאָה to מוֹרָא suggests that the term could be understood as a reference to the city's awesome or fearsome character. In the larger context of Zeph 3:1-20, which portrays the process by which YHWH purges the city so that it becomes the holy center of creation to which all nations come to offer tribute to YHWH, such terminological ambiguity hints to the audience concerning the coming change in the city's character and role.[13]

11   See B. Jongeling, "Jeux de Mots en Sophonie III 1 et 3?" *VT* 21 (1971) 541–47. For methodological discussion of the role of metaphor in prophetic literature, see Anders Jørgen Bjørndalen, *Untersuchungen zur allegorischen Rede der Propheten Amos und Jesaja* (BZAW 165; Berlin: de Gruyter, 1986); Gören Eidevall, *Grapes in the Desert: Metaphors, Models and*

Themes in Hosea 4–14 (ConBOT 43; Stockholm: Almqvist & Wiksell, 1996); Birgette Seiffert, *Metaphorisches Reden von Gott im Hoseabuch* (FRLANT 166; Göttingen: Vandenhoeck & Ruprecht, 1996).

12   See GKC, §75rr.

13   Cf. Ben Zvi, *Zephaniah*, 184–85, who recognizes the

Much the same may be said about the second participle employed to characterize the city, וְנִגְאָלָה, "and defiled." Again, the form is a *niphal* feminine singular participle derived from the root גאל II, "to defile." The root is attested elsewhere in the Hebrew Bible in both *niphal* (Isa 59:3; Lam 4:14) and other stems (Mal 1:7; Ezra 2:62; Neh 7:64; Isa 63:3; Dan 1:8), although it is considered to be a relatively late term related to the root געל, "to loathe." The present *niphal* participle is the only example of this particular form in the Hebrew Bible. Nevertheless, the form points once again to the ambiguity of the term in that the root גאל I, means "to redeem." Although גאל I does not appear as a *niphal* feminine participle elsewhere in the Bible, it does appear in other formulations of the *niphal* stem (Lev 25:49, 54; 27:20, 27, 28, 33; Isa 52:3) to refer to fields, slaves, holy things, and Jerusalem that have been redeemed. Thus the potential association of the present וְנִגְאָלָה with a form of the root גאל I suggests that the city should be considered both "defiled" and "redeemed," which of course points to the ultimate transition of the status of the city as one moves from the beginning of Zeph 3:1-20 to its conclusion.

The third expression employed to characterize the city, הָעִיר הַיּוֹנָה, "the oppressing city," likewise employs a *qal* feminine singular participle, הַיּוֹנָה. The case for ambiguity is less clear here because the term derives from the root ינה, "to oppress," well attested throughout the Bible, but there is no analogous verbal form that might suggest a positive characterization of the city. Nevertheless, the term הַיּוֹנָה is analogous to two other terms in the Bible, the noun יוֹנָה, "dove," and the proper name יוֹנָה, "Jonah." Although the prophet Jonah ben Amittai is mentioned as a ninth-century Israelite prophet from the reign of Jeroboam ben Joash of Israel (2 Kgs 14:25), no particular significance can be attached to this association as the prophet has nothing to do with Jerusalem or other concerns from the book of Zephaniah. Furthermore, the book of Jonah, which does address the question of Nineveh's fate, appears to have been written during the early Persian period at a much later time than Zephaniah.[14] The association of the present verb with the noun for "dove" is noteworthy, however, in that doves are hardly considered to be symbols for evil anywhere in the Hebrew Bible. Rather, they are employed to convey deliverance from the flood in the time of Noah (Gen 8:8, 9, 10, 11, 12), silliness or indecisiveness (Hos 7:11), beauty (Cant 1:15; 4:1), a term of endearment (Cant 2:14; 5:2; 6:9; Ps 56:1), symbols for returning exiles (Isa 60:8; Hos 11:11), and so on. Of course, the dove is also to be offered as a holy sacrifice at the altar of the Jerusalem Temple (Lev 1:14; 5:7, 11; 12:6; Num 6:10; etc.). In all these cases, the dove does not represent a threat; rather, it represents a positive image, particularly in relation to the return of exiles to Jerusalem that is highlighted as a central motif in the portrayal of Jerusalem's restoration in Zeph 3:19-20. This last reference is particularly striking in relation to Jerusalem's characterization as the oppressing city in that Jerusalem's oppressors (Heb. מֹעֲנַיִךְ, "your oppressors") are the ones who will bring the city's exiles home. Nevertheless, the expression in 3:1 cannot be justified philologically as "dove," since the term הַיּוֹנָה is formulated with a definite article. This requires that the term be read as an adjective of הָעִיר, "the city," a role for which the noun "dove" can hardly qualify. Like the examples of "contemptuous/fearsome" and "defiled/redeemed" cited above, it only suggests the transformation of the city as articulated throughout the balance of the text.

Of course, these ambiguities have had their impact on the versions, prompting them to read the verse either as a reference to Nineveh or as a positive characterization of Jerusalem or Nineveh.[15] Thus the LXX reads, "Woe, O remarkable and redeemed one, the dove city," or "Woe, O remarkable and redeemed one. The dove did not listen. . . ." The characterization of the city as "remarkable" reads מֻרְאָה as a *hophal* form of the root ראה, "to see," which suggests a reference to Nineveh's greatness or to Jerusalem's designation as Moriah, like-

ambiguity of the term but sees it only as a device that channels the attention of the audience to the indictment of the city; cf. Ryou, *Zephaniah's Oracles*, 260–61, who likewise reads the term only in relation to the city's indictment.

14 See my commentary on Jonah in Sweeney, *Twelve Prophets*, 301–34.

15 See esp. Vlaardingerbroek, *Zephaniah*, 170–71; cf. Gerleman, *Zephanja*, 46–48.

wise derived from the root ראה (2 Chr 3:1; Gen 22:14). The Peshitta follows suit by reading the verse as: "Woe, O famous and redeemed city, the city of Jonah." It clearly understands the city as Nineveh, as indicated by its reading of היונה in reference to the prophet and book Jonah, and by its addition of "and he shall say" at the end of Zeph 2:15 to portray 3:1-4 as the statement that passersby will make when they see the destroyed city of Nineveh. The Vulgate also follows the LXX to a certain extent by reading, "Woe, O provocative and redeemed city of the dove," apparently in reference to Jerusalem.[16] Targum Jonathan reads independently, "Woe, O she who hurries and is redeemed [or, 'and falls apart'], the city which multiplies provocations," apparently in reference to Nineveh.

■ **2** The ambiguities of the language in v. 1 begin to subside as v. 2 employs much more explicit language to level accusations against the still unnamed city. Although the formulation of the prophet's language shifts from the direct address of the initial הוֹי statement to the third person characterization of the anonymous city, the shift in language continues the ambiguous portrayal of the preceding verse in that the form suggests to the prophet's Jerusalemite and Judean audience that they are not addressed when indeed they constitute the population of the "contentious and defiled" city. The identity of the city becomes apparent only in v. 2b, and then only by virtue of the prophet's statement that the city did not trust or draw near to YHWH, here identified as its G-d. Although later tradents might argue that YHWH is indeed the G-d of Nineveh, such contentions require the support of other biblical books such as Nahum or Jonah (and perhaps even Isaiah) that clearly portray Nineveh under the control of YHWH. Although the seeds of such claims might appear in the book of Zephaniah, it is by no means clear that the prophet or the book holds that Nineveh should be condemned for not trusting YHWH or drawing near to YHWH as its G-d. It is clear, however, that the book holds that Jerusalem and Judah should be expected to adhere to YHWH as demonstrated by the accusations leveled in 1:2-18 against those in Jerusalem and Judah. Nevertheless, the ambiguities of the language employed within this oracle, the claims made by other biblical books, and the theological perspectives of Alexandrian Judaism (see LXX) and the early Syrian church (see Peshitta) apparently prompt the reading of this oracle in reference to Nineveh centuries after the lifetime of the prophet Zephaniah.

The initial paired statement of v. 2a points clearly to the refusal of the city to listen to anyone or to accept any sort of correction or moral discipline. The statement, "it/she did not listen to a voice," employs the verbal root שמע, "to hear," together with the preposition ב, "in, with, by," and the noun קוֹל, "voice," which is generally taken as an idiom that means "to listen to, obey."[17] Normally, the identity of the party whose voice is to be heeded is specified, but no such specification is made in the present verse. Most interpreters point to the specific mention of YHWH in v. 2b as a means to identify YHWH as the party that the city does not obey, but the nonspecific formulation of v. 2a also indicates that the city is not prepared to listen to anyone. Much the same applies to the second element of the pair, "she/it did not take instruction." The statement employs the term מוּסָר, "chastisement, correction, discipline, instruction," which is rooted in the wisdom traditions where it refers to the moral discipline or instruction that parents convey to their children (Prov 1:8; 4:1; 13:1), teachers to their students (Prov 1:2, 7; 15:33; 23:23), G-d to people (Prov 3:11; Job 5:17). The term also appears frequently in the prophets (esp. Jeremiah) to convey similar notions (Jer 2:30; 5:3; 7:28; 17:23; 32:33; Isa 26:16; Ezek 5:15; see below on Zeph 3:7).[18] Many have noted the parallel between Zeph 3:2a and Jer 7:28, "and you said unto them, 'This is the nation that did not listen to the voice of YHWH (לֹא שָׁמְעוּ בְּקוֹל ה״) and that did not take instruction (וְלֹא לָקְחוּ מוּסָר); truth has perished, it is cut off from their mouth."[19] Although it is tempting to argue that perhaps Jeremiah is dependent on Zephaniah, no clear grounds for such a contention are apparent.

16   Gerleman, *Zephanja*, 48.

17   See BDB, 1034; 1 Sam 8:7; Deut 4:30; Jer 3:13.

18   For a full study of the term מוּסָר, see James Alvin Sanders, "Suffering as Divine Discipline in the Old Testament and Post-Biblical Judaism," *Colgate Rochester Divinity School Bulletin* 28 (1955).

19   E.g., Ben Zvi, *Zephaniah*, 188.

As noted above, the statements in v. 2b that the city did not trust in YHWH or draw near to its G-d clearly identify it as Jerusalem. Much like the oracles concerning the nations in Amos 1–2, which draw the audience in by condemning Israel's various enemies only to focus ultimately on Israel itself,[20] the present oracle concerning Jerusalem builds on the preceding oracles concerning the nations and the ambiguities of Zeph 3:1-2a in order to capture the audience's attention and sympathy only to target Jerusalem as the object of YHWH's statements. Unlike Amos 1–2, however, the rhetorical ploy is not employed here to involve the audience in self-condemnation; rather, it is to gain the audience's attention for the prophet's claim that YHWH is about to change the fortunes of Jerusalem to make it the holy center of creation at large and the nations in particular. In order to accomplish that, however, the prophet must account for Jerusalem's suffering at the hands of the Assyrians from the late eighth century on. He does so by claiming that Jerusalem refused to listen to G-d and was punished. But as the balance of the passage is designed to demonstrate, the purge that will purify Jerusalem for its central role is at hand, presumably in Josiah's reform program.

The expressions employed in this passage do not appear to be technical expressions. The statement, "in YHWH it/she did not trust," employs the verb בטח, which appears frequently throughout the Psalms and other books to convey a basic relationship with YHWH on the part of human beings (see Pss 9:11; 21:8; 22:5, 6; 25:2; 26:1; 28:7; 32:10; 37:3; 40:4; 55:24; 56:5, 12; 62:9; 84:13; 91:2; 112:7; 115:9, 10, 11; 125:1; 143:8; cf. 2 Kgs 18:5; 19:10; Isa 37:10; 26:3, 4; Jer 17:7; 39:18; Prov 16:20; 29:25; 1 Chr 5:20).[21] Likewise, although the following statement, "unto her/its G-d, she/it did not draw near,"

is sometimes understood as a reference to cultic worship of YHWH based on the occurrence of the verb קרב, "to draw near" (cf. Ezek 40:46; 45:4; Num 1:51; 3:10, 38; 18:7),[22] the term merely conveys approach to various parties for any number of purposes. The technical term for approaching the altar to offer sacrifice is generally the *hiphil* form of the verb (see Exod 29:4, 8; 40:12, 14; Lev 3:6; 7:35; 8:6, 13, 24; Num 8:9, 10; 16:5, 9, 10; etc.), not the *qal* stative form that appears here.

■ **3** Verses 3 and 4 then shift to a pointed critique of various state officials, including the so-called "officials" or "princes" (שָׂרִים), "judges" (שֹׁפְטִים), "prophets" (נְבִיאִים), and "priests" (כֹּהֲנִים). As noted above, the "officials" and "judges" mentioned in v. 3 are metaphorically portrayed as "roaring lions" and "evening wolves" in order to demonstrate their rapaciousness in abusing the people for whose welfare they are responsible. The prophets and priests mentioned in v. 4 are directly accused of deliberately abusing their official roles. Again, the king is not mentioned in the list of officials, very likely because the text lays the groundwork for a purge of Judean officials as part of King Josiah's reform program. Alternatively, the accusations made in this text are designed to prompt those who hold official positions in Josiah's Judah to exercise full responsibility in carrying out the duties of their respective offices.

A number of scholars have noted the parallel between Zeph 3:3-4 and Ezek 22:23-31,[23] in which Ezekiel condemns the prophets, priests, and officials of Judah in language very much like that of Zeph 3:3-4; that is, Ezekiel compares the prophets to roaring lions who devour prey, states that the priests have done violence to YHWH's Torah and profaned holiness, and compares the officials to wolves who also devour prey, shed blood, and take bribes. Because Ezekiel does not mention the

---

20 See Sweeney, *Twelve Prophets*, 200–218, on Amos 1–2.

21 Cf. Ben Zvi, *Zephaniah*, 188, who cites these verses to demonstrate that the expression presupposes blessing on the part of those who trust in YHWH.

22 E.g., R. L. Smith, *Micah–Malachi*, 138; Seybold, *Zephanja*, 111.

23 E.g., Michael Fishbane, *Biblical Interpretation in Ancient Israel* (Oxford: Clarendon, 1985) 461–63; Ben Zvi, *Zephaniah*, 196–205; Vlaardingerbroek, *Zephaniah*, 169; Edler, *Kerygma*, 150–54; Zimmerli, *Ezekiel 1*, 465–70; D. H. Müller, "Der Prophet

Ezechiel entlehnt eine Stelle des Propheten Zephanja und glossiert sie," *WZKM* 19 (1905) 263–70.

judges that appear in Zeph 3:3-4, some have supposed that Ezekiel and Zephaniah are dependent on a third source that each reworked differently.[24] It should be noted, however, that Ezekiel portrays the crimes of the officials as those of corrupt judges. Furthermore, the book of Ezekiel never refers to judges. In that the Mosaic tradition in Exod 18:21-23 makes very clear that judges are to be chosen from among the officials of the people, it would appear that Ezekiel 22 presupposes both Zeph 3:3-4 and Exod 18:21-23, especially since Ezekiel is well known as an erudite individual who constantly cites earlier texts and traditions from both the Bible and the general ancient Near Eastern world. Reference to judges in the context of Ezekiel 22 would be unnecessary, as they are already addressed by reference to the officials.

As noted in the discussion of Zeph 1:8, the Hebrew term שַׂר is a relatively common and general term for an official or person who is granted some sort of leadership responsibility. The term is frequently translated as "prince," in part because of the cognate Akkadian term *šarru*, "king," but this is somewhat misleading, as the term does not necessarily convey royal identity. It is frequently employed in a military context, where it designates "commanders" or "captains" of various sized units, for example, "commanders of fifties" (2 Kgs 1:9-14; Isa 3:3), "commanders of hundreds" (1 Sam 22:7; 8:12), "commanders of thousands" (1 Sam 17:18), as well as "commanders of the chariotry" (1 Kgs 22:31; 2 Chr 18:30), "commanders of his cavalry" (1 Kgs 9:22; 2 Chr 8:9), "commanders of the army" (Gen 21:22; 26:26; 1 Sam 12:9), "commanders of wars" (2 Chr 32:6), and so on. The term may also be employed to designate the chiefs or heads of other official classes, such as "the captain of the guards" (Gen 37:36; cf. 1 Kgs 14:27), "the chief of the cupbearers" (Gen 40:2), "the chief of the bakers" (Gen 40:2), "the chief of the prison house" (Gen 39:21), "the chief of livestock" (Gen 47:6), "the chiefs of taxes/labor" or "taskmasters" (Exod 1:11), as well as chiefs of various sorts of religious classes, including "the chiefs of priests" (Ezra 8:24; 2 Chr 36:14), "the chiefs of the Levites" (1 Chr 15:16; 2 Chr 35:9), "the chiefs of holiness" in reference to the courses of priests (1 Chr 24:5), and so on. The term also designates various civil or governmental roles, such as "the officials of the peo-

ple" (Ezek 11:1; 2 Chr 24:23), "the chiefs of the tribes" (1 Chr 27:22; 29:6), "the chiefs of Judah" (Neh 12:31), "the heads of families" (Ezra 8:29; 1 Chr 29:6), "a ruler of a state/district" (1 Kgs 20:18; Esth 1:3), "the commander of a city" (Judg 9:30), "the commander of a citadel/ capital" (Neh 7:2), or general officials working under the king or other authority (1 Chr 22:17; Ezra 8:20; 1 Kgs 4:2; 2 Kgs 24:12; Jer 34:21). They may also have judicial authority (Exod 18:21; Deut 1:15; Hos 5:10; Isa 1:23). The precise role in which the term is employed here is not explicit, but the earlier reference to them together with the "sons of the king" in Zeph 1:8 and the present listing of priests in 3:4 suggests that they might be considered as some sort of officials who exercise authority on behalf of the king. Certainly, their metaphorical portrayal as "roaring lions" conveys Judean identity, insofar as the lion is the symbol of the tribe of Judah and of royalty (Gen 49:8-12; cf. Amos 1:2). As noted above, the roaring lion portrays a lion that has taken prey (Amos 3:4, 8). Insofar as the officials are responsible for the welfare of the people, the image of a lion taking prey conveys the image of an official who feeds off of the very people whom he is charged to protect, thus violating fundamental principles of justice for the "officials" of the state (cf. Exod 18:21, which defines the qualities of the officials set as judges over the people as "men who fear G-d," "are trustworthy," and who "hate dishonest gain"; cf. Exod 23:1-8; Deut 16:18-20). Of course, the charge of such abuse of office points to a purge, whether real or threatened, as a means to carry out the reform program of King Josiah.

Verse 2b then turns to the characterization of the judges as "wolves of the evening," who "do not leave anything until morning." The grouping of the judges together with the above-named officials makes a great deal of sense, since Exod 18:21-23 indicates that the judges are to be chosen from among the officials of the people. In any case, the judges would have the same responsibilities as the officials for the welfare of the people and for carrying out justice (see Exod 23:1-8; Deut 16:18-20). Likewise, the metaphorical portrayal of the judges as "evening wolves" conveys a similar image of the abuse of power to that of the roaring lions in v. 2a. Wolves are predators, who often take their prey under

---

24 E.g., Ben Zvi, *Zephaniah*, 204–5.

cover of darkness when they are unlikely to be confronted or when they outnumber their prey and can expect little resistance. It is an appropriate metaphor for the present context.

Nevertheless, there has been a great deal of discussion of the "evening wolves" (זְאֵבֵי עֶרֶב), both because the phrase also appears in Hab 1:8 and because the LXX renders it as "wolves of Arabia" (Greek ὡς λύκοι τῆς Ἀραβίας, "like wolves of Arabia"). The root of the difficulty apparently lies in understanding the logical consistency in the relationship between the terms "evening" and "morning" in the verse; why should evening wolves be portrayed as remaining until morning? It is also rooted in the appearance of the term זְאֵב עֲרָבוֹת, "wolf of the deserts/steppes," in Jer 5:6. Despite the fact that the Hebrew text is supported by the Murabbaʿat text, TJ, Peshitta, and Vulgate, there have been persistent attempts to emend the text, generally in accordance with Jer 5:6.[25] Indeed, some argue that the supposed original עֲרָבָה/עֲרָבוֹת, "steppes/steppe," was emended to עֶרֶב, "evening," under the influence of the reference to "morning" at the end of the verse, and that the entire expression, "evening wolves," was then secondarily introduced into Hab 1:8.[26] Such a contention hardly makes sense, though, as it presupposes that a more difficult term was created for Zeph 3:3 from an easily understood term that appears in Jer 5:6, and that the difficult term was then read into an otherwise understandable text in Habakkuk. It would appear that the LXX translators misread the text in relation to Jer 5:6, which reflects a common experience with wolves (and coyotes) in both the ancient and modern worlds: wolves come from the desert, often identified as Arabia in the ancient world, just as they continue to come down from the San Gabriel Mountains into the suburbs of southern California when they are unable to find food in their usual haunts. Because they are nocturnal and tend to avoid confrontation, they normally appear at night or at daybreak. When they do appear in areas of human habitation, however, they tend to be more desperate—after all, they only come when they are unable to find food elsewhere—and they can be dangerous when confronted and trapped. When they are especially desperate, they tend to devour anything they come upon. This would explain the phrase, "they do not leave anything until morning."

Scholars have had a difficult time understanding the verb לֹא גָרְמוּ, "they do not leave." The verb גרם is a *hapax legomenon* in biblical Hebrew that means "to cut off, reserve," which seems not to make full sense in the present context. The issue is further complicated by the occurrence of the noun גֶּרֶם, "bone" (Gen 49:14; 2 Kgs 19:3; Prov 17:22; 25:15), which has prompted suggestions that the term means "to gnaw to the bone" or the like. Nevertheless, the verb is well attested in Rabbinic Hebrew, and the meaning "to drag along, carry with it, cause," does make sense in the present context as wolves tend to roam and eat throughout the night, but they then return home at daybreak when the darkness no longer conceals their activities. It is an appropriate metaphor for dishonest judges who act on the presumption that no one will reveal their perversion of justice.

Ezekiel 22:27 combines and elaborates on Zephaniah's statements concerning the officials and the judges by stating that the officials "within it are like wolves tearing the prey, shedding blood, destroying lives to get dishonest gain." Earlier, in Ezek 22:25, the passage condemns the prophets for acting "like a roaring lion tearing the prey, devouring human lives, taking treasure and precious things, and making widows."

■ **4** The critique of Judean officials continues in v. 4 with charges that the prophets and the priests have abused their offices by failing to carry out their duties with integrity. The pairing of these offices, like that of the officials and judges in v. 3, makes some sense as both prophets and priests are concerned professionally with representing and communicating the will of YHWH. In many cases, prophets may act in relation to the sanctuary as oracle diviners[27] (see the role of Moses

25 Given the role that Jer 5:6 plays in this discussion, it is noteworthy that LXX Jer 5:6 does not preserve a reading of "wolf of the desert," but instead reads as "and a wolf (has destroyed them) even to their houses" (καὶ λύκος ἕως τῶν οἰκιῶν ὠλόθρευσεν αὐτούς).

26 Karl Elliger, "Das Ende der 'Abendwölfe' in Zeph 3,3 Hab 1,8," in Walter Baumgartner et al., eds., *Festschrift Alfred Bertholet zum 80. Geburtstag* (Tübingen: Mohr [Siebeck], 1950) 158–75. For other proposals, see Meinrad Stenzel, "Zum Verständnis von Zeph. III 3B," *VT* 1 (1951) 303–5; Jongeling, "Jeux."

27 Note that prophets were frequently associated with temples in the ancient Near East; see Lester L.

as portrayed in Exod 34:29-35 and Samuel in 1 Samuel 1–3; 7–12; 16; cf. Ezekiel, esp. chaps. 1–3, whose prophecies are based on his visions of the ark from the inner sanctuary of the Jerusalem Temple[28]) or as Levitical singers/prophets in the Second Temple liturgy (see the portrayal of Levitical singers as prophets in the books of Chronicles; 1 Chronicles 25; 2 Chronicles 20; 29, etc.).[29] Although it was clearly not necessary to be a priest or associated with a sanctuary to be a prophet in ancient Israel/Judah,[30] various priestly figures in addition to those mentioned above, such as Jeremiah and Zechariah, also functioned as prophets.[31]

The prophets are charged with being "wanton" and "men of treacheries." The term פֹּחֲזִים, "wanton," is based on the root פחז, "to be wanton, reckless," which appears elsewhere as פַּחַז, "wanton, reckless," to describe Reuben's untrustworthy character in taking his father's concubine (Gen 49:4; cf. 35:22), and as פַּחֲזוּת, "recklessness," to describe prophets labeled by Jeremiah as false and lying (Jer 23:32). Indeed, the credibility of prophets was an issue in ancient Israel and Judah (e.g., Deut 18:9-22; 1 Kings 13; 22) as well as in the rest of the ancient world, especially in the period of the late Judean monarchy and the Babylonian exile when the threats against Jerusalem and ultimately its destruction raised questions about the validity of prophetic claims that YHWH would protect Jerusalem (see Jeremiah 23; 27–28).[32] The designation of prophets as אַנְשֵׁי בֹּגְדוֹת, "men of treacheries," employs the root בגד, "to be treacherous," which appears in various forms throughout the Hebrew Bible in reference to deceit and deliberate betrayal (e.g., Exod 21:8; Judg 9:3; Isa 21:2; 24:16; 33:1; Jer 3:7, 10; 12:1; Pss 59:6; 78:57; Job 6:15; Lam 1:2). By the time of Josiah's reign, the credibility of prophets who argued that YHWH would protect Jerusalem had been challenged by the rise of the Assyrian Empire and its domination of Judah for nearly a century, but the collapse of Assyria in the late seventh century would have prompted a rereading of earlier prophets to support Josiah's efforts at restoration.[33]

Ezek 22:28 expands on these statements by claiming that the prophets have metaphorically "smeared whitewash on their behalf" and that they have been "seeing false visions and divining lies" by stating, "'Thus says YHWH' when YHWH has not spoken."

Verse 4b characterizes the priests as those "who profane holiness" (חִלְּלוּ־קֹדֶשׁ). The priests are charged with creating, maintaining, and teaching what is holy in the world; this statement charges them with complete abandonment of their expected role (see Lev 21:6; 2 Chr 23:6; 31:8; Ezra 8:28; cf. Exod 28:36; 39:30, which describe the headgear of the high priest inscribed with the statement, "Holy to YHWH"). The statement that "they have corrupted Torah" (חָמְסוּ תוֹרָה) likewise charges

Grabbe, "Prophets, Priests, Diviners and Sages in Ancient Israel," in Heather A. McKay and David J. A. Clines, eds., *Of Prophets' Visions and the Wisdom of Sages* (Fest. R. N. Whybray; JSOTSup 162; Sheffield: Sheffield Academic Press, 1993) 43–62; Frederick H. Cryer, *Divination in Ancient Israel and Its Near Eastern Environment: A Socio-Historical Investigation* (JSOTSup 142; Sheffield: Sheffield Academic Press, 1994).

28 See Marvin A. Sweeney, "Ezekiel: Zadokite Priest and Visionary Prophet of the Exile," *SBLSP, 2000* (Atlanta: Society of Biblical Literature, 2000) 728–51; idem, "The Latter Prophets," in Steven L. McKenzie and M. Patrick Graham, eds., *The Hebrew Bible Today: An Introduction to Critical Issues* (Louisville: Westminster John Knox, 1998) 69–94, esp. 88–94.

29 See David L. Petersen, *Late Israelite Prophecy: Studies in Deutero-Prophetic Literature and in Chronicles* (SBLMS 23; Missoula, Mont.: Scholars Press, 1977) 55–96; Raymond Jacques Tournay, *Seeing and Hearing God with the Psalms: The Prophetic Liturgy of the Second Temple in Jerusalem* (JSOTSup 118; Sheffield: Sheffield Academic Press, 1991).

30 See, e.g., the discussion of the social role of the prophet in Joseph Blenkinsopp, *A History of Prophecy in Israel* (rev. ed.; Louisville: Westminster John Knox, 1996) 30–39; David L. Petersen, *The Roles of Israel's Prophets* (JSOTSup 17; Sheffield: JSOT Press, 1981); Robert L. Wilson, *Prophecy and Society in Ancient Israel* (Philadelphia: Fortress Press, 1980).

31 Sweeney, "Latter Prophets," 81–88; idem, "Jeremiah," in David N. Freedman et al., eds., *Eerdmans Dictionary of the Bible* (Grand Rapids: Eerdmans, 2000) 686–89.

32 For discussion, see, e.g., James A. Sanders, "Hermeneutics in True and False Prophecy," in George W. Coats and Burke O. Long, eds., *Canon and Authority* (Philadelphia: Fortress Press, 1977) 21–41.

33 See Sweeney, *King Josiah*.

the priests with failing to fulfill properly one of their fundamental functions, that is, the proper teaching or communication of YHWH's will in the world. The term תּוֹרָה, frequently mistranslated as "law" under the influence of Paul's writings in the NT, properly means "instruction," particularly divine instruction, in that it derives from the *hiphil* form of the root ירה, "to guide."[34] It is employed in the Hebrew Bible to refer to the instruction of a mother (Prov 1:8; 6:20, 23), a father (3:1; 4:2; 7:2), the sages (13:14; 28:4, 7, 9; 29:18), a poet (Ps 78:1), and a wife (Prov 31:26). More frequently, it refers to divine instruction (Job 22:22; Isa 1:10; 2:2; 5:24; 8:16, 20; 30:9; Jer 8:8; Mic 4:4), especially concerning holy matters that the priesthood is expected to teach (Hos 2:11; Mal 2:6, 7, 8, 9; Ezek 22:26; 2 Chr 15:3; cf. Lev 10:10-11). It includes the various bodies of law or legal instruction that appear throughout the Pentateuch; fundamentally, it is the priests who are expected to convey properly YHWH's Torah by answering the questions of

the people (see Hag 2:10-19) and to read the Torah to them every seventh year at the Festival of Sukkot (Deut 31:9-13; cf. Nehemiah 8). The verb חמס means literally "to treat violently, wrongly," and it appears elsewhere in reference to the mistreatment of widows and orphans (Lam 2:6), Job (Job 21:27), and general mistreatment (Prov 8:36).

The same expressions employed here to describe the misconduct of the priests appear in Ezek 22:26, a text that apparently elaborates on the present statement: "they have done violence to my Torah and have profaned my holy things." Ezek 22:26 expands on Zephaniah's formulation, however, by stating that the priests make no distinction between the holy and the profane, the clean and unclean, and they disregard YHWH's Sabbaths.

---

34   See Louis Isaac Rabinowitz, "Torah: The Term," *EncJud* 15:1235–36.

Translation

5 YHWH is righteous in her midst;[a]
　　he does not do iniquity.[b]
Morning by morning he gives forth his law
　　　to the light; it does not fail;[c]
　　and he does not know iniquity, shame.[d]

6 "I have cut off nations;[e]
　　their corner fortifications are demolished.[f]
I have ruined their streets
　　so that no one passes;
their cities are wasted,
　　without anyone, no one inhabits.[g]

7 I have said, 'Surely, fear me,
　　take[h] instruction,'
and her habitation shall not be cut off[i]
　　because of all that I have visited upon
　　　her.
Indeed, they worked even harder to corrupt
　　all their deeds.[j]

8 Therefore, wait for me,"[k] utterance of
　　YHWH,
　　"for the day when I arise for prey.[l]
For my judgment is to gather nations,
　　to assemble kingdoms,
to pour out upon them my wrath,
　　all my hot anger,
for in the fire of my jealousy,
　　all the earth will be consumed.[m]

9 For then I will transform (the languages of)
　　the nations
　　into a pure speech,[n]
to call,[o] all of them, in the name of YHWH,
　　to serve him with one accord.

10 From across the rivers of Cush,[p]
my supplicants, the daughter of my dis-
　　persed,[q] will present my grain offer-
　　ing.

11 In that day you will not be ashamed of all of
　　your deeds[r]
　　by which you rebelled against me.[s]
For then I shall remove from your midst
　　your proud exultant ones,
so that you will not again be arrogant
　　in my holy mountain.

12 And I shall cause to remain in your midst
　　a people humble and lowly,
and they will take refuge[t] in the name of
　　YHWH.

13 The remnant of Israel[u] will not commit iniq-
　　uity
　　and they will not speak a lie,
and there will not be found in their mouth
　　a deceitful tongue,
for they will graze and lie down,[v]
　　and no one frightens them."

a　TJ, יוי זכאה אמר לאשריה שכינתיה בגוה, "YHWH, the
righteous one, has said/promised to cause his
Shekinah [Presence] to dwell in her midst."

b　TJ, לית קדמוהי למעבד שקר, "it is not before him to
act falsely."

c　TJ, הא כנהור צפרא דאזיל ותקיף כין דיניה נפיק לאפרש
ולא מתעכב, "Behold, like the light of the morning
which does and is firm, so his judgment goes out
forever and it is not detained"; cf. Peshitta, bṣprᵓ
wbṣprᵓ dynwhy yhb bnwhrᵓ wlᵓ mšwḥr, "Every morning
his law he gives in the light and he does not tarry."

d　Note that LXX Vaticanus reads only, "morning by
morning he gives his judgment, and not injustice in
strife," but several MSS and early church traditions
(Freer Codex, Vg, 449', Theophilus Antiochensis,
Gildas Sapiens) add, εις φως, "unto light," after "he
gives his judgment." Other MSS (22, 48, 86^mg, Syro-
hexapla^mg) read the full text as, εις φως και ουκ
αβερκρυβη (επερ. 48) και ουκ εγνω (pl.
Syrohexapla^mg) αδικιαν εν απαιτησει (απατ. 58;
omit εν απαιτ. 239), "unto light, and it is not hidden, and he does not know injustice in extortion,"
immediately following "he gives his judgment."
Many other MSS and traditions read with the MT.
See the textual notes to v. 5 in Ziegler, *Duodecim
Prophetae*, 281.

e　MT reads the last statement as וְלֹא־יוֹדֵעַ עַוָּל בֹּשֶׁת; cf.
Mur 20:36, עֹול [לֹא נֶעְדרן. Many, including TJ
and Peshitta, read עַוָּל as the subject of the verb:
"but the iniquitous one does not know shame,"
which is grammatically correct and understands the
statement as a means to contrast those who do evil
with YHWH. Nevertheless, a reference to the iniquitous as subject seems out of place in this context.
The reading proposed here, like the LXX, takes both
עַוָּל and בֹּשֶׁת as objects of the verb for which YHWH
serves as subject. Lacking firm textual evidence,
one may only speculate that one of these terms may
have been a gloss on the other (cf. Gerleman,
Zephanja, 51; Ryou, *Zephaniah's Oracles*, 61–62) or
that עַוָּל may have been the misplaced subject of לֹא
נֶעְדר, thus, "and the iniquitous one is not hidden,
and he [YHWH] does not know shame." Cf. Vulgate, *nescivit autem iniquus confusionem*, "he does not
know, but the perverse is confused." Note that the
LXX tradition reads בשת as both νῖκος (= νείκος),
"strife," and ἀπαίτησις, "extortion" (see note a
above). Since νῖκος (= νείκος) presupposes that בֹּשֶׁת
should be read as a form of the verb בוס, "to tram-
ple," or perhaps the verb בזה, "to despise," and
ἀπαίτησις presupposes that בשת should be read as
a form of the verb בזז, "to despoil," it appears that
there was some difficulty in rendering the term בֹּשֶׁת
in relation to the preceding עַוָּל. The readings pre-

served in the Greek tradition apparently represent different approaches to resolving this problem; cf. Gerleman, *Zephanja*, 52.

f   MT, גוֹיִם הִכְרַתִּי, "I have cut off nations"; cf. LXX, ἐν διαφθορᾷ κατέσπασα ἐπερηφάνους, "In destruction, I have brought down the arrogant," apparently reading this statement in relation to the Day of YHWH tradition in Isa 2:6-21, which stresses the downfall of the arrogant in the earth.

g   Cf. Peshitta, *ʾwbdt ʿmmʾ wʾthblt dwyʾ*, "I have destroyed the nations, and I have destroyed the misery," apparently involves an inner Syriac corruption of *zwytʾ*, "corner," to *dwytʾ*, "misery" (Ryou, *Zephaniah's Oracles*, 63; Gerleman, *Zephanja*, 53; Rudolph, *Zephanja*, 286). Note that פִּנּוֹתָם, "their corners/corner fortifications," may also be read in relation to Aramaic forms of the verb פנה, which can mean, "to turn, pervert" (see Jastrow, *Dictionary* 2:1187).

h   See the reading of 8HevXIIgr 23:36-38, ἀπ]ώ[λοντο αἱ πόλεις αὐτῶν παρὰ μὴ ὑπάρ]χ[ε]ιν ἄνδ[ρα διὰ τοῦ μὴ εἶναι κατοιχ]οῦντα, "Destroyed [are their cities so that no] ma[n exists, so that no one inha]bits" (see Tov, *Greek Minor Prophets*, 65).

i   Peshitta adds, *wmny*, "and from me (take instruction)."

j   MT, מְעוֹנָה לֹא־יִכָּרֵת, "and her inhabitation shall not be cut off"; the Murabbaʿat scroll is lacking for all of v. 7. Cf. LXX, καὶ οὐ μὴ ἐξολεθρευθῆτε ἐξ ὀφθαλμῶν αὐτῆς, "and you shall not be cut off from its eyes," apparently reading Heb. מְעוֹנָה, "its habitation," as מֵעֵינָה, "from its eye," which only requires a shift from *waw* to *yod*, which are often confused because of the similarity of their orthography in antiquity. See also Peshitta, which reads, *wlʾ nʾbd mn ʿynyh klmdn dpqdt ʿlyh*, "and there shall not be destroyed from her eyes everything that I decreed upon her." Cf. 8HevXIIgr 23:39-40, [καὶ οὐ ἡ π]ηγὴ [αὐ]τῆς, "[and not h]er [wa]ters," which apparently reads Heb. מעינה as the orthographically identical "her spring" instead of "her eye" (note that Tov's reconstruction clearly does not fill the gap in the papyrus). TJ reads, מְדוֹרֵהוֹן, "their inhabitation," and Vulgate reads, *habitaculum eius*, "its inhabitation" with MT. For discussion see Gerleman, *Zephanja*, 53-54; Ryou, *Zephaniah's Oracles*, 65-66.

k   MT, עֲלִילוֹתָם כֹּל הִשְׁחִיתוּ הִשְׁכִּימוּ אָכֵן, "indeed, they rose early, they corrupted all their deeds"; Murabbaʿat lacks v. 7 due to scroll damage. Cf. LXX, ἑτοιμάζου ὄρθρισον διέφθαρται πᾶσα ἡ ἐπιφυλλὶς αὐτῶν, "get ready, rise early, all their grapes/gleanings are destroyed." The LXX apparently reads אָכֵן as an Aramaic *aphel* (cf. Hebrew *hiphil*) imperative of the root כון, "to prepare" (cf. Peshitta below; but see also 8HevXIIgr below, which clearly reads הִשְׁכִּימוּ in the same sense), the *hiphil* perfect of הִשְׁכִּימוּ as the

hiphil masculine plural imperative (which requires no change in consonants), and עֲלִילוֹתָם as "their grapes/gleanings," which can be orthographically identical, i.e., עֹלֵלוֹת, "gleanings," as opposed to עֲלִילוֹת, "deeds." The LXX apparently reads the statements in relation to punishments that have already been visited upon the people. Cf. 8HevXIIgr 23:41-42, Διὰ τοῦτο ὀ[ρθρίσατε διαφθείρ]ατε πάντα τὰ ἐπιτ[ηδεύματα αὐτῶν, "Therefore, be ready, their pursuits are destroyed," which reads הִשְׁכִּימוּ as an imperative, "be ready/get up early," and הִשְׁחִיתוּ as a perfect form with כֹּל עֲלִילוֹתָם as its subject; Peshitta, *ʾttybw wqrbw whblw klhyn ṣnʿhwn*, "and they made ready, and they proceeded, and they corrupted all of their doings." TJ and Vulgate read the verse like the MT.

l   Cf. TJ, בכן סברו למימרי, "Therefore, look for my *Memra*."

m   Cf. Vulgate, *in die resurrectionis meae in futuram*, "in the day of my resurrection in the future," which is clearly motivated by theological concerns. Cf. TJ, ליום אתגליותי למדן, "for the day that I am revealed to judge."

n   Cf. TJ, יסופון כל רשעי ארעא, "all the wicked of the earth shall come to an end."

o   MT, בְרוּרָה שָׂפָה אֶל־עַמִּים אֶהְפֹּךְ אָז־כִּי, "for then I will change unto nations a pure/select language"; Mur 21:3, ברורה שפה העמים על[, "upon the nations a pure/select language." Cf. LXX, ὅτι τότε μεταστρέψω ἐπὶ λαοὺς γλῶσσαν εἰς γενεὰν αὐτῆς, "for I will change upon the peoples a tongue unto her generation/coming into being," apparently reading בְרוּרָה as a form of the root ברא, "to create," with a feminine singular pronominal suffix. Such a reading would apparently presuppose that the language of the nations is changed back to its singular form prior to the time of the tower of Babel episode (Gen 11:1-9) when all the earth (v. 9) was created.

p   MT, לִקְרֹא, "to call"; cf. TJ, לצלאה, "to pray."

q   MT, כּוּשׁ, "Cush (Ethiopia)"; Mur 21:4, כוש, "Cush (Ethiopia)"; cf. LXX, Αἰθιοπίας, "Ethiopia"; TJ, הודו, "India"; Peshitta, *dkwš*, "of Cush"; Vulgate, *Aethiopiae*, "of Ethiopia."

r   MT, בַּת־פּוּצַי עֲתָרַי, "my supplicants, the daughter of my dispersion," may well represent an early gloss of one term upon the other since the two expressions appear to stand in an appositional relationship (cf. Gerleman, *Zephanja*, 57). Cf. Mur 21:4, עתרי בת פוצי, "my supplicants, the daughter of my dispersion," which clearly includes both terms. Vaticanus lacks the phrases altogether, reading, "From across the rivers of Ethiopia, they will bring my offering," but later traditions read, προσδέξομαι ἐν διεσπαμένοις, "I will receive my dispersed ones," perhaps reading עתרי as a form of the verb עטר, "to surround, protect" (cf. Ziegler, *Duodecim Prophetae*, 282). The two expressions are also lacking in the Peshitta, which reads simply, "From across the rivers of Cush, bringing to me sacrifices." Nevertheless, the absence of these expressions in Vaticanus and Peshitta leave the following statement concerning the presentation of offerings to YHWH without a clear subject. Cf. TJ, גלות עמי דאתגליאו, "the exile of my people which was exiled," which clearly struggles with the phrase, but presupposes the two expressions, and Vulgate, *inde supplices mei filii dispersiorum meorum*, "from them are my supplicants, daughters of my dispersion."

s   MT, עֲלִילֹתַיִךְ, "your deeds"; cf. TJ, עובדך בישא, "your evil deeds."

t   MT, בִּי, "against me"; cf. TJ, במימרי, "against my *Memra*."

u   MT, וְחָסוּ, "and they will take refuge"; cf. Mur 21:7, וחסו, "and they will take refuge"; LXX, καὶ εὐλαβηθήσονται, "and they shall pay reverence"; TJ, ויתרחצון, "and they shall trust"; Peshitta, *wnsbrwn*, "and they shall trust"; Vulgate, *et sperabunt*, "and looking to."

v   The initial οἱ κατάλοιποι τοῦ Ισραηλ, "and those who remain of Israel," must function as the subject of the preceding phrase in v. 12, that is, "and those who remain of Israel shall pay reverence to the name of the L-rd." The following statement begins with καί, "and," which marks the beginning of a new syntactical unit, that is, "and they shall not do injustice." See Gerleman, *Zephanja*, 60.

w   Cf. TJ, ארי אנון יתפרנסון וישרון, "for they shall support themselves and lie down," which eliminates any suggestion of the activity of sheep.

Form and Setting

Zephaniah 3:5-13 constitutes the second subunit of the prophet's exhortative speech in 3:1-20 in which he presents a scenario by which YHWH will restore Jerusalem as the holy center of the nations. As noted above, the chapter begins with the prophet's woe oracle in 3:1-4 in which he articulates the reasons for Jerusalem's punishment, continues in 3:5-13 with the prophet's presentation of YHWH's speech concerning divine plans to see to Jerusalem's restoration by gathering the nations and changing them so that they will recognize YHWH and restore Jerusalem, and concludes in 3:14-20 with the prophet's summons to rejoice directed to Jerusalem and Israel in view of the coming restoration. Zephaniah 3:5-13 plays the key role within this larger structure in that it asserts YHWH's righteousness (v. 5) as a means to introduce YHWH's statements concerning Jerusalem's coming restoration.

There are a number of reasons for the demarcation of this passage. First, v. 5 lacks an introductory syntactical connector that would join it to vv. 1-4. Second, the reference to YHWH as subject in v. 5 shifts the focus of attention from Jerusalem, which is the subject of vv. 1-4. Although some might argue that the third person feminine singular pronoun references to Jerusalem in v. 5 tie it to vv. 1-4, which explicitly mention the city,[1] the shift in subject to YHWH must override this feature to demonstrate that v. 5 forms the introduction to a new subunit within the larger text structure of vv. 1-20. Third, although v. 6 employs first person pronouns to portray YHWH as the speaker in contrast to the third person references to YHWH in v. 5 and vv. 1-4, the presence of the oracular formula in v. 8 demonstrates that the prophet is the primary speaker in this passage who presents YHWH's words to the audience. Fourth, 3:5 articulates the premise that YHWH is righteous and not evil, which the presentation of YHWH's speech in vv. 6-12 is designed to demonstrate. Furthermore, the assertion of YHWH's righteousness contrasts markedly with the portrayal of the wicked city and its corrupt officials in vv. 1-4. Many have argued that v. 5 is a secondary redactional addition because of its shift in theme, the portrayal of the speaker, and its supposed concluding function in relation to vv. 1-4,[2] but these considerations indicate that v. 5 is the introduction to the second stage of the prophet's discourse in vv. 1-20 in which he attempts to persuade his audience that YHWH is righteous and intends to restore Jerusalem now that its period of punishment is nearly concluded. Following the

---

1   E.g., Ryou, *Zephaniah's Oracles*, 265 n. 282; Edler, *Kerygma*, 95. cf. Vlaardingerbroek, *Zephaniah*, 168.

2   Ryou, *Zephaniah's Oracles* 305–6; Edler, *Kerygma*, 95–96; Vlaardingerbroek, *Zephaniah*, 168; Langhor, "Sophonie," 18; Horst, *Propheten*, 197; Elliger, *Zephanja*, 76.

presentation of YHWH's speech in vv. 6-12, v. 13 presents the prophet's statements once again with an objective third person announcement of the coming security of the remnant of Israel that sums up and concludes the statements made by YHWH in vv. 6-12. Verse 14 then begins an entirely new subunit within 3:1-20, as indicated by the prophet's syntactically independent direct address to the city of Jerusalem calling for her to rejoice at her impending restoration.

Indeed, the internal structure and thematic development of 3:5-13 demonstrate the overall rhetorical strategy of the passage.[3] Verse 5 begins the prophet's discourse with the assertion of YHWH's righteousness and a denial that YHWH is capable of acting deceitfully or treacherously. The prophet's statements draw on the imagery of daybreak, insofar as the morning light is employed to illustrate YHWH's righteousness. This of course recalls the daily morning liturgy of sacrifice and prayer that opens each day in the temple to portray the daily creation of the world beginning with light (Exod 29:38-46, esp. 39; Num 28:1-9, esp. 4; cf. Gen 1:3-5; Psalm 104). In essence, the prophet's statements draw on the constancy of creation, particularly the order of night and day, to point to YHWH's reliability and righteousness. Jerusalemite and Judean tradition states that YHWH will protect the city of Jerusalem as the holy center of creation,[4] and the created order of the natural world testifies to YHWH's reliability. In this respect, the passage emerges as an example of a theodicy that attempts to demonstrate YHWH's righteousness in the face of evil.[5]

The passage then shifts to the prophet's presentation of YHWH's speech in vv. 6-12. As noted above, the oracular formula in v. 8 demonstrates that the prophet is the primary speaker in these verses and, together with the first person formulation employed throughout the speech, that the prophet here conveys the words of YHWH. Overall, YHWH's speech is formulated as an exhortation in that it calls on the audience to wait for the day when YHWH will take action to gather the nations and to restore Jerusalem (v. 8),[6] but it also employs elements of the disputation form in order to argue its case persuasively.[7] In general, the disputation form is an argumentative speech form in which the speaker attempts to dispute a contention of an audience and prompt them to accept a countercontention. Three basic elements appear within the deep structure of the disputation: (1) the thesis to be disputed; (2) the counterthesis for which the speaker argues; and (3) the argumentation proper. The thesis to be disputed is the contention that YHWH is evil. This has already appeared explicitly in the programmatic v. 5, but it appears in YHWH's speech as well in that it argues that by corrupting their ways the people and not YHWH are wicked and thus responsible for the misfortunes that have befallen them as punishment from YHWH (3:7b; cf. 3:1-4). This thesis is also implicit in YHWH's initial statements of responsibility for the destruction leveled against the nations and their cities. The counterthesis of course is that YHWH is righteous. This contention is implicit in the above-mentioned statement that the people corrupted their ways, but it is also apparent in v. 7a, in which YHWH states that in the past, YHWH had instructed Jerusalem to "fear me, take instruction," and that its habitation would not be cut off, but that Jerusalem had declined to do so. Again, the implication is that Jerusalem had suffered punishment for this failure and was therefore responsible for its own troubles. Both the thesis and the counterthesis thus appear in vv. 6-7, in which YHWH reviews the past relationship

3 Cf. Sweeney, "Form-Critical Reassessment," 402, which differs in minor details from the present analysis.

4 E.g., Psalms 2; 46; 47; 48; 89; 110; 132.

5 Cf. Psalm 89, which raises similar questions with regard to the house of David.

6 For discussion of the exhortation form, see Sweeney, *Isaiah 1–39*, 520; Hunter, *Seek the Lord*; K. Arvid Tångberg, *Die prophetische Mahnrede* (FRLANT 143; Göttingen: Vandenhoeck & Ruprecht, 1987); G. Warmuth, *Das Mahnwort* (BBET 1; Frankfurt: Lang, 1976); Thomas M. Raitt,

"The Prophetic Summons to Repentance," *ZAW* 83 (1971) 30–49; Hans W. Wolff, "Das Thema 'Umkehr' in der alttestamentlichen Prophetie," *ZThK* 48 (1951) 129–48; cf. Floyd, *Minor Prophets*, 235.

7 Sweeney, *Isaiah 1–39*, 519; Donald F. Murray, "The Rhetoric of Disputation: Re-examination of a Prophetic Genre," *JSOT* 38 (1987) 95–121; Adrian Graffy, *A Prophet Confronts His People* (AnBib 104; Rome: Biblical Institute Press, 1984).

with Jerusalem: YHWH had called on Jerusalem to show fear and take instruction, but it had refused to do so. Verse 6 relates YHWH's actions in destroying the nations and their cities, and v. 7 relates YHWH's statements to Jerusalem together with Jerusalem's reaction to those statements.

Verses 8-12, introduced by לָכֵן, "therefore," then focus on the future realization of YHWH's righteousness in the form of Jerusalem's (and Israel's) restoration. This constitutes the basic argumentation on behalf of the counterthesis, that is, YHWH is righteous and the future restoration of Jerusalem will bear this out.

The first portion of this passage in vv. 8-10 focuses on YHWH's actions concerning the nations. It begins with the prophet's presentation of YHWH's command to the audience, "wait for me, for the day when I arise as a witness" (v. 8a), followed by three כִּי clauses, each of which articulates a reason for the audience to wait for YHWH (vv. 8b-9). The clause in v. 8bα states YHWH's decision to gather nations and pour out the wrath of judgment upon them. The clause in v. 8bβ reiterates this sentiment with a statement that YHWH's fiery jealousy will consume the entire earth. The clause in v. 9 then states that YHWH will change the speech of the nations of the world so that they might call on YHWH. Finally, v. 10 sums up this subunit by portraying the now changed nations as YHWH's supplicants, who will bring offerings to Jerusalem from across the rivers of Cush/Ethiopia.

The second portion of this passage in vv. 11-12 then focuses on YHWH's actions in relation to Jerusalem. The subunit begins with the well-known formula בַּיּוֹם הַהוּא, "in that day," to indicate the future time when the coming scenario will be realized.[8] Again, the basic internal structure of this subunit begins with YHWH's assertion, formulated as a direct second person feminine singular address to Jerusalem, that she need not be ashamed of her deeds by which she rebelled against YHWH (v. 11a). The reason for this assertion then appears in the form of a כִּי clause in vv. 11b-12: YHWH promises to remove Jerusalem's arrogance (v. 11b), leaving a humble and lowly remnant in Jerusalem that will take refuge in YHWH's name (v. 12). YHWH's words

entail a continued purge of the city, but they point to its conclusion and to a secure future for the remnant of the people.

Having concluded the presentation of YHWH's speech in vv. 6-12, which is designed to demonstrate future security for the people of Jerusalem, in 3:13 the prophet then reverts to his own speech, which provides the basic structure for the subunit 3:5-13 within the larger structure of 3:1-20. Here the prophet reiterates YHWH's words in vv. 11-12, that is, the remnant of Israel will no longer act iniquitously, speak lies, or engage in deceit (v. 13a). The כִּי clause in v. 13b indicates instead that the remnant of Israel will be secure like sheep lying down in their pastures. Such a contention not only builds on and clarifies the specific meaning of YHWH's own statements in vv. 11-12, it also resolves the issue of the iniquity, evil, and deceit claimed for Jerusalem in vv. 7b and 1-4, by which v. 5 makes direct comparison with the character of YHWH. In this manner, YHWH's righteous character is both vindicated and confirmed in contrast to the past character claimed for Jerusalem and its ultimate transformation by means of YHWH's purge.

The social setting for such a discourse must be identified as the Jerusalem Temple, as indicated by the initial references to the morning liturgy of the temple in v. 5 and by the portrayal of the nations bringing offerings to YHWH in v. 10. Indeed, such a setting conforms well to the model of Josiah's restoration, which is centered in the purification of the temple as the holy center of Jerusalem, Israel, and the world at large. Likewise, the portrayal of YHWH's purge of the arrogant (vv. 11-12) points to Josiah's restoration program with its call for the purge of Jerusalem and Judah, which of course is designed to motivate reform on the part of the people and their major social institutions. Finally, the portrayal of the gathering of the nations for punishment and the presentation of YHWH's offerings from beyond the rivers of Cush points to a fundamental change in the relationship to the nations: they will no longer threaten Jerusalem/Israel, but will instead recognize YHWH and bring offerings to Jerusalem. The reference to Cush is

---

8   For discussion of this formula, see DeVries, *From Old Revelation*, 36, 206, 255, 300, 302, 320, although he mistakenly argues that this passage is the result of later redaction in light of the experience of the exile and restoration (203–5).

particularly noteworthy insofar as it seems to point to Egypt as the source for recognition of YHWH by the nations. This would be a remarkable fulfillment of the purposes of the exodus from Egypt as portrayed in biblical narrative, that is, not only the redemption of Israel from Egyptian bondage, but the recognition of YHWH by Egypt and the other nations as well (see Exod 5:2; 7:5, 17; 8:10; 9:14; 14:18; 15:11-18; Isa 19:16-25). In this regard, the above-mentioned rise of Saite Egypt and its incursions into territories ruled by the Assyrians in the mid-seventh century must have played a crucial role in the prophet's thinking concerning Josiah's reform; that is, the rise of Saite Egypt signaled YHWH's intentions to bring down the Assyrian Empire and to restore Jerusalem and Israel following the long period of its submission to Assyria. Just as all creation participated by means of the plagues and sea in the overthrow of Egypt at the time of the exodus, so all creation would participate in the gathering of the nations (Zeph 3:8; 1:2-3) as the Egyptians would come to recognize YHWH as sovereign of the entire earth in the time of Zephaniah and Josiah.

3:5-7

■ **5** As noted above, 3:5 provides the basic premise concerning YHWH's righteousness that the following presentation of YHWH's speech in vv. 6-12 is designed to demonstrate. The verse does relate to the preceding material in vv. 1-4 in that the expression בְּקִרְבָּהּ, "in its/her midst," appears in both v. 5 and v. 3 in reference to the contentious city, Jerusalem, mentioned at the outset of 3:1-4. It is also related by the contrast posed within v. 5 between the righteous YHWH and those who do iniquity, which in turn highlights the contrast between YHWH and the corrupt officials of the contentious city that are named in vv. 3-4. Nevertheless, this does not require that v. 5 forms the conclusion to vv. 1-4. Instead, the absence of a syntactical connection at the beginning of v. 5 and its focus on YHWH as the subject of concern, whose words are presented by the prophet in the following vv. 6-12, point to its role as the introduction to the

next subunit of the text that is concerned with demonstrating YHWH's righteousness by pointing to YHWH's plans to restore Jerusalem and the remnant of Israel at the center of the nations. Indeed, the third person feminine singular reference to the city/Jerusalem in v. 5 also relates to the third person feminine singular references to the city in the expressions מְעוֹנָהּ, "her habitation," and עָלֶיהָ, "upon/against her," in v. 7 and the second feminine singular address forms employed in reference to the city throughout YHWH's speech in vv. 6-12. The repeated references to בְּקִרְבֵּךְ, "in your midst" (vv. 11, 12), are particularly noteworthy. Likewise, the prophet's statement in v. 13 that "the remnant of Israel will not do iniquity (לֹא־יַעֲשׂוּ עַוְלָה)" recalls the similar statement in v. 5 that YHWH "will not do iniquity (לֹא־יַעֲשֶׂה עַוְלָה). The reference to YHWH's daily מִשְׁפָּט, "law, judgment, justice," points forward to YHWH's "decision" (מִשְׁפָּט) to gather nations in v. 8, and the references to the "morning" and "shame" in v. 5 point to the early rising of Jerusalem's wicked one in v. 7 and to YHWH's instructions that she should no more be ashamed in v. 10 because the wicked are to be purged from her midst. Clearly, v. 5 anticipates the material in vv. 6-13. In this respect, the references in v. 5 to the concerns of vv. 1-4 point to the relationship of two subunits, vv. 5-13 and vv. 1-4, within the larger structure of 3:1-20.

The major concern of v. 5 is to assert YHWH's righteousness. In that the experience of approximately a century of Assyrian domination from the late eighth through the late seventh centuries would call YHWH's power and righteousness into question, the verse is ultimately concerned with the issue of theodicy. Such a concern is apparent in the use of the term צַדִּיק, "righteous," which is commonly employed in a judicial setting to designate one who is vindicated or acquitted in court (Exod 23:7, 8; Deut 16:19; 25:1; 1 Kgs 8:32; 2 Chr 6:23; Isa 5:23; 29:21, etc.) as opposed to one who is condemned or convicted of a crime and designated רָשָׁע, "wicked" (Exod 23:7; Deut 25:1; 1 Kgs 8:32; 2 Chr 6:23; Isa 5:23, etc.).[9] Although עַוְלָה, "iniquity," is a far more general term (see Ps 64:7; Job 6:29; 11:14; 15:16; 22:23; 24:20; 36:33; Ezek 28:15; Prov 22:8; Hos 10:13), the following

---

9   Cf. Ben Zvi, *Zephaniah*, 207–8. For discussion of the legal terminology, see George W. Ramsey, "Speech Forms in Hebrew Law and Prophetic Oracles," *JBL*   96 (1977) 45–58; Hans-Joachim Boecker, *Redeformen des Rechtlebens im alten Testament* (WMANT 14; Neukirchen-Vluyn: Neukirchener Verlag, 1970).

parallel statement that YHWH "does not do iniquity" (לֹא־יַעֲשֶׂה עַוְלָה) also has potential legal connotations as indicated by the appearance of its masculine form in Lev 19:15, "You shall do no injustice (עָוֶל) in judgment (בְּמִשְׁפָּט)." Such connotations appear to underlie Jehoshaphat's instructions to his newly appointed judges in 2 Chr 19:7, "and now let the fear of G-d be upon you; observe and act (accordingly), for there is not with YHWH our G-d iniquity (עַוְלָה), showing favor, or taking bribes." The term can also appear in liturgical contexts to assert YHWH's righteousness, for example, Ps 92:16, which asserts that the role of the "righteous" (צַדִּיק) is "to declare that YHWH is upright, my rock, and there is no iniquity (עַוְלָתָה) in him."

Indeed, scholars have noted the association of the language of v. 5 with liturgical statements in the Psalms,[10] and many have used this as a justification for declaring all or part of v. 5 to be a secondary addition to this text.[11] But such a view overlooks the rhetorical function of this verse within the larger context of 3:5-13 or 3:1-20 as articulated here, as well as the social setting of the temple in which the prophet's presentation of YHWH's speech would most likely be placed. The temple provides a primary venue for public speakers, particularly prophets, who wish to comment on YHWH's character, actions, righteousness or lack thereof, and so on (see Jeremiah 7; cf. Amos 7–9, which presupposes that Amos speaks at the Bethel temple[12]). Furthermore, since Zephaniah appears to have been an early supporter of Josiah's reform program, the temple would provide a natural setting for the delivery of these oracles. The use of language that appears commonly in the Psalms would be expected in such a setting.

Zephaniah's comments, for example, that YHWH renders judgment each morning, appear to presuppose the daily morning liturgy of the temple.[13] The statement that YHWH's law "is not hidden" reinforces the initial contention that YHWH "gives his law to the light each morning."[14] The temple liturgy begins each morning, presumably at dawn, with the daily morning sacrifice (see Exod 29:38-46; Num 28:1-9; Lev 6:1-5, esp. v. 4), the incense offerings (Exod 30:7), and freewill offerings (Exod 36:3). It is also designated as a time for prayer (Pss 5:4; 88:14) and hymnic praise for G-d (Pss 59:17; 92:3). Since the temple is conceived in ancient Judean thought to be the center of the cosmos from which cre-

---

10   E.g., Ben Zvi, *Zephaniah*, 206–7.

11   See Ryou, *Zephaniah's Oracles*, 305, who cites parallels to Pss 11:7; 92:16; 129:4; 145:17; Isa 50:4; 51:4; Deut 32:4; Dan 9:14, most of which may be related to a liturgical setting, as part of his contention that v. 5 is a redactional addition to this text.

12   For discussion of Amos 7–9, see Sweeney, *Twelve Prophets*, 249–74.

13   See 1 Chronicles 16, which relates various psalms sung at the time that the ark is brought to Jerusalem. Although this text is generally believed to represent a postexilic conceptualization of the entry of the ark into Jerusalem, 2 Sam 6:5 likewise relates the dancing and music that preceded the ark as it was brought into Jerusalem. See also 2 Kgs 11:14, which relates music in the temple at the coronation of Joash ben Jehoahaz/Ahaziah as king of Judah.

14   Ryou, *Zephaniah's Oracles*, 59–61, 124–25, argues that לָאוֹר, "to the light," must be read as the first element of a clause that includes the following לֹא נֶעְדָּר, "he/it is not lacking." This requires that לָאוֹר be read as a temporal formula analogous to בַּבֹּקֶר בַּבֹּקֶר, "morning by morning/every morning," at the beginning of v. 5b and that YHWH be considered the subject of the statement, i.e., "every dawn he does not fail" (p. 16). Ryou's argument is based on the preference for reading the two statements of v. 5bα as syntactic parallels and the difficulties evident in the LXX reading of the verse. The MT reading, however, takes לָאוֹר as the indirect object of the preceding statement, i.e., "every morning, he [YHWH] brings his law to light," which is presupposed by the other versions. Although attractive on syntactical grounds, Ryou's proposal must be rejected for two basic reasons. First, it is not clear why לָאוֹר should refer to the dawn, especially since the preposition ל is fundamentally directional even though it can sometimes function in a temporal sense. Second, the subject of לֹא נֶעְדָּר is מִשְׁפָּטוֹ, "his law," as indicated by the *niphal* construction of the verb. If YHWH gives law, it is not clear why YHWH should be considered hidden or lacking at dawn; the issues of YHWH's righteousness or giving law do not impinge on YHWH's absence. Even if YHWH were iniquitous, as the preceding statement suggests, YHWH would still be present. But if YHWH gives law to the light, it is clear that it (YHWH's law) would not be hidden or lacking. Note the similar statement in Ps 19:5b-7 (quoted in the commentary below) that "nothing is hidden from its [the sun's] heat." It is not YHWH who is

ation proceeds, the morning liturgy would celebrate YHWH's creation of the world by pointing to light as the first act of creation (see Gen 1:3-5).[15] A number of the psalms extol YHWH as creator of the world (e.g., Psalms 8; 19; 33; 104). Solar imagery frequently permeates the psalms as a means to describe YHWH's role as creator of the world (Psalms 8; 19; 104; cf. Habakkuk 3), and YHWH's role as creator is frequently correlated with YHWH's role as the giver of justice, law, wise counsel, and so on (Psalms 8; 19; 33). Psalm 19 is particularly noteworthy in this regard. It begins by extolling YHWH as creator, with a special emphasis on solar imagery to express that role: "in them [the heavens] he has placed a tent for the sun, and it goes out like a bridegroom from his wedding canopy and like a man rejoices to run a course; from the end of the heavens is its going out, and its circuit is to their end, and nothing is hidden from its heat" (vv. 5b-7). Immediately following this portrayal of the created order through the imagery of the sun is a series of verses that extol YHWH's Torah, decrees, precepts, and so on: "The Torah of YHWH is perfect, restoring the soul; the testimony of YHWH is sure, making the simple wise; the precepts of YHWH are upright, rejoicing the heart; the commandment of YHWH is pure, giving light to the eyes," and so on (vv. 8-9).

The statements in Zeph 3:5 clearly reflect a similar conceptualization of YHWH, YHWH's righteousness, YHWH's law, and YHWH's role as creator, beginning with light, which in turn is correlated with justice. Of course, we do not know what liturgical traditions would have been employed in the temple during Josiah's reign, but these parallels would indicate that Zephaniah draws on such liturgical traditions in formulating an argument that YHWH is righteous. Certainly, the concern with theodicy is well known in the Psalms (e.g., Psalms 37; 60; 79; 83; 89; 85; 108; 137).[16] It is therefore hardly sur-

prising that such an issue would appear in prophetic texts that draw on liturgical traditions.

Verse 5bβ is frequently understood to provide a contrast with YHWH by stating, "and the iniquitous one does not know shame." This is problematic, however, in that the statement appears to be parallel to v. 5aβ, which states that YHWH "does not do iniquity." Since all segments of v. 5 focus on YHWH as the subject of action, it is not entirely clear why v. 5bβ should shift to one who is iniquitous as the subject. It is also not clear why the text should state that the iniquitous do not know shame; does this imply that YHWH does or should? Most scholars who maintain this view do so on three grounds: (1) the premise that v. 5 is the conclusion to vv. 1-4; (2) the expression is meant to recall the charges leveled against Jerusalem's officials in vv. 3-4; (3) the introductory *waw* of the statement is asseverative, indicating a contradiction in the behavior of the iniquitous in that they know no shame despite the light of YHWH's justice. The role of v. 5 as the introduction to vv. 6-13 is noted above. Furthermore, the poetic structure of the passage appears to call for YHWH as the subject of this statement as well. The current masoretic pointing and punctuation of the verse requires that the masculine singular noun עַוָּל, "iniquitous one," be read as the subject of the masculine singular verb יוֹדֵעַ, "he knows," and that the feminine singular noun בֹּשֶׁת, "shame," be read as the object of the verb. One may speculate that if עַוָּל was pointed as עָוֶל, "injustice," it would convey a meaning similar to בֹּשֶׁת. Each could then easily serve as the object of the verb; indeed, they would stand in an appositional syntactical relationship in which "shame" defines the meaning of "injustice," or "injustice" would link "shame" to the preceding statement in vv. 5aβ that YHWH "does not do iniquity." In such a scenario, עול would enter the text as a gloss based on עוֹלָה in v. 5aβ. No unambiguous

not hidden from the sun's heat but all that YHWH has created.

15 For discussion of the temple as the center of creation, see esp. Levenson, "Temple"; idem, *Sinai*; idem, "The Jerusalem Temple in Devotional and Visionary Experience," in Arthur Green, ed., *Jewish Spirituality: From the Bible Through the Middle Ages* (New York: Crossroad, 1988) 32-61; Moshe Weinfeld, "Zion and Jerusalem as Religious and Political Capital: Ideology and Utopia," in Richard E. Fried-

man, ed., *The Poet and the Historian: Essays in Literary and Historical Biblical Criticism* (HSS 26; Chico, Calif.: Scholars Press, 1983) 75-115.

16 See Michael Emmendörffer, *Der ferne Gott. Eine Untersuchung der alttestamentlichen Volkklagelieder vor dem Hintergrund der Mesopotamischen Literatur* (FAT 21; Tübingen: Mohr [Siebeck], 1998).

evidence for such a contention exists. It is noteworthy, therefore, that both the LXX and Vulgate read YHWH as the subject of the statement rather than the anonymous iniquitous one: "and he does not know injustice in extortion" (LXX), and "he does not know, but the perverse is confused" (Vulgate). Given the lack of clear evidence for the reconstruction of such a gloss, however, the statement that "the iniquitous one does not know shame" must be taken as a link, like בְּקִרְבָּהּ noted above that marks the transition of a new subunit in 3:5-13 within the larger literary structure of 3:1-20.

■ **6** The appearance of first person singular pronouns indicates that v. 6 begins the speech by YHWH presented by the prophet in vv. 6-12. As noted above, the appearance of the oracular formula "utterance of YHWH" in v. 8 indicates that the prophet is the primary speaker of the passage and that he conveys YHWH's words. Likewise, YHWH's speech is formulated as both an exhortation to take refuge in YHWH (see v. 12) and a disputation to demonstrate to the people the principles articulated in v. 5: that YHWH is righteous and that YHWH continues to function as the creator who gives law each morning.

In order to demonstrate the contentions of v. 5, it is necessary to prove that YHWH is responsible for all the punishment that has befallen Israel and Judah, that YHWH was compelled to bring punishment on Israel and Judah because they had acted contrary to YHWH's will, that YHWH would bring punishment upon the nations as well for failing to adhere to YHWH's will, and that the ultimate outcome of the process of punishment would be the restoration of Israel and Judah around Jerusalem at the center of creation.

YHWH's speech is designed to articulate all of these points. It begins in v. 6 with YHWH's assertions that YHWH is responsible for cutting off nations, destroying their defensive towers, ruining their streets, and leaving their cities devastated and without inhabitants. At this point, YHWH focuses on the punishment of the nations in order to demonstrate complete mastery of creation; that is, even though YHWH is the G-d of Israel and Judah, YHWH maintains power over all the nations by virtue of YHWH's role as creator.[17] Such a contention is particularly important in the present context because it demonstrates YHWH's complete control over events in the world of creation and indicates that Israel's and Judah's suffering was part of a deliberate plan on YHWH's part to restore Jerusalem as the pristine center of creation. In this respect, YHWH's punishment against the nations is parallel to that of YHWH's punishment against Israel and Judah. Nevertheless, the following material indicates that the results for both the nations and Israel/Judah differ within the same scenario; that is, the remnant of Israel/Judah stands at the center of a purified or chastised creation, and the nations come to Jerusalem to call on YHWH and bring offerings (vv. 9-10). The statement apparently anticipates the downfall of Assyria (cf. 2:13-15), but it also points to the previously mentioned threats posed against other nations, such as Philistia, Moab, and Ammon, as well as the downfall of Cush (2:4, 5-7, 6-11, 12). Again, the rise of Saite Egypt and the Neo-Babylonian Empire in the mid- to late seventh century appears to underlie this statement.

Although the verse clearly portrays YHWH's punishment against the nations, the parallel with Israel's/Judah's punishment has rendered it somewhat ambiguous; Israel and Judah appear to be included among the nations that have suffered punishment. The ambiguity is reinforced by the appearance of language very similar to that of v. 6 in the book of Jeremiah that relates to the punishment of Jerusalem. Thus Jer 2:15 states, "its [Israel's] cities are in ruins, without inhabitant"; Jer 4:7 states concerning Jerusalem and Judah, "he [a destroyer of nations] has gone out from his place to make your land a waste; your cities will be in ruins without inhabitant"; Jer 9:11 states, "and I [YHWH] will make the towns of Judah a desolation without inhabitant."[18] One

---

17　Cf. the book of Nahum, which makes a similar argument based on the downfall of Nineveh (Marvin A. Sweeney, "Concerning the Structure and Generic Character of the Book of Nahum," *ZAW* 102 [1992] 364–77).

18　See Ben Zvi, *Zephaniah*, 213–14; cf. Jer 26:9, which employs similar language in reference to Shiloh.

should recognize, however, that Zephaniah and Jeremiah are two different prophets and books with distinct agendas: Jeremiah is concerned with interpreting Jerusalem's and Judah's downfall at the hands of Babylonia, whereas Zephaniah is concerned with motivating its audience to adhere to YHWH in anticipation of the collapse of Assyria and the rise of Egypt.[19] Such ambiguity appears to motivate unjustified readings of this verse as a statement of YHWH's judgment against Jerusalem.[20] This ambiguity also apparently lies behind the LXX rendition of the initial statement of the passage: "In destruction, I have brought down the arrogant," apparently reading גֵּאִים "arrogant, proud," in place of גּוֹיִם, "nations." The effect is to eliminate the nations as the objects of YHWH's punishment in order to portray a worldwide judgment that includes both Israel and the nations. Such a scenario is suggested by Isa 2:6-21, which portrays YHWH's judgment against all who are high or arrogant (note the use of גאה, "arrogant," in Isa 2:12), including both Israel and the nations.

■ **7** The interpretation of this verse has been complicated by the perception that it is designed to announce the punishment of Jerusalem. This understanding is based in part on the perceptions of its readers who presuppose the realities of the Babylonian exile and expect that Zephaniah must be read in relation to that experience. It is also based in part on the LXX's reading of מְעוֹנָה, "her habitation," as ἐξ ὀφθαλμῶν αὐτῆς (=מֵעֵינֶיהָ), "from her eyes," which results in a reading of the verse as: "and there shall not be cut off from her eyes all that I have visited [i.e., punishment] upon them," that is,

Jerusalem will yet see YHWH's punishment.[21] A similar reading appears in the Peshitta: "and there shall not be destroyed from her eyes (ʿynyh) everything that I decreed upon her." Berlin has already pointed to the inconsistency that such a reading entails within the present context, which is concerned not with the punishment of Jerusalem but with the gathering of the nations.[22] She rightly notes that the intent here is to avert punishment for Jerusalem. Nevertheless, her own attempt to emend מְעוֹנָה to מֵעֲוֺנָהּ, "from her guilt/punishment," must be rejected for lack of textual evidence and because it too perpetuates a reading of the verse in relation to the upcoming Babylonian exile.

Thus far, interpreters have taken insufficient account of the character of this text, including the reading of מְעוֹנָה found in the MT and presupposed by both the Targum and the Vulgate, as a component of a persuasive discourse that is designed to convince a late-seventh-century Jerusalemite audience that YHWH will act to restore the city as the center of creation and the nations.[23] Indeed, no one in this setting is aware of the Babylonian exile; rather, the people of Jerusalem in this period would be aware of a long period of Assyrian hegemony, the apparent weakening of the Assyrian Empire, and the resulting threats posed to Assyrian territories as the empire continues to weaken. Clearly, change was taking place, and the result could well be beneficial for Jerusalem and Judah. As noted in v. 6, YHWH asserts responsibility for the destruction of nations that is taking place in this period. In v. 7 YHWH recalls earlier statements to Jerusalem, here addressed in

---

19 See esp. Richard Coggins, "An Alternative Prophetic Tradition?" in Richard Coggins, Anthony Phillips, and Michael Knibb, eds., *Israel's Prophetic Tradition: Essays in Honour of Peter Ackroyd* (Cambridge: Cambridge Univ. Press, 1982) 77–94, who warns against the assumption that contemporary prophets share the same basic message or viewpoint and calls instead for recognition of the unique characteristics of each.

20 E.g., Roberts, *Zephaniah*, 214. Note that his reading is based on an emendation of גּוֹיִם, "nations," to גּוֹיָם, "their nation" (i.e., Judah) because the reading does not fit the context (pp. 208–9).

21 For scholars who accept this emendation, see Floyd, *Minor Prophets*, 230 (implicit in his structure analysis); Bennett, "Zephaniah," 695, 696; Ryou, *Zepha-*

niah's Oracles, 65; Roberts, *Zephaniah*, 209; Renaud, *Sophonie*, 242; Keller, *Sophonie*, 208; Edler, *Kerygma* 161; Rudolph, *Zephanja*, 286; Horst, *Propheten*, 196; Elliger, *Zephanja*, 76; Junker, *Sophonia*, 84; Sellin, *Zwölfprophetenbuch*, 438; Nowack, *Propheten*, 303; van Hoonacker, *Prophètes*, 530; J. M. P. Smith, *Zephaniah*, 242–46; Marti, *Dodekapropheton*, 373–74; Wellhausen, *Propheten*, 157.

22 Berlin, *Zephaniah*, 131–32, esp. 132.

23 Several interpreters accept the MT reading, but persist in reading the verse as a reference to Jerusalem's coming punishment; see, e.g., Vlaardingerbroek, *Zephaniah*, 183; Seybold, *Zephanja*, 112; R. L. Smith, *Micah–Malachi*, 139, 140; Ball, *Zephaniah*, 167–70.

second person feminine singular forms (cf. 3:1-4, which characterizes the city with third feminine singular forms, and 3:14-19, which likewise uses second feminine singular address forms for Jerusalem), that Jerusalem "should fear me and take instruction." YHWH's statement continues with the assertion, "and her habitation shall not be cut off (because of) all that I have visited upon her." Afterward, YHWH reverts to a third person masculine characterization of the city by noting the eagerness of its people not to take instruction and instead to "corrupt their deeds."

Several crucial factors must be considered in reading this verse. First, interpreters have been unable to identify a precise source for the citation of YHWH's statement, "surely, fear me, take instruction." Although the concern with the fear of YHWH and the need to accept YHWH's instruction run rampant throughout the Bible, the absence of a precise source for this statement has prompted scholars to propose that "I have said" (אָמַרְתִּי) actually means "I thought," "I intended," and so on.[24] Alternatively, it has prompted others to maintain that the addressee of this text is not Jerusalem but rather the nations.[25] In this case, YHWH's statement becomes a sort of aside in the larger concern with YHWH's punishment of the nations. But this statement is germane to the persuasive character of this speech. YHWH's credibility is on the line, as indicated already in relation to v. 5. In this case, YHWH tells the Jerusalemite audience that YHWH's punishments were not intended to destroy the city of Jerusalem, and the implicit claim is that the city in fact was not destroyed during the course of the Assyrian occupation. This in itself was remarkable for a city that had revolted against the Assyrians in the time of Hezekiah. The normal Assyrian policy was to destroy rebellious cities and to deport their populations as they

had done in Damascus, Samaria, and others, when those cities rebelled against Assyrian authority.[26] Indeed, Jerusalem's survival during Sennacherib's 701 invasion of Judah became the basic premise for the Isaian traditions (Isaiah 36–39; 2 Kings 19–20) concerning YHWH's protection of the city.[27] It is noteworthy, therefore, that, in contrast to other prophetic traditions such as Micah (see Mic 3:12), Isaiah never states that YHWH will destroy Jerusalem. Instead, the entire Isaian tradition emphasizes YHWH's fealty to the city and attempts to restore it as the center of creation—much like the book of Zephaniah.[28]

With this in mind, it is noteworthy that concern with the fear of YHWH and the taking of instruction appears in Isa 8:11, "For YHWH spoke thus to me while his hand was strong upon me, and he warned/instructed me [וְיִסְּרֵנִי, from the root יסר of מוּסָר, 'instruction'] not to walk in the way of this people saying, 'Do not call conspiracy all that this people calls conspiracy, and do not fear what it fears, or be in dread, but YHWH Sebaot, him you shall regard as holy; let him be your fear [מוֹרַאֲ, from the root ירא, 'to fear'], and let him be your dread." This passage states the concerns both with YHWH's instruction and with the fear of YHWH as articulated in Zeph 3:7. Indeed, it appears immediately prior to Isaiah's famous call in Isa 8:16-17 to "bind up the testimony, seal the teaching among my disciples. I will wait for YHWH, who is hiding his face from the house of Jacob, and I will hope in him." This statement is related to several others in 29:11-12; 30:8; and 34:16-17 that are concerned with writing and reading the book of Isaiah in order to await the fulfillment of its oracles.[29] Although the last passage appears to be much later than the others, all point to a concern to read the book of Isaiah and to interpret it in relation to later times. It

24   E.g., Vlaardingerbroek, *Zephaniah,*182.

25   E.g., Ben Zvi, *Zephaniah,* 214–15. Note that when taken as a whole, the LXX translation actually does read the verse in relation to the nations: "I said, so fear me and accept instruction and you shall not cut off from its eye as much as all that I have brought punishment on *them* [i.e., the nations]."

26   See Bustenay Oded, *Mass Deportations and Deportees in the Assyrian Empire* (Wiesbaden: Harrassowitz, 1979).

27   See Sweeney, *Isaiah 1–39,* 460–88; Ronald E. Clements, *Isaiah and the Deliverance of Jerusalem: A*

Study in the Interpretation of Prophecy in the Old Testament (JSOTSup 13; Sheffield: JSOT Press, 1980).

28   See Christopher Seitz, *Zion's Final Destiny: The Development of the Book of Isaiah* (Minneapolis: Fortress Press, 1991).

29   For discussion of each of these passages, see Sweeney, *Isaiah 1–39,* 165–88, 373–86, 386–401, 437–47.

appears that one of the times in which Isaiah was read was in relation to the reform of King Josiah. Isaiah and other prophets were reread—and frequently rewritten—as prophetic witnesses that pointed forward to their fulfillment in the reign and reform of King Josiah of Judah.[30] In that Zephaniah seems to rely heavily on the Isaian traditions, Zephaniah was apparently one of those readers who understood Isaiah's oracles to be fulfilled in his own time. In this case, Zephaniah's argument depends on the earlier Isaian tradition; that is, YHWH had brought punishment on Jerusalem for the people's actions but YHWH would not destroy the city, and YHWH would restore Jerusalem once the punishment was complete. In Zephaniah's view, that time had come in his own day.

Second, the statement, "all that I visited upon her," does indeed refer to punishment. A number of scholars have attempted to argue that the meaning of the expression פָּקַדְתִּי, "I visited, punished, examined, mustered," cannot refer to YHWH's punishment but to the injunctions or instruction that YHWH had "laid upon" or expected of Jerusalem (cf. Job 36:23; 2 Chr 36:23; Ezra 1:2).[31] Thus the statement would reinforce the view that YHWH's intention in this speech was to condemn Jerusalem, reading in emended form, "and there will not be cut off from her eyes/sight all that I have laid upon/enjoined her." This fails to consider both the persuasive and the retrospective viewpoints of the preceding statements, especially the contentions that YHWH had called on Jerusalem to fear YHWH and to accept instruction together with YHWH's pledge not to destroy the city but only to bring punishment upon it. It would appear that the verse is designed to reconcile two potentially competing viewpoints: that YHWH had sworn to protect Jerusalem and that YHWH had brought punishment upon the city. Such a combination is inherent in the Isaiah tradition, and Zephaniah appears to rely on it here in articulating a viewpoint that YHWH sought to punish Jerusalem, but not to destroy it, so that the city could serve divine plans to demonstrate sovereignty over all creation and nations. In such a case, the prophet calls on the audience to accept this viewpoint as part of an

overall argumentative strategy to convince the audience to return to YHWH (2:1-3) and to wait for the time of YHWH's action to bring this plan into being (3:8).

Third, the statement in v. 7b, "Indeed, they worked even harder to corrupt their ways," often serves as justification for the contention that v. 7 is ultimately concerned with condemning Jerusalem. Indeed, it is well suited for such a role in that it asserts the wrongdoing of the people of the city. Nevertheless, the reason for its inclusion here must be considered, especially in view of the absence elsewhere in this passage to condemn Jerusalem or to bring punishment upon it. In a context that is concerned with YHWH's credibility and with YHWH's plans to gather the nations to demonstrate that credibility, the reference to Jerusalem's wrongdoing does not provide the justification for the future punishment of Jerusalem. Instead, it provides the justification for Jerusalem's past punishment. It also points to the present obstacle to the prophet's rhetorical goal: the people do not adhere to YHWH's expectations because they do not consider YHWH to be a credible deity. A century of Assyrian domination and the devastation of their country would certainly call YHWH's credibility into question. But in articulating the people's reaction to YHWH's past calls to fear YHWH and to accept instruction, the prophet lays the basis for the following call, placed in the mouth of YHWH, to wait for YHWH (v. 8) so that the people can see that YHWH planned Jerusalem's punishment as part of a larger scenario in which the nations would recognize YHWH's power and come to Jerusalem, now to be restored by YHWH to its proper role, in order to demonstrate that recognition. In essence, the prophet's reference to Jerusalem's past wrongdoing provides an important basis for the calls to wait for YHWH (3:8) and to seek YHWH before it is too late (2:1-3).

---

30 For a comprehensive discussion of this issue, including Zephaniah, see Sweeney, *King Josiah*.

31 See, e.g., Wellhausen, *Propheten*, 157; J. M. P. Smith, *Zephaniah*, 242.

3:8-13

■ **8** YHWH's call to "wait for me" expresses the primary rhetorical goal of the speech presented in vv. 6-12 in that it addresses the audience directly in order to demand action from it. YHWH's demand depends on the preceding statements concerning both the destruction of nations (v. 6) and YHWH's prior statements concerning Jerusalem's ignoring divine calls to fear YHWH and accept instruction (v. 7), since the present call to wait for YHWH points to YHWH's intentions to bring punishment on the nations, prompt them to acknowledge YHWH, and thereby restore Jerusalem to its place at the center of creation.

The interpretation of this passage has suffered markedly from the mistaken belief among its many readers that the passage must articulate judgment against Jerusalem.[32] Indeed, the initial particle, לָכֵן, "therefore," typically introduces the formal announcement of punishment within the structure of the prophetic judgment speech.[33] Although judgment is a motif in this passage, the judgment is directed against the nations, not against Jerusalem. The interpretation is also complicated by several key readings in the versions that have prompted several unwarranted textual emendations. But the differences among the versions point to their own struggles to understand this text, and often to modify in order to suit their own conceptions of what the text has to say. Nevertheless, the persuasive character of this speech and its basic focus on YHWH's actions against the nations point to a reading in which YHWH attempts to convince the Jerusalemite/Judean audience that (1) YHWH is a credible deity who indeed exercises power over the nations despite Jerusalem's past suffering, and (2) that YHWH's past statements concerning the basic security of the city despite its suffering are about to be realized.

Scholars have noted that the particle לָכֵן, "therefore," normally introduces the announcement of punishment in the typical form of the prophetic speech. Following the articulation of the various improper actions that constitute the grounds or reasons for the punishment, the particle לָכֵן highlights the consequential nature of the punishment, which is warranted because of the aforementioned acts. Thus the prophetic judgment speech form correlates the initial articulation of the grounds for punishment and the punishment itself. But such is not the case in vv. 7 and 8. Whereas v. 7 concerns the actions of Jerusalem in corrupting its deeds, v. 8 concerns YHWH's gathering of the nations. In the present context, Jerusalem's actions in v. 7 can hardly constitute the grounds for the punishment of the nations. Indeed, Jerusalem had already suffered punishment at the hands of the Assyrians, conceived as YHWH's agents in the prophetic traditions of Isaiah (cf. Isaiah 5–12). The particle לָכֵן therefore does express consequentiality but must be of a different nature. In this case, it points to YHWH's need to demonstrate to Jerusalem that YHWH's past assurances of Jerusalem's continuity, even in the midst of its own punishment, are credible.

YHWH's exhortative statement, חַכּוּ־לִי, "wait for me," must also be considered. This statement has proved to be particularly problematic because of its masculine imperative address form, which differs markedly from the second feminine singular address form employed for Jerusalem in v. 7 (see also the feminine singular characterization of the city in vv. 1-4, 11-12a, and 14-19). Because the imperative is correctly judged to be an address to Jerusalem, the LXX modified it to the Greek aorist imperative singular form, ὑπόμεινόν με, "wait for me," apparently to produce a consistent address form.[34] Interestingly, both the LXX and Vulgate read the verse not as an indication of YHWH's judgment against

---

32 See, e.g., the discussions in Ben Zvi, *Zephaniah*, 219–24; Ryou, *Zephaniah's Oracles*, 306–8; Vlaardingerbroek, *Zephaniah*, 179–81, 184; Renaud, *Sophonie*, 243–45; Roberts, *Zephaniah*, 214–16; Rudolph, *Zephanja*, 289–90.

33 For discussion of the formal features of the prophetic judgment speech, see Sweeney, *Isaiah 1–39*, 533–34; Claus Westermann, *Basic Forms of Prophetic Speech* (Louisville: Westminster John Knox, 1991) 129–209.

34 Note that contra Ben Zvi, *Zephaniah*, 219 n. 711, the Peshitta text reads, *skw ly*, "wait for me," a *pael* masculine plural imperative form of the verb *skʾ*, "to wait." The Vulgate, however, does read the imperative as the singular *expecta me*, "expect/wait for me," as opposed to the plural *expectate me*.

Jerusalem, but as a statement of YHWH's judgment against the nations that is to be witnessed by Jerusalem. Nevertheless, the emendation to the singular form often serves as a justification for claims that the purpose of the passage is to announce judgment against Jerusalem. In general, the verb חכה is employed to express the expectation of positive events rather than judgment (see Isa 30:18; 64:3; Hab 2:3; Pss 33:20; 106:13; cf. Job 3:21). It is noteworthy that the verb חכה, "to wait," also appears in Isaiah's earlier statements concerning his decision to wait for the future realization of YHWH's plans: "bind up the testimony, seal the Torah, and I will wait for YHWH (וְחִכִּיתִי לֹ)), who hides his face from the house of Jacob, and I will hope for him" (Isa 8:16-17). As noted above, the present statements in Zephaniah appear to take up Isaiah's earlier language concerning the need to wait for the future realization of YHWH's promises of security for Jerusalem. In Zephaniah's view, that time had come.

The shift from second person feminine singular characterization of Jerusalem to second masculine plural characterization therefore cannot be resolved by claims for textual emendation. The shift is apparently based on a distinction between the character of the city itself as "the daughter of Zion" (Zeph 3:14), which is always portrayed with feminine singular references, and the "remnant of Israel," which is left inside the city and is always characterized with masculine plural forms (3:12-13). Such a view is consistent with the claims that Jerusalem would have to be purified of its apostates by sacrifice on the Day of YHWH in 1:2-18.

The oracular formula נְאֻם־ה״, "utterance of YHWH," in v. 8a[4-5] functions in its typical role to certify that these statements are oracular statements from YHWH.[35] It thereby serves the persuasive function of the prophet's presentation of YHWH's speech by asserting the validity of the source of its claims.

The second portion of YHWH's initial exhortational statement, "for the day when I arise for prey," is a temporal clause that defines the period of time that YHWH calls on the audience to wait. Of course, one does not know when that time might be, but the context of the book of Zephaniah, particularly the oracles concerning the nations and its use of the Day of YHWH motif to express YHWH's impending actions, suggests that the time would be the present time of Josiah's early reign. The expression לְעַד, "for prey/booty," is particularly controversial, because it suggests that YHWH is about to take victims. Both the LXX and the Peshitta read the term as לְעֵד, "for a witness": "until the day of my rising unto witness (εἰς μαρτύριον)" (LXX) and "until the day that I rise for a witness (lshdwtʾ)" (Peshitta). Apparently, both traditions understand the phrase in reference to YHWH's role as judge against the nations (cf. Jer 29:23; Mic 1:2; Mal 3:5; Ps 50:7, for YHWH's role as judicial witness). The Targum appears to presuppose a similar interpretation in reference to YHWH's role as judge: "for the day of my being revealed for judgment (למדן)."[36] Most interpreters therefore accept the emendations to לְעֵד.[37] The Vulgate reads the expression as לְעַד, but chooses the alternative meaning of the term in reference to "time" or "eternity,"[38] and renders the phrase in rela-

35 See Sweeney, *Isaiah 1–39,* 546.
36 See Churgin, *Targum Jonathan,* 109/337, for discussion of the Targum's reading in relation to *Pesiq. R.* 34: "It is sworn before me, that everyone who waits for my kingdom, I myself witness for him to good, as it is said, 'for the day of my rising as a witness.'" Churgin also notes *Exod. Rab.* 17, "But for the future to come he stands and judges his world in standing . . . as it is written, 'Therefore wait for me in the day of my rising for a time.'"
37 See Ryou, *Zephaniah's Oracles,* 67–68; Floyd, *Minor Prophets,* 233; Bennett, "Zephaniah," 696; Roberts, *Zephaniah,* 209–10; Renaud, *Sophonie,* 242; R. L. Smith, *Micah–Malachi,* 139; Rudolph, *Zephanja,* 287; Ball, *Zephaniah,* 172; Keller, *Sophonie,* 210; Edler, *Kerygma,* 166–67; Horst, *Propheten,* 196; Elliger,

Zephanja, 77; Junker, *Sophonia,* 84; Sellin, *Zwölf-prophetenbuch,* 438; Nowack, *Propheten,* 304; van Hoonacker, *Prophètes,* 531; J. M. P. Smith, *Zephaniah,* 247, 253; Marti, *Dodekapropheton,* 374; Wellhausen, *Propheten,* 158; Schwally, "Sefanjâ," 201–2.
38 For similar temporal understandings of the term, see Berlin, *Zephaniah,* 133; Seybold, *Zephanja,* 112, 113.

tion to the resurrection of Jesus: "in my resurrection in the future." Indeed, Jerome attributes this understanding to his rabbinical teachers.[39]

Nevertheless, both of these interpretations miss an essential point: YHWH is coming to gather the nations and to pour out wrath upon them. In such a context, the statement that YHWH is rising "for prey" makes a great deal of sense (cf. Gen 49:27; Isa 33:23).[40] In this regard, YHWH acts as an executioner or warrior who comes to take bloody action against the nations who are now YHWH's victims, much like those in Jerusalem/Judah who are charged with rejecting YHWH (cf. 1:14-18).

Verse 8b contains two כִּי clauses (and a third appears in v. 9) that specify the reasons why the audience should wait for YHWH. The first builds on YHWH's judicial character, introduced by the basic premise of the exhortation/disputation expressed in v. 5 that YHWH gives "his law/decision (מִשְׁפָּטוֹ) each morning," by stating that YHWH's "decision" or "judgment" (מִשְׁפָּטִי, "my decision/judgment") is to gather nations and to assemble kingdoms. The verbs אָסַף, "to gather," and קָבַץ, "to assemble," may be used in the general sense of assembling people for any particular purpose (אָסַף and קָבַץ together, Gen 29:22; Exod 3:16; 4:29; Num 11:16, 24; 21:16; Josh 2:18; 1 Sam 5:8, 11; 2 Kgs 23:1; Joel 2:16; Isa 11:12; Hab 2:5; Ezek 11:17). The terms may also be used in relation to the harvesting, gathering, or collection of agricultural produce (אָסַף, Exod 23:10, 16; Lev 23:39; 25:3, 20; Deut 11:14; 16:13; 28:38; Isa 17:5; Jer 40:10, 12; Job 39:12; Ps 39:7; קָבַץ, Gen 41:35, 48) and other forms of material gain, such as booty, money, and so on (אָסַף, 2 Kgs 22:24; 2 Chr 24:11; קָבַץ, Deut 13:17; cf. 2 Chr 24:5; Ezek 16:31). They may be used to describe assembly for battle (אָסַף, Num 21:23; Judg 11:20; 1 Sam 17:1; 2 Sam 10:17; 12:29; Zech 14:2; קָבַץ, Judg 12:4; 1 Sam 7:5; 28:1; 29:1; 2 Sam 2:30; 1 Kgs 20:1; 2 Kgs 6:24), destruction (אָסַף, 1 Sam 15:6; Ezek 34:29; Jer 8:13), or judgment by YHWH (קָבַץ, Ezek 22:20). Indeed, the following refer-

ences to YHWH's wrath, anger, and zeal clearly indicate that the nations are to be judged and punished. In this sense, the use of the verb אָסַף points back to YHWH's initial statements of the book: "I will surely gather all from upon the face of the earth . . . I will gather human and animal, I will gather the bird of the heavens and the fish of the sea" (Zeph 1:2-3a). This, of course, is in keeping with the general perspective of the oracles concerning the nations in 2:4, 5-15. But there is also an ironic quality to YHWH's statements in that the verb קָבַץ is also frequently employed in the Hebrew Bible in reference to YHWH's gathering the dispersed or exiled people of Israel and Judah (Mic 2:12; 4:6; Jer 31:10; Zech 10:8; Isa 54:7; 56:8; Deut 30:3, 4; Jer 23:3; 29:14; 31:8; etc.; cf. Isa 40:11), sometimes in combination with אָסַף (e.g., Mic 2:12; 4:6; Isa 11:12). Indeed, the verbs אָסַף and קָבַץ appear at the end of the book in Zeph 3:18, 19 to express Jerusalem's/Israel's restoration. Thus the announcement that YHWH will "gather/assemble" nations expresses both judgment and restoration. The irony appears in that the judgment of the nations leads to the restoration of Jerusalem at their center, and as a result the nations too will be restored.

This scenario has an impact on the reading of עֲלֵיהֶם, "upon them," in the phrase, "to pour out upon them my wrath." Because of the prevailing view that this oracle must announce judgment against Jerusalem, Judah, and Israel, some interpreters maintain that the third person masculine plural pronominal suffix הֶם-, "them," must be emended to the second masculine plural pronominal suffix כֶם-, "you," so that the phrase continues the second person masculine plural address form employed in the exhortation, "wait for me," in v. 8a.[41] Rudolph goes so far as to argue that the original עֲלֵיכֶם was deliberately changed to עֲלֵיהֶם in the Second Temple period in order to divert judgment from Israel to the nations who were to serve as G-d's instrument of punishment.[42] This is sheer invention on Rudolph's part. There is no textual

39 See Ben Zvi, *Zephaniah*, 222 n. 722; Churgin, *Targum Jonathan*, 109/337, who cites the statement from *Exod. Rab.* 17 cited in n. 5 above, which provides a temporal understanding of the term. For discussion of the interpretation of this verse in relation to resurrection by Jerome and other early church fathers, see Vlaardingerbroek, *Zephaniah*, 185.

40 Cf. Ben Zvi, *Zephaniah*, 220–23; Vlaardingerbroek, *Zephaniah*, 184–86.

41 E.g., Rudolph, *Zephanja*, 287, 290; Edler, *Kerygma*, 161.

42 Rudolph, *Zephanja*, 290.

support for such an emendation, and it conflicts with the clear statements by YHWH in v. 8b that announce judgment against the nations. Insofar as the addressee of YHWH's speech is Jerusalem/Judah, and it speaks objectively about the nations in third person plural perspective, it is entirely appropriate that the third person masculine plural pronominal suffix in עֲלֵיהֶם be retained.

Finally, the second כִּי clause of v. 8, "for in the fire of my jealousy, all the earth will be consumed," expresses YHWH's decision to pass judgment on the entire earth. This phrase is often viewed as a later addition to the text because of its supposed eschatological perspective and because it appears in identical form in 1:18aβ.[43] Nevertheless, it should be viewed as intrinsic to this text. There is no textual evidence for its omission, and by correlating YHWH's statements against the nations with those directed against the wicked of Judah in chap. 1, it points to the comprehensive nature of YHWH's judgment applied against both the nations and Israel prior to the reestablishment of Jerusalem at the center of the nations and creation. Indeed, such a perspective that both Israel and the nations will suffer punishment prior to the placement of Jerusalem as the holy center of creation to which the nations will come to honor YHWH is characteristic of the book of Isaiah, in contrast to Micah and Zechariah, which envision Israel's defeat of the nations prior to their coming to Jerusalem to recognize YHWH.[44] The relationship with Isaiah is particularly important, especially with regard to the relationship between this text and Isaiah 8–9, because a similar statement appears in Isa 9:6b, "from now until eternity, the zeal of YHWH Sebaot will do this," which concludes the sequence of material in which Isaiah expresses his willingness to seal up the testimony and wait for the future realization of his prophetic oracles. Once again, the book of Zephaniah employs references to the Isaian tradition to assert that that time has come. It should be noted that TJ apparently noted the problem of YHWH's claim to destroy the entire earth and specified, "for the

fire of my retribution, all the wicked of the land will come to an end" (cf. Gen 18:22-33, in which Abraham challenges YHWH's proposal to destroy all of Sodom and Gomorrah by pointing out that there might be some righteous people within).

■ 9 A number of scholars maintain that vv. 9-10 are secondary additions that point to an eschatological scenario in which the nations will be transformed so that they speak a common language, employ that language to recognize and serve YHWH as the sovereign of all creation, and return exiled Jews to Jerusalem. The basic reason for such a position is that the scenario of restoration at the hands of the nations following a period of Israel's dispersion must derive from the late exilic or Persian (early postexilic) periods. The argument depends in large measure on contentions that 3:6-10 is concerned with judgment against Jerusalem, and that v. 9 marks an important shift in concern to the nations. It also depends on the appearance of the introductory transitional particle combination כִּי־אָז, "for then," in v. 9 and the clear dependence on the tower of Babel tradition in Gen 11:1-9 and Isaiah's oracles concerning Egypt in Isaiah 18–19. Indeed, Steck contends that the eschatological perspectives of vv. 9-10 were added so that Zephaniah could be incorporated into the book of the Twelve Prophets as a whole.[45]

Nevertheless, the contention that vv. 9-10 are postexilic additions to the text of Zephaniah must be rejected. First, the above analysis demonstrates that vv. 5 and 6-8 are concerned not with YHWH's judgment against Jerusalem or Israel, but with YHWH's actions against the nations as part of an exhortative and disputational rhetorical strategy that is designed to convince the seventh-century Jerusalemite/Judean audience that YHWH will maintain the security of Jerusalem/Judah despite the punitive measures that are taken against them. In short, there is no fundamental shift in theme from judgment against Jerusalem to judgment against the nations.[46] Even for those who contend that v. 9 repre-

---

43 E.g., Renaud, *Sophonie,* 245.

44 See Marvin A. Sweeney, "Micah's Debate with Isaiah," *JSOT* 93 (2001) 111–24; idem, *Twelve Prophets,* 559–706.

45 Odil Hannes Steck, "Zu Zef 3,9-10," *BZ* 34 (1990) 90–95; cf. James D. Nogalski, *Literary Precursors to the Book of the Twelve* (BZAW 217; Berlin: de

Gruyter, 1993) 171–215, for discussion of Zephaniah's place in the book of the Twelve.

46 It is noteworthy that this argument often depends on the emendation of עֲלֵיהֶם, "upon them" (i.e., upon the nations), in v. 8 to עֲלֵיכֶם, "upon you" (i.e., upon the people of Jerusalem/Israel). See, e.g., Edler, *Kerygma,* 21–22, 57–60. But see the discus-

sents a shift from the portrayal in v. 8 of full judgment against the nations, the purification or purging of the nations portrayed here is consistent with the purification or purging of Jerusalem and Judah proposed in 1:2-18 and 2:1-3. Both Jerusalem/Judah and the nations share in YHWH's actions to prepare for the recognition of YHWH's sovereignty throughout all creation.

Second, the particle combination כִּי־אָז, "for then," does not therefore mark the beginning of a new redactional unit; indeed, this argument actually depends on the alleged thematic shift in the passage. Instead, the particles merely indicate a temporal transition that marks the contents of vv. 9-10 as a consequence of the actions stated in the two earlier כִּי clauses of v. 8b, that is, YHWH's decision is to gather the nations and pour out wrath against them (v. 8b) and YHWH's wrath will consume all of the earth (v. 8b). The expanded particle כִּי־אָז points to vv. 9-10 as the climactic elements in the reasons given for the basic exhortation of the passage in v. 8a, "wait for me. . . ."[47]

Third, v. 9 appears to depend on the tower of Babel tradition in Gen 11:1-9 in which the nations were scattered throughout the earth and their languages confused as a result of their attempts to build a tower that would enable them to reach heaven. Indeed, the verb פּוּץ, "to scatter," which appears in v. 10 as part of the phrase "daughter of my dispersion (פּוּצַי)," also appears in the nations' statement as to why they wanted to build the tower in the first place: "and they said, 'Come and let us build for ourselves a tower with its top in the heavens, and we will make for ourselves a name, lest we be scattered (נָפוּץ) upon the face of the earth'" (Gen 11:4). It appears once again in the statement of YHWH's action against the nations: "and YHWH scattered (וַיָּפֶץ ה״) them from there upon the face of all the earth, and they ceased to build the city" (Gen 11:8). The dependence of Zeph 3:9-10 on this tradition can hardly be taken as an indication of its late date. The tower of Babel narrative in Gen 11:1-9 is generally recognized as a J-stratum nar-

rative, which most scholars date to the earliest stages of pentateuchal composition, that is, in the tenth-ninth centuries BCE.[48] Although the Pentateuch had likely not achieved its final form by the mid-seventh century, the tower of Babel tradition would presumably have been available for use by Zephaniah.

Fourth, v. 10 draws on Isaiah's oracles concerning Egypt in Isaiah 18–19. This is clear from the use of the phrase, "from across the rivers of Cush" (מֵעֵבֶר לְנַהֲרֵי־כוּשׁ), which appears in Isa 18:1 as part of the specification of the destination of ambassadors sent from Jerusalem: "Woe, land of whirring wings that is beyond the rivers of Cush (אֲשֶׁר מֵעֵבֶר לְנַהֲרֵי־כוּשׁ)." It is also evident from the portrayal of YHWH's "suppliants" (עֲתָרַי, "my suppliants") who bring YHWH's offering (יוֹבִלוּן מִנְחָתִי, "[who] present my grain offering") and the portrayal in Isa 18:7 of gifts presented by the Egyptians/Ethiopians to YHWH: "At that time gifts will be brought (יוּבַל־שַׁי) to YHWH Sebaot by a people tall and smooth . . . to Mount Zion, the place of the name of YHWH Sebaot." Other correspondences include the use of the term שָׂפָה, literally "lip," as a term for "language" in both v. 9 and Isa 19:18. Again, the argument that Zeph 3:9-10 is postexilic depends in part on dating the Isaian Egyptian oracles to a relatively late date in the exilic or postexilic period. But I argue that the Egyptian oracles in Isa 18:1-7 and 19:1-17 must be placed in relation to the efforts of King Hoshea of Israel to gain support from Pharaoh So of Egypt for his revolt against Assyria in 724 (cf. 2 Kgs 17:4), that the material in Isa 19:18-25 must be dated to the reign of King Manasseh (786–742), and that 20:1-6, which closes out the material in 19:1-25, must date to the reign of Josiah.[49] If this is the case, the Egyptian/Ethiopian oracles in Isaiah 18–19 were available in the mid-seventh century. Indeed, the assignment of 20:1-6, which is linked literarily to Isaiah 19, to the time of Josiah, indicates an effort to read these oracles in relation to Josiah's reform.[50]

---

sion of this statement above, where I reject this emendation.

47   Cf. Roberts, *Zephaniah*, 216.

48   See, e.g., Otto Kaiser, *Introduction to the Old Testament: A Presentation of its Results and Problems* (Minneapolis: Augsburg, 1975) 86; J. Alberto Soggin, *Introduction to the Old Testament* (3d ed.; OTL;

Philadelphia: Westminster, 1989) 116.

49   For detailed discussion of this material with bibliography, see Sweeney, *Isaiah 1–39*, 252–76.

50   See also Sweeney, *King Josiah*.

Fifth, the portrayal of Egyptians or Ethiopians as supplicants to YHWH in the mid-seventh century points once again to the perception that the defeat of the Twenty-fifth Ethiopian Dynasty, the withdrawal of the Assyrians from Egypt, and the rise of Saite Dynasty marked YHWH's actions to bring down the Assyrian Empire and to restore Judah. In this early period, Saite moves would have marked Egypt as a potential ally of Judah against the Assyrians; after all, they had attempted to function in this role during the Assyrian invasions of the late eighth century. In such a scenario, the Egyptian moves into Philistia in the mid-seventh century and the portrayal of their offering gifts to YHWH, perhaps as overtures to relations with Jerusalem, would have been seen as a fulfillment of Isaiah's earlier oracles in Josiah's early reign.[51]

Verse 9 therefore emerges as Zephaniah's attempt to portray YHWH's projected punishment against the nations as a purge like that envisioned for Jerusalem and Judah in 1:2-18. It also emerges as a reversal of the scattering of the nations in the tower of Babel tradition now found in Gen 11:1-9. Many have noted that Mur 21:3 reads על העמים, "upon the peoples," instead of MT אֶל־עַמִּים, "unto peoples." Murabbaʿat therefore offers a more stylistically pleasing rendition of the verse, which seems to underlie TJ (על עממיא) and Peshitta (ʿl ʿmmʾ), both of which employ a form of עַל and the definite article, but the definite article is lacking in LXX ἐπὶ λαοὺς, although Greek ἐπὶ could render Hebrew עַל; see also Vulgate populis, which lacks both עַל and a definite article in keeping with Latin style). Thus the MT reading appears to be preferable, and Murabbaʿat may be a concession to style.[52]

The expression שָׂפָה בְרוּרָה apparently refers to a pure or special speech necessary so that the nations may all speak a common language, unlike the variety of languages that they speak in empirical reality or, from the view of tradition, in the aftermath of the tower of Babel incident. As noted above, the term שָׂפָה means literally "lip, edge" but it may be used metaphorically for "language" elsewhere in the Hebrew Bible (see Gen 11:1, 6,

7, 9; Ps 81:6; Ezek 3:5, 6; Isa 33:19; 28:11; 19:18). The term בְרוּרָה means "pure, select, elect." It derives from the root ברר, which refers to the purification or purging of rebels (Ezek 20:38), pure or sincere speech (Job 33:3), pure or polished arrows (Isa 49:2), testing or proving by G-d (Qoh 3:18), and select men such as brave men (1 Chr 7:40), porters (1 Chr 9:22), musicians (1 Chr 16:41), and even sheep (Neh 5:18). The range of meanings suggests a special speech, in contrast to the common languages spoken by the nations, that will enable them to speak together to YHWH. The term's associations with purity and purging relate well to a context that calls for punishment against the nations that renders them fit to approach G-d. It is noteworthy that the LXX reads the term as γλῶσσαν εἰς γενεάν, "a tongue unto their generation/coming into being," which seems to derive בְרוּרָה from the root ברא, "to create."[53] This is apparently a reference to the created state of human beings and their speech prior to the tower of Babel incident in the eyes of the LXX translator.

Finally, v. 9b points to the goal of the punishment and the purge of the nations, so that they might all call on YHWH and serve YHWH with one effort. The calling on YHWH by the nations appears ironically to portray YHWH's desire that the nations call on YHWH rather than build a tower (Gen 11:1-9), and it calls to mind the notice in Gen 4:26, "at that time people began to call on the name of YHWH," as well as Isa 19:18, "on that day there will be five cities in the land of Egypt that speak the language of Canaan and swear allegiance to YHWH Sebaot. One of these will be called the city of the sun." The reference to serving YHWH with "one shoulder" (שְׁכֶם אֶחָד) is an idiomatic reference to serving YHWH with "one effort, accord." The LXX and Peshitta employ a variation on the metaphor by referring to "one yoke" (Greek ὑπὸ ζυγὸν ἕνα; Syriac bnyr ḥd).[54]

■ **10** Despite the absence of a clear syntactical link, v. 10 continues the portrayal of the nations' recognition of YHWH begun in v. 9. As noted in the discussion of v. 9 above, v. 10 draws heavily on the Isaian oracles concerning Egypt and Ethiopia in Isa 18:1-7 and 19:1-25 in that

---

51 For further discussion of the perspective of v. 10, see below.

52 Note that the construction אֶל עַמִּים also appears in Isa 49:22; Ezek 3:6, whereas עַל־הָעַמִּים appears only in Isa 62:10.

53 Contra Gerleman, *Zephanja*, 57.

54 Cf. ibid.

it employs the phrase "from across the rivers of Cush" that appears in Isa 18:1, the image of the Egyptians or Ethiopians presenting gifts to YHWH in 18:7, and the use of the term שָׂפָה in reference to language in 19:18. In addition, 19:16-25 lays out a scenario in which Egypt will be smitten by YHWH and ultimately come to recognize YHWH together with Assyria and Israel. It is noteworthy that 19:21 notes explicitly that the Egyptians will offer מִנְחָה, "grain offering," to YHWH together with other types of offerings and sacrifices, and that 19:22 refers to Egypt's making supplications to YHWH (lit. "and there will be supplicating for them," וְנֶעְתַּר לָהֶם). As noted in the discussion of v. 9, Isa 18:1-7 and 19:1-17 date to the time of Hoshea, 19:18-25 dates to the time of Manasseh, and 20:1-6 dates to the time of Josiah. Insofar as Isaiah 20 points to a Josian reading of this material, it would appear that the references to Egypt's sending tribute to YHWH in 18:1-7 and the internal conflict within Egypt in 19:1-15 would refer to the conflicts in which the Egyptian Saite Dynasty—with the aid of its ally, Assyria—established its rule over all of Egypt in place of the Twenty-fifth Ethiopian Dynasty. Since the Saite Pharaoh Psamtek ultimately moved into Philistia and reportedly undertook a twenty-nine-year siege of Ashdod, it seems likely that he would also have sent ambassadors and gifts to Jerusalem as a means to open relations.[55] Whether his intent was to establish a cooperative arrangement or to enforce his control over Judah must remain uncertain. Nevertheless, such moves, especially in the context of Assyria's own internal conflicts and its withdrawal from Egypt and southwestern Asia, would have signaled to Jerusalem that YHWH was indeed acting to remove the Assyrian oppressors, and that Egypt might well be an agent for accomplishing this. In such a scenario, Isaiah's earlier oracles would be read in relation to the early reign of Josiah, and they would point to a reversal of Egypt's traditional role vis-à-vis Israel as expressed in the exodus tradition; that is, whereas Egypt had played the role of Israel's oppressor in the exodus, YHWH's actions against Egypt had their intended effect and the Egyptians were now also ready to recognize YHWH. That this relationship soured in the latter years of Josiah's reign, when Neco ultimately put Josiah to death, does not impinge upon perceptions of a changing world order in which Egypt would rise and Assyria would fall in the early reign of Josiah. After nearly a century of Assyrian oppression, anything that led to the downfall of Assyria would be understood as a blessing from YHWH.

Although v. 10 clearly appears in a context that focuses on YHWH's actions in relation to the nations, interpreters have frequently argued that v. 10 is a postexilic addition to the text that focuses either on the nations' eschatological recognition of YHWH or on the return of Israel's or Judah's exiles to Jerusalem.[56] The postexilic setting for this verse is dismissed above in the discussion of the setting of vv. 9-10. Nevertheless, some further observations are necessary.

First, the term עֲתָרַי, "my supplicants," is a unique form of the root עתר, "to pray, supplicate." It is a relatively common term employed in reference to worship or entreaty of YHWH, and could easily refer to Judean or Israelite worshipers of YHWH. Nevertheless, the intertextual relationship between Zeph 3:9-10 and Isaiah 18–19 and the general focus on the nations in Zeph 3:8b-10 points to the use of the term in reference to the nations who will recognize YHWH, specifically Egypt or the lands beyond the rivers of Cush. Because this verse points to an understanding that Isaiah 18–19 are fulfilled, the supplicants must be from Egypt or Ethiopia.

Second, the expression בַּת־פּוּצַי, "daughter of my dispersion/scattering," is generally taken to be a reference to the exiles of Israel or Judah, and could therefore derive only from the exilic or postexilic period.[57] Again, such an interpretation overlooks the context of this passage, which points to an understanding of this term in reference to the nations. It is therefore noteworthy that, although the verb פוץ sometimes refers to Israel's/ Judah's exiles in the Babylonian or Persian periods (e.g., Ezek 34:5, 6; Zech 13:7), the verb is commonly employed in reference to YHWH's defeat of enemies (1 Sam 11:11;

55   See Herodotus 2.157; cf. Redford, *Egypt*, 441–46.
56   Schwally, "Sefanjâ," 202–4; Marti, *Dodekapropheton*, 374–75; J. M. P. Smith, *Zephaniah*, 248–50; Elliger, *Zephanja*, 80–81; Horst, *Propheten*, 199; Edler, *Kerygma*, 57–60; Renaud, *Sophonie*, 247–49; Steck, "Zu Zef 3,9-10."
57   See the discussions in Ben Zvi, *Zephaniah*, 227–30; Vlaardingerbroek, *Zephaniah*, 195–96.

Num 10:35; Ps 68:2). Indeed, Num 10:35 preserves a rather well-known tradition that employs the verb in relation to the ark and its role as a war palladium in early Israelite tradition: "Rise, O YHWH, let your enemies be scattered (וְיָפֻצוּ אֹיְבֶיךָ), and your foes flee before you" (cf. Ps 68:2, "Let G-d rise up; let his enemies be scattered [יָפוּצוּ אוֹיְבָיו]"). Both Num 10:35 and Psalm 68 were apparently well known in ancient Israel and Judah; it therefore seems unlikely that the use of the verb פוץ would automatically refer to Israelite or Judean exiles, especially since the context in Zeph 3:8b-10 points to such a concern with the nations.

Third, there has also been some speculation that either or both terms may represent a gloss in the text.[58] This seems unlikely, as Mur 21:4 clearly includes both expressions just as they appear in the MT. The root of the issue apparently lies in the Old Greek text of the LXX as represented in Vaticanus, which omits both expressions: "From across the rivers of Ethiopia, they will offer my sacrifices," which in turn is followed by the Peshitta: "From across the rivers of Cush, bringing to me sacrifices." Both readings specify no subject that identifies the party making the offerings, although v. 9 would seem to require that the nations would present the offering in keeping with the Hebrew text. A variety of later Greek traditions include the statement, "(From across the rivers of Ethiopia), I will receive my dispersed ones,[59] (they will offer my sacrifices)," which indicates that the phrases were read in relation to an Israelite/Judean exile or diaspora. This would suggest that the expressions were omitted from the early LXX tradition (and likewise from the Peshitta) because such a statement would have created tension in the text, and elsewhere the LXX of Zephaniah is known to make such stylistic emendations. Both TJ and the Vulgate include both expressions in their renditions of the verse.

Finally, the language employed for the presentation of the offering to YHWH, יוֹבִלוּ מִנְחָתִי, "they will present my offering," points to a formal procession of offering.

The verb יבל, "to conduct, bear along," generally conveys a formal processional action (see Pss 68:30; 76:12).[60] The term מִנְחָה, "gift, offering, tribute," can refer to gifts in general (e.g., Gen 32:14, 19, 21; 33:10; Ps 20:4; Num 29:39) or to tribute (e.g., Judg 13:15, 17; 2 Sam 8:2, 6; 1 Kgs 5:1; 2 Kgs 17:3, 4). More frequently, it refers to offerings made to G-d, whether grain or meat (Gen 4:3, 4, 5; Num 16:15; 1 Sam 2:17; 26:19; Isa 1:13), although it designates the grain offering in Priestly texts (e.g., Exod 30:9; 40:29; Lev 7:37; 23:37; Num 18:9; 29:39; cf. Josh 22:23, 39). When read in relation to the expectation that the nations will employ their newly purified or selected language "to call on the name of YHWH" in v. 9, it seems most likely that the "offering" envisioned here is to be presented at the temple in order to acknowledge YHWH and Jerusalem as the center of creation.

■ 11 Although the introductory formula, בַּיּוֹם הַהוּא, "in that day," is frequently viewed as an indication of redactional work,[61] the first person form of vv. 11-12 demonstrates that the words are formulated as part of the prophet's presentation of YHWH's speech that begins in v. 6. There is some literary tension, however, in that YHWH addresses Jerusalem with second person feminine address forms in contrast to the masculine plural address forms of v. 8. Nevertheless, the combination of feminine singular and masculine plural references in v. 12 indicates that the second feminine singular forms (e.g., בְּקִרְבֵּךְ, "in your midst") are employed in reference to the city of Jerusalem itself whereas the masculine plural forms (e.g., וְחָסוּ, "and they will take refuge") are employed for the people of Jerusalem who will constitute the remnant of Israel. Furthermore, the contention that Jerusalem should no longer feel shame because YHWH will remove the arrogant from her midst builds on the prophet's prior statements concerning the corruption of Jerusalem's officials in 3:1-4 and YHWH's reiteration in 3:7 of past statements that the city would be secure despite its punishment and that its people con-

---

58 See the work cited in n. 25 above.

59 The rendition of עֲתָרַי as προσδέχομαι, "I will receive," apparently presupposes a form of the root עתר, "to surround, protect." Note that the root in Aramaic often means "to surround, guard, protect" (Jastrow, *Dictionary* 2:1064–65), and the Assyrian root *etēru* means "to spare, rescue" (BDB, 742).

60 See BDB, 384–85.

61 E.g., Ben Zvi, *Zephaniah*, 230; Vlaardingerbroek, *Zephaniah*, 199–200; for general discussion see DeVries, *From Old Revelation*, 38–63, esp. 36 (cf. 195, 206).

tinued to corrupt their ways. The reference to "that day" relates to the day when YHWH will arise mentioned in 3:8. Thus v. 11 takes up YHWH's projected plans for Jerusalem and the remnant of Israel once actions against the nations are completed. This points to the conclusion of the sequence in v. 13, which posits that no one (i.e., from the nations) will molest the purged remnant of Israel (in Jerusalem).

The initial statement of this sequence, "you will not be ashamed of all your deeds, by which you rebelled against me," constitutes the basic proposition that will be elaborated upon throughout the balance of the material in vv. 11b-13. The issue has nothing to do with guilt or lack thereof; YHWH's statement in v. 8 has already expressed the notion that Jerusalem will survive despite the actions of its people. Verse 11a fully acknowledges or asserts the rebellious nature of the people's actions by employing the verb פשע, which normally designates both religious rebellion against YHWH (see, e.g., Isa 1:28; 46:8; 48:8; 53:12; Hos 14:10; Amos 4:4) and political rebellion against a king or other power figures (see, e.g., 1 Kgs 12:19; 2 Kgs 1:1; 3:5, 7; 8:22).[62] It apparently does so deliberately so that it might build on the assertion of v. 8 that Jerusalem will survive despite the actions of its people. As vv. 11b-13 indicate, YHWH will undertake a purge of the city to remove its arrogant elements so that the city's survival will be ensured. As Ben Zvi notes, the expressions "you will not be ashamed" and "they will take refuge in the (name of) YHWH" form a syntagmatic pair in Pss 25:20; 31:2; 71:1 (cf. Pss 22:6; 25:2; Job 6:20), in which the psalmist typically calls on YHWH to grant refuge so that the speaker will not be put to shame.[63] By splitting this typical combination, placing YHWH's assurance that Jerusalem need not be ashamed at the outset of the subunit (v. 11a) and stating that the people's refuge in YHWH will constitute the outcome of YHWH's forming a remnant of Israel (v. 12b), the present passage points to the realization of this liturgical plea. Such a contention further serves the rhetorical goals of the passage—and indeed of the book

as a whole—to convince the audience to seek YHWH (2:3) now that YHWH's power is manifested in the world.

YHWH's statement in v. 11b concerning the intention to purge Jerusalem of its arrogant elements apparently draws on the Isaian tradition. It begins with the particle combination כִּי־אָז, "for then," which expresses both cause, that is, the reason that Jerusalem need not feel shame, and temporal consequence in that it points to YHWH's future actions (cf. the use of the same particle combination in v. 9). The verb אָסִיר, "I will remove," appears also in Isa 1:25, "and I will remove (וְאָסִירָה) your dross," as part of a larger oracle in Isa 1:21-26, which employs the metaphor of refining or purifying metal to portray YHWH's intentions to purge Jerusalem of its evil and undesirable elements.

The expression עַלִּיזֵי גַּאֲוָתֵךְ, "your proud exultant ones," likewise draws on terminology that typically appears in Isaiah, beginning with the same basic expression, עַלִּיזֵי גַּאֲוָתִי, "my proud exultant ones," in Isa 13:3 that refers to YHWH's warriors, as well as references to "the exultant city," קִרְיָה עַלִּיזָה, in 22:2 (Jerusalem) and 32:13 (Jerusalem) or simply "the exultant (city)," in 23:7 (Tyre). The noun עַלִּיזִים, "exultant ones," appears in 24:8 to designate those in the land whose rejoicing comes to an end with YHWH's punishment, and the verb עלז appears in 5:14 to describe those who will go down to Sheol. Although 13:3 and 24:8 are likely later compositions from the sixth century,[64] the use of the term עַלִּיז and its derivatives is clearly characteristic of the Isaian tradition, especially to designate those in Israel who are to be punished by YHWH. The reference in 32:13 is particularly instructive in relation to Zeph 3:11 because Isaiah 32 is a composition from the period of King Josiah that projects the restoration of the exultant city following its period of punishment.[65]

Although it is not so closely associated with Isaiah as עַלִּיז, the term גַּאֲוָה, "pride, proud," also appears frequently in the book (besides Isa 13:3) in reference to the pride of the northern kingdom of Israel, that is, "in

---

62   For a full discussion of the various forms of this term, see Rolf Knierim, *Die Hauptbegriffe für Sünde im Alten Testament* (Gütersloh: Mohn, 1967) 113-84.

63   Ben Zvi, *Zephaniah*, 231; cf. Berlin, *Zephaniah*, 136.

64   See Sweeney, *Isaiah 1-39*, 229-35, 316-20.

65   Ibid., 415-18.

pride and arrogance they held back" (9:8); YHWH's actions against Babylon, "I will put an end to the pride of the arrogant" (13:11); the pride of Moab, "we have heard of the pride of Moab—how proud he is—of his arrogance, his pride, and his insolence" (16:6); and again concerning the pride of Moab, "their pride will be laid low" (25:11). Again, 13:11 and 25:11 are later, but the expression appears frequently in Isaiah. Likewise, related terms such as גֵּאֶה, "arrogance" (2:12), גָּאוֹן, "splendor, excellence" (2:10, 19, 21; 14:11; see also the occurrence of the term in later passages: 4:2; 13:11, 19; 24:14; 49:19; 50:44; 60:15), and גֵּאוּת, "majesty" (9:17; 12:5; and the later 26:10), appear throughout the book.

Similar observations may be made concerning the term גְּבֹהָה, "haughty," in the phrase, "and you shall no longer be haughty (לֹא־תוֹסִפִי לְגָבְהָה עוֹד) in my holy mountain,"[66] in Zeph 3:11b. The term is based in the root גבה, which makes its appearance throughout Isaiah (Isa 2:11, 15, 17; 3:16; 5:15, 16; 7:11; 10:33; 30:25) to designate arrogant people or actions deserving of punishment.

The concentration of the various terms for arrogance and pride in Isa 2:6-21 is particularly important for understanding Zeph 3:11 because it points to YHWH's actions against all that is proud, arrogant, exalted, and so on, on the Day of YHWH, which is precisely the scenario articulated in Zephaniah and particularly in 3:11-13. It is no accident that the book of Isaiah is a primary source for articulating the notion that YHWH's punishment against Jerusalem or Israel will leave a remnant of the people that will ultimately serve as the basis for

Israel's restoration (see Isa 4:2-6; 6:1-13; 7:1-9; 10:20-26; 37:30-32). Again, the Josianic period compositions in 7:1-9 and 37:30-32 indicate that Isaiah's message of the remnant was understood to be fulfilled with the restoration of the Judean kingdom under King Josiah.[67] Note also that the Josian era passage in 11:1-16[68] includes the passage, "they will not hurt or destroy on all my holy mountain (בְּכָל־הַר קָדְשִׁי)," which relates to the concluding phrase, "in my holy mountain" (בְּהַר קָדְשִׁי) in Zeph 3:11.

■ 12 Verse 12 continues the sentiments expressed by the presentation of YHWH's speech in v. 11 by announcing the formation of the remnant of Israel as a result of YHWH's purge of the nation and the world at large.[69] The introductory waw-consecutive verbal form, וְהִשְׁאַרְתִּי, "and I shall cause to remain," the first person singular subject, and the second feminine singular addressee (i.e., Jerusalem) mark this verse as a continuation of YHWH's speech in v. 11. The absence of a syntactical connector prior to שְׁאֵרִית יִשְׂרָאֵל, "the remnant of Israel," however, does not demonstrate that v. 12 closes the speech; rather, it indicates that v. 13 forms the climactic rhetorical goal of the speech in that it defines the characteristics of the remnant of Israel.[70]

Essentially, v. 12 states that YHWH will create a remnant defined as "a people humble and lowly (עַם עָנִי וָדָל) . . . will take refuge in the name of YHWH (וְחָסוּ בְשֵׁם ה')." This statement has prompted considerable interest in the use of Zephaniah for contemporary theology, especially with regard to concern for and identification with the poor in Christianity based on historical models

66 Cf. Isa 23:12, "you will no longer exult (לֹא־תוֹסִיפִי עוֹד לַעֲלוֹז), O oppressed, virgin daughter of Sidon," which employs the same basic phraseology, but with a different expression for pride, as in Zeph 3:11b.

67 For the dating of these passages, see Sweeney, Isaiah 1–39, 149–59, 476–85. See also Sweeney, King Josiah, 234–55, for general discussion of the Josianic redaction of Isaiah.

68 For the date of Isaiah 11, see Sweeney, Isaiah 1–39, 203–10; idem, "Jesse's New Shoot in Isaiah 11: A Josianic Reading of the Prophet," in Richard D. Weis and David M. Carr, eds., A Gift of God in Due Season: Essays on Scripture and Community in Honor of James A. Sanders (JSOTSup 225; Sheffield: Sheffield Academic Press, 1996) 103–18.

69 For discussion of the remnant concept in the book

of Zephaniah, see George W. Anderson, "The Idea of the Remnant in the Book of Zephaniah," ASTI 11 (1977–78) 11–14; Greg A. King, "The Remnant in Zephaniah," BSac 151 (October–December 1994) 414–27. See also George W. Anderson, "Some Observations on the Old Testament Doctrine of the Remnant," Transactions of the Glasgow University Oriental Society 23 (1969–70) 1–10.

70 For further discussion see the treatment of v. 13 below.

presented in the book.[71] There is sometimes a tendency to oversimplify the issue by claiming that Zephaniah addresses a class conflict between the poor and the powerful elite in ancient Judean society and identifies with the poor by calling for the overthrow of the elite. Although class conflict was surely endemic in ancient Judean society, such a conceptualization may draw overmuch on contemporary issues or models of class conflict and economic exploitation. The issue needs to be considered, however, in relation to the social and political realities of ancient Judah in the mid-seventh century and the rhetorical concerns of the book.

Indeed, there is evidence that ancient Judah suffered massive destruction of its population as a result of the Assyrian invasions of the late eighth century and that the Judean monarchs, Manasseh, Amon, and Josiah, were faced with the task of rebuilding the rural Judean farming population and its social structure.[72] Under Manasseh, the Judean population was forced to shift eastward and southward, away from the fertile Shephelah and into the Judean highlands and Negev wilderness, as Assyria established its industrial and commercial sphere of influence in the coastal plain of Philistia and the former territories of Judah in the Shephelah.[73] But as Manasseh and his circle of advisors in Jerusalem were closely identified with Assyrian interests, particularly as Assyrian power waxed during the first half of the seventh century, opposition against his rule began to grow among the Judean rural population that was forced to bear the brunt of the Assyrian attack and later was displaced by Assyrian interests and heavily taxed to supply the necessary tribute to support Assyria. As the Assyrian Empire began to decline in the mid-seventh century, the increasingly powerful role of the so-called עַם־הָאָרֶץ, "people of the land," became evident in the failed coup

against Manasseh's son Amon (see 2 Kgs 21:19-26). The assassination of Amon was apparently carried out by members of the royal entourage in Jerusalem, who likely saw the decline of Assyria as an opportunity for revolt. But the coup was quickly put down by the עַם־הָאָרֶץ, who had suffered considerably in past attempts by the Judean monarchs to revolt against Assyria, and Amon's young son Josiah was placed on the throne. Although Josiah subsequently steered the country toward independence from Assyria when he reached the age of majority, he did not do so by direct confrontation with the Assyrians—that path had proved disastrous in the past. Instead, he took a more passive approach that would protect his people and waited until it was clear that Assyria would be able to do little about Judean assertions of independence, as the Assyrian army had to be concerned with the threat posed to the empire by the Babylonians and Medes to the east. Such a strategy was not unlike that of Hezekiah, in that it relied on a relationship with Babylonia, but it meant that Judah would not be involved in direct military confrontation with the Assyrians. Furthermore, the attention and greater rights given to the poor of the land in Deuteronomy, widely believed to be a lawcode promulgated if not written under the influence of Josiah,[74] indicates that Josiah succeeded in building a new alliance between the house of David and the עַם־הָאָרֶץ of Judah. Certainly, the placement by the עַם־הָאָרֶץ of Josiah's son Jehoahaz on the throne after his death signals such support, especially since he was removed and exiled by the Egyptians because he was perceived to continue his father's pro-Babylonian policy over against the Egyptians (see 2 Kgs 23:31-35).

---

71 See Gilberto Gorgulho, "Zefanja und die historische Bedeutung der Armen," *EvTh* 51 (1991) 81–92; Weigl, *Zefanja,* 214; Frank Crüsemann, "Israel, die Völker und die Armen," in Walter Dietrich and Milton Schwantes, eds., *Der Tag wird kommen. Ein interkontextuelles Gespräch über das Buch des Propheten Zefanja* (SBS 170; Stuttgart: Katholisches Bibelwerk, 1996) 123–33.

72 See esp. Baruch Halpern, "Jerusalem and the Lineages in the Seventh Century BCE: Kinship and the Rise of Individual Moral Liability," in Baruch Halpern and Deborah W. Hobson, eds., *Law and*

Ideology in Monarchic Israel (JSOTSup 124; Sheffield: Sheffield Academic Press, 1991) 11–107.

73 Israel Finkelstein, "The Archaeology of the Days of Manasseh," in Michael D. Coogan, J. Cheryl Exum, and Lawrence E. Stager, eds., *Scripture and Other Artifacts: Essays on the Bible and Archaeology in Honor of Philip J. King* (Louisville: Westminster John Knox, 1994) 119–87; Gitin, "Tel Miqne-Ekron."

74 For discussion of this issue, see Sweeney, *King Josiah,* 137–69; Moshe Weinfeld, *Deuteronomy and the Deuteronomic School* (1972; reprinted Winona Lake, Ind.: Eisenbrauns, 1992).

It is against this background that the designation of the remnant as "a people humble and lowly" must be read. Such language signals Josiah's identification with the Judean עַם־הָאָרֶץ, who would be portrayed as humble and lowly over against the royal court in Jerusalem that had been so closely identified with Manasseh's (forced) collaboration with the Assyrian Empire. Indeed, the call for a purge of Judah—especially its officials (Zeph 1:2-18; 3:1-4) who were identified with Assyrian interests—and the characterization of those to be purged as arrogant, proud, haughty, and so on, in v. 11, would well serve Josiah's interest to reform and reconstitute his state in an effort to assert its freedom from Assyrian control. One may debate whether the rural Judean population was poor; indeed, the use of designations such as "humble," "lowly," "righteous," and so on is designed to assert a certain moral (and political) superiority of one party over another. It must be noted, however, that the people of the land played a considerable role in designating the kings of Israel prior to the reign of Solomon, but they played little role from Solomon's reign on.[75] It may also be debated whether such a purge entailed the full removal of these officials or a persuasive attempt to convince the targets of the critique to join in Josiah's new program.[76]

It is also noteworthy that the terminology עָנִי וָדָל, "humble and lowly," plays an important role in the Isaian tradition. The terms appear together in the context of Isaiah's accusations against those in Israel who abuse power to oppress the poor: "Woe to you who decree evil decrees and write oppressive documents, to turn aside the lowly/needy (דַּלִּים) from judicial due process and to rob the humble/poor of my people (עֲנִיֵּי עַמִּי) of law." Similar references to such concern for the humble/poor and lowly/needy also appear in Isa 3:14, 15, and 29:19

(see also the later 26:6). The terms also play an important role in defining the characteristics of the ideal Davidic monarch articulated in 11:1-16, a text attributed to the Josian rereading of the Isaian tradition: "and he shall judge the lowly (דַּלִּים) with righteousness, and he shall arbitrate with integrity for the humble of the land (עַנְוֵי אָרֶץ)" (see further 32:7, which is also attributed to the Josian redaction of Isaiah).[77] Again, Zephaniah appears to draw heavily on Isaian motifs and language, both from Isaiah ben Amoz and from the Josian redaction of Isaiah, in formulating his own oracles in support of Josiah's reform program.

Finally, Ben Zvi notes the unusual reference to YHWH's "name" in the phrase, "and they will take refuge in the name of YHWH," as opposed to the more customary phrase found in the Psalms, "to take refuge in YHWH" (see Pss 22:6; 25:2; 71:1).[78] It is therefore noteworthy that interest in the name of YHWH is especially characteristic of Deuteronomy, which emphasizes that the central sanctuary is "the place where YHWH chooses to cause his name to dwell" (Deut 12:5, 11; 14:23; 16:2, 6, 11; 26:2). Since an early form of Deuteronomy also appears to have played an important role in Josiah's program,[79] this phrase also seems to indicate Zephaniah's dependence on literature employed to support Josiah's reform.

■ 13 The present form of v. 13 in the MT lacks any syntactical connection with the preceding material in v. 12, and this lack of connection raises questions concerning its relationship to the presentation of YHWH's speech in vv. 6-12. The problem is compounded by the absence of first person forms that would clearly identify it as speech by YHWH or of third person references to YHWH that would signal a shift to speech by the prophet. The LXX has apparently sought to resolve this issue by reading the

---

75 Note that the people or the elders apparently designated Saul (1 Sam 10:17-27; 11:1-15) and David (2 Sam 2:1-4; 5:1-5) as king (note that they also requested that Gideon serve as king, Judg 8:22-28), and that they apparently approved David's choice of Solomon (1 Kgs 2:38-40). Nevertheless, the people of Judah appear to play little role in the selection of Davidic monarchs until the coup against Amon and, prior to that, Athaliah's attempted coup against the Davidic house (2 Kings 11). For discussion see Sweeney, *King Josiah*, 105–6.

76 Note 2 Kgs 23:20, which indicates that Josiah exe-

cuted the priests of the high places of the land outside Jerusalem, but this does not indicate that similar lethal means were employed within Jerusalem.

77 See Sweeney, *Isaiah 1–39*, 203–10, 415–19; idem, *King Josiah*, 234–55, for the dating of these texts.

78 Ben Zvi, *Zephaniah*, 231.

79 Sweeney, *King Josiah*, 137–68.

initial expression of the verse, שְׁאֵרִית יִשְׂרָאֵל, "remnant of Israel," as the subject of the preceding clause in v. 12b, "and the remnants of Israel shall pay honor to the name of the L-rd, and they shall not do injustice. . . ." By serving as the subject of v. 12b and of v. 13, the expression "remnant of Israel" is then associated with a statement that includes a third person reference to YHWH, which then identifies vv. 12b-13 as speech by the prophet. Such a move is unjustified,[80] however, as the resulting chain of statements would require a *waw*-conjunctive formulation for the following material, that is, "and they will not do (וְלֹא יַעֲשׂוּ) iniquity, . . ." in order to associate it with other *waw*-consecutive verbal formations that would constitute this proposed subunit. Although the Greek text does supply the conjunction καί at this point to make its understanding of the relationship clear, reading καὶ οὐ ποιήσουσιν ἀδικίαν, "and they will not do injustice," the Hebrew text lacks any conjunction for this clause and reads simply, לֹא יַעֲשׂוּ עַוְלָה, "they will not do iniquity." Given the absence of a syntactical relationship with v. 12b, the expression "remnant of Israel" must function as the subject of v. 13.[81] The expression שְׁאֵרִית יִשְׂרָאֵל is grammatically singular and the verbs are plural, but the expression functions collectively to serve as the subject of the verbs.[82]

The identity of the speaker in v. 13 is not entirely certain. Nevertheless, the verse serves as the climax, either of YHWH's own speech or of the prophet's presentation of YHWH's speech, in that it defines the characteristics of the remnant of Israel that remains following YHWH's purge of both Israel and the nations. The internal references in the verse suggest that the prophet is indeed the speaker, because the verse alludes to statements in Zephaniah outside the immediate context of YHWH's speech in vv. 6-12. The initial statement that "the remnant of Israel will not do iniquity" (שְׁאֵרִית יִשְׂרָאֵל לֹא יַעֲשׂוּ עַוְלָה), for example, corresponds to the prophet's statement in v. 5 that introduces YHWH's speech, that is, "YHWH is righteous in its/her midst, he does not do

iniquity (לֹא יַעֲשֶׂה עַוְלָה)." The statements that the remnant of Israel "will not speak a lie" and that "there will not be found in their mouth a deceitful tongue" echo the earlier statements by the prophet that "its/her prophets are wanton, men of treachery" (3:4a) and by YHWH that they (those who leap over the threshold) "fill the house of their L-rd with violence and deceit" (1:9b). Likewise, the pastoral metaphor that portrays the remnant of Israel as flocks that "graze and lie down, and no one frightens them," picks up earlier imagery in the prophet's statements concerning Philistia that portrays the remnant of the house of Judah as sheep that will graze in the houses of Ashkelon and lie down in the evening (2:7). Overall, the verse appears to cite the prophet's statements in the immediate context of chap. 3 as well as in the oracle concerning Philistia. The only possible allusion to a statement by YHWH is the reference to deceit, but even this is covered by the prophet's statement in 3:4. Of course, these observations do not demonstrate that the prophet is the speaker in this verse, but they point to the likelihood that this is the case. Verse 13 would then function as the prophet's summation of YHWH's speech in vv. 6-12 (within the larger context of the book) and thereby prepare the hearer/reader for the next component of YHWH's speech in vv. 14-20.

Many interpreters have noted that the expression "remnant of Israel" seems to introduce a new element in Zephaniah insofar as other statements concerning the remnant of the nation refer to Judah (2:7), the unspecified "my people/my nation" (2:9), and even the remnant of Baal (1:4). The name Israel does not appear elsewhere in Zephaniah, and this has prompted suggestions that the expression "remnant of Israel" is a later addition to the text that is designed to point to eschatological hopes for the restoration of all Israel.[83] Such a contention, however, overlooks the fact that a major component of Josiah's program of restoration was to extend Davidic rule over the territory of the former northern kingdom

---

80 Contra Gerleman, *Zephanja*, 60; Vlaardingerbroek, *Zephaniah*, 203–4; Rudolph, *Zephanja*, 292; Roberts, *Zephaniah*, 210; Renaud, *Sophonie*, 250; Sellin, *Zwölfprophetenbuch*, 440; J. M. P. Smith, *Zephaniah*, 251–52; Marti, *Dodekapropheton*, 375–76.

81 Cf. Weigl, *Zefanja*, 201.

82 See GKC, §145b-g.

83 E.g., Edler, *Kerygma*, 109–10, who considers the expression to be a gloss.

of Israel as well as Judah and thereby to reunite all Israel under the rule of the Davidic monarchy. Such a move of course would restore the old Davidic/Solomonic empire. Since v. 13 forms the climactic statement of the prophet's presentation of YHWH's words concerning the restoration of Jerusalem at the center of creation, it makes a great deal of sense to employ the term "remnant of Israel"; Israel, rather than Judah or any other component of Israel, is the ideal entity that will constitute YHWH's nation centered around Jerusalem and the temple.

The moral characteristics of the people are also worthy of note. Many have focused on these terms as indications of moral or ethical purity on the part of the restored remnant of Israel. This understanding has important implications for establishing the social setting of these oracles, as such moral purity is required of those who would enter the temple precincts for the worship of YHWH. The so-called entrance liturgies in Psalms 15 and 24 (see also Isa 33:14-16) define the moral characteristics of those who would enter the temple, "O YHWH, who may abide in your tent? Who may dwell on your holy mountain? Those who walk blamelessly, and do what is right, and speak the truth from their heart; who do not slander with their tongue, and do no evil to their friends, nor take up a reproach against their neighbors" (Ps 15:1-3).[84] Likewise, Ps 24:3-4 states, "Who shall ascend the hill of YHWH? And who shall stand in his holy place? Those who have clean hands and pure hearts, who do not lift up their souls to what is false, and do not swear deceitfully." A simple

comparison the language indicates that the qualities articulated in Zeph 3:13 and in the entrance psalms are analogous; even the references to YHWH's holy mountain/hill pick up the similar reference in 3:12.

It would seem then that 3:13 states the characteristics of the remnant of Israel in an effort to demonstrate that the remnant is fit for entry into the temple. Since the balance of the book is concerned with purging the nation in the course of sacrifice to mark the celebration of the Day of YHWH at the Jerusalem Temple, this verse marks the point at which the purge has achieved its goals and the temple celebration can commence. Such concerns correspond to those of Josiah's reform once again in that the purification of the temple and the purge of the nation portrayed in the narrative accounts of his reign (2 Kings 23) point to similar efforts to purify the nation so that it might engage in proper worship of YHWH at the Jerusalem Temple. Again, the pastoral imagery employed to portray the resulting tranquility of the people appears also in Isa 11:1-16, previously noted as a part of the Josian rereading of Isaiah, which presents images of the wolf living in peace with the lamb, the leopard lying down with the kid, the calf, lion, and fatling together, and so on (see Isa 11:6-9). Such a scene appears to replicate the tranquility and peace of the garden of Eden, which is precisely the imagery conveyed by the temple in Jerusalem with its depiction of the plants, animals, cherubim, and so on of the garden of Eden (see 1 Kings 6).[85]

---

84   For discussion of the entrance liturgy, see Sweeney, *Isaiah 1–39*, 520; Klaus Koch, "Tempeleinlassliturgien und Dekaloge," in Rolf Rendtorff and Klaus Koch, eds., *Studien zur Theologie der alttestamentlichen Überlieferungen* (Fest. G. von Rad; Neukirchen-Vluyn: Neukirchener Verlag, 1961) 45–60. For discussion of Psalms 15 and 24, see esp. Gerstenberger, *Psalms, Part 1,* 86–89, 117–19.

85   Note the use of similar language to portray the tranquility and security, generally for the nation at large, in Lev 26:6; Jer 30:10; 46:27; Ezek 34:28; 39:26; Mic 4:4; Job 11:19; cf. Deut 28:26; Isa 17:2; Jer 7:33; Nah 2:12; Ben Zvi, *Zephaniah,* 238.

3

3:14-20 The Prophet's Exhortation to Jerusalem: YHWH Will Establish Jerusalem as Holy Center of Creation

Translation

14 Sing, O Daughter Zion![a]
Shout, O Israel![b]
Rejoice and exult with a full heart,
O Daughter Jerusalem!
15 YHWH has removed your judgment,[c]
he has turned aside your enemy.[d]
The King of Israel, YHWH, is in your midst,[e]
you need not fear evil again![f]
16 On that day, it will be said to Jerusalem,[g]
"Do not fear,[h] O Zion,[i]
Do not let your hands be slack,
17 YHWH, your G-d, is in your midst,[j] a warrior who delivers;[k]
he rejoices over you in delight,[l]
he plows with his love,[m]
he dances over you with singing![n]
18 Those who have suffered from the appointed time when I punished you
were[o] a burden upon her, a reproach.[p]
19 Behold, I am dealing with all who oppress you at that time,[q]
and I shall deliver the lame, and the outcast I shall collect.
And I shall appoint their shame for praise and for renown
in all the earth.[r]
20 In that time I shall bring you[s]
and in the time when I gather you,
indeed, I shall appoint you for renown and for praise
among all the peoples of the earth,
when I restore your captivity/fortunes[t]
before your eyes," says YHWH.

a MT reads, בַּת־צִיּוֹן, "O Daughter Zion"; cf. TJ, כנשתא דציאן, "O Synagogue of Zion."
b MT reads, יִשְׂרָאֵל, "O Israel"; cf. LXX, *θύγατερ Ιερουσαλεμ*, "O Daughter Jerusalem."
c MT reads, הֵסִיר ה״ מִשְׁפָּטַיִךְ, "YHWH has removed your judgments"; cf. LXX, *πειεῖλε κύριος τὰ ἀδικήματά σου*, "The L-rd is stripping off your iniquities"; TJ, דייני שקרא מגויך אגלי יי״, "YHWH has exiled the false judges from your midst"; Peshitta, *ʾʿbr mryʾ dynyky*, "The L-rd has removed your judgments"; Vulgate, *abstulit Dominus iudicium tuum*, "The L-rd has removed your judgments."
d MT reads, פִּנָּה אֹיְבֵךְ, "he has turned aside your enemies"; cf. Mur 21:11, פנה איביך, "he has turned aside your enemies"; LXX, *λελύτρωταί σε ἐκ χειρὸς ἐχθρῶν σου*, "he has ransomed you from the hand of your enemies"; Peshitta, *wʾprq mnky bʿldbbyky*, "and he has driven away from you your enemies."
e Cf. TJ, מלכיה דישראל יי״ אמר לאשראה שכינתיה בגויך, "The King of Israel, YHWH, has promised to cause his Shekinah to dwell in your midst."
f MT reads, לֹא־תִירְאִי רָע עוֹד, "you need not fear evil again," clearly reading the verb תיראי as a form of the verbal root ירא, "to fear"; cf. LXX, *οὐκ ὄψῃ κακὰ οὐκέτι*, "you will not see evil any longer," and Peshitta, *twb lʾ thzyn byštʾ*, "you will not again see evil," both of which read תיראי as a form of the root ראה, "to see."
g Cf. LXX, *ἐρεῖ κύριος τῇ Ιερουσαλημ*, "the L-rd will say to Jerusalem."
h Cf. LXX, *θάρσει*, "take courage."
i Cf. Peshitta, *wlṣhywn*, "and to Zion."
j Cf. TJ, יי״ אלקרך אמר לאשראה שכינתיה בגויך, "YHWH your G-d has promised to cause his Shekinah to dwell in your midst."
k MT, גִּבּוֹר יוֹשִׁיעַ, "a warrior who delivers"; cf. TJ, גיבר פריק, "a mighty redeemer."
l MT reads, יָשִׂישׂ עָלַיִךְ בְּשִׂמְחָה, "he will rejoice over you with joy"; cf. Peshitta, *nbsmky bhdtʾ*, "he will make you glad with joy."
m MT reads, יַחֲרִישׁ בְּאַהֲבָתוֹ, "he plows with his love" or "he will be silent with his love"; cf. LXX, *καὶ καινιεῖ σε ἐν τῇ ἀγαπήσει αὐτοῦ*, "and he will renew you with his love"; and Peshitta, *whdtky bhwbh*, "and he renews you with his love," both of which read the enigmatic verb יחריש as יחדיש, requiring only the substitution of ד for the similarly formed ר. See also TJ, יכבוש על חובך ברחמתיה, "he will pardon your sins in his mercy," which understands יַחֲרִישׁ as a reference to G-d's silence and thus forgiveness in the face of wrongdoing.
n Cf. LXX, *ἐν τέρψει ὡς ἐν ἡμέρᾳ ἑορτῆς*, "in delight as in a day of feasting/holiday"; Peshitta, *btšbwhtʾ ʾyk dbywmʾ dʿdʿʾdʾ*, "in praise as in a day of festival."
o MT reads, נוּגֵי מִמּוֹעֵד אָסַפְתִּי מִמֵּךְ הָיוּ, "those who have

suffered from the appointed time (when) I gathered from you were"; cf. LXX, καὶ συνάξω τοὺς συντετριμμένους οὐαί, "and I shall gather those who are crushed. Woe/Alas . . ."; TJ, דהוו מעכבין ביך זמני מועדיך ארחיקית מויך, "those who were delaying among you the times of your holidays, I shall make far from your midst. Woe . . ."; Peshitta, w²ᶜbr mnky ᵓylyn dmmllyn hww, "and I shall remove from you those who were speaking (reproaches against you)."

p   MT reads, מַשְׂאֵת עָלֶיהָ חֶרְפָּה, "(they were) a burden upon her, a reproach"; cf. LXX, οὐαί τίς ἔλαβεν ἐπʼ αὐτὴν ὀνειδισμόν, "Alas! Who takes upon her a reproach?"; TJ, וי עליהון על דהוו נטלין זינהון לקבליך, ומחסדין ליך, "Woe upon them, for they were carrying their armament against you and shaming you"; Peshitta, dmmllyn hww ᶜlyky ḥsdᵓ, "those who were speaking reproaches against you."

q   So MT, הִנְנִי עֹשֶׂה אֶת־כָּל־מְעַנַּיִךְ בָּעֵת הַהִיא; cf. LXX, ἰδοὺ ἐγὼ ποιῶ ἐν σοὶ ἕνεκα σοῦ ἐν τῷ καιρῷ ἐκείνῳ λέγει κύριος, "Behold, I am working in you for your sake in that day says the L-rd"; TJ, האנא עביד ההוא גמירא עם כל משעבדך בעדנא, "Behold, I am making a full end with all who were enslaving you at that

time"; Peshitta, hᵓ ᶜbd ᵓnᵓ lklhwn bd mmkkyn bgwky bzbn² hw, "Behold, I am acting against all of them because (they were) humbling in your midst in that time"; Vulgate, ecce ego interficiam omnes qui adflixerunt te in tempore illo, "Behold, I am doing away with all who afflict you in that time."

r   MT reads, בְּכָל־הָאָרֶץ בָּשְׁתָּם, "in all the earth, their shame"; cf. LXX, ἐν πάσῃ τῇ γῇ, "in all the earth"; TJ, בכל ארע בהתתהון, "in all the land of their shame"; Peshitta, bklh ᵓrᶜdbhtthwn, "in all the land where they were shamed"; Vulgate, in omni terra confusionis eorum, "in all the land of your confusion."

s   Cf. LXX, καὶ καταισχυνθήσονται ἐν τῷ καιρῷ ἐκείνῳ ὅταν καλῶς ὑμῖν ποιήσω, "and they will be put to shame in that day when I shall do good for you."

t   So MT, בְּשׁוּבִי אֶת־שְׁבוּתֵיכֶם; cf. LXX, ἐν τῷ ἐπιστρέφειν με τὴν αἰχμαλωσίαν ὑμῶν, "in my returning your captivity"; TJ, כד אתיב ית גלותכון, "when I return your exile"; Peshitta, m² dmhpk ²n² šbytkwn, "when I return your captivity"; Vulgate, cum convertero captivitatem, "when I restore your captivity."

Form and Setting

Zephaniah 3:14-20 constitutes the third basic subunit of the prophet's exhortative speech in 3:1-20 in which he lays out the scenario by which YHWH will establish Jerusalem as the holy center of all creation and the nations. Whereas 3:1-4 relates the reasons for Jerusalem's punishment and 3:5-13 relates YHWH's plans to prompt the nations to recognize Jerusalem, 3:14-20 presents the prophet's exhortative address to Jerusalem in which he conveys YHWH's oracle of reassurance to the city concerning its coming restoration and role at the center of the nations. The passage thereby provides the climactic capstone to the prophet's speech in 3:1-20 that is designed to persuade its audience that Jerusalem's oppression under the Assyrians is about to come to an end and that the city will now take its place as YHWH's holy city, metaphorically expressed with language that suggests Jerusalem's role as YHWH's bride. Indeed, the passage provides a fitting conclusion to the prophet's parenetic speech in 2:1—3:20 in which he attempts to persuade his audience to seek YHWH,

that is, to join in with those who would purge the city and nation of its purported pagan elements under the auspices of King Josiah's program of national and religious reform.

The passage is easily demarcated by both its form and contents. It begins in vv. 14-15 with second person feminine singular address forms directed by the prophet to Jerusalem and to Israel at large, here addressed as בַּת־צִיּוֹן, "Daughter Zion," יִשְׂרָאֵל, "Israel," and בַּת־יְרוּשָׁלַם, "Daughter Jerusalem." Although a similar address form appears in 3:11, it is subsumed into the overall structure of the prophet's presentation of YHWH's statements concerning the purging of the nations—and indeed of Jerusalem as well—so that the city could be recognized for its new role. The address forms in vv. 14-15, however, are syntactically independent from the preceding block of material, and the shift to a call for rejoicing in v. 14, while simultaneously acknowledging divine pardon and protection in v. 15, marks a new rhetorical stage in the prophet's speech that points to the final realization of the promises of restoration that have been implicit in the speech from the beginning. The reference to YHWH in v. 15 makes clear that the prophet is the speaker. Furthermore, various features of vv. 16-20 indicate that the prophet remains the speaker throughout, including the third person references to Jerusalem in v. 16a, the third person references to YHWH in v. 17, the third person feminine singular reference to the city in v. 18b, and the YHWH speech formula in v. 20bβ[5-6]. Although syntactic breaks appear at the beginning of vv. 16, 17, 18, 19, and 20, these verses as a whole elaborate on the basic postulates of v. 15. These postulates include (1) YHWH has removed Jerusalem's judgments and turned aside her enemies; (2) YHWH is king in her midst; (3) Jerusalem need not fear any longer. Verses 16-20 elaborate on these postulates by piecing together, within the framework of the prophet's speech, objective statements concerning the city's future (v. 16a-bα[1-4]) and addresses to the city by both the prophet (vv. 16bα[5-6]β-17) and by YHWH (vv. 18-20) concerning Jerusalem's coming restoration and recognition. In this scenario, the references to "that day" in v. 16 and "that time" in vv. 19 and 20 aid in tying the unit together and serving its persuasive or rhetorical goals by providing a clear focus on the future realization of YHWH's promises. Of course, the subunit closes with the conclusion of the book in v. 20.

The structure of 3:14-20 appears to be based on the generic pattern of the hymn or psalm of praise, which includes both a summons to praise or rejoice and the reasons for such praise or rejoicing.[1] Nevertheless, the present context adapts this genre to a prophetic setting by presenting the prophet as the primary speaker of the passage who conveys YHWH's words and by including references to the future realization of reasons for the summons.[2] The first major component of the passage appears in 3:14, which constitutes a summons to rejoice addressed by the prophet to Jerusalem and Israel at large.[3] Indeed, the reference to Israel is crucial to the overall goals of this passage in that the restoration of Jerusalem entails the restoration of the city at the center of a restored Israel and the entire world. Verses 18-20

below make this clear by referring to the shame of those who have been oppressed and the return of the lame and outcast in the overall scenario of the restoration of Jerusalem's fortunes or captivity. Verse 14 employs second person feminine singular imperative verbs, including רָנִּי, "sing," שִׂמְחִי, "rejoice," and עָלְזִי, "exult," which are directed to Jerusalem, characterized either as "Daughter Zion" or "Daughter Jerusalem." One masculine plural imperative, הָרִיעוּ, "blow a horn," appears, but this accommodates the characterization of the addressee as "Israel." Verse 14 then constitutes the basic rhetorical or parenetical premise of vv. 14-20: it calls on the audience to celebrate.

Verses 15-20 then constitute the second basic component of 3:14-20 by providing the reasons why the audience should celebrate. Many interpreters restrict this function to v. 15 alone,[4] but such a decision overlooks the function of vv. 16-20 in relation to v. 15. Verse 15 provides the basic reason why the audience should celebrate: YHWH has eliminated Jerusalem's judgments and enemies so that the city no longer stands under threat, and YHWH, now identified as the king of Israel, stands in the midst of the city so that it need no longer fear. Beginning with the concluding instruction to Jerusalem that she need not fear, vv. 16-20 then elaborate on the basic contentions of v. 15, beginning with the premise that Jerusalem need no longer fear and moving on to address YHWH's presence in Jerusalem and rejoicing over her, the elimination of the city's oppression, the return of her exiles, and the granting of praise and renown.

The key to the internal structure of vv. 16-20 appears to lie in the recognition that the passage constitutes the prophet's presentation of two sets of addresses to the city, both his own and that of YHWH. The passage begins with the prophet's introduction to both of these addresses in v. 16aα-β[1-2], "on that day it shall be said to Jerusalem," which portrays their realization at a future day. The two addresses to the city, the first by the

---

1   For discussion of the psalm of praise or hymn, see Gerstenberger, *Psalms, Part 1*, 16–19.

2   Cf. Frank Crüsemann, *Studien zur Formgeschichte von Hymnus und Danklied in Israel* (WMANT 32; Neukirchen-Vluyn: Neukirchener Verlag, 1969) 55–65.

3   Cf. Floyd, *Minor Prophets*, 243–44.

4   E.g., Striek, *Zephanjabuch*, 210–16; cf. Floyd, *Minor Prophets*, 239–40.

prophet in vv. 16aβ³⁻⁴-17 and the second by YHWH in vv. 18-20, then follow.

The prophet's address to Jerusalem begins in vv. 16aβ³⁻⁴-17 with a version of the reassurance formula expressed as a direct address in v. 16aβ³⁻⁴-b, "Do not fear, O Zion, do not let your hands be slack."[5] This statement reiterates that of v. 15bβ, and thereby establishes a relationship with the preceding unit. Although many have seen this as justification to consider v. 16 (and the pericope at large) as a later addition,[6] the presence of the reassurance formula here merely signals an interest in elaborating on or developing the basic premises articulated in v. 15. This is accomplished in v. 17 in which the prophet describes YHWH's joy over Zion as part of his (the prophet's) efforts to demonstrate why Zion need no longer fear. Overall, the imagery is that of jubilation, although the enigmatic statement, "he will plow/be silent in his love," indicates that the metaphorical reuniting of bride and groom also contributes to the scenario (see the discussion of this statement below; cf. Isaiah 54; Jeremiah 2; Hos 3:1-5).

The prophet's presentation of YHWH's address to the city then follows in vv. 18-20. Although the bulk of this passage is formulated as YHWH's first person direct address to Jerusalem, the role of the prophet as the one who conveys YHWH's statements is evident in the concluding speech formula of v. 20bβ⁵⁻⁶, "אָמַר ה׳, "said YHWH," and perhaps in the third person reference to Jerusalem in v. 18bβ²⁻³, עָלֶיהָ חֶרְפָּה, "upon her, a shame." Although the status of this reference is uncertain, it may constitute a gloss (see discussion of this verse below). Apart from the framework statements by the prophet, YHWH's address to Jerusalem includes three basic components, each of which constitutes a syntactically self-contained subunit of the whole. The first appears in v. 18, which is philologically difficult (see the discussion below), but which asserts the premise that Jerusalem's past punishment, inflicted by YHWH, constitutes a burden or shame for her. This point is made in order to pro-

vide the basis for a portrayal of the transformation of the city's fortunes in the succeeding verses. Thus the second component of YHWH's speech appears in v. 19, in which YHWH states the intention to deal with the city's oppression at the specified future time (v. 19a). A series of waw-consecutive statements then follows in v. 19b, which outlines YHWH's plans to deliver the lame, gather the outcast, and appoint both for praise and fame throughout all the land in which they had been shamed. Finally, v. 20 reiterates and clarifies the statements made in v. 19 in that it too states YHWH's intentions to bring in and gather the city, grant it fame and praise throughout the land, and return from its captivity. Because v. 20 repeats the contentions of v. 19, it may well be the product of a later writer who sought to clarify the somewhat enigmatic statements of v. 19.[7]

Many scholars contend that 3:14-20, in whole or in part, is the product of the postexilic redaction of the book, based largely on its generic features, for example, the summons to praise, the reassurance formula, and its exhortative character, as well as on its fundamental concern with the restoration of Jerusalem following a period of punishment and exile.[8] Such features and concerns, however, hardly constitute a firm basis for a postexilic dating. Scholars must recall that the Babylonian exile was not the only exile faced by ancient Israel and Judah in antiquity—indeed, the outlook of modern readers is profoundly influenced by the Babylonian destruction of Jerusalem and the exile of its inhabitants. The destruction of northern Israel in the period of Assyrian hegemony, the subsequent deportation of much of its population, the loss of a great deal of Judean territory, and the exile—whether voluntary or not—of many Judeans, must also be considered as a fundamental reality faced by ancient Judeans. In the present case, the overall scenario of Jerusalem's restoration and the return of its exiles must be considered in relation to King Josiah's reform, when the opportunity for such restoration and return seemed to have arrived. Again,

---

5   For discussion of the reassurance formula and its context in the oracle of salvation, see Sweeney, *Isaiah 1–39*, 547; Edgar Conrad, *Fear Not Warrior: A Study of the ʾal tîrâ Pericopes in the Hebrew Scriptures* (BJS 75; Chico, Calif.: Scholars Press, 1985).

6   E.g., Striek, *Zephanjabuch*, 39–45, and the literature cited there.

7   Cf. Edler, *Kerygma*, 98–99.

8   E.g., Striek, *Zephanjabuch*, 39–45; Edler, *Kerygma*, 60–67, 98–99; Seybold, *Zephanja*, 114, 115–19; Renaud, *Sophonie*, 253–59; Rudolph, *Zephanja*, 297–300; Vlaardingerbroek, *Zephaniah*, 194.

the promise of such restoration would play an important role in the persuasive goals of the present text insofar as such an idyllic scenario would prompt the late-seventh-century Judean audience to conclude that support for the king's program represented a ripe opportunity to restore Judah's—and Israel's—sovereignty and greatness. In view of the passage's dependence on the hymn or psalm of praise genre, the sociohistorical setting for this passage, and indeed for the book of Zephaniah as a whole, must be sought in the early years of Josiah's reform. Although the exact relation of the prophets to the temple ritual is not entirely certain in the period of the late monarchy,[9] it seems likely that Zephaniah's oracles were delivered either as a formal part of a temple liturgy that was designed to support the king's reform program or in association with formal temple worship; that is, the prophet employed liturgical genres to deliver his oracles at a time for cultic observance at the temple.

■ **14** Verse 14 constitutes a version of the formal summons to praise that is characteristic of the hymns or psalms of praise that were performed as part of the temple liturgy to give praise to YHWH.[10] The passage employs four imperatives that call on the addressees to sing/shout for joy, shout/blow a trumpet, rejoice, and exult as a result of YHWH's actions on behalf of Jerusalem/Israel that will be outlined in the subsequent verses of the passage. The verbs appear to be characteristic of the typical summons, and they occur often in prophetic texts that are rooted in the hymns.

The first verb, רָנִּי, "sing, shout for joy," is a *qal* feminine singular imperative form of the root רנן directed to

the feminine singular "Daughter Zion." Normally, the Psalms employ *piel* forms of this verb (Pss 5:12; 67:5; 90:14; 92:5; 98:4; 149:5; 132:9; 145:7; 132:16; 51:16; 59:17; 33:1; 20:6; 63:8; 89:13; 95:1; 84:3; 96:12 [= 1 Chr 16:33]; 98:8; 71:23), and the *piel* form appears in some prophetic texts as well (Jer 31:12; 51:48; Isa 26:19; 35:2; 52:8), all of which have cultic associations. Otherwise, the *qal* form of the verb appears only once in the Psalms (Ps 35:27),[11] but it appears frequently in prophetic contexts (Jer 31:7; Isa 12:6; 24:14; 54:1; 44:23; 49:13; 42:11; 35:6; 61:7; Zech 2:14), which suggests that the *qal* form is characteristic of prophetic attempts to emulate the hymn rather than of the hymn itself.[12]

The second verb, הָרִיעוּ, "shout, blow a trumpet," is a *hiphil* masculine plural imperative form of the root רוע directed to the collective addressee Israel. Although the verb appears in a number of Psalms that praise YHWH (Pss 47:2; 66:1; 81:2; 95:1, 2; 98:4, 6; 100:1; cf. 41:12) and in narratives that relate such contexts (1 Sam 4:5; Ezra 3:11, 13), it appears to be quite at home in narratives and other texts that depict battle and triumph over enemies (e.g., Josh 6:5, 10, 16, 20; Judg 7:21; 1 Sam 17:52; Isa 42:13; 2 Chr 13:12, 15; Num 10:7, 9; Hos 5:8; Joel 2:1; Jer 50:15). Insofar as v. 15 specifically points to YHWH's turning aside Jerusalem's/Israel's enemies as a basis for praise, the context appears to provide the basis for the choice of this verb.

The paired feminine singular imperatives שִׂמְחִי וְעָלְזִי, "rejoice and exult," here directed to "Daughter Jerusalem," appear elsewhere only in Jer 50:11, where they depict the rejoicing of Babylonians who plunder Israel

---

9   By the time of the Second Temple, prophets appear to have played a formal role in the performance of the temple liturgy (see Raymond Jacques Tournay, *Seeing and Hearing God with the Psalms: The Prophetic Liturgy of the Second Temple in Jerusalem* [JSOTSup 118; Sheffield: Sheffield Academic Press, 1991]; David L. Petersen, *Late Israelite Prophecy: Studies in Deutero-Prophetic Literature and in Chronicles* [SBLMS 23; Missoula, Mont.: Scholars Press, 1977]). Various images of prophets as oracle diviners, e.g., Moses (Exod 32:7-11; 34:29-35), Samuel (1 Samuel 1–3), Isaiah (Isaiah 37), and Ezekiel (Ezek 14:1), suggest some relationship to the temple, but the evidence is ambiguous. Moses, Isaiah, and Ezekiel appear to be located outside the tabernacle or temple precincts. Jeremiah's famous temple sermon (Jeremiah 7) may

have been possible because of his identity as an Elide priest rather than as a prophet. Nevertheless, Samuel's activities at Shiloh and the presumption that Amos was a professional prophet at Bethel (see Amos 7:10-17) suggest some role for prophetic activity in the temple precincts.

10   Gerstenberger, *Psalms, Part 1,* 16–19; Crüsemann, *Studien*; Claus Westermann, *Praise and Lament in the Psalms* (Atlanta: John Knox, 1981).

11   Cf. Lam 2:19, where the verb is employed in reference to crying out in distress.

12   Cf. Ben Zvi, *Zephaniah,* 239.

and Judah. Otherwise, the verbs appear individually in a variety of contexts as basic terms to express joy and exultation. The verb שמח depicts religious rejoicing in Pss 21:2; 32:11; 9:3; 48:12; 119:74; 96:11; 97:1; 1 Sam 2:1; Deut 12:7, 12, 18; 16:11; 27:7; 1 Sam 11:15; Joel 2:23; 2 Chr 29:36; 1 Chr 29:9; 16:10, 31; Isa 9:2; Lev 23:40. The verb עלז appears in similar contexts in Pss 149:5; 68:5; 28:7; Hab 3:18.

The feminine characterization of the addressees as "Daughter Zion" and "Daughter Jerusalem" takes up a characteristic ancient Mediterranean depiction of a city as a woman or the bride of a deity.[13] Cities and nations are characteristically designated in this fashion throughout the Bible, for example, "daughter Tyre" (Ps 45:13), "daughter Babel" (Isa 47:1; Zech 2:11), "daughter Tarshish" (Isa 23:10), "daughter Sidon" (Isa 23:12), "daughter Dibon" (Jer 48:18), and "daughter Edom" (Lam 4:21, 22). The expression "Daughter Zion" as a designation for Jerusalem appears in Isa 1:8; 10:32; 16:1; 62:11; Mic 1:13; 4:8, 10, 13; Jer 4:31; 6:2, 23; Zech 2:14; 9:9; Ps 9:15; Lam 1:6; 2:1, 4; 4:22; cf. Lam 2:8, 10, 13, 18; 2 Kgs 19:21; Isa 37:22; 52:2. The expression "Daughter Jerusalem" appears in 2 Kgs 19:21; Isa 37:22; Mic 4:8; Lam 2:13, 15. The characterization of the city in this fashion also draws on the traditions of Israel as YHWH's bride (cf. Hosea 1–3; Jeremiah 2; Ezekiel 16; Isaiah 49–54), especially since YHWH's rejoicing over the redeemed Jerusalem is portrayed in explicitly sexual terms in v. 17b.

The imagery focuses especially on Jerusalem as the addressee, which points to Josiah's interest in the purging of the city to serve as the holy center of the nation and the world, but the reference to Israel as addressee is also noteworthy. Although the inconsistency in gender appears to have agitated the LXX translator, who rendered "Israel" here as "Daughter Jerusalem" in keeping with the concluding reference to the addressee in the verse, the choice of "Israel" here appears to be deliberate. The ideology of Jerusalem as the site of the temple and the holy center of Israel of course demands such a choice, as the restoration of the city is the necessary prerequisite for the restoration of the nation at large.[14] In that Josiah's reform was intended to lead to the purification and restoration of Jerusalem as a prelude to the restoration of Davidic rule over all Israel, the reference to the masculine Israel together with the feminine "Daughter Zion" and "Daughter Jerusalem" appears to make eminent sense.

■ 15 Verse 15 introduces the second component of this textual block that takes up the reasons why the audience should rejoice and praise YHWH. Although many scholars see vv. 14-15 as a single unit distinct from vv. 16-20, v. 15 both provides the fundamental reason for praise of YHWH and introduces vv. 16-20, which elaborate on it.[15]

Verse 15 begins with the statement that "YHWH has removed your judgment (מִשְׁפָּטַיִךְ)." Although the term מִשְׁפָּט can convey a variety of meanings related to judgment or justice, such as "law," "justice," "judgment," "court case," and so on, the context requires that it signify legal judgment or the execution of sentence against the city of Jerusalem or Israel at large (cf. 3:8; Deut 32:41; Isa 4:4; Ezek 5:8; Hos 5:1, 11; 10:4; cf. Exod 21:1, 31; 24:3; Deut 7:12).[16] The statement thereby characterizes the suffering endured by Jerusalem/Israel at the hands of the Assyrians during the eighth-seventh centuries as a legal judgment or punishment by YHWH for wrongs committed in the past. Indeed, such a conceptualization is entirely consistent with prophetic traditions that understand disaster to be a form of punishment

13   See Klaus Baltzer, "Stadt-Tyche oder Zion-Jerusalem," in Jutta Hausmann and Hans-Jürgen Zobel, eds., Alttestamentlicher Glaube und biblische Theologie. Festschrift für Horst Dietrich Preuss (Stuttgart: Kohlhammer, 1992) 114–19.

14   See Levenson, "Temple"; idem, Sinai.

15   See Striek, Zephanjabuch, 210–16; Floyd, Minor Prophets, 239–40; Vlaardingerbroek, Zephaniah, 193–94; Weigl, Zefanja, 218; Edler, Kerygma, 60–66; Ben Zvi, Zephaniah, 322–25; Seybold, Zephanja, 115; Günter Krinetzki, Zefanjastudien: Motiv- und Traditionskritik + Kompositions- und Redaktionskritik

(Regensburger Studien zur Theologie 7; Frankfurt am Main: Lang, 1977) 36; Rudolph, Zephanja, 297; Horst, Propheten, 199; Elliger, Zephanja, 77; J. M. P. Smith, Zephaniah, 256; Schwally, "Sefanjâ," 205–10.

16   For discussion see Hans-Joachim Boecker, Redeformen des Rechtslebens im Alten Testament (2d ed.; WMANT 14; Neukirchen-Vluyn: Neukirchener Verlag, 1970).

brought upon the nation by YHWH (see the so-called trial speeches in Isaiah 1; Jeremiah 2; Hosea 4; Micah 6).[17] In this case, however, the prophet maintains that YHWH has removed or reversed the sentence, which indicates that the period of judgment is fulfilled or at least at an end (cf. Isa 40:2, which expresses similar notions concerning the fulfillment of Israel's punishment). Although some have attempted to understand the term as a plural,[18] such an understanding is unnecessary as a single judgment or sentence can account for Jerusalem's/Israel's suffering at the hands of the Assyrians. It is noteworthy that the LXX and TJ read this term as a plural, but both are interpretive. The LXX reads the statement as, "The L-rd is stripping off your iniquities (τὰ ἀδικήματα σου)," which understands it as a reference to Jerusalem's sins rather than to its punishment (cf. Peshitta). Targum Jonathan reads, "YHWH has exiled the false judges from your midst," which likewise elliptically reads the verse as a reference to those within the city who sinned rather than to the city's punishment.

The statement that YHWH "has turned aside your enemy" provides a parallel, especially since prophetic texts presuppose YHWH's actions to raise up a foreign enemy to execute judgment against Israel (e.g., Isaiah 5). In this case, the removal of the enemy coincides with the removal of judgment against the nation. Although there have been attempts to emend the singular אֹיְבֵךְ, "your enemy," to a plural in keeping with the reading of the Murabbaʿat manuscript, LXX, and Peshitta, such an emendation is unnecessary, as Assyria was the major agent of Israel's and Judah's oppression throughout the late eighth and seventh centuries. At the time of Josiah's reign, the anticipated downfall of Assyria provided the impetus for restoration and the perception that YHWH was acting to restore Jerusalem and Israel.[19]

The statement that "the King of Israel, YHWH, is in your midst," provides the rationale for the two prior statements concerning the elimination of the nation's judgment and enemy. Clearly, the image of the (human) king's presence in the city conveys a sense of security in the ancient world, which is metaphorically employed to depict YHWH's protection of Jerusalem from danger. Of course, such a depiction of the divine king in the city would coincide nicely with the restoration or reassertion of Davidic royal authority in the time of Josiah; that is, Josiah's royal presence and protection in the city represents YHWH's royal presence and protection in keeping with the basic postulates of Davidic ideology (see Psalm 2; 2 Samuel 7). Curiously, however, such a statement presupposes divine absence at a time of judgment. This notion is implicit in the earlier Isaian tradition, in which the prophet states that YHWH will hide the divine face from Israel at a time when the nation was suffering invasion from the Assyrians (Isa 8:17). It likewise appears in the later Ezekiel tradition, which portrays YHWH's abandonment of the Jerusalem Temple as part of a larger depiction of judgment and the destruction of Jerusalem (see Ezekiel 8–11). Both traditions clearly address the problem of theodicy in that they both attempt to justify the suffering of Jerusalem/Israel and the failure of YHWH to protect as a consequence of sin. Much the same may be said for the present statement in Zephaniah; that is, YHWH returns to the city after having left it to its punishment for wrongdoing. In all cases, YHWH's absence and failure to protect is justified by the claim that the people had sinned. Such a claim entails that those who suffered must have deserved their punishment, but such theological justifications for suffering are coming under increasing questioning as a result of the modern experience of the Shoah or Holocaust. Modern theologians, including both Jews and Christians, are increasingly and justifiably reluctant to claim that suffering is the result of wrongdoing because such a contention would thereby entail that all who perished in the Shoah (or who suffered in other contexts) deserved their fate.[20] Although such theological premises might be questionable in the present, such

17   Sweeney, *Isaiah 1–39*, 541–42; Boecker, *Redeformen*; J. Harvey, *Le plaidoyer prophétique contre Israël après la rupture de l'alliance* (Montreal: Bellarmin, 1967); Kirsten Nielsen, *YHWH as Prosecutor and Judge* (JSOTSup 9; Sheffield: JSOT Press, 1978).

18   See Ben Zvi, *Zephaniah*, 242, for discussion and bibliography.

19   See ibid., 240–41, for discussion.

20   For discussion see, e.g., Steven Katz, *Post-Holocaust Dialogues* (New York: New York Univ. Press, 1985); Clark Williamson, *A Guest in the House of Israel* (Louisville: Westminster John Knox, 1992).

assertions in Zephaniah and the other prophets must be understood as attempts to assume responsibility for one's own fate, and thereby represent an attempt to chart a course of action, that is, observance of the will of YHWH, as a means to guard against such suffering in the future.

Finally, v. 15 concludes with a statement based in the formal reassurance formula, "you need not fear evil again." The reassurance formula, אַל תִּירָא, "do not fear," is a typical feature of the salvation oracle, which promises deliverance from adversity or future security (e.g., Gen 15:1; 35:17; 1 Sam 22:23; Isa 7:4-9; 37:6-7; 40:9; 41:10; Job 5:21-22).[21] In the present instance, it reinforces the prophet's message that the punishment of Jerusalem is now at an end and that the city is about to be restored to its proper role at the center of creation. As noted above, both the LXX and Peshitta read the verbal root ראה, "to see," rather than ירא, "to fear," that is, "you shall not see evil any longer." This reading entails only the elimination of the letter *yod* from תִּירָא, "you shall fear," so that the verb reads תִּרְאִי, "you shall see." Such a reading may be explained by the fact that the two verbs look and sound nearly alike.

■ **16** Verse 16 introduces a block of material in vv. 16-20 that elaborates on the prophet's preceding statement in v. 15 concerning the basis for his summons to praise in v. 14. Although many scholars have raised questions concerning the identity of the party that will speak the following words of comfort to Jerusalem,[22] the formulation of these verses indicates that the prophet is the speaker throughout and that he conveys both his own words of comfort to Zion in vv. 16aβ⁵⁻⁶-17 and those of YHWH in vv. 18-20bβ¹⁻⁴.

The verse begins with the prophet's introduction to his words and those by YHWH with a modified form of the typical בַּיּוֹם הַהוּא formula in v. 16aαβ¹⁻², "On that day, it will be said to Jerusalem." Many scholars have assumed that this formula is a clear sign of later redac-

tional activity,[23] and the manner in which the following statements by the prophet take up the themes of vv. 14-15, that is, the reassurance formula, the reference to YHWH's presence in the city's midst, and the general portrayal of rejoicing, has reinforced the conclusion that this material is the product of later redaction.[24] Such a view is unwarranted. The בַּיּוֹם הַהוּא formula is not a secure sign of later redaction. Such a conclusion is based on the view that many passages introduced by the formula in the preexilic prophetic books point to a future time of salvation in striking contrast to the themes of punishment that were taken to be characteristic of the "authentic" words of the preexilic prophets. In addition, such portrayals of salvation were taken to be eschatological visions that had little to do with the contemporary historical realities of the prophet in question. Such a view imposes a theological prejudgment that preexilic prophets could only speak messages of judgment and exilic or postexilic prophets spoke messages of salvation, because the historical experience of their respective periods warranted such statements. This is a rather wooden view of prophecy that conceives prophets as capable of speaking only about what has taken place in historical reality rather than about what is possible, and it certainly ignores the rhetorical or persuasive dimensions of prophetic speech; a portrayal of an idyllic future is frequently essential in order to enable the prophet to convince his/her audience that his/her message or assessment of the present situation is cogent. In the present case, Zephaniah attempts to convince his audience to accept and participate in Josiah's reform. An idyllic portrayal of Jerusalem's secure and peaceful future is essential to his efforts. It is hardly eschatological; instead, it speaks to the possibilities of peace that Jerusalemites of the seventh century would have longed for after years of Assyrian oppression.

21 See Sweeney, *Isaiah 1–39,* 547; Conrad, *Fear Not Warrior.*

22 E.g., Vlaardingerbroek, *Zephaniah,* 212; Keller, *Sophonie,* 214. Note that LXX indicates that YHWH will be the speaker, but this conflicts with the third person reference to YHWH in v. 17.

23 Most recently, DeVries, *From Old Revelation,* esp. 38–63, 203–5.

24 See Floyd, *Minor Prophets,* 243; Vlaardingerbroek, *Zephaniah,* 210; Ben Zvi, *Zephaniah,* 245–46; Renaud, *Sophonie,* 253–57; Rudolph, *Zephanja,* 298; Horst, *Propheten,* 200; Nowack, *Propheten,* 306.

Furthermore, a number of scholars have noted links between Zephaniah's use of the reassurance formula and the general portrayal of Jerusalem's restoration and that of Deutero-Isaiah and Joel as a basis for claiming that the Zephanian verses are dependent on the Isaian and Joel traditions (see Isa 41:10, 14; 43:1, 5; 44:1; 54:4; Joel 2:21).[25] Such an argument can hardly be employed, however, as recent studies have demonstrated conclusively both Deutero-Isaiah's and Joel's dependence on earlier tradition.[26] If there is a direct relationship between these texts, then Deutero-Isaiah and Joel are likely to be dependent on Zephaniah rather than vice versa.

Finally, the formula בַּיּוֹם הַהוּא hardly indicates an eschatological future. From a semantic perspective, the expression merely indicates a future time, not an eschatological event. Even though it may well point to the time of the realization of the Day of YHWH, the analysis of the Day of YHWH in Zephaniah 1 above indicates that the day would be realized with the success of Josiah's reform. It should be noted that the prophet's parenetic speech in 2:1–3:20 begins with references to the Day of YHWH in 2:1-3, and clearly indicates that his goal is to persuade his audience to accept his call to seek YHWH. In this case, seeking YHWH entails acceptance of the king's reform and restoration program, which is intended to restore Jerusalem to its role as the holy center of Israel and, by extension, of the world.

The prophet's own statement to Jerusalem then follows in vv. 16bβ[3-4]-17. One cannot be entirely certain whether he expects to utter these words himself to the city at the future time when its security will be realized or if he anticipates that someone else will make the statement, but the intensity and directness of his persuasive efforts throughout the book—and especially in 2:1–3:20—suggests that he expects an immediate response from his audience. This would of course entail that he would expect to see this time of restoration himself and that he would be able to utter these words. In any case, he utters them at the time that he makes his appeal to his audience. Although they repeat the themes of vv. 14-

15, as noted above, they seem to add relatively little to the preceding statements other than an extended portrayal of the scenario already described. This suggests that these statements are not the product of later redaction, that is, there is no effort here to modify or clarify the preceding statements, as is the case in the redactional material of v. 20 below (see the discussion of 3:20 and its relationship to 3:18-19 below). It merely serves the oral setting and persuasive goals of the prophet's speech insofar as he repeats his primary statements in order to drive home his point to the audience. Nothing of true substance changes from vv. 14-15 to vv. 16-17.

The prophet's statement begins with a reiteration of the reassurance formula, "Do not fear (אַל־תִּירְאִי), O Zion," from the prophet's earlier statement in v. 15bβ. As noted above, the reassurance formula is a typical feature of prophetic oracles of salvation, especially when the oracle announces deliverance from an enemy or other threat, in this case, the end of Assyrian oppression and the inauguration of Jerusalem's (and Israel's) restoration as an independent entity under YHWH and the Davidic king. The following statement, "do not let your hands be slack (אַל־יִרְפּוּ יָדָיִךְ)," employs an idiom that appears periodically throughout the Bible to express the need to take courage and act, whether in the face of adversity or in the face of opportunity (see 2 Sam 4:1; Isa 13:7; Jer 6:24; 50:43; Ezek 7:17; 21:12; Ezra 4:4; Neh 6:9; 2 Chr 15:7).[27] In the present instance, it provides a fitting complement to the prophet's early use of the reassurance formula. Since it focuses on the city's actions, it also serves the rhetorical goals of the passage by metaphorically calling on the audience to act.

■ 17 The prophet's words continue in v. 17 with a series of statements that speak of YHWH's presence in the city and the resulting joy of their renewed relationship.

The first statement, "YHWH, your G-d, is in your midst," reiterates the earlier statement of v. 15bα, "the King of Israel, YHWH, is in your midst." Whereas the earlier statement emphasized YHWH's role as king, v. 17 emphasizes YHWH's role as a saving hero by adding the

25 E.g., Striek, *Zephanjabuch,* 39–41.
26 Benjamin Sommer, *A Prophet Reads Scripture: Allusion in Isaiah 40–66* (Stanford: Stanford Univ. Press, 1998); Willey, *Remember;* Siegfried Bergler, *Joel als Schriftinterpret* (BEATAJ 16; Frankfurt am Main: Lang, 1988); Sweeney, *Twelve Prophets,* 145–87.
27 See Berlin, *Zephaniah,* 144; Vlaardingerbroek, *Zephaniah,* 213.

appellation גִּבּוֹר יוֹשִׁיעַ, "a warrior who delivers/brings victory."[28] Although interpreters are sometimes uncomfortable with the military connotations of such an expression,[29] especially in the context of a passage that speaks of the coming of peace, it must be recalled that the coming era of peace is the direct result of the impending downfall of the Assyrian Empire, which subjugated Judah and much of the rest of the ancient Near East by military force. The deliverance of Israel from Egypt at the time of the exodus or from Sisera and Hazor in the time of the judges is conceived in similar terms (see Exodus 15; Judges 5). Thus it is noteworthy that the book of Nahum, produced late in the reign of Josiah following the defeat of Nineveh by the Babylonians and Medes, likewise portrays YHWH as the powerful warrior who brought down this evil foe.[30] In this regard, the characterization of YHWH as a delivering warrior also relates well to the use of the reassurance formula, which appears frequently in contexts to reassure its addressee that a threat has passed (see Isa 7:4-9; 10:20-26).

Verse 17b then turns to the general rejoicing that will take place as YHWH and Jerusalem renew their relationship. The depiction employs general terms and images for joy and exultation, but the overall image is based in a marriage metaphor that depicts the reunion of husband, YHWH, and wife, Jerusalem, after a period of separation. The key to this image lies in the enigmatic statement of v. 17bα[4-5], יַחֲרִישׁ בְּאַהֲבָתוֹ, here translated as, "he plows with his love."[31] The problem with this statement lies in the interpretation of the verb חרשׁ, which can mean, "to be silent, dumb, speechless," or "to engrave, plow, devise." Most interpreters render the verb according to the first meaning. Ben Zvi identifies three primary possibilities: (1) the love of G-d is too tender for expression; (2) G-d will be satisfied, that is, at rest or silent; and (3) G-d is silent concerning the sins of the people.[32] Although none of these proposals has provided a satisfactory explanation for YHWH's silent love at a time of exultation, scholars have been reluctant to look to the second meaning of the root חרשׁ because of difficulties in relating the meaning "to engrave," "to plow," "to devise" to the context of love and celebration. The difficulties with the term are so great that the LXX and Peshitta read the verb as חרשׁ, "to renew," so that the phrase reads, "he will renew (you) with his love." Of course, such a reading requires the introduction of "you" as the object of the verb. No object is attested in the Hebrew text, and the Murabbaʿat scroll confirms the reading of the root חרשׁ.

The metaphorical dimensions of the term חרשׁ, however, need to be considered. The term is employed metaphorically for plowing with a number of different meanings. Thus Hos 10:11 states, "Judah must plow, Jacob must harrow for himself," in a context in which YHWH calls for Judah and Israel to take action to act righteously rather than contrary to YHWH's will. The ethical connotations thus become clear in Hos 10:13, "you have plowed wickedness, you have reaped injustice." Likewise, Job 4:8 reads, "As I have seen, those who plow iniquity and sow trouble reap the same." Ps 129:3 employs the term as an expression for oppression: "the plowers plowed upon my back, they made furrows long." Most interesting for the present passage is Samson's accusation in Judg 14:18 that the Philistines had discovered the meaning of his riddle from his wife: "If you had not plowed with my heifer, you would not have found out my riddle." Here the term clearly conveys interaction between the Philistine men and his Philistine wife, and even suggests Samson's belief that something more than

---

28 This translation presupposes an implicit relative clause between the two expressions, the absence of which is often a characteristic of archaic or archaizing poetry. See GKC, §155a-n, which characterizes this syntactical feature as coordination rather than as the omission of the relative pronoun.

29 Cf., e.g., Ben Zvi, *Zephaniah*, 247–49.

30 For analysis of Nahum, see Marvin A. Sweeney, "Concerning the Structure and Generic Character of the Book of Nahum," *ZAW* 104 (1992) 364–77; idem, *King Josiah*, 198–207; idem, *Twelve Prophets*, 417–49.

31 See also Marvin A. Sweeney, "Metaphor and Rhetorical Strategy in Zephaniah," in Timothy Sandoval and Carleen Mandolfo, eds., *Relating to the Text: Interdisciplinary and Form-Critical Insights on the Bible* (JSOTSup; Sheffield: Sheffield Academic Press, forthcoming).

32 Ben Zvi, *Zephaniah*, 251.

mere conversation, perhaps with intimations of a sexual relationship, had passed between them.[33] In all cases, the term conveys some form of action other than plowing on the part of its subjects. Given the metaphorical dimensions of the verb חרשׁ, especially in relation to the interaction between the Philistine men and Samson's wife, and the general scenario of rejoicing and the renewal of the relationship between the "warrior" YHWH and the clearly female "Daughter Zion" of 3:14-20, it seems reasonable to conclude that the expression, "he plows with his love," expresses the renewal of that relationship. Such a conceptualization would draw on the well-known tradition of Israel/Zion as YHWH's bride to portray YHWH's return to his long-forsaken bride (see Hosea 2; Jeremiah 2; Isaiah 49–54; Ezekiel 16).[34] It would also contrast markedly to YHWH's "expulsion" or "divorce" of the Philistine cities noted above in 2:4.[35]

■ **18** The prophet's presentation of YHWH's statements to Jerusalem begins in v. 18. Although YHWH's identity as the speaker is clear from the first person formulation of the speech in vv. 18-20, the concluding YHWH speech formula at the end of v. 20 indicates that the prophet is the primary speaker who conveys YHWH's words.

YHWH's speech represents an attempt to grapple theologically with the realities of Judah's and Israel's subjugation and suffering during the Assyrian period in light of the decline of Assyrian power. Overall, it attempts to justify Assyria's domination of Judah from the latter portion of the eighth century through the mid-seventh century by claiming that the Assyrians were brought by YHWH as a means to punish Judah for purported wrongdoing. But with the decline of Assyrian power, YHWH's speech asserts that the time of punishment is over, Jerusalem and Judah have paid their debts, and the time for restoration is at hand, requiring that the city be purged of any lingering wrongdoing so that the city may resume its role at the center of creation.

Verse 18 provides the introduction to YHWH's speech by asserting that those who had suffered punishment or exile were to be considered as a sort of sacrifice or offering that was presumably necessary to purge the city of its sins. Indeed, v. 18 is one of the most difficult statements in the book of Zephaniah, and it has provoked a wide variety of readings both among the ancient versions of the book and its modern interpreters,[36] but a close examination of the forms of expression employed within the verse makes this understanding clear.

Problems emerge at the outset of the verse in relation to the expression נוּגֵי מִמּוֹעֵד, which is generally understood as a reference to cultic celebration based on the appearance of the term מוֹעֵד, "appointed time, festival."[37] The term נוּגֵי conveys suffering or oppression, as

---

33 Cf. Tammi J. Schneider, *Judges* (Berit Olam; Collegeville, Minn.: Liturgical Press, 2000), 211.

34 For discussion of the various iterations of these images and traditions, see Yvonne Sherwood, *The Prostitute and the Prophet: Hosea's Marriage in Literary-Theoretical Perspective* (JSOTSup 212; GCT 2; Sheffield: Sheffield Academic Press, 1996); Marie-Theres Wacker, *Figurationen des Weiblichen im Hosea-Buch* (Herders biblische Studien 8; Freiburg: Herder, 1996); A. R. Pete Diamond and Kathleen M. O'Connor, "Unfaithful Passions: Coding Women Coding Men in Jeremiah 2-3 (4.2)," in A. R. Pete Diamond, Kathleen M. O'Connor, and Louis Stuhlman, eds., *Troubling Jeremiah* (JSOTSup 260; Sheffield: Sheffield Academic Press, 2000) 123–45; Patricia Tull Willey, "The Servant of YHWH and Daughter of Zion: Alternating Visions of YHWH's Community," *SBLSP, 1995* (ed. Eugene H. Lovering Jr.; Atlanta: Scholars Press, 1995) 267–303; Julie Galambush, *Jerusalem in the Book of Ezekiel: The City as YHWH's Wife* (SBLDS 130; Atlanta: Scholars

Press, 1992). See also Marvin A. Sweeney, "On *ûmᵉśôś* in Isaiah 8.6," in Phillip R. Davies and David J. A. Clines, eds., *Among the Prophets: Language, Image and Structure in the Prophetic Writings* (JSOTSup 144; Sheffield: Sheffield Academic Press, 1993) 42–54, which notes similar images pertaining to rape in Isa 8:6-8 and marriage in Isa 66:10-14, both of which employ forms of the root שׂושׂ, "to rejoice," as in Zeph 3:17.

35 See Zalcman, "Ambiguity," and the discussion of 2:4 above.

36 For an overview of ancient and modern readings of this verse, see esp. Ball, *Zephaniah,* 187–93.

37 See further Sweeney, "Metaphor."

it is a *niphal* masculine plural construct particle derived from the root יגה, which can mean "to suffer, be aggrieved" (cf. Lam 1:4), or "to be thrust away, expelled" (cf. the *hiphil* form of this verb in 2 Sam 20:13). Although the appearance of the preposition מִן, "from," with מוֹעֵד is unusual in a construct relationship, it is possible in Hebrew (cf. Gen 3:22; Isa 28:9; Jer 23:23; Ezek 13:2; Hos 7:5).[38] The resulting translation, "those who were aggrieved/thrust out from the festival,"[39] however, seems to make little sense in the present context, especially when read in relation to the following statement, אָסַפְתִּי מִמֵּךְ, "I have gathered from you." Various attempts have been made to follow the LXX and Peshitta, which read the phrase in relation to v. 17,[40] but difficulties in reconciling the image of those who suffer with the rejoicing depicted in v. 17 demonstrate the futility of such efforts.

Consideration of the following material is essential for a proper reading of this verse, particularly the verb הָיוּ, "they were." Following the expression אָסַפְתִּי מִמֵּךְ, this verb has caused considerable difficulties, since it seems to have been left hanging without an appropriate referent. Consequently, the LXX and TJ, despite their other differences, agree in reading the verb as the particle הוֹי, "Woe, Alas!" which requires the transposition of the letters *waw* and *yod*. Of course, such a reading is probably interpretive, as the Murabbaʿat manuscript appears to confirm the reading of the verb.[41]

Nevertheless, one should note that the expression נוּגֵי מִמּוֹעֵד provides the only possible subject for the verb הָיוּ. This would suggest that the basic phrase was meant to read, "Those who are aggrieved/have suffered from the appointed time/festival . . . were. . . ." Such a reading of course raises questions concerning the role of the phrase אָסַפְתִּי מִמֵּךְ, "I punished you," literally, "I have gathered from you." As noted in the discussion of the verb אסף in 1:2, 3; 3:8, it clearly refers to YHWH's actions to punish, destroy, or remove those who are sub-

ject to divine judgment. The second person feminine singular pronoun would have to refer to Jerusalem in keeping with the overall context of 3:14-20. Such an understanding suggests that the phrase is intended to modify the preceding נוּגֵי מִמּוֹעֵד; it refers to those who are aggrieved or who have suffered as those whom YHWH has "gathered from you" or those in Jerusalem whom YHWH has punished. This would require a relative pronoun, but we have already observed in the expression גִּבּוֹר יוֹשִׁיעַ, "a warrior who delivers," in v. 17 above that the writer of this passage is capable of dispensing with the relative pronoun. Thus the phrase would read, "those who are aggrieved/have suffered from the appointed time/festival which I gathered from you were . . . ," which remains somewhat difficult. Further observations are in order.

Although many have understood מוֹעֵד to refer to a festival,[42] the term itself means simply "appointed time," which can refer to festivals or to other fixed times, such as the time that YHWH will return to Abraham and Sarah (Gen 17:21; 18:14; 21:2), the appointed place of battle between Israel and Ai (Josh 8:14), the time appointed for waiting by Samuel (1 Sam 13:8), the time that the Shunammite woman will bear a son (2 Kgs 4:6, 17), the appointed times of the stork (Jer 8:7), the time that Habakkuk's vision will be realized (Hab 2:3), and the appointed time of the end (Dan 8:19; 11:27, 29, 35). Clearly, the term refers to appointed times of importance other than festivals. The last two examples are especially important because both appear in reference to times of divine judgment or intervention in human affairs. Such an understanding is particularly important in relation to the phrase אָסַפְתִּי מִמֵּךְ, "I punished/gathered from you," which also refers to divine judgment in Zephaniah. This would suggest that both phrases refer to those who suffered judgment from YHWH in the book of Zephaniah, that is, נוּגֵי מִמּוֹעֵד refers to those who suffered punishment or exile at YHWH's appointed time of

---

38 GKC, §130a; Vlaardingerbroek, *Zephaniah*, 215.

39 Such a reading is adopted by TJ, which reads the verse as an indictment of those who obstructed the proper observance of the festivals of Judaism in the late Second Temple period. For discussion of this reading, see Robert P. Gordon, *Studies in the Targum to the Twelve Prophets: From Nahum to Malachi* (VTSup 51; Leiden: Brill, 1994) 49–52.

40 E.g., Gerleman, *Zephanja*, 63.

41 Note, however, that there is a gap in the MS at this point, leaving only a disputed reading of the final letter *waw* (see Milik, *Murabbaʿat*, 202).

42 E.g., Ben Zvi, *Zephaniah*, 253.

judgment, and אָסַפְתִּי מִמֵּךְ refers to them as those who were gathered by YHWH. Thus the phrase would read, "those who have suffered from the appointed time when I punished/gathered from you were. . . ."

The conclusion of the statement remains to be considered. Clearly, the noun מַשְׂאֵת, "burden," stands as the predicate noun of the verb הָיוּ, so that those who suffered from the appointed time of YHWH's punishment are identified as a "burden." This expression has also prompted difficulties, in part because of the following expression ("upon her a reproach") and because the exact significance of a burden in the context of a passage that calls for rejoicing is unclear. Derived from the root נשׂא, "to rise, lift up," the term is often employed in reference to more specialized meanings, such as a signal (Judg 20:38; Jer 6:1), the uplifting of hands in prayer (Ps 141:2), a portion of a meal carried to the table of a king or other superior (Gen 43:34; 2 Sam 11:8; 19:43; Jer 40:5; Esth 2:18), an enforced gift or tax (Amos 5:11), and offerings, taxes, or sacred contributions (2 Chr 24:6, 9; Ezek 20:40). These last several meanings are particularly important for the present context because they indicate the sense of a gift, tax, or offering that was made to YHWH. This would suggest that those who suffered punishment from YHWH in 3:18 are here conceived of as an offering or obligation paid to YHWH as part of the process of punishment that would ultimately purge the city.

Such a meaning certainly relates to the following phrase, עָלֶיהָ חֶרְפָּה, "upon her, a reproach," which apparently understands those who were punished by YHWH to constitute a reproach upon the city. Nevertheless, the phrase is problematic because its third person feminine singular reference to Jerusalem disrupts the pattern of second person feminine singular address forms employed for Jerusalem throughout the bulk of 3:14-20. Two explanations are possible. First, the phrase could be the prophet's own third person aside, which aids in explaining the significance of the preceding statement by YHWH. In such a case, the form of the statement would correspond to the prophet's introductory statement in v. 16aαβ[1-2], which he employs to introduce his own words and those of YHWH: "on that day it will be said to Jerusalem. . . ." Alternatively, the phrase is an

early gloss meant to specify the meaning of the term מַשְׂאֵת, which can be somewhat enigmatic as an offering to YHWH. The use of the term חֶרְפָּה, "reproach," would therefore reinforce the punitive connotations of the expression. Nevertheless, one should note that the Murabbaʿat manuscript includes the expression עליה חרפה.

In sum, v. 18 appears to rationalize YHWH's punishment or purge of Jerusalem and Judah in terms and imagery like that found in Zephaniah 1, that is, those who were punished and perhaps exiled from the land are considered as a sort of offering to YHWH, not unlike those who are to be sacrificed on the Day of YHWH in Zephaniah 1. Such a statement thereby prepares the audience to accept the punishment already suffered by the nations as an act of divine righteousness that prepares for the restoration or return of those punished and exiled in vv. 19-20. Of course, the assertion that those who were punished are to be considered as a sort of national offering would be rejected in modern theology in the aftermath of the Shoah and other tragedies. Nevertheless, the assertion here must be recognized as an attempt at theodicy, or maintaining the righteousness and efficaciousness of YHWH in the aftermath of a national tragedy in the eighth and seventh centuries; that is, the writer of Zephaniah chooses not to charge YHWH with wrongdoing as a means to explain Judah's suffering but to maintain that the nation itself was responsible for its experience.

■ **19** Having provided a rationale for the suffering of the nation, YHWH's speech then shifts to the coming scenario of restoration in vv. 19-20. Scholars frequently maintain that these verses are postexilic additions to the text because of both the threefold appearance of the temporal formula בָּעֵת הַהִיא, "at/in that time," which is understood as a reference to the time of the eschaton, and the general scenario of the return of Israel's and Judah's exiles, which could only presuppose the time of the restoration following the Babylonian exile.[43] Neither of these criteria alone, however, is sufficient to establish the postexilic dating of these verses. The expression בָּעֵת הַהִיא in and of itself does not convey eschatological content, but only refers to a time in the future. Likewise, as indicated above, seventh-century Judah would have

43   E.g., DeVries, *From Old Revelation*, 64–74, 202–5.

been quite concerned with the issue of returning exiles from both Israel and Judah as many fled the Assyrian invasions of the late eighth century and the oppression of anti-Assyrian elements in Judah during the early-seventh-century reign of Manasseh. Furthermore, many Judean territories, such as those in the Shephelah, had been stripped away by the Assyrians, and elements of the Israelite and Judean population had been resettled in areas such as Philistia, particularly the city of Ekron, where they were put to work by the Assyrians to produce olive oil for the empire. With the decline of Assyria in the mid-seventh century, the opportunity to restore those territories and people to a newly resurgent Davidic kingdom would have been of utmost concern.

Verse 19 begins with YHWH's statement, הִנְנִי עֹשֶׂה אֶת־כָּל־מְעַנַּיִךְ בָּעֵת הַהִיא, "Behold, I am dealing with/doing all those who oppress you in that time." This statement has caused considerable problems for interpreters from the time of the LXX, which renders the passage, "Behold, I am working in you for your sake in that day, says the L-rd." Since the basic text is supported by both the Murabbaʿat manuscript and 4QXII[b],[44] the LXX reading must be seen as an interpretive rendition that attempts to resolve problems in understanding the text.[45] Much the same may be said for TJ: "Behold, I am making a full end with all who were enslaving you at that time"; the Peshitta: "Behold, I am acting for all of them who were humbling/oppressing in your midst in that time"; and the Vulgate: "Behold, I am doing away with all who afflict in that time." Each version represents a different approach for interpreting the verb עשׂה, "doing," which constitutes the primary problem in interpreting this passage. Semantically speaking, the verb conveys simple action without specifying the nature of the action. Hence the LXX reads the verb as a reference to YHWH's

actions on behalf of Jerusalem, which appears to be the primary intent of the passage as a whole. Targum Jonathan reads the verb as a reference to YHWH's destruction of those who oppress Jerusalem, again in keeping with the general intent of the passage. The Peshitta and Vulgate took similar, although more literal, stances in coming to similar conclusions. Although the use of the verb is vague, Ezek 22:14 and 23:25 provide examples of the use of the verb עשׂה in reference to punitive action taken against the people of Judah.[46] Because of the semantic meaning of the verb, it appears to refer to "dealing with" someone. In the case of 3:19, the phrase is therefore best understood as a reference to YHWH's efforts to bring punishment upon Jerusalem's oppressors: "Behold, I am dealing with all who oppress you at that time."

The second phrase of this verse takes up the return of the exiles, here described as "the lame" (הַצֹּלֵעָה) and "the outcast/expelled" (הַנִּדָּחָה). Again, scholars have noted the similarity between this statement and that of Mic 4:6-7, "In that day, utterance of YHWH, 'I will gather the lame (הַצֹּלֵעָה), and the outcast (הַנִּדָּחָה) I will assemble, and those whom I have wronged, and I will make the lame for a remnant and the one who is far off for a strong nation,'" to argue for the late dating of Zeph 3:19 since the Zephanian text must be dependent on the Mican text.[47] An analysis of Micah 4–5, however, indicates that it is an exilic or postexilic text, as indicated by its own reference to exile in Babylonia (Mic 4:10) and by its use of other texts from Isa 2:2-4 in Mic 4:1-5 and Isa 2:6-21 in Mic 5:14.[48] If there is a deliberate intertextual association between the two texts, then Mic 4:6-7 would have to be dependent on Zeph 3:19 and not vice versa. In such a case, 3:19 could easily be considered a seventh-century text. In this regard, it is noteworthy that the

---

44 The text in 4QXII[b], however, is quite fragmentary, preserving only the largely uncertain, [אתכל מעניך]; see Fuller, "Twelve," 235 and plate XLIII.

45 Cf. Gerleman, *Zephanja*, 65, who claims that LXX is of no help.

46 See J. M. P. Smith, *Zephaniah*, 259 (who notes Ezek 23:29; Jer 21:2; and Ps 109:21 as well); Rudolph, *Zephanja*, 294; Ben Zvi, *Zephaniah*, 256; Berlin, *Zephaniah*, 147; Vlaardingerbroek, *Zephaniah*, 217; Renaud, *Sophonie*, 258 (who notes Ezek 23:29 as well); Roberts, *Zephaniah*, 221; cf. Gerleman,

Zephanja, 65, who noted the possibility offered by the use of the verb עשׂה in Ezek 22:14.

47 Ben Zvi, *Zephaniah*, 256–58.

48 For discussion see Sweeney, *Twelve Prophets*, 376–93.

terms הַצֹּלֵעָה and הַנִּדָּחָה are both formulated as feminine singular participles, that is, "she that is lame" and "she that is outcast," in keeping with the feminine singular characterization of Jerusalem as "Daughter Zion" and "Daughter Jerusalem" throughout 3:14-20. Similar characterization is employed for Jerusalem in Micah 4, although it does not become apparent until Mic 4:8, after the quotation of the terms in question.

The concluding phrase of the verse, "and I shall appoint them for praise and for renown [lit. 'a name'] in all the earth/land where they were shamed," presents an image of honor for the exiles that is designed to highlight the contrast between their new circumstances and their prior shamed and despised state. Some have noted that the expression וְשַׂמְתִּים, "and I will set/appoint them," is syntactically inconsistent because it employs a masculine plural suffix pronoun to refer to the two preceding feminine singular referents.[49] Consequently, they propose to take the final *mem* as an enclitic that points forward to בָּשְׁתָּם, "their shame," the concluding expression of v. 19. The statement would then read, "and I shall appoint their shame for praise and for renown in all the earth." The shift from feminine singular to masculine plural pronoun referents presents little problem since the characterization of Jerusalem in 3:14-20 includes both the feminine singular "Daughter Zion"/ "Daughter Jerusalem" and the masculine plural "Israel" (see 3:14). Although the "lame" and the "outcast" are formulated as feminine singular characters, they clearly serve as metaphors for all Israel throughout these verses; the use of the masculine plural pronominal suffixes in v. 19 simply makes this clear.

Finally, the concluding expression, בָּשְׁתָּם, "their shame," has also provoked discussion because of its potentially problematic syntactical role. One would expect that the expression would stand in a construct relationship with the preceding term, but this is impossible due to the presence of the definite article in the expression בְּכָל־הָאָרֶץ, "in all the land/earth." Nevertheless, TJ and the Vulgate read in this fashion. Alternatively, the expression could be an example of another case in which the relative pronoun is absent as in v. 17 ("a warrior who delivers") and v. 18 ("a burden, upon her a reproach") above. Peshitta chooses this approach:

"in all the land where they were shamed." The LXX translator, perhaps recognizing the difficulties in both approaches, read the phrase as the introduction to v. 20: "and they will be put to shame in that day. . . ." Nevertheless, the proposal noted above to read בָּשְׁתָּם in relation to the preceding וְשַׂמְתִּים appears to resolve the difficulty, despite its unusual syntactical structure. The notion that exile was a shame on the nation underlies the reference to the "reproach" that characterizes all who had suffered in v. 18. It may be that the present phrase provided motivation for the gloss in v. 18, as suggested above.

■ **20** Finally, v. 20 provides the climax for 3:14, and indeed for both the parenetic speech in 2:1—3:20 and even the book as a whole, by pointing to the future restoration and recognition of Jerusalem and the return of its exiles. It is striking that the verse reiterates v. 19 nearly point for point, although some differences are apparent. First, the addressee is characterized with second person masculine plural suffix pronouns in contrast to the feminine singular characterization of v. 19. Second, there is no sense of shame attached to the exiles or to those who have suffered. Third, the somewhat metaphorical references to the return of the nation's exiles in v. 19 are here made explicit. Altogether, it would appear that v. 20 clarifies the somewhat vaguely formulated and grammatically problematic v. 19 with clear, straightforward, and unproblematic statements that YHWH will restore the nation and its exiles. On the one hand, this could be a sign that v. 20 is a redactional gloss that was added to eliminate the uncertainties of v. 19. Alternatively, it is indeed the climax of the subunit 3:14-20 and the book as a whole that addresses the audience as Israel (cf. 3:14) directly in the masculine plural and states unambiguously that the nation will be restored and its exiles returned. Such a statement would naturally provide the climactic and concluding point in a parenetic speech that was designed to enlist the audience's support for King Josiah's program of national restoration and religious reform.

Scholars have noted the somewhat unusual appearance of the particle כִּי at the beginning of v. 20b.[50] Following the initial expression of v. 20a, "in that time I shall bring you in and the time when I gather you," the

---

49   E.g., Berlin, *Zephaniah*, 147; Sabottka, *Zephanja*, 139.   50   E.g., Vlaardingerbroek, *Zephaniah*, 218–19.

presence of the כִּי seems somewhat perplexing if it is to be taken in its usual causative sense. It should be noted, however, that the preceding statement is hardly complete, especially since the second element of the phrase is based on the infinitive construct קַבְּצִי, "(and in the time) when I gather (you)." Although infinitive constructs can function as finite verbs, the presence of the כִּי immediately following v. 20a may explain why the author chose an infinitive construct phrase for v. 20aβ in contrast to the finite verbal phrase of v. 20aα: "in that time I shall bring you." Given the infinitive construct formulation of v. 20aβ and its introductory conjunction, it can function syntactically only as an introduction to what follows.[51] In this case, the כִּי at the beginning of v. 20b must be an asseverative כִּי that conveys emphasis rather than causation: "and in the time when I gather you, indeed, I shall appoint you for renown and for praise among all the peoples of the earth." In this case, the כִּי emphasizes YHWH's promise to grant renown and praise to Israel when it is restored. Consequently, the first two statements are not vv. 20a and 20bα as indicated by the strophic arrangement of *BHS;* rather, the two basic elements are v. 20aα and 20aβ-bα, "in that time I shall bring you," and "in the time when I gather you, indeed, I shall appoint you for renown and for praise among all the peoples of the earth."

Two problems remain. First, the statement in v. 20aα, "in that time I shall bring you," has no indirect object;

that is, to where will YHWH bring you? The versions made various attempts to deal with this problem. The LXX reads, "and they shall be put to shame in that day when I will do good for you." Targum Jonathan reads, "at that time I will bring you in." Peshitta reads, "at that time I will bring you again." Vulgate allows the text to stand, "In that time I shall bring you." The Murabbaʿat text confirms the MT. Nevertheless, all of these readings must be considered as attempts to interpret the text rather than as witnesses to an original reading. Given the parallel in content between v. 20aα and 20aβ, this might suggest that v. 20aα was also meant to serve as an introductory temporal clause: "at the time (when) I shall bring you and at the time of my gathering you, indeed, I shall appoint you for renown and for praise among all the peoples of the earth." Second, a concluding temporal clause then follows as indicated by the use of the infinitive construct verb: "when I restore (בְּשׁוּבִי) your captivity/fortunes to your eyes."[52] This would suggest an attempt to specify the introductory references to "bring you" and "gather you" in relation to the restoration of the exiles and Jerusalem's fortunes so that no ambiguity remains. Israel's exiles are coming home.

Finally, as noted above, the concluding speech formula אָמַר ה׳, "says YHWH," together with the prophet's introductory statement in v. 16aαβ[1-2], identifies the whole of vv. 16-20 as a speech by the prophet in which he conveys both his own words and those of YHWH.

---

51 Cf. Roberts, *Zephaniah,* 221.

52 The problems associated with the expression "to restore captivity/fortunes" have been discussed in relation to Zeph 2:7 above. Note that the versions unanimously read the statement as a reference to the return of the exiles. Nevertheless, Job 42:10 indicates that the expression can refer more gener-

ally to a restoration of fortunes (cf. Berlin, *Zephaniah,* 148). It is noteworthy that, in contrast to Zeph 2:7, the Masoretes indicated no alternative reading for the expression שׁוּב שְׁבוּת. Ben Zvi, *Zephaniah,* 260, notes that the distinction in meaning between "restoring exiles" and "restoring fortunes" is "hardly significant."

Bibliography

1. Commentaries

J. Wellhausen
Die Kleinen Propheten (Berlin: de Gruyter, ³1898, ⁴1963).

Karl Marti
Das Dodekapropheton (KHAT XIII; Tübingen: Mohr [Siebeck], 1904).

A. van Hoonacker
Les Douze Petits Prophètes (EB; Paris: Gabalda, 1908).

John Merlin Powis Smith, William Hayes Ward, and Julius A. Bewer
A Critical and Exegetical Commentary on Micah, Zephaniah, Nahum, Habakkuk, Obadiah, and Joel (ICC; Edinburgh: T & T Clark, 1911, 1985).

W. Nowack
Die Kleinen Propheten (HKAT III/4; Göttingen: Vandenhoeck & Ruprecht, 1922).

Ernst Sellin
Das Zwölfprophetenbuch (2d-3d eds.; 2 vols.; KAT XII; Leipzig: Deichert, 1930).

Hubert Junker
Die Zwölf Kleinen Propheten. II. Hälfte: Nahum, Habakuk, Sophonia, Aggäus, Zacharias, Malachias (HSAT VIII/3.II; Bonn: Hanstein, 1938).

A. Cohen
The Twelve Prophets (Soncino Books of the Bible; London: Soncino, ¹1948, ²1957).

Karl Elliger
Die Propheten Nahum, Habakuk, Zephanja, Haggai, Sacharja, Maleachi (ATD 25/2; Göttingen: Vandenhoeck & Ruprecht, ¹1949, ⁸1982).

Charles L. Taylor Jr., and Howard Thurman
"The Book of Zephaniah," pp. 1005-34. In George Arthur Buttrick et al., eds., *The Interpreter's Bible*, vol. 6: *Lamentations; Ezekiel; Daniel; Hosea; Joel; Amos; Obadiah; Jonah; Micah; Nahum; Habakkuk; Zephaniah; Haggai; Zechariah; Malachi* (Nashville: Abingdon, 1956).

A. Deissler and M. Delcor
La sainte Bible. Tome VIII (1ʳᵉ partie): Les Petits Prophètes (Paris: Letouzey & Ané, 1961).

J. H. Eaton
Obadiah, Nahum, Habakkuk and Zephaniah (Torch Bible Commentaries; London: SCM, 1961).

Th. H. Robinson and F. Horst
Die Zwölf Kleinen Propheten (3d ed.; HAT 14; Tübingen: Mohr [Siebeck], 1964).

René Vuilleumier and Carl-A. Keller
Michée, Nahoum, Habacuc, Sophonie (CAT XIb; Neuchâtel: Delachaux et Niestlé, 1971).

Wilhelm Rudolph
Micha–Nahum–Habakuk–Zephanja (KAT XIII/3; Gütersloh: Mohn, 1975).

John D. W. Watts
The Books of Joel, Obadiah, Jonah, Nahum, Habakkuk and Zephaniah (Cambridge Bible Commentary; Cambridge: Cambridge Univ. Press, 1975).

A. S. van der Woude
Habakuk, Zefanja (POT; Nijkerk: Callenbach, 1978).

Ralph Smith
Micah–Malachi (WBC 32; Waco: Word, 1984).

Elizabeth Achtemeier
Nahum–Malachi (Interpretation; Atlanta: John Knox, 1986).

B. Renaud
Michée–Sophonie–Nahum (Sources bibliques; Paris: Gabalda, 1987).

Mária Eszenyei Széles
Habakkuk and Zephaniah: Wrath and Mercy (International Theological Commentary; Grand Rapids: Eerdmans, 1987).

Elizabeth Achtemeier
"Zephaniah," pp. 742-744. In James L. Mays et al., eds., *Harper's Bible Commentary* (San Francisco: Harper & Row, 1988).

Alfons Deissler
Zwölf Propheten III: Zefanja, Haggai, Sacharja, Maleachi (Die Neue Echter Bibel; Würzburg: Echter, 1988).

David W. Baker
Nahum, Habakkuk, Zephaniah (Tyndale Old Testament Commentaries; Downers Grove, Ill.; InterVarsity Press, 1988).

O. Palmer Robertson
The Books of Nahum, Habakkuk, and Zephaniah (New International Commentary on the Old Testament; Grand Rapids: Eerdmans, 1990).

J. J. M. Roberts
Nahum, Habakkuk, and Zephaniah (OTL; Louisville: Westminster John Knox, 1991).

Klaus Seybold
Nahum, Habakuk, Zephanja (ZBK 24.2; Zürich: Theologischer Verlag, 1991).

Adele Berlin
Zephaniah (AB 25A; New York: Doubleday, 1994).

Robert A. Bennett
"The Book of Zephaniah," pp. 657-704. In Leander E. Keck et al., eds., *The New Interpreter's Bible*, vol. 7: *Introduction to Apocalyptic Literature; Daniel; Additions to Daniel; Hosea; Joel; Amos; Obadiah; Jonah; Micah; Nahum; Habakkuk; Zephaniah; Haggai; Zechariah; Malachi* (Nashville: Abingdon, 1996).

William P. Brown

Obadiah through Malachi (Westminster Bible Companion; Louisville: Westminster John Knox, 1996).

Johannes Vlaardingerbroek

Zephaniah (Historical Commentary on the Old Testament; Leuven: Peeters, 1999).

Michael H. Floyd

Minor Prophets, Part 2 (FOTL 22; Grand Rapids: Eerdmans, 2000).

Marvin A. Sweeney

The Twelve Prophets (2 vols.; Berit Olam: Collegeville, Minn.: Liturgical Press, 2000).

Margaret S. Odell

"Zephaniah," pp. 671–74. In James L. Mays et al., eds., *HarperCollins Bible Commentary* (New York: HarperSanFranciso, 2000).

2. Text Editions

Allegro, John M. *Qumrân Cave 4. I (4Q158–4Q186).* DJD 5. Oxford: Clarendon, 1968.

Barthélemy, D., J. T. Milik, et al. *Qumran Cave I.* DJD 1. Oxford: Clarendeon, 1955.

Benoit, P., O.P., J. T. Milik, and R. de Vaux. *Les Grottes de Murabbaʿat.* 2 vols. DJD 2. Oxford: Clarendon, 1961.

Dold, Alban. *Prophetentexte in Vulgata-Übersetzung nach der ältesten Handschriften-Überlieferung der St. Galler Palimpseste No 193 und No 567.* Texte und Arbeiten I.1/2. Beuron: Erzabtei Beuron, 1917.

Elliger, Karl, and Wilhelm Rudolph. *Biblia Hebraica Stuttgartensia.* 3d ed. Stuttgart: Deutsche Bibelanstalt, 1987.

Heisz, Abr. *Eine anonyme arabische Uebersetzung und Erklärung der Propheten Zephanja, Haggai und Zecharja.* Berlin: Itzkowski, 1902.

Löfgren, Oscar. *Jona, Nahum, Habakuk, Zephanja, Haggai, Sacharja, und Maleachi Äthiopisch.* Uppsala: Almqvist & Wiksells, 1930.

Mason, Rex. *Zephaniah, Habakkuk, Joel.* OTG. Sheffield: JSOT Press, 1994.

Pauli, Ioannis, PP. II. *Biblia Sacra iuxta latinam vulgatam versionem ad codicum fidem. Liber Duodecim Prophetarum.* Rome: Libreria Editrice Vaticana, 1987.

Peshitta Institute, The. *Vetus Testamentum Syriace iuxta simplicem syrorum versionen. Pars III, fasciculus iv: Dodekapropheton-Daniel-Bel-Draco.* Leiden: Brill, 1980.

Rahlfs, Alfred. *Septuaginta.* 2 vols. Stuttgart: Württembergische Bibelanstalt, 1935.

Sperber, Alexander. *The Bible in Aramaic.* Vol. 3: *The Latter Prophets according to Targum Jonathan.* Leiden: Brill, 1962.

Till, Walter C. *Die Achmîmische Version der Zwölf Kleinen Propheten (Codex Rainerianus, Wien).* Hauniae: Gyldendalske Boghandel-Nordisk Forlag, 1927.

Tov, Emanuel, et al. *The Greek Minor Prophets Scroll from Naḥal Ḥever (8ḤevXIIgr).* DJD 8; Oxford: Clarendon, 1990.

Ulrich, Eugene, et al. *Qumran Cave 4. X: The Prophets.* DJD 15. Oxford: Clarendon, 1997.

Weber, Robertus. *Biblia Sacra iuxta vulgatum versionem.* Stuttgart: Deutsche Bibelanstalt, 1969.

Ziegler, Joseph. *Septuaginta: Vetus Testamentum Graecum.* Vol. 13: *Duodecim Prophetae.* 3d ed. Göttingen: Vandenhoeck & Ruprecht, 1984.

3. General Studies

Anderson, George W. "The Idea of the Remnant in the Book of Zephaniah." *ASTI* 11 (1977–78) 11–14.

Anderson, R. W., Jr. "Zephaniah ben Cushi and Cush of Benjamin: Traces of Cushite Presence in Syria-Palestine," pp. 45–70. In Steven W. Holloway and Lowell K. Handy, eds. *The Pitcher Is Broken: Memorial Essays for Gösta W. Ahlström.* JSOTSup 190. Sheffield: Sheffield Academic Press, 1995.

Bacher, W. "Zu Zephanja 2,4." *ZAW* 11 (1891) 185–86.

Bachmann, J. "Zur Textkritik des Propheten Zephanja." *ThStK* 67 (1894) 641–55.

Ball, Ivan J., Jr. "The Rhetorical Shape of Zephaniah," pp. 155–65. In Edgar W. Conrad and E. G. Newing, eds. *Perspectives on Language and Text: Essays and Poems in Honor of Francis I. Andersen's Sixtieth Birthday.* Winona Lake, Ind.: Eisenbrauns, 1987.

——. *Zephaniah: A Rhetorical Study.* Berkeley: BIBAL, ¹1972, ²1988.

Barthélemy, Dominique. *Les Devanciers d'Aquila.* VTSup 10. Leiden: Brill, 1963.

——, et al. *Critique textuelle de l'ancien Testament. Tome 3: Ézéchiel, Daniel et les 12 Prophètes.* OBO 50/3. Göttingen: Vandenhoeck & Ruprecht, 1992.

Barton, John. "The Canonical Meaning of the Book of the Twelve," pp. 59–73. In J. Barton and D. J. Reimer, eds., *After the Exile: Essays in Honour of Rex Mason.* Macon, Ga.: Mercer Univ. Press, 1996.

Ben Zvi, Ehud. *A Historical-Critical Study of the Book of Zephaniah.* BZAW 198. Berlin: de Gruyter, 1991.

Berlin, Adele. "Zephaniah's Oracles against the Nations and an Israelite Cultural Myth," pp. 175–84. In Astrid B. Beck et al., eds. *Fortunate the Eyes That See: Essays in Honor of David Noel Freedman.* Grand Rapids: Eerdmans, 1995.

Bewer, Julius A. "Textual Suggestions on Isa. 2:6, 66:3, Zeph. 2:2, 5." *JBL* 27 (1908) 163–66.

Bič, Miloš. *Trois prophètes dans un temps de ténèbres: Sophonie–Nahum–Habaquq.* Lectio divina 48. Paris: Cerf, 1968.

Bosshard, Erich. "Beobachtungen zum Zwölfprophetenbuch." *BN* 40 (1987) 30–62.

Brin, Gerson. "The Title בן (ה)מלך and Its Parallels: The Significance and Evaluation of an Official Title." *AION* 29 (1969) 432–65.

Budde, Karl. "Eine folgenschwere Redaction des Zwölfprophetenbuchs." *ZAW* 39 (1922) 218–29.

Calès, Jean. "L'authenticité de Sophonie, II, 11 et son contexte primitif." *Recherches de science religieuse* 10 (1920) 355–57.

Cathcart, Kevin J. "*bōšet* in Zephaniah 3:5." *JNSL* 12 (1984) 35–39.

Cathcart, Kevin J., and Robert P. Gordon. *The Targum of the Minor Prophets.* Aramaic Bible 14. Wilmington, Del.: Glazier, 1989.

Cazelles, Henri. "Sophonie, Jérémie, et les Scythes en Palestine." *RB* 74 (1967) 24–44.

——. "Zephaniah, Jeremiah, and the Scythians in Palestine," pp. 129–49. In Leo G. Perdue and Brian W. Kovacs, eds. *A Prophet to the Nations: Essays in Jeremiah Studies.* Winona Lake, Ind.: Eisenbrauns, 1984.

Christensen, Duane L. "Zephaniah 2:4-15: A Theological Basis for Josiah's Program of Political Expansion." *CBQ* 46 (1984) 669–82.

Churgin, Pinkhos. *Targum Jonathan to the Prophets.* 1927; reprinted New York: KTAV, 1983.

Collins, Terence. *The Mantle of Elijah: The Redaction Criticism of the Prophetical Books.* BibSem 20. Sheffield: JSOT Press, 1993.

De Roche, Michael. "Zephaniah I 2-3: The 'Sweeping' of Creation." *VT* 30 (1980) 104–9.

Dietrich, Walter, and Milton Schwantes, eds. *Der Tag wird kommen: Ein interkontextuelles Gespräch über das Buch des Propheten Zefanja.* SBS 170. Stuttgart: Katholisches Bibelwerk, 1996.

Donner, Herbert. "Die Schwellenhüpfer: Beobachtungen zu Zephanja 1,8f." *JSS* 15 (1970) 42–55.

Duhm, Bernhard. "Anmerkungen zu den Zwölfpropheten. 4. Buch Zephanja." *ZAW* 31 (1911) 93–100.

Edler, Rainer. *Das Kerygma des Propheten Zefanja.* Freiburger theologische Studien 120. Freiburg: Herder, 1984.

Efros, L. "Textual Notes on the Hebrew Bible." *JAOS* 45 (1925) 152–54.

Elliger, Karl. "Das Ende der 'Abendwölfe' in Zeph 3,3 Hab 1,8," pp. 158–75. In Walter Baumgartner et al., eds., *Festschrift Alfred Bertholet zum 80. Geburtstag.* Tübingen: Mohr (Siebeck), 1950.

Fagnani, C. P. "The Structure of the Text of the Book of Zephaniah," pp. 260–77. In *Old Testament and Semitic Studies in Memory of W. R. Harper,* vol. 2. 2 vols. Chicago: Univ. of Chicago Press, 1908.

Ferguson, H. "The Historical Testimony of the Prophet Zephaniah." *JBL* (1883) 42–59.

Florit, Josep Ribera. "La versión aramaica de Profeta Sofonías." *Estudios Bíblicos* 40 (1982) 127–58.

Fuller, Russell. "The Form and Formation of the Book of the Twelve: The Evidence from the Judean Desert," pp. 86–101. In James W. Watts and Paul R. House, eds., *Forming Prophetic Literature: Essays on Isaiah and the Twelve in Honor of John D. W. Watts.* JSOTSup 235. Sheffield: Sheffield Academic Press, 1996.

——. "The Text of the Twelve Minor Prophets." *CurBS* 7 (1999) 81–95.

Gaster, Theodore H. "Two Textual Emendations. Zephaniah iii.17." *ExpT* 78 (1966–67) 267.

Gelston, A. *The Peshitta of the Twelve Prophets.* Oxford: Clarendon, 1987.

Gerleman, Gillis. *Zephanja. Textkritisch und literarkritisch untersucht.* Lund: Gleerup, 1942.

Ginsberg, H. L. "Gleanings in First Isaiah," pp. 245–59. In Moshe Davis, ed., *Mordecai M. Kaplan Jubilee Volume.* 2 vols. New York: Jewish Theological Seminary, 1953.

Gordon, Robert P. *Studies in the Targum to the Twelve Prophets: From Nahum to Malachi.* VTSup 51. Leiden: Brill, 1994.

Gorgulho, Gilberto. "Zefanja und die historische Bedeutung der Armen." *EvTh* 51 (1991) 81–92.

Gray, John. "A Metaphor from Building in Zephaniah ii 1." *VT* 3 (1953) 404–7.

Greenfield, J. C. "A Hapax Legomenon: ממשק חרול," pp. 79–82. In Sheldon R. Brunswick, ed., *Studies in Judaica, Karaitica and Islamica. Presented to Leon Nemoy on His Eightieth Birthday.* Tel Aviv: Bar-Ilan Univ. Press, 1982.

Haak, Robert D. "'Cush' in Zephaniah," pp. 238–51. In Steven W. Holloway and Lowell K. Handy, eds. *The Pitcher Is Broken: Memorial Essays for Gösta W. Ahlström.* JSOTSup 190. Sheffield: Sheffield Academic Press, 1995.

Harrison, C. R., Jr. "The Unity of the Minor Prophets in the Septuagint." *BIOSCS* 21 (1988) 55–72.

Haupt, Paul. "Pelican and Bittern." *JBL* 39 (1920) 158–61, 171.

——. "The Prototype of the Dies Irae." *JBL* 38 (1919) 142–51.

Heller, J. "Zephanias Ahnenreihe (Eine redaktionsgeschichtliche Bemerkung zu Zeph. I 1)." *VT* 21 (1971) 102–4.

Herrmann, Johannes, and Friedrich Baumgärtel. "Die Septuaginta zum Zwölfprophetenbuch das Werk zweier Übersetzer," pp. 32–38. In Johannes Herrmann and Friedrich Baumgärtel, eds., *Beiträge zur Entstehungsgeschichte der Septuaginta.* Berlin: Kohlhammer, 1923.

Hoffmann, Yair. "The Day of the Lord as a Concept and a Term in the Prophetic Literature." *ZAW* 93 (1981) 37–50.

——. *The Prophecies against Foreign Nations in the Bible* (Hebrew). Tel Aviv: Tel Aviv Univ. Press, 1977.

House, Paul R. "Dramatic Coherence in Nahum, Habakkuk, and Zephaniah," pp. 195–208. In James W. Watts and Paul R. House, eds., *Forming Prophetic Literature: Essays on Isaiah and the Twelve in Honor of John D. W. Watts.* JSOTSup 235. Sheffield: Sheffield Academic Press, 1996.

——. *The Unity of the Twelve.* JSOTSup 97; BLS 27. Sheffield: Almond, 1990.

——. *Zephaniah: A Prophetic Drama.* JSOTSup 69. BLS 69. Sheffield: Almond, 1988.

Hunter, A. Vanlier. *Seek the Lord! A Study of the Meaning and Function of the Exhortations in Amos, Hosea, Isaiah, Micah, and Zephaniah.* Baltimore: St. Mary's Seminary and University, 1982.

Hyatt, J. Philip. "The Date and Background of Zephaniah." *JNES* 7 (1948) 25–29.

Ihromi. "Die Häufung der Verben des Jubelns in Zephanja III 14f, 16-18: *rnn rwᶜ ᶜlz sws* und *gil*." *VT* 33 (1983) 106–10.

Irsigler, Hubert. "Äquivalenz in Poesie. Die kontextuellen Synoyme *saᶜaqā–yalalā–šibr gedu(w)l* in Zef 1,10c.d.e." *BZ* 22 (1978) 221–35.

———. *Gottesgericht und Jahwetag. Die Komposition Zef 1,1–2,3, untersucht auf der Grundlage der Literarkritik des Zefanjabuches.* ATSAT 3. St. Ottilien: EOS, 1977.

Jeppesen, Knud. "Zephaniah I 5b." *VT* 31 (1981) 372–73.

Jones, Barry Alan. *The Formation of the Book of the Twelve: A Study in Text and Canon.* SBLDS 149. Atlanta: Scholars Press, 1995.

Jongeling, B. "Jeux de Mots en Sophonie III 1 et 3?" *VT* 21 (1971) 541–47.

Kapelrud, Arvid S. "Eschatology in Micah and Zephaniah," pp. 255–62. In Maurice Carrez, Joseph Doré, and Pierre Grelot, eds. *De la Tôrah au Messie.* Fest. H. Cazelles. Paris: Desclée, 1981.

———. *The Message of the Prophet Zephaniah: Morphology and Ideas.* Oslo: Universitetsforlaget, 1975.

King, Greg A. "The Day of the Lord in Zephaniah." *BSac* 152 (1995) 16–32.

———. "The Remnant in Zephaniah." *BSac* 151 (1994) 414–27.

Köhler, Ludwig. "Emendationen. e) Zeph 2,2," 176, in Karl Budde, ed., *Vom Alten Testament: Karl Marti zum siebzigsten Geburtstage gewidmet.* BZAW 41. Giessen: Töpelmann, 1925.

Krinetzki, Günther. *Zefanjastudien: Motiv- und Traditionskritik + Kompositions- und Redaktionskritik.* Regensburger Studien zur Theologie 7. Frankfurt am Main: Lang, 1977.

Kselman, John S. "A Note on Jer 49,20 and Ze 2,6-7." *CBQ* 32 (1970) 579–81.

Langhor, Guy. "Le livre de Sophonie et la critique d'authenticité." *EThL* 52 (1976) 1–27.

———. "Rédaction et composition du livre de Sophonie." *Mus* 89 (1976) 51–73.

Lohfink, Norbert, S.J. "Zefanja und das Israel der Armen." *BK* 39 (1984) 100–108.

———. "Zephaniah and the Church of the Poor." *TD* 32 (1985) 113–18.

Loretz, O. "Theologie des Zephanja-Buches." *UF* 5 (1973) 219–28.

Mendecki, Norbert. "Deuteronomistische Redaktion von Zef 3,18-20?" *BN* 60 (1991) 27–32.

Muraoka, Takamitsu. "In Defence of the Unity of the Septuagint Minor Prophets." *AJBI* 15 (1989) 25–36.

Nel, P. J. "Structural and Conceptual Strategy in Zephaniah, Chapter 1." *JNSL* 15 (1989) 155–67.

Nogalski, James D. *Literary Precursors to the Book of the Twelve.* BZAW 217. Berlin: de Gruyter, 1993.

———. *Redactional Processes in the Book of the Twelve.* BZAW 218. Berlin: de Gruyter, 1993.

Nogalski, James D., and Marvin A. Sweeney, eds. *Reading and Hearing the Book of the Twelve.* SBLSymS 15. Altanta: Society of Biblical Literature, 2000.

Oeming, Manfred. "Gericht Gottes und Geschicke der Völker nach Zef 3,1-13." *Theologische Quartalschrift* 167 (1987) 289–300.

Olivier, J. P. J. "A Possible Interpretation of the Word *siyyâ* in Zeph. 2,13." *JNSL* 8 (1980) 95–97.

Renaud, B. "Le livre de Sophonie: Le jour de Yahweh thème structurant de la synthèse rédactionelle." *RevScRel* 60 (1986) 1–33.

Rose, M. "'Atheismus' als Wohlstandserachtung? (Zephanja 1,2)." *Theologische Zeitschrift* 37 (1981) 193–208.

Ryou, Daniel Hojoon. *Zephaniah's Oracles Against the Nations: A Synchronic and Diachronic Study of Zephaniah 2:1–3:8.* BibIntSer 13. Leiden: Brill, 1995.

Sabottka, Liudger. *Zephanja: Versuch einer Neuübersetzung mit philologischer Kommentar.* BibOr 25. Rome: Biblical Institute Press, 1972.

Scharbert, Josef. "Zefanja und die Reform des Joschija," pp. 237–53. In Lothar Ruppert, Peter Weimer, and Erich Zenger, eds. *Künder des Wortes. Beiträge zur Theologie der Propheten.* Würzburg: Echter, 1982.

Schart, Aaron. *Die Entstehung des Zwölfprophetenbuchs.* BZAW 260. Berlin: de Gruyter, 1998.

Schneider, Dale. "The Unity of the Book of the Twelve." Ph.D. diss. Yale University, 1979.

Schunk, K.-D. "Juda in der Verkündigung des Propheten Zefanja," pp. 174–79. In J. Hausmann and H.-J. Zobel, eds. *Alttestamentlicher Glaube und biblische Theologie: Festschrift für Horst Dietrich Preuss.* Stuttgart: Kohlhammer, 1992.

Schwally, Friedrich. "Das Buch Sefanjâ, eine historisch-kritische Untersuchung." *ZAW* 10 (1890) 165–240.

Seybold, Klaus. *Satirische Prophetie: Studien zum Buch Zefanja.* SBS 120. Stuttgart: Katholisches Bibelwerk, 1985.

———. "Text und Textauslegung in Zef 2,1-3." *BN* 25 (1984) 49–54.

———. "Die Verwendung der Bildmotive in der Prophetie Zefanjas," pp. 30–54. In Helga Weippert, Klaus Seybold, and Manfred Weippert, eds. *Beiträge zur prophetischen Bildsprache in Israel und Assyrien.* OBO 64. Göttingen: Vandenhoeck & Ruprecht, 1985.

Smith, Louise Pettibone, and Ernest R. Lacheman. "The Authorship of the Book of Zephaniah." *JNES* 9 (1950) 137–42.

Smolar, Leivy, and Moses Aberbach. *Studies in Targum Jonathan to the Prophets.* Reprinted New York: KTAV, 1983.

Steck, Odil Hannes. *Der Abschluss der Prophetie im Alten Testament: Ein Versuch zur Frage der Vorgeschichte des Kanons.* BTS 17. Neukirchen-Vluyn: Neukirchener, 1991.

——. "Zu Zef 3,9-10." *BZ* 34 (1990) 90–95.

Stenzel, Meinrad. "Zum Verständnis von Zeph. III 3B." *VT* 1 (1951) 303–5.

Striek, Marco. *Das vordeuteronomistische Zephanjabuch.* BBET 29. Frankfurt am Main: Lang, 1999.

Sweeney, Marvin A. "A Form-Critical Reassessment of the Book of Zephaniah." *CBQ* 53 (1991) 388–408.

——. "Metaphor and Rhetorical Strategy in Zephaniah." In Timothy Sandoval and Carleen Mandolfo, eds., *Relating to the Text: Interdisciplinary and Form-Critical Insights on the Bible.* JSOTSup; Sheffield: Sheffield Academic Press, forthcoming.

Thomas, D. Winton. "A Pun on the Name Ashdod in Zephaniah ii 4." *ExpT* 74 (1962–63) 63.

Tsevat, Matitiahu. "Some Biblical Notes." *HUCA* 24 (1952–53) 111–12.

van der Woude, Adam S. "Bemerkungen zu einigen umstrittenen Stellen im Zwölfprophetenbuch. Zefanja 3:3b," p. 496. In A. Caquot and M. Delcor, eds., *Mélanges bibliques et orientaux.* Fest. Henri Cazelles; AOAT 212. Neukirchen-Vluyn: Neukirchener, 1981.

——. "Predikte Zefanja een wereldgericht?" *NedThT* 20 (1965–66) 1–16.

Watts, James W., and Paul R. House, eds. *Forming Prophetic Literature: Essays on Isaiah and the Twelve in Honor of J. D. W. Watts.* JSOTSup 235. Sheffield: Sheffield Academic Press, 1996.

Weigl, Michael. *Zefanja und "Israel der Armen." Eine Untersuchung zur Theologie des Buches Zefanja.* ÖBSt 13. Klosterneuburg: Österreichische Katholisches Bibelwerk, 1994.

Williams, Donald L. "The Date of Zephaniah." *JBL* 82 (1963) 77–88.

Winckler, H. "Zum Alten Testament—חבלהים (Zeph. 2,5)," pp. 232–33. In *Altorientalische Forschungen III.* Leipzig: Pfeiffer, 1906.

Wolff, Ronald E. "The Editing of the Book of the Twelve." *ZAW* 53 (1935) 90–129.

Zalcman, Lawrence. "Ambiguity and Assonance in Zephaniah ii 4." *VT* 36 (1986) 365–70.

——. "*Di sera*, Desert, Dessert." *ExpT* 91 (1979–80) 311.

Zandstra, Sidney. *The Witness of the Vulgate, Peshitta and Septuagint to the Text of Zephaniah.* Contributions to Oriental History and Philology 4. 1909. Reprinted New York: AMS, 1966.

Ziegler, Joesph. *Sylloge: Gesammelte Aufsätze zur Septuaginta.* Mittheilungen des Septuaginta-Unternehmens 10. Göttingen: Vandenhoeck & Ruprecht, 1971.

Index

c / New Testament

Matthew
    13:41   41

Romans
    2:16   2

1 Corinthians
    3:13   2

1 Thessalonians
    5:2   2

2 Thessalonians
    2:2   2

2 Timothy
    1:12   2
    1:18   2
    4:8   2

Revelation
    6:17   41
    14:5   41
    16:1   41

d / Greco-Roman Literature

Herodotus
Persian Wars
    2.157   121

2. Subjects

3. Authors

Aberbach, Moses
29, 32, 74, 91, 152

Aejmalaeus, Anneli
112, 121

Aharoni, Yohanan
26, 146, 147

Ahlström, Gösta
17, 83

Albrektson, Bertil
80

Alexander, Philip S.
29

Allegro, John
29

Alt, Albrecht
18, 91

Anderson, Gary A.
75,103

Anderson, George W.
188

Anderson, Roger W.,
Jr.
48

Appelbaum, S.
24

Avigad, Nahman
9, 26, 45, 67, 76,
89, 90

Avi-Yonah, Michael
24, 34, 89

Bacher, Wilhelm
32

Bachmann, J.
64

Ball, Ivan J., Jr.
62, 78, 98, 111,
114, 116, 141, 146,
158, 176, 180, 203

Baltzer, Klaus
198

Bar-Adon, Pessah
26

Baron, Salo Wittmayer
10, 11

Barr, James
132, 152

Barth, Jacob
59

Barthélemy,
Dominique
26, 27, 28, 30

Baumann, Gerlinde
16

Baumgärtel, Friedrich
21, 62

Beit-Arieh, Itzhaq
147

Ben-Hayyim, Zeev
10

Ben Zvi, Ehud
1, 6, 48, 58, 61, 63,
64, 66, 68, 70, 72,
77, 78, 85, 87, 89,
95, 97, 99, 101,
102, 104, 111, 114,
116, 117, 118, 120,
121, 126, 127, 128,
142, 143, 146, 155,
158, 159, 161, 162,
163, 172, 173, 175,
177, 179, 181, 185,
186, 187, 190, 192,
197, 198, 199, 200,
202, 204, 206, 208

Bennett, Robert A.
49, 51, 96, 111,
148, 158, 176, 180

Berger, Samuel
39

Bergler, Siegfried
97, 100, 201

Berlin, Adele
5, 17, 61, 64, 68,
71, 72, 86, 88, 95,
97, 101, 111, 114,
116, 120, 128, 130,
140, 153, 158, 176,
180, 187, 201, 206,
207, 208

Betlyon, John W.
92

Bickerman, Elias
19, 23

Biddle, Mark
106

Bjørndalen, Anders
159

Blenkinsopp, Joseph
13, 165

Boecker, Hans-Joachim
172, 198, 199

Bonnard, P.-E.
155

Bracke, John M.
131, 132

Brin, G.
84

Brinkman, John
15, 54, 151

Brown, William P.
66

Budde, Karl
86

Cathcart, Kevin J.
29, 31, 32, 45, 52,
73, 74, 79, 82

Černý, Ladislav
52

Childs, Brevard S.
107, 134, 141

Christensen, Duane
14, 146

Churgin, Pinkhos
29, 30, 31, 34, 65,
180

Clements, Ronald E.
177

Cogan, Mordecai
67, 68

Coggins, Richard
176

Conrad, Edgar W.
196

Coote, Robert
137

Crawford, Timothy G.
4

Crenshaw, James L.
66, 100

Cresson, Bruce C.
147

Crüsemann, Frank
189, 195

Cryer, Frederick H.
57, 165

Daiches, S.
56

Dalman, Gustav H.
66

Dearman, J. Andrew
18, 135, 137

De Lagarde, Paul
20

De Roche, Michael
57, 62

De Vaux, Roland
28

Dever, William G.
67

DeVries, Simon J.
82, 83, 88, 93, 171,
186, 200, 205

Dhorme, Paul
59, 86

Diamond, A. R. Pete
203

Dijkstra, Meindert
137

Dirksen, Peter B.
34, 35

Dold, Alban
39

Donner, Herbert
15, 82, 86, 87

Dotan, Aaron
3, 10

Dothan, Trude
91

Driver, Samuel Rolles
59, 86

Edler, Rainer
72, 88, 92, 95, 101,

222

Designer's Notes

In the design of the visual aspects of *Hermeneia,* consideration has been given to relating the form to the content by symbolic means.

The letters of the logotype *Hermeneia* are a fusion of forms alluding simultaneously to Hebrew (dotted vowel markings) and Greek (geometric round shapes) letter forms. In their modern treatment they remind us of the electronic age as well, the vantage point from which this investigation of the past begins.

The Lion of Judah used as visual identification for the series is based on the Seal of Shema. The version for *Hermeneia* is again a fusion of Hebrew calligraphic forms, especially the legs of the lion, and Greek elements characterized by the geometric. In the sequence of arcs, which can be understood as scroll-like images, the first is the lion's mouth. It is reasserted and accelerated in the whorl and returns in the aggressively arched tail: tradition is passed from one age to the next, rediscovered and re-formed.

"Who is worthy to open the scroll and break its seals. . . ."

Then one of the elders said to me

"weep not; lo, the Lion of the tribe of David,
the Root of David, has conquered,
so that he can open the scroll and
its seven seals."

Rev. 5:2, 5

To celebrate the signal achievement in biblical scholarship which *Hermeneia* represents, the entire series will by its color constitute a signal on the theologian's bookshelf: the Old Testament will be bound in yellow and the New Testament in red, traceable to a commonly used color coding for synagogue and church in medieval painting; in pure color terms, varying degrees of intensity of the warm segment of the color spectrum. The colors interpenetrate when the binding color for the Old Testament is used to imprint volumes from the New and vice versa.

Wherever possible, a photograph of the oldest extant manuscript, or a historically significant document pertaining to the biblical sources, will be displayed on the end papers of each volume to give a feel for the tangible reality and beauty of the source material.

The title-page motifs are expressive derivations from the Hermeneia logotype, repeated seven times to form a matrix and debossed on the cover of each volume. These sifted-out elements will be seen to be in their exact positions within the parent matrix.

Horizontal markings at gradated levels on the spine will assist in grouping the volumes according to these conventional categories.

The type has been set with unjustified right margins so as to preserve the internal consistency of word spacing. This is a major factor in both legibility and aesthetic quality; the resultant uneven line endings are only slight impairments to legibility by comparison. In this respect the type resembles the handwritten manuscripts where the quality of the calligraphic writing is dependent on establishing and holding to integral spacing patterns.

All of the type faces in common use today have been designed between AD 1500 and the present. For the biblical text a face was chosen which does not arbitrarily date the text, but rather one which is uncompromisingly modern and unembellished so that its feel is of the universal. The type style is Univers 65 by Adrian Frutiger.

The expository texts and footnotes are set in Baskerville, chosen for its compatibility with the many brief Greek and Hebrew insertions. The double-column format and the shorter line length facilitate speed reading and the wide margins to the left of footnotes provide for the scholar's own notations.

Kenneth Hiebert

Category of biblical writing,
key symbolic characteristic,
and volumes so identified.

1

Law
(boundaries described)
  Genesis
  Exodus
  Leviticus
  Numbers
  Deuteronomy

2

History
(trek through time and space)
  Joshua
  Judges
  Ruth
  1 Samuel
  2 Samuel
  1 Kings
  2 Kings
  1 Chronicles
  2 Chronicles
  Ezra
  Nehemiah
  Esther

3

Poetry
(lyric emotional expression)
  Job
  Psalms
  Proverbs
  Ecclesiastes
  Song of Songs

4

Prophets
(inspired seers)
  Isaiah
  Jeremiah
  Lamentations
  Ezekiel
  Daniel
  Hosea
  Joel
  Amos
  Obadiah
  Jonah
  Micah
  Nahum
  Habakkuk
  Zephaniah
  Haggai
  Zechariah
  Malachi

5

New Testament Narrative
(focus on One)
  Matthew
  Mark
  Luke
  John
  Acts

6

Epistles
(directed instruction)
  Romans
  1 Corinthians
  2 Corinthians
  Galatians
  Ephesians
  Philippians
  Colossians
  1 Thessalonians
  2 Thessalonians
  1 Timothy
  2 Timothy
  Titus
  Philemon
  Hebrews
  James
  1 Peter
  2 Peter
  1 John
  2 John
  3 John
  Jude

7

Apocalypse
(vision of the future)
  Revelation

8

Extracanonical Writings
(peripheral records)